Complete
Digital Photography
Eighth Edition

Ben Long

Cengage Learning PTR

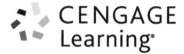
CENGAGE
Learning®

Professional • Technical • Reference

Australia • Brazil • Japan • Korea • Mexico • Singapore • Spain • United Kingdom • United States

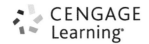

CENGAGE Learning

Professional • Technical • Reference

Complete Digital Photography
Eighth Edition
Ben Long

Publisher and General Manager,
Cengage Learning PTR:
Stacy L. Hiquet

Associate Director of Marketing:
Sarah Panella

Manager of Editorial Services:
Heather Talbot

Product Manager: Heather Hurley

Project and Copy Editor: Marta Justak

Technical Reviewer: Jim Long

Interior Layout: Jill Flores

Cover Designer: Mike Tanamachi

Indexer: Larry Sweazy

Proofreader: Sue Boshers

For product information and technology assistance, contact us at
Cengage Learning Customer & Sales Support, 1-800-354-9706

For permission to use material from this text or product,
submit all requests online at **cengage.com/permissions**
Further permissions questions can be emailed to
permissionrequest@cengage.com

Library of Congress Control Number: 2014945696

ISBN-13: 978-1-305-25872-3

ISBN-10: 1-305-25872-X

Cengage Learning PTR
20 Channel Center Street
Boston, MA 02210
USA

Cengage Learning is a leading provider of customized learning solutions with office locations around the globe, including Singapore, the United Kingdom, Australia, Mexico, Brazil, and Japan. Locate your local office at: **international.cengage.com/region**

Cengage Learning products are represented in Canada by Nelson Education, Ltd. For your lifelong learning solutions, visit **cengageptr.com**

Visit our corporate website at **cengage.com**

Printed in Canada
1 2 3 4 5 6 7 16 15 14

Acknowledgments

There are a lot of changes and additions in this revision of *Complete Digital Photography, Eighth Edition* and many of them are there because, once again, my dad, Jim Long, did such a thorough job of technical editing.

I was also thrilled to have the production team of Marta Justak and Jill Flores again, who applied their considerable talent and care to making this such a nice book. Finally, thanks to Stacy Hiquet for giving us the go-ahead to move this book forward ahead of schedule.

About the Author

Ben Long is a San Francisco-based photographer and writer. The author of over a dozen books on digital photography and digital video, he has been a longtime contributor to many magazines, including *MacWeek*, *MacUser*, *Macworld UK*, and more. He is currently a senior contributing editor for *Macworld* magazine, a senior editor at CreativePro.com, and has created many best-selling photography instruction courses for Lynda.com. His photography clients have included 20th Century Fox, Blue Note Records, Global Business Network, the San Francisco Jazz Festival, the Pickle Family Circus, and Grammy-nominated jazz musicians Don Byron and Dafnis Prieto. Long has taught and lectured on photography around the world. He also dabbles in computer programming, and has written image editing utilities that are in use in the Smithsonian, the British Museum, and the White House.

Contents

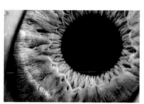

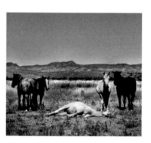

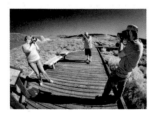

3

Camera Anatomy 36

Holding and Controlling Your Camera

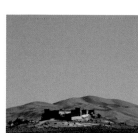

4 Image Transfer 74

Building a Workstation and Transferring from Your Camera

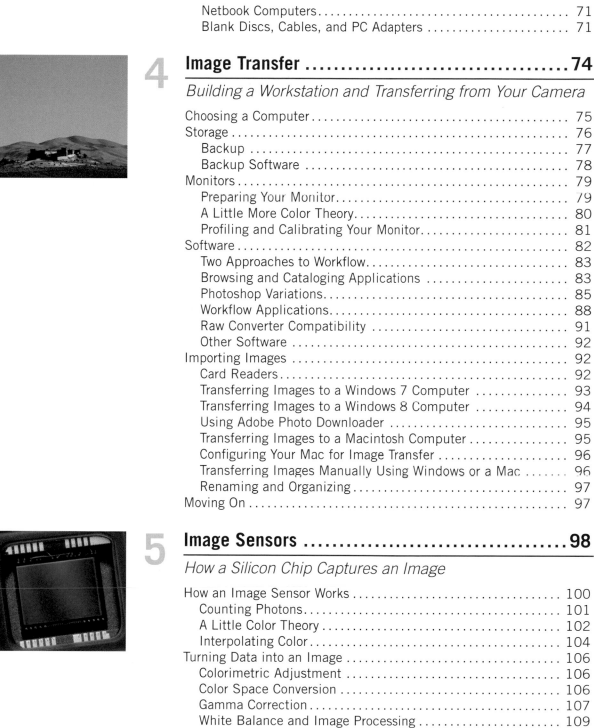

5 Image Sensors 98

How a Silicon Chip Captures an Image

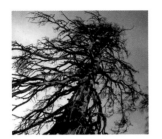

6 Exposure Basics................................ 112

The Fundamental Theory of Exposure

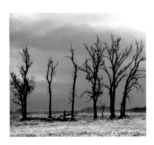

7 Program Mode.................................. 128

Taking Control of Exposure, Focus, and More

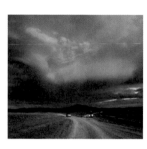

8 Advanced Exposure 168

*Learning More About Your Light Meter and
Exposure Controls*

9 Finding and Composing a Photo 198

Learning the Art of Photography

10 Lighting 246

The Process of Controlling Light

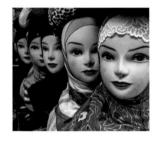

11 Raw Shooting.................................. 264

Gaining More Editing Power Through Raw Format

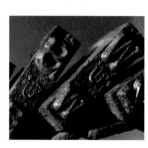

12 Special Shooting................................ 274

Camera Features and Techniques for Specific Situations

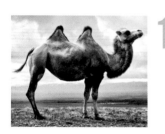

13 Workflow 326

Managing Your Images and Starting Postproduction

14 Editing Workflows and First Steps 364

Understanding the Order of Edits and Making Your First Adjustments

15 Correcting Tone 386

Ensuring That White, Black, and Overall Contrast Are Correct

16 Correcting Color................................. 416

Repairing, Improving, and Changing Color

17 Selective Editing and Masks..................... 438

Making Edits to Specific Parts of an Image

18 Photoshop Adjustment Layers 468

Advanced Tools for Adjustments and Corrections

19 Black-and-White Conversion 484

Turning Your Color Images into Black-and-White Images

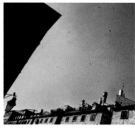

20 Layers, Retouching, and Special Effects 498

*Additional Editing Tools and Concepts for Improving
Your Images*

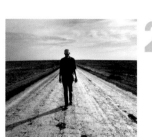

21 Panoramic Stitching and HDR Merging. 526

How to Process These Multi-Shot Effects

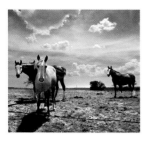

22 Output 544

Taking Your Images to Print or Electronic Output

Introduction

In 1990, I began using version 1 of a new piece of software called Photoshop. Adobe, at that time, was best-known for PostScript—the page description language that was used in most laser printers. It would be nice to write about how using that first version was a startling experience that instantly changed my ideas about photography and image editing, but there had already been image editing programs around, most notably Silicon Beach's Digital Darkroom. Adobe did not create the digital image editing market, but over the next 10 years they absolutely defined and ultimately dominated it.

During those years, I enjoyed working through the addition of layers, Adjustment Layers, Camera Raw, and many more features. Through all those features, though, Photoshop remained built around the document-centric Open/Save paradigm of late 1980s software. As processing power, memory, and storage increased, Adobe kept pace as best they could, but ultimately it was not possible to change Photoshop's basic design. And so they created Lightroom, which eschewed the old-fashioned architecture of Photoshop for one that is much speedier and more flexible.

In the previous seven editions of this book, I have used Photoshop as the basis for all of the postproduction tutorials. With this edition, that has all changed. In the latter chapters of this book, you will find that I now offer Lightroom as the basis for postproduction workflow and editing. Photoshop is far from obsolete, though, and it's still the perfect tool of choice for many image editing options—it still touches the majority of the images that I print—and so a lot of Photoshop training remains.

The good news is that Lightroom is an ideal workflow tool, so if you follow the examples and practices set forth in this book, you'll find yourself with a robust, comprehensive, and very capable postproduction workflow.

On Learning Photography

In the 1980s, the graphic design world went through an enormous change. Aldus, Incorporated released PageMaker 1.0, and Adobe Systems, Inc. unveiled the first PostScript laser printer. The result was "desktop publishing." And with desktop publishing came a lot of really bad, ugly designs.

What desktop publishing technology did was to give anyone instant craft ability. Whereas graphic design had traditionally required a lot of skill with a lot of manual tools, tools that required years of practice to use well, desktop publishing gave everyone the ability to instantly draw a straight line. Suddenly, people who had never had any interest in graphic design thought "I know how to use these new, digital tools, therefore I'm a graphic designer." Mostly, what they did was reveal that graphic design requires much more than simply knowing the craft.

The advent of digital cameras and Photoshop had the same effect on photography. With their automatic features and instant feedback, digital cameras didn't require the extensive theoretical understanding that you had to have to use a film camera. And with Photoshop, the complex chemistries and tricky practices of the darkroom were reduced to push-button simplicity. Suddenly, everyone was buying a camera and a computer and proclaiming themselves "photographers."

I've been writing about and teaching photography since the beginning of the digital era, and for many years, I found that students were focused on learning Photoshop or some other image editing program. But over the last few years, I've been noticing a change. Just as graphic designers eventually reclaimed their profession from the "desktop publishing revolution," now more people seem to understand that learning to use an image editor is not the same thing as learning photography.

As the novelty of the ease of digital technology has worn off, people are getting back to the essential questions of making a good photo: How do I recognize interesting subject matter? How do I translate that into an interesting image? What do I need to do to capture that translation?

Because of that, this book is far more than a book about theory and button-pushing. In these pages, you'll find a lot of instruction on the "softer" more "artistic" concepts that you need to understand to be a good photographer.

One of the best ways to improve as a photographer is to cast a learned eye on other photos. There are more people shooting now than ever, and as more people recognize that it takes something besides good button pushing to get a good image, the number of nice photos in the world only increases.

It's a good time to be a photographer, and the changes in this latest edition will help you go as deep as you want to go into the art and craft of the photographic discipline.

How This Book Is Organized

This book is aimed at photographers of all levels. Photographic technology, whether digital or film, sees the world very differently from your eyes, and it's important to understand how your camera's results will differ from your visual experience at the scene. Therefore, Chapter 1, "Eyes, Brains, Lights, and Images," leads you through an exploration of your visual sense and how it differs from your camera. Many of the concepts in this chapter will become critical when you learn more about exposure.

Chapters 2 and 3, "Getting to Know Your Camera" and "Camera Anatomy," serve to familiarize you with your camera. Like any tool, you'll get better results from your camera if you know how to use it well, and these chapters should get you up to speed with all those buttons and dials.

To assess the results of the exercises in Chapters 2 and 3, you'll need to move your images into your computer. Chapter 4, "Image Transfer," will walk you through the process of importing images from your camera.

The great film photographers of the past didn't just understand composition and exposure theory, they also had detailed understanding of the chemistry of their film and darkroom technologies. It was this understanding that provided them with such fine control over their final result. Digital photographers similarly benefit from an understanding of digital image capture, so Chapter 5, "Image Sensors" walks you through the basics of how the guts of your digital camera work.

Chapters 6, 7, and 8—"Exposure Basics," "Program Mode," and "Advanced Exposure"—provide a thorough, detailed series of lessons in exposure theory. Starting with the most basic concerns and controls, you'll progress steadily up to the most advanced exposure features of your camera and learn how these tools can be used to broaden your expressive palette.

Chapter 9, "Finding and Composing a Photo," gives you a break from the technical concerns of shooting, and offers a lengthy discussion of how you go about finding a potential subject, and how to craft that subject into a final image. Photography is a discipline that rewards constant practice and experimentation, and this chapter will provide you with an understanding of the nontechnical subjects that you will explore for the rest of your photographic life.

Just about any digital camera you buy these days will have a built-in flash unit, and learning to use it can be tricky. Chapter 10, "Lighting," will walk you through the process of modifying light using flashes and reflectors.

All SLRs and many point-and-shoot cameras offer the ability to shoot in raw format, which provides several advantages over the JPEG shooting that your camera defaults to. Chapter 11, "Raw Shooting," discusses the particular advantages of raw shooting and addresses specific concerns that you'll face when shooting in raw mode.

Chapter 12, "Special Shooting," takes the detailed understanding of shooting that you glean from the first 11 chapters, and applies it to specific situations. In this chapter, you'll learn to shoot sporting events, theatrical events, how to shoot in low light, and much more.

With Chapters 13 and 14, "Workflow" and "Editing Workflows and First Steps," your postproduction education will begin, starting with a discussion of what workflow is and why it matters.

As you'll learn in the workflow chapters, one of your first image editing tasks is to correct tone, so Chapter 15, "Correcting Tone," will walk you through basic tonal adjustments. This is followed by Chapter 16, "Correcting Color."

Chapter 17, "Selective Editing and Masks," presents some of the most important tools that you'll add to your editing arsenal. With masks, you can make localized edits and adjustments, and good masking skills can be crucial to getting the results you want.

Adjustment Layers give Photoshop users a very simple way to work with masks. Chapter 18, "Photoshop Adjustment Layers," will show you the ins and outs of Adjustment Layers, as well as introduce you to other techniques for applying edits and adjustments to specific parts of an image. These tools augment Lightroom's built-in masking and provide valuable localized editing controls.

Black-and-white processing is given a detailed discussion in Chapter 19, "Black-and-White Conversion," while layers and other special effects and retouching tools are covered in Chapter 20, "Layers, Retouching, and Special Effects."

Panoramic stitching and HDR (high dynamic range) merging are covered in Chapter 21, "Panoramic Stitching and HDR Merging." These lessons build on the panoramic and HDR shooting discussions that are introduced in Chapter 12.

Finally, the last stage of your workflow is covered in Chapter 22, "Output," where you'll learn how to turn your finished images into files for email, Web pages, or archival prints.

However, this book offers you much more than what's printed on these pages. Throughout the book, you'll find Web links to movies and additional PDF documents that you can download. These resources will provide you with further discussions, examples, and tutorials on a wide variety of topics.

What You Need

Obviously, to take pictures you need a camera, and this book assumes that you already have one. The postproduction chapters of this book are built around Adobe Photoshop and Lightroom, and you can download demos of each from *www.adobe.com/downloads*. However, most image editing programs use similar interfaces, so you should find that the editing lessons herein translate very easily to many other image editing programs.

The Photoshop tutorials are built around the latest version of Photoshop (as of this writing), which is Photoshop CC. Most of the tutorials will work on earlier versions, and Photoshop Elements can easily be used for the book's tutorial sections. Because of the changes introduced in Photoshop CS6, some tutorials won't work well with previous versions. For those, you can download compatible tutorials from the companion website.

Finally, you need to have some curiosity about photography and the world in general. As with any art form, photography is a process of exploration. There's no recipe for a good photo, and while I recommend some specific ways of doing things, it's very rare that my recommendations are the best for everybody. Don't ever stop exploring on your own and trying to find the methods that work best for you.

There are many more tutorials, reviews, essays, and articles at the book's companion website *www.completedigitalphotography.com*. You can also email me through the site by clicking on the Contact Us link.

Glossary

Photography has always involved a lot of jargon and technical terms, and to help you with those I've built a glossary on the companion website. You can find it at *www.completedigital photography.com/glossary*.

Companion Website Downloads

You may download the companion website files from *www.completedigitalphotography.com/ CDP8*.

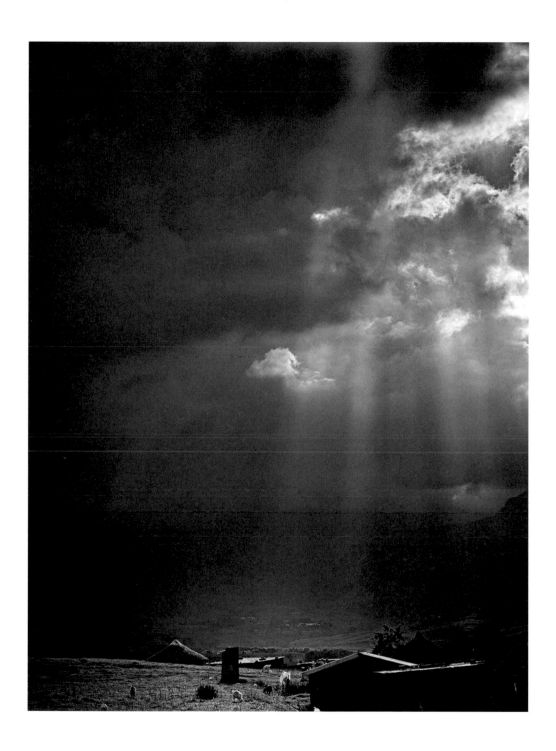

1

EYES, BRAINS, LIGHTS, AND IMAGES

Understanding How You See

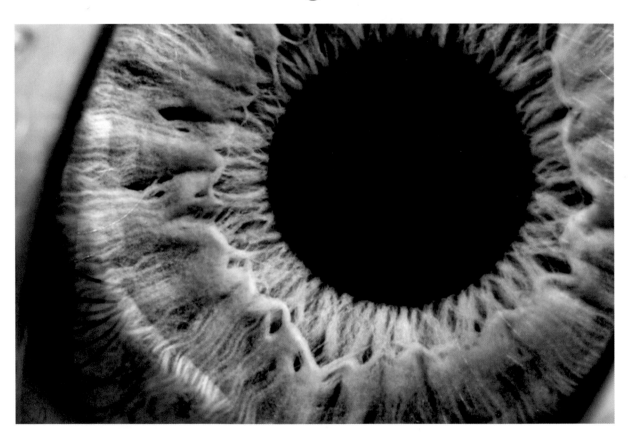

C

onsider, for a moment, a piece of film.

To make a piece of film, a thin strip of translucent celluloid is covered with a gelatin emulsion that includes crystals of silver halide. Silver halide is light sensitive, and when light strikes silver halide crystals, the crystals undergo a chemical change. As more light strikes a particular area of the silver halide–covered film, that area goes through more changes. When the film is developed, those chemically changed silver halide crystals turn into grains of silver. Where more silver halide is exposed to light, more metallic silver grains appear. The silver crystals, though, are dark, so areas that are exposed to more light get darker and darker—in other words, lighter areas of the original scene are represented as darker concentrations of silver. Thus, a negative image is created, as shown in Figure 1.1.

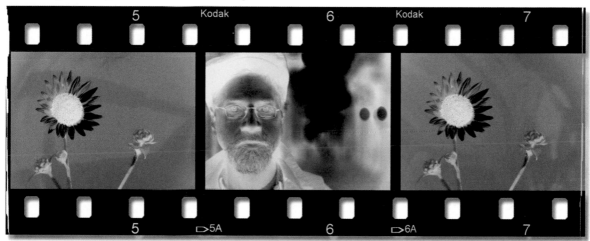

Figure 1.1 After a piece of film is developed, it contains a negative image.

If you project that negative image onto a photographic paper that is coated with silver halide crystals, the same chemical process occurs. A latent image is captured by the silver halide crystals on the paper, and when developed, the photon-activated crystals are turned into black metallic silver. But because the image is a negative, this time the original lighter areas collect fewer silver halide crystals. The practical upshot is that a positive image is produced.

One of the things that is amazing about this technology is that a single piece of film is both an imaging medium and a storage device. What's more, the negatives and prints that are produced can be very durable.

The image sensor that you'll find inside a digital camera also exploits the light sensitivity of certain elements. Instead of silver, though, a digital image sensor uses a special type of electronic circuit. For each pixel on the sensor's surface, there is a capacitor attached to a photodiode. A capacitor is simply a device that can store an electric charge, while a photodiode is a device that conducts or allows current to flow when it is exposed to light. Before capturing an image, the capacitor is given an electrical charge. When the photodiode is struck by light, the photodiode drains some of the charge from its attached capacitor. Just as silver halide crystals clump together in proportion to the amount of light that strikes them, a photodiode will reduce the charge on the capacitor in direct proportion to the number of photons that it was exposed to.

Your camera's image sensor is covered with these circuits—one for each pixel in your final image. By measuring the voltages across the surface of the image sensor, your camera can find out how much light struck each location. Your camera then passes this information to an onboard computer, which analyzes and interprets it to yield a full-color digital image, which is then stored on a memory card. All of this (and more) happens so quickly that your camera can capture multiple images in a single second.

Digital image sensors are incredibly sensitive to light. To understand how sensitive they are, just look at images from the Hubble telescope. The digital image sensors in this giant, orbiting telescope can yield images by capturing photons that have traveled through space for billions of years.

Both film and digital image sensors are amazing technologies, and they have improved dramatically over the years, thanks to the work of untold numbers of brilliant engineers. Both technologies allow for the capture and creation of striking, finely detailed, color-rich images.

And both pale in comparison to the imaging properties of the human eye.

The fact is, as amazing as our current imaging technologies are, there are many things that the human eye does much better, and a few things that the eye can do that analog and digital imaging technology can't do at all.

How Your Eyes See

Like a piece of film, or a digital image sensor, your eye has a light-sensitive area called the *retina* (see Figure 1.2).

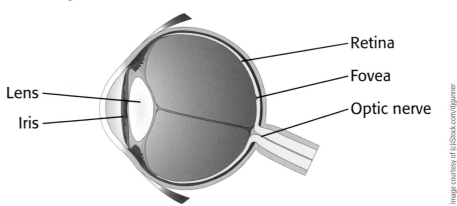

Figure 1.2

The eye is a lot like a camera. It focuses light with a lens, controls exposure with an iris, and has an imaging medium, the retina.

Located at the back of the eye, the retina contains four different kinds of light-sensitive cells: rods and three different types of cones. Cones are the color-sensitive cells, and most of them are found in a tiny region called the *fovea*. Less than one millimeter in diameter, the fovea is responsible not only for color, but also for sharpness and almost all of your spatial sensitivity. Cones can only detect light that strikes them straight on, which means that only well-focused light will activate them.

The fovea is very small yet contains all of the cells that generate your focused vision. Consequently, only a tiny bit of your field of view is in focus at any given time. This may come as a bit of a surprise, but of your whole field of view, only an area about the size of your thumbnail is actually in focus.

To test this, try an experiment. With this book held at arm's length, place your thumb on the page in the middle of a paragraph. Without moving your eyes, pay attention to the text around your thumb. While the area right next to your thumb might be in focus (it might not, depending on the size of your thumb), you probably can't read the text that's just a little farther away. Without moving your eyes, take your thumb off the page and note that the text where your thumb was is now in focus.

That thumb-sized focused area is the extent of your foveal vision. However, you perceive a full field of view of focused color vision because you subconsciously move your eyes around to sample your entire field of view. Your brain then assembles all of these samples into what you perceive as a fully focused, full-color visual sense.

Because they only respond to light coming from a single angle, cones (the light sensitive cells in the fovea) are not very light-sensitive, and as light levels decrease, colors become muted, and the rods in your eyes take over.

Rods cover the rest of the retina—about 98 to 99 percent of it—and they see only in monochrome. However, they can be triggered by light coming from just about any direction, which makes them incredibly sensitive to light. A rod that has been given time to adapt to the dark can detect a single photon of light—this means that, in good conditions, you could see the light of a candle from 17 miles away. But because rods are not located in the fovea, they don't yield as focused an image as what you see when your foveal vision is active.

Your rods are what we consider *peripheral vision*, and while your peripheral vision is not super sharp, it is great for seeing dim objects in low light. If you've ever spent any time making astronomical observations through a telescope, then you might already know that, often, the only way to see a very dim object is to avert your eyes from it. When you point your peripheral, rod-based vision at a very dim subject, you often see the object better—not necessarily sharper, but brighter. In fact, you may not be able to see the object at all unless you look away from it.

Your rod vision can also come in handy when walking in the dark. Next time you're out in the country, away from bright lights, take a walk outside. If possible, get off the pavement and put your feet on some less even terrain. If you keep your eyes focused directly ahead of you and don't move them while you walk, you'll probably find that your peripheral vision reveals a tremendous amount of detail on the path in front of you. Some of the things you see might disappear if you look directly at them, because your rod vision does a much better job in the dark than your foveal vision. If you practice this technique, you'll probably find that it's easier to walk in the dark using your peripheral vision than it is to use a flashlight, which completely wipes out your low-light vision and confines what you see to only the area lit up by the light.

Understanding the light sensitivity of your own eyes, and how to exploit that sensitivity, can be handy in low-light shooting situations when it can be difficult to identify subject matter and composition.

Of course, these days we spend most of our time in well-lit areas, moving through a full-color world.

Transmitting Color to the Brain

Earlier, I mentioned that there are three types of cones. Each type is sensitive to a different wavelength of color. One type is sensitive to red, another to green, and the third to blue. These colors are the additive primaries of light. As they are mixed together, they create other colors (see Figure 1.3).

If you mix equal amounts of red, green, and blue, the result is white. Varying amounts of each of these primaries allow you to create all of the other colors that the human eye can perceive.

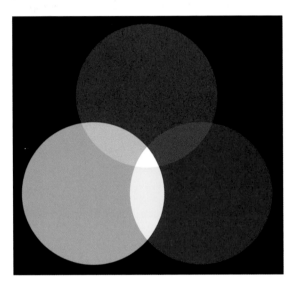

Figure 1.3

Red, green, and blue—the three additive primary colors of light—can be mixed together to create other colors. As you combine them, the resulting color gets lighter, eventually becoming white. Note also that where the colors overlap, they create the secondary primary colors—cyan, magenta, and yellow. These are the primary colors of ink.

The Different Primary Sets

In grade school, you might have learned some different primary colors, such as yellow. Yellow, cyan, and magenta are the primary colors of pigment, which are different from the light primaries. Unlike the primary colors of light, if you mix equal amounts of the primary colors of pigment, you get black. Because of this, we say that pigment colors are subtractive, while the colors of light are additive.

The total number of colors that the eye can perceive is not known for certain. Current research suggests a number from 2.3 million to 10 million different colors.

Like a digital camera, rods and cones generate electrical impulses when exposed to light. These signals are separated into two channels, one for brightness, and one for color, and both are transmitted to the brain via the optic nerve. The brightness channel contains far more information than the color channel, which might be one reason that black-and-white images are so compelling—they're composed exclusively of the type of information that the human visual system is the most sensitive to.

Once these signals get to the visual cortex in the brain, they get processed in many different ways. You can see one result of this processing by looking at something white.

If you've replaced any of the incandescent light bulbs in your house with compact fluorescents, you might have noticed how the compact fluorescents have a different color. They are what we call a "cooler" light, because they cast a light that's bluer than the warmer red light created by a tungsten bulb. Different types of light have different inherent colors, but your brain is able to compensate for this by automatically adapting so that color looks correct in any type of light, no matter what its color is.

For example, you might read this book under tungsten lighting and see the pages as white. However, if you carry it into your fluorescently lit kitchen, it will still look white, even though fluorescent light is much bluer than tungsten light. It will continue to appear white if you take it out into bright sun, into shade, or look at it under sodium vapor lights at night.

The brain is able to correct color in this way because it understands that a piece of paper is supposed to be white. In other words, you don't see these pages as white because of a purely optical process. While your eyes are incredibly sensitive to light and collect a good amount of visual data, a full 80 percent of what you perceive with your eyes is generated by your brain!

Based on your experience, memory, and expectations, your brain imposes a model of the world onto the visual signals that it receives from your eyes. At the simplest level, this model allows your brain to correct color, but it can also dramatically change your perception of objects in the world.

You can immediately feel how much the brain is involved in your visual sense simply by looking at an optical illusion. Optical illusions occur when your brain's model, or expectation, doesn't quite match the data coming from your eyes. The brain gets confused, and your sense of what you're seeing becomes more ambiguous.

One of the simplest examples is shown in Figure 1.4.

Your brain recognizes some lines that seem to indicate a particular thing, a cube, and so it tells you "Oh yeah, I know what that is, that's a cube." Except that it's not a cube, it's merely some lines on the page, even though those lines are describing a shape very similar to a cube. So, at some point in the process of trying to reconcile "cube" with the set of lines that you're seeing, the brain gets tripped up, and your perception of the object becomes less certain. The cube appears to change orientation as the brain tries to sort out what it's seeing. Ultimately, of course, your brain is simply wrong—the image is merely flat lines on paper.

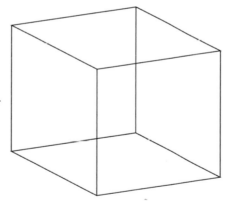

Figure 1.4

Your brain knows enough about the overall shape of these two-dimensional lines to assume that they represent a three-dimensional object—a cube. Of course, your brain is wrong. This isn't actually a 3D object, so there's not really enough information for your brain to correctly render a fully realized cube. As it struggles to reconcile what it's seeing with what it *thinks* the object is, the cube appears to flip back and forth.

Figure 1.5 shows another example, an optical illusion created by MIT researcher Edward H. Adelson.

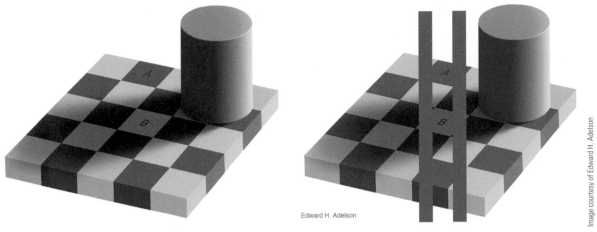

Figure 1.5 While the checkered squares appear to be alternating colors, squares A and B are actually the same color. In fact, your brain "corrects" the B square to make it fit an expectation that isn't true. The right figure shows that the two squares are actually the same color.

Light and Dark

Camera makers have yet to devise any kind of technology that can perform the type of sophisticated color adaptation that your eyes pull off. When you throw in the fact that the eye also provides extremely fast, silent autofocus with a range from a few centimeters all the way to infinity, it becomes obvious that current camera technology lags far behind the capability of the human eye.

The good news is that none of these facts mean that you can't take beautiful, compelling images. However, it is important to understand that your eyes see a world that your camera can't necessarily capture. Understanding the differences between what your eyes can see and what your camera can capture is an essential step for taking better pictures.

The most significant difference between the eye and any camera is the range of brightness that your eye can perceive. Just as your camera can alter the amount of light that strikes its image sensor by changing the size of its aperture, your eye can alter the amount of light that strikes its retina by closing the iris. Your eye controls brightness, or exposure, by opening and closing its iris, or pupil, to limit the amount of light that strikes the retina. It does this automatically as you look at brighter and darker things, and as the light in a scene changes.

Dynamic range is the measure of the darkest to lightest tones that can be captured by a device. Your eye can manage in very dark, moonless nights guided only by starlight, as well as in harsh, glaring sunlight. If you express this difference as a ratio, then the total dynamic range of the human eye is about a billion to one—the brightest thing you can perceive is about a billion times brighter than the darkest thing.

Photographers use a different way to measure light. Every time the amount of light in a scene doubles, photographers say that the scene has brightened by one *stop*, or *f-stop*. Conversely, if you cut the amount of light in a scene in half, then the scene has darkened by one stop. *Every doubling or halving of light is measured as one stop.* Using this measure, the human eye can perceive a total dynamic range of about 30 stops. However, you can't perceive this entire range at once. As you know, your eyes have to adjust to darkness and to emerging from darkness into bright light. So, while your eyes have the ability to perceive 30 stops of light, at any given time, they can only discern a dynamic range of about 15 stops. That is, the darkest thing and brightest thing in the scene can be about 15 stops apart. By comparison, a digital camera has a total dynamic range of 10 to 12 f-stops, and in any particular scene, you can expect to capture a range of about 5 to 9 stops.

Because the eye can see so much more dynamic range than your camera can, you will often have to make decisions about what part of the range you want to capture in a scene.

For example, consider Figure 1.6. In real life, the bottom of the canyon and the blue of the sky were visible to the eye. However, because the camera has a smaller dynamic range than the eye, it could capture only some of the range of light. It was not possible to shoot a single exposure that would properly expose both the depths of the canyon and the bright sky above. Although we can see detail in the sky in the first image, we see no detail in the canyon. In the second image, we have the exact opposite problem.

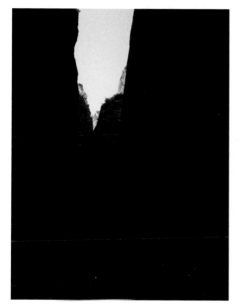 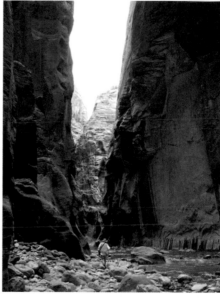

Figure 1.6 Because of the huge range of light to dark in this canyon, it was not possible to take a single exposure that captured both the bottom of the canyon and the sky above.

Learning to recognize when your camera will see things differently than your eye is an essential skill that will come with practice. In this book, you'll learn how to compensate for your camera's dynamic range deficiencies so that you can get images that are closer to how you actually see a scene. But to use these skills effectively, you first have to be able to recognize when dynamic range is a problem.

Summing Up

Offering continuous autofocus from a few centimeters to infinity, real-time color adaptation for different types of lights, a tremendous dynamic range, silent operation, and easy portability, your eyes trump modern camera technology in a number of ways. But, by understanding what we've discussed here, you'll be better able to work around the limitations of your camera.

However, there are a few ways that your camera outperforms the human eye. First, you can change the lens on it. Sure, modern surgical techniques allow lens replacement in the eye, but it's not the sort of thing you want to do every day, and you can't swap your eye's lens out for one with more magnification or a wider field of view.

Your eyes are used for more than just creating pretty pictures, of course. They serve a valuable role in balance, locomotion, and general survival. As such, they need to work quickly to provide you with a constantly updated stream of visual information. With a camera, though, you can choose to spend more time gathering light to create a single image. If you take, for example, 15 seconds for an exposure, then you'll produce an image with a tremendous amount of detail that you can't see with your naked eye.

How to Learn Photography

A title such as "How to Learn Photography" might be a little presumptuous, so I'll qualify it here by saying that the approach used in this book is *a* way to learn photography, but it's one that, after years of teaching and writing, I have found works very well.

The study of photography covers two major domains: craft, which is the study of the mechanics of making a good image (or to put it in simpler terms: the button pushing) and artistry, which encompasses the study of recognizing and understanding what makes a good image. In this book, we're going to cover both domains.

As in any discipline, craft and art inform each other. When you have more sophisticated craft skills, your artistic eye will change, and you will begin to recognize more potential images. Similarly, as your artistic side becomes more developed, you will come to understand the relevance and importance of more areas of photographic craft.

While some people have a predisposition to both the art and craft side of photography, both domains are simply skills that can be learned by anybody. Sometimes, people resist the idea that "art" is simply a skill that can be learned, but I believe it is. Some people seem more "artistic" because they simply have an innate understanding of certain processes, which the rest of us have to learn. The most important thing to understand is that both domains require practice. Lots of practice. This is a theme that I will harp on throughout this book, and at various places I will encourage you to go out and practice particular things.

Because this book is intended for shooters of many skill levels, the next chapter is going to begin with a very basic study of the craft. If you're already beyond this level, give it a quick skim and feel free to move on. The goal in the next couple of chapters is to get the basic skills down that will be required for more advanced work in the rest of the book.

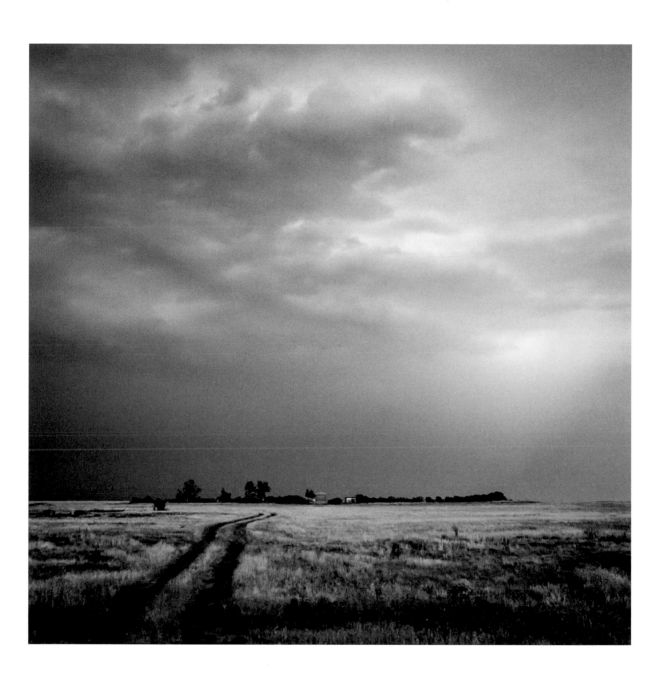

2

GETTING TO KNOW YOUR CAMERA

Using Auto Mode for Snapshot Shooting

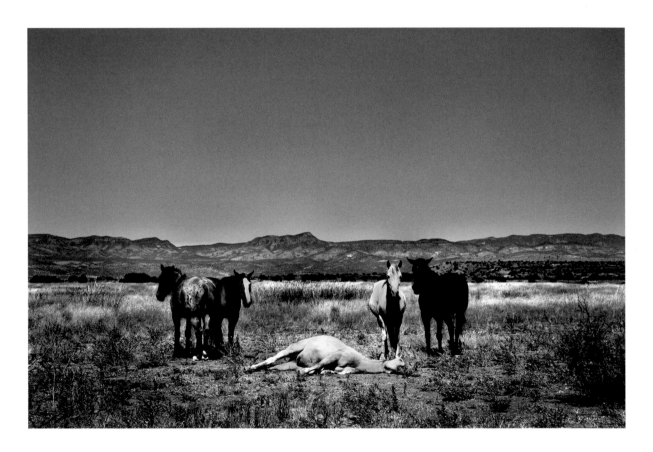

Twenty or so years ago, if you had gone camera shopping, you would have been able to buy an all-manual camera for a fairly reasonable amount of money. If you wanted to add a bunch of automatic features, though, you would have expected to pay a lot more.

Things are very different today. Now, for a very reasonable amount of money, you can get an all-automatic camera with far more automation than any camera of 20 years ago. But if you want to start adding manual features, you'll have to pay a lot more.

Whether you work with an inexpensive point-and-shoot or an expensive SLR, your camera will have a fully automatic mode. In this mode, it will make all of the critical decisions required to take a good photo. It will focus, select exposure settings, calculate correct color, and make many other important decisions.

Auto mode can't compose your shot for you, of course, and there's no guarantee that it will always make the best decision, creatively, but in general, auto modes on cameras today are *extremely* capable, and will almost always make very good—and often the best—decisions.

Because auto modes do such a good job, they provide an excellent way to practice some fundamental skills. With them, you can start shooting right away and then activate more advanced features later. In this chapter, we're going to take advantage of auto mode so that you can begin practicing shooting right now. Along the way, you're going to get an introduction to some fundamental photographic concepts. We'll build on these core skills throughout the rest of the book. If you're a more advanced user, there may not be anything new for you in this chapter, but give it a skim anyway. If it seems way below your skill level, don't worry, we'll soon be moving on to more advanced topics.

Camera Basics

Before we get shooting, it's important that you know some fundamental things about your camera. You've probably dealt with all of these already, but just to be sure we're on the same page, let's work through some basic camera anatomy.

All cameras are different, so I can't speak to the specifics of your particular model, but if you have your camera manual in hand, you should be able to follow along with this section and figure out the equivalent controls on your camera. You'll also learn some terms here that we'll be using throughout the rest of this book.

Point-and-Shoot or SLR

The digital camera market is divided into two major categories: point-and-shoot cameras and single lens reflex, or SLR cameras. While both types share many features, and both are capable of producing great images, they vary significantly in their capabilities and the way you use them.

Point-and-Shoots

The term *point-and-shoot* covers a huge range of sizes, body designs, and capabilities. While some people think point-and-shoot implies "lower quality" or "underfeatured," this isn't necessarily true, so don't be prejudiced by this term. These days, point-and-shoot digital cameras can have pro-quality lenses, possess extensive feature sets, and produce excellent images.

Point-and-shoot cameras come in a huge range of sizes and designs, but if you have one, it probably looks something like one of the cameras shown in Figure 2.1.

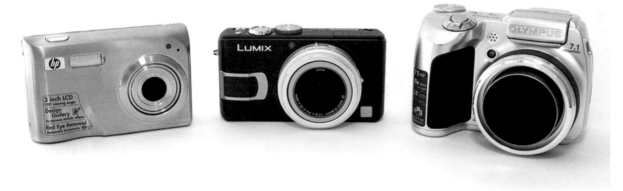

Figure 2.1   Point-and-shoot cameras run the gamut from tiny, easily pocketable cameras to larger units with longer lenses, more controls, and advanced features.

With a point-and-shoot camera, you usually use the LCD screen on the back of the camera as your viewfinder. With it, you can frame your shot and check the camera's current status. Menu settings and other control readouts are also displayed on the LCD. Some point-and-shoot cameras also include an *optical viewfinder,* which is a small window you can look through to frame your shot.

Your point-and-shoot probably also has a built-in flash, and depending on how sophisticated it is, it might have any number of additional buttons and controls. We'll discuss these in more detail later.

Point-and-shoot cameras with optical viewfinders have two lenses. Your viewfinder looks through one, while the other is used to focus light onto the image sensor (Figure 2.2).

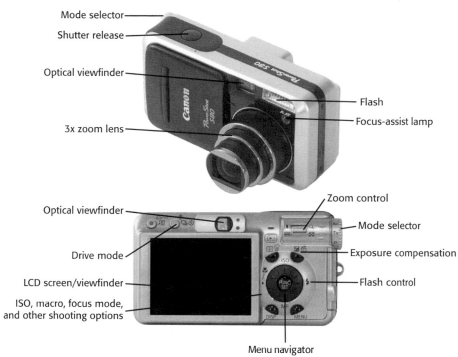

Mode selector
Shutter release
Optical viewfinder
3x zoom lens

Flash
Focus-assist lamp

Optical viewfinder
Drive mode
LCD screen/viewfinder
ISO, macro, focus mode, and other shooting options

Zoom control
Mode selector
Exposure compensation
Flash control

Menu navigator

Figure 2.2

On a point-and-shoot camera with an optical viewfinder, you look through one lens, but the camera's image sensor looks through a second lens. On an SLR, you look through the same lens that the image sensor uses.

Cell Phone Cameras

A few years ago, if you had told me I would be covering cell phone cameras in this book I would have laughed at you. But many cell phone cameras now deliver image quality far beyond what was available in point-and-shoots (and SLRs!) from years gone by. While not all cell phones pack good cameras, there are now plenty of smart phones that do, and much of what is covered in this book is directly applicable to those devices. At the time of this writing, cell phone cameras offer features and image quality that put them squarely in the realm of "mid-range point-and-shoot cameras."

SLR

SLR, or *single lens reflex*, means that your camera's viewfinder looks through the same lens that is used to focus light onto the image sensor inside the camera body (see Figure 2.3). The advantage of an SLR viewfinder is that it shows a much more accurate framing than the viewfinder on a typical point-and-shoot camera, and it shows the effects of any filters or lens attachments that you might have added.

Similar to a point-and-shoot, many SLRs allow you to use their LCD screens as a viewfinder; however, the optical viewfinder on an SLR will always be much brighter and clearer than what you see on an LCD screen on any camera.

Almost all digital SLRs use removable lenses, meaning you can change to a different type of lens at any time. In addition, you can add specialty lenses, such as tilt-and-shift lenses for architectural photography or telescope mounts for astronomical photography. The option to change lenses also means that you can improve image quality by investing in better (and usually more expensive) lenses.

SLRs also offer other more professional features than their point-and-shoot counterparts, such as more sophisticated focus mechanisms, faster performance, the ability to shoot raw format, advanced external flash systems, body designs tailored to rugged environments, and more (see Figure 2.3).

Both of these camera types have their advantages and disadvantages, and I'm not trying to argue that you should use one over another. Rather, at this point you should simply identify which type of camera you have and understand the terms that are mentioned here.

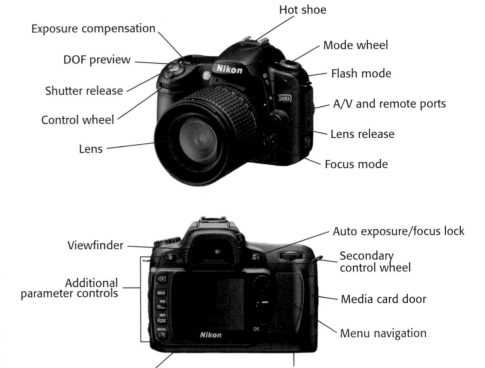

Figure 2.3

Most SLRs feature a design similar to this Nikon camera and variations of these controls. On some cameras, some of these features are accessible through dedicated buttons, while on other cameras, these features are controlled via menu options.

Mirrorless Cameras

Sitting between SLRs and point-and-shoots is a category of camera that has many of the quality and usability advantages of an SLR, but is closer to the size of a point-and-shoot. Similar to an SLR, *mirrorless cameras* have removable lenses and larger image sensors, as well as high-end features such as full manual controls. But mirrorless cameras are smaller than even the tiniest SLR, making them much easier to tote around (see Figure 2.4).

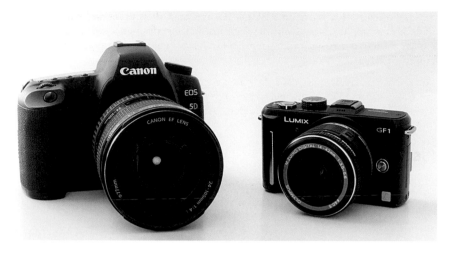

Figure 2.4

Micro Four Thirds cameras, such as the Panasonic GF1 on the right, are just one type of a category of camera that offers removable lenses and excellent image quality in a far smaller package than a typical SLR.

The dominant mirrorless cameras at the time of this writing conform to the Micro Four Thirds specification. Olympus and Panasonic both make Micro Four Thirds cameras; however, Nikon and Fuji are also making their own mirrorless cameras, which use a different lens mount than Micro Four Thirds.

Compared to a point-and-shoot, a mirrorless camera offers better image quality and more control. However, note that unlike an SLR, it won't offer optical viewfinders—only electronic LCD viewfinders.

Compact Interchangeable Lens Cameras

The camera industry has struggled with what to call this category of camera. At the time of the last edition of this book, compact interchangeable lens cameras, or CILC, was the name that was gaining traction. While you'll still occasionally see that term, most people now refer to these cameras simply as mirrorless. Technically, point-and-shoots are also mirrorless, of course.

Battery, Media Card, Power Switch

Your camera requires a battery to operate, and you should know how to install and remove the battery, as well as how to charge it.

A media card is also required by your camera. This is a small memory chip that your camera uses to store images while you're shooting. You need to know how to insert and remove the media card.

Finally, your camera should have a power switch on it somewhere, which you use—obviously—to turn the camera on and off.

These are all covered in your camera's owner's manual, and if you have any doubt or confusion about any of these controls, check out your manual now.

Don't Drop That Camera!

Your camera probably also came with a shoulder or wrist strap, along with instructions on how to attach it to your camera. Take my advice and install the strap! Dropping is not good for any camera (and hitting the ground is even worse), and a strap is the easiest way to prevent a potentially damaging camera drop.

Shooting in Auto Mode

Unless it's an older, extremely simple model, your camera will have a mechanism for choosing a *shooting mode*. The shooting mode you choose determines which decisions the camera will make and which decisions will be left up to you.

In Auto mode, the camera will make most, if not all, decisions. On all cameras, Auto mode will determine the essential exposure settings, as well as many other important parameters, such as whether the flash should fire. Some cameras will even automatically detect if you need to be in a different mode, for example, if your subject is smiling, if the camera is shaking, and more.

To shoot in Auto mode, follow these steps.

Setting Your Camera to Auto Mode

If you don't already know how to change the shooting mode on your camera, find the control now. On some cameras, it will be a physical dial on the camera body. On other cameras, particularly small cameras that don't have room for a lot of physical controls, it might be an option that you configure using a menu (see Figure 2.5).

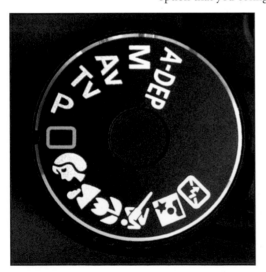
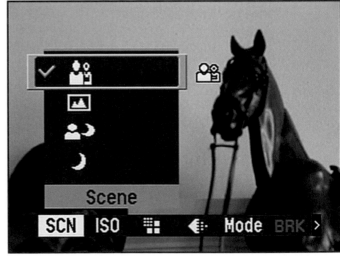

Figure 2.5 Some cameras have physical dials that let you select different shooting modes; others require a trip into the camera's menu system to change modes.

Consult your camera's manual if you can't find the mode control. Look for "shooting mode," "mode," "Auto mode," or a similar term. If you still can't find it, and you're working with an inexpensive point-and-shoot camera, then your camera may not have a shooting mode control. Rather, it might simply be in Auto mode all the time. Most automatic modes are named some variation of *Auto*.

Canon Auto Mode

Most Canon SLRs use an icon of a green box to indicate Auto mode.

If you're working with an SLR, then you'll need to check one more setting. SLR lenses can be set to either auto or manual focus, usually using a switch on the lens. If your lens has such a switch, make sure that it's set to autofocus, which is usually designated A (see Figure 2.6).

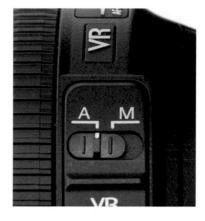

Figure 2.6 If you're using an SLR, your lens should have a switch on it somewhere that lets you change the lens from autofocus to manual focus. Make sure that it's set to autofocus, which is usually designated "A" or "AF."

Smart Phone Camera Modes

The camera apps on most smart phones do not have modes—they simply work in Auto mode all the time. Some third-party apps might provide special scene modes that apply post-processing effects to your images, but these will still be full auto exposure modes.

Framing Your Shot

You probably already know this step: look through the viewfinder and frame your shot. If your camera has a zoom lens, then you can zoom to frame tighter or wider. Don't worry too much right now about composition, as we'll discuss composition in detail in Chapter 9, "Finding and Composing a Photo."

Focal Length

If you wear glasses, then you already know that as your eyes get worse, you have to get thicker glasses because a thicker lens provides more magnification. Camera lenses work the same way. The longer the lens, the more magnification it provides.

With camera lenses, the length of the lens is measured in millimeters, and is referred to as the *focal length* of the lens. A longer focal length means a more telephoto lens, which means more magnification and less field of view. So a 200mm lens provides a greater telephoto capacity than a 50mm lens (see Figure 2.7).

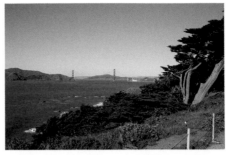

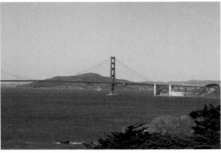
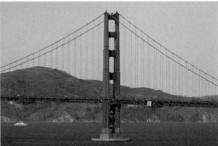

Magnification also affects the field of view of a lens. A lens with more magnification yields an image with a narrower field of view. You can see this in Figure 2.7. At 300mm, we see a fairly narrow field of view, encompassing just one tower of the bridge. At the much shorter 24mm focal length, we see a tremendously wide field of view, which encompasses the entire bridge and much of the surrounding countryside and water.

How to Press the Shutter Button

After you frame your shot, you're ready to take the picture. Pressing the shutter button may seem very simple, but proper use of the shutter button is a critical process to understand because it's how you control your camera's autofocus and metering features.

With your shot framed, press the shutter button down *halfway*. You should feel a halfway point, where the shutter button kind of stops. With a half-press of the shutter button, the camera's autofocus mechanism will analyze your scene to try to determine what the subject is. It will then lock focus on that subject.

Once it locks focus, a few things may happen, depending on your camera. Autofocus systems typically have different points in the frame that they can focus on, and many viewfinders show you the actual points. Once the camera has picked a point, the camera will usually highlight its choice. In an SLR, you'll see this in the viewfinder, while with a point-and-shoot camera, you'll usually only see this in the LCD viewfinder. (You won't see it in the optical viewfinder, if your point-and-shoot camera has one.)

Some cameras only have one focus point, usually in the center of the frame. But these days, most cameras have multiple focus points. This allows the autofocus system to accommodate more complex compositions, such as a person standing to the side of the frame.

A lens is focused to a specific distance, so everything in the scene at that distance will be in focus. (As you'll see later, objects closer or farther than that distance might also be in focus, depending on your camera's aperture setting.) Your scene might include several potential subjects that are all positioned at the same distance. If this is the case, then the camera might light up focus points on each of those subjects. It's telling you that they will all be in focus because they are all at the same distance. As long as one of these points is on the subject you want, then your camera has focused correctly (see Figure 2.8).

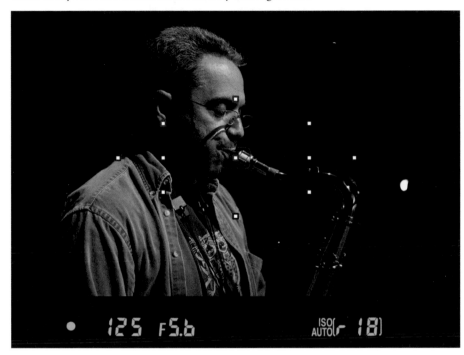

Figure 2.8

When you half-press the shutter button to autofocus, your camera will let you know when it has locked focus. Here, focus points are lighting up red in the viewfinder to indicate where the camera has decided to focus.

After the camera has focused, it will probably also beep, and will possibly show a "go" indicator of some kind, which is usually a green light in the viewfinder or on the LCD display. At this point, you can press the shutter button the rest of the way to take the shot.

It is *crucial* that you use this "half-press, wait, full-press" process when using an autofocus camera. If you wait until the precise moment when you want to take the shot, and then mash the button down all the way, you'll most likely miss the moment you were hoping to capture, because the camera will have to focus, meter, and perform a bunch of other calculations before it can fire. All of these processes take time, so it's essential that you engage in the pre-focus step of pushing the shutter button down halfway to give the camera time to take its measurements.

Easy Does It with the Shutter Button

When the camera has indicated that it has locked focus, and you're ready to press the shutter button all the way, gently squeeze the button. If you jab at it, you might jar the camera and end up shaking it enough to soften the image.

After you take the shot, your camera will display the resulting image on its LCD screen, allowing you to review it. Many cameras also give you the option of deleting the image during this review, by simply pressing the delete button.

Managing Flash in Auto Mode

As mentioned earlier, in Auto mode your camera will most likely automatically decide when to fire the flash. If it analyzes the scene and decides that it would benefit from some additional illumination, then it will fire the flash. There will be times when using a flash is inappropriate—say at a performance or in front of a glass window. However, if Auto mode has decided to use the flash, it can be stubborn about giving up on the idea.

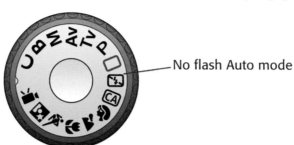

No flash Auto mode

Figure 2.9

This mode provides all of the features of Auto mode without any flash. It's ideal when you want the ease of Auto mode, but are shooting in a location where flash isn't appropriate.

Your camera might have a special "no-flash" Auto mode that gives you all of the features of Auto mode except for automatic flash selection. To select it, you might have something like the mode shown in Figure 2.9.

Similarly, on a point-and-shoot camera, you might be able to activate a special flash cancel mode. You usually reach this by pressing the flash button (the one with the lightning bolt on it) until your LCD screen displays that same lightning bolt with a circle and a line through it.

If you're working with an SLR that *doesn't* have a no-flash Auto mode, then you'll need to follow this procedure for canceling the flash:

1. Half-press the shutter button to meter and focus. If the camera thinks flash is necessary, it will pop up the flash.

2. While still holding the shutter button down halfway, push the flash back down to close it.

3. Now press the shutter button the rest of the way to take your shot.

Finally, if none of these methods seem to work for you, check your camera's manual for details on how to deactivate or cancel the flash. As you'll see later, there are other modes that still give you a lot of automatic features, but also provide control of the flash.

Using Auto Mode in Low Light

In a low-light situation, you might see some strange flashes coming from the camera's built-in flash or even a bright light shining into your scene from a lamp on the front of the camera. Like your eye, your camera's autofocus system needs a certain amount of light before it can "see" well enough to focus. Therefore, in low-light situations, many cameras employ their built-in flash or a built-in "focus-assist light" to brighten up the scene so that the autofocus mechanism can work.

If, after you half-press the shutter button, your camera *doesn't* beep or indicate that the focus has been locked, then the scene might be too dark for the camera to achieve focus, or your camera might be confused by the composition. Release the shutter button, try a slight reframing, and then half-press again.

Reset Your Camera

If you don't hear a beep when the camera autofocuses, or if you don't see an image review after you take a shot, there's a chance that these features on your camera have been disabled or altered. Consult your manual for how to re-enable them. Your camera might also have a reset feature, which will restore all settings to their factory defaults. After a reset, you can slowly customize the camera as you learn about different features.

Adjusting the Focus of the Viewfinder

If you have an SLR, or a point-and-shoot camera with an optical viewfinder, and you find that the image still looks fuzzy after the camera has locked focus, then there's a chance that the *diopter* control on your viewfinder needs adjustment. The diopter is usually a small knob next to the viewfinder (see Figure 2.10). As you turn it, you should see the image get sharper or softer. If you wear glasses, you can remove your glasses and adjust the diopter to compensate, providing you with a way of shooting, glasses-free. Note that if your eyes are bad enough, the diopter may not be able to compensate.

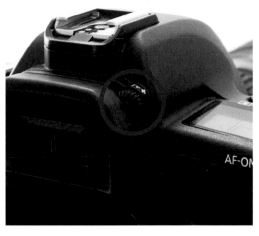

Figure 2.10

A diopter wheel lets you adjust your optical viewfinder to compensate for your own vision.

Practice Shots

What we've covered here are the basics of shooting: compose, half-press the shutter to focus, and then squeeze to shoot. This is the process that you'll use no matter what shooting mode you're working in.

Spend some time shooting in Auto mode to get a feel for the shutter and basic camera controls.

Shutter Speed and Status

Exposure is a topic we'll be covering and discussing in great detail throughout this book. At the simplest level, exposure is simply a measure of how much light the image sensor in your camera is exposed to during the shot. If there's too much light, then your image will be too bright, and many details will be washed out to complete white. If there's not enough light, then your image will be too dark, and many details will be lost in dark shadows (see Figure 2.11). Your camera provides three different mechanisms for controlling exposure: shutter speed, aperture, and ISO. In addition to controlling how bright or dark your image is, these mechanisms also provide you with some creative options. Throughout the rest of this book, you'll learn the details of these mechanisms and creative options, but for right now, your goal is to develop an important habit.

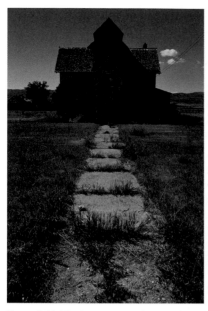
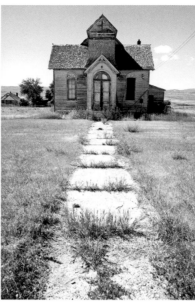
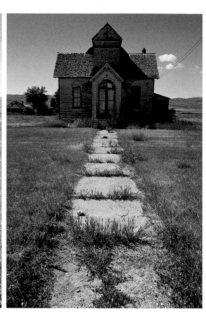

Figure 2.11 The first image is underexposed. It's too dark, and details in the shadow areas have gone to black. The second image has the opposite problem. It's overexposed, and it is so bright that the highlight areas have gone to white. The third image has a good, overall brightness level—both the shadows and highlights are preserved.

The shutter in your camera is a little curtain that sits in front of the image sensor. It opens and closes very quickly to control how much light passes through to the sensor. *Shutter speed* is a measure of how many seconds the shutter stays open. When the shutter is open longer, more light passes through, and your image gets brighter. But if the shutter is open long enough, moving objects in your image will get blurrier. In addition, with a longer shutter speed, any motion of the camera will result in a soft or outright blurry image. In other words, if your hands are a little shaky, your image could end up soft if your shutter speed is too slow (see Figure 2.12).

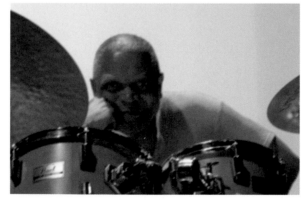

Figure 2.12

This image is a little soft because this venue was dark enough that the camera selected a slower shutter speed. The shutter speed was slow enough that the natural shakiness of my hands blurred the image.

Typically, a scene in bright sunlight, shot with a fairly typical lens, will require a shutter speed around 1/60th of a second. Shutter speeds can range tremendously, from 1/8000th of a second to whole minutes or even hours.

Reading Shutter Speed

As you learned in the last section, when you half-press the shutter button, your camera uses its autofocus mechanism to choose and focus on a subject in your scene. It also selects exposure settings: shutter speed, aperture, and ISO. When it beeps to indicate focus lock, it will also probably display its chosen shutter speed and aperture, either in the viewfinder or on the camera's LCD screen.

Shutter Speed Display

Some older, very simple point-and-shoots won't display shutter speed and aperture. These days, though, most cameras do.

Some cameras have two LCD screens, the large screen used for image playback and composition, and a smaller screen that is dedicated to showing camera status. SLRs typically show chosen exposure settings both in the viewfinder and on one of these LCD screens. Point-and-shoot cameras normally only show exposure settings on the LCD viewfinder screen.

Shutter speed and aperture are usually listed side-by-side with shutter speed appearing first. Because shutter speeds are almost always fractional—1/100th of a second, for example—some shutter speed displays only show the denominator of the fraction. So, if your camera has chosen a shutter speed of 1/125th of a second, your camera might show a shutter speed readout of 125 (see Figure 2.13).

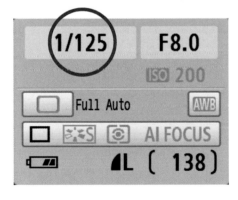
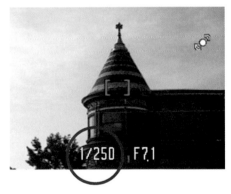
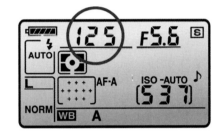

Figure 2.13

Your camera might display exposure information in one or more different ways. Clockwise from upper left, you can see the readout in a typical SLR viewfinder, the readout on a dedicated status screen, the readout from the status presented on a rear LCD screen, and the status shown on a typical point-and-shoot LCD viewfinder. Note that sometimes shutter speed is shown as a denominator only.

Find the shutter speed display on your camera and then try this exercise:

1. Point the camera at a window or bright light and press the shutter button halfway down to lock focus and calculate an exposure. The camera should display its chosen shutter speed and aperture on one of its displays.

2. Now release the shutter and point the camera at a darker subject—a shadow under a table, for example. Then press the shutter button halfway down. You should now see a slower shutter speed. Because the darker scene requires more light, the camera has chosen a longer shutter speed. Remember, a longer shutter speed allows more light.

The habit that you need to develop right now is to always pay attention to that shutter speed number when you're shooting, because if the number goes too low, there's a chance your image will be soft or blurry.

Every time you half-press the shutter button, take note of the shutter speed that the camera has chosen. In Chapter 7, "Program Mode," we'll learn how to calculate the lowest shutter speed that you can use in a given situation. For now, just assume that if the shutter speed drops below 1/60th of a second, there's a chance that your image will be soft due to camera shake.

I've often had beginning students say "This picture is out of focus, why isn't my camera working?" when in fact the image *was* properly focused, but the shutter speed was slow enough that handheld shaking rendered the image soft. There *are* things you can do when shutter speed goes too slow for sharp shooting. For now, your goal is to get in the habit of always knowing at what shutter speed you're shooting.

Check Once in Non-Changing Light

In general, if the light in your scene stays the same, your shutter speed probably won't change from shot to shot. So, if you're trying to shoot quickly in a situation where the light's not changing—a sporting event, for example—then you probably only need to check shutter speed when you start shooting. After you've determined it's acceptable, you can simply keep shooting with only an occasional check-in.

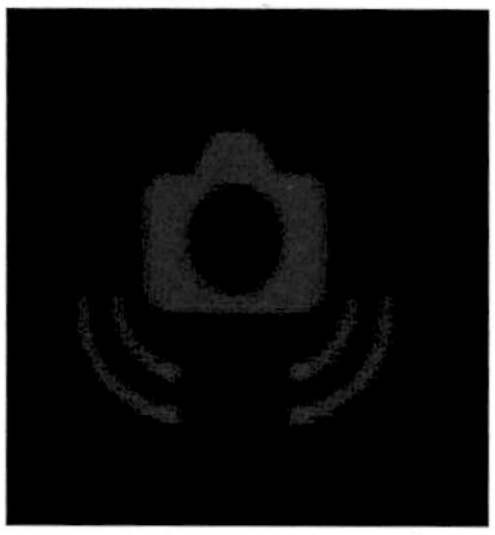

Figure 2.14

On some cameras, when the camera is forced to a shutter speed that's not fast enough for stable handheld shooting, a shake warning of some kind will appear on the LCD screen.

When Shutter Speed Can't Go Low Enough

If the light is such that your camera can't get a shutter speed that it thinks is fast enough to ensure a good handheld shot, then it might flash some kind of "shaky camera" indicator in the viewfinder (see Figure 2.14). Or it might flash the shutter speed or aperture readout to indicate that the current image will be over- or underexposed.

Playing Back Your Images

As you've already seen, your camera gives you a brief review after you shoot an image. Your camera might even provide settings that allow you to shorten or extend this review time. But when you're ready for a serious review of your images, you'll want to use your camera's playback function.

Your camera should have a play control that switches the camera into Playback mode for reviewing your images. On some cameras, Playback is a mode, just like Auto mode, and is selected using the same mode control that you use to select Auto mode.

Once you're in Playback mode, you should be able to navigate through your images. You might also be able to zoom into your images and pan about them or zoom out to view multiple images as thumbnails (see Figure 2.15). Finally, you should also be able to delete images that you don't want. Some cameras also let you lock images to prevent accidental deleting. Consult your camera manual to learn more about these features.

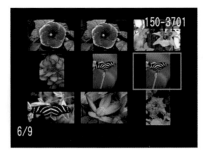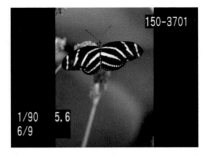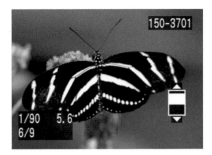

Figure 2.15 The Playback modes on many cameras let you zoom out to see thumbnail views of all of the images on a card or zoom in and pan to see a close-up view of an individual image.

Your camera might also display data about the images you've shot (Figure 2.16). In addition to the image number, your camera might show other data, such as the image quality setting and the shutter speed and aperture. If you review an image and see that it looks kind of soft, you can check the shutter speed to see if that might have been the problem.

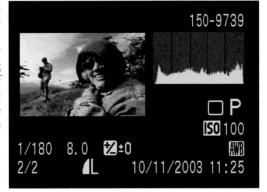

Figure 2.16

Many cameras also let you view a data display that shows data about an image, including exposure and shooting parameters, and an important aid called the *histogram*.

Leaving Playback Mode

On many cameras, you can leave Playback mode and return to shooting mode simply by giving the shutter button a half-press. This means that you can switch back to shooting quickly after reviewing shots. If your camera requires you to change a mode dial or other control to return to shooting, it will be harder to switch quickly between playback and shooting. This is something to consider when shopping for a camera.

Touch Screen Playback Controls

Many cameras these days, including some SLRs, provide touch screens. In addition to letting you control many shooting functions via the touch screen, these cameras also usually provide playback controls that are very similar to what you'll find on a smartphone or tablet. For example, you can usually swipe left and right on the screen to navigate images and pinch to zoom in and out. Unfortunately, these cameras often don't provide any kind of on-screen indication that such features are available, so you'll need to check your camera manual or simply experiment to learn all of the touch-screen playback features on your specific model.

Using Scene Modes

Auto mode can do a very good job of making critical decisions for you. In fact, for 80–90 percent of the images you take, Auto mode will probably be all that you need.

However, Auto mode knows nothing about the subject matter in your scene. Consequently, it's incapable of making any kind of creative decisions or even of knowing when it might need to bias its decision-making to be able to capture, say, a fast-moving object.

Many cameras, therefore, have additional Auto modes called *Scene modes*. These special shooting modes automatically bias certain decisions to be more appropriate to specific types of subject matter.

For example, a Sports mode will err on the side of faster shutter speeds, to better freeze fast-moving action.

Scene modes are typically accessed using the same control that you used to select Auto (see Figure 2.17).

Figure 2.17

If your camera has a mode dial, then it might have options for Scene modes, which bias the camera's decisions so that it calculates more appropriate exposures for specific shooting situations.

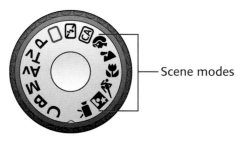

Scene modes

Different cameras provide different assortments of scene modes, but most cameras typically have at least these modes:

◆ **Portrait mode.** Very often, when shooting a portrait, you want to blur out the background, to bring more attention to the foreground. In Portrait mode, the camera will choose exposure settings that will help soften the background (refer to Figure 2.18).

◆ **Landscape mode.** This is typically the opposite of portrait. When shooting a landscape, you want to ensure that everything in the scene is in focus. This mode will choose settings that will ensure that objects both near and far are in focus.

◆ **Close-up mode.** This mode is used for shooting small objects, flowers, or close-ups of products. Close-up mode selects specific focusing modes and exposure options.

◆ **Sand and Snow mode.** If you're shooting a scene that includes lots of white, such as a beach or snow-covered field, then this mode can help ensure that the whites in the scene actually appear white.

Figure 2.18

In the upper image, everything in the scene is in focus. In the lower image, the camera was switched to Portrait mode, which chose exposure settings that caused the background to blur out. The result is a subject who commands more attention.

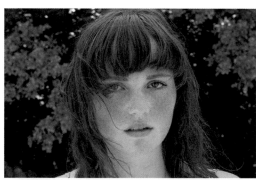

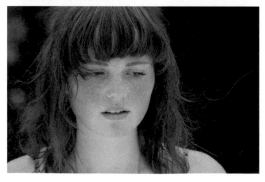

◆ **Sports mode.** As mentioned earlier, Sports mode will bias toward fast, motion-stopping shutter speeds. On some cameras, Sports mode will also engage a *servo autofocus*, which can track a moving subject to ensure that it's always in focus, and Burst mode so that you can simply hold down the button to shoot multiple shots.

◆ **Night Portrait mode.** The flash on your camera has a limited range—and on a small camera, a *very* limited range. If you're shooting in very low light with your flash, the flash will *only* illuminate subjects within its range. Everything else in the frame will be dark. Night Portrait mode causes the camera to fire the flash but also use a slow shutter speed to expose elements properly that are outside of the flash range (see Figures 2.19 and 2.20).

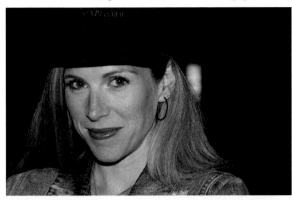

Figure 2.19

If you take a flash picture at night, you'll usually end up with a well-exposed subject on a background that is completely black. On most cameras, the range of the flash is only around 10 feet. Objects beyond that distance will not be illuminated by the flash.

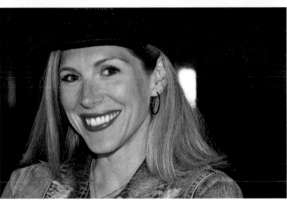

Figure 2.20

Night Portrait mode combines the flash with a longer shutter speed so that both your subject and background are well exposed.

Tell Your Night Portrait Subjects to Hold Still!

Because Night Portrait modes use a slow shutter speed, it's important to tell your subjects to stay still after the flash has fired. Ask them not to move until you say it's okay.

Learn This Feature!

If your camera has a Night Portrait mode (or an equivalent), you'll probably find it to be one of the most useful features on your camera. If your camera doesn't have a specific Night Portrait mode, don't worry, because you can probably achieve the same result through manual control.

Your camera might have all, some, or none of these Scene modes, or additional modes not mentioned here. Since most smaller point-and-shoot cameras lack manual features, they often come with a *huge* assortment of Scene modes, usually accessed from a menu of some kind (see Figure 2.21). These modes will cover everything from low light to different lighting types, and on and on. Consult your camera manual for details on how to access Scene modes and what they do.

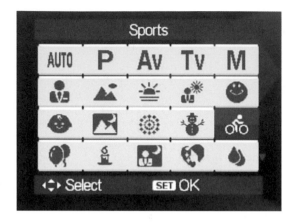

Figure 2.21

Many point-and-shoot cameras are loaded with Scene modes, tailored to very specific situations. On smaller cameras, this is often the only manual control that you have. Note that some cameras lump Scene modes and shooting modes together, as in this case, where Program and Priority modes are alongside specialized Scene modes.

Not All Features Will Be Available

When you shoot in Auto mode or a Scene mode, some features of your camera will be locked out. For example, in Auto mode, you probably won't be allowed to change white balance or ISO. If you find a feature you can't use, this means that you'll need to change to a different mode. For now, though, stick with Auto and Scene modes. We'll cover all of the other modes and controls as we work forward.

Snapshot Tips

One of the best things about Auto mode is that since it takes care of the technical burden of shooting, you can focus on handling the camera and composing shots. Here are some quick tips for improving your shots.

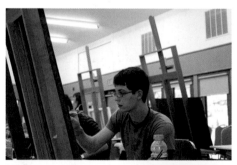

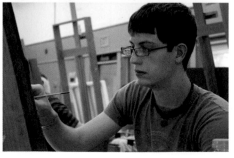

Figure 2.22

Don't waste space in the frame! Try to put only the things that matter in your shot. This image works much better without all that extra, empty headroom.

Pay Attention to Headroom—Fill the Frame

When shooting a portrait or a candid snapshot of someone, you usually don't need a lot of headroom, unless you want to show something specific above your subject's head.

For example, in this image, the extra headroom doesn't add anything to the picture. In fact, it's kind of distracting, and takes up space that could be used to show a larger image of the person (see Figure 2.22).

A better approach is to fill the frame with more of the person. You can see a better view of them, and you still have enough background to get an idea of their environment. Most importantly, you have no trouble identifying the subject of the image. By getting in tighter, you're focusing the viewer's attention.

"Fill the frame" is one of the most important compositional rules you can learn. Don't waste space in the frame. Empty space in your image is space that could be used to get a better view of your subject.

Don't Be Afraid to Get in Close

You don't have to show a person's entire face or head. Don't be afraid to crop the person and get in close for a very personal shot (see Figure 2.23).

You can get close by either standing physically close to the person or by standing farther away and zooming in. However, as you'll see later, these two options produce very different images, so you'll want to think about which approach is right for your subject.

A general rule when cropping a person is not to crop them at a joint. Rather than cropping them at the knees, crop them mid-thigh or mid-shin. Elbows, wrists, waist, and especially ankles follow the same rule.

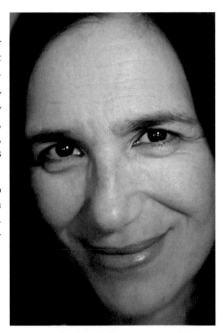

Figure 2.23

When shooting portraits, don't be afraid to get in close. You don't have to show a person's whole head. It's fine to crop.

Lead Your Subject

When shooting a portrait of someone who is looking off frame, consider leading the subject, as shown in Figure 2.24. When someone's looking out of the frame, we're more interested in the space that's in front of him than the space that's behind him. Even if we can't see what it is he is looking at, we still want to feel extra space that sits in the direction he is looking.

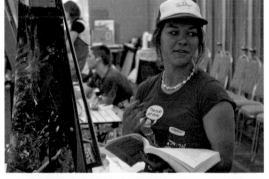

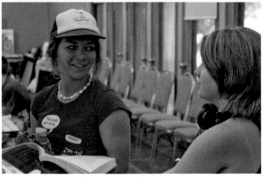

Figure 2.24

When shooting someone looking off frame, "lead" the person by placing some space in front of her.

Remember: Your Knees Can Bend

It's easy to forget about that third dimension that you can move in, so you might end up shooting all of your shots while standing up. But often, the best perspective is down low. Don't forget that you can bend your knees (or even lie on the ground) to get a different angle. Getting down low is especially important when shooting children and animals, since it puts you at a more personable, eye-to-eye relationship with them (see Figure 2.25).

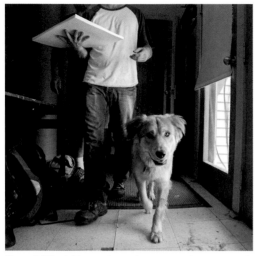
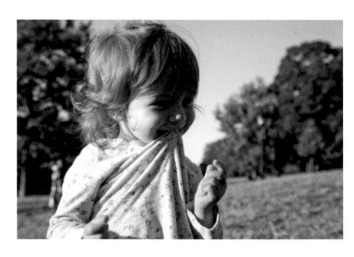

Figure 2.25 Children and animals live low to the ground. Often, the best pictures of them occur down at their altitude.

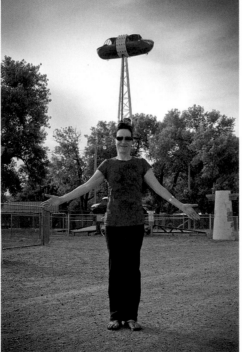

Watch the Background

Don't just pay attention to your subjects, remember that they're also standing in front of something. Make sure there's nothing "sticking out" of their heads or juxtaposed in a distracting way (see Figure 2.26).

Figure 2.26

Pay attention to the foreground/ background relationship in your scene to ensure that objects aren't juxtaposed in strange ways. One of the best ways to do this is to trace your eyes around the edge of the frame.

Watch Out for Backlighting

This tip is loosely related to the previous tip. Be careful about shooting your subject in front of a brightly lit background, such as a window or shooting into the sun. While there are times when you can use such an approach to great effect, for simple snapshots, you'll get better results by managing the backlight in your shots.

If you find yourself shooting someone in front of a window or a bright light, try to move them or yourself so that the light is not directly behind them, or try using your camera's fill flash (see Figure 2.27).

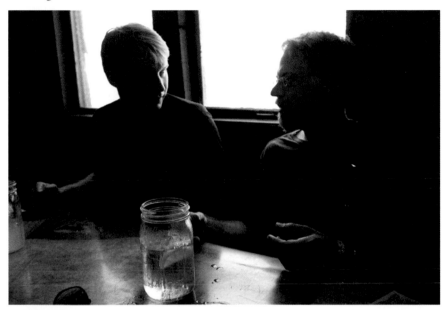

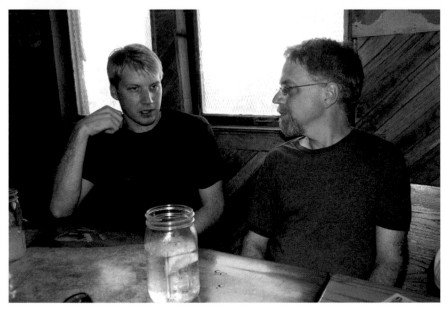

Figure 2.27

This image has a problem with backlighting, which can be corrected with the use of a flash.

The problem with bright lights in the background of a shot is that they confuse the camera's light meter. When there's a bright light in the background, the camera meters to expose that bright light properly, which usually means that the foreground is left underexposed and appears too dark.

In Auto mode, your camera might recognize such a situation and fire the flash automatically. The flash will serve to light up the foreground, creating a more even exposure with the background.

Later, you'll learn more about metering, as well as other strategies for handling backlighting. For now, even if you aren't sure exactly how to handle such a situation, at least start learning to recognize when you're shooting in this type of difficult lighting condition.

Understand Flash Range

Remember that the flash on your camera has a limited range. Anything beyond the range of the flash will not be illuminated at all. So, if you're standing at night across the street from a person or building and you shoot a picture with the flash popped up, you'll probably get a shot that's just a circle of illumination in front of you. The person and building might still be in complete darkness.

For that situation, flash is not the answer. Instead, you'll need to employ some low-light shooting strategies, which we'll discuss in Chapter 12, "Special Shooting."

Coverage

Many people think that an expert photographer sees a scene or subject, thinks about how to best frame and expose it, and then takes a picture of it. Describe this to any "experts" or "professional" photographers, and they'll probably laugh at you.

The fact is, even the most accomplished photographer rarely shoots only one exposure of a subject. Instead, photographers *work* their subject—something we'll be discussing a lot in this book.

Very often, the only way to find the best composition of a scene is to move around it. Get closer and farther, stand on your tiptoes, squat down low, and circle the scene. Look through the viewfinder through all those movements and shoot the whole time.

It's okay to review your shots and then try again. Photography is like sculpture: you can't always visualize the finished shot right away. Instead, you have to "sculpt" the scene and try different vantage points until you find an angle that makes the most interesting composition and that has the nicest play of shadow, light, and color.

It is *very* rare that, when a subject catches your eye, you just happen to be standing in the very best spot in the world (and that you also happen to be exactly the right height) to shoot the best possible image.

So, as you continue your practice, be sure to shoot broad coverage of your scene. Stay moving, play with distance and angle, and pay attention to how the relationship of the objects in your scene changes as you move around.

You may be surprised to find that the final images that you like best are very different from what you originally envisioned as the best picture.

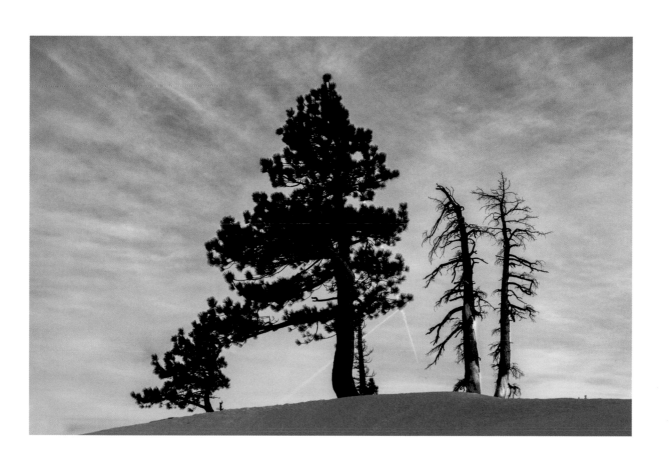

3

CAMERA ANATOMY

Holding and Controlling Your Camera

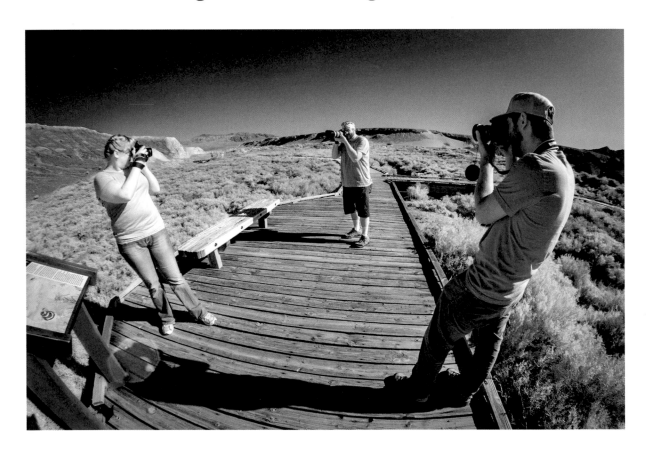

Photography is a physical act. In addition to the physical act of seeing, you have to manipulate your camera to get the framing and settings that you want. If you're in a rapidly changing situation, or if you've spotted a scene that's soon going to change, then you have to be able to make changes to your camera's settings very quickly. For these reasons, it's essential that you have a thorough familiarity and understanding of your camera's controls.

Just as artisans need to know how to coax the behavior they want from their tools, you need to understand what the different settings on your camera do and why you might want to configure them in a particular way. Just as importantly, you need to be able to make these adjustments quickly and efficiently without breaking the "flow" of your shooting.

In this chapter, we're going to build on what you learned in Chapter 2, "Getting to Know Your Camera," and take a deeper look at the handling of your camera. Along the way, you'll learn a little more about its inner workings.

Point-and-Shoots and SLRs Revisited

In the last chapter, you learned some of the very high-level differences between a point-and-shoot camera and an SLR. However, for a more useful understanding of the strengths and weaknesses of both types of cameras, we need to go a little deeper into the fundamental characteristics of both types of cameras.

A Very Fancy Box

When you strip it down to its most basic construction, a digital camera is no different than a film camera from 150 years ago, because all cameras have certain things in common. Whether it's a digital or film camera, has fully automatic controls or is completely manual, all camera designs start with a lightproof box. On one side of this box sits a lens for focusing light, and on the opposite side of the box sits the *focal plane*—the area that the lens focuses onto. The focal plane holds a light-sensitive recording medium of some kind. In a film camera, this would be a piece of film of any type. In an 18th-century camera obscura, this might have been a big piece of paper—the "photographer" would trace over the projected image to create a drawing or painting. In a digital camera, the focal plane houses a digital image sensor.

Everything else on a camera is simply there to add convenience for the photographer. Film cameras, for example, might add the capability to hold rolls of film and have a mechanism to advance the film roll to a new, unexposed area of film. This saves the photographer the trouble of hassling with changing the film every time he wants to take an image. Light meters, autofocus systems, and LCD screens—all of these items serve to make things easier for the photographer. As far as actual image capture goes, though, all you really need is a lightproof box, a recording medium, and a lens.

One Camera, Hold the Lens

Actually, you don't necessarily even need a lens. A pinhole camera simply uses a pinhole in the camera body in place of the lens. Thanks to the physics of light, this pinhole projects an inverted image onto the focal plane.

What an Image Sensor Does

An image sensor is a special type of light-sensitive silicon chip. Currently, there are two major types of image sensors available: the charge-coupled device (CCD) and the complementary metal oxide semiconductor (CMOS). When you take a picture, the light falling on the image sensor is sampled and converted into electrical signals. (For those of you who keep track of such things, the sampling rate of a sensor is basically the number of pixels on the sensor.) After the image sensor is exposed, these signals are boosted by an amplifier and sent to an analog-to-digital converter that turns the signals into digits. These numbers are then sent to an onboard computer for processing. Once the computer has calculated the final image, the new image data is stored on a memory card (see Figure 3.1).

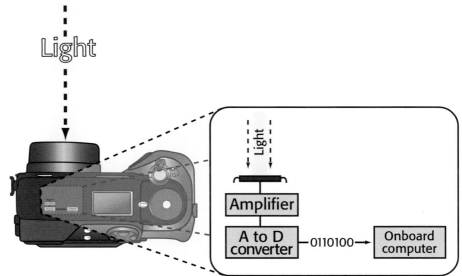

Figure 3.1

Light passes into a digital camera, just as it would in a film camera. However, instead of hitting a piece of film, it is digitized by a computer chip and passed to an onboard computer to create an image.

Later, we'll look at what the onboard computer does with the image data that it gets off the sensor.

Point-and-Shoot Design

From a camera design perspective, one of the great advantages that digital cameras have over film cameras is that digital image sensors can be made extremely small. Whereas a piece of 35mm film is 36mm wide, the image sensor in a typical point-and-shoot camera is only 5mm wide (see Figure 3.2). Thanks to this small sensor size and the fact that a digital camera doesn't need a mechanism for holding and moving film, digital cameras can be made extremely small.

No matter what their size and shape, a digital point-and-shoot camera is still built around a lightproof box with a digital image sensor on one side and a lens on the other.

As light falls on the image sensor, the camera turns it into an image and passes that image on to the LCD screen, which is why you can use the LCD screen as a viewfinder. Because it's a purely digital process to get the image to the screen—rather than having an optical process of bouncing light around inside the camera body—point-and-shoot cameras can have fairly radical designs.

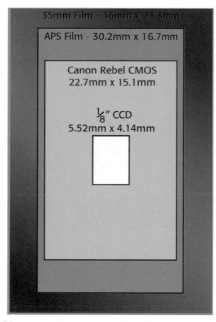

Figure 3.2

Most image sensors are very small, particularly when compared to the size of 35mm film. The 1/8" sensor size is typical of what's found in a point-and-shoot camera.

A point-and-shoot camera with an optical viewfinder uses an entirely separate lens for the viewfinder. So the main camera lens is used to expose the sensor, while the optical viewfinder looks through a second lens (see Figure 3.3).

One downside to this scheme is that, because you're not looking through the same lens that the image sensor is looking through, you're not necessarily seeing the exact image that will be recorded. If you're using lens filters or extensions—such as a telephoto or wide-angle extension—you won't be able to see the effects of these lens add-ons through your viewfinder.

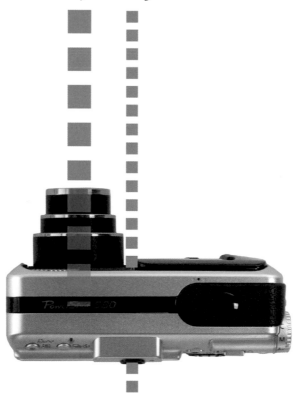

Figure 3.3

In most point-and-shoot cameras, the light passing through the camera's lens falls onto the focal plane. If the camera has an optical viewfinder, it uses a completely different light path, meaning that what you see in the viewfinder is not exactly what's landing on the image sensor.

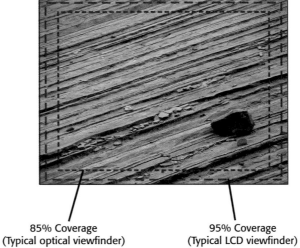

85% Coverage
(Typical optical viewfinder)

95% Coverage
(Typical LCD viewfinder)

Also, note that the optical viewfinders on most point-and-shoot cameras typically only show you around 80–85 percent of what will be in your final image. By contrast, the LCD screen shows you 98–100 percent of your composition (see Figure 3.4). What's more, the crop in the optical viewfinder might not be uniform. In other words, it won't necessarily crop out of the center of the frame.

Small size is obviously a great advantage to a point-and-shoot camera. After all, it doesn't matter how good your camera is if it's so big that you never carry it with you. A small point-and-shoot can be stuck in a pocket easily any time you head out the door, and many point-and-shoots these days yield excellent image quality and pack great lenses and features.

SLR Design

A single lens reflex camera has only a single lens, which is used both as a viewfinder and to expose the focal plane. Because you're looking through the same lens that exposes the sensor, you get a very accurate view of the image you will capture. However, in a digital camera, the image sensor sits directly behind the lens. With the image sensor there, you can't simply place a viewfinder directly behind the lens because the image sensor blocks the light path. Instead, a little bit of extra engineering is required.

If you look at the profile of your SLR, you'll see that the lens is sitting much lower than the viewfinder. If you were to saw your camera in half, down the middle, you would see that the image sensor and shutter sit directly behind the lens, and in front of the shutter, you would find a mirror set at a 45° angle. This mirror bounces the light from the lens up toward the top of the camera. There, the light enters either a prism or a complicated arrangement of mirrors, where it is redirected out through the viewfinder (see Figure 3.5).

As you might have already noticed, with the mirror sitting between the lens and the image sensor, there's no way that the sensor can see out the lens. This is what the "reflex" part of SLR is all about.

When you press the shutter button, the camera flips the mirror up so that it's completely out of the way of the image sensor. Then the shutter is opened, the sensor is exposed, the shutter closes, and the mirror falls back down. This is why the viewfinder blacks out when you take a picture—with the mirror up, the light is no longer being directed up to the viewfinder. Part of the distinctive sound of an SLR is the extra noise that is made when the mirror flips up and down.

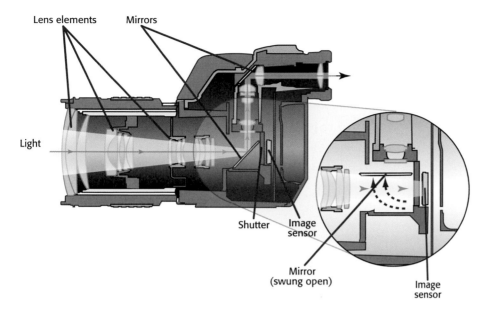

Lens elements Mirrors

Light

Shutter Image sensor

Mirror (swung open)

Image sensor

Figure 3.5

In an SLR camera, light passing through the lens is bounced off a mirror and up into the viewfinder. This through-the-lens (TTL) light path ensures that you are seeing the same thing the camera sees. When you press the shutter-release button, the mirror is flipped up so the light can pass onto the image sensor.

If you take the lens off your camera, you can see the mirror itself. It sits inside the mirror chamber (see Figure 3.6). Tilt the camera and look at the top of the mirror chamber, and you'll see where the light gets bounced up into the pentaprism.

Because they look directly through the lens, SLR viewfinders present a much brighter, clearer view than the optical viewfinders on point-and-shoot cameras, which look through separate, low-quality optics.

SLR viewfinders typically show you around 98 percent of your final image, and because you are looking through the same lens the image sensor looks through, you can see the effects of any filters or lens extensions you may have installed on your lens. SLR viewfinders usually include status displays that show exposure information and other camera settings. Because you can see your image and all your settings in the same viewfinder, you're free to concentrate on shooting.

Today, most SLRs offer the ability to use the LCD screen as a viewfinder, an option called Live View.

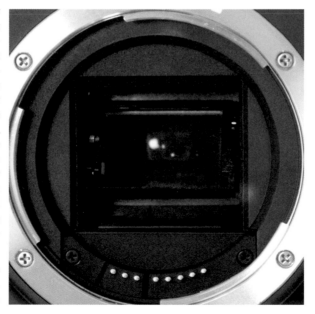

Figure 3.6

If you take the lens off your SLR, you can see the mirror sitting in the mirror chamber. Tilt the camera and look toward the top of the mirror chamber to see up into the pentaprism (or pentamirror, depending on which your camera has).

Mirrorless Cameras

Many of the mirrorless cameras discussed in Chapter 2, and some fancier point-and-shoot cameras, have an SLR appearance, but don't actually have a true single-lens reflex design. Although many of these cameras have a viewfinder positioned just like a real SLR, the viewfinder is not optical. Rather, it is an electronic viewfinder—a little LCD screen—just like you'd find on a video camcorder. Usually referred to as a *through-the-lens* or *TTL* viewfinder, these mechanisms look through the same lens that is used to expose the image sensor, and they show the same image as the LCD screen on the back of the camera. Although this is a terrific advantage over the optical viewfinder found on a typical point-and-shoot camera, an electronic viewfinder (EVF) is far inferior to a true SLR viewfinder.

Electronic TTL viewfinders lack the clarity and resolution of an SLR viewfinder, which makes manually focusing extremely difficult and can be distracting when framing. To their credit, they offer extensive feedback of the camera's current settings and, unlike an external LCD screen, can be seen in bright sunlight. In the last year, EVFs have improved remarkably and are now beginning to rival optical viewfinders in terms of clarity and sharpness. If you're considering a camera with a TTL electronic viewfinder, then you should definitely try the camera before you make your final decision.

Other Cameras with Electronic Viewfinders

There are other cameras that have electronic viewfinders similar to what you'll find in a mirrorless camera. Their viewfinders have the same issues as those described above.

Buying a Camera

If you've been looking to buy a new camera (either because you're new to photography or because you're upgrading from an older camera), then the information in this chapter and the last should help.

Camera Parts

Throughout the shooting chapters of this book, I'll be referring to specific controls that you might need to activate or modify to get particular results. Since this book can't address the interface specifics of every camera in the world, this section will teach you some broad concepts and help you find out for yourself how your camera's interface is set up. As you read the following sections, identify each of the parts and controls on your camera. It's a good idea to have your camera's manual with you through this section, and it doesn't matter if your camera is an SLR or a point-and-shoot. Spending some time at home learning the function of each button and dial on your camera and where to access specific controls will help you shoot quickly and efficiently in the field.

The Lens

It may sound a little patronizing to ask you to identify the lens on your camera, but bear with me for a moment, as there are some less obvious things that you might not know about your camera's optics. On most cameras, the lens is fairly conspicuous—it's the big round thing that sticks off the front of the camera body.

On small point-and-shoot cameras, the lens may retract into the camera body and not be visible until you activate the camera. If your camera has such an automatic mechanism, then it might have a built-in lens covering that opens and closes as the lens extends (see Figure 3.7).

It's important to understand that these automatic lens coverings can be somewhat fragile. If they get jabbed with something, such as a ball point pen that's floating loose in your camera bag, they can be damaged in a way that will prevent them from opening or closing, and possibly in a way that will keep the lens from extending and retracting. If this happens, you'll have to send the camera to a service center for repairs.

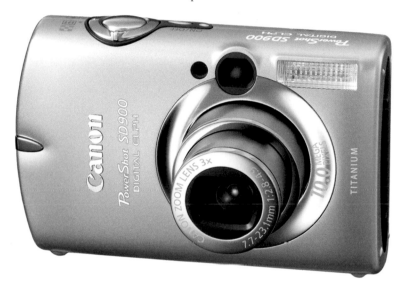

Figure 3.7

This camera has a lens that automatically retracts into the camera body when the camera is powered down. It also has a lens cap that automatically opens and closes when the lens extends and retracts.

You need to be careful with all lenses, but be especially cautious with mechanized, extensible lenses, as they can be fragile.

Some advanced point-and-shoot cameras allow you to attach optional lens accessories, such as filter holders or wide-angle and telephoto add-ons. Consult your manual for details.

Hidden Lenses

If your camera doesn't have any kind of visible lens—just an opening on the front of the camera—but it still offers a zoom feature, then most likely the lens is mounted vertically inside the camera body (see Figure 3.8). A prism or mirror is used to bounce the light that enters the lens opening down into the vertically positioned lens.

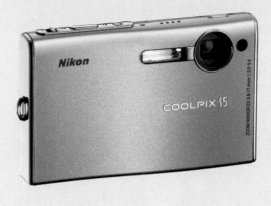

Figure 3.8

If your camera can zoom, but there's no visible lens on the outside of the camera, then most likely the lens is positioned vertically within the camera body.

Stabilization

Many lenses include image stabilization hardware. These mechanisms track the jitter you produce with your hands and automatically alter the optical properties of the lens to counteract the effects of that jitter. If you jitter to the left, the lens alters itself to bend the light passing through the lens back to the right to counteract the jitter. Image stabilization is not meant to be a substitute for a tripod. Instead, it provides enough stability to make it easier to frame a shot when using an extreme telephoto lens, and can allow you to shoot in much lower light, with slower shutter speeds, without worrying about hand shake.

If your camera has this feature, it might provide a switch on the lens for turning it on and off. (Later, we'll discuss why you might want to turn it off.) Some point-and-shoot cameras also have a stabilization feature and offer a menu control for activating and deactivating stabilization.

Note that a stabilization feature on a lens will drain your camera's battery faster. On many cameras, stabilization doesn't kick in until you half-press the shutter button, so if your battery is running low, you'll want to minimize the time you spend with the shutter button held down, or you'll want to turn off stabilization altogether. On other cameras, stabilization doesn't activate until a full shutter press, which will conserve battery. However, when shooting with a long lens, stabilization can help with framing your shot. If it doesn't activate until you fully press the shutter, then it won't offer any aid while composing.

Some higher-end lenses include two modes of stabilization. One stabilizes the lens as described here, while the second mode stabilizes only the vertical axis, enabling you to pan the camera smoothly. If you're panning with the idea of blurring out the background of a moving subject, such as a racecar, single-axis stabilization can be very handy.

With some older stabilization systems, you should deactivate the stabilizer when your camera is mounted on a tripod, as the system can be confused when you pan or tilt. Most new systems don't have this trouble, but if you're tripod-mounted, you might want to deactivate stabilization simply to save battery power. If you're shooting extremely close (macro shooting), then stabilization offers no advantage, so you might as well turn it off to save power.

Some curious stabilization trivia: When you half-press the shutter button to focus, you'll probably hear the stabilization system kick in, and you should see its effects in the viewfinder. However, what you're seeing is possibly not the full stabilization effect that your camera can muster. That doesn't kick in until you press the shutter completely, the reason being that your camera maker doesn't want you to get motion sickness.

Motion sickness occurs when the information that your eyes send to your brain conflicts with the information that your inner ear sends to your brain. So, if your ear is saying that you're moving, but your eyes are saying, "No, everything's perfectly stable," then you can end up with motion sickness. Apparently, with early stabilization systems, people felt queasy when looking through a stabilized viewfinder for a length of time.

Newer stabilization systems should be free of any nausea-inducing traits.

Stabilized Sensors

While some vendors, such as Canon and Nikon, make lenses that have built-in stabilizing mechanisms, a few vendors, such as Sony, Pentax, and Olympus, have opted to stabilize the image sensor itself. In these cameras, the sensor sits on a movable plate that can shift from side-to-side and up and down to compensate for any jitter introduced by your hand.

The advantage of a stabilized sensor is that it will work with any lens you attach to the camera. The disadvantage is that stabilization mechanisms usually need to be tweaked to work optimally with a particular lens. Consequently, you'll typically find that sensor stabilization methods don't yield as much of a stabilizing effect as stabilized lenses. In addition, with a stabilized sensor, the stabilization occurs *after* you've looked at the image, which means that a stabilized sensor offers no advantage when trying to shoot with a very long telephoto lens. A stabilized lens, on the other hand, provides a steady view while framing, which can make telephoto shooting much easier.

Digital Zoom

Most point-and-shoot cameras also include a digital zoom feature. Before we get into how a digital zoom works, you'll want to follow this simple procedure.

> **Step 1:** Turn off the digital zoom feature.

> **Step 2:** Don't ever turn it on again.

That's it! You're done and can now go on to the next section.

However, if you're curious about the digital zoom feature on your camera (which you're never going to use), here's how it works.

Obviously, the camera cannot digitally increase its focal length, so a digital zoom feature works by cropping the image and then scaling that cropped area up to the full size of the frame. The problem with most digital zooms is that they use bad interpolation algorithms when they scale up, so they tend to produce jagged, blocky images. Consequently, rather than using a digital zoom, it's much better to shoot the image with your camera's maximum optical zoom and then crop and enlarge it yourself using an image editor. Most image editors provide more sophisticated interpolation options, and since most cameras today pack huge pixel counts, you can do a lot of cropping and enlarging in your image editor.

There are four occasions when a digital zoom can prove useful:

◆ If you don't have any image editing software that is capable of cropping and upsampling.

◆ If you don't want to magnify the JPEG artifacts in your image. Because the camera enlarges your image *before* compressing, digital zooms don't worsen any JPEG artifacts. Enlarging the image in an image editor will do so.

◆ If you're shooting at one of the camera's lower resolutions, digital zoom may not degrade your image. Most of the time, when you shoot at a lower resolution, the camera simply shoots at full resolution and then downsamples. Because there's more resolution to start with, using a digital zoom on a lower-resolution image often produces fine results.

◆ If you absolutely need a close-up of something that is beyond the range of your camera's optical zoom, and you don't care about image quality.

If you must use a digital zoom feature, you ideally want to have one that offers good interpolation and provides a continuous range of zooming rather than fixed zoom ratios.

When digital zoom is active, the zoom indicator on the camera's LCD screen will be divided into separate optical and digital regions, and the camera might even pause before going into digital zoom, to prevent you from accidentally zooming digitally. In the end, it's best to just turn it off and forget about it.

SLR Lenses

If you're using an SLR, then your lens is most likely removable, usually by pressing and holding a lens release button while you twist the lens. Changing lenses in the field can require a bit of coordination as you try to hold two lenses and your camera, but a neck strap can make this much easier, because you won't have to worry about the camera falling.

Your SLR lens probably also has a focus ring, which allows you to focus the lens manually by simply turning the ring. Some cameras require you to put the lens into Manual Focus mode by flipping a manual focus switch. Others offer a manual focus override that automatically activates when you turn the focus ring.

These days, most digital SLRs come with some kind of starter lens as part of a kit. These "kit" lenses are often very capable, decent lenses that offer a good zoom range. As your photography skills improve, you might find that you want something more. One of the great advantages of an SLR is that you can choose lenses tailored to the type of shooting you like to do and to the image quality level you want. For example, if you mostly shoot sports or wildlife, you might want to get longer, more telephoto lenses, while landscape shooters might invest in lenses on the other end of the spectrum. If you plan on printing your images very large, then you might need lenses that yield excellent sharpness, because large printing often reveals image flaws caused by weak optics.

Lenses fall into two categories: zoom lenses, which allow you to vary focal length to go from wide angle to telephoto, and prime lenses, which have a fixed focal length.

Prime lenses are sometimes sharper than the same focal length in a zoom lens, but zoom lenses let you carry the equivalent of a huge number of prime lenses.

Focal Length Multipliers—35mm Equivalency

All lenses project a circular image onto the focal plane. The film or image sensor that's sitting on the focal plane records a rectangular crop from the middle of that circle. Obviously, a larger sensor records a larger crop (see Figure 3.9). Because of this, the same lens placed on a camera with a different sensor size will yield a different field of view.

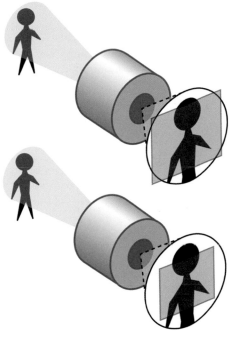

The 35mm frame size has been the standard for so long that experienced photographers tend to think in terms of 35mm when they consider a particular focal length. On a 35mm film camera, a 50mm lens is considered a "normal" lens (that is, one with a field of view that's roughly equivalent to what the naked eye sees), while a 200mm is considered telephoto and 28mm is considered wide angle. When you attach those same lenses to cameras with smaller sensors, they have a field of view that is more telephoto than what they'd have on a 35mm film camera. In other words, when you place a 50mm lens on a camera with a sensor that is smaller than a piece of 35mm film, it might end up having the equivalent field of view of a 70mm lens on a 35mm camera.

Figure 3.9

Your lens projects a circular image, but your camera's image sensor crops a rectangular portion out of that image. The amount that is cropped depends on the size of the sensor. This is why different sensor sizes yield different fields of view for any given focal length.

The sensor in a point-and-shoot camera is so small that camera makers can get away with using lenses that have very short focal lengths—usually in the 8–15mm range. In 35mm terms, 8–15mm is insanely wide-angle, but on a small point-and-shoot, it might be the equivalent of a fairly normal zoom range.

If you want to know the 35mm field-of-view equivalency on a camera that uses a smaller sensor, then you must multiply the actual focal length of the lens by a multiplication factor. Fortunately, with point-and-shoot cameras, if your manual doesn't list the multiplication factor, it will probably list the equivalent 35mm focal length range.

This cropping factor can be advantageous for shooters who like using very long telephoto lenses. For example, if you stick a 300mm lens on a Canon EOS Digital Rebel series camera, which has a 1.6x focal length multiplier, you'll have the same field of view as a 480mm lens. If you like shooting with wide-angle lenses, though, things are a different story. A 24mm lens—a very wide lens on a full-frame camera—will have a full-frame equivalent field of view of 36mm, which is not very wide.

Cropped Versus Full-Frame Sensors

Most digital SLRs have an image sensor that's smaller than a piece of 35mm film; these are known as *cropped sensors*. There are also digital SLRs that have a full-frame sensor, which is the size of a piece of 35mm film. When you put a lens on a camera with a full-frame sensor, you don't have to apply any kind of 35mm equivalency. With their larger area, full-frame sensors allow for very high pixel counts. At the time of this writing you can buy a Nikon D800, which has a pixel count of 36 megapixels. Because of their bigger mirrors and viewfinders, full-frame cameras also tend to have larger, brighter viewfinders than SLRs equipped with cropped sensors. As you'll learn later, cameras with full-frame sensors also have some properties that give you some different creative choices.

Lenses that work on full-frame cameras will also work on cropped-sensor cameras. Both Canon and Nikon, as well as third-party lens manufacturers like Tamron and Sigma, make a selection of lenses that are designed specifically for cropped-sensor cameras. These lenses are smaller and lighter than equivalent full-frame lenses, and they will not work on a full-frame camera. Canon denotes their cropped-sensor lenses with an S moniker, while Nikon tags theirs with DX.

The reason cropped-sensor lenses won't work on full frame cameras is that their rear element sits farther back than the rear element on a full-frame lens. Because cropped sensor cameras have smaller mirrors, this protruding element can fit in the body of a cropped sensor camera (see Figure 3.10). They also do not typically project an image circle large enough to cover a full frame sensor.

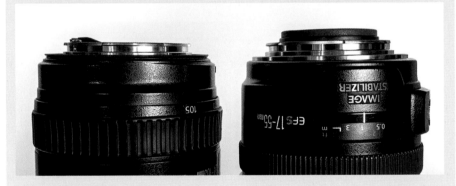

Figure 3.10 The image on the left shows the camera mount of a lens that can fit on either full-frame or cropped-sensor cameras. Because the right-hand mount protrudes further into the camera body, it will only work on cameras with a cropped sensor.

Basic Controls

You should already know where the most basic controls on your camera are: power switch, shutter button, and zoom control.

- ◆ **Power switch.** This might be a button, a sliding switch, or a rocker switch of some kind. Some power switches also have additional functions. For example, on Nikon SLRs, the power switch also lets you turn on the light for the top-mounted LCD screen. Some cameras place the depth of field preview control on the power switch.

◆ **Shutter button.** We discussed the shutter button in detail in Chapter 2, so you should already be comfortable with where it is and how to use it to control autofocus.

◆ **Zoom control.** If you're using a point-and-shoot camera, there will be an electronic zoom control somewhere on the camera's body. Often, it is a rocker switch that surrounds the shutter button. Other cameras have simple buttons on the back of the camera body. These days, most vendors are using the icons shown in Figure 3.11 to indicate zoom. If you're using an SLR, then you'll control zooming by turning a ring on the camera's lens. You'll learn more about this later.

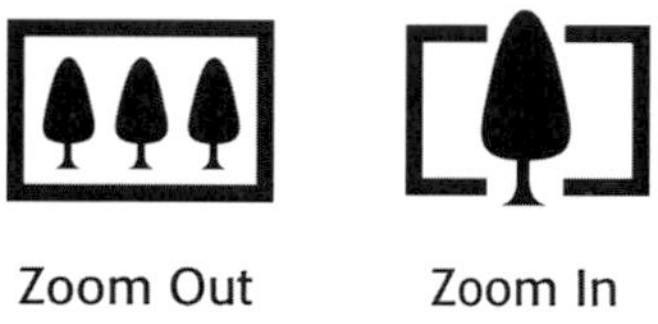

Zoom Out   **Zoom In**

Figure 3.11

Most cameras use icons like these to indicate zooming out and in.

Mode Selection

If you worked through Chapter 2, you should already be familiar with your camera's mode selection control. This is the dial or menu option that you'll use to set the camera's shooting mode. As explained earlier, the mode you choose determines what the camera will control automatically and what will be left up to you. We'll be working with Auto mode later in this chapter, and moving on to other modes starting in Chapter 7, "Program Mode."

Some cameras use their mode selection controls to activate video features, specialized functions like panoramic shooting, or even image playback.

Status Display

The status display is another feature that you probably already know, but I'm calling it out here to make certain that you understand what I mean when I refer to your camera's "status display." There are a *lot* of settings to keep track of on your camera, from shutter speed and aperture to image size, format, and white balance settings. On all cameras, these settings are shown in a status display of some kind. You saw examples of different status displays in Chapter 2 when you learned how to read the camera's shutter speed choice.

Most cameras also provide a control that lets you deactivate the status display or cycle through different configurations of status information (see Figure 3.12). This control is usually a button called *Display* or *DISP*. Pressing the button repeatedly will show different status screens and probably offer the option of turning the screen off altogether, which can be important when shooting in low-light venues such as concerts and performances.

More advanced SLRs will usually have a second LCD screen mounted on the top of the camera or above the main LCD.

On your camera's status display, make sure that you know where shutter speed and aperture are displayed. You'll learn what the rest of the status readouts mean as we work through more features.

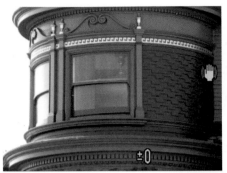
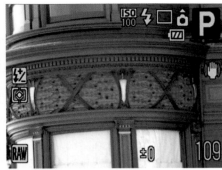

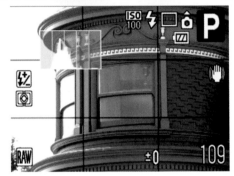

Figure 3.12

Some cameras allow you to display different amounts of status information while shooting. Some cameras include a very bare screen, a screen with basic exposure information, and additional screens with more advanced features, such as a grid and Live Histogram.

LCD Screens

One of the decisions you'll need to make when shopping for an SLR is whether you want a dedicated status display. A dedicated status display is an additional LCD screen mounted on top of the camera, and it is usually easier to read in bright daylight. It also requires a physically larger camera body. Consequently, cameras that use their main LCD for a status display are often smaller and lighter. If you opt for one of these smaller models, look for a camera that has a sensor that automatically detects when you are looking through the viewfinder. These cameras will automatically shut off the camera's rear LCD so that it doesn't shine in your eyes while looking through the viewfinder.

Shooting Controls

Autofocus and zooming will be the shooting controls that you'll use most often, but your camera probably also has some other very important shooting features, including multiple light meters, several autofocus modes, flash, burst modes, and many more options and controls.

Usually, these primary shooting controls are grouped together (see Figure 3.13).

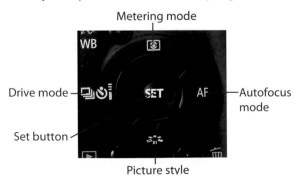

Metering mode

WB

Drive mode — SET   AF —Autofocus mode

Set button

Picture style

Figure 3.13

Most cameras group essential shooting configuration controls together, either in a collection of buttons or in a menu.

On smaller point-and-shoot cameras, there's not always enough room for external buttons for these controls. Instead, these cameras usually offer a button you can press to bring up a simple menu for configuring these critical features (see Figure 3.14). On some cameras, this is listed as a *Function*, or *Func* button. On other cameras, the menu is always visible on-screen, and you simply use a navigation control to select and configure parameters.

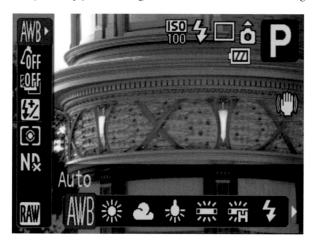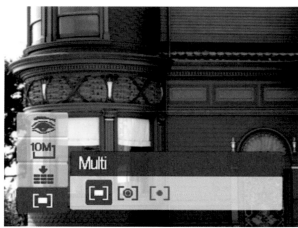

Figure 3.14 Some cameras have a dedicated Function button (sometimes labeled *Func*), which provides a menu of commonly used functions, like meter selection. Function menus provide quick access and keep you from having to tunnel into the full menu system.

The controls on most SLRs are operated by a combination of buttons and control wheels—usually a wheel near the shutter button and another on the back of the camera. Consult your camera manual for details on how these controls are used.

Menu Activation and Navigation

All cameras have a menu system that is used for configuring everything from the current date and time to important shooting parameters. Your camera should have a Menu button on it somewhere, as well as navigation controls for selecting and altering different menu item choices.

In general, the items found in the menu system are features that you probably don't need quick access to while shooting. Rather, they're lower-level settings that you change less often or features that are not used every day.

Flash System

Your camera might have a flash, which will either be built in to the camera's body or housed in a pop-up unit. If your camera has a pop-up flash, then there's probably a button that will release the flash. Popping up the flash also tells the camera to use the flash. Pressing the flash back down deactivates the flash.

Somewhere on the camera should be a flash mode control, which will have a little lightning bolt icon next to it. This feature provides you with some control over how and when the camera will fire its flash.

The front of your camera might also have a window that looks sort of like the flash or possibly like a lens. This is most likely a focus-assist lamp, which was discussed in Chapter 2.

Your camera might also have a hot shoe on the top of the camera body. This is a mount that you can use to attach an external flash unit. The "hot" in "hot shoe" means that there are electrical contacts in the mount that allow the camera to communicate with the flash.

Playback Controls

In Chapter 2, we took a quick look at the basics of image playback, so you should already know how to activate the Playback mode on your camera, as well as how to navigate from one image to another, and possibly how to zoom in and out and delete images.

In addition to these controls, your camera might provide some other handy functions. Check your manual to find out if your camera offers these features:

- ◆ **Image info and histogram display.** When reviewing an image, there should be a way that you can view one or more pages of data about the image. In addition to the date and time that the image was shot, you should also be able to see the exposure settings that were used and possibly a histogram, which we'll explore in more detail throughout this book.

- ◆ **Image jumping.** If you've got a big card with lots of images on it, scrolling through each individual image can be tedious. Some cameras allow you to jump through 10, 20, or even 100 at a time. Other cameras will let you automatically jump around images based on the date and time stamps stored with each image (see Figure 3.15).

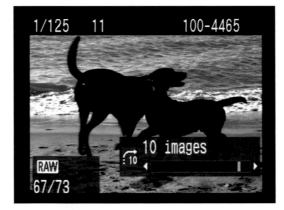

Figure 3.15

In Playback mode, your camera might provide a facility for jumping through your images in large batches.

- ◆ **Deleting and locking images.** These features were discussed in Chapter 2. If you didn't track them down at the time, it's worth looking into them now. Some cameras also allow you to delete an image when it appears for review immediately after you shoot it. Usually, a simple press of the Delete or Erase button while the image review is showing is all you need to do.

- ◆ **Changing the brightness of your LCD screen.** Some cameras let you change screen brightness. If you're having trouble seeing your images in bright daylight, look for a brightness control in your camera's main menu.

Erasing images gives you a way to free up space on your card, if you find yourself running out of room. Deleting bad shots can also help speed up your postproduction workflow. If a shot is blatantly bad—your finger was in front of the lens, for example— go ahead and delete the image so that you don't have it cluttering up your workflow later. If you're in a situation that demands speedy shooting, you shouldn't waste time sorting and deleting images, but if you have some downtime, dumping bad images can make things easier later.

When you rotate the camera to shoot in a vertical orientation, your camera most likely detects this rotation (unless the camera is very old) and notes it in the image file. Your camera might offer options that control how to deal with this rotation. Depending on how this option is set, your camera may or may not fill the whole LCD screen with the image, but instead show a smaller, rotated version.

Other, specialized playback features abound, from the ability to create slideshows in the camera to face detection features that allow you to zoom in easily and pan from face to face within an image to check focus. We won't go into detail on these specialized features, but you might want to examine your camera's capabilities to determine if they're anything you're interested in or might use.

Finally, you can connect most cameras to a TV, allowing you to view your images on a larger screen or present slideshows to a group of people. Your camera should have come with a cable for patching into either an SD or HD TV, or possibly both. If you're traveling, reviewing images on a TV can be a nice way of assessing your shooting, if you don't have a computer with you.

Recovering Deleted Images

There might come an occasion when you accidentally delete an image or even all the images on your card. Static electricity, bad card readers, broken cameras, and other hardware or environmental conditions could also cause a card to "crash," leaving you with lost images. Fortunately, it is often possible to recover deleted images from a media card through the use of special software.

Image recovery is possible because when you delete an image, the camera doesn't actually write zeroes over the image data on the card. Instead, it simply erases that image's entry from the directory of files that are stored on the card. Recovery software works by finding deleted image data on the card and rebuilding the card's directory to point to that data. If you have accidentally deleted one or more images that you want to recover, you should not shoot any more images with that card to insure that the deleted image is not written over with a new image.

A crashed card might simply be a card whose directory has gotten corrupted. Recovery software can rebuild the directory, allowing you to regain access to your images.

File recovery software on your desktop computer works the same way, but you'll need recovery software designed specifically for flash memory cards if you want to try to recover images from your camera's card. The software you use on your desktop computer most likely won't work.

My preference for recovery software is PhotoRescue from *www.datarescue.com*. You can download a free, fully functional copy from their website. This free version will let you analyze your card, and it will show you any recoverable images. If you see images you want, you can then pay to unlock the software and perform the recovery.

Configuring Your Camera

Keeping track of all of your camera's controls and settings can feel overwhelming. Fortunately, many of the settings on your camera are not "everyday" settings. Rather, they're basic configuration parameters you'll probably change once and then rarely touch again. For this section, grab your camera manual and follow along. When we're done, you'll have a better understanding of some fundamental configurations.

Date and Time

Your camera has a clock in it, and when you first powered up the camera it probably asked you to set the date and time. Every time you take a picture, the current date and time are stored in the resulting image file, giving you a record of exactly when each picture was shot.

Your camera might also have a setting for indicating the time zone you're in. As you travel, you can change it to the local time zone. If you forget to change the time while traveling, know that some image editing software will automatically adjust the time stamp of images to compensate for shooting in a different time zone. Some cameras allow you to store a home time and then indicate a separate "current" time zone. Consult your manual for details.

Image Size and Compression

Your camera probably provides a number of different size and compression choices. The point of having options for size and compression is to allow you to manage the space on your storage card better and ultimately to manage the space on your computer's hard drive.

Image size is simply the dimensions, in pixels, of the image the camera will create. A 10-megapixel camera, for example, typically offers a maximum pixel count of roughly 3648 × 2736 pixels, along with options for shooting at lower pixel counts. So you might get a 7-megapixel option (3072 × 2304), a 4-megapixel option (2304 × 1728), and a VGA option (640 × 480 pixels).

By default, most cameras compress the images you shoot using an algorithm called *JPEG*. This is the same type of compression that is often applied to images that you see on the Web, and your camera probably offers several levels of compression. The problem with JPEG compression is that while it can do an exceptional job of reducing the storage requirements of a big image, it can also visibly degrade your image. Blocky patterns in your image are the result of too much JPEG compression.

When it comes to compression, it's best to always shoot with the lowest compression level (highest quality). JPEG artifacts are difficult, if not impossible, to remove later, so try to avoid them altogether. If you're shooting in raw format, this won't be a concern.

Nowadays, with storage so cheap, there's almost no reason not to shoot at full size with the least possible compression, even if you only plan to upload your images to the Web. Full-size images will have to be resized before being posted to the Web, but the extra size gives you the option of later repurposing your images for print or for cropping and enlarging part of the image. After all, you never know what use you might one day find for an image. Most of the time it's best to set your size and compression to their highest-quality settings and then leave them there.

However, there might be times when you want to change these settings—if you're on a long shoot and you begin to run out of storage, for example. Or if you're shooting for a particular type of output—posting a product shot to eBay, for example—and you don't want to spend a lot of time resizing your images later, then setting the size in-camera might be a good time-saver.

Which size option is best depends on how you will output your images. If your images are destined for the Web, you might be able to get away with 640 × 480 resolution. The correct image size for print depends on the type of printer to which you'll be outputting and the final print size of your image. We'll discuss these issues in detail when we talk about output.

Obviously, choosing the largest image size with the lowest compression setting means you won't be able to fit as many images onto your storage card. If you run short on storage when you're in the field, you might want to switch to different image size and compression settings.

◆ If your destination is the Web, you can afford to lower the camera's resolution (and hope you never want to print any of your images).

◆ If your final destination is print, you should keep your resolution the same but increase your compression (and hope the artifacting isn't too bad).

Storage Is Cheap and Easy

Storage is one of those few problems you can solve easily by spending additional money. If you want to ensure that you can always shoot at the highest quality your camera allows, you should invest in more storage.

Some cameras do not allow you to adjust image size and compression separately. Instead, they offer a menu of predefined combinations. In Figure 3.16, the camera shows options for full resolution with high quality (low compression), full resolution with low quality (high compression), the same options for medium and small resolution, and finally raw format. Next are options for raw format, plus a separate JPEG file, and then finally raw only.

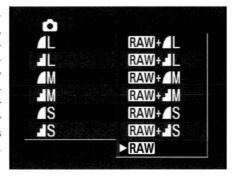

Figure 3.16

A typical image size menu. In this menu, you can select between three different sizes, each with a choice of two compression (quality) settings, raw format plus a JPEG, or just raw format.

File Format

Although JPEG is the default format for all digital cameras, many models also offer some additional uncompressed formats. Uncompressed files take up substantially more space than JPEGs, but are free from the blocky artifacts that JPEG images sometimes possess. They might also afford you more editing latitude and allow some edits that simply aren't possible in JPEG files. Your camera probably supports one or all of the following formats:

◆ **Raw.** If your camera supports it, raw is the preferred choice for uncompressed shooting, and we'll cover raw in detail later. If you don't want to shoot in JPEG format, and your camera offers both TIFF and raw options, it's better to choose raw. Raw files are smaller than TIFF files and offer much more editing flexibility.

◆ **Raw + JPEG.** Some cameras can simultaneously store images in raw and JPEG mode. We'll discuss the merits and drawbacks of this later.

◆ **TIFF.** TIFF files are a standard, uncompressed file format that just about every graphics program can read. TIFF files are useful for those times when you want to greatly enlarge an area or part of an area and simply can't afford to see any JPEG artifacts.

You'll probably rarely change image size and compression unless you start to run out of storage. You might change file format more often, although beginning digital photographers might want to stick with JPEG before complicating matters with raw options.

Image Processing Parameters

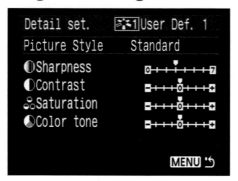

Most cameras provide special menu options for controlling some image processing functions such as contrast, saturation, and sharpness (see Figure 3.17). These adjustments are applied to JPEG or TIFF files in-camera after you shoot. They're really nothing more than the same type of image editing operations you might perform later, using your image editor on your computer. In most cases, these options offer a simple slider control that gives you a choice of three to five different levels for each setting.

If you regularly find yourself making a particular change in postproduction—for example, consistently increasing or decreasing the saturation, bumping up the contrast, or sharpening your images—then adjusting your camera's image processing parameters might save you from having to perform these additional editing steps. This can greatly simplify your postproduction workflow. Just as film photographers used to choose a particular type of film for its contrast and color characteristics, you can use these settings so that your camera shoots images with a particular look.

The downside to these settings is that they sometimes "use up" some of your editing latitude, meaning that later you won't be able to make as many edits before encountering visible problems in your image.

Sharpening is a particularly dangerous setting because it is possible to sharpen an image too much, and it's impossible to remove oversharpening later.

Of course, if you want to change these features regularly, that's fine. You might, for example, discover that one contrast setting works very well indoors, while another works better outdoors. Or perhaps you have a job where the client wants images to look "antique." In that case, you might choose to dial down the saturation for the duration of the shoot.

Many cameras provide the option to store sets of parameters so you can quickly reconfigure an entire batch of settings with a single menu option.

Raw Not Affected

Remember: If you're shooting raw, these parameters have no effect. However, the image that's displayed on your camera's LCD after you shoot *might* be processed with these settings. As such, it can appear that changing these types of settings is altering your raw file. They're not doing that. They're simply altering the image the camera builds for playback.

Alternately, you can choose settings that apply as few changes as possible, with the idea that you'll perform all editing and corrections later. Many cameras offer a "neutral" setting that performs very little adjustment. As your image editing skills improve, you'll probably find that this is the best option.

Other Features

Your camera might have lots of other features, ranging from ones that you want to use regularly to others that you won't use at all, and still others that are worth knowing about, just in case you find yourself in the type of situation that they're designed for. Some handy utility features to look for are the following:

◆ **Sound.** Sometimes referred to as *Beep*, your camera probably has a mechanism for turning off any beeps and sounds it might make. For shooting during performances or in museums or in other places where silent shooting is necessary, this can be an essential option. Note that on an SLR, while you can turn off the electronic beeps and sounds, you can't silence the sound of the shutter and mirror. However some SLRs offer special modes that yield a quieter shutter at the expense of slower burst speed.

◆ **Aspect ratio.** The ratio of an image's length to its width is called the *aspect ratio*. Most point-and-shoot digital cameras use the same 4:3 aspect ratio that your computer screen and standard definition television might use, but some—and almost all SLRs— use the 3:2 aspect ratio of 35mm film (see Figure 3.18).

Some cameras offer a choice of either aspect ratio. However, many of these cameras achieve the wider 3:2 aspect ratio by simply shooting a cropped version of the camera's native 4:3 ratio. Therefore, when you shoot 3:2, you're shooting images with fewer pixels. It's often better to simply shoot 4:3 and crop the image later.

Some cameras also offer an even wider 16:9 aspect ratio, just like what you'll find on an HD TV. Usually, this change is achieved through cropping, but some cameras actually offer a 16:9 image sensor. Square is another handy aspect ratio option that offers its own set of composition challenges and advantages.

There is no "right" or "wrong" aspect ratio, and the more you shoot, the more you may develop a preference.

◆ **Viewfinder overlays.** Some cameras, especially Nikons, offer the ability to superimpose grids and other shooting aids in the viewfinder. Some cameras also offer virtual levels for ensuring that your shots are level.

◆ **Customization.** Your camera might allow for customization of its interface. Some cameras let you change the function of specific buttons and dials on the camera or build custom menus that contain only features you want. Once you learn your camera's features, you may want to employ customization options to facilitate easier access to the features you use most.

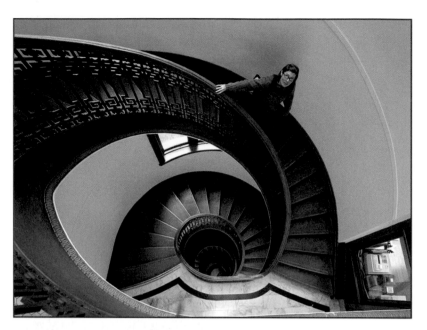

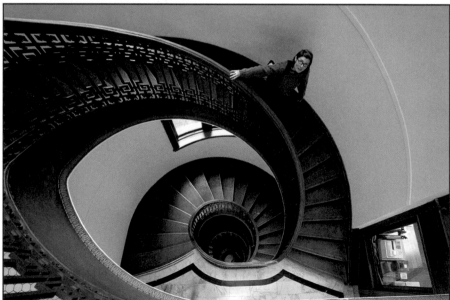

Figure 3.18

Most digital cameras use the same 4:3 aspect ratio as your computer monitor (as shown in the top image). Most digital SLR cameras use the 3:2 aspect ratio of 35mm film (as shown in the lower image).

◆ **Sleep.** Your camera probably has a Sleep mode that causes it to switch to a low-power setting if you don't use it for a while. Most cameras doze off if you don't use them for 30 seconds. This is fine for everyday, snapshot shooting, but it can be a real bother if you're shooting portraits or other studio work that requires a long setup. For these occasions, you might want to change the sleep time to its maximum (15 to 30 minutes). If you know you're going to be away from the camera for a bit, turn off the LCD screen to conserve power.

Holding the Camera

While holding a camera might seem fairly straightforward, good form can be critical for preventing soft images brought about by a shaky hand. Paying attention to a few simple guidelines about grip and posture will improve your chances of getting sharp images and reduce neck and back strain after a day of carrying a heavy camera bag.

The Grip

Holding a typical point-and-shoot is pretty simple. Just get a sturdy grip on the camera and position it so that you can see the LCD screen.

Because an SLR weighs more, and is a potentially awkward shape, you need to be careful to hold it in a way that allows for good stability. To guarantee the most stable hold, your left hand should go underneath the lens barrel where it connects to the camera (see Figure 3.19). When you cradle the camera this way, you'll have an easier time holding the camera for longer periods of time. With your finger on the shutter release, you shouldn't have any trouble reaching the control buttons on the back of the camera with your thumb.

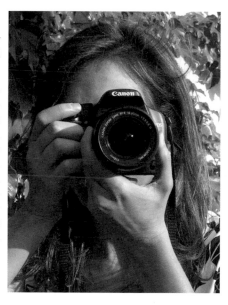

Figure 3.19

When holding an SLR, support the lens with your left hand to provide a stable platform for holding the camera.

Feet, Elbows, and Neck

No matter what your shooting conditions, from simple street or event shooting to more complex shooting in harsh environments, keeping your camera stable is an essential part of shooting sharp images and having maximum creative control.

Many people believe that if you're shooting with a fast shutter speed, you don't have to worry about camera stability, but camera shake can impact your images even at very fast shutter speeds. What's more, camera stability becomes more important if you're shooting with a camera that has a very high pixel count. A camera with 10 or 12 megapixels is capable of revealing the softness that can be caused by very fine camera shake and vibration.

While tripods and monopods are the obvious solutions for stabilizing your camera, there are also tricks you can employ when shooting handheld to achieve better stability. As you practice your handheld shooting, you'll get more adept at keeping your camera steady. Here are some tips you can use to improve your camera stability when shooting by hand.

Keep your elbows in. Holding your elbows against your sides provides much better stability than holding them out and away from your body (see Figure 3.20). Practice this enough, and you'll get so used to feeling your elbows tucked into your body while shooting (as if you're being hugged) that it should feel weird when you don't shoot this way.

This is especially true when shooting with the camera in portrait orientation. When shooting vertically, many people use the position shown in Figure 3.21. If you turn the camera the other way, though, you can keep your elbows against your body for greater stability. It's also more comfortable, albeit it doesn't give you that cool "gotta get the shot" look.

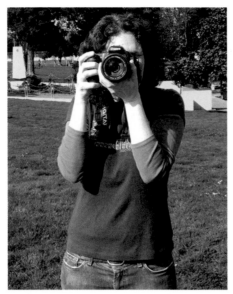 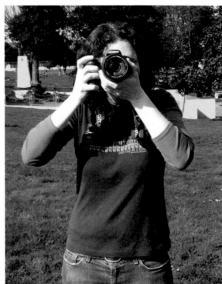

Figure 3.20

You'll get a much more stable hold on the camera if you keep your elbows at your side to stabilize your arms.

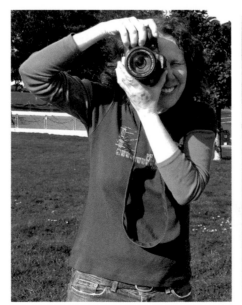 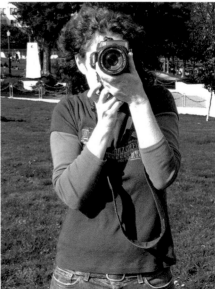

Figure 3.21

The "elbows in" rule also applies to shooting in Portrait mode. In the right-hand image, the photographer has a much more stable position than she does in the left, with her elbows akimbo.

When using a camera with an optical viewfinder, always lift the camera all the way to your face (see Figure 3.22). You may think that you're doing this, but many people lift the camera partway to their face and then push their neck forward to close the gap. In addition to giving you bad posture and possibly contributing as much to back pain as a heavy camera bag on your shoulder, jutting your neck forward is a less stable position.

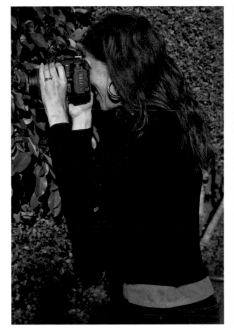 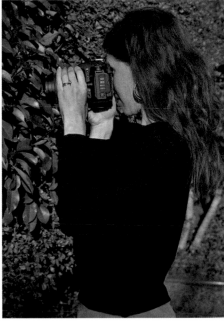

Figure 3.22

You'll get a more stable shot and have less neck pain if you bring the camera all the way to your eye, rather than pushing your neck forward.

More Practice with Auto

We've covered a lot of technical details in this chapter, with the goal of learning to use your camera quickly and efficiently. In the field, quick use of the camera is often what makes the difference between capturing a "decisive moment" and getting a boring shot.

As we move on to more advanced shooting topics, you can keep practicing in Auto mode. Using a camera's fully automatic mode does not mean you're some kind of photographic wimp. The automatic modes on most cameras are very powerful, and having the camera make technical decisions for you can free you up to focus on content and composition. We're still not ready for a formal composition lesson, but here are some exercises to try right now before moving on to the next chapter.

Shoot with a Fixed Focal Length

Using a zoom lens is a great way to become lazy. As you'll see later, there can be a great difference in images shot from different locations, but with a zoom lens, you tend to root in one place, rather than staying on the move. Here are three quick exercises that will get you seeing and thinking in a different way.

◆ **Full Wide.** Zoom your lens out to full wide, leave it there, and spend a few hours shooting. Instead of zooming to frame a different shot, you'll have to move around and reposition yourself, and this might lead you to discover shots you hadn't recognized earlier. Be aware that you may not be able to visualize or recognize potential scenes when limited to a wide focal length, because your eyes don't see this way. So, if you think you spot something even vaguely interesting, look at it through the camera. If it turns out to be a dull image, you don't have to take the shot, but there's no harm in taking a look through the camera. It's important to learn that when you look through the viewfinder, you might see potential shots that you don't recognize when looking with the naked eye.

◆ **Full Tele.** Now zoom to the longest focal length of your lens and do the same exercise. Remember, no zooming!

◆ **Normal.** Set your zoom lens to somewhere in the middle so that it shows roughly the same focal length as the naked eye. On most digital SLRs, this will be around 30mm. On a full-frame SLR, this will be 50mm. Since most point-and-shoot cameras don't have lens markings, you'll have to find this field of view by hand. Some of the most famous, celebrated photos of all time have been shot with a 50mm lens. The great French photographer Henri Cartier-Bresson worked exclusively with a 50—if it's good enough for him, the rest of us should be able to manage.

Set your camera at this focal length and spend a few hours shooting. Again, no zooming! Some SLR lenses show a dot on the zoom ring to indicate where normal is.

Obviously, if you're using an SLR with prime lenses—that is, lenses that don't zoom—then you get this type of shooting experience all the time. These exercises are a way for you to learn some of the advantages and disadvantages of shooting with a fixed focal length lens. Mostly, they should get you used to the feeling of "working a shot." This kind of movement and exploration is how you should always work, whether you have a zoom lens or not.

For Those Times When You're "Not Seeing Any Images"

On field trips, I'll occasionally have a student come up and say that they're "not seeing anything." I'll follow them around for a while and find that they're walking around and looking at a lot of things, but *never* raising the camera to their eye. Great photographers often don't recognize an image until they look through the camera, so don't expect shots to just leap out at you while you're walking around. Don't be shy about constantly raising the camera to your eye to check things out. You might be surprised by what you find.

Camera Care and Maintenance

Basic digital camera care is pretty simple, and is just what you'd expect for any electronic or optical device. Don't drop it, don't smash it into things, keep it dry, and keep it clean.

In this section, we'll look at some specific maintenance issues and care concerns.

Batteries and Power

Older rechargeable batteries had an annoying habit of developing a "memory," which limited how much charge they could hold. Modern rechargeables don't have this problem, and you can feel free to "top off" your rechargeable batteries any time you want—there's no need to completely drain them before you put them on the charger. That said, for the first couple of charges, it's good to drain the battery completely before you charge it up. Doing this every so often will "condition" the battery so that it performs better over its lifetime.

Rechargeable batteries eventually wear out, so if you notice that your battery is not holding a charge for very long, you might need to replace it.

If you're planning a long trip and won't have access to power, then you might want to carry multiple batteries. You can buy additional batteries for your camera from most major camera vendors. You might also find that there are third-party battery options for your camera. While your camera manufacturer will likely warn you that using such batteries can damage your camera, I've never had any trouble using third-party batteries, and they're often much cheaper than the batteries sold by camera manufacturers.

You might also be able to find a third-party charging solution for your batteries. Third-party chargers are often cheaper than the battery chargers sold by your camera maker, and they are also usually smaller, lighter, and sometimes come with additional options such as car cigarette lighter adapters.

Other remote power options include solar chargers, such as those made by Solio (*www.solio.com*) (see Figure 3.23).

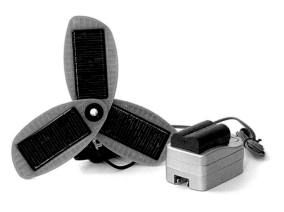

Figure 3.23

If you have a car charger for your camera battery, you can easily charge it while driving or connect it to a portable solar charger.

Obviously, when you travel abroad, you'll need to buy the appropriate adapters and converters to power your charger and any other equipment you might choose to bring along. Most camera chargers will work on any voltage from 100 to 240 volts, so all you'll need to bring is an adapter for the particular plug style that's used at your destination. The back of your camera's charger should indicate the voltage range that it can use.

Finally, be aware that cold temperatures will noticeably shorten battery life. If you're shooting outside in below-freezing temperatures, your batteries will probably die quickly. You can often squeeze a little more power out of them by taking them out of the camera and warming them up inside your pocket. This might sound hard to believe, but it's true. A few minutes inside your coat can often get you an additional dozen pictures. Don't put the whole camera in your pocket because the temperature change might fog your camera's lens or viewfinder.

Lens Cleaning

Given how critical your camera's lens is to the photographic process, it's obviously important to keep it clean. The good news is that tiny specks and splotches on your lens are often not visible to the camera, since it might focus *past* the debris on the end of the lens. Still, there's nothing wrong with erring on the side of caution and keeping your lens as clean as possible.

Any camera or eyeglasses store will sell lens papers or lens cloths. These are the best way to keep your lens clean. Disposable lens papers are a better alternative than lens cloths, because it's difficult to keep a lens cloth clean while carrying it around.

You will rarely, if ever, need to use any kind of liquid lens cleaner, but if you do—perhaps there's a spot that won't come off easily—be sure to use one designed for cleaning fine optics. Don't just grab a bottle of Windex and start squirting, as this can damage the anti-glare coatings on the end of your lens.

Also, don't clean your lens with your shirt or any other article of clothing that you might be wearing. While it may look clean, the cloth might be hiding abrasive particles or dirt that could scratch your lens.

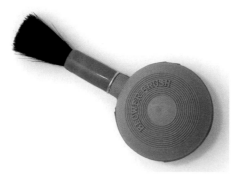

Be careful when using compressed air to clean your lens; the liquid propellant used in the can could spray onto your lens. Hold the air can completely upright to avoid spraying propellant. A blower brush, available at any camera store, is a good tool for lens and camera cleaning (see Figure 3.24).

If you're an SLR user, remember to clean both ends of the lens. Again, a blower brush is the best way to deal with the camera end of the lens.

Figure 3.24

Use a blower brush for cleaning dust off the ends of your lenses.

UV Filters

One of the best ways to protect your lens investment is to attach a UV or skylight filter to the end of your lens. These filters don't alter the appearance of your image at all, and they provide valuable protection to the end of your lens. In addition to safeguarding against scratches and dirt, a filter can even protect the lens in the event you fall or drop it.

When shopping for a filter, be sure to spend a little extra for a multicoated filter. This will ensure that you're getting a filter with optical properties that won't degrade your lens.

Sensor Cleaning

If you have a digital SLR with removable lenses, then you might one day encounter the problem of sensor dust. When you take the lens off your camera, the sensor chamber is exposed to the elements in a way that it never is with a point-and-shoot camera. With the lens off, it's possible for dust and other debris to get on the image sensor, and this dust can be visible in your final image.

The pixels on a digital image sensor are very, very small. On a 10-megapixel point-and-shoot camera, 10 million of them are crammed into an area smaller than your fingernail. Because they're so small, it doesn't take a very big piece of dust to obscure thousands of them, leaving a dark smudge or spot in your final image (see Figure 3.25).

The sensor itself is not actually directly exposed to the outside world, since it sits behind a clear glass filter. In many newer SLRs, a built-in cleaning mechanism automatically vibrates this filter every time you turn the camera on or off, in an attempt to remove dust. A piece of sticky material below the filter traps any fallen dust so that it doesn't float around the sensor chamber.

Whether or not your camera includes built-in sensor cleaning, you should take precautions to keep your sensor clean. Where sensor dust is concerned, prevention can be very effective.

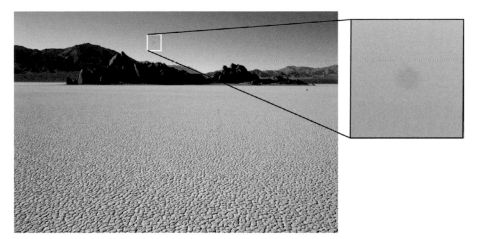

Figure 3.25

If you see spots or smudges in the same place on multiple images, you could be facing a sensor dust problem.

Most of the dust that lands on your sensor is delivered by the end of the lens—the end that attaches to your camera. So keeping your lenses clean is a good way to keep your sensor clean. Before you go out on a shoot, use a blower bulb or blower brush (but never compressed air) to blow out the camera end of your lens.

When changing lenses, try to use gravity in your favor. Keep the camera pointed down and don't remove one lens until you have the other lens in-hand, ready to attach. It might feel like it requires three hands, but if you hang the camera around your neck and practice, you'll develop the coordination to make speedy lens changes.

Dusty New Camera

If you have lots of dust problems when you first get your camera, this might be the result of some of the materials inside the sensor chamber shedding residues of different kinds. This should abate after a few months.

When you remove a lens, always put the end caps on before you put the camera in any kind of bag, and be very careful to keep the cap itself clean. This will keep the camera-end of your lens clean, which will reduce the chance of transferring dust to the sensor via the lens.

It's easy to tell if you have a sensor dust problem because you'll see the same smudge or spot appearing in the same place from one image to the next. If you see a spec or smudge in the same place in every image, then you probably need to clean your sensor. If you want to be sure, then put your camera in manual focus, point it at a blank white wall (or clear blue sky), defocus the lens, and take a picture. Bring this image into your image editor and increase the contrast using a Levels adjustment. (You'll learn how to do this in Chapter 15, "Correcting Tone.") Any dust problems should be readily apparent.

To clean your sensor, you'll need special cleaning tools and a little time. If you're not comfortable with this type of endeavor, you can send your camera to its manufacturer for cleaning. Consult your camera maker's website to find a nearby service center.

There are two types of cleaning: dry and wet. Dry cleaning involves using a special brush to remove debris from your sensor, while wet cleaning involves special swabs and chemicals for removing particularly stubborn particles. You can find both types of products and excellent sensor cleaning tutorials at *www.visibledust.com*. The Visible Dust Corporation has a long history of making cleaning materials for high-end microscopes and other optical devices, and they make top-notch products.

Don't Spray Compressed Air into Your SLR's Body!

Never, ever use compressed air to clean your sensor! The propellants used in cans of compressed air can leave a physical residue that can permanently mar your sensor.

Carrying a Long Lens

If you're an SLR user, then one of the easiest ways to protect your lenses is to follow this very simple tip. When you have a long lens mounted on your camera, pay attention to how you hang the camera on your shoulder. There's a big difference between the two approaches shown in Figure 3.26.

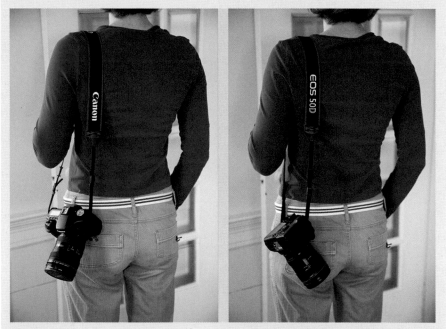

Figure 3.26 You can hang your camera over your shoulder with the lens facing out, where it can bump into things, or tuck it into your back, which keeps it much safer.

In addition to keeping the lens hidden behind you, where there's less chance of it bumping into something, you'll find that your camera moves much less. Also, the camera is less noticeable from the front, making it easier to approach people without scaring them.

Whether you're walking around town or scrambling up a trail, keeping your lens tucked into your back provides more stable carrying and more security for your expensive glass.

Water and Digital Cameras

Digital cameras and water definitely do not mix. Although a few sprinkles are nothing to worry about, you absolutely do *not* want to submerge your camera. If your camera goes in the drink, fish it out immediately and do everything you can to get it dry. Immediately remove the battery and media card; open all port covers, lids, and flaps, and wipe off any water you can see, no matter how small. Set the camera in a warm place and do *not* turn it on until you're sure the camera has had time to dry, both inside and out. At the least, give it a couple of days to dry.

After drying off the camera, some people suggest covering it completely with uncooked rice. Leave the camera covered for at least a day. The rice will act like a desiccant and absorb moisture from the camera. If the camera in question is an SLR, you'll obviously want to put the body cap on before ladling on the rice.

If you know you're going to be using your camera in potentially wet situations (kayaking, canoeing, taking your convertible to the car wash), consider buying a dry bag, which is a sealable, waterproof bag that will keep your camera dry even if it gets submerged.

Your camera should be fine in light rain, as long as it doesn't get completely soaked. If you plan to spend all day in the rain, or are shooting in very heavy rain, try sticking your camera in a Ziploc bag. You'll still be able to access the controls, and you can always cut a hole for the lens (see Figure 3.27).

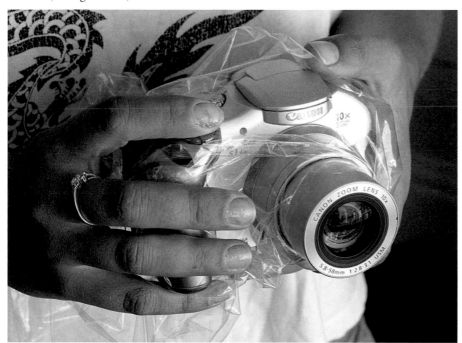

Figure 3.27

If you're shooting in light rain, consider using a Ziploc bag to protect your camera. Be forewarned that your camera is very sensitive to cold and damp.

One thing to note about rain: while a digital camera is an electronic device, it can be used in light rain. You don't want to take it out in a torrential downpour, but sprinkling and light showers should be fine, if you work to keep it as dry as you can. Some higher-end SLRs are weather-sealed, which allows them to be used in more extreme environments, and some point-and-shoots are designed to be so waterproof that they can be submerged.

Weather Sealing Is Only as Good as Your Lens ▬▬▬▬▬

If you have a higher-end SLR that offers a weather-sealed body, be aware that if you don't have a lens that offers a weather-sealed gasket where it joins the camera body, then your camera is no longer weatherproof. If you plan on shooting in very rugged environments, you'll need to choose your lenses with weatherproofing in mind.

Cold Weather

Shooting in cold weather presents a number of problems for the digital photographer. First, there are the LCDs on your camera. Remember that the "L" in LCD stands for liquid. As temperatures drop, your LCD will become far less "L," and the last thing you want is for it to turn into a solid crystal display. Although the LCD won't necessarily be damaged by cold weather, it might prove to be unusable.

Other, smaller electronic components might actually be damaged if you try to use them in cold weather. Extreme cold might cause small electronic components to expand or contract enough that using them will cause them to break. Your camera's documentation should list a range of operating temperatures, and although you *might* be able to push these an extra 20° on the cold end, it's safe to say that such use won't be covered by your warranty.

Even if you're shooting within your camera's proscribed operating temperatures, be very careful when you move the camera from cold temperatures to warm. Walking into a heated house from a day of shooting in the snow can cause potentially damaging condensation to form inside the camera. If you know you're going to be shooting in cold weather, take a Ziploc bag with you. Before you go into a warm building, put the camera in the bag and zip it up. Once inside, give the camera 20 or 30 minutes to warm up to room temperature before you let it out of the bag. If you don't have a bag, be sure not to turn it on until any condensation has had time to evaporate.

If the temperature is cold enough to freeze your camera, it's probably cold enough that you'll be wearing gloves. Because gloves tend to reduce your manual dexterity, be absolutely certain your camera has a neck or wrist strap and that it's securely attached to some part of your body.

In addition, if you're shooting in icy, slippery conditions where you might be prone to falling, attach a UV filter to the end of your lens. This will add an extra level of scratch and shatter protection that might save your lens in the event of a fall.

If temperatures are very low, then the warmth of your face will also present a problem. When you raise your eye to the viewfinder, there's a good chance that the viewfinder will fog and become completely opaque. If that happens, lower the camera and wait for the viewfinder to clear. Then try to shoot without pressing your eye completely to the viewfinder. Alternately, you can switch to Live View. And remember that batteries can be greatly affected by cold weather.

Hot Weather and Digital Cameras

Hot weather can also affect your camera, because as your camera heats up, noise in your images increases. If you're shooting in hot weather, this can cause a visible increase of stuck pixel noise—bright white pixels scattered about your image. This is especially problematic if you're in a hot environment, in direct sunlight, with a black camera.

You might also notice the LCD screen acting a little sluggish. Screen redraw may look weird, and some or all of the screen might appear black. Many LCD screens are not reliable above 32°C (90°F). If your screen appears to be overheating, turn off your camera and try to get it somewhere where it can cool down. If you must shoot in high temperatures, consider keeping your camera in some type of dry cooler (an ice chest with some blue ice) until you're ready to shoot.

If you haven't exceeded the camera's recommended operating temperature, but your LCD has overheated and isn't working, it's probably safe to keep shooting using the camera's optical viewfinder (if it has one). Turn off the picture-review function because your LCD won't be visible anyway.

Media Cards

There are a few things you should know about removable media cards. Obviously, these cards are fragile, so treat them with care. Also, consider the following issues:

◆ **The bigger the card's capacity, the more power it takes to keep it running.** Consequently, in theory, smaller cards use less battery. Although it's difficult to tell if this has any bearing in the real world, switching to a smaller-capacity card when your batteries run low might garner you a few extra shots.

◆ **Larger-capacity cards generate more heat.** If you're using a tiny camera, which tends to get hot simply because of its design, it might be worth sticking to smaller-capacity cards since excess heat can make your images noisier.

◆ **If something goes wrong with a larger-capacity card, you'll lose more images than you would if you had been using a smaller capacity card.** Therefore, it might be worth buying a number of smaller cards instead of one big one.

◆ **X-rays don't seem to matter.** So feel free to take your camera with you to the airport, dentist, or thoracic surgeon.

SD and CompactFlash Considerations

SecureDigital or *SD* cards come in three varieties: regular SD cards, SDHC cards, which support capacities up to 32GB and offer faster transfer times, and SDXC, which offer capacities up to 2TB. While all three types of cards have the same form factor, be aware that SDHC and SDXC cards will only work if your camera specifically supports those formats. An older camera might not. This same caveat is true for SD card readers. Regular SD cards should work in any camera or reader with an SD slot.

CompactFlash cards now come in a variant called *UDMA (Ultra Direct Memory Access)*. If you have a camera that supports UDMA cards, then you might find that they work faster than regular CompactFlash cards. If you put a UDMA card in a camera that doesn't support UDMA, it will still work, but there's a chance it will be slower than the fastest, regular CompactFlash cards.

Media cards all come in different speeds. When we speak of access speed for a media card, we are referring to how quickly data can be read from the card and written to the card. Read and write speed is usually not the same. Cards with faster read speeds will transfer data to your computer more quickly, while cards with faster write speeds will allow you to shoot longer bursts more often, as well as to shoot higher quality video.

These days, SD cards are labeled with a class rating that indicates the minimum speed that the card can sustain when transferring data. A class 2 card will be able to sustain 2MB of sustained data transfer, while a Class 4 card can sustain 4MB. Class 8 and 10 can sustain 8 and 10MB, respectively.

Note that this is the minimum rate that the card can maintain. Each class might actually be able to burst data out at a faster rate.

As a still photographer, card speed won't be a huge issue for you unless you regularly shoot large bursts of images and need your camera to be able to offload that data quickly to facilitate more shooting. Faster cards are more expensive, so you might find that you would like to have a mix of speeds: Slow cards for bulk, regular shooting, and a couple of fast cards for times when you find yourself shooting quantities of image bursts.

Additional Storage Options

Earlier in this chapter, you read about some image size/compression strategies for saving media. Although these practices can make your storage go farther, the ideal solution is simply to buy more media cards. The price of media cards continues to drop, but if you tend to shoot *lots* of images, or if you're planning an extended trip, consider some of these storage alternatives.

Laptop Computers

If you plan on taking a long trip, you can augment your media cards with a laptop computer. In addition to giving you a place to store images, you'll have a complete darkroom with you. With a laptop and your favorite image editing application, you can assess right away whether your day's shooting was successful and determine if you need to reshoot something. What's more, if you begin organizing in the field—sorting, keywording, choosing select images—then you'll have a leg up on your postproduction when you get home. In fact, if you've got enough downtime on your trip, you might arrive home with your postproduction chores finished!

Tablets

A tablet computer might provide you with a good amount of image editing power. Bear in mind that you probably won't be able to use the same software that you use for your desktop workflow, and more importantly, you won't have as much storage as you have with a laptop computer. If you shoot raw, the limited storage on a tablet may be a deal breaker. If you're a JPEG shooter, then a tablet might be a more viable option. No matter what format you shoot, you'll need to look carefully at your postproduction workflow and evaluate how a tablet can fit into it.

Portable Battery-Powered Hard Drives

If you don't feel like lugging around your laptop computer, consider a stand-alone battery-powered hard drive device such as the HyperDrive ColorSpace UDMA2 shown in Figure 3.28. Measuring roughly the same size as a paperback book, these battery-powered devices contain a hard drive, a media slot, and an LCD screen. Simply insert the media from your camera into the slot, and you can back up your images to the internal drive. You can then put the card back into your camera, erase it, and start shooting again. These types of devices also allow you to view and delete images, build slideshows that can be output to a TV via a standard video out port, and even listen to MP3s. Because they're built around standard laptop computer hard drives, these devices deliver a much cheaper price-per-megabyte than any type of flash card.

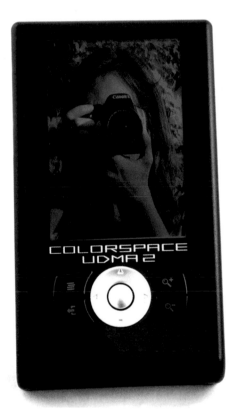

Figure 3.28

The HyperDrive ColorSpace UDMA2 gives you a portable battery-powered hard drive with built-in media slots and an operating system that makes it easy to transfer images, as well as review images and play slideshows.

Netbook Computers

Netbooks are small, light, and inexpensive. While they may not pack a screen that's big enough for serious image editing, they do come with lots of storage, and you can also use them for email and Web browsing, media playback, and all your usual laptop computer chores.

Blank Discs, Cables, and PC Adapters

Finally, you can simply carry around some blank CDs or DVDs and all of your camera's connectivity options. Then you need only find a service bureau, an Internet café, or a friend with a computer to burn your camera's images to your blanks. Obviously, your service bureau or friend will need a burner and the appropriate port. If they're running an older operating system that doesn't automatically download images, you'll need to bring the transfer software provided with your camera.

Hedge Your Bets by Offloading

Even if you have a very large storage card—one that can hold all the pictures you might conceivably need to shoot—it's still a good idea to offload some images from time to time. Media cards can crash, and backing up to another form of media is a good way to ensure that you won't lose all your images in the event of a storage crash. If you have the space, consider making more than one backup.

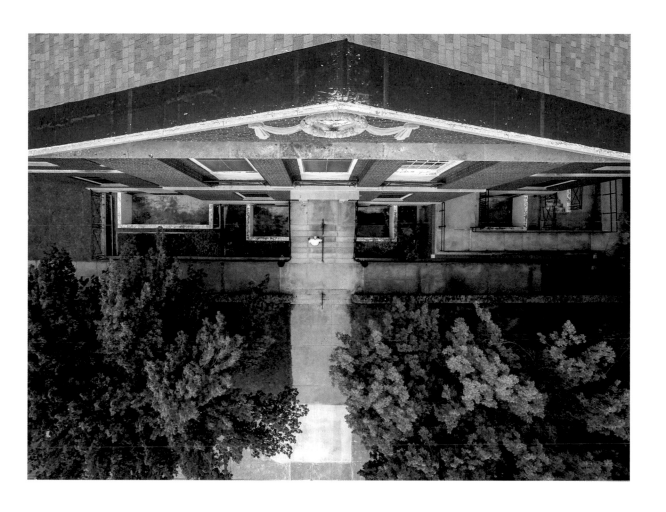

4

IMAGE TRANSFER

Building a Workstation and Transferring from Your Camera

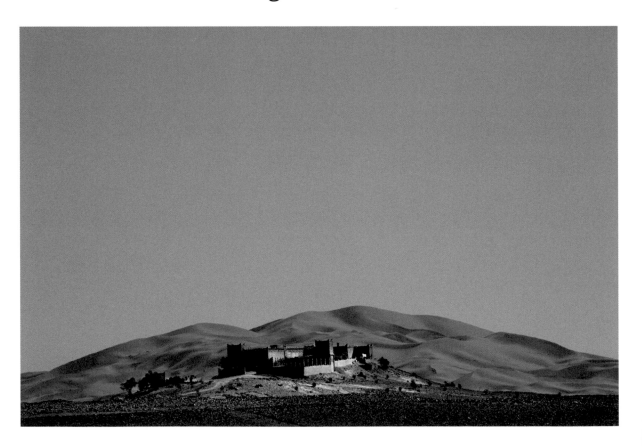

Digital cameras offer tremendous dynamic range and low-light performance that no film can match, but one of their best attributes is that you can quickly and easily get images out of the camera and start your postproduction process. This process begins when you transfer images from your camera to your computer.

In this chapter, we're going to take a quick look at image transfer, so that you can start working with the images that you've been shooting. In later chapters, we'll take a very detailed look at *workflow*, the exact steps that you need to get your image from the camera to a finished print. Here, we're simply going to discuss strategies and practices for getting your images copied to your computer, and that discussion will begin with a quick look at what makes a good digital photography workstation.

Choosing a Computer

When I wrote the first edition of this book, computer choice was a fairly delicate issue because the computing power of the day was somewhat limited when it came to image editing. These days, things are much easier for the simple fact that even entry-level computers are *very* fast, and storage is extremely cheap.

That said, there will be a performance difference between a new, top-of-the-line computer and a lesser model. This will be especially pronounced if you use a camera that has a sensor that packs a lot of pixels—25 megapixels or higher. However, we're talking about a level of performance difference that is more luxury than necessity.

One thing that's changed a lot in the last few years is that more image editing applications take advantage of the extra processing power that can be provided by a video card. The video card in your computer provides the interface between the computer and your monitor, and these cards often have their own dedicated graphics processing computers on board. These *graphics processing units*, or *GPUs*, can provide an extra processing kick for those programs that exploit them. The latest versions of Adobe Photoshop and Lightroom can exploit a GPU to improve performance.

RAM is also an important consideration when working with digital images. If scrolling or zooming your images is slow, or if you see images paint in chunks onto the screen, then you might want to consider adding more RAM.

For editing images in Photoshop, Adobe recommends a RAM size equal to two to three times the size of your typical image.

This is why you need a lot of RAM for image editing. For maximum performance, you'll want a RAM level closer to 20 times the size of your image. In addition, remember that your OS and other applications will also need some memory, so don't base your RAM needs on Photoshop alone (see Figure 4.1).

In the end, if you're on a budget, you might want to consider paying for a slightly slower, less-expensive processor and putting the money you save into more RAM.

Fortunately, RAM is cheap, so you should be able to easily outfit your computer with at least the recommended RAM specs provided by your image editing applications. You can always add more RAM later if you find that your current memory capacity is too low.

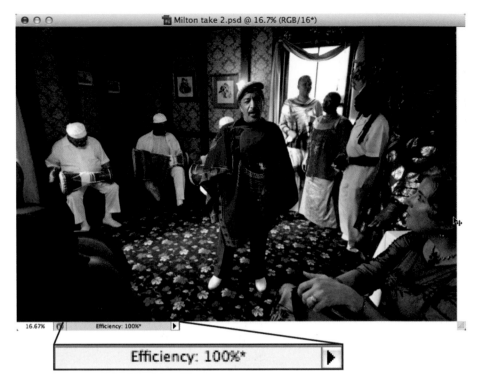

Figure 4.1

If Photoshop's Efficiency meter drops below 100 percent, you know that it can no longer keep all of its image data in RAM, which can lead to slower performance. By default, that Efficiency gauge box shows the current image's file size. Click on the arrow to the right of the box, and you can select other things to display, including the Efficiency meter.

Storage

The bad news is that digital images can take up a lot of space. The good news is that hard disk storage is cheap. Simply put, the more storage you have, the better. Bear in mind that you'll need space for your OS, your image editing applications, and any other software you plan on using, and that's all *before* you've shot any pictures. However, a 500GB drive should keep you editing for a while.

If you have a desktop, tower-type computer, then the cheapest way to add storage is to put additional drives into the tower's internal drive bays (assuming it has any available). If you're using a laptop computer, or a desktop computer such as an iMac, which doesn't have drive bays, then you'll have to add storage using external hard drives.

Most external drives plug into the USB-2 or USB-3 port on your computer, though some can connect via FireWire, Thunderbolt, or eSATA. Find out what kind of interface you have before you go drive shopping. Small 2.5" drives like the one shown in the center of Figure 4.2 are great for portable use, because they don't require any external power connector. Instead, a single USB-2, USB-3, or FireWire cable provides both the data connection and power. Larger 3.5" drives require a separate power supply. The advantage to 3.5" drives is that they come in larger capacities and have a much lower price per gigabyte.

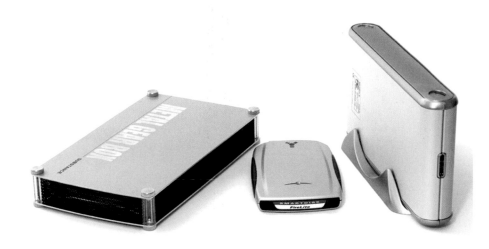

Figure 4.2

External drives make excellent storage add-ons for backup or additional workspace. Small 2.5" drives, like the one in the center, can take their power from the same cable that is used to connect the drive to the computer, making them ideal for taking on the road. Larger drives require separate power, but offer much larger capacities and better price per gigabyte.

Thunderbolt drives can be daisy-chained—as you need more storage, you can plug new drives into the Thunderbolt connectors on your current drives. USB-2 and USB-3 drives require a free port on your computer, although you can add a USB hub to gain more ports. USB hubs come powered and unpowered. (Powered ones simply have an external power supply of their own.)

Note that hard drives that do not have external power supplies will need to be plugged into a powered USB port. The ports built in to your computer are powered, so that's not a problem. If you're plugging one of these drives into a hub, it will have to be a powered hub.

USB-3 Drives

USB-3 drives are now widely available. USB-3 offers faster transfer speeds, but only if you have a USB-3 port on your computer. USB-3 drives use a different type of connector, but the USB-3 specification, and its connector, is backward-compatible with USB-2. So you can plug USB-3 drives into a USB-2 port and use them at USB-2 speeds.

Backup

Hopefully, you haven't already learned this the hard way, but eventually a hard drive will fail. A hard drive is a mechanical device with a lot of moving parts, and after a while, all that disk spinning and drive head moving takes its toll and a mechanical failure occurs. When this happens, your drive will most likely become unusable. While there are services that can attempt to get your data off the drive, they usually charge around $1,000 with no guarantee of success.

Of course, other things can happen to your drives—they can be lost, stolen, and so on. The best and only way to ensure that you don't lose images is to diligently back up your files, and the easiest way to back up is to buy additional hard drives. You can then simply copy your image folders to your backup drive or use backup software.

RAID

You can configure multiple hard drives into a *RAID*, or *redundant array of independent disks*. RAIDs can be configured in several different ways, the most common methods being designated with the labels RAID0 through RAID6. The different categories of RAIDs provide different degrees of speed (how fast data is written to or read from them) and fault tolerance (the ability to recover data if a drive fails).

RAID0 uses "striping" without parity. (*Parity* simply means that some extra bits are written out to facilitate different recovery options, in the event of a failure.) "Striping" means that successive blocks of data are alternated between two drives. This makes for very speedy access, because while one drive is reading a block of data, the other drive can be preparing to read the next block. But, since neither drive contains all of the data, if one drive is lost, all the data is lost. RAID0 provides an increase in speed, but no increase in fault tolerance.

RAID1 uses "mirroring." This means that all the data is written to both drives, so if one drive fails, all the data can be recovered from the other drive. RAID1 provides a high degree of fault tolerance but little or no increase in speed. RAID2 through RAID6 utilize striping with parity. These configurations provide various combinations of increased speed and fault tolerance, with RAID6 using dual parity, which gives it the capability to recover from the loss of two drives.

Many operating systems offer software-based RAID implementations, usually levels 0, 1, and 5 but sometimes others. Many motherboards and drive controllers offer hardware or firmware implementations. If you decide to use one of these, be aware that RAID0 provides no fault tolerance; if you lose one of your two RAID drives, you have lost all your data. Any of the other implementations will provide fault tolerance.

Data Robotics has created a nonstandard RAID implementation, which they call *BeyondRaid*. It is available in their "Drobo" products, which is an incredibly easy-to-use package. A multiple-drive enclosure, the Drobo lets you add and remove drives easily, and doesn't require drives to be the same size. Intelligent software built into the device takes care of keeping your data redundant.

If you're comfortable with the process of assembling a PC, then you should consider an unRAID, an excellent, low-cost solution that offers the same kind of fault tolerance that RAID and Drobo systems do. It can use mixed drive sizes and can be expanded one drive at a time. If you have any spare PC hardware around, it can be a very cost-effective solution. You can learn more about it here: *www.completedigitalphotography.com/unraid*.

Remember that all of these systems provide a high degree of fault tolerance but are not bulletproof. Two drives can fail at the same time (more likely if they are the same model and the same age), and drive controllers or power supplies can fail in such a way as to corrupt the data on all drives connected to them. All of these redundant systems provide a huge increase in fault tolerance over storage on a single drive. You must decide whether or not you want to back up the data on your array onto drives in a second enclosure (or perhaps on removable drives).

Backup Software

There are a number of backup programs that make short work of backing up your data. What you ideally want is software that will perform a progressive backup, which means that the only files copied are files that have been changed since the last backup. This is much faster than a system that re-copies files that haven't been altered. Some backup programs will even let you return to any of several different states. So, if you've backed up three times over the last month, these programs will let you return to any of those backup states.

During our discussion of workflow, we'll cover the details of when you should back up.

Monitors

You're going to be spending a lot of time staring at your computer screen, so it's important to choose wisely when you select a monitor. While it's possible to get a large LCD screen for relatively low cost, as a photographer, you have some color and contrast concerns that can really only be satisfied by a higher-quality display.

Hunt down reviews and, if possible, try to see the screen in person before you buy it. You want a bright display with good sharpness, a wide viewing angle, and as broad a contrast range as you can get. If you're working with a laptop, try to avoid glossy screens because the extra gloss can obscure shadow details, and the extra reflections can make color assessment difficult.

Preparing Your Monitor

If you've ever stood in the TV department of an appliance store, you've seen firsthand how an image can differ from screen to screen. And, as you may have already discovered, prints can often look very different from the image on your computer monitor. *Monitor profiling* and *calibration* is the process of tuning your system so that your printed output better matches what you see on-screen, so that the same image will appear consistent from one screen to another. How much effort you spend on this process depends on how picky you are, what kind of workflow you expect to have, and what kind of gear you use.

Fortunately, there's been a lot of good work done to improve color consistency from screen to print, so getting good results from your printer is not as complicated as it used to be. With the current generation of printer drivers from Epson, Canon, and HP, you can get very good results by simply using the automatic color-correction features built into the printer drivers. Note that these drivers probably won't produce prints that match the color on your monitor exactly, but you'll likely find that with practice, you'll learn how things on your screen correspond to what comes out of your printer. For example, you'll get better at eyeballing when shadows in an image are too dark.

However, your screen will never *exactly* match your printed output, simply because the two technologies are very different. Your monitor and printer use different primary colors, which mix together in very different ways. Adding to the problem is the fact that your monitor is a self-illuminated display that generates its own light, while a photographic print is a reflective media that bounces light from another source. Finally, your monitor probably has a much wider gamut, or range of displayable colors, than does any printer that you'll find.

All of these parameters combine to create a very tricky situation for your computer. Trying to display an image in the same way that it will print is very tough. As such, you'll never get your monitor and prints to match exactly. However, with a little care, you can get them very close, which means you can greatly reduce the number of test prints that you need to make.

If you've ever worked in a darkroom, you know that it takes a fair number of test prints to discover exactly what printing exposure is best for a particular image. The same is true when printing digitally, but through calibration and profiling it is possible to greatly reduce the number of test prints. If you're frustrated with the wasted ink and paper that you have to go through to make test prints, just bear in mind that it's still much more cost effective than working in a chemical darkroom. And, as the technology improves, we may one day have much better screen-to-printer fidelity.

Online Printing Services

If all you're looking for is snapshot output, then you may be better off using an online printing service or a drugstore service. These often deliver simple 4" × 6" output at a much more affordable rate than you can get from your desktop printer.

In the following section, we'll discuss monitor profiling and a few basics of color management. We'll have much more to say about this subject in Chapter 22, "Output," when we discuss printing.

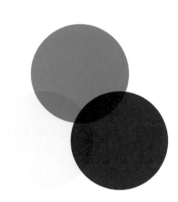

Figure 4.3

The primary colors of ink are cyan, magenta, and yellow. These colors differ from the primary colors of light—red, green, and blue—that your camera uses to create images. This difference is one of the things that makes monitor/printer calibration so complicated.

A Little More Color Theory

As you learned earlier, light mixes together in an additive process so that as colors are added together they appear more and more white. Ink, on the other hand, mixes in a subtractive manner. That is, as colors are mixed, they appear darker. While the primary colors of light—the fundamental colors from which all other colors can be made—are red, green, and blue, the primary colors of ink are cyan, magenta, and yellow (see Figure 4.3).

This difference in the way colors are made is what makes accurate matching of your monitor and printer so difficult. Each time you print, your computer has to figure out how to take your image—which it represents as a combination of red, green, and blue light—and convert it into the mix of cyan, magenta, and yellow ink that your printer expects.

Special K—Why Printers Add Black

As you might already know, color printing uses four colors: cyan, magenta, yellow, and black. (Some printing processes add additional colors, but they all include these four.) Black is not a primary color, of course, but black ink is added to the mix because it is impossible to create perfectly pure ink pigments. Therefore, although the theory says that if you mix cyan, magenta, and yellow together you will eventually get black, the truth is you'll just get very dark brown because of impurities in the color pigments of your inks. Adding a little black ink is the only way to get true black. This is why most color printing is a four-color process called *CMYK*.

As if converting colors between these two different color spaces weren't difficult enough, accurate color reproduction is further complicated by the fact that not every monitor is the same. There are a number of reasons why, ranging from differences in color adjustments on each monitor to differences in age to differences in manufacturing. This is why a digital image or Web page on your monitor might look completely different on someone else's monitor.

Printers have their own collection of troubles. Each manufacturer might take a different approach to reproducing colors, and different brands of ink and types of paper have their own unique color qualities as well. Fortunately, with just a few steps, you can greatly improve color consistency.

Profiling and Calibrating Your Monitor

To improve color consistency across multiple devices, a group of camera, software, and display vendors created the International Color Consortium. The ICC has defined a standard method of profiling printers and monitors. An ICC profile is a small text file that contains a description of the color and contrast properties of a device. These descriptions can be used by software in your computer to adjust color on-the-fly as it passes from one device to another. The color in your document is never actually altered. Instead, it is temporarily modified in an attempt to preserve consistency from one device to another. Consequently, your image should appear consistent as you move it from computer to computer and from screen to printer.

This type of color management only works well when you have controllable viewing conditions and accurate, high-quality profiles for your monitor and printer. We'll talk about printer profiles when we discuss output. Right now, it's time to consider your monitor profile.

The Macintosh operating system includes a software monitor calibrator that lets you create a monitor profile by eye. (Go to System Preferences > Displays, click the Color tab, press the Calibrate button, and follow the on-screen instructions.) If you're using Photoshop on Windows, it should include calibration capability in its drivers. These programs yield profiles that are better than using no profile at all, but if you're going to bother with color management, it's best to use a hardware profiler to create a monitor profile.

There are several relatively inexpensive profilers on the market, ranging from the $99 PANTONE hueyPRO or ColorVision Spyder2express ($79), to more expensive systems such as the $169 Spyder3Pro (see Figure 4.4) or the $249 Spyder3Elite.

These gizmos provide you with a piece of hardware that you attach or hang in front of your monitor. The included software then uses the device to measure the color and contrast properties of your monitor, and then it generates a profile—a small data file—that you install on your computer. The higher-priced profilers do a better job than the less expensive

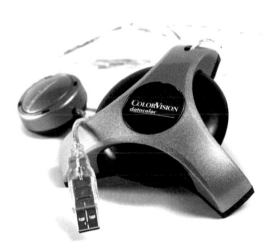

Figure 4.4

The ColorVision Spyder is just one of several different monitor calibrator/profilers. After hanging the device in front of your monitor, you use special included software to build a profile automatically.

units, and their software provides more configuration options. However, even a $79 device will be better than no calibration or "eyeballed" calibration. The money you invest in a calibrator will more than pay for itself in saved ink and paper.

All these devices include detailed instructions on their use, as well as guides for getting better results. In general, the process is automatic and painless, and you'll probably want to reprofile at least once a month (more if your monitor is older).

Monitor Calibration Tips

Before you calibrate your monitor, whether by eye or with a hardware calibrator, let the monitor warm up for half an hour or so. This will give it time to get up to its usual operating temperature. For best results, turn down the lights in the room and block any reflections or glare that might be striking the monitor.

Set your desktop background or pattern to a neutral gray. (When you do any precise color manipulation or editing, you should set your desktop to gray to keep your eyes from getting confused.) If you want to get really picky, it's a good idea to move any large, brightly colored objects out of your field of view. In general, you want your working space to be neutrally colored.

Before you invest too much in calibration hardware, remember that not every monitor is capable of being calibrated. If your monitor lacks controls for altering contrast and brightness, then you probably won't have much luck calibrating it. In general, you won't have much calibration latitude on laptop displays, iMacs, Apple Cinema Displays, and other affordable LCD screens. CRTs fare much better, as do high-end LCD screens.

Software

Image editing and correction is a critical part of the photography process, but it's important to understand that corrections and adjustments are just one part of your postproduction process. Sorting, organizing, and selecting your choice images is often a bigger chore than any type of special effects or digital correction. In fact, if you do your job right while you're shooting, then you might not have to do much, if any, correction and manipulation later.

We'll discuss postproduction in detail in the second half of this book; however, the basic workflow goes like this: import your images from your camera or media card, identify the select images that you think are the keepers, apply metadata and keywords to your images to ease organization, adjust and correct your selects, output your images, back up and then archive.

The tutorials in this book are built around Adobe Photoshop Lightroom and Photoshop CC. Demo versions of both of these programs can be downloaded from Adobe's website. I chose Lightroom for these demos because it's an excellent image editor and organizational tool, but also because when it comes to specific types of edits, you'll find that most other image editors use controls like those that Adobe designed for the original Photoshop. So the things you'll learn in Lightroom and Photoshop will apply to most other editing tools. Even if you don't go on with either of these applications, the lessons you learn in this book should carry over to other image editing programs.

However, there are a lot of applications out there that can help with various parts of your postproduction process. Over the next few pages, I'm going to give you a brief overview of the postproduction landscape. You'll learn about the workflow issues you'll face and what tools are available to help with these issues.

What About the Software That Shipped with My Camera?

Most cameras ship with some combination of image editing, importing, and image browsing software. If your camera can shoot in raw format, then it might come bundled with a raw conversion program of some kind. Some cameras are bundled with popular apps such as Photoshop Elements, but most include proprietary applications developed by the camera manufacturer.

In general, it's safe to say that these bundled apps are not as good as many inexpensive third-party alternatives. However, if you can't afford or don't have access to other applications, the bundled software will probably work fine.

Two Approaches to Workflow

When it comes to choosing software (and an overall workflow approach), you have two choices. The first is a "manual" process that uses a few different applications in conjunction with your computer's file manager. In this approach, you will use the following procedures:

- ◆ Copy images to your computer.

- ◆ Organize your images by placing them in folders. Using the file manager on your computer, you will find, move, copy, and rename images, and perform any other organizational tasks.

- ◆ Use browsing software to view thumbnails and previews of all of the images in a folder.

- ◆ Launch images from your browser or open images from your file manager into an image editing application.

- ◆ Output your images and then back up and archive the files using backup software or your program's file manager.

Alternatively, you can use a dedicated workflow application. Programs like Adobe Photoshop Lightroom and Apple's iPhoto take care of importing and organizing for you, giving you a one-stop location for organizing, editing, backup, and more. Dedicated workflow applications include image editing features, and often these are the only editing tools you need to get the job done. To facilitate working with other programs, such as Photoshop, these tools also allow you to launch images directly into another application.

The advantage of the first manual approach is that it provides tremendous flexibility. You can organize images however you want and use any tool you like for any part of your workflow. The advantage to the second approach is that it might be easier if you're not comfortable with managing files on your own. Also, dedicated workflow tools like Lightroom make it much easier to search and update your archive as it grows. You might also find that even simple postproduction tasks go quicker because you don't have to hassle with opening, saving, and organizing files. Finally, these applications also make short work out of outputting websites and books, and exporting to social media and photo sharing sites.

In the next section, we'll take a quick look at some of the applications you'll need if you want to piece together a workflow using the first approach.

Browsing and Cataloging Applications

While your file manager might provide good tools for copying, moving, deleting, and organizing files, it probably doesn't provide much of a facility for previewing images. With a browser application, you can view a folder of images as thumbnails, rather than as simple file names and icons. These thumbnails can usually be made larger or smaller, and most browsers also provide a way to view a larger preview.

Browser applications typically provide a lot of other image-related utility features, such as image rotation, batch renaming, metadata viewing and editing, and the capability to create folders and move and copy files. Many browsers also offer import features, raw conversion, and batch-processing capabilities that allow you to speed up your workflow. Some browser programs provide limited image editing and correction tools, but most assume that you'll perform serious editing in a separate, dedicated image editing program.

A browser serves as a halfway point between your file manager and image editor. While a browser provides viewing, editing, and metadata controls that aren't available in your file manager, it still relies on the directory system and file architecture provided by your OS. In other words, it's just a different way of viewing the folders and documents that you see in the file manager. You can think of it as a more photo-friendly front end. By comparison, work-flow applications like Lightroom maintain their own database of images and file structure, and they manage the copying, moving, and organization of images for you.

If you don't want to commit to a workflow application like Lightroom, then a browser pro-gram will be an essential tool for viewing, sorting, and launching images into your image editor. Some cross-platform browser applications include the following:

◆ **Adobe Bridge,** which has shipped with Photoshop since version CS2, offers all the browser features you'd expect, wrapped up in an interface that integrates seamlessly with the other apps in the Adobe Creative Cloud (Photoshop, Illustrator, InDesign, and so on). What's more, it provides access to Photoshop Camera Raw for raw con-version and offers excellent batch-processing capabilities. That said, Bridge is slow to search large collections of images, and it may have a limited lifespan. At the time of this writing, Adobe has placed Bridge in "maintenance mode," meaning there will be no additions or changes to the application, only bug fixes.

◆ **Camera Bits Photo Mechanic** provides most of the features you'd want in a browser, including capturing, renaming, raw conversion, metadata editing, and much more. In addition, the program provides batch processing features, the ability to import from multiple cards simultaneously, and extremely fast performance. If you work on short deadlines or have older hardware, Photo Mechanic's speedy performance might be the deal-making feature for you.

A cataloging application allows you to create a catalog of any folder or volume. Because you ultimately might end up with more images than you have hard drive space for, you'll want to organize images onto different hard drives or recordable disks. A cataloging application provides you with a way of keeping track of which images are located where. You can browse through thumbnails in the catalog to find the image you're looking for, and the catalog will list the location of the image. You can then go find that particular volume—be it a hard drive or recordable disk—and retrieve the image.

Cataloging applications typically provide extensive mechanisms for editing the metadata of images, as well as tools for searching and sorting images based on this metadata. You can also share catalogs with friends or coworkers so that they can browse your library.

Some very good cross-platform catalog programs that provide all the expected cataloging features include the following:

◆ **Extensis Portfolio** offers excellent features including the ability to view full-screen previews of any cataloged image, support for dozens of raw formats, batch file conversion features, one-click CD archiving, folder syncing, and excellent Web publishing features.

◆ **Phase One Media Pro** also provides excellent cataloging features with superb Web output, very speedy performance, the ability to create stand-alone viewer documents, and much more (see Figure 4.5).

◆ **Canto Cumulus** is a high-end cataloging system that offers a sophisticated client/server architecture that is ideal for workgroups and large publishing organizations. If you want to create complex multiuser photo/print production workflows, then Cumulus might be the tool for you.

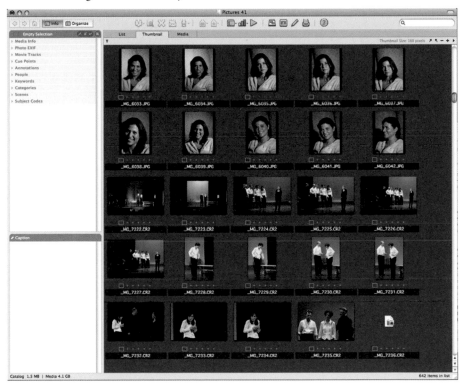

Figure 4.5

Phase One Media Pro is a fine example of an image-cataloging program. With it, you can easily create catalog documents of folders, hard drives, or CDs and DVDs.

Photoshop Variations

Everyone knows you can use an image editing program like Photoshop to make wild changes to an image. Of course, what you'll use it for the most are less obvious edits. Cropping, tone and color adjustments, and maybe the occasional retouching are the editing tasks you'll perform the most.

However, even what appear to be "simple" color and tone adjustments can be hard to pull off, which is why an advanced image editor provides so many different ways of making these adjustments. In addition to the adjustments, you might also want the capability to make edits to just one part of an image, to stitch panoramic images, and more.

We'll be doing some tutorial work in Adobe Photoshop, and if you choose to use it you should know that it comes in two variants:

◆ **Adobe Photoshop CC.** Photoshop offers an enormous selection of tools, wrapped up in a very good interface, and all of it is built on top of an excellent color engine that yields professional-quality results. You'll be hard-pressed to find a feature that Photoshop doesn't have, but if you do find yourself wanting additional features, you'll probably be able to hunt down a third-party Photoshop plug-in that adds that functionality to the program. While this depth makes Photoshop hard to beat in head-to-head feature comparisons, it also makes for a program that can be fairly intimidating.

Photoshop is not just for photographers. The program has extensive Web development features, prepress tools, compositing and special effects features, scientific analysis features, and more. The fact is, most photographers don't need the bulk of the features included in the program. Fortunately, if you keep this in mind as you learn Photoshop, you should find that you can safely ignore the features you don't need, and you can easily customize Photoshop's interface to hide the features you don't want.

Photoshop is an industry unto itself, so you should have no trouble finding all sorts of resources for learning the program, from books to websites to training videos to classes. Also, Photoshop comes bundled with Bridge, making the package a complete workflow solution.

Photoshop is currently available via subscription at a variety of extremely reasonable price points.

◆ **Photoshop Elements.** This is a stripped-down, under-$100 version of Photoshop that offers all the essential photography features that you'll need. Photoshop Elements uses an interface similar to Photoshop CC's interface, so you get all of the advantages of Photoshop's UI design and most of the higher-end package's most important features and performance characteristics. What you *don't* get are some tools that you may or may not need. For example, Elements lacks the capability to work with CMYK images—the type of images you need to create if you're going to output to a professional offset press. You also cannot use Elements to edit and view individual color channels. As you'll see later, this can be important because channel editing is a necessary feature for creating certain types of effects. Finally, Elements does not include some of Photoshop CC's more advanced editing tools, such as high-end masking and black-and-white conversion features, and offers no automation capabilities.

Elements is a great way to get into Photoshop. If you need more power later, you can always upgrade to the full version, which shares most of the Elements interface.

Nondestructive Editing

Earlier, you learned that an image is composed of a number of pixels represented by numeric values. In most image editors, when you make an adjustment, the color values of the adjusted pixels are altered to reflect your changes. In a *nondestructive editing* system, actual pixel values are never altered. Instead, a description of any edit that you make is stored in a list. Any time the computer needs to display, output, or print the image, the original pixel values are processed according to the instructions stored in the list of edits (see Figure 4.6).

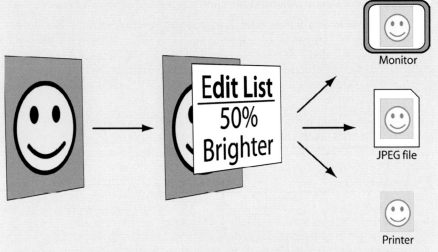

Figure 4.6 In a nondestructive editing system, all edits that you make are kept in a list. In real time, the editing software takes your original image data, processes it according to the instructions in the list, and then outputs it to your monitor, printer, or to a file.

The advantage of a nondestructive editing system is that you can undo any edit at any time. You can also go back and alter the *parameters* of any edit at any time, making a nondestructive system far more flexible than a destructive editor. Photoshop's Adjustment Layers (which you'll learn about in detail later) are a form of nondestructive editing. Adobe's Photoshop Camera Raw, Lightroom, and Apple's iPhoto offer completely nondestructive editing.

Why You Want a Pressure-Sensitive Tablet

If you routinely use the paint brush, rubber stamp (clone), or dodge and burn tools in your image editor, or if you do a lot of masking work, then you should seriously consider investing in a pressure-sensitive tablet. Tablets like the Wacom Bamboo Pen shown in Figure 4.7 provide a drawing surface and electronic stylus that do a great job of mimicking the experience of working with real-world tools.

With a pressure-sensitive stylus, when you push harder your brush gets bigger, or changes color, or becomes more opaque, all depending on how the software you're using is configured.

Some people find the "look at screen/draw on lap or tabletop" coordination to be a little confusing at first, but after only one or two sessions, you'll wonder how you ever managed to paint with a mouse or trackpad.

Wacom is the market leader, and with good reason. Their tablets are incredibly well designed and include excellent software. What's more, all the major image editing applications support Wacom's pressure sensitivity.

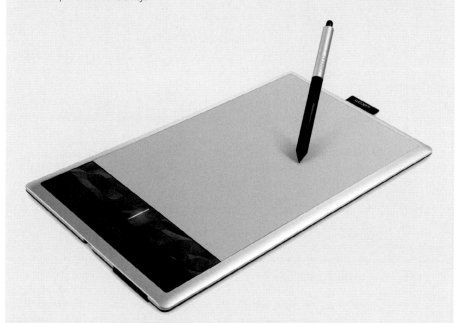

Figure 4.7 A pressure-sensitive tablet like this Wacom Bamboo Pen makes any brush, retouching, or masking operation much easier.

Workflow Applications

Workflow applications help you with the sorting, cataloging, organization, and archiving of your images, provide image editing tools of their own, and also give you a way to launch into the editing phase of your workflow. With a workflow application, you won't need a browser or cataloging application, and you will probably spend less time in the file manager of your operating system. Also, your workflow will be identical whether you work with JPEG or raw files. Listed below are descriptions of the most popular workflow applications.

◆ **Adobe Bridge.** Bridge has been around for a while, and has always offered good browsing features, meaning you can point Bridge at a folder and quickly see thumbnails of all the images contained within (see Figure 4.8). Bridge also lets you copy and move files, see large previews, compare images, zoom in close to assess fine details, and much more. With Bridge, you can quickly launch images into Photoshop and batch-process your images, making it simple to apply the same edits to huge groups of images. Bridge also allows you to build virtual albums (called *Collections*), providing a way to keep your library organized as it grows. Bridge currently ships with Adobe Photoshop.

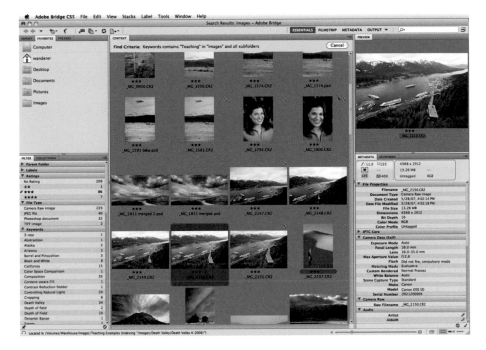

Figure 4.8

Adobe Bridge provides everything you need to build a complete workflow around Adobe Photoshop.

◆ **Photoshop Lightroom.** Available for both Mac and Windows, Photoshop Lightroom offers importing, sorting, comparing, organizing, keywording, editing, raw conversion, Web page output, and printing, all in a single application that provides different virtual "rooms" for each task (see Figure 4.9). Lightroom's strongest advantages are an entirely nondestructive editing approach and the fact that it's built around Photoshop Camera Raw for raw conversion. This means that it supports a tremendous number of raw formats and provides all the tools you expect to find in a good raw converter.

Current users of Photoshop Camera Raw will find it easy to switch to Lightroom, while the huge number of third-party websites and books devoted to the product make it possible for novices to get up to speed quickly.

Lightroom also has excellent Photoshop integration, making it simple to jump from editing in Lightroom to performing all of your usual Photoshop edits, and all without having to hassle with file management of any kind.

You can download a free 30-day, fully functional trial version of Lightroom for Mac or Windows at *www.adobe.com/go/trylightroom*.

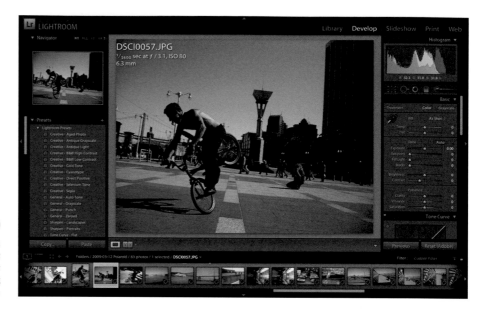

Figure 4.9

Adobe Photoshop Lightroom provides a single application that offers an integrated environment for importing, sorting, applying metadata, editing, and output.

◆ **Aperture.** Apple invented the photography workflow genre with Aperture (you might even be able to argue that they invented it with iPhoto), a Mac-only product that combines all of the expected workflow features, including nondestructive editing, and adds book printing, automatic backup, tethered shooting, multicard importing, scriptability, and more. Aperture's raw converter is first-rate and includes good editing tools (see Figure 4.10). Its biggest strength is its exceptional interface, which allows for a fluid, ever-changing workflow. With Aperture, you're never stuck in any particular mode, making it easy to work the way you want to work and the way that is best for the particular images that you're processing.

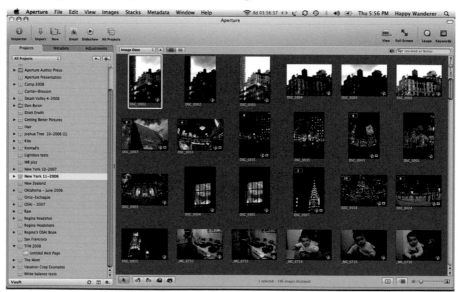

Figure 4.10

Apple's Aperture offers a full assortment of workflow tools wrapped up in an excellent, fluid, nonmodal interface.

On the downside, Aperture's Photoshop integration is not as strong as Lightroom's or Bridge's. Aperture performs much of its editing work using the graphics-processing unit on your computer's video card. As such, it's very important to check that your Mac is Aperture compatible.

Aperture Discontinued

Just as this book was going to press, Apple announced that it was discontinuing development of Aperture. This application will be replaced by a new one that will be bundled with future versions of the OS.

Apple iPhoto

If you're a Mac user, you have another workflow management option in the form of iPhoto. Bundled free with all new Macs, or available separately from the Apple App Store, iPhoto is a very good image management, editing, organization, and output tool (Figure 4.11). iPhoto provides all the workflow management features that most users will need, including importing, organizing, keywording, editing, and output. iPhoto supports JPEGs and raw files, providing you with the same workflow no matter what type of file you're working with. If you're a Mac user, it's worth giving iPhoto a close look before you invest in any additional software.

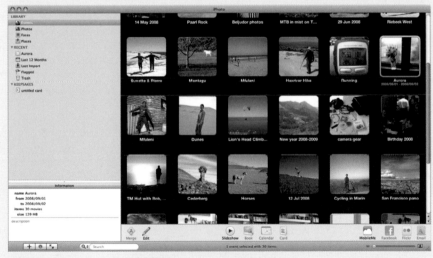

Figure 4.11 Apple's iPhoto is bundled with all Macs and provides an excellent workflow and editing solution. Because it's free and very capable, it's worth taking a close look at iPhoto before investing in other software.

Raw Converter Compatibility

If you plan on using raw, then you'll need to be sure that your raw conversion or workflow application supports your particular camera. A raw converter must have a special profile for your specific type of raw-capable camera. If your application doesn't specifically say that it works with the raw files from your camera of choice, then you'll need to consider a different program. Right now, Photoshop Camera Raw (which is built into Photoshop, Photoshop

Elements, and Photoshop Lightroom) supports far more raw formats than any other converter, although any of the major raw conversion apps will support all of the popular cameras.

Most software vendors are diligent about releasing updates to support cameras as they're released, but it can sometimes take a while for these updates to appear.

Other Software

Finally, there might be other utilities and applications that you'll find a use for. Panoramic stitching software can be used to turn multiple shots into a single, wide panorama; special high dynamic range software can be used to turn multiple exposures into a single image with expanded dynamic range; and file recovery software can be used to recover images from cards you've accidentally erased. We'll cover all of these in more detail throughout this book.

Importing Images

Every image you shoot is stored on your camera's media card as an individual file. The file is a document just like you might create on your computer. Importing (some people call this step *ingesting*, but that sounds a little too biological for me) is simply the process of copying those image files from your camera's media card to your computer. To import, you can connect your camera to your computer via a cable (usually a USB cable) or take the media card out of your camera and put it into a media card reader attached to your computer.

Card Readers

Depending on its interface, a media card reader can be faster than plugging your camera into your computer to transfer images, and it doesn't drain your camera battery. Also, most card readers support lots of different formats, so if you have more than one camera (say, an SLR and a small point-and-shoot) that use different formats, then you need to carry only one card reader and a cable.

Check Your SD and CompactFlash Reader Carefully

If you're shopping for an SD card reader, be aware that some cameras that support SD also support a newer, faster, higher-capacity format called SDHC. If you're using any *SDHC* cards, you'll need to be sure to get a reader that can read SDHC. Similarly, if you use UDMA CompactFlash cards, you'll want to be sure to get a UDMA card reader.

Handling an Unreadable Card

Sometimes, you might find that a card that has always worked fine in your card reader suddenly doesn't read. If this happens, put the card back in the camera and see whether you can view images on the camera's screen. If you can, then you know that the camera can read the card just fine. Plug the camera into your computer and try transferring the images that way. It will usually work. When you're done, format the card. This will usually get the card working with your card reader again.

Transferring Images to a Windows 7 Computer

In Windows 7, when a camera or card reader is plugged in, you'll see the dialog box shown in Figure 4.12.

The "Import pictures and videos" option copies images from your camera or media card to the Pictures directory, and it allows you to customize the import process. After the import is complete, the pictures are displayed on the *Imported Pictures and Videos* screen (Figure 4.13).

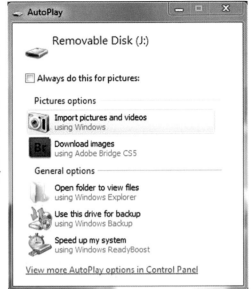

Figure 4.12

When you insert a card reader or camera into your Windows 7 computer, you'll see this dialog box.

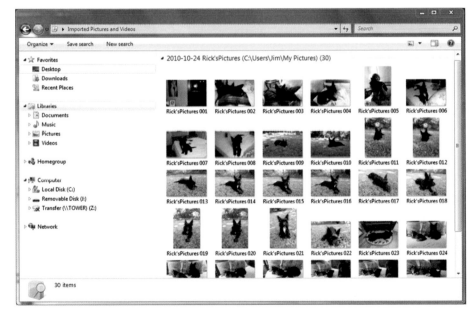

Figure 4.13

After importing, your images are shown in the Imported Pictures and Videos viewer.

Clicking on one of the images on this screen will open the Windows Photo Viewer, which allows you to view all of the pictures in the directory (Figure 4.14).

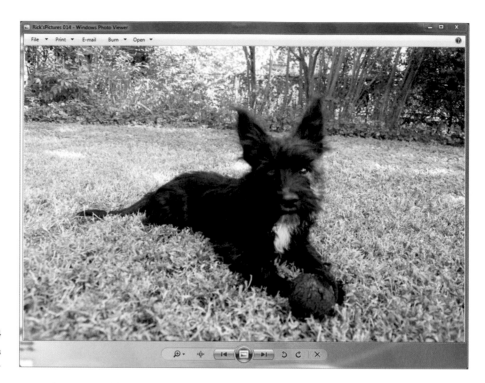

Figure 4.14

Clicking on a thumbnail brings up the Windows Photo Viewer.

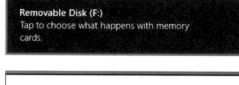

Transferring Images to a Windows 8 Computer

In Windows 8, when a camera or card reader is plugged in, you'll see a sequence of two dialog boxes shown in Figure 4.15.

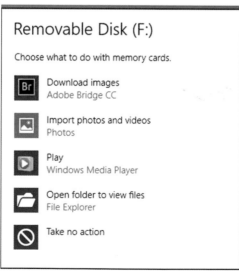

Figure 4.15

When you insert a card reader or camera into your Windows 8 computer, you'll see this sequence of dialog boxes. With the second box you can choose how you want Windows to import your images.

If you choose "Import photos and videos," you will see a screen similar to Figure 4.16, and you will be able to select which images to import.

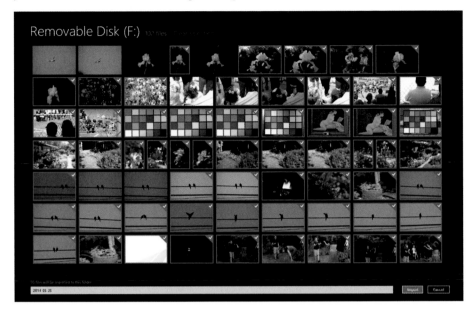

Figure 4.16

With this screen, you can import all of the images on the card (the default), or you can clear the selection and click on the ones you want to import.

Changing Media Card Preferences

If you set an "Always do this for pictures" option in Windows 7 or simply made a selection in Windows 8 and decided later that you want to change it, go to the Control Panel, and then select Hardware and Sound. Find the AutoPlay, which will bring up the screen for changing the default settings for media or devices. For Windows 7, you can edit the Pictures category to select a different option, or choose "Ask me every time" to get Windows to present you with a dialog box of choices. For Windows 8, you edit the Memory card category.

Using Adobe Photo Downloader

Adobe Photoshop Elements and Adobe Photoshop CS both include a Photo Downloader application that you can configure to launch automatically when a camera or card reader is attached to your computer.

Photo Downloader lets you choose a location to store your files, and it can automatically create subfolders based on the date and time stamp of each image. Photo Downloader can also rename your images from the meaningless names your camera creates to something more intelligible.

If you use a Photoshop-based workflow, this might be the way to go.

Transferring Images to a Macintosh Computer

Transferring images to your Mac is very simple, and you have a number of options for determining what happens when you attach the camera or card reader.

Depending on when you bought your Mac, you might have a copy of iPhoto, Apple's image organizing and editing program. iPhoto is very good, and can handle the transfer of images from your media card, and help you with the rest of your workflow, from organizing to editing to output. Be aware that iPhoto imports your images into its own library system. If you want to manage the location of your images on your own, then you'll want to skip iPhoto.

If your Mac doesn't have it, you can buy the latest version from the Apple App Store.

Every Mac ships with a copy of Image Capture, a utility that helps manage the transfer of images into your computer. Image Capture has no editing or organizational features—its sole purpose is to get images copied onto your hard drive. Once they're there, you can decide what to do with them.

Configuring Your Mac for Image Transfer

You can tell your Mac what you want to have happen when you plug in a camera or a media card reader. This makes it simple to choose what software you want to use to transfer your images.

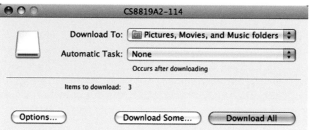

Figure 4.17

All Macs ship with Image Capture, which provides a simple way to manage the transfer of images from a camera or media card reader.

In your Applications folder there should be a program called *Image Capture*. By default, it will open automatically any time you plug in a camera or card reader, and will present a window for managing the transfer of images (see Figure 4.17).

With Image Capture, you can choose where you want your images downloaded and what to do after they've copied. If you press the Download Some button, you can even select specific images to copy.

Image Capture also lets you specify what you want your Mac to do when you plug in a card reader or camera. If you go to the Image Capture menu and choose Preferences, you'll see a pop-up menu that lets you select which application you want to have launched whenever a camera or a media card reader is plugged into your Mac.

The menu will list iPhoto (if you have it), Image Capture, and possibly other applications if you have them installed. If you have a program installed that you'd like to use, but you don't see it listed, choose Other. Image Capture will present you with a dialog box that allows you to pick the program you'd like to use.

Finally, if you'd like complete manual control, you can choose No Application.

Transferring Images Manually Using Windows or a Mac

For complete manual control of your image transfers, configure your computer to do nothing when a camera or card reader is plugged in. When you attach a card reader or camera, it will appear on your desktop (or in Windows Explorer on Windows), just as if it were a hard drive, leaving you free to copy files as you please.

The advantage to this approach is that it puts you in control of where files are placed, so you can create a folder structure on your drive that makes the most sense to you.

The downside is that, depending on which version of your operating system you're using, you won't necessarily be able to see thumbnail previews of your images before you transfer them, which means you won't be able to pick and choose which images to copy. Obviously, you can always sort through them later.

To transfer images manually:

1. Plug in the camera or card reader.

2. When the camera or card reader icon appears on your desktop, open it up. You should see a folder inside called *DCIM*. There might be some other folders, but DCIM is the only one you need to worry about. It is the standard location that camera vendors have agreed upon for storing images.

3. Inside the DCIM folder, you will find additional folders, usually named with some combination of numbers and the make of your camera (i.e., "100NIKON"). Depending on how many images you've shot, there may be more. Open each folder and copy its contents to your desired location.

Renaming and Organizing

Depending on your workflow, your archiving scheme, and your final output needs, you might need to rename your image files. Your camera generates fairly meaningless names, but if you'll be searching and sorting your images using any kind of thumbnail viewer, file names may not be so relevant. But, if you like to search for specific images by file name, you'll probably want to rename them. Some people use elaborate naming schemes that include shoot dates, project numbers, and so on.

If you attach metadata and keywords to your images, which we'll explore later, file names aren't so important, as you can search your image library for specific metadata tags. Similarly, if your operating system lets you search by date, you may not need to include dates in your naming schemes. The decision to rename might become easier for you after you've considered some of the other workflow steps.

Adobe Bridge provides very good batch renaming commands, as do Camera Bits Photo Mechanic, Nikon Capture NX, and Adobe Lightroom.

When it comes to organizing, you can choose to arrange your images into folders and subfolders using your file manager. Image browsers like Adobe Bridge and Photo Mechanic can help you with this step, too. Programs like iPhoto or Lightroom manage organization for you, so the underlying folder structure might not be as critical to your workflow with those applications.

Moving On

Obviously, there are a lot more details that have to be understood in order to make a functional photo workflow. The goal here was to help you understand an overview of what your workflow will ultimately be and provide you with enough information so that you can start transferring your images and reviewing them on your computer as you continue to study exposure, composition, and other fundamentals of photography.

In the next chapter, we're going to take a technical detour that will lay the foundation for some of the exposure work that we'll do in later chapters.

5

IMAGE SENSORS

How a Silicon Chip Captures an Image

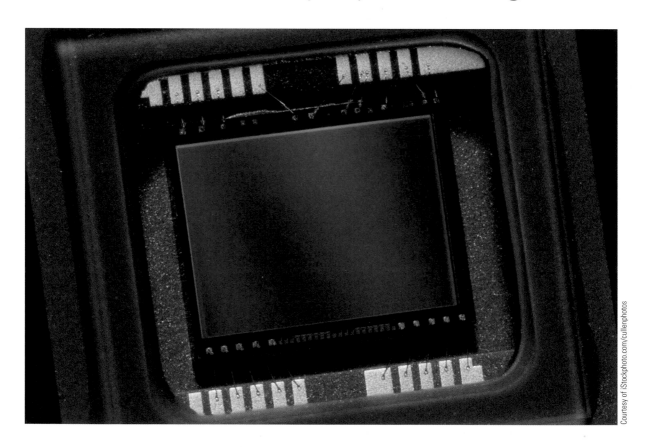

In the old days, photographers made their own photographic papers, films, and developing chemicals. Whether it was to achieve a particular style or texture or to gain more control over their printing processes, photographers such as Ansel Adams, Alfred Stieglitz, and Eduard Steichen had to know a good deal about chemistry to create their prints. Similarly, to really understand how to get the most out of your digital camera, it's important to understand some of the technology behind it. In this chapter, you're going to learn about how the image sensor inside your digital camera works, but first you need to have a basic understanding of the *digitizing* process.

The "real" world in which we live is an *analog* world. Light and sound come to us as continuous analog waves that our senses interpret. Unfortunately, it's very difficult to invent a technology that can record a continuous analog wave accurately. For example, you can cut a continuous wave into a vinyl record, but because of the limitations of this storage process, the resulting recording is often noisy, scratchy, and unable to capture a full range of sound.

Storing a series of numbers, on the other hand, is much simpler. You can carve them in stone, write them on paper, burn them to a DVD, or in the case of digital cameras, record them to small electronic memory chips. Moreover, no matter how you store them, as long as you don't make any mistakes when recording or copying them, you'll suffer no loss of data or quality as you move those numbers from place to place. Therefore, if you can find a way to represent something in the real world as a series of numbers, you can store those numbers very easily using your chosen recording medium.

The process of converting something into numbers (or digits) is called *digitizing*. The first step in digitizing is to divide your subject into distinct units. In the case of a digital camera, these units are called *picture elements*, or *pixels*. Your camera's image sensor is divided into a grid of pixels. When you take a picture, the sensor is exposed to light, and the light is sampled at each pixel in the grid. How fine your grid is (that is, what *resolution* it has) varies depending on the sophistication of your equipment.

Next, each sampled pixel in the grid is analyzed to determine how "full" it is; that is, a corresponding numeric value is assigned that represents that pixel's contents. The result is a representation composed entirely of "digits" or numbers, hence the term *digit*izing. Finally, these numeric values are stored on some type of storage medium.

Figure 5.1 is a simple image composed entirely of black-and-white pixels. As you can see, it's very easy to assign a 1 or a 0 to each pixel to represent the image. Because it takes only a single *bit* to represent each pixel, this image is called a *one-bit image*.

In the example shown in Figure 5.1, the individual samples can be only 0 or 1 because we are storing only one bit of information per pixel. If you want to record more than simple black-and-white images, you need to be able to specify more levels of gray—that is, we need to have more choices than just 0 or 1. By going to a higher *bit depth*—let's say 8 bits, which allows for 256 different values—you can record more information, as seen in Figure 5.2.

With 256 shades from which to choose, you can represent a finer degree of detail than you could with only two choices. Capturing a full color image is more complicated, and you'll learn about that later in this chapter.

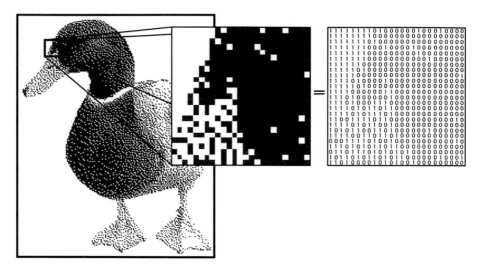

Figure 5.1

Each pixel in this one-bit image is represented by a 1 or a 0.

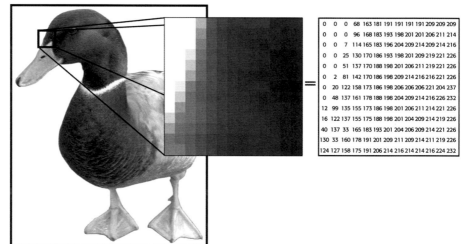

Figure 5.2

By storing bigger numbers for each pixel, we can store much more than simple black-and-white dots. With the ability to use gray pixels, the image looks much more realistic.

To sum up, two of the factors that determine the quality of a digitizing process are the number of pixels you capture and the dynamic range (how wide a range of levels you have for each pixel).

Many other factors affect the quality of a digitized image, from your camera's lens to its compression software. Before exploring these questions, let's look at how your camera manages all of this sampling, measuring, and storage. Understanding how your camera perceives, captures, and stores color information will make certain types of editing operations easier later on and help you to understand some of the terms you'll encounter when shopping for a camera.

How an Image Sensor Works

As you learned earlier, all cameras have certain things in common: they include a lightproof body, a lens, and a recording medium. In the 150+ years since the invention of photography, digital photography represents the first fundamental change in how a camera works. Sure, there have been a lot of advances along the way—color, roll film, light meters, autofocus, on-board flash, and much more—but through it all, the image was always recorded using a chemical process, usually onto a piece of celluloid film. Digital photography marks the first time that a nonchemical recording medium has been employed.

George Smith and Willard Boyle were two engineers employed by Bell Labs. The story goes that one day in late October, the two men spent about an hour sketching out an idea for a new type of semiconductor that could be used for computer memory and for the creation of a solid-state, tubeless video camera. The year was 1969, and in that hour, the two men invented the *charge-coupled device*, or CCD.

Roughly a year later, Bell Labs created a solid-state video camera using Smith and Boyle's new chip. Although their original intention was to build a simple camera that could be used in a video-telephone device, they soon built a camera that was good enough for broadcast television.

Since then, CCDs have been used in everything from cameras to fax machines. Because video cameras don't require a lot of pixels (only half a million or so), the CCD worked great for creating video-quality images. For printing pictures, though, you need millions and millions of pixels. Consequently, it wasn't until the mid-1990s that CCDs could be manufactured with enough pixels to compete with photographic film.

Counting Photons

The image sensor in your digital camera is a silicon chip that is covered with a grid of small electrodes called *photosites*, one for each pixel (see Figure 5.3). Each photosite contains a photodiode and a capacitor (as mentioned in Chapter 1, "Eyes, Brains, Lights, and Images") along with other electronic components, depending upon the type of sensor.

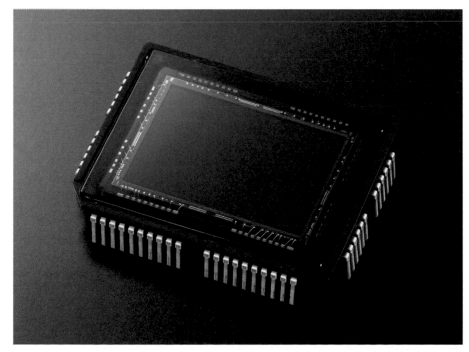

Figure 5.3

The sensor from a Nikon D70 has an imaging area of 23.7mm by 15.6mm.

When you turn your camera on, it places a uniform charge, or voltage, onto the capacitor at each photosite of its image sensor. When light strikes a particular photosite, it causes the photodiode to drain some of the charge from the capacitor. The amount of drained charge is directly proportional to the number of photons that strikes the photodiode.

By measuring the reduction in voltage at a particular photosite, your camera is able to determine how much light hit that particular site during the exposure. As described previously, this measurement is then converted into a number by an analog-to-digital converter.

Most cameras use either a 12-bit or 14-bit analog-to-digital converter, which means that the value from each photosite is converted into a 12- or 14-bit number. In the case of a 12-bit converter, this produces a number between 0 and 4,096; with a 14-bit converter, you get a number between 0 and 16,384. Note that an analog-to-digital converter with a higher bit depth (one with a wider range of numbers) doesn't give your sensor a larger dynamic range. The brightest and darkest colors the sensor can represent remain the same, but the extra bit depth does mean that the camera will produce finer gradations within that dynamic range. As you'll see later, how many bits get used in your final image depends on the format in which you save the image.

The term *CCD* is derived from the way the camera reads the charges of the individual photosites. After exposing the CCD, the charges on the first row of photosites are transferred to a read-out register where they are amplified and then sent to an analog-to-digital converter. Each row of charges is electrically coupled to the next row so that after one row has been read and deleted, all of the other rows move down to fill the now empty space (see Figure 5.4).

In a CMOS sensor, each photosite can be read individually without the need for shifting.

Photosites are sensitive only to how much light they receive; they know nothing about color. To achieve color, some additional computing is required.

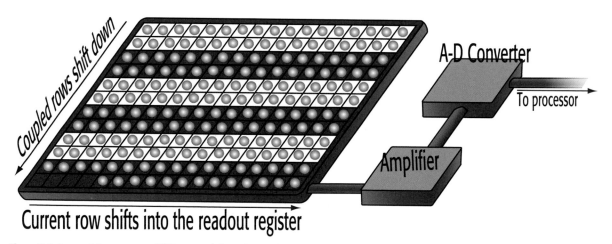

Figure 5.4 Rows of photosites on a CCD are coupled together. As the bottom row of photosites is read off the bottom of the CCD, all of the rows above it shift down. This is the "coupled" in charge-coupled device.

A Little Color Theory

In 1869, James Clerk Maxwell asked photographer Thomas Sutton (the inventor of the SLR camera) to take three black-and-white photographs of a tartan ribbon. Maxwell wanted to test a theory he had about a possible method for creating color photographs. He asked Sutton to place a different filter over the camera for each shot: first, a red filter; then a green; and then a blue. After the film was developed, Maxwell projected all three black-and-white pictures onto a screen using three projectors fitted with the same filters that were used to shoot the photos. When the images were projected directly on top of each other, the images combined and Maxell had the world's first color photo.

Needless to say, this process was hardly speedy or convenient. Unfortunately, it took another 30 years to turn Maxwell's discovery into a commercially viable product. This happened in 1903, when the Lumière brothers used red, green, and blue dyes to color grains of starch that could be applied to glass plates to create color images. They called their process *autochrome*, and it was the first successful color printing process.

If you read Chapter 1, then those three colors should be familiar to you; they're the additive primary colors of light, which can be mixed together to create all other colors. They're also the same three primaries that your eyes are sensitive to.

Note that Maxwell did not discover light's additive properties. Newton had done similar experiments long before, but Maxwell was the first to apply the properties to photography.

A digital image is composed of three different black-and-white images, which are combined to create a full-color image. The image shown in Figure 5.5 is called an *RGB* image because it uses red, green, and blue channels to create a color image.

This story is not just a trivial history lesson. Understanding that your full color images are composed of separate channels will come in very handy later when you start editing. Very often, you'll correct color casts and adjust your images by viewing and manipulating individual color channels.

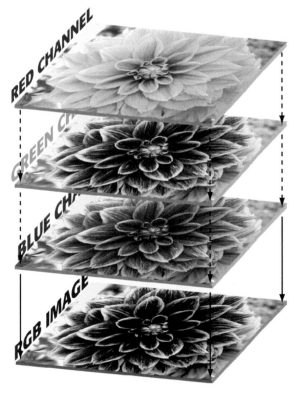

Figure 5.5

In a digital image, three separate red, green, and blue channels are combined to create a final, full-color picture.

You Say "Black and White," I Say "Grayscale"

Although film photographers use the term *black-and-white* to denote an image that lacks color, in the digital world it's better to use the term *grayscale*. A black-and-white image would be one that contained only black or white pixels, which is different from an image that is made up of varying shades of gray.

In the century and a half since Maxwell's discovery, many other ways of representing color have been discovered. For example, another model called *L*A*B color* (also known as *Lab color*) uses one channel for lightness information, another channel for greenness or redness, and a third channel for blueness or yellowness. In addition, there is the cyan, magenta, yellow, and black (CMYK) model that printers use.

Each of these approaches is called a *color model*, and each model has a particular *gamut*, or range, of colors it can display. Some gamuts are more appropriate to certain tasks than others, and all are smaller than the range of colors your eye can perceive.

We'll deal more with gamuts and color models in later chapters. For now, it's important to understand that digital photos are made up of separate red, green, and blue channels that combine to create a color image.

Interpolating Color

By measuring photons, an image sensor can determine how much light has struck each part of its surface, but the data that comes off the sensor doesn't contain any information about color. At its heart, an image sensor is purely a grayscale device. To produce a color image, it must perform a type of interpolation (which is a fancy word for "very educated guess").

Each photosite on your camera's image sensor is covered by a filter—red, green, or blue. This combination of filters is called a *color filter array*, and most image sensors use a filter pattern like the one shown in Figure 5.6, called the *Bayer Pattern*.

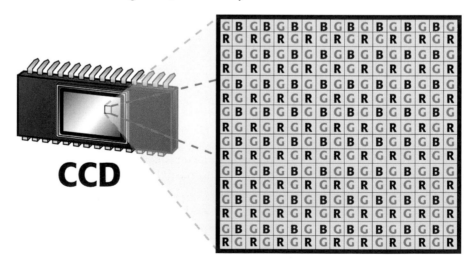

Figure 5.6

To see color, alternating pixels on an image sensor are covered with a different colored filter. The color filter array shown here is called the *Bayer Pattern*.

With these filters, the image sensor can produce separate, incomplete red, green, and blue images. The images are incomplete because the red image, for example, is missing all of the pixels that were covered with a blue filter, whereas the blue filter is missing all of the pixels that were covered with a red filter. Both the red and blue images are missing the vast number of green-filtered pixels.

The camera can calculate the color of any given pixel by analyzing all of the adjacent pixels. For example, if you look at a particular pixel and see that the pixel to the immediate left of it is a bright red pixel, the pixel to the right is a bright blue pixel, and the pixels above and below are bright green, then the pixel in question is probably white. Why? As you learned earlier, if you mix equal amounts of red, green, and blue light together, you get white light. (By the way, if you're wondering why there are so many more green pixels than red or blue pixels, it's because the eye is more sensitive to green. Consequently, it's better to have as much green information as possible.)

This process of interpolating is called *demosaicing*, and different vendors employ different approaches to the demosaicing process. For example, many cameras look at only immediately adjacent pixels, but some cameras analyze a region up to 9×9 pixels.

Some cameras use a different type of color filter array. Some use a cyan, yellow, green, and magenta filter, while others use a red, green, blue, and emerald filter. These require demosaicing, just like an RGB filter.

In some of their cameras, Fuji takes a different approach to demosaicing. Most cameras are fitted with a special filter, which sits directly in front of the image sensor. This filter blurs the image slightly to help smear colors around on the sensor surface, which eases the demosaicing process. The Fuji XTrans sensor uses a randomized pattern of red, green, and blue color filters, which eliminates the need for the low-pass filter, thus producing sharper images straight off the sensor.

After the demosaicing process is complete, each pixel is now a full-color sample, comprised of a combination of red, blue, and green components. Typically, each of these components is represented as an eight-bit number; thus, a full-color image requires 24 bits per pixel.

As you've seen, image sensors are often very small, sometimes as small as 1/4 or 1/2 inch (6 or 12mm, respectively). By comparison, a single frame of 35mm film is 36×23.3mm. The fact that image sensors can be so small is the main reason why digital cameras can be so tiny. By packing more and more photosites onto an image sensor, chipmakers can increase the sensor's pixel count. However, there is a price to pay for this. To pack more photosites onto the surface of the chip, the individual sites have to be made much smaller. As each site gets smaller, its ability to collect light is compromised because it doesn't have as much physical space to catch passing photons. This limitation results in a chip with a poor *signal-to-noise ratio*; that is, the amount of good data the chip collects—the signal—is muddied by the amount of noise—noise from the camera's electronics, noise from other nearby electrical sources, noise from cosmic rays raining down from space—that the chip collects.

In your final image, this signal-to-noise confusion can manifest as grainy patterns in your image—visible noise like what you see on a TV channel filled with static—or other annoying artifacts.

To improve the light-collecting capability of tiny photosites, most chipmakers position tiny microlenses over each photosite. These lenses focus the light more tightly into the photosite in an effort to improve the signal-to-noise ratio. However, these lenses can cause problems of their own in the form of artifacts in your final image.

Image sensors suffer from another problem that film lacks. If too much light hits a particular photosite, it can spill over into adjacent photosites. If the camera's software isn't smart enough to recognize that this has happened, you will see a *blooming* artifact (smearing colors or flared highlights) in your final image. Blooming is more prevalent in a physically smaller image sensor with higher resolution because the photosites are packed more tightly together. This problem is not insurmountable, and even if your image does suffer from blooming problems from time to time, these artifacts won't necessarily be visible in your final prints.

Extra Pixels

Not all of the photosites in an image sensor are used for recording your image. Some are used to assess the black levels in your image; others are used for determining white balance. Finally, some pixels are masked away altogether. For example, if the sensor has a square array of pixels but your camera manufacturer wants to create a camera that shoots rectangular images, the manufacturer will mask out some of the pixels on the edge of the sensor to get the picture shape they want.

Turning Data into an Image

Before the light from your lens ever strikes the sensor, it is passed through several filters. These include an infrared filter and a low-pass filter. (Some cameras use a very slight infrared filter, making them ideal for infrared photography, as you'll see later.) The infrared filter prevents false colors, which can be caused by infrared light that is not visible to the human eye. The low-pass filter helps prevent artifacts (such as moiré patterns) from being created during the digitizing process. Many photographers turn pale when they hear this, particularly those who have just spent lots of money on very sharp lenses. But, as you will see, this softening can be corrected later, either in the camera or during postprocessing.

After you take a picture, the data is read off the image sensor, amplified, passed through an analog-to-digital converter, and then passed to your camera's on-board processor. There, it is demosaiced to produce a color image. However, straight demosaicing does not produce an accurate, attractive color image. A little more calculation is required by the camera's on-board computer.

Colorimetric Adjustment

First, the image goes through a "colorimetric adjustment." During demosaicing, the camera's processor knows that a particular pixel was red or green or blue (or whatever colors were used in the color filter array), but it doesn't know which precise shades of those primary colors were used in the filters. So the color needs to be skewed slightly to compensate for the specific color qualities of the color filter array.

Color Space Conversion

At this stage, your camera knows a lot about what color each pixel in your image is. For example, it might know that one particular pixel is 100 percent of a particular shade of chartreuse. But what exactly does 100 percent mean? For this number to be meaningful, some boundaries need to be defined, so your image is mapped into a color space.

A *color space* is simply a mathematical model that can be used to represent colors. Some color spaces are larger than others, and so they might allow for more variation in a particular color—reds, for example. In other words, "100 percent red" in one color space might be a different shade from "100 percent red" in another color space. Without a color space, your image would be a fairly meaningless array of numbers. Your camera probably provides a choice of two different color spaces: sRGB and Adobe RGB (see Figure 5.7). You'll learn much more about color space choices later.

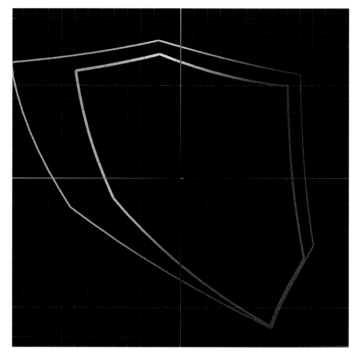

Figure 5.7

This graph shows the colors defined by both the Adobe RGB and sRGB color spaces. The bigger ring is Adobe RGB, which can hold all of the same colors as sRGB and a good deal more. While the range of purples and blues are mostly the same, Adobe RGB can hold a much greater range of greens.

Gamma Correction

In an imaging chip, when twice as much light hits a single pixel, twice as much change in voltage is produced. In other words, the response of the pixels to light is linear—increase the light, and you get a linear change in voltage. Your eyes don't work this way. When you increase brightness, your eyes register a logarithmic increase, rather than a linear increase. So a doubling of light does not make you perceive a scene as being twice as bright.

The practical upshot of all of this is that your eyes are able to see a lot of really fine detail in shadow and highlight areas. As an example, consider the upper image in Figure 5.8. This grayscale ramp goes from black to white in a linear fashion. This is how your camera sees a change in brightness.

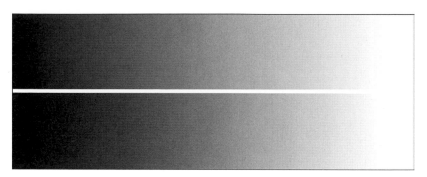

Figure 5.8

The upper ramp makes a linear progression from black to white. This is how your digital camera's sensor sees the world. The lower ramp makes a nonlinear progression. This is the type of light response your eyes have.

The lower image goes from black to white in a nonlinear fashion. Notice that there is much more variation in the lower fourth and upper fourth of the nonlinear ramp. In other words, the shadows and highlights have been expanded to show more variation.

Because of their nonlinear nature, your eyes tend to expand the shadow and highlight areas, registering more subtle changes and allowing you to see more detail. As we'll discover in many places in this book, your eyes are extremely sensitive to subtle changes in contrast—much more than they are to changes in color. This is because the light-sensitive portion of your eye is composed mostly of luminance-sensitive rods, while only a tiny part is composed of color-sensitive cones.

In order to get accurate brightness values—to expand the highlights and shadows so they appear more like what your eye is used to—your camera applies a mathematical curve to all its brightness values. This is called a *gamma curve*, sometimes called *gamma correction* (see Figure 5.9).

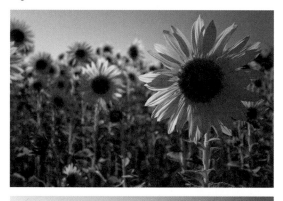

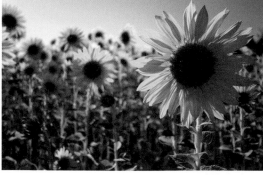

Figure 5.9

The upper image shows this picture before gamma correction. Note the difference in overall contrast. As with the gray ramp in Figure 5.8, the lower, gamma-corrected image has darker shadows and more varied highlights.

White Balance and Image Processing

As discussed in Chapter 1, your eye has the incredible ability to adjust its color perception so that colors are accurate under different types of lights. Like a piece of film (which must be formulated for specific types of light), a digital image sensor cannot automatically adapt to different types of light. Instead, the image data from the sensor must be calibrated to the type of light you're shooting in, which is a process called *white balance*.

The camera might also allow you to select several other adjustments, from contrast to brightness to color saturation. These adjustments are just like the ones you might apply in an image editor and are usually applied after the white balancing adjustment.

Sharpening and Noise Reduction

Finally, many cameras employ some type of noise reduction algorithm to reduce unwanted noise in your image, and almost all cameras perform some type of sharpening in order to compensate for the softening caused by the low-pass filter.

JPEG Compression and Saving

At this point in the process, your camera has processed the image and is ready to save it to the camera's media card. Before saving, it applies JPEG compression, to save space and to speed the write-time.

All this processing takes place as soon as your image has been shot, and as you might imagine, it can take a while to perform all these calculations. I mean "take a while" in computer terms, but even though your camera's processor is very speedy, it can still be overwhelmed with image processing. To counter this, most cameras include an extra memory buffer that allows them to cache a few images for processing, freeing up the camera for immediate shooting.

The procedure described here is what is required to turn the image data your camera captures into a final image. When you shoot in JPEG mode, all of the processing that you just read about happens in your camera's on-board computer. In Chapter 11, "Raw Shooting," you'll learn about another option, raw format shooting.

How JPEG Compression Works

After your image has been processed, it's ready to be stored on whatever storage medium is provided by your camera. While there are many different storage options for camera makers to choose from, they all have one thing in common: they're finite. Consequently, to make the most of the available storage, cameras compress their images, usually using a type of compression called *JPEG*.

Created by the *Joint Photographic Experts Group*, JPEG is a powerful algorithm that can greatly reduce the size of a photo but at the cost of image quality. Consequently, JPEG is referred to as a *lossy* compression format.

When saving in JPEG mode, the camera first converts the image data from its original 12- or 14-bit format down to an 8-bit format, reducing the range of brightness levels from 4,096 (12 bits) or 16,384 (14 bits) all the way down to 256. Once the data is in 8-bit mode, the camera is ready to start compressing.

Most cameras offer two forms of JPEG compression: a low-quality option that visibly degrades an image but offers compression ratios of 10 or 20:1, and a high-quality option that performs a good amount of compression—usually around 4:1—but without severely degrading your image. Some cameras offer an even finer JPEG compression that cuts file sizes while producing images that are indistinguishable from uncompressed originals. In most cases, you'll probably find that any artifacts introduced by higher-quality JPEG compression are not visible in your final prints.

JPEG compression works by exploiting the fact that human vision is more sensitive to changes in brightness than to changes in color. To JPEG-compress an image, your camera first converts the image into a color space where each pixel is expressed using a chrominance (color) value and a luminance (brightness) value.

Next, the chrominance values are analyzed in blocks of 8 × 8 pixels. The color in each 64-pixel area is averaged so that any slight (and hopefully imperceptible) change in color is removed, a process known as *quantization*. Note that because the averaging is performed only on the chrominance channel, all the luminance information in the image—the information your eye is most sensitive to—is preserved.

After quantization, a nonlossy compression algorithm is applied to the entire image. In the *very* simplest terms, a nonlossy compression scheme works something like this: rather than encoding AAAAAABBBBBCCC, you simply encode 6A5B3C. After quantization, the chrominance information in your image will be more uniform, and larger chunks of similar data will be available, meaning that this final compression step will be more effective.

What does all this mean to your image? Figure 5.10 shows an image that has been overcompressed. As you can see, areas of flat color or smooth gradations have turned into rectangular chunks, whereas contrast in areas of high detail has been boosted too high. Fortunately, most digital cameras offer much better compression quality than what you see here in Figure 5.10.

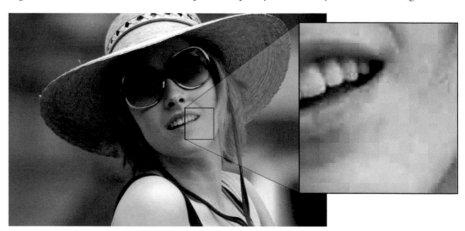

Figure 5.10

This image has been compressed far too much, as can be seen from the nasty JPEG artifacts.

Meanwhile…Back in the Real World

If the information in this chapter seems unnecessary, it's probably because when you buy a film camera you don't have to worry about imaging technology—it's included in the film you use. However, if you're serious about photography, you probably do need to spend some time considering the merits of different films. And, just as you need a little knowledge of film chemistry to assess the quality of a particular film stock, the topics covered in this chapter will help you better test a particular camera. You'll also find some of these concepts coming up again when we talk about solving particular image editing troubles.

Your camera is more than just an image sensor, and throughout the rest of the shooting chapters, you'll learn about the other components, controls, and mechanisms on your camera.

Note that if you're shooting raw, some of what you learned in this chapter will be a little different. You'll learn about raw shooting in Chapter 11.

Pixels, Revisited

Pixel is a term we'll be using a lot, so here's a summary of what we've covered so far with regard to pixels. Pixel stands for *picture element*, and is used to refer to any individual unit of information in a raster image. A *raster image* is simply an image that's made up of colored dots. So the image on your computer screen is a raster image made up of pixels, and your digital camera produces a raster image of different-colored pixels.

Earlier, you learned about the photosites on an image sensor. There is one photosite for each pixel in the resulting image.

A pixel's color is represented as a numerical value. The range of color that any single pixel can be is limited only by the amount of memory that your imaging device devotes to that pixel. With 24 bits, you can count from 0 to roughly 16 million, which means that any pixel on your screen can be one of roughly 16 million colors.

6

EXPOSURE BASICS

The Fundamental Theory of Exposure

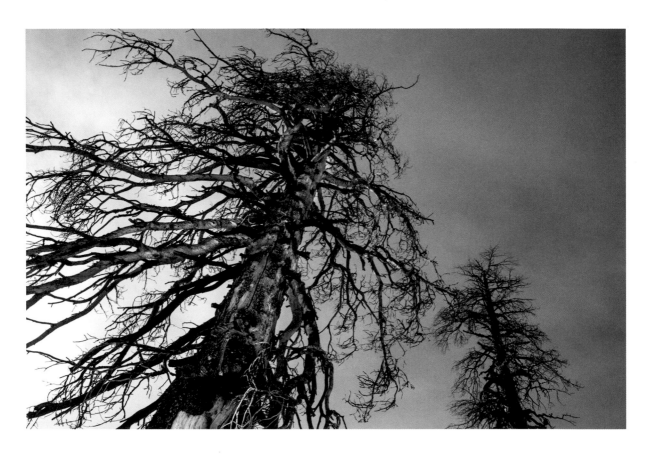

While photographic technology has changed dramatically over the last century and a half, one thing has remained the same: the physics of light still works just as it did when the first cameras were invented in the 19th century. This means that the basic skills that all photographers must learn have remained constant throughout the development of photographic technology.

In this chapter, we're going to look at some fundamental exposure theory. This is the sort of stuff that, only 25 years ago, you *had* to learn to be able to take good pictures. Nowadays, with the adept automatic modes provided by digital cameras, you don't actually have to know this stuff to get good results with your camera. However, as capable as automatic modes have become, an automatic mechanism may be confused by some situations simply because there's no way for it to know what the final image is that you are envisioning when you frame a shot. With an understanding of the exposure concepts presented in this chapter, you'll be able to work around the limitations that can confuse your camera's automatic features and achieve results that may not be possible with an automatic function.

Stops

In Chapter 1, "Eyes, Brains, Lights, and Images," you learned that a stop is a measure of light. Every time the light in a scene is doubled, we say the amount of light has increased by one stop. Conversely, a halving of light means the light has decreased by one stop. This is a term that will be used extensively throughout the rest of this book and for the rest of your photographic career. Experienced photographers are often able to recognize, by eye, how many stops of brightening or darkening have occurred in a scene or image. Good photography doesn't require this skill, but you *do* need to understand the term "stop," especially as we deepen our exposure discussion here, and in Chapter 7, "Program Mode."

Over- and Underexposure Defined

At the simplest level, though, the effect of exposure choice is fairly easy to understand. If you turn out the lights in your house in the middle of the night, your eye won't be able to gather enough light to see very much. In other words, the inside of your house will be underexposed.

Conversely, when a doctor shines a bright light in your eyes, you probably can't see anything at all, because the sensors in your eyes will go into overdrive. In other words, your field of view will be overexposed.

A digital image sensor (or a piece of film) works the same way. If a scene is underexposed, either because there's not enough light or because you choose bad exposure settings, then the scene will be too dark. If you overexpose a scene, then the resulting image will be too bright. See Figure 6.1 for some examples.

Both over- and underexposure can even be a problem in a single image, as some areas in an image might be overexposed, while others will be underexposed (see Figure 6.2).

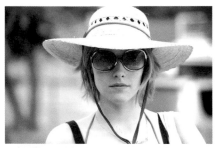

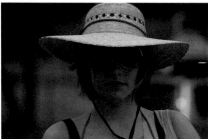

Figure 6.1

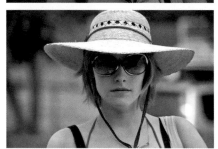

The first image is overexposed. Note how the bright areas of the hat have been blown out to complete white. The middle image is plainly underexposed. It's too dark overall, and the shadowy areas under the hat are going to complete black. The third image has a nice overall exposure with highlights that contain details and shadows that aren't too dark.

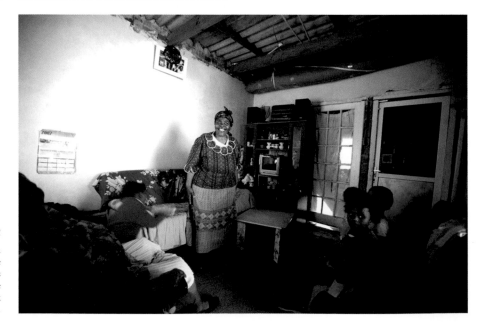

Figure 6.2

This image suffers from both over- and underexposure. The wall and some other highlights are overexposed to complete white, while the shadows are dark and murky.

As a photographer, one of your primary concerns is to make sure that you choose settings that expose the camera's image sensor to an amount of light that will render a scene that is neither too bright nor too dark—that is, neither over- nor underexposed.

As you'll see in Chapter 7, there might be other times when you choose to intentionally over- or underexpose your images.

Exposure Control Mechanisms

Your camera provides two mechanical mechanisms for controlling the amount of light that strikes the image sensor: the shutter and the aperture.

The shutter is like a little door that opens and closes very quickly to control how much light passes through to the image sensor. Shutter speed is a measure of how long the shutter stays open, as measured in seconds. Because shutter speeds in most situations are very quick, you'll most often see shutter speeds that are fractions of a second—1/60th, 1/125th, 1/1000th, and so on. A faster shutter speed exposes the sensor to *less* light.

In an SLR, the shutter is composed of two curtains. The first curtain opens to expose the sensor, while the second curtain follows to close the opening. When using a fast shutter speed, the sensor will not be completely revealed at any particular time because the second curtain will start following the first curtain almost immediately. This creates a quickly moving slit that exposes the sensor.

You can see a movie of this whole process in action in the Chapter 6 section of the companion website at *www.completedigitalphotography.com/CDP8*.

On many point-and-shoot cameras, there is no mechanical shutter. Instead, the sensor is simply turned on for the desired amount of time. Because there's no shutter moving around, the camera can actually capture a picture without making a sound. Most cameras beep or play a recorded shutter sound to let you know that the shot has been taken. This kind of feedback is helpful, but your camera probably allows you to disable the sound for times when you want to shoot silently.

The second mechanism for controlling light is a mechanical iris, or aperture. This concept should be familiar to you, since your eyes have irises that open and close as light levels change. If you've ever walked out of a dark movie theater in the middle of the day, then you've experienced what happens when your irises are open too wide; you must wait for them to close down so that your field of view is no longer overexposed.

The iris in your camera is composed of a series of interlocking metal leaves. The iris opening can be expanded and contracted to make a bigger or smaller opening (see Figure 6.3).

With a wider aperture, more light gets to the image sensor.

As you learned earlier, the shutter is held in the camera body, just in front of the image sensor. The iris is part of the lens. It's positioned at the end of the lens, near the mount that attaches the lens to the camera body.

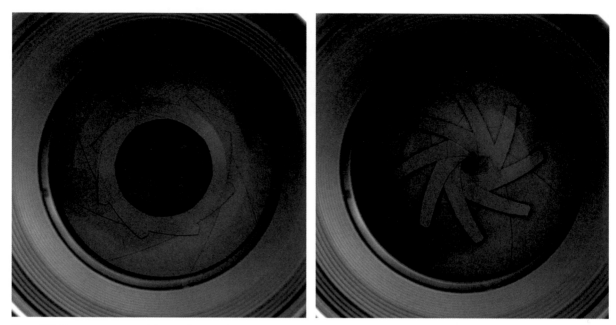

Figure 6.3 The iris in your camera's lens can be opened and closed to allow more or less light to pass through to the sensor.

Shutter Speed

To recap: Shutter speeds are measured in seconds, and a longer shutter speed exposes the image sensor to light for a longer time than a shorter shutter speed. Shutter speeds can range from 30 seconds up to 1/8000th of a second, depending on your camera's capabilities, and you can even create longer exposures lasting minutes, hours, or even days.

In the auto shooting that you did in Chapter 2, "Getting to Know Your Camera," the camera calculated an appropriate shutter speed for you automatically and showed it to you in its status display.

As mentioned in Chapter 2, the shutter speed display on your camera shows the denominator part of the current shutter speed. So, if you see "100" on the shutter speed display, then the camera is set to 1/100th of a second.

Most cameras go down to about a fourth of a second, which reads as 4 on the shutter. From there, most cameras switch to a display that shows seconds and tenths of seconds. So you might see 0.3, which reads as 3 tenths of a second. As you continue to slow the shutter, you might see 1.6. On Canon cameras, you'll likely see something like 1"6, which is meant to be read as 1.6 seconds.

The shutter speed on most cameras tops out at 30 seconds; however, many cameras also include a Bulb setting. This will either be a dedicated mode that you can switch to using the same control that you use to select other shooting modes, or it will come after the 30-second mark on the shutter speed selector.

In Bulb mode, which is usually indicated with a B or the word Bulb, the shutter will remain open for as long as you hold the shutter button down. This allows you to shoot exposures longer than 30 seconds.

Aperture

The size of the aperture is controlled automatically by the camera when you shoot in certain modes, including Auto. However, as you'll see later, it can also be controlled manually. Aperture size is measured in f-stops, and like shutter speed, an f-stop number is often fractional, so you'll see f-stops with values like f5.6, f8, or f11 (see Figure 6.4).

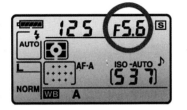

Figure 6.4

This typical camera readout is showing an aperture choice of f5.6.

An f-stop is a measure of the ratio of the focal length of the lens to the size of the aperture. Apertures are circular, so because you're dealing with the area of a circle, the math can yield fractional numbers. Don't worry about understanding that ratio; you don't have to know the math to use f-stop values effectively.

Less Is More

Now the tricky part: f-stops can be a little unintuitive at first because of the way that they're measured. A larger f-stop number, say 16, indicates a *smaller* opening. For example, Figure 6.5 shows two lens apertures, one set to f-stop 8 and another set to f4.

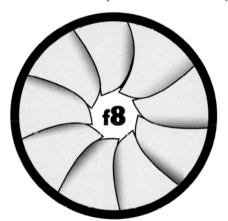
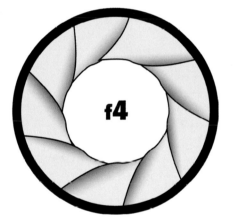

Figure 6.5

Here's a representation of two apertures, one set to f8 and the other set to f4. As you can see, the higher number corresponds to more closure, or a smaller opening.

When you choose a higher f-stop number, the aperture stops more light. With a lower f-stop number, the aperture is larger, and less light is stopped. Unfortunately, there's no real sure-fire way to learn this; you just have to memorize it. Over time, it will become intuitive, and we'll be doing more aperture work later in the book.

Aperture Experiment

If you are nearsighted enough to need glasses, try this quick little depth-of-field experiment. Take off your glasses and curl up your index finger against your thumb. You should be able to curl your finger tight enough to create a tiny little hole in the curve of your index finger. If you look through the hole without your glasses, you will probably find that everything is in focus. This hole is a very tiny aperture, and therefore provides very deep depth of field—deep enough, in fact, that it can correct your vision. On the downside, it doesn't let a lot of light through, so unless you're in bright daylight, you might not be able to see anything well enough to determine if it's in focus. The next time you're confused about how aperture relates to depth of field, remember this test.

Throughout the rest of this book, I'll use a few aperture-related terms. When I speak of "stopping down a lens," I mean choosing a smaller aperture (larger f-number). "Opening up the lens" means choosing a larger aperture (smaller f-number). "Shooting full wide" means to choose the largest possible aperture (the one with the smallest number).

Not all lenses can open up to the same aperture. Creating a lens that can open very wide requires a lot of high-quality glass, so you might find that some of your lenses only open to, say f4, while other lenses can open to f2, or even wider. The maximum aperture that your lens can open to will be written on the front ring of the lens.

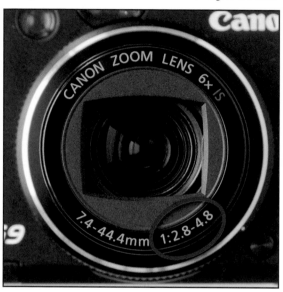

Figure 6.6

The lens on this Canon G9 indicates that it has maximum apertures of 2.8 at full wide to 4.8 at full telephoto.

If you're using a zoom lens, be aware that the largest possible aperture can vary, depending on the focal length you've chosen. For example, if you look at the front of your lens where the brand name and a bunch of numbers are printed, you might see something like "1:3.5-5.6." This tells you the aperture range, from full wide to full telephoto. On such a lens, the widest aperture you could use when zoomed all the way out would be f3.5. At full telephoto, the widest aperture would be f5.6. As you zoom through the focal length range, the maximum aperture available will change from 3.5 to 5.6 (see Figure 6.6).

Other zoom lenses might have a constant maximum aperture across the entire zoom range. It's a complicated engineering prospect to make a small zoom lens that has a constant maximum aperture, so lenses with a constant aperture are usually larger and often more expensive. The advantage of a zoom lens with a constant aperture is that you'll always know what your widest aperture will be because your lens won't close down as you zoom in.

A lens with a wider maximum aperture than another lens is said to be *faster*. In general, when someone talks about the speed of a lens—"Look at this really expensive, very fast 50mm lens that I just bought!"—they're referring to the fact that its maximum aperture can be very wide.

Why There Are Two Ways to Control Light

What you've learned here is that there are two ways by which you can limit the amount of light that hits the sensor: you can change the amount of time that the shutter is open, and you can change the size of the aperture in the lens so that it creates a bigger or smaller opening. But why are there two mechanisms for controlling light? If your concern is just to ensure that the image is neither too bright nor too dark, wouldn't one mechanism be enough?

If good exposure were only a matter of brightness, then yes, one mechanism would be plenty, but because of the physics of light, there can be a big difference in your final image, depending on whether you control exposure using shutter speed or aperture. In fact, after compositional decisions, the bulk of your creative power as a photographer comes from how you choose to manipulate shutter speed and aperture.

How Shutter Speed Choice Affects Your Image

The effect of shutter speed is pretty intuitive. As you choose a faster shutter speed, you gain more ability to freeze the motion in your scene. That is, when the shutter is open for a very short time, a moving subject will be frozen. When the shutter is open for a longer time, a moving subject will be blurred and smeary.

You were introduced to this idea in Chapter 2 when you learned that a faster shutter speed could be necessary to prevent blurring caused by a shaky hand.

You may think that blurry and smeared is inherently bad, and that you will always want your images sharp and clear, but consider Figure 6.7.

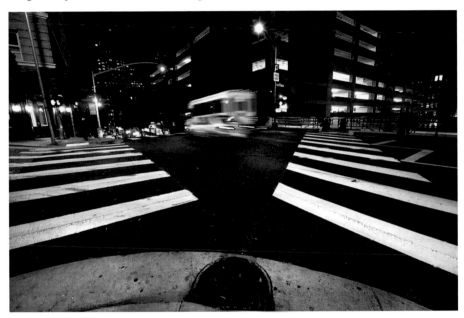

Figure 6.7

This image was shot with a slower shutter speed with the goal of blurring the truck's motion.

By choosing a slower shutter speed, the truck was blurred as it moved through the frame. If I had used a faster shutter speed, and rendered the truck perfectly sharp, then it might have appeared as if it were simply parked in the street. To truly convey what was going on in the scene, I needed to endow a sense of motion by carefully using motion blur. To get this shot, I had to make a concentrated effort to hold the camera steady. During a slow shutter speed, any camera motion will result in blur throughout the image. If you're shooting in very windy conditions, with a telephoto lens, or in a location where you can't get stable footing, then shooting with a slow shutter speed might not be possible. Of course, a tripod will help in any of these circumstances.

In addition to blurring motion to reveal the action of a scene, you might choose to blur elements in an image for more creative effect. Intentional blur allows you to add a level of abstraction to your image, and that's often more interesting than a more "literal" interpretation of a scene (see Figure 6.8).

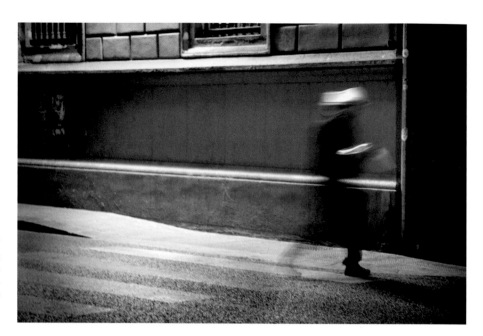

Figure 6.8

I intentionally blurred the
motion of the person in this
scene, because I thought a
smeary, ghostly figure would be
more interesting than a sharp,
perfectly-rendered figure.

Depth of Field—How Aperture Choice Affects Your Image

Choosing a smaller aperture will keep more light from getting to the sensor. But changing aperture has another effect on your image. As you go to a smaller aperture, the *depth of field* in your image gets deeper. Depth of field is simply a measure of how much of your image is in focus, as shown in Figure 6.9.

Depth of field is measured around the distance at which you're focused. So, if you've selected an aperture that gives you 10 feet of depth of field, then an area 10 feet deep will be in focus, centered on the distance where you focused.

It's very important to understand that focus is not always *evenly* centered on your focus point. At very close distances, depth of field will extend equally in front of and behind your focus point. But as the distance to your point of focus increases, the depth of field will increase more *behind* your subject. We'll discuss this in more detail later. For now, remember the one-thirds/two-thirds rule, which states that about one-third of your available depth will be in front of the point of focus and the other two-thirds will be behind it (see Figure 6.10).

While it may seem like it would be best to have everything in your image in focus, there are times when having a sharply focused background can distract the viewer from your foreground subject. Portraits are the most common example of when to use shallow depth of field. If you choose a larger aperture for a portrait, you'll create a softer background that will bring more attention to the subject of the portrait (refer back to Figure 2.18 in Chapter 2).

So, just as you can use shutter speed to control motion stopping, you will sometimes want to consider when a depth of field change can be used to better express the subject or scene that you're shooting.

Also, know that every lens has an aperture "sweet spot." If you stop down too far, you might suffer a noticeable sharpness penalty. Depending on how big you intend to print your final image, this loss of sharpness may not be visible.

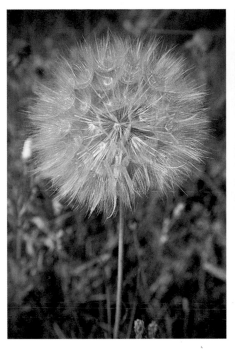 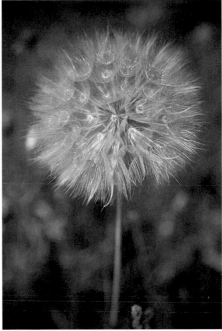

Figure 6.9

The image on the left has more depth of field—the focus stays sharp all the way into the distance. It was shot with a smaller aperture than the image on the right, which has a shallower depth of field. Focus drops off into the distance.

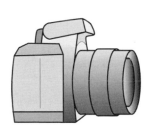 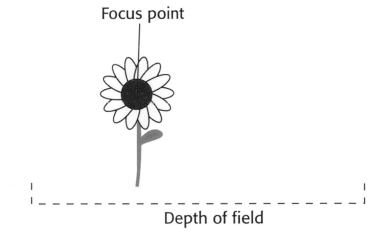

Figure 6.10 Depth of field is measured from your point of focus, not from the end of the lens. About one-third of your depth of field lies in front of the focus point, with the rest falling behind.

This softening occurs because as light rays pass through a small opening, they begin to diverge and interfere with one another. This diffraction keeps them from all focusing at the appropriate locations.

To test your own lenses for their sharpness sweet spot, shoot the same image at a range of apertures from biggest to smallest and then compare the results in your image editor. You'll probably find that there is a noticeable drop-off in sharpness near the edges of your aperture range. On an SLR with a smaller sensor, you usually won't want to go much past f8. On a full-frame SLR, f11 is about as small as you'll want to go. However, everyone has his or her own idea of what is acceptably sharp, so it's worth doing some tests of your own. Find a scene with fine detail and shoot it at a range of apertures. Take the results into your image editor and see if you can spot a sharpness drop-off at a particular aperture.

Shutter Speed/Aperture Balance

Being able to blur motion or shoot with a shallower depth of field provides a tremendous amount of creative latitude. However, if you choose a longer shutter speed to create a blurrier sense of motion in a picture, then your image might end up overexposed. The slower speed will allow too much light to hit the sensor, and your image could end up too bright.

You can compensate for a slower shutter speed by using a smaller aperture. (Depending on what mode you're in, your camera will do this for you.) A smaller aperture will allow less light to pass through the lens, and will restore a correct level of brightness to your image. Of course, a smaller aperture might mean more depth of field. So, if you want to blur the motion, have a shallower depth of field, *and* a scene that is properly bright, then you might have a problem. Balancing all of these factors is one of the obstacles you'll face as a photographer. (Are you beginning to see why there are *two* mechanisms for controlling light?)

Conversely, if you need a fast shutter speed to stop motion, then you can open the aperture wider. With a wider aperture, more light will pass through the lens, so you can get away with faster shutter speeds, but your image will have a shallower depth of field.

To better understand this balance, you have to learn a new term, *reciprocity*.

Reciprocity

Earlier, you learned that a stop is a measure of light. When you double the amount of light that hits the sensor, we say that you have increased the amount of light exposure by one stop. Conversely, if you halve the light, you decrease the exposure by one stop.

Consider these shutter speeds:

> 1/60 1/120 1/250 1/500 1/1000 1/2000 1/4000

Each one is half (roughly) the previous shutter speed. In other words, there is a one-stop difference in the amount of light exposure generated by each successive speed.

Now look at this list of apertures:

> f4 f5.6 f8 f11 f16 f22

Because most of us aren't familiar with calculating the area of a circle, the relationship between these numbers isn't so obvious. But trust me when I say that each one represents an opening that's twice as big as the previous one. In other words, there's a difference of one stop of light exposure between each successive aperture in this list.

When you encounter a situation where you need to balance motion-stopping power with depth of field and overall illumination, you can take advantage of the fact that both shutter speed and aperture can be adjusted by the same amount in opposite directions. In other words, the two values have a reciprocal relationship (see Figure 6.11).

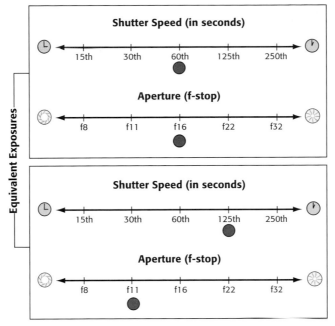

Figure 6.11

Because of the reciprocal nature of exposure parameters, if you change one parameter in one direction, you can move the other parameter in the opposite direction and still achieve the same overall exposure. In other words, both of the exposure settings shown in this chart result in the same amount of light striking the sensor.

For example, let's say your camera recommends an exposure of 1/500th of a second at f8. Because it can't make any creative decisions, it has no idea how much motion stopping or depth of field you might want, so it simply tries to recommend a shutter speed and aperture combination that will give you a good level of illumination and allow for a sharp image when shooting handheld.

If you decide that you want more motion-stopping power, so you increase the shutter speed from 1/500th to 1/1000th (one stop), you'll run the risk of darkening your image. You can compensate for that darkening by opening your aperture from f8 to f5.6 (one stop) (refer to Figure 6.11).

This reciprocal relationship means there are many different shutter speed/aperture combinations that yield the same overall exposure. That is, many combinations of shutter speed and aperture produce the same level of brightness in the final image. However, some combinations might produce an image with more depth of field than others, while others might yield an image that has blurrier motion.

For now, don't worry about how you control all of this on your camera. At this point, the goal is to understand the concepts.

ISO—the Third Exposure Parameter

One of the great advantages of shooting digitally is that you have an additional parameter that you can change to control exposure.

As you learned earlier, after the image sensor in a camera is exposed, the data is read off the sensor in the form of electrical voltages. These voltage levels are very, very small, so the first thing that happens to them is that they are amplified so that they can be measured more easily. As you amplify the voltages more, the sensor effectively becomes more light sensitive, because dimmer light levels will be boosted.

ISO is a standard for measuring the sensitivity of film. (ISO stands for *International Standards Organization*, the committee that specifies the standard.) Digital vendors adopted this standard early on as a way of specifying the sensitivity of an image sensor. When you increase the ISO setting on your camera, you're essentially making the sensor more light sensitive. As it becomes more sensitive, it will require less exposure to be able to "see" a scene, which will allow you to shoot in very low light levels. The ability to raise your ISO also gives you more latitude for changing shutter speed or aperture because all three parameters share a reciprocal relationship.

Reciprocal ISOs

If your camera offers the ability to change ISO, and most do these days, then you probably will have a range of settings that goes something like this:

100 200 400 800 1600

As should be obvious, like aperture and shutter speed, each successive ISO setting is double the previous one, meaning there's a one-stop difference between each ISO. So, if you end up in a situation where your shutter speed and aperture choices have left your scene underexposed by a stop, you can increase your ISO setting by one stop to compensate.

For example, say your camera is set to ISO 100, and you meter a scene and find that the camera wants a shutter speed of 1/25th of a second—too slow for handheld shooting. If you increase to ISO 200, then your shutter speed will halve to 1/50th of a second. Increase to ISO 400, and you'll get your shutter speed to a zippy 1/100th of a second—fast enough for stable handheld shooting.

Adjusting ISO allows you to buy yourself more shutter speed or aperture latitude for times when you need more motion stopping power or depth-of-field control. Some cameras offer a wider range of ISOs than what you see here. On some cameras, ISO 50 is an option, while others push the opposite end of the scale offering ISOs over 100,000. We'll learn more of the details of ISO later.

ISO and Noise

You might be tempted to just leave your ISO set high all the time, to ensure that you always get a fast shutter speed. Unfortunately, there's a price to pay for higher ISO—as you increase ISO, your images will get noisier. (Look ahead to Figures 7.27 and 7.28 in Chapter 7 for examples of noise.)

Bad noise troubles can ruin an otherwise great image, so it's important to always keep your ISO as low as you can get away with.

Fractional Stops

If you're coming from the film world, and you learned to shoot on a manual camera, then you might not recognize all of the shutter speeds and aperture choices on your digital camera. In the old days, shutter speed and aperture controls used the progression of settings that we've looked at here, with one stop of exposure difference between each setting. Like your digital camera, the range was usually wider than what I've shown.

It is possible, though, to adjust shutter speed and aperture by intervals that are smaller than a whole stop. By default, your camera probably adjusts in one-third stop intervals. So, as you adjust the shutter speed control on your camera, you might see a progression that goes like this:

1/15 1/20 1/25 **1/30** 1/40 1/50 **1/60** 1/80 1/100 **1/125** 1/160 1/200

Here, the one-stop increments are in bold. The other values are increases of one-third of a stop. All the same reciprocal rules apply when dealing with fractional stops. These fractional values give you a more granular, finer level of aperture control.

On most cameras, apertures also progress in third-stop increments, as do ISOs.

Confused by "Speed"

The word *speed* comes up a lot when speaking of photography because it can be used to describe three different things: the quickness with which the shutter opens and closes, the maximum aperture of a lens, and the sensitivity of the image sensor (ISO). As you become more comfortable with these concepts, you should have no trouble determining which meaning is being used at any given time.

Summing Up

The relationship between shutter speed, aperture, and ISO setting can be confusing to new photographers. Hopefully, the chart in Figure 6.12 will clarify some of the information presented here.

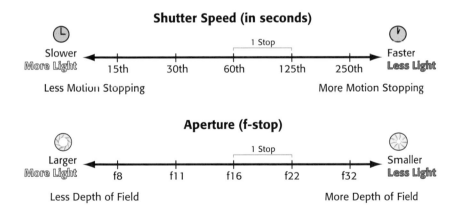

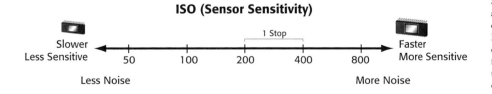

Figure 6.12

Shutter speed, aperture, and ISO are the three exposure parameters over which you have control. Each provides a different way of controlling the exposure in the final image. Each adjustment, in turn, affects your image in different ways.

Remember, if you move any one of these parameters in one direction, you must move one of the others in the opposite direction to maintain equivalent exposure, because all three parameters are reciprocally related. Of course, you can choose to move one parameter or another without moving any others to create an intentional over- or underexposure. Later, we'll learn why you might want to do this.

Returning to Auto Mode

Now that you've learned about the mechanisms that control exposure, let's look again at the Auto mode on your camera. As you learned in Chapter 2, when you press the shutter button halfway down, the camera focuses and calculates exposure settings—aperture and shutter speed. If your camera is set to an auto ISO mode, then the camera may alter ISO as well. The result *should* be an exposure that is neither too bright nor too dark.

Once the camera has calculated these values and autofocused, it displays its choices, either in the viewfinder on the rear LCD, on a status LCD, or possibly in all of these locations. These numbers should make a little more sense to you now.

As you've seen, many combinations of shutter speed and aperture settings yield the same overall exposure. The camera's algorithms are designed to take the safest possible combination. That is, a shutter speed and aperture that will yield a good overall exposure without risking handheld shake from a slow shutter speed or image softness from an extreme aperture.

Later, you'll learn about one additional effect of your exposure choices, and that has to do with tonality—how light and dark particular images are—and how much editing latitude an image has.

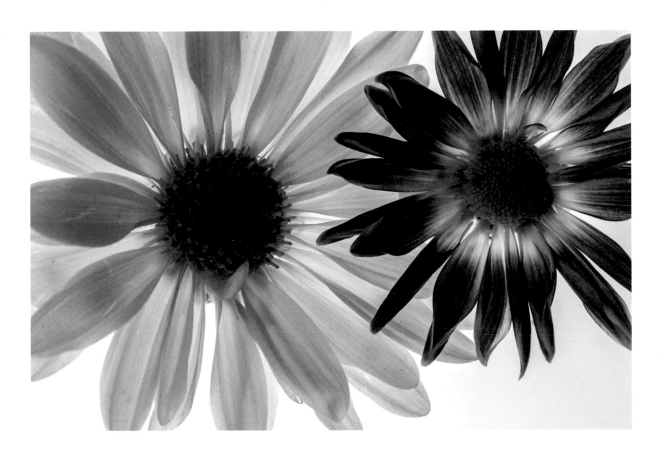

7

PROGRAM MODE

Taking Control of Exposure, Focus, and More

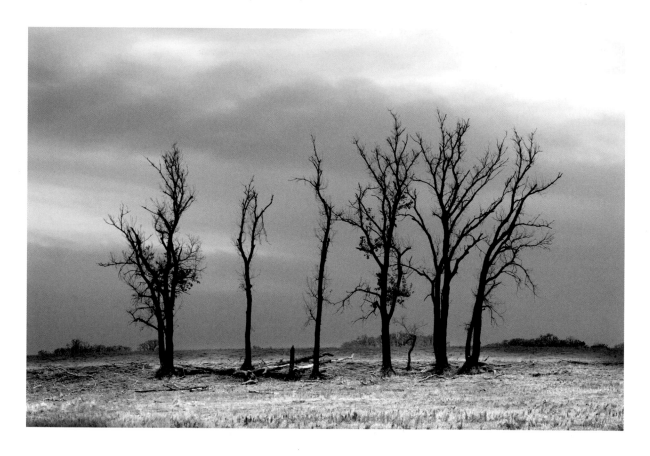

Your camera may be blistering with buttons and dials, or it might have a long list of menu options and functions, or maybe even have both lots of controls and lots of menu options. Most of these controls simply manipulate the three exposure settings that you learned about in the last chapter.

Shutter speed, aperture, and ISO are the three critical decisions that all photos require, and most of the controls on your camera simply provide you with different ways to manipulate these parameters. Some controls allow you to change how the camera calculates these parameters, while others enable you to perform slight modifications to these three crucial settings. The good news is that, while there are still a lot of things to learn about shooting, most of them will involve nothing more than different ways of manipulating these three properties.

So far in this book, I've asked you to practice shooting in Auto mode. All digital cameras include an auto mode, and when you use it, the camera automatically selects a shutter speed, aperture, and possibly ISO setting for you, based on what its light meter reports about your scene. As you've probably discovered, for many situations Auto mode does a very good job. There are times, though, when its decisions don't yield images that match your creative vision. Or you might find lighting situations that sometimes confuse your camera's Auto mode. Fortunately, most cameras provide a way for you to take more control and configure some or all of the camera's settings yourself.

In this chapter, we're going to switch from Auto to Program mode, which provides some additional manual overrides. We're also going to learn more about autofocus and some other camera subsystems. We're still deeply in the realm of "craft" here, because you must know how to control your camera before you can begin to apply an artistic sensibility to your images.

Switching to Program Mode

If you followed along during Chapter 2, "Getting to Know Your Camera," you should have found the mechanism that your camera provides for changing modes. Look at your camera's mode control and see if it has a P on it. This stands for Program mode.

Program mode is a lot like Auto mode because it automatically calculates aperture and shutter speed, and possibly ISO, but it also allows for a fair amount of manual override. In most Program modes, you'll be able to control white balance, Flash mode, and apply changes to aperture and shutter speed. In addition, you'll most likely be able to choose whether you're shooting single shots or bursts of images; you'll have control of the camera's autofocus system and much more. Depending on the controls on your camera, you might actually have as much manual control in Program mode as you have in some manual modes on your camera.

Most of the features that you'll see in this chapter will also be available in the additional modes that we'll discuss later. If your camera doesn't have a particular feature discussed here, just skip that section and move on to the next.

Focusing Revisited

With the Auto mode practice that you got earlier, you should now be pretty comfortable with the autofocus mechanism on your camera, as well as the practice of prefocusing, which is the process of pressing the button halfway down to autofocus. If you didn't read Chapter 2, go back now and review the section called "How to Press the Shutter Button." To use the autofocus system on your camera effectively, prefocusing has to be second nature.

While modern autofocus systems are very good, they can be confused in certain situations, so there will be times when you'll need to override or take manual control of your camera's focus. Fortunately, most cameras provide a number of focusing options.

How Autofocus Works

These days, most cameras use a passive autofocus system—most often a contrast detection system. You should be able to find out what type of system your camera uses by simply looking at the specifications table in your camera's manual. For example, your camera might specify its autofocus system as a "TTL contrast detection autofocus."

Contrast-detecting autofocus systems work by focusing the lens until the image has as much contrast as possible. The idea is that a low-contrast image is a blurry image. Therefore, by increasing contrast, the camera increases sharpness. The top image in Figure 7.1 shows an out-of-focus image. Look at the individual pixels up close, and you'll see that there is very little change from one pixel to the next. That is, the pixels have little contrast between them. In the bottom image in Figure 7.1, a sharp image, you can see that individual pixels have a more dramatic change in contrast from pixel to pixel.

When you press the shutter release halfway, a passive autofocus camera takes an initial reading of the contrast in your shot. It then focuses the lens closer and checks the contrast again. If contrast has increased, the camera continues focusing inward until the contrast decreases. With a decrease in focus, the camera knows it has gone too far and can step back to the correct focus.

Many variables can affect this process, such as the camera's capability to detect contrast, the precision with which it can move its lens, and the speed at which it can go through the entire procedure. Theoretically, a camera with more autofocus steps can achieve a more precise focus position, and therefore, it can achieve better focus. However, point-and-shoot digital cameras typically have *very* deep depths of field, so tiny changes in focus usually aren't that important. Moreover, most of the steps in an autofocus system are centered around very close (macro) ranges, where they tend to be needed and where depth of field offers less compensation, so a camera that provides more autofocus steps will probably not yield significantly better performance in everyday use.

The *TTL* part means *through the lens*. In other words, the camera's sensor looks through the camera's lens to focus, as opposed to systems that have a separate sensor outside the lens. TTL systems are superior because they're more accurate.

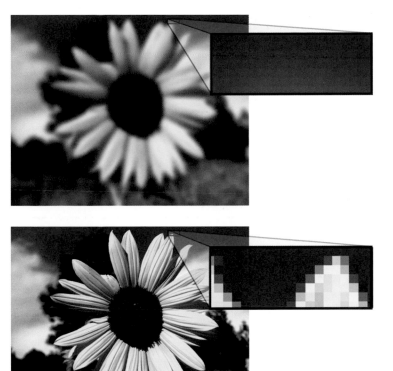

Figure 7.1

If you look closely at the pixels in the top, blurry image, you'll see that there is very little change in tone from one to the next, meaning that there is little contrast between them. In the bottom image, there is a big contrast change from pixel to pixel. This is why searching for high contrast is a good way to detect focus.

Contrast detection is largely a function of the available light in your scene. If the area in which you're pointing your camera is too dark, or is uniformly colored, your camera won't be able to detect any contrast and will be unable to determine focus. Today, many cameras include an *automatic focus-assist lamp* (also known as an autofocus-assist lamp) that shines a light onto your scene if the camera can't detect focus. By lighting up the scene, your camera's autofocus mechanism can "see" better. Some cameras use a normal white-light focus-assist lamp, whereas others use a less-intrusive red lamp. Some cameras will use their built-in flash, firing a rapid series of short bursts to illuminate the scene enough to detect focus.

A passive autofocus mechanism has many advantages, including the following:

◆ Passive autofocus systems work with any filters or lens attachments you might be using, because they look through the camera's lens to calculate focus.

◆ They can work through windows, water, or other transparent materials.

◆ They have no distance limitation, although your camera's autofocus-assist lamp will have some type of limiting distance.

On the downside, passive systems do require light in your scene and a subject that has enough detail to produce contrast. However, these limitations are minor, and as you'll see later, you can usually work around them using one of several techniques.

Other Autofocus Mechanisms

If you have a higher-end digital SLR, your camera might use a more advanced form of autofocus called *phase difference*, or *phase detection*. Phase detection autofocus is a passive TTL metering system that uses a complex arrangement of prisms and two tiny CCD arrays that are placed next to the focal plane. Both CCDs see the same part of the image, but one CCD looks through the left edge of the lens and the other looks through the right edge.

When the lens is focused too close, the image in the left edge of the CCD will be slightly to the left of the right-edge CCD. When the lens is focused too far, the opposite occurs. By analyzing the two images and determining the difference in shift between them, the camera can calculate which way to move the lens and how far it needs to go.

Phase difference systems are incredibly accurate and generally speedy. In addition, many of these systems are capable of focusing in near darkness. On the downside, some phase difference autofocus mechanisms become less reliable at apertures below f5.6, because as the aperture gets smaller, the CCDs lose their line of sight out of the lens and the mechanism can become confused. In general, though, these systems, whether single- or multispot, are by far the most accurate, quickest autofocus mechanisms available.

Some lower-end cameras use an active autofocus mechanism that employs an infrared beam to measure the distance to your subject; your camera then sets the focus accordingly. It's called an "active" system because the camera actively emits a signal to measure distance.

Although active autofocus mechanisms work fairly well, they have a number of limitations.

- ◆ You must have a clear line of sight between you and your subject. Bars in a zoo, fence posts, or other obstructions can keep the camera from measuring distance accurately.

- ◆ Because the infrared beam is not originating from the lens, the camera might not calculate focus correctly if you're using any type of lens attachment, such as a wide-angle or telephoto adapter. Consequently, most cameras with active autofocus mechanisms don't provide for such attachments.

- ◆ If you're standing close to another strong infrared source, such as a hot campfire or a birthday cake covered with candles, the heat from that source can confuse the camera's autofocus mechanism.

On the positive side, active autofocus systems work just fine in the dark.

Autofocus Modes

Your camera might provide a few Autofocus mode choices, which are completely independent of the shooting modes that we've already talked about. Autofocus modes typically change the approach that the camera takes for identifying a subject.

Focus Points

Obviously, you want your autofocusing system to focus on the subject of your image, not on something else in the scene. Therefore, most autofocus systems have a focusing zone or spot that determines which part of the image will be analyzed for focus. On a simple camera, this will be a small area in the middle of the frame, and it's usually marked with crosshairs or a box.

If your subject isn't in the middle of the frame, there's a good chance your camera will focus on the background of your image, leaving the foreground soft or outright blurry (see Figure 7.2).

Because your subject isn't always in the middle of your image, most cameras offer multiple focus zones. A camera with multiple focus spots analyzes several different points in your image to determine where your subject

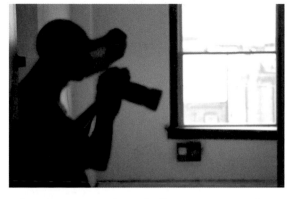

Figure 7.2

I wanted to focus on the woman in the foreground, but the camera focused on the wall in the distance.

might be. Once it has decided where the subject is, it analyzes the focus spot or spots closest to that subject to calculate focus. This process allows you to frame your image as you like without having to worry about your subject being in the middle of the frame.

Modern autofocus systems are very good at identifying the subject in a scene, but it's still possible for them to mess up. Therefore, it's important to pay attention to where the camera is focusing. When the camera locks focus, it will illuminate or flash the focus point or points it chose (see Figure 7.3). Get in the habit of paying attention to its choice. If it chooses the wrong spot, you'll need to try again.

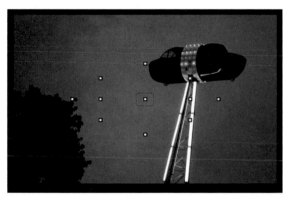

Figure 7.3

There are several potential subjects for the camera to focus on in this image—the carnival ride, obviously, but also the tree on the left and the sky in the background. Fortunately, the camera has picked the correct one. You can see what distance it has chosen to focus at by the focus points that it has lit up.

Sometimes your camera will light up several focus points at once. Remember that when you focus a lens, you're focusing it on a plane that's a particular distance from the camera. When your camera identifies the subject, it lights up any focus points that sit on that subject, but it also lights up any other points that sit on other objects *that are at the same distance as your subject*.

When multiple spots light up, the only thing you need to worry about is whether there's a lit focus point on the subject that you want in focus.

Different cameras offer different numbers of focus points. A less expensive camera might offer 7, for example, while a more expensive one might offer more than 20.

Because automatic mechanisms can't always choose the correct focus point, most cameras offer the option of manually selecting a focus point, which ensures that your autofocus mechanism analyzes the right area. You should have some type of control that will let you cycle through each of the camera's focus points (see Figure 7.4).

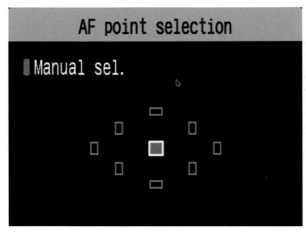 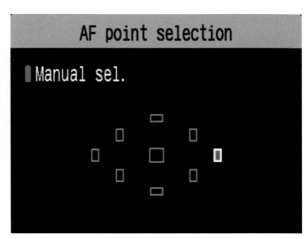

Figure 7.4 Your camera should provide some sort of mechanism for manually selecting a focus point.

When to Manually Choose a Focus Point

Certain types of scenes might consistently confuse an autofocus system. Landscape scenes can often yield bad focus point choices, as can shots of a still life, such as a picture of a product you want to post on eBay. You can solve all of these problems with manual focus point selection.

In addition to using the LCD display to choose a focus point (as shown in the previous example), your camera might also show your focus point choice in the camera's viewfinder or on the status LCD screen. Consult your manual for details.

Center-Point Focusing (for SLRs and Point-and-Shoots)

Most cameras with multispot autofocus mechanisms also allow you to put the camera into a single, Center-Spot Focusing mode (sometimes called *spot focus*), which forces the camera to behave like a single-spot autofocus camera. Very often, single-spot focus is the most reliable, fastest way to focus when creating an unusual composition. If your camera only offers a single focus point, then you'll find yourself using the following technique a lot. Even if your camera has multiple points, you may find that this technique is an effective way to work.

Say your camera is set for center focus (or only has a center focus point), and you want to focus on something on the right side of the frame. If you frame your shot the way you want it and half-press the shutter button, your camera will likely focus on the background, rather than on the subject at the side of the frame. In these situations, you need to employ the following technique:

1. Point the camera's center focusing target at your subject.

2. Press the shutter button halfway to lock focus.

3. While holding down the shutter button, reframe your shot to your desired framing. When you press the button the rest of the way, the camera will take the picture using the focus it initially calculated.

Figure 7.5 shows an example of this method.

If your camera has multiple focus spots, you might have been able to frame this image as desired. On a good autofocus system, the camera will properly identify the arrow as the subject and select the appropriate spot. You'll want to experiment with your camera's focus system to determine how good a job it does at identifying the subject in a scene.

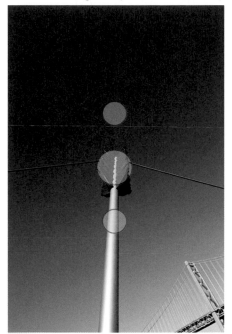 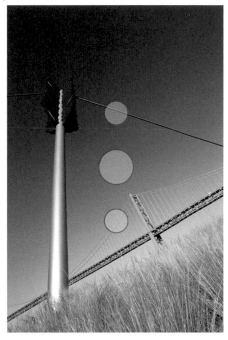

Figure 7.5

To keep the camera from focusing on the sky, the camera's focusing target was pointed at the arrow, and the shutter release was pressed down halfway to lock the focus. The image was reframed, and the picture was shot with the correct focus.

One advantage of choosing a center-based approach is that you always know where the camera is going to focus. If you're trying to shoot quickly, it can sometimes be quicker to lock focus and reframe, as described previously, rather than to worry about focusing and assessing whether the camera chose the right spot or not.

Be aware, though, that there are some potential pitfalls to a center focusing technique.

In addition to calculating focus, when you press down your shutter button halfway, your camera calculates exposure and white balance (if you're using automatic white balance). If the lighting in your frame is substantially different after you reframe from what it was when you locked focus, your camera's exposure could be off. (As you'll see in the next chapter, you can sometimes use this exposure change to your advantage.)

Camera manufacturers have come up with two solutions for these problems. The first is a separate exposure lock button that allows you to lock your camera's exposure and focus independently. Different exposure lock features work in different ways, but most allow you to do something like this: frame your shot, measure and lock the exposure, move your camera and lock focus on your subject, and then return to your final framing with everything ready to go. In the next chapter, we'll explore the vagaries of metering when reframing. Consult your camera's manual to learn about its exposure lock feature.

What to Do If Your Autofocus Won't Lock Focus

Autofocus mechanisms can get confused if you're trying to focus on something with low contrast. You might hear the lens searching back and forth, and the image in the viewfinder

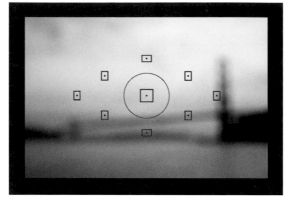

will swing in and out of focus, as the camera tries to hone in on the correct focus distance. This usually happens either because the camera's focus points are on a part of the scene that lacks contrast, or because they're centered on a textureless object (see Figure 7.6).

When this happens, you must use the same focus and reframe technique that you saw earlier.

Figure 7.6

Since all of the focus points are sitting on fog, which has no contrast, the camera can't focus.

1. Frame your shot so that the camera's focus points sit on something that's the same distance as your desired focus and then press the shutter button halfway to lock focus.

2. With the button held halfway down, reframe to your desired composition.

3. Take the shot (see Figure 7.7).

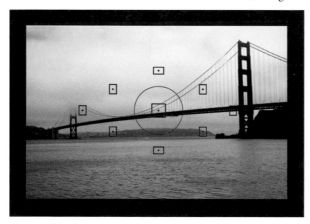 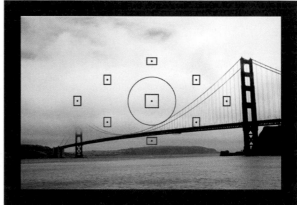

Figure 7.7 To focus on the bridge, I tilted down until the camera's focus spots were on the bridge, which has some contrast on it. I then half-pressed to lock focus and reframed to take the shot.

If your camera uses a TTL contrast-detection focusing system, the center focusing spot (no matter how many focus zones the camera has) is usually a dual-axis zone. That is, it examines contrast along both a horizontal and vertical axis. If the camera has multiple focus spots, there's a good chance that the other zones are single-axis zones, which measure only contrast (and, therefore, focus) along a horizontal axis. For locking focus on horizontal subjects, such as horizons, a single-axis zone can be problematic. For these situations, you might want to force the camera to use its center dual-axis zone.

Autofocus in Low Light

Sometimes, your scene might lack contrast because there's not much light around. In these cases, the camera may have trouble locking focus. To give the autofocus system some help, your camera might light up its autofocus-assist lamp or flash its built-in flash. This extra light can help the camera lock focus.

Note that if you're using a camera that has a pop-up flash for autofocus assist, you might have to pop the flash up manually to enable this feature. If you don't want the flash to fire during your shot, you'll have to do the following.

1. Pop up the flash.

2. Press the shutter button down halfway to focus. The camera will fire the flash to light up the scene and help the autofocus system. Once focus is locked, the camera will beep as normal.

3. Continue to hold the shutter button down halfway, while you close the flash.

4. Take your shot.

Be aware that a focus-assist light or flash has limited range, so it won't help if you're shooting a landscape shot or something far away. But if you're taking a portrait or snapshot, you should be fine. You might want to warn your subject that the camera is going to shine a light or flash at them, although these days most people are used to weird lights coming out of cameras.

Alternately, if you're using an SLR that has a lens with an Autofocus/Manual focus switch on its lens, you can let the camera use the flash to assist focus and then switch the lens to manual focus. Close the flash and then shoot.

If the focus-assist light doesn't solve your focus problem, try the focus and reframe trick shown earlier. Very often, you can find a bright highlight, or a reflection in a dark scene, and focus on that, if it's at the right distance.

Face Detection Autofocus

Operating on the assumption that a face is usually a subject, face detection autofocus systems identify a face in your scene and then set focus on that subject. For portraits and quick snapshots involving people, this can be an ideal focusing mode.

Usually, a box or crosshair is placed on the detected face. If multiple faces are detected, the camera will probably provide a way to cycle through each face to the one you want to focus on. If all of the faces are the same distance from the camera, then it doesn't matter which one you pick.

Some face detection systems offer special modes for shooting groups of people. Others offer the additional feature of smile detection, which only shoots when the subject is smiling.

A variation of this feature tells the camera not to shoot until the camera is held still. This can be a great option for self-portraits where you have to hold the camera at arm's length, pointed at yourself. Before you rely on these features for a once-in-a-lifetime shot, experiment with them a little bit to see how to operate them and how effective they are.

Continuous Autofocus

Your camera might have a continuous autofocus mode, which automatically refocuses every time you move or zoom the camera. With continuous autofocus, your camera stands a much better chance of being ready to shoot at any time. However, continuous autofocus can drain your battery and sometimes be distracting, because you will constantly hear the lens working. If your camera has a speedy autofocus, you might find little advantage to a continuous mechanism.

Focus Tracking—Sometimes Called "Servo Tracking"

If your camera provides a Servo Focus, or Focus Tracking mode, you have an easy way of keeping a moving subject in focus. Servo Focus is a special focus mode that automatically tracks a moving object and keeps it in focus, even as you reframe the shot.

To use most Servo Focus mechanisms, you activate the Servo mode and then focus on your subject as you normally would. Continue to hold the shutter button down halfway, and the camera will continually refocus and adjust its exposure as your subject moves.

Note that, because the camera is continuously focusing, it most likely will never beep or show you any of its normal "focus lock" indicators. So you can simply take the shot whenever you want. If the camera has not managed to lock focus, or is currently changing focus, then there might be a slight lag before the shutter is tripped.

Some cameras offer multiple variations of Servo Focus for different types of moving subjects. For example, you might have a Servo option tailored specifically to subjects that accelerate and decelerate quickly and another that's tailored to subjects that suddenly change directions. Other modes might be well suited to subjects that are entering the frame or to situations where the moving subject might be passing behind a still object.

For sports or wildlife shooting, Servo Focus can be a lifesaver. However, you'll want to experiment with your camera's Servo Focus to determine its effectiveness before you commit to using it during an important event (see Figure 7.8).

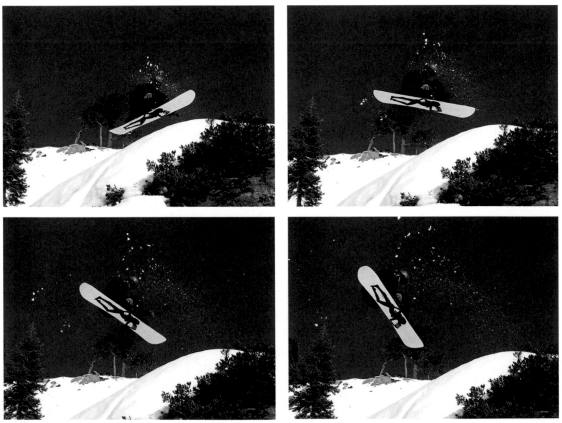

Figure 7.8 A Servo Focus mode will keep your subject in focus even if it, or the camera, is moving.

Autofocus on a Cell Phone Camera

Cell phone cameras use contrast detection autofocus, and many offer the same advanced face detection features that you'll find in a dedicated point-and-shoot or SLR. While most of them lack focus spots or manual focus features, many smart phones allow you to simply tap on the screen to select where you want to focus. This feature provides a way to create more complex compositions.

On many phones, tapping to select a particular focus point also impacts exposure.

Manual Focus

Your camera's autofocus system is probably all the focusing control you'll ever need. However, if you run into a situation where your camera can't autofocus and you can't work around it, or if you have a particularly "creative" shot you want to compose, you might need to resort to your camera's manual focus.

On point-and-shoot cameras, manual focus is often a special focus mode that you have to activate. On an SLR, you usually activate manual focus by simply switching the AF/MF switch on the camera's lens, as you saw in Chapter 2.

Manual Focus on an SLR

Because SLR lenses all have focus rings on them, as well as bright viewfinders, manually focusing is fairly easy. On some lenses, you must first switch the lens to manual focus before the focus ring will work. On other lenses, manual focus will automatically work as soon as you turn the ring. So, if you don't like the results from the camera's autofocus, you can simply turn the focus ring to refocus.

Manual Focus on a Point-and-Shoot

Manual focus on a point-and-shoot camera can be difficult. The controls for changing focus distance are often weak, while the LCD screen might be too small to reveal accurate focus. Fortunately, because of their small sensor size, and because auto exposure mechanisms are sometimes biased toward smaller apertures, you often don't have to worry about your focus being dead-on, because your depth of field will be deep enough that everything in your image will be sharp (assuming that your focus is in the ballpark).

To ease manual focus, some cameras provide a special zoomed view that shows an enlarged crop of the center of your image. This can make it easier to assess focus (see Figure 7.9).

Even if your camera doesn't have a full manual focus control, it might have a Landscape scene mode, which probably locks focus on infinity, in addition to aiming for a deeper depth of field. This feature can make for speedier shooting when working with distance subjects. However, note that many scene modes require you to shoot JPEG files, so if you prefer to shoot raw, this isn't the best option for locking focus.

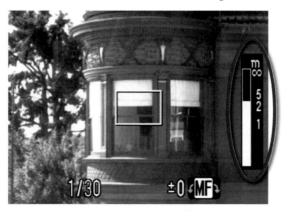

Figure 7.9

If your point-and-shoot camera offers a manual focus feature, it should provide some kind of indicator of focus. It might also allow you to display a magnified section of your image.

Consult your camera's manual for details on manual focus and explore its scene modes to determine which ones might serve as useful manual focus controls.

When to Use Manual Focus

If you use an SLR, then manual focus is much easier than it is on a point-and-shoot camera. Manual focus can often be very handy, and you'll want to think about it during situations like the following:

◆ If your autofocus system isn't working because the light is too low or because your scene lacks contrast, consider switching to manual focus. Manually focusing in low light can be hard, simply because it's difficult to see when your subject is in focus, but it's worth a try.

◆ Manual focus can speed your shooting when working with a subject that isn't changing, such as a sit-down portrait. Set focus once, and then as long as neither you nor your subject moves forward or backward, you can continue to shoot without refocusing. This can greatly speed up shooting. This is also a great technique for still life and product shots, and sometimes works with landscapes.

◆ When shooting moving objects, some people find manual focus to be faster than autofocus. Once you've focused, any changes in focus as the subject moves will probably be fairly small. Many of the people who think this, though, are very experienced shooters with a lot of practice. Or they're just the type of people who like to show off.

With my SLR, I will often use a combination of auto and manual focus. For example, if I'm shooting a landscape and have set my camera on a tripod, or if I'm shooting someone on a stage, and I know neither of us will move, then I'll let my camera autofocus. Once it's focused, I'll switch the lens over to manual focus. Then I know that I'm focused at the right distance, and because I'm set to manual focus, the camera won't change that focus. This also works well for product shots.

This technique is also good for times when you're shooting in extremely low light—outside in the woods, for example—and your camera won't lock focus. In these situations, try using a flashlight to illuminate your subject. If you have a cell phone, or some other point light source, place it in the scene at the distance you want to focus on. After you've achieved focus, switch the lens to manual focus and remove the light source from your scene. You're now ready to shoot.

Finally, you can always guess at the focus if your lens has distance markings. Either pace off or eyeball the distance to your subject and then set the lens to that distance (see Figure 7.10).

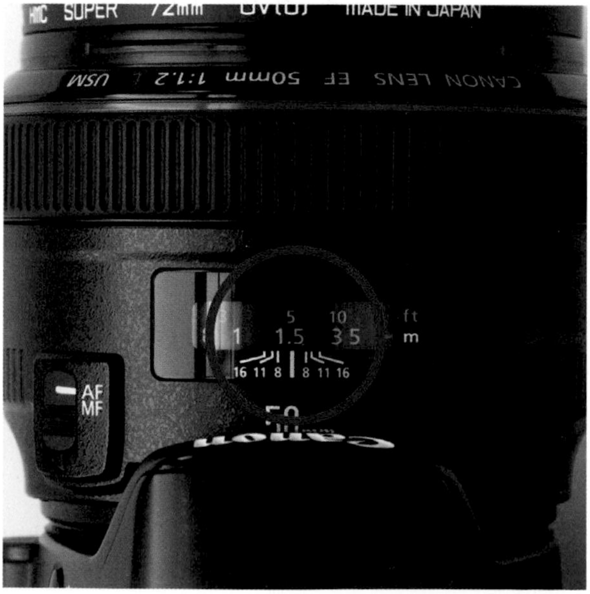

Figure 7.10

Many SLR lenses include markings that indicate the distance that the lens is focused on.

Evaluating Focus

One of the great advantages of a digital camera is its ability to display your picture immediately after shooting. However, at the time of this writing, even the highest-quality camera-mounted LCD is not good enough to check focus accurately, even when zooming in close to the recorded image.

If you're not sure whether your shot was in focus, try again. If the light is so low that you have to shoot manually, then shoot multiple shots with slight variations of focus.

Finally, if the lighting allows, switch to a smaller aperture. As you've learned, with a smaller aperture, you have deeper depth of field, which means more of your image will be in focus. You'll learn how to change aperture later.

The Eyes Have It When Focusing

People relate very strongly to the eyes in an image, so when shooting portraits, be certain that your subject's eyes are in focus. Everything else in the image can be soft, but if the eyes are in focus, you can still have a compelling image. If need be, place the focus point of your camera directly on your subject's eyes. If you're shooting with a very shallow depth of field, it's especially important to have the eyes in focus.

The Golden Rule of Focus

If there's any one rule to using an autofocus camera, it's simply to pay attention to where the camera has chosen to focus. If your camera has a single-spot focusing system that sometimes requires you to lock focus and reframe, be sure to look for any potential metering and white balance troubles before you shoot. If your camera has a multispot focusing system, be certain it has chosen the correct subject and focusing zone. When using Face Detection on a shot containing multiple people, be sure to pay attention to which face has been selected.

As long as you remember that focus matters (and it's easy to forget this critical point, when shooting in a hurry), you will get home with sharp images.

Shutter Speed and Aperture Can Also Affect Focus

To ensure sharp images, you also want to be sure that your shutter speed is fast enough to freeze any motion in the scene, and that your depth of field is deep enough to render all that you want in focus. So you need to pay attention to your shutter speed and aperture, as well as your autofocus system.

Shutter Lag Even with Prefocusing

Shutter lag is a slight delay between the time you press the shutter button all the way down (after prefocusing first, of course) and when the camera takes the shot. Unfortunately, some cameras have a bit of a shutter lag even if you've already pressed down the shutter release halfway to go through the prefocusing step. There's really nothing you can do to work around this problem except to learn how long the lag is so you can try to anticipate when you need to press the shutter to capture the action you want. Another option is to switch to your camera's Burst mode (sometimes referred to as Drive) and shoot a series of images with the hope that one of them will capture the moment you were looking for. We'll look at bursts later in this chapter.

White Balance

Different types of light shine with different color qualities. Direct sunlight, for example, is very blue, while tungsten light is very orange. As you learned in Chapter 1, "Eyes, Brains, Lights, and Images," your eyes have the amazing ability to move among different types of light, yet still perceive colors in the same way. Blue looks blue whether you're in sunlight or a lamp-lit room. Your eyes can even understand mixed lighting conditions—sunlight shining through a window into a fluorescent-lit room, for example.

Unlike your eyes, a digital image sensor is not as sophisticated. When you shoot under different types of light, the same color might vary from one photo to the next, due to the changing lighting conditions. An image sensor simply captures light and passes it to the camera's on-board computer for processing. It's up to that computer to interpret the color correctly for the particular type of light in which you are shooting. For it to perform this interpretation correctly, the camera's computer needs to determine or be told what type of light is striking your subject. Fortunately, there's a very easy way to perform this calibration.

In grade school, you probably learned how droplets of rain can act like tiny prisms. As they scatter the sunlight passing through them, a rainbow is formed. From this, you learned that the light that you see is actually made up of a bunch of independent color components, the Roy G. Biv collection of red, orange, yellow, green, blue, indigo, and violet. These colors combine to create the white light that you normally see.

The idea with white balancing is that if a camera can reproduce white accurately, it can represent any other color accurately. Once your camera knows what in your scene is supposed to be white, it can determine the type of light in your scene and accurately reproduce any other color. Figure 7.11 shows the same scene shot several times, each with a different white balance setting.

You Say "Color," I Say "Color Temperature"

The color of a specific light is measured as a temperature using the Kelvin scale. For example, direct sunlight has a color temperature of 5500°K. You will often see photographers referring to the *color temperature* of a light source, and your camera's white balance setting might even prompt you to enter the color temperature of the current light.

The reason light color is defined as temperature is because of something called *black body radiation*. If you heat a black object, it will begin to change color. As it gets hotter, it will progress through a spectrum of colors from red through orange, then yellow, white, and blue-white. The color corresponds to the temperature at which the object has been heated. This, then, is why light is measured as a temperature.

One thing to note, as the temperature increases, the color shifts toward blue. So higher temperatures actually yield colors that are traditionally referred to as "cooler."

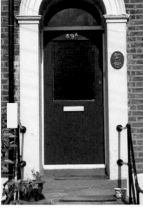

Auto White Balance

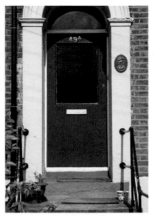

Cloudy White Balance

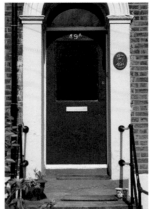

Fluorescent White Balance

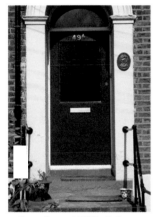

Incandescent White Balance

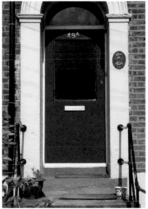

Shadow White Balance

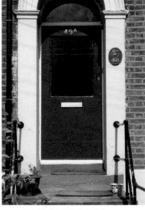

Sunlight White Balance

Figure 7.11

Although film photographers need to select a film that is balanced for the type of light in which they'll be shooting, digital photographers need to make certain their cameras are properly white balanced for the current light. If you use the wrong white balance setting, your images will have strange color casts that can be difficult to remove.

Auto and Preset White Balance

Every time you take your camera into a new lighting situation, you need to consider how to white balance for that light. Proper white balance is essential to getting accurate color, and the only equivalent it has in the film world is the choice you make when you buy a particular type of film. Consequently, whether you're new to photography or you're an experienced film photographer, you must learn to start thinking about white balance!

All cameras have an automatic white balance feature, and depending on the quality of your camera, this might be all you need to get accurate white balance. The simplest automatic white balance mechanisms look for the brightest point in your shot, assume that that point is white, and then use that white value as a reference to balance accordingly. More sophisticated automatic white balancers perform a complex analysis of many different areas in your image. Both mechanisms are surprisingly effective, and you'll almost always get very good color with auto white balance when shooting in direct sunlight, and decent color in other lighting conditions. However, even a few clouds can confuse an auto white balance mechanism, and in other types of light you may find that your auto white balance works poorly.

Fortunately, most cameras offer preset white balance configurations for different lighting conditions—Daylight, Tungsten, Fluorescent, and possibly a Cloudy or Overcast setting. (Tungsten is sometimes called "Incandescent" or "Indoors.") Because there are two different temperatures of fluorescent lights—"cool white" and "warm white"—some cameras offer separate settings for each fluorescent color.

Figure 7.12

Some cameras use manual white balance controls that are measured in degrees Kelvin. If your camera simply presents a list of temperatures, here are the types of lights to which those temperatures correspond.

White Balance in K°	
2700°K	-	Tungsten
3000°K	-	Halogen
4000°K	-	Flourescent
4500°K	-	Flourescent
5500°K	-	Sunlight
6500°K	-	Cloudy
7500°K	-	Shade

Other cameras will actually specify white balance presets in degrees Kelvin. Be sure you understand which setting corresponds to which type of light (see Figure 7.12).

These white balance presets are usually more accurate than automatic white balance in the situations for which they're designed. However, you can't always be sure that your lighting situation is exactly the color temperature your camera's preset is expecting. For these situations, some cameras offer white balance fine-tuning that allows you to alter a preset white balance to be warmer or cooler.

Manual White Balance

In general, you can expect your camera's auto white balance to do very well in direct sunlight. For other instances, you can try white balance presets, which may not be tuned exactly right for the light you're trying to shoot in. Therefore, for the absolute best results under any lighting situation—and especially under mixed lighting—you'll want to use your camera's manual white balance.

To use a manual white balance control, hold a white object, such as a piece of paper, in front of the camera and activate the camera's manual white balance feature. The camera will study that white object and calculate a white balance based on the light in your scene.

Measure the Right Light with the Right White

When you manually white balance, be sure to hold your white card in the light that is hitting your subject. This is particularly critical in a studio situation where your camera might be sitting in very different light from your subject, or if you're standing outside in the sun, but you've placed a subject in the shade.

On some cameras, you set manual white balance by pointing the camera at a white object and then pressing a special button. On others, you take a picture of the white object and then tell the camera to use that image as the white reference. The advantage to the second approach is that you can store white pictures shot in different lighting situations and switch between them very easily. Check your camera's manual for more details.

Figure 7.13 shows an image shot with auto white balance in the shade. The color is not wildly out of whack, but it's too cool, and the flesh tones are not accurate. In the second image, the model held up a piece of white paper, and the camera's manual white balance feature was used to calculate white balance. The third image was taken using that manual white balance setting. As you can see, it's much warmer, with more accurate flesh tones.

For this technique to work, the white piece of paper *must* be in the same light as your subject. For example, in Figure 7.13 the camera was positioned outside of the shade, in direct sunlight. If the paper were held directly in front of the camera, you would have ended up with a white balance calculation based on direct sun rather than on shade.

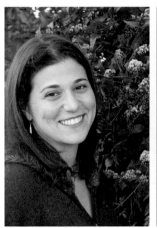 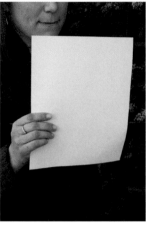 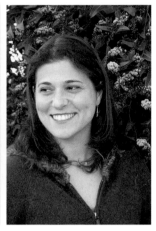

Figure 7.13

The first image was shot with auto white balance. For the second image, the model held up a white piece of paper. The camera was told to use this image to set a manual white balance, and then took the third image, which is much more accurate.

Take some test pictures with your camera to learn more about its white balance peculiarities. This will give you a better idea of when you need to white balance manually.

Change Manual White Balance Every Time You Change Light ━━━

After you've manually white balanced, you can continue to use that white balance setting as long as your lighting doesn't change. It your lighting changes, you'll need to white balance again.

Assessing White Balance

To make the LCD screen on a camera more visible in bright light, most cameras increase the brightness and color saturation of the images they show on-screen. This means that it's not actually possible to see accurate color in the images on your camera's LCD screen. While the screen is probably good enough to spot something like the bad shady white balance you saw in Figure 7.13, very subtle problems will not be detectable. Later, you'll learn how to assess white balance using a tool in your camera called a *histogram*.

As you use your camera more, you'll learn how accurate its automatic white balance and preset options are.

White Balance Shift

There will be times when neither auto white balance nor the white balance presets on your camera will be right for your situation. Unfortunately, sometimes manual white balance is not an option—perhaps you don't have a white object with you, or you can't get an object placed within the light in your scene. For these instances, some cameras provide a white balance shift option.

White balance shift lets you bias the white balance presets in your camera to skew color more toward green, magenta, blue, or amber. These are very subtle adjustments—too subtle to show up in the printing process shown in this book. But they can serve to improve the overall color tone of your image if you're printing on a photo printer.

Bring Your Light Balancing Experience

Film shooters who are used to balancing light in a scene using colored filters will have an easier time with white balance shift features. White balance shift lets you apply similar color adjustments to your images. Like color filters, white balance shift uses the mireds scale, a unit of measure for specifying color density, for its adjustments.

If you're only shooting a single shot, hassling with white balance shift isn't worth the time. But let's say you're shooting an event, and upon arriving at the location, you take a couple of test shots to determine what white balance looks best in the available lighting. If you decide that all of the images are a little too cool, or too warm, or have a weird color shift of some kind, you could dial in a white balance shift and all of your images would be correct when you shot them, saving you a tremendous amount of time in your image editor later.

To be honest, though, this is not a feature that you will use very often, if at all, for the simple fact that manual white balance and raw shooting, which you'll learn about later, are much easier solutions.

Eyeballing White Balance in Live View

If you find yourself in a situation where you need to manually white balance, but it's not possible, then you might be able to get a decent manual white balance by eye. For this to work, you need a camera that allows you to specify white balance in degrees Kelvin.

1. Put your camera into Live View mode and frame your shot.

2. Activate the camera's white balance control and select the option to choose a white balance by Kelvin degrees.

3. As you dial through different temperatures, you'll see the image on the LCD screen change color. Select a temperature that looks right, and you're ready to shoot.

This won't necessarily get you a perfectly accurate white balance, but it should get you in the ballpark.

White Balance Bracketing

Some cameras offer a white balance bracketing feature, which provides you with an additional way to tackle troublesome white balance situations.

Bracketing is the process of shooting multiple exposures of the same scene with slightly different settings. Bracketing is most often used for varying exposure, but some cameras include an option for bracketing white balance.

When you activate the white balance bracketing feature, the next shot you take will be made using your chosen white balance. The shot you take after that will be shot with the same white balance, but one that has been shifted to be more blue/amber (blue in the shadows, amber in the highlights). The shot after that will be biased toward magenta/green.

This process of shooting more white balance coverage simply improves your chances of getting a good white balance when shooting in tricky lighting.

Avoid White Balance Concerns Altogether

Finally, there's another way to ease your white balance concerns, which is to shoot in raw format, if your camera provides it. Raw does not obviate the need for white balance, but with a raw file, you can alter the white balance of an image later, just as if you were back at the location, changing settings on your camera.

Getting white balance correct in your camera means less editing hassle later, but correcting white balance in a raw file is very easy, and you'll learn more about it later in this book.

White Balance Aids

While the manual white balance image in Figure 7.13 looks much better, it's still not perfect. Overall, the color is a little yellowish. Even though manual white balance is almost always better than auto, there are some simple things you can do to improve it even more.

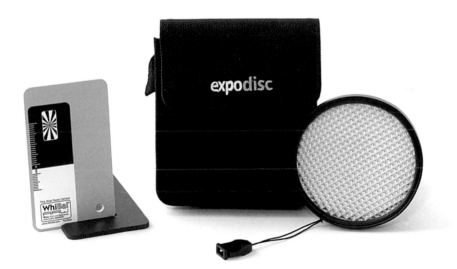

Figure 7.14

These two white balance aids can greatly improve the accuracy of your manual white balance operations. On the left is the WhiBal white balance reference card and on the right is the ExpoDisc.

The ExpoDisc shown in Figure 7.14 is a white balance aid that works in conjunction with your camera's manual white balance. When you're ready to manually white balance, you place the ExpoDisc over the end of your lens and point your camera at your light source. Then you take a white balance reference shot and use this as the source of your manual white balance. Really, the ExpoDisc is nothing more than a substitute for a white piece of paper. However, the white balance derived from the ExpoDisc-generated shot is often more accurate than what you'll get off a piece of paper, as you can see in Figure 7.15.

You can pick up an ExpoDisc for 50 bucks and you can learn more about them, including detailed tutorials on how to use them, at *www.expoimaging.com*.

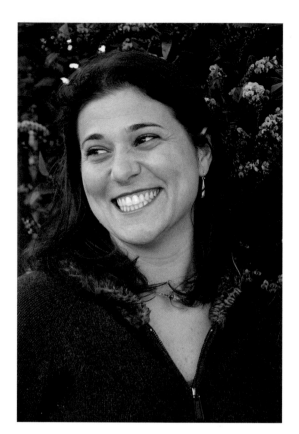

Figure 7.15

For this image, I used the
ExpoDisc to perform my manual
white balance. As you can see, it's
more accurate than the in-camera
manual white balance shown in
Figure 7.13.

While the ExpoDisc lets you get accurate color right out of the camera, it requires you to position the camera at your subject's location and then point back to your light source. This can be difficult if your light source is an on-camera flash or if you're standing in shade while your subject is illuminated. A white balance reference card such as the WhiBal card shown in Figure 7.14 provides a simple way to correct white balance *after* you've taken the shot. To use the WhiBal card, you place it within your light field, just as you do with a normal white balance reference, and then take a picture using auto white balance. Next, remove the card and shoot your shots, also using auto white balance (see Figure 7.16). Later, you can use your image editor to correct the white balance using your reference image. We'll discuss how to do this later in the book.

A white balance reference card even works well for street shooting. If you find yourself in a weird lighting situation, just hold the card in front of the camera and take a shot. You can use that image later to correct the other shots you took in that light. Or if the situation you're in is changing rapidly, take the shot you want first and then grab the WhiBal shot afterward. Working with the WhiBal card offers the quickest way to record white balance (see Figure 7.17).

The WhiBal card is available from *www.michaeltapesdesign.com* and sells for around $30.

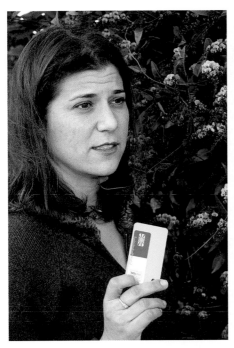
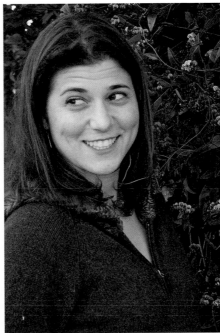

Figure 7 .16

In the left image, the model is holding the WhiBal white balance reference. I took a picture and then removed the card. In the image editor, I used that reference image to correct the color in the right-hand image, resulting in a very accurate white balance.

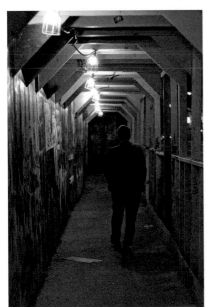
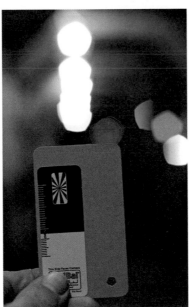
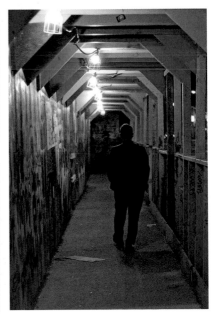

Figure 7.17 While walking down the street late at night, I took the shot on the left. Because I knew that auto white balance would be inaccurate, I immediately held up my WhiBal card and took a shot of it. Later, I used the WhiBal image to correct the color in my original shot.

Don't Plan on Correcting Bad White Balance

It can take a lot of work to correct a bad white balance (see Figure 7.18). The color shifts that occur from incorrect white balance don't affect all the colors in an image equally— for example, the highlights in an image might be shifted more than the shadows. Consequently, you won't be able to do a simple global correction. Moreover, as you'll see later, by the time you're done correcting the white balance, you might have used up so much of your image's editing potential that it will be difficult to perform further corrections and adjustments without introducing artifacts. In the end, it's best to shoot with the most accurate white balance your camera can manage.

If you're shooting in Raw mode, you might feel like you don't need to worry about white balance, since raw files allow you to set white balance after the fact, without using up any of your editing latitude. This is true, but shooting with bad white balance means you'll have to do additional corrections and adjustments later. Shooting as cleanly as possible in-camera will greatly speed your workflow. Also, though raw images allow for fine white balance control, it can still be difficult to determine the correct white balance in postproduction.

No matter what format you're shooting in, you may decide that you don't need to worry about white balance because you're ultimately going for a stylized look, not realistic color. That's fine, but you never know how you might want to repurpose your images later. Having accurate white balance will give you a record of what the real color was and still allow you to perform your stylized adjustments.

For all these reasons, it's important to give thought to white balance while shooting.

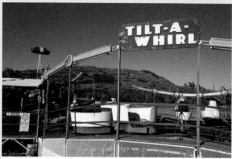
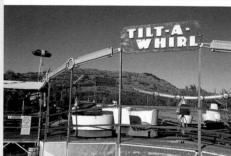
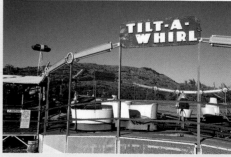

Figure 7.18

The top image was accidentally shot with Tungsten white balance (instead of auto or daylight). The middle image shows my attempts to correct the color. Although the image is improved, completely removing the bad color casts is extremely difficult and results in an image with bad posterizing artifacts (which are difficult to see at this print size). The bottom image was shot with a correct white balance. As you can see, white balance choice is not to be taken lightly, because correcting it later is extremely difficult.

Cell Phone Cameras and White Balance

Cell phone cameras don't usually provide white balance controls. (The fact is I've never seen a cell phone camera with a white balance control and am only hedging just in case someone releases one by the time this book sees print.) Fortunately, a good cell phone camera will provide enough image editing latitude for you to make some effective white balance correction in post, either on the phone or in your computer. For example, if a portrait shot in the shade looks too cool, warming it up shouldn't be a problem.

Sometimes the white balance in an image can be thrown off (on any camera) by a large field of color in the frame. If you're shooting something against a bright red wall or on a deep green lawn, you might be able to get better white balance by framing out some of that dominant color.

Since white balance control on a cell phone camera is limited, your best option is to learn some good correction tools and play with them enough to learn how much white balance correction latitude you have with your particular cell phone camera.

Drive Mode

Sometimes referred to as *Burst mode*, the Drive modes on different cameras work at different speeds, but they all have one thing in common: as long as you hold down the button, the camera will keep shooting.

Drive mode is most useful when you're shooting action scenes such as performances and sporting events, or wild animals, or any moment where you're concerned that your reflexes won't be fast enough to grab the decisive moment. When you use Drive mode, you can shoot a burst of images and pick out the best one later (see Figure 7.19).

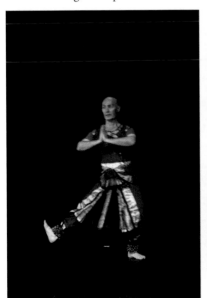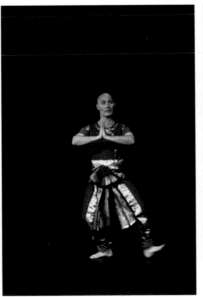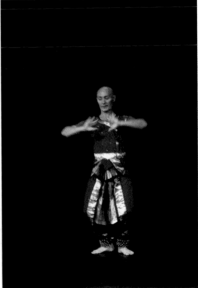

Figure 7.19 Drive mode is ideal for shooting any type of action, because it allows you to shoot a burst of images to capture a specific moment.

Drive mode can also be useful for everyday events, especially when shooting candid shots of people. Because people's expressions can change very subtly from one moment to the next, shooting a burst of images lets you shoot a range of subtle expressions (see Figure 7.20).

Some cameras can burst very quickly, zipping through five to seven pictures per second. Cameras designed specifically for sports shooting might even manage to go faster. Casio makes point-and-shoot cameras that can shoot 30 full-resolution images per second. Other cameras will clock slower burst speeds, sometimes dropping to 1.5 to 2 frames per second. Still, even this slow speed can be useful in some situations.

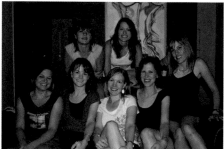
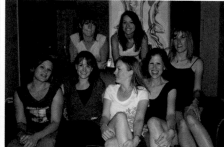
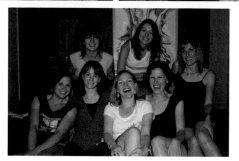

Figure 7.20

When shooting groups of people, it's tough identifying the precise moment when everyone's eyes will be open, and they'll all have good expressions. With Drive mode, you can easily shoot a burst and then pick out the best image.

Shooting in Drive Mode

First, activate your camera's Drive mode. Note that some cameras offer multiple Drive modes with different speeds. For example, they might have a slow Drive mode that can capture three frames per second and a faster mode that manages five. The slower mode will let you maintain a burst over a longer period of time, while the faster mode will shoot more often. If your subject is not moving quickly, the slower burst speed captures more variety.

In Drive mode, as long as you hold the shutter button down, the camera will continue to shoot, bursting away at whatever speed it can manage. If your autofocus is set to servo, then the camera will refocus on moving objects while it bursts.

While your camera might be able to capture a bunch of shots in one second, it can't write them out to the storage card that quickly. To get around this problem, the camera contains a big memory buffer. As you shoot more images, they are quickly stuffed into the buffer, to free up the camera for more shooting.

Most cameras with a Drive mode have some kind of readout that tells you how much space is left in the internal buffer (see Figure 7.21).

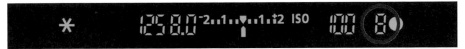

Figure 7.21 Most cameras have some kind of readout that shows how many shots are available in the current buffer. When this number gets to zero, you have to wait for the camera to clear out buffer space.

The camera does not wait until the buffer is full before it starts writing. It continuously writes as you shoot, but when the counter hits zero, the camera will stop shooting. If you continue to hold the button down, the camera will shoot again as soon as some space is available, but you'll probably only get one shot off before you experience another pause.

If you lift your finger off the button for a few seconds, to give the camera time to dump more images, the number of shots that can be taken at full speed will go back up.

In practice, buffer limitations probably won't be a problem, because you'll rarely shoot long bursts. But it's still a good idea to keep an eye on the buffer number and to shoot small bursts with breaks in between. If the "big play" is about to unfold, don't just start bursting with the idea that you'll get the whole thing. Wait until the critical moment is as close as possible and then start your burst.

Image format affects the number of images the buffer can hold. For example, you can fit more low-resolution JPEG images into the buffer than raw files. Also note that the time it takes the camera to write out images is partly dependent on the speed of the memory card you're using. If you find yourself shooting a lot of bursts and having to wait for the camera to finish writing, then you should consider buying faster cards.

Drive Mode and Image Review

When you shoot in Drive mode, the camera does not display each image on the LCD screen. Instead, it waits until you're done with the burst and then displays the last image you shot.

Continuous Flash Shots

Most cameras can't use a flash when shooting in a Burst mode, because there isn't enough time for the flash to recharge. However, some cameras can manage roughly one frame per second when shooting with the built-in flash. If you regularly need to shoot with bursts of flash shots, you might want to shop for a camera with a good flash burst speed.

Don't Let Drive Mode Make You Lazy

While Drive mode can be a great way to capture a specific moment in a complex, rapidly changing scene, don't become too dependent on it. Learning to shoot in Single Frame mode is a very important skill that will greatly improve your ability to recognize the "decisive moment" in a scene. What's more, depending on the speed of your camera's burst feature, the decisive moment may happen between frames. Consequently, being practiced at recognizing, anticipating, and capturing single frames can be an essential skill for shooting dynamic scenes.

Self-Timer

At some point, you've probably owned a camera that had a self-timer on it. You know: you set the timer and then run as fast as you can to try to get in the shot and look natural in the five seconds or so that you have before the camera fires. Most digital cameras have this type of feature.

Your camera might offer a few self-timer options, such as the following:

◆ **Self-timer.** Press the button, wait the specified interval, and the camera takes a picture. These options usually have a fairly long interval, such as 10 seconds.

◆ **Self-timer with variable delay.** Some cameras with variable delay let you specify any amount of delay, while others simply include an additional interval, usually a very short one, like two seconds.

◆ **Self-timer continuous.** Some cameras can be configured so that when the self-timer fires, a burst of two or three shots will be taken rather than a single shot. This can be handy when shooting groups of people, for the reasons mentioned earlier.

The 10-second interval is designed to give you enough time to get in front of the camera. The 2-second timer is not for self-portraits, but for when you want to take a shot with minimal camera contact. Any time you handle the camera, you risk introducing shake that can cause your images to be soft. This is especially problematic when shooting exposures around one-half to five seconds. In these instances, you'll get the sharpest image if you put the camera on a tripod and use a self-timer. A two-second timer gives the camera enough time to stop vibrating, but doesn't delay so long as to be tedious. This is a good approach for low-light photos, astrophotography, or photos where you're using a small aperture for deep depth of field, and so must use a long shutter speed.

Self-Timer and Self-Portraits

If you want to shoot a solo self-portrait, bear in mind that focus can be tricky. When you half-press the shutter button, the camera will focus on whatever might be behind where you intend to stand (since you'll be behind the camera), which could be a long way away. After you press the shutter button down all the way and run in front of the camera, the focus won't change—it will still be locked on the distant point that it focused on when you half-pressed the button.

To compensate for this, tilt the camera down and focus on the spot on the ground where you plan to stand. In fact, you might want to mark the spot beforehand. Press the shutter halfway to lock focus; then frame your shot and press the rest of the way to start the timer.

With the camera focused, trip the shutter and move to the marked spot, and you should get good focus. To improve your chances, select a small aperture to increase the depth of field. That way, if the focus is off by a foot or two, your image will still most likely be in focus (see Figure 7.22).

If you're shooting with an SLR, your camera might have come with an eyepiece cover attached to its strap. Without your face in front of the viewfinder, light can filter in through the viewfinder and throw off the camera's exposure. By covering the viewfinder with the eyepiece cover, you can protect the exposure from stray light (see Figure 7.23).

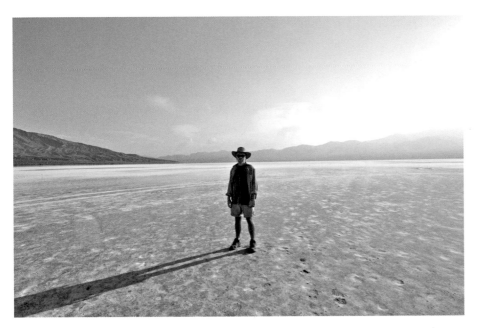

Figure 7.22

To shoot this self-portrait, I focused on a spot on the ground where I planned to stand. Then I switched the camera to manual focus to lock that focus and pressed the self-timer.

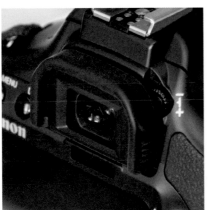

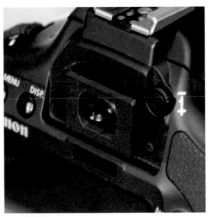

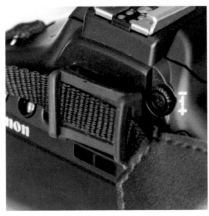

Figure 7.23

To use the eyepiece cover, remove the eyepiece and then fit the cover (which is usually attached to the camera strap) over the eyepiece mount.

Remote Controls

In the old days, you could attach something called a *cable release* to the shutter button of your camera. This was a long cord with a little plunger mechanism running through it. When you pressed the button at the top, the plunger was pushed forward, and a pin came out the other end and pushed the shutter button.

Since digital cameras all have electronic shutters, you no longer need such a crude mechanical device. Instead, you get to use an expensive electronic device.

If you have a point-and-shoot camera, it might provide an option for a separate wireless remote control, or, if you're lucky, it might even have come bundled with one. These controls usually include a shutter button and possibly a zoom control. A wireless remote is a great fix for the self-portrait problem described earlier.

Most SLRs include a port for attaching a cabled remote control of some kind. These remotes vary in features, but all include a shutter button. Some might also include a long-exposure timer, which allows you to program an exposure of a particular duration, or a lock feature, for using Bulb mode. Others might include an intervalometer, which allows you to shoot time-lapse movies (see Figure 7.24).

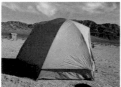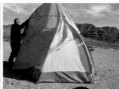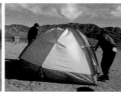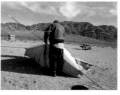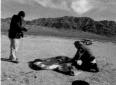

Figure 7.24 Some stills from a time-lapse movie, shot with a Canon G9, which features a built-in time-lapse feature.

An *intervalometer* will automatically take a shot at a given interval. Some intervalometers also let you specify the number of frames you want taken at each interval. This feature allows you to perform a time-lapse bracketed sequence when used in conjunction with your camera's Auto Bracketing mode. (It also allows you to shoot time-lapse HDR movies.)

The shutter button on all remote controls works just like the shutter button on your real camera: press the button halfway to autofocus and then press it the rest of the way to shoot.

Remote controls are great for self-portraits or for any time when you want to keep your hands off the camera to reduce vibration. They are also good for portrait shooting, because you can stay out from behind the camera and maintain eye contact with your subject.

Third-Party Remotes

The remote controls sold by your camera maker can be pricey, so you might want to look for a third-party alternative. If you have an SLR, you'll probably be able to find lots of third-party remote control alternatives, from simple wired remotes all the way to sophisticated remotes with intervalometers.

You can probably also find third-party wireless remotes for your SLR. These remotes include a receiving unit that you plug into the remote port on your camera and a small handheld unit for tripping the shutter.

Cell Phone Camera Remotes

There are a number of third-party cell phone camera remotes for both iPhones and Android phones. Most work via Bluetooth, which means they're wireless and have decent range. Another option is to find a camera app that provides a self-timer feature or remote trigger of some kind. For example, some camera apps can be configured to trip the shutter at the sound of a whistle or loud noise, providing you with a way of firing the shutter from in front of the camera (though you might have a strange, puckered expression in the resulting picture).

Tethered Shooting

Your in-camera histogram provides an excellent way to judge your exposure, while your camera's LCD screen lets you see your exact composition. Your computer, though, has a much larger monitor than your camera, and offers software tools that provide far more powerful image analysis. To take advantage of your computer's larger screen and more advanced software, you might want to consider tethering your camera to your computer *while* shooting.

When tethered, every image you shoot will automatically be moved to your computer and displayed on-screen. This allows you to assess focus, color, and tone more easily, and then adjust your shot and reshoot.

Your tethering software might also allow you to control your camera. Many tethering programs let you see and adjust all exposure parameters, and then fire the shutter. So, once you get your shot set, you can return to your computer and try different exposures—and immediately see the results—without having to run back and forth between the camera and computer. Some can even show you the view through the viewfinder, giving you the option of full remote composition, exposure control, and shutter firing.

Tethered shooting is ideal for studio work, where you tend to set the camera in place and alter lighting and exposure. For live action studio work, such as portraiture, tethering is a boon both because of the better view afforded by a real monitor and because your client can see your shots as you work.

If you're willing to lug a computer and relevant power, then you can even work tethered in the field. When shooting wildlife, you can hide your camera and control it from a blind or more distant location. Sports shooters often tether because it affords them the chance to install a camera in a difficult location, such as directly above a basketball goal.

Most cameras capable of tethered shooting ship with software that handles the real-time transfer to the computer. For more details, consult the software manual that came with your camera. These days, most cameras tether using USB cables.

A variation of tethered shooting is to connect the video out port of your camera to a TV.

Manual Override with Program Shift (Flexible Program)

You've already learned about the effects that different shutter speed and aperture choices have on your final image. Earlier, you saw that by controlling shutter speed, you could choose how much you wanted to freeze or blur motion, and that by controlling aperture, you could choose how much you wanted to blur out the background. You also learned that these parameters have a reciprocal relationship. If you change one, you can change the other to compensate.

Most SLRs, and quite a few point-and-shoots, provide a lot of different ways to change shutter speed and aperture, allowing you to take complete creative control of motion stopping and depth of field.

Your camera's light meter aims for a shutter speed that is appropriate for handheld shooting and an aperture that's not so small that you'll suffer a sharpness penalty. (Remember, your lens has an aperture "sweet spot" when it comes to sharpness.) But as you've learned, many different combinations of shutter speed and aperture yield the same exposure. Some of these combinations will have a faster or slower shutter speed and conversely, a larger or smaller aperture.

Some cameras provide a feature that allows you to cycle automatically through reciprocal exposures after the camera has metered. Normally, it's very simple: half-press the shutter to meter and then use your camera's program shift equivalent to cycle through all the other combinations of shutter speed and aperture that yield that same exposure.

Other Names for Program Shift

Canon, Olympus, and Panasonic call this feature *Program Shift*, while Nikon and Fuji call it *Flexible Program*, and Sony calls it *Manual Shift*. Other cameras have the feature, but may not give it a specific name. Check your manual to see if your camera has such a feature and to find out how to control it.

If you press the shutter halfway to meter, and the camera yields a reading of 1/125th at f7.1, and you then move your Program Shift feature one notch, the meter reading changes to 1/200th at f6.3. Another move gives you 1/250th at f5, and so on. Each of these exposures is equivalent—that is, they all yield the same overall brightness—but as you continue to shift, your shutter speed is getting faster, which gives you more motion-stopping power. The aperture is also getting wider, which might yield a shallower depth of field.

Here's a real-world example. The first image in Figure 7.25 shows the scene as the camera chose to meter it. It chose f11 at 1/400th of a second, and the resulting image has good overall illumination. However, I was curious to see what the image might look like with a shallower depth of field, so I took another shot. I pressed the shutter button halfway down to meter, and again the camera showed f11 at 1/400th. I then turned the Program Shift control on my camera until the aperture was open as wide as possible (that is, until the smallest f-number appeared). On this particular lens, at this particular focal length, the widest aperture was f5. The camera showed that, at this aperture, the exposure would be 1/2000th of a second. These two combinations, f11 at 1/400th and f5 at 1/2000th, end up yielding the same overall illumination. But the second exposure has shallower depth of field, as you can see in the second image.

By using Program Shift, I have effectively taken an important level of manual control without having to leave Program mode.

Your camera's Program Shift feature (if it has one) probably doesn't work in Auto mode, but should be active in Program mode. This means that, in addition to the full benefits of Auto mode, you've got Program Shift as a manual override for choosing a faster or slower shutter speed, or bigger or smaller aperture, all while maintaining a correct exposure. This allows you to quickly select a particular parameter without having to leave Program mode.

Say you're out shooting in Program mode and a portrait opportunity suddenly presents itself. You can meter just as you always would, and then use Program Shift to quickly change to a metering with a very wide aperture (low f-stop number) to blur out the background. You haven't changed any kind of mode—you're still in Program mode—so with your next image you'll be back to your camera's normal Program mode behavior.

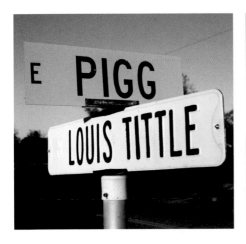 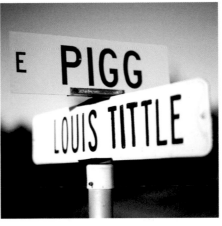

Figure 7.25

These two images have the same overall exposure, but in the second image, I used my camera's Program Shift feature to dial in a wider aperture, to yield shallower depth of field. Most importantly, I didn't have to leave Program mode to get this manual control.

This is a great feature, and an easy way to mix auto and manual shooting very quickly, so it's worth tracking it down in your camera manual.

Calculating a Safe Shutter Speed for Handheld Shooting

Once you start fiddling with shutter speed (which you can do with the Program Shift feature), you have to be very careful about the shutter speed you choose. If you pick a shutter speed that's too low, you'll run the risk of getting blurry images due to camera shake. Even when you're shooting in Auto mode, you still need to know when the shutter speed that the camera has chosen is too low for reliable handheld shooting.

The generally accepted rule for what makes a shutter speed acceptable for handheld shooting is to simply take one over your current focal length. So, if you're shooting with a 50mm lens (or a zoom lens set to 50mm), you shouldn't shoot any slower than 1/50th of a second. If you're shooting with a focal length of 200mm, you shouldn't shoot with a shutter speed slower than 1/200th.

The idea is that, as the image is magnified when you zoom in, so too is any motion within the frame. Thus, you have to use a faster shutter speed as you go to a longer focal length because any motion is magnified.

On a point-and-shoot camera, you may not have a readout that tells you what your current focal length is. However, these cameras will usually have a hand-holding warning indicator, which will show if the camera thinks that your shutter speed is too slow for safe handheld shooting at the current focal length.

If you're shooting with a digital SLR, you'll be able to determine your current focal length by simply looking at your lens. However, as you learned earlier, lenses on a digital SLR are often subject to a focal length multiplier that changes the effective crop of the lens at a given focal length. If your lens has a focal length multiplier of 1.6, you'll first need to multiply your current focal length by 1.6 and then perform your calculation.

Stabilization and Shutter Speed

In Chapter 3, "Camera Anatomy," you learned about stabilized lenses, which include technology that allows them to smooth out the vibration and jitters that come from your hands. Most stabilizers are rated in terms of how many stops of stabilization they provide. For example, a three-stop stabilizer lets you shoot with a shutter speed that is three stops lower than what you could shoot at with a nonstabilized lens. Figure 7.26 details how three stops of stabilization affects your minimum handheld shutter speed.

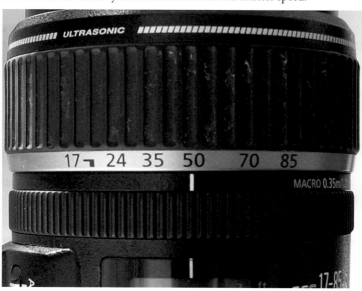

Figure 7.26

This 17–85mm lens is currently set to a focal length of 50mm. However, this lens is attached to a Canon EOS SLR that has a focal length multiple of 1.6. Therefore, the crop of this lens is equivalent to 50 × 1.6, or 80mm. The minimum shutter speed for sharp handheld shooting is 1/80th of a second. However, because the lens has a three-stop image stabilizing system, you might be able to get away with shooting as low as 1/10th (80 ÷ 2 = 40; 40 ÷ 2 = 20; 20 ÷ 2 = 10, or three halvings, which means three stops).

Do You Really Need to Calculate Handheld Shutter Speed?

Suddenly, it may sound like shutter speed is an incredibly complicated thing. If the last bit of calculation scared you, don't worry, this is not something you'll have to consider on every shot you take. The only time you need to start thinking about calculating handheld shutter speed is if you're in low light.

If you're out shooting at dusk with a 100mm lens, and you notice that the camera has chosen a shutter speed of 1/60th of a second, you should recognize that 1/60th is a little slow for a lens that long, because according to the handheld shooting rule, you shouldn't be shooting slower than 1/100th of a second.

Similarly, if you walk into a dark auditorium to shoot a play or concert, you should meter the scene—look through the camera and press the shutter button halfway, and see what kind of shutter speed the camera picks. Once you know what the camera is suggesting for a shutter speed, you'll have a better idea of how long a lens you can use.

When you see that your shutter speeds are going long, you'll want to be extra careful to hold the camera steady. If you have a tripod or monopod with you, get it out. Otherwise, see if there's a place you can rest the camera.

Assessing Exposure with Your Ears

By now, you should have a good idea of what your camera's shutter sounds like. As shutter speed gets slower, you can hear the delay between when the shutter opens and closes. Listening to the sound of your shutter can be an easy way to keep track of when your shutter speed might have dropped too low for handheld shooting. Also, you might notice that the viewfinder stays blacked out for longer. If you hear a slow shutter speed, you'll want to consider reshooting the shot with a more appropriate shutter speed.

Changing ISO

If your camera picks a shutter speed that is too low for handheld shooting, you have several options. By the time the camera has set the shutter speed down low, it's probably already opened the aperture all the way, so the odds are you won't be able to compensate for the slow shutter by going to a wider aperture. However, don't forget that you have a third exposure control: ISO.

In the previous chapter, you learned that the ISO setting controls how light sensitive the camera's sensor is. A higher ISO number means the sensor is effectively more light sensitive, which allows you to use shorter shutter speeds and smaller apertures. For times when you need lots of motion-stopping power or deeper depth of field, the ability to increase your ISO can make the difference between getting and missing the shot that you want. Increasing ISO is also a great option when your camera has chosen a shutter speed that's too slow for steady handheld shooting. In fact, the image sensors in some digital cameras are so sensitive that you can dial the ISO up to a level that allows you to shoot in much lower light than you could ever manage with film.

When your shutter speed dips down low, it's time to raise the ISO. For example, say you're shooting with a 100mm lens at ISO 100, and your camera's meter has selected a shutter speed of 1/60th of a second. If you increase ISO to 200, you will gain one stop of sensitivity, and your camera will compensate by doubling the shutter speed to 1/120th—plenty fast for handheld shooting.

Or perhaps you're shooting with a 100mm lens at ISO 100, and it's now half an hour later than the first shot, and your camera is metering at 1/30th of a second. If you switch to ISO 200, shutter speed will go to 1/60th of a second—still too slow. If you go to ISO 400, you'll be back up to 1/120th of a second, well within the realm of safe handheld shooting.

As mentioned earlier, you'll also want to employ all the techniques that you can to stabilize the camera.

Remember to Breathe

When trying to hold the camera steady—which is especially important when using a slow shutter speed—remember to squeeze the trigger gently. Use the posture tips we discussed earlier, and don't hold your breath. Holding your breath actually makes you shakier. Take a breath, let it out, and squeeze the shutter release. If possible, try to find something to lean against or that you can use to steady the camera.

If a faster ISO offers better low-light performance and the ability to shoot with really fast shutter speeds and narrow apertures whenever you need them, why shouldn't you just leave the camera on ISO 1600 all the time?

Earlier, you learned that the camera increases ISO by boosting the amplification of the voltages that are read off the sensor after an image is shot. Unfortunately, anytime you amplify any type of electrical signal, you increase any noise in the signal along with the data you're trying to read. Noise is just what you think it is—the extraneous, static signals that you hear on a radio. Noise is generated by components in the camera, by other electrical sources in the room, and even by the stray cosmic ray that might be passing through you and the rest of the planet. The practical upshot of this is that as you increase the ISO of the camera, you also increase the noise (grainy patterns that sometimes look a lot like film grain) in your image.

You always want to shoot at the lowest ISO that you can to ensure that you don't introduce extraneous noise. On most new SLRs, you'll probably find that there's very little difference in the amount of noise you see in an ISO 100 to 400 image. So you can safely choose these ISOs and see no discernible noise increase.

These cameras will possibly see a visible increase in noise as ISO climbs from there, but it's still very low and very usable.

With their smaller sensors, point-and-shoot cameras don't fare as well when ISO is raised, but they can still take good shots. No matter what type of camera you have, do some experiments at higher ISO to determine if your camera yields images with acceptable levels of noise.

Sometimes a bit of texture can add a lot of atmosphere to an image, so noise may not be a problem. Most importantly, just because noise is visible on-screen doesn't mean it will show up in print. By the time you've scaled your image to your desired output size and the printer has processed it, the noise might be far less visible.

Two Kinds of Noise

Digital cameras generate two different kinds of noise: luminance noise and chrominance noise. Not all cameras produce both, and not all produce both at the same time. Luminance noise is simply noisy patterns of changing luminance—bright speckles that appear in your image, usually in the shadow tones (see Figure 7.27).

Chrominance noise appears as splotchy patterns of color, also usually in the shadow tones. Usually, chrominance noise appears as red or magenta splotches, but the color, splotch size, and density varies from camera to camera (see Figure 7.28).

Of the two, luminance noise is the less egregious, partly because it looks the most like film grain or texture. Color noise looks very "digital" somehow, and is extremely difficult to remove. Different cameras produce different amounts of noise, and some digital cameras produce "prettier" noise than others. Noise will always get worse as you increase ISO, and usually gets worse as light levels are lower.

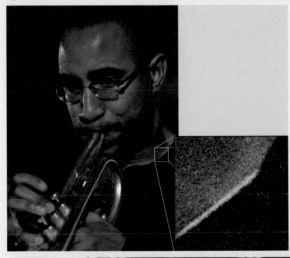

Figure 7.27

Luminance noise appears as speckled patterns of varied luminance. If you have to have noise, this is the preferable type, as it looks more like a film texture-type grain.

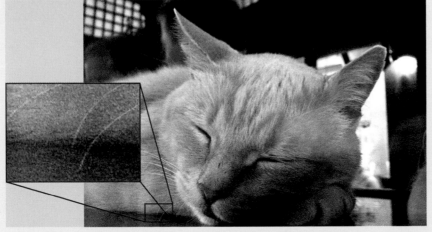

Figure 7.28 Chrominance noise appears in your image as varying patterns of color. Chrominance noise has no film counterpart, so it looks very "digital." It's extremely difficult to remove.

ISO Changes in Bright Light

In addition to allowing you to shoot in lower light levels, an increase in ISO can also buy you some shutter speed and aperture latitude.

For example, let's say you're trying to shoot a close-up of a flower on a windy day. Your meter has recommended 1/125th of a second at f3.5—the widest possible aperture on the lens you're using. This is great because it gives you the shallow depth of field that you want, but unfortunately it's so windy that 1/125th of a second is resulting in an image that's too blurry. Increasing the shutter speed by two stops to 1/1000, will leave the image underexposed, because the camera's aperture can't be opened any further.

If you increase the ISO from 100 to 400 (a two-stop difference), you'll have enough exposure latitude to make your shutter speed change and get your shot.

Remember to Change Back!

When you raise your ISO for a particular situation, it's critical that you remember to change it back! If you're shooting in a dark environment at ISO 1600 and then move into bright daylight, your images will have extra noise if you don't remember to change your ISO back to something more appropriate. Try to get in the habit of always thinking about what ISO you're set for when you enter a new lighting environment.

Auto ISO

Many cameras now provide an Auto ISO setting, which tries to calculate an ISO setting automatically. These mechanisms aim to keep ISO as low as possible, but your camera will know to kick in a higher ISO if shutter speed goes too low for acceptable handheld shooting.

Assess Your Camera's Noise

Different cameras perform differently at a given ISO. Before you go shooting in a low light environment it's a good idea to test your camera's noise response at high ISO. Don't worry, there's nothing complicated about this. All you have to do is take some shots in low light at a range of ISOs and see what you think of the quality of the resulting image.

On my SLR, I find that ISO 3200 is completely usable and ISO 6400 and 12,800 are acceptable in a pinch. Knowing that I don't want to push beyond 3200 if I don't have to is a valuable piece of information when I'm shooting in low light and trying to pick a shutter speed.

When evaluating images, remember to evaluate them in the format that you will be delivering them in. If that's a small image on a Web page, then assess your images that way. If it's an 8×10 inch print, then use such prints for your evaluation. Simply judging by what's on your monitor may be misleading.

JPEG Exposure Tips

If you're shooting in JPEG or TIFF mode (we haven't yet discussed shooting in Raw mode, but we'll get to that later), here are two simple things to keep in mind when choosing an exposure:

◆ **Protect your highlights!** Overexposed highlights are ugly! They're big, empty areas of white that are boring and distracting, so when choosing an exposure, be sure to pick one that won't overexpose the highlights in your image. While you want to have shadow detail, it's always better to risk losing shadow detail to be sure you've preserved highlight detail. A dark, black shadow will be less noticeable and distracting than a blown-out highlight.

◆ **Usually, a slight bit of underexposure will yield slightly better saturation.** In typical, evenly lit daylight and indoor situations, leaving your camera set to −.3 stops will produce slightly "punchier" images. However, if you're in a bright location or shooting something with a lot of white, you'll want to adjust your exposure accordingly.

Obviously, these two factors must be balanced with any other exposure concerns you're juggling (depth of field, motion stopping, tone mapping, and so on).

Fractional ISO Numbers

Like shutter speed and aperture, when you increase ISO by one stop, the ISO number doubles. Thus, increasing from ISO 100 to 200 is a change of one stop. Some cameras, though, allow you to change ISO in fractions of a stop. For example, you might be able to change from 200 to 250, a change of 1/3 of a stop.

Most cameras that offer fractional stop increases also provide the option to change the interval, usually choosing between 1/3 and 1/2 of a stop. Here you can see 1/3 stop ISO settings. Full stop settings are listed in bold.

100 125 160 **200** 250 320 **400** 500 640 **800** 1000 1250 **1600**

Putting It All Together

We've covered a lot of topics in this chapter, and it may sound like a lot to remember, but with just a little practice you'll find that the issues covered here will become second nature. With experience, you'll learn when you need to change the Autofocus mode on your camera and what the different modes are best for.

Similarly, with white balance, you'll come to recognize when you're in a situation that will trip up your camera's white balance mechanism—shade, for example—and you will know to use a preset or manual setting.

Drive modes and self-timers can be lifesavers when you need them, but you probably won't find yourself using them all the time. Like manual white balance and Servo Focus, these are features that are aimed at very specific problems. Now that you know these options are there, you can fall back on them when necessary.

Of all the items in this chapter, the two that you will use most often are Program Shift and ISO change. As you learned, Program Shift gives you important manual overrides without having to give up the convenience of Program mode's automatic features. With it, you can take creative control of shutter speed and aperture.

In Chapter 2, you were encouraged to get in the habit of noting shutter speed while shooting. In this chapter, you learned how to know when shutter speed has gone too low for stable handheld shooting and how you can use ISO to get your shutter speed back up to acceptable handheld levels. These are essential skills that you'll use constantly.

Many people think that Program mode is for beginners, but I shoot regularly in Program mode. For everyday shooting, Program mode can provide everything I need. When it's time for the occasional manual override, Program Shift gives me the power to make a shutter speed or aperture change. If I know for sure that I'll be shooting a number of frames that have very specific aperture or shutter speed needs, then I'll switch to a more manual mode, so that I don't have to constantly use Program Shift to get where I want to be. (You'll learn about those modes in the next chapter.) But Program mode is not something you'll use while learning and then leave behind. It's a powerful, important tool in your photography arsenal.

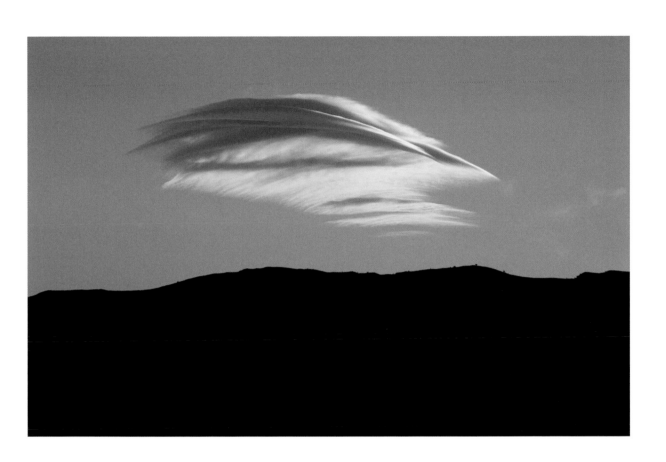

8

ADVANCED EXPOSURE

Learning More About Your Light Meter and Exposure Controls

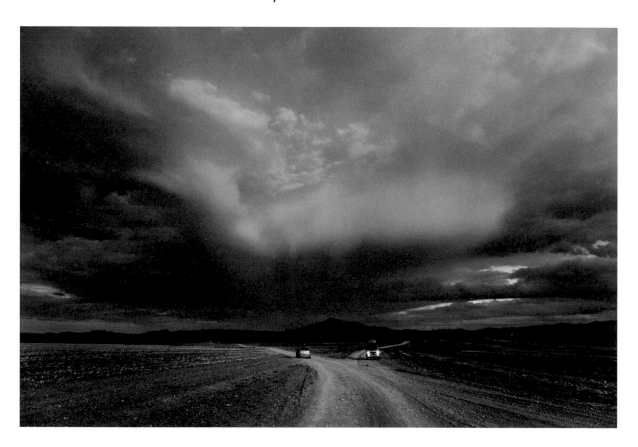

According to Ansel Adams, when famed photographer Margaret Bourke-White was shooting, she would simply set her camera on 1/100th of a second and then shoot the same image over and over using every aperture her camera could manage. This, combined with her tremendous compositional skill, ensured that at least one of her images would come out the way she envisioned.

Although digital cameras make Bourke-White's approach far more cost-effective than it was with film, a much better practice is to spend some time learning how to use the tools and features found on your camera intelligently to ensure that you get a good shot with only one or two exposures.

At the simplest level, your exposure choice governs whether your image will be too bright or too dark. In this regard, your camera's automatic meter will almost always do a good job of keeping your image well exposed, but your choice of exposure also provides a tremendous degree of creative control. In the last chapter, you were introduced to the effects that different exposure decisions have on your final image. In this chapter, we'll explore metering and exposure in greater detail.

In these days of fancy digital image editors, many people think, "Why should I worry so much about exposure? I can just fix it in the computer later." That may or may not be true because it is possible to shoot images that have problems that can't be fixed. So you stand a better chance of coming home with good images if you work to get exposure right in-camera. What's more, as you learn more about exposure and what your camera is capable of, you'll begin to notice scenes that you might not have recognized as potential photos before. As you'll learn when we get into postproduction, there's a finite amount of editing that can be performed on an image before it begins to visibly degrade. If you get the exposure right in-camera, you won't have to make these types of broad, potentially damaging edits. Finally, image editing takes time. Shooting with an accurate exposure will mean less postproduction work and a more efficient workflow.

The Light Meter Revisited

Any time you half-press the shutter button on your camera, the light meter activates. It measures the light in your scene and calculates a shutter speed and aperture (and ISO, if your camera is set to Auto ISO). By this point, you should be familiar with the process of metering, and hopefully have been practicing what we've covered in previous chapters. If so, then you might have discovered already that the automatic meter in your camera *can* be confused. When this happens, it won't calculate the best exposure for your scene. Consider the image shown in Figure 8.1.

The meter has chosen settings that will expose the bright sky properly in the background, both because it's such a large feature in the scene and because the meter tries its best to avoid overexposure. However, exposing for the brightness in the sky has resulted in the subject's face ending up too dark. This is the most common bad metering problem, but you will find other issues that occur as a result of bad metering. In addition to highlights that blow out to complete white, bad metering can yield an inability to show black objects as truly black.

Figure 8.1

This image suffers from bad backlighting, which has left the subject's face in shadow.

There are many ways to solve metering problems. You can use your camera's manual overrides to compensate for what the camera has metered, but this requires you to know how much compensation to use, which is a difficult thing to judge by eye.

Fortunately, most cameras include several different Metering modes. These modes take different approaches to measuring the light in your scene, and some are more appropriate to some situations than others. Your camera might have some, or all, of these modes. Consult your manual to learn what modes your camera provides and how to select them.

- ◆ **Matrix meter** (sometimes called *Evaluative* or *Multisegment*). A Matrix meter divides your image into a grid and takes a separate meter reading for each cell in the grid. These cells are then analyzed to determine an exposure setting (see Figure 8.2).

Figure 8.2

Most cameras offer some form of Matrix metering, which samples light from all parts of your image to come up with a final exposure calculation.

The exact number of cells varies greatly from camera to camera, and the total number is not nearly as important as how well the camera processes the data it gathers from those cells. Matrix metering algorithms are very closely guarded trade secrets, and different cameras take different factors into consideration. Some might consider the autofocus point that has been selected, depth of field, brightness differential across the image, and possibly even color content.

Matrix metering is the best choice for most situations and is certainly the best option when you're simply trying to get a quick shot using your camera's automatic features. However, as you saw earlier, there will be times when you'll need to make some adjustments to your Matrix meter reading.

- ◆ **Center-weighted averaging.** A variation of Matrix metering, Center-weighted averaging also divides your image into a grid of cells, but when analyzing the readings, a Center-weighted metering system gives preference to the cells in the middle of the image. Typically, the middle 80 percent of the cells are considered more important than the outlying regions (see Figure 8.3).

Figure 8.3

In a Center-weighted averaging meter, readings are taken from the entire scene, but more statistical weight is given to the cells in the middle.

Center-weighted metering is designed for those times when your subject is in the middle of your frame and your background contains bright lights, dark shadows, or other extreme lighting situations that might throw off the metering in the center of your image.

◆ **Partial metering.** This setting meters only the cells in the center of your scene. The size of the area is usually about 10 percent of the total scene. Like Center-weighted metering, Partial metering also provides a way to address backlighting troubles. Because Partial metering completely ignores the cells that sit outside of the metered area, it's often better than Center-weighted averaging when dealing with extreme backlighting problems, as shown in Figure 8.4.

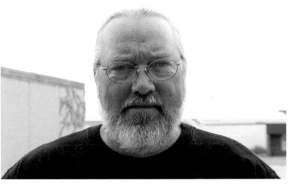

Figure 8.4

With Partial metering, I can fix the backlighting problem that you saw in Figure 8.1.

◆ **Spot metering.** A Spot meter measures only a small area of your image, usually the center. The metering from this area is the only information used to calculate an exposure. This area is much smaller than what a typical Partial meter will provide, and it doesn't take any other areas of the image into account. Spot meters allow you to get very precise readings of particular areas of an image and are the best choice when there's something in a scene—a highlight or small detail—that you want to ensure is properly exposed. Place the center of your viewfinder on that detail when you meter, and the camera will calculate an exposure that will render that area properly. Depending on the scene, the rest of your image may or may not be exposed properly. Spot and Partial meters are often ideal for shooting performers on a stage, where the stage lighting can confuse a Matrix meter.

Locking Exposure

Different SLRs (and some advanced point-and-shoots) handle exposure locking in different ways. For example, on Nikon SLRs, if you press the shutter button halfway down, hold it, and reframe, the camera will automatically re-meter your scene and choose new exposure settings. In other words, the camera doesn't lock exposure automatically.

Canon cameras work this same way *if* you're using Partial, Center-weight, or Spot metering—that is, they will continuously re-meter as you reframe, even with the shutter button held down. However, if you're in Evaluative metering, then when you half-press the shutter button, the exposure will lock, and will not change as you reframe.

Other brands will work differently, but it's easy enough to figure out how your camera works:

◆ Frame a shot with a bright subject.

◆ Press and hold the shutter button. Take note of the exposure settings.

◆ Reframe so that the majority of the frame is filled with dark areas and note if the exposure settings change.

If the exposure settings do not change, then you know your camera locks exposure when the shutter button is held down. You should try this experiment in each metering mode.

Most SLRs also include an exposure lock button that allows you to lock exposure so that it doesn't change when you move the camera around. However, many SLRs also include the ability to reprogram this button and change the behavior of the shutter button.

For example, using a custom function setting in most Canon and Nikon SLRs, you can set up the camera so that when the shutter button is half pressed, the camera meters, *but does not focus*. In this configuration, you use a button on the back of the camera to activate autofocus. This gives you separate control of metering and focus with separate locks for each.

For maximum flexibility—especially if you tend to focus and reframe a lot—configuring your camera this way can be very useful.

Consult your camera manual for details. Look for entries on exposure lock, focus lock, and custom functions relating to both of these subjects. (You'll sometimes see exposure lock listed as "AE Lock.")

What Your Light Meter Meters

Your light meter does only one thing: it measures the luminance of the light reflected by your subject. (Luminance is the same thing as brightness.) Whether it measures the luminance of the entire scene or just a part of it depends on the type of meter you are using.

Figure 8.5 shows an equal number of black-and-white boxes. If you were to measure this illustration with a light meter, you would find that it is reflecting 18 percent of the light that is striking it. Yes, it might seem like it should be reflecting 50 percent of the light, but it's not. The luminance of most scenes averages out to be the same as these boxes—that is, most scenes in the real world reflect 18 percent of the light that strikes them.

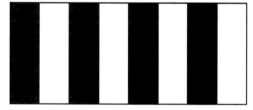

Figure 8.5

Although each of these squares is black or white, the entire field of boxes meters as 18 percent or middle gray.

Because this is a measure of luminance only (not color), you can also think of this 18 percent reflectance as a shade of gray. Therefore, this particular amount of reflectance is known to photographers as 18 percent gray or middle gray.

The most important thing to know about your camera's light meter is that it always assumes it is pointed at something that is 18 percent gray. In other words, your light meter calculates an exposure recommendation that will accurately reproduce middle gray under your current lighting. Because a typical scene reflects 18 percent of the light that hits it, this assumption is usually fairly accurate. Obviously, if the lighting in your scene suddenly changes, the readings will no longer be accurate (even if the scene is still reflecting 18 percent of that light), and you'll have to re-meter.

However, because your scene might not be exactly 18 percent gray, to get the best results from your light meter, you'll want to meter off something that is middle gray, such as an 18 percent gray card. Readily available at any photo supply store, you can simply place this card in your scene and use it as the subject for your metering. That said, modern light meters can do a very good job, so gray cards are not as necessary as they once were. Personally, I wouldn't invest in a gray card until I'd spent a fair amount of time with my camera, explored its various metering options, and determined if there were consistent times when my meter failed me. If so, then a gray card might be a fix.

Unfortunately, although 18 percent gray is often a good assumption, it's not always correct. For example, the left image in Figure 8.6 was shot using the camera's default metering. The image is neither too bright nor too dark—in other words, the meter did a good job of picking an exposure that yields a good overall result. However, the black statue appears a little grayer than it did in real life. This is because the camera is *assuming* that the statue is gray, so it is calculating an exposure that will correctly render the statue as *gray*.

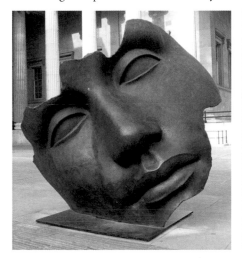 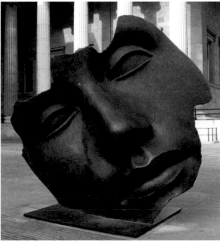

Figure 8.6

Here, the left image looks good, but the camera's default metering did not render the statue in its true black tone. By underexposing, I was able to produce a truer representation in the right image.

In the second figure, I underexposed the image to render the statue in its true, blacker tone. (Note that by underexposing, I also got a better rendering of the brightly lit columns in the background. Because they're not overexposed anymore, you can see more detail on them.) In other words, I took the camera's initial metering as a starting point and then modified it to capture a range of tones that is more accurate.

Note that this adjustment does not mean that there's something wrong with my light meter. The light meter was actually doing what it's supposed to do: calculate an exposure that's correct for a middle gray scene. The problem is that, in this case, my scene is not middle gray, it's darker.

Just as I underexposed to restore the blacks in the image, if you're shooting something white—or if you're in a white environment, such as snow—you might need to overexpose to correctly render white objects as white, rather than as middle gray. However, while this used to be a must-do practice when shooting bright scenes, such as snow-field landscapes or white sand beaches, today's meters are much better at evaluating these situations, so overexposure is rarely needed.

Colors have a luminance, or tone, just as black-and-white images do, and therefore need the same type of compensation for accurate reproduction. For example, look at Figure 8.7. The left image was shot with the camera's recommended metering, whereas the right image was underexposed by a third of a stop because the blue color of the carnival ride was a bit darker than 18 percent gray. Simply put, by overexposing your images, your colors will become lighter; underexposing will make your colors darker. Such adjustments allow you to either restore the right color to the objects in your scene, or intentionally boost or decrease the saturation of objects within your scene.

As stated earlier, your camera's light meter generates exposure settings that create an adequate picture. In general, your camera's meter will yield images with good color and proper exposure throughout the shadows and highlights. However, because of your light meter's assumptions, your picture might come out lacking details in some highlights or shadows. Or it might look a little flat, because darker or lighter tones will all be rendered as middle tones. With some simple exposure adjustments, you can turn these images from adequate to exceptional, yielding pictures with improved color accuracy, contrast, and saturation (or tonal accuracy and contrast, if you're shooting black and white).

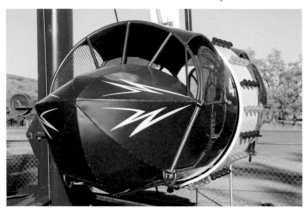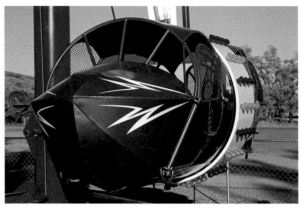

Figure 8.7 Through careful choice of exposure when shooting, you can capture images with better color saturation.

Note that the way you choose to create an over- or underexposure has no impact on the overall tonal adjustment. If you choose to change shutter speed, aperture, or some combination of both, you'll get the same tonal alteration in your final image. Which method you choose might depend on other exposure needs that you have—motion stopping or depth of field, for example. You'll learn more about this when we cover exposure controls later in this chapter.

The Risks of Over- and Underexposure

When you start fiddling with the camera's carefully calculated exposure settings, you'll risk over- or underexposing your scene to the point where bright things blow out to complete white or dark shadows fall to complete black. When an area in an image goes to all white or all black, it becomes an area with no detail.

This isn't so bad where shadows are concerned because a black shadow simply looks like an area that's too dark to see. Unless the shadowy area has some detail that you really want to keep, letting a shadow darken is not too terrible (see Figure 8.8).

Overexposed highlights, on the other hand, are almost always distracting. An area of complete white acts like a magnet for the viewer's eye, and it can sometimes upstage your subject (see Figure 8.9).

At times, it's worth overexposing a highlight to get better tonality on your subject. In Figure 8.10, the clouds are completely blown out, but this was necessary to get good exposure on the subjects' faces. Because of the composition and the strength of the faces, the overexposure is not too distracting.

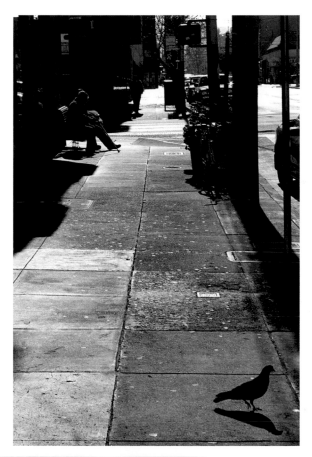

Figure 8.8

A lot of the shadows in this image have gone to complete black. Detail-less shadows, though, are not necessarily a detriment. In this case, they don't contain detail that I'm interested in, and the dark silhouettes work well.

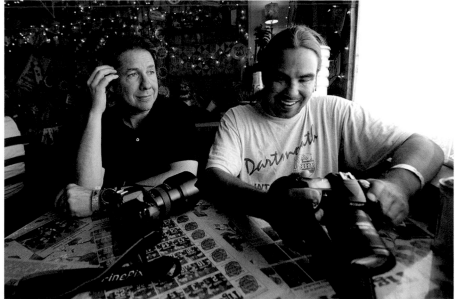

Figure 8.9

The overexposed window in this image is a big distraction. It acts like a magnet for the viewer's eye, and upstages our subjects.

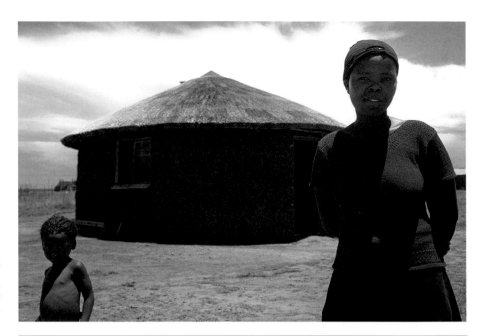

Figure 8.10

There will be times when you might have to sacrifice highlight detail to get good tonality and detail on your subject.

Electronic Viewfinders and Metering

Using your camera's LCD screen as a viewfinder presents a significant limitation that you should be aware of. While your eye can see a huge range of light to dark, your camera can only capture a fraction of that range, and the image shown on your camera's LCD is even more limited (Figure 8.11).

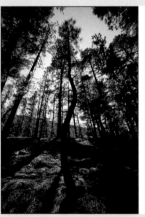
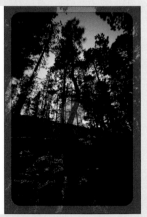

Figure 8.11

The image on the left shows how this scene looks to your eye and how the camera will ultimately capture it. The image on the right shows how it looks through the more limited dynamic range of an LCD viewfinder. Since you can't see all the details, it can be more difficult to judge composition while looking at the viewfinder.

Therefore, when using an LCD or electronic viewfinder, it's very important to keep one eye on the actual scene. This will help you assess what tones you have to work with, and it will remind you that there might be more detail in the scene than your camera is showing you.

Of course, you can also just take a shot and look at the resulting image on your screen to determine whether you got what you want. If you don't like what you see, you can adjust your exposure and try again. The important thing is simply to be aware that your LCD viewfinder is showing you a narrower range of tones than what you see and what the camera will actually capture.

Adjusting Exposure

As you've seen, there are many creative options to weigh and decisions to make when you choose an exposure for an image. For example, you might know that you want a shallow depth of field, so you will select a wide aperture. However, perhaps your images include many dark-colored objects that you feel need to be underexposed. At this point, you would probably choose to adopt a shorter shutter speed, rather than a smaller aperture, to preserve your shallow depth of field. Of course, if there are some fast-moving objects in your scene you were hoping to blur, you'll have to consider just how much you can speed up your shutter speed. All these different factors must be weighed and balanced.

Once you've made your decisions, you can begin to use your camera's settings to adjust your exposure accordingly. Fortunately, even if you have a less-expensive camera, you probably have enough controls to make some simple adjustments.

In this section, we'll cover all the ways you can adjust exposure on your digital camera. Which adjustments to make will depend on your image, and which controls to use to make your adjustment will depend on which exposure characteristics you want to change and which you want to preserve.

Exposure Compensation

These days, almost all digital cameras, from simple point-and-shoots to high-end digital SLRs, provide exposure compensation controls. Even some camera phones now include an exposure compensation feature!

With exposure compensation, you can specify an amount of over- or underexposure. Most cameras let you adjust exposure compensation in 1/2 or 1/3-stop increments, and allow you to over- or underexpose by up to two stops (see Figure 8.12).

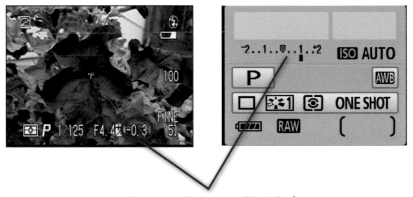

Exposure Compensation Display

Figure 8.12

Different cameras show exposure compensation settings in different ways. On the left, the camera is simply providing a numeric readout of the amount of exposure compensation (–.3 stops). The display on the right is showing exposure compensation of +1 stop.

What's great about exposure compensation is that it lets you think in purely relative terms with no concern for a specific shutter speed or aperture. For example, if you decide your scene needs to be underexposed by a stop to properly render some black objects, simply press the minus exposure button twice (assuming your exposure compensation increments in half stops). Your camera will meter as normal to determine its usual adequate exposure, but will then shoot at one stop under that exposure. Exposure compensation controls are the quickest and easiest way (and on some cameras, the only way) to make exposure adjustments.

On many cameras, the fully automatic mode will not provide access to exposure compensation, so you'll have to switch to Program mode (or your camera's equivalent).

Most cameras try to achieve the requested change in exposure by changing shutter speed. When this isn't possible, either because the camera's shutter can't go any faster or because slowing the shutter speed would risk blurring the image, the camera will make changes to aperture. Sometimes, the camera will make slight changes to shutter speed and aperture and ISO (if you're set to an Auto ISO setting), so that no single parameter is adjusted too much. Fortunately, these changes are usually minor enough that you won't see any change in the camera's ability to freeze motion or in the image's depth of field or amount of noise.

Exposure compensation controls are powerful tools, and you will continue to use them even after you've learned some of the other exposure controls at your disposal (see Figure 8.13). Get comfortable with your camera's exposure compensation controls, learn how to use them quickly, and begin learning how to recognize how much compensation is necessary for different situations. Because there are no hard-and-fast rules for over- or underexposing, you have to go out and practice!

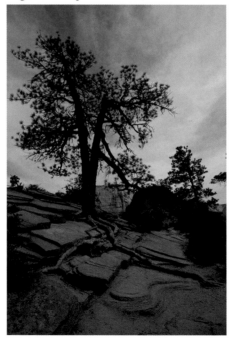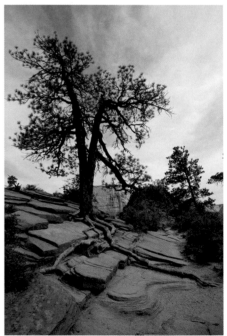

Figure 8.13

Because of the bright sky, the camera's default metering left the tree just a little dark, so I dialed in +2/3 of a stop of exposure compensation to produce the image on the right, which has a slightly brighter tree. I've lost a tiny bit of detail in the clouds, but in this case it's acceptable. I didn't have any particular depth of field ideas about this image, so I wasn't worried about the camera altering depth of field.

Adjusting Exposure on a Cell Phone Camera

Most cell phones lack any kind of exposure compensation control. However, if your phone camera lets you tap on the screen to set a focus point, be aware that it's probably also Spot metering on that scene. This is great in high-dynamic situations such as a person standing in front of a window. By default, the camera will expose so that the bright highlights in the window are properly exposed, which will leave your subject's face in shadow. Tap on their face and the phone should expose for the face. The windows will blow out but at least the darker areas will be visible. This is the extent of the exposure control that you have on most cell phone cameras. Note that some applications let you independently set focus and exposure.

Exposure Compensation and Program Shift

In the last chapter, you learned about Program Shift, which lets you automatically change between reciprocal exposures after the camera has metered. With Program Shift, you can switch quickly to a different shutter speed or aperture, while maintaining the correct exposure.

Because Program Shift always changes to a reciprocal exposure, it will never result in an over- or underexposure. However, as you've learned, there are times when you *want* to over- or underexpose, perhaps to improve the tone of a color. For these times, you can dial in an exposure compensation, and you can easily use these two features together.

For example, perhaps you decide to meter and then use Program Shift to switch to a wider aperture because you want a shallower depth of field. But maybe you're shooting something dark and want a little bit of underexposure to render the proper tone. If you dial in −1/3 of a stop of exposure compensation, you can still get both your wide aperture *and* your underexposure. In many cases, these two controls will provide all of the manual power you need.

Fixing a Consistent Exposure Problem

I was shooting in Zion National Park recently, and noticed that my camera was consistently overexposing. It wasn't a camera I'd used very much, and I wasn't sure if this was simply a characteristic of this camera. Whatever the cause, the overexposure was consistent, so I just dialed in a −.3 exposure compensation and left it there. As you can see in Figure 8.14, this was a very slight adjustment, but it served to keep the images from being quite so "hot."

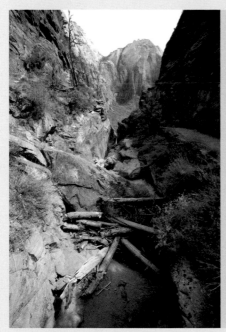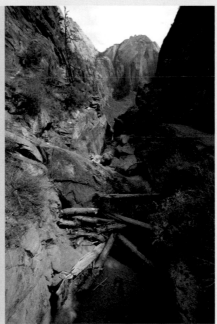

Figure 8.14 Exposure compensation is also an easy way to deal with repeating exposure problems. A −.3 exposure compensation was all I needed to improve this scene, and since my camera had been repeatedly overexposing, I just left this adjustment dialed in.

Of course, lighting changes with time of day and as you move around, so you'll want to check in with your exposures to ensure that any adjustment you've dialed in is still helpful.

Controlling Exposure with Your Light Meter

Using a built-in light meter, you can force an over- or underexposure by pointing the camera at something darker or lighter. Meter off a darker subject, and your camera will overexpose. Meter off a lighter subject, and you'll get an underexposure (see Figure 8.15). However, because your camera will probably lock focus at the same time as exposure, you'll need to be certain you are metering off something that is at the same distance as the image you would like to have in focus, or use your camera's exposure lock feature (if it has one).

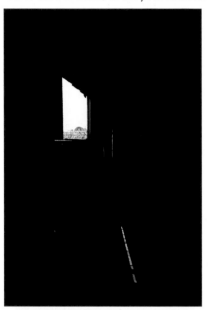 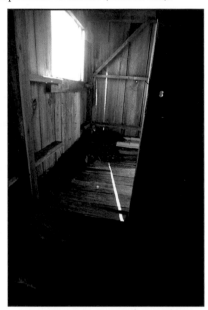

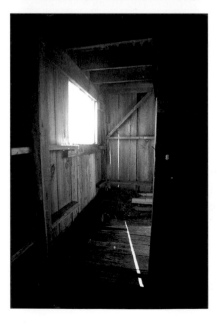 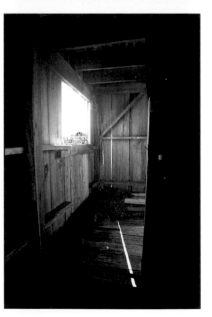

Figure 8.15

The upper-left image was exposed using the camera's default metering, which exposed for the window, leaving the rest of the room in darkness. By tilting the camera down, as shown in the upper-right picture, I was able to force the camera to meter more accurately for the dark tones in the image, resulting in the lower-left picture. Finally, I cut the properly exposed window from the dark frame and then composited it with the well-exposed image to produce the final composite shown in the lower right.

For cameras that lack more sophisticated manual controls, such as small point-and-shoots, this may be your best option for trying to control exposure. Obviously, with this technique you have no control as to whether the camera changes shutter speed or aperture, but you can make an image brighter or darker using this approach.

Even if your camera *does* have manual controls, this technique can be handy in a pinch, when you need to shoot quickly and want to get a lighter or darker exposure.

Understanding Exposure Locking

This technique is basically a variation of the focus and reframing technique that you learned in the last chapter. As you saw earlier, some cameras will automatically re-meter as you reframe, and others won't. For this technique to work, you'll need to understand how and when your camera locks exposure.

Priority Modes

Priority modes provide a great balance of manual control with some automatic assistance. In a Priority mode, you choose either the shutter speed or the aperture you want, and the camera will calculate the corresponding value that is required to ensure a good exposure. For example, in Shutter Priority, you define a shutter speed, and the camera calculates the correct corresponding aperture. In Aperture Priority, you pick the aperture you want, and the camera calculates a correct shutter speed.

Typically, you'll select Shutter Priority when you want to control motion and Aperture Priority when you want to control depth of field. For example, if you're shooting landscapes and know that you're going to want a deep depth of field all day long, you can set the camera on Aperture Priority, dial in f11, and be assured that every shot will be taken with that aperture.

Or, if you're shooting a sporting event and know that you want lots of motion-stopping power, you can select Shutter Priority and set the shutter speed to something quick, like 1/1000th of a second.

Priority modes are a great way of taking some manual control, while still allowing your camera's sophisticated metering to stay involved in the choice of exposure settings (see Figure 8.16).

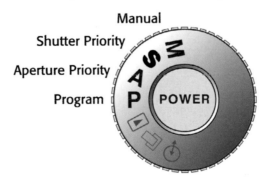

Figure 8.16

If your camera provides Priority modes, you'll most likely see something like this on the camera's mode dial or in its mode menu.

Canon's Goofy Mode Names

I shoot with a Canon SLR, so you can trust me when I say that Canon has stupid labels for their Priority modes. On a Canon mode dial, Shutter Priority mode is listed as Tv while Aperture Priority is listed as Av. Av is somewhat intuitive—you can just remember "Aperture value." For Tv, just try to think of it as "Time value."

Using a Priority mode is simple: after switching to the appropriate mode, select the aperture or shutter speed that's appropriate for what you're trying to achieve. When you half-press the shutter button to meter, the camera will calculate the corresponding other value.

Most cameras will warn you when they think you've chosen an exposure combination that will result in over- or underexposure. Don't worry, the camera will still shoot the picture; these warnings are simply there to tell you that your settings don't conform to the camera's idea of a good picture. Check your manual for details on how your camera indicates a bad exposure combination.

Priority Modes and Exposure Compensation

When you use exposure compensation in Auto or Program mode, you have no control over how it achieves its compensation—it might adjust shutter speed, aperture, or both. If you want to maintain control of a specific parameter, put your camera into the appropriate Priority mode. For example, if your camera is in Shutter Priority mode, any exposure compensation adjustments will be made by altering aperture (and ISO if you're in Auto ISO mode), ensuring that you retain control of shutter speed. In Aperture Priority, compensation will be achieved through shutter speed changes (and again, possibly ISO).

Manual Mode

Manual mode gives you control of both aperture and shutter speed. However, because some digital cameras have cumbersome manual controls, you might find it easier to simply use a Priority mode. In Manual mode, your camera should have one control for choosing shutter speed and another for choosing aperture. You can set these to anything you want and still take a picture, which means that in Manual mode it is possible to take an image with very bad exposure.

Fortunately, you can still use your light meter when in Manual mode. On most cameras, when you use Manual mode, the same display that is normally used to show exposure compensation will serve as a guide to whether or not your exposure is good. When you half-press the shutter button, instead of choosing a shutter speed and aperture (since you will already have done that by hand), the camera will meter your scene and show you whether your chosen settings are under- or overexposed or okay.

For example, Figure 8.17 first shows a typical in-viewfinder status display. You can see that I've set shutter speed to 1/125th and aperture to f8. After pressing the shutter button down halfway, the Exposure Compensation shows +1 stop, indicating that the meter has determined that the current settings are overexposed by one stop. If you're trying to intentionally overexpose, you can leave them this way. Instead, I adjusted the exposure settings one stop down by increasing the shutter speed from 1/125th to 1/250. This faster shutter speed lets in one stop less light, and now the meter shows a good exposure.

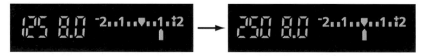

Figure 8.17 Here, in Manual mode, the camera is telling me that my initial exposure settings will yield an image that's overexposed by a stop. After a simple adjustment, the meter reads a good exposure.

On most meters, if your over- or underexposure is beyond two stops, the indicator will flash.

Obviously, readouts can differ on different cameras, so check your camera manual to learn exactly how yours works. You'll also need to learn how to adjust both shutter speed and aperture when shooting in Manual mode. Again, your manual will detail these controls for you.

Manual Mode Practice, or "Shoot Photos the Old-Fashioned Way"

If your camera has a Manual mode, you might be interested in trying a truly all-manual exercise.

In the very old days, before light meters, photographers had to calculate exposure by hand (or rather, by eye). A lot of experience was necessary to properly assess exposure for a complicated scene, but there were a number of tricks that eased the process. If you're comfortable with your camera's manual controls, you can give this type of shooting a try.

In most cases, when shooting in bright sunlight, you can use the "sunny 16 rule" for calculating exposure. Set the aperture on f16 and use a shutter speed equal to 1 over your ISO. In other words, if you're shooting at ISO 100, you would set the aperture to f16 and shutter speed to 1/100th of a second. If you're shooting at ISO 400, you would set the aperture to f16 and shutter speed to 1/400th. Those settings should produce an image with correct brightness when shooting in bright sunlight.

The sunny 16 rule gives you a good baseline for calculating an exposure. From this baseline, you can think about how to over- or underexpose to compensate for lighting situations that aren't completely sunny or for times when you need to alter an exposure to improve the tone.

For example, say it's a sunny day, but you're shooting in shade using ISO 100, and you think it might be shady enough to reduce the overall brightness of the scene by one stop. How do you know it's one stop? After a while, you would know this by experience. When you're starting out, you have to guess. Because your scene is one stop darker than bright sunlight, you need to overexpose.

Overexposure means you need more light. If you slow your shutter speed down by one stop, you'd get more light, but then you'd be shooting at 1/50th of a second, which might be too slow for handheld shooting. (Remember, because of the sunny 16 rule, at ISO 100 your baseline shutter speed is 1/100th, so one stop down would be to cut your shutter speed in half, to 1/50th.) A better approach might be to open your aperture wider. As you know, lower f numbers mean a wider aperture, so you could switch from f16 to f11, a widening of one stop. (Consult the list of apertures that you saw in Chapter 6, "Exposure Basics," if you're unsure as to what a one-stop aperture change is.)

Another option would be to leave the shutter speed and aperture where they are and increase the ISO to 200.

Now let's complicate things further and say that you're shooting in shade that's one stop darker than bright sun, but you want a shallow depth of field. Because you need to overexpose by one stop, you've already decided to widen your aperture, so you're shooting at 1/100th of a second at f11. But you want an even wider aperture to ensure a shallow depth of field. If you just keep opening the aperture, you'll continue to brighten the exposure. So, as you widen the aperture, you'll want to make a corresponding shutter speed adjustment. Changing from f11 to f8 opens the aperture one more stop. To preserve your overall exposure, change your shutter speed from 1/100th to 1/200th. Opening from f8 to f5.6 gets your aperture one stop wider, so you move your shutter speed to 1/400th. Finally, your lens can go one stop wider, so you open to f4 and make a corresponding shutter speed shift to 1/800th. Now you've got a wide aperture for shallow depth of field, and you've preserved your one stop of overexposure to compensate for the shade.

Trying a few shots this way in Manual mode gets you deep into the interrelationship between shutter speed, aperture, and ISO, and can be good practice. Fortunately, for everyday shooting, your light meter does all of this thinking for you.

Which Method Should You Use?

You've learned a number of different methods for controlling exposure here. Hopefully, along the way you've also learned that there's no one method that is ideal for every situation. You should have seen that underneath each of these methods, there's still just aperture, shutter speed, and ISO. Each of the modes and techniques discussed here simply provides a different way of controlling those three parameters, and you should have seen that the actual controls in each mode or method are pretty simple.

There's no "magic" to a Priority mode, and there's no picture you can take with a Priority or Auto mode that you can't take with a Manual mode. Similarly, Manual mode does not open up some extra power that you can't achieve in Auto mode. But, in some instances, one or another will make it easier to get the results you want.

Your goal is to understand the use of shutter speed and aperture, as well as how they're related. Your choice of exposure control method will be fairly obvious if you have a good understanding of what each exposure parameter is used for and how they interrelate.

There's no hierarchy to shooting modes. You don't start in Auto mode, then graduate to Priority modes, and then one day become so sophisticated that you finally switch to Manual mode and never use anything else. Rather, your goal is to simply understand exposure theory well enough that you can recognize which mode is going to provide the control that you need for the specific shooting situation that you're in.

If you're trying to shoot fast-moving subject matter, then you'll probably opt for Shutter Priority mode. If you're shooting landscapes, street scenes, or portraits—any situation where you want depth of field control—then Aperture Priority is probably your best bet. I frequently use Program mode if I know that a mid-range aperture setting will be fine, and I want to shoot quickly. Manual mode is handy if you're working in extremely low light or if you're using an external light meter.

The point is, you want an understanding of all of these modes, so that you can choose the one that is best for your current shooting situation.

In-Camera Histograms

First, the bad news. The LCD viewfinder on your camera will greatly increase the brightness, and possibly color contrast and saturation, in any image you view. This is because the camera's designers want to ensure that the image on the viewfinder is visible in bright, direct sunlight. Because of this, your camera's LCD screen does not present an accurate representation of what the colors and tones in your image actually look like. This means that when you shoot an image and then look at the results on the viewfinder, you won't necessarily be able to spot over- or underexposure or assess contrast and color.

The good news is that if your camera includes a built-in histogram, you can easily determine if your image has certain exposure problems. Not all cameras have histograms, but your camera's manual should make it easy to determine how to activate the histogram view for any image you've taken.

Figure 8.18 shows a histogram display from a Canon SLR. In addition to displaying the histogram, the thumbnail display flashes any areas that have clipped highlights or shadows.

You'll be spending a lot of time with histograms when you start postproduction, so an understanding of the use of a histogram is very important. But histograms can also help you when you're shooting by making it easier to identify when you've selected a good exposure.

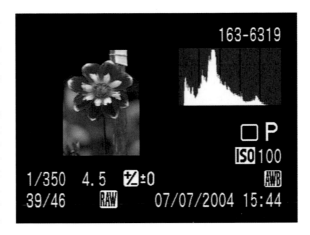

Figure 8.18

Many cameras can display a histogram of any image you've shot. In addition to this histogram, this display from a Canon SLR shows date, time, and all exposure parameters. In over- or underexposed images, the display also flashes areas in the image thumbnail that are "clipped" in the histogram.

Histograms Defined

A histogram is a simple graph of the distribution of all the tones in your image. Histograms can be easily created by most image editing applications, and they are a great way to understand exposure.

Look at Figure 8.19 and its accompanying histogram.

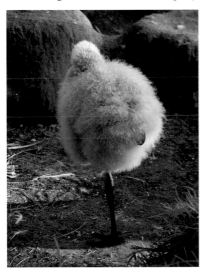

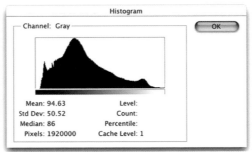

Figure 8.19

With a histogram, you can analyze your images to determine which type of exposure corrections they might need.

A histogram is simply a bar chart showing how much of each shade of gray is present in the image, with each vertical line representing one shade. Black is at the far left, and white is at the far right.

From the histogram, you can see that the image in Figure 8.19 is fairly well exposed. It has a good range of tones from black to light gray, which means it has a lot of contrast. Most of the tones are distributed toward the lower end because of the dark grays and shadows in the background. However, even though the background is dark, there is still a good range of middle gray tones and lighter tones from the gray of the baby flamingo.

Notice that the shadow areas do not clip. That is, they curve down to nothing by the time the graph reaches the left side. This means that the shadowy details in the image have not gone to solid black. In fact, there is very little solid black in the image at all. Also notice that there are a large number of tones overall, meaning the image has a good dynamic range, and therefore a lot of editing potential. Although the brighter areas are a little weak, you can correct for this in your image editor.

Now, look at Figure 8.20.

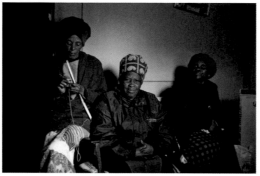

Figure 8.20

An underexposed image has a characteristic histogram.

You can probably tell by looking at Figure 8.20 that the image is underexposed, but the histogram still provides some interesting information. As you can see, there is no white in this image at all and very little medium gray, but at the lower end there is a preponderance of solid black. Notice that the shadow areas don't curve down to black as they do in Figure 8.19. Rather, they are "clipped" off the edge of the histogram—the image is so dark and underexposed that many of the darkest tones have piled up on the very left end of the histogram. In a well-exposed image, the shadow areas would be spread over a larger number of darker tones with only a little solid black. If you look in the shadow areas of the image, you'll see that they look completely black, rather than having any variation or range in their dark tones. In other words, the shadows have lost detail.

In a grayscale image, a histogram is literally a graph of the gray tones in an image. As you saw earlier, colors have a tone that roughly corresponds to the tonal qualities of a shade of gray. When you take a histogram of a color image, the resulting graph shows a composite of the red, green, and blue channels in the image. The practical upshot is a graph that is still an accurate gauge of the contrast and tonal information in your image.

An image that is overexposed will exhibit a similar histogram but be weighted on the other end with tones grouped in the white areas and with clipped highlights (see Figure 8.21).

The histogram is an exceptional exposure tool for shooting in a difficult lighting situation. Set your exposure, shoot a test shot, and then take a quick look at the image's histogram. If you see clipped highlights or shadows, you'll need to try a different exposure and shoot again.

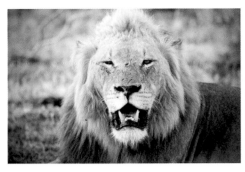
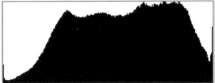

Figure 8.21

An overexposed image—the tones are weighted to the right of the histogram. In this image, you can see that the highlights are clipped—they get cut off by the right side of the histogram. In the image, the white parts of the lion's face have blown out to complete, detail-less white.

Assessing Contrast

In addition to spotting over- and underexposure problems, you can use your camera's histogram to determine the amount of contrast in an image. Take a look at Figure 8.22.

The image has little contrast and appears "flat." A quick look at the histogram shows why. Most of the tones are grouped in the middle of the graph—they don't cover a broad range.

After consulting this histogram, you would know that it was worth trying a second, additional exposure. In this case, I shot the image again with one stop of overexposure (see Figure 8.23). (I applied the overexposure using the exposure compensation control, because I didn't have specific shutter speed or aperture needs.)

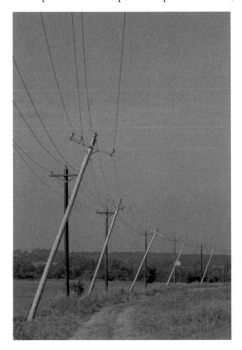

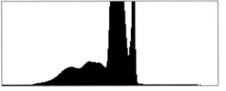

Figure 8.22

A low-contrast histogram will not show a wide spread of data. In this image, there's little distance between the darkest to lightest tones.

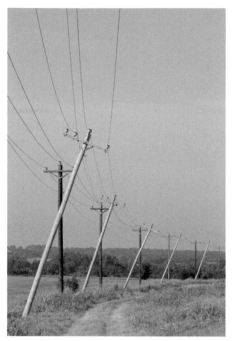

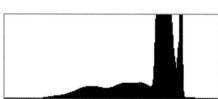

Figure 8.23

I dialed in a one-stop overexposure and shot again. This time the histogram shows more contrast. With this greater amount of data, I'll have more editing latitude when I start making adjustments and corrections.

Histogram Thought Experiment

If you were to take Figure 8.23 and flip it horizontally to create a mirror image—that is, the telephone poles would be on the right side of the screen, tilting to the left—how would the histogram change? If you answered "it wouldn't change at all," you're correct. There is no "geographic" correspondence between a location in the image and a location on the histogram. The histogram simply shows the distribution of tones. When the image is flipped, the same number of each tone still exists, so the histogram looks identical.

Note, though, that some images show a low-contrast histogram because they actually don't have much contrast in them. The histogram for Figure 8.24, for example, shows mostly dark tones. There's not a huge range of tonal information in the image because the image is mostly a dark background. So there's no way I could actually capture more contrast from this image. However, the histogram can still tell me whether I've clipped the highlights or shadows.

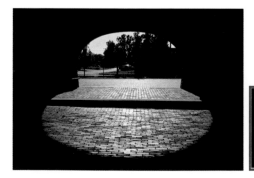

Figure 8.24

This histogram shows low contrast because there's simply not much contrast in this image. It's mostly a dark background.

Don't Worry About the Shape of the Histogram

There is no right or wrong shape to a histogram, so don't worry about the overall shape of the pile of tones. As long as you have good contrast, and nothing is clipping, you have a healthy histogram. Bear in mind that some images are low-contrast scenes, so getting a very "contrasty" histogram may not be possible.

Live Histogram

If your camera has a live histogram feature, like the one shown in Figure 8.25, then you can watch the histogram *while* you change exposures.

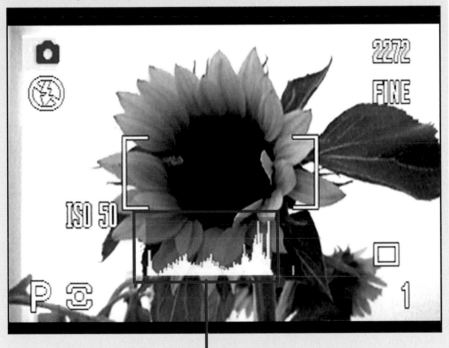

Live histogram display

Figure 8.25 A live histogram display (shown here directly beneath the focusing target) can make it easier to determine the correct exposure. A live histogram is particularly useful for cameras that lack optical viewfinders, because LCD viewfinders don't always provide a full view of an image's dynamic range.

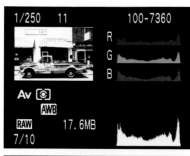

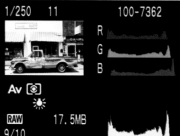

The Three-Channel Histogram

Your histogram can't tell you too much about the color in your image, but if your camera displays a three-channel histogram, you might be able to get a sense for bad white balance. A three-channel histogram simply shows a separate histogram for each color channel (red, green, and blue). If the three channels are way out of registration, there's a chance your image has a white balance problem (see Figure 8.26). Note, though, that this is a difficult thing to assess, because sometimes images simply have very different amounts of different colors, which can also skew your histogram.

Figure 8.26

A three-channel histogram can sometimes help identify white balance troubles in the field. If the three channels are way out of registration with each other, then there's a chance that your image will have a visible white balance issue. The second image was shot with an incorrect tungsten white balance setting.

Recording Your Exposure Settings

To really understand exposure, how it works, and what decisions to make, you must practice. However, for your practice to do you any good, you need a record of what exposure settings you used for each image. In the old days, you had to carry around a notebook and record your exposure settings by hand. You can still do that, of course, and make any other notes you feel are important to remember, but the odds are that your camera will remember your settings for you, because most digital cameras record a number of shooting parameters along with the image data. Figure 8.27 shows the information stored by a Nikon point-and-shoot camera.

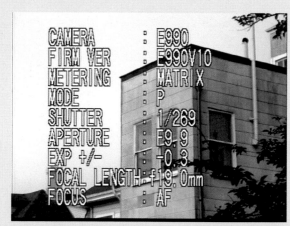

Figure 8.27

Most cameras will store a record of all the parameters you used for each shot. This data is stored with the file and can be read using special software.

This information is stored using a standard format called *Exchangeable Image File (EXIF)*, which was created by the Japan Electronic Industry Development Association in 1995. If your digital camera is EXIF compatible (and most are), all its files are EXIF files, whether they use JPEG or TIFF compression.

Bracketing

While it's important to understand all the exposure theory we've discussed here, there's a very simple practice you can employ to help ensure that you get a correct exposure, no matter what shooting situation you're in.

Bracketing is the process of shooting extra exposures above and below your target exposure to give yourself a margin of error in your exposure calculation or adjustment. If you've made a somewhat accurate, educated guess about exposure, one of your bracketed images will most likely be good, even if your original guess was off. Bracketing is a tried-and-true practice of film photographers.

For example, if you're shooting a scene with a big mix of bright and dark tones, then you might want to bracket your shots. Or, if you're shooting a very bright or very dark object, and you aren't sure how to expose to render the tones properly, then bracketing may be your answer.

The great thing about EXIF files is that their image data can be read by any program, even if that program isn't specifically EXIF compatible. The EXIF data is simply stored in the header information of the file, so any application that can read JPEG or TIFF files can still read an EXIF-compatible file.

These days, most image editing, cataloging, and browsing applications allow you to look at an image's EXIF data (as shown in Figure 8.28). As you'll see later, this data is often very helpful when editing.

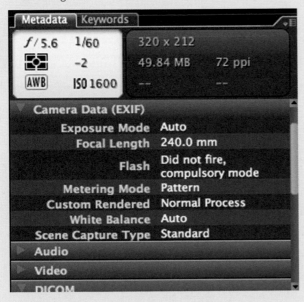

Figure 8.28

Adobe Bridge displays an EXIF readout for each image you select.

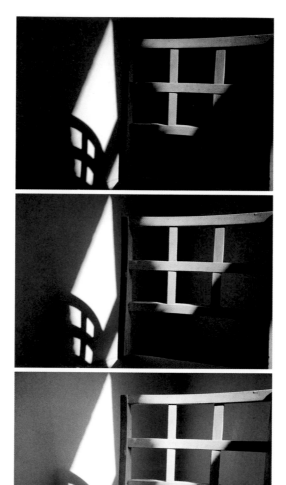

The easiest way to bracket is with your exposure compensation control. Take a shot, dial in an underexposure, and shoot again. Then do the same with an overexposure. There's no right or wrong exposure interval to use, and you can shoot as many images as you want (see Figure 8.29).

As always, with exposure compensation, you'll have no way to control *how* the camera achieves its over- or underexposure, so you may want to switch to a Priority mode for your bracketing, to maintain control over the exposure parameter that matters for your shot.

Bracketing does *not* make you an amateur, and it doesn't mean you don't know what you're doing, or that you're cheating. Some of the best photographers in history bracketed very heavily.

Obviously, bracketing is not a viable option when you're shooting action shots or any sort of fleeting moment. But for landscapes, still lifes, portraits, and other unchanging static scenes, bracketing can mean the difference between a usable shot and a poorly exposed shot.

Figure 8.29

This is a bracketed set of images of the same scene. The top image was shot underexposed by one stop, the second image is exposed as the camera metered it, and the third is overexposed by one stop.

Auto Bracketing

Many digital cameras offer autobracketing features, which let the camera take care of bracketing for you. For example, Figure 8.30 shows the Auto Exposure Bracketing menu control from a Canon digital SLR, which lets you dial in a bracketing range. Here, we've chosen a three-step bracket with one-stop intervals. When you press the shutter, the camera will shoot an image at the recommended metering and then automatically adjust for one stop of underexposure. This setting will be used for the next shot, while the shot after that will automatically be set for one stop of overexposure.

If you activate the camera's Drive (or Burst) mode, you can simply press and hold the shutter release for three shots, and the camera will shoot an autobracketed set. This is a great way of knocking off an entire bracketed set quickly. I used Burst and Autobracket to shoot the three images in Figure 8.31. I chose to bracket that scene because I knew that the bright sky and darker foreground could confuse the camera's meter. Anytime you shoot a scene with a big variation from brightest

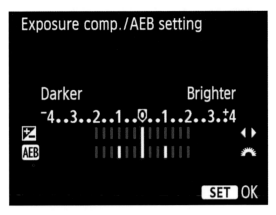

Figure 8.30

An autobracketing setting lets you specify how many shots in the bracket and what interval you want between each exposure.

to darkest (a scene with a lot of dynamic range), there's a chance your meter will miscalculate. In this case, it proved to be a good idea, as the first shot—the one taken with the camera's normal metering—was too bright. The highlights, especially in the sky, were overexposed. The second, underexposed image worked the best.

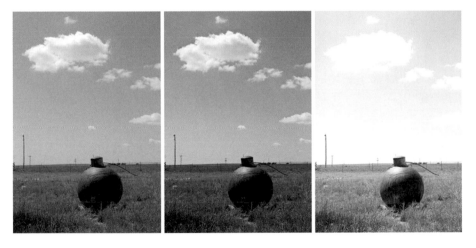

Figure 8.31

I used autobracketing to shoot this scene because I knew that the high dynamic range here was a tricky metering situation, and that one of the images would come out properly exposed.

Saving Space While Bracketing

With digital bracketing, you don't have to worry about the waste and expense of shooting extra film. However, if storage is a concern, you might want to examine your bracketed set. After shooting, quickly check the histogram for each image using your camera's LCD. You can then throw out the images that are obviously poorly exposed.

Your camera might offer additional autobracketing features. Some cameras, for example, offer a two-stop autobracket. This can be handy for a situation where you know that overexposure is a bad idea, but that underexposure might yield a better image. So, with a two-stop bracket, you could shoot a regular and an underexposed image. Other cameras allow a five-step bracket, which provides you with the capability to shoot a huge exposure range very easily.

When autobracketing, your camera will employ its usual procedure for determining whether it should achieve its exposure adjustment through shutter speed changes, aperture, or both. If you want to force it to make its changes through either aperture or shutter speed adjustments only, then you'll need to put your camera into a Priority mode and configure it accordingly.

Why It's Best to Capture as Much Image Data as Possible

As you've just seen, you can use the histogram to determine how much data you've captured. An image with a lot of data will have more tones across its histogram. Obviously, some images—an albino in white swim trunks standing in front of an igloo—are not going to have a wide range of data. But an image with more tones will allow you to make more edits before you visibly degrade the image.

Later, you'll learn how your editing operations expand and contract the data in a particular tonal range. As this data gets squished and stretched, tones can become posterized.

Posterizing is the process of reducing the number of tones in an image. The image retains its dynamic range—that is, the brightest and darkest tones remain the same—but the number of intervening tones is reduced.

Figure 8.32 shows a grayscale ramp that goes from black to white, using 256 different shades. The second image shows the same ramp from black to white, but it has been posterized down to 16 colors.

After a little editing, you may be able to spot some posterization problems in your image, like the ones in Figure 8.33. Note that the gradient of the shadow underneath his collar is not a smooth ramp.

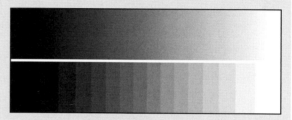

Figure 8.32 This grayscale ramp has been posterized to 16 colors. It still spans black to white, but there are now only 16 gradations between full black and full white. Posterizing is the process of reducing the number of tones that are used to represent an image, and posterization is especially ugly in areas of transition like a gradient.

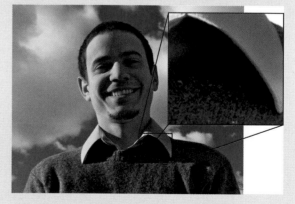

Figure 8.33

In this image, you can see posterization of shadow tones underneath the man's shirt collar. This posterization has occurred because there wasn't enough image data in the image to support the amount of editing applied to the shadows.

An image with more tonal information in it is less prone to these types of artifacts. Capturing more image data will prevent these troubles and make for more editing flexibility later. The histogram is your key to determining how much data you've captured.

Scene Modes Revisited

In Chapter 2, "Getting to Know Your Camera," you were introduced to Scene modes, special modes that bias your camera's decision-making process so that it's more appropriate to specific types of scenes. If you're shooting with a high-end SLR, then your camera might not offer any Scene modes. Most mid-range cameras, though, offer Scene modes, and smaller point-and-shoots typically offer *lots* of them, in lieu of more advanced manual controls. Now that you've had some study of shutter speed and aperture, let's revisit some of the most basic Scene modes and take a more technical look at what they're doing.

- ◆ **Portrait mode.** This mode attempts to blur out the background of an image, in order to bring more focus to the subject. As you've learned, this can be achieved by using a wide aperture (which has a low f number). A wider aperture yields an image with shallower depth of field. Your Portrait mode might also activate face detection automatically and possibly smile and blink detection.

- ◆ **Landscape mode.** When shooting a landscape, you usually want everything in the scene to be in focus, which means a very deep depth of field. Deep depth of field means a very small aperture. Landscape modes will also often lock focus on infinity.

- ◆ **Sand and Snow mode.** As you've learned, white colors sometimes need to be overexposed so that they don't end up gray in your final image. Sand and Snow mode will calculate overexposures that will render whites as they should be.

Be aware, too, that when you're shooting in a Scene mode, not all of your camera's features will be available. Like Auto mode, Scene modes lock out a lot of your camera's functions. If you try to change a setting that is not allowed, you might see a warning of some kind (see Figure 8.34).

As an exercise, it can be interesting to look through the Scene modes on your camera to see if you can determine what they might be doing, exposure-wise, in their approach to the situations they're tailored for. Bear in mind that some Scene modes may not alter exposure at all, but will activate instead other features such as Special Drive or Focus modes, or they might apply a lot of tone and color adjustments.

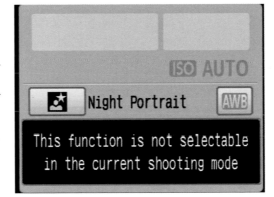

Figure 8.34

You can't access all of your camera's functions when using some Scene modes. If you try to use one that's not allowed, your camera will probably warn you.

Image Processing Parameters Revisited

In Chapter 3, "Camera Anatomy," you learned about the image processing parameters that your camera might provide. (These features were also covered briefly in Chapter 5, "Image Sensors.") These are the sharpness, saturation, contrast, and possibly other adjustments that your camera makes to any JPEG or TIFF image that it shoots.

These settings never affect shutter speed, aperture, ISO, metering, focus mode, or any other shooting parameters. As explained earlier, they are image adjustment processes that the computer in your camera performs *after* the image has been shot. They are no different than adjustments that you would make in your computer using a program like Photoshop.

Personally, I prefer to make my edits myself, using an image editor, but as I explained in Chapter 3, there are times when letting the camera perform these adjustments will speed up your workflow.

Different vendors have different names for these settings. Canon calls them *Picture Styles*, while Nikon refers to them as *Picture Controls*. Some cameras don't have a specific name for them; rather, they are simply parameters that appear in a menu.

Canon Picture Styles and Nikon Picture Controls actually offer more adjustment power than what you'll see in the in-camera menus. With both of these features, you can define complex image editing profiles that include subtle color shifts of specific colors, complex contrast adjustments, and more. Both vendors provide editing programs that you can use on your desktop computer to create additional Picture Styles or Picture Controls that you can then download to your camera (see Figure 8.35).

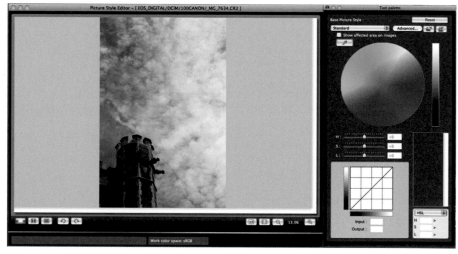

Figure 8.35

Both Canon and Nikon provide applications for your desktop computer, which allow you to create new image processing profiles for your camera.

Again, to determine if this functionality is useful to you, you'll need to think about your workflow. Creating a custom setting like this can be very handy if you need to crank out images quickly without doing *any* postproduction editing. For wedding and event shooters who routinely shoot the same subject matter under roughly the same lighting conditions, this can be a great feature. But for most of us who are willing to spend some time editing individual images, it makes more sense to make adjustments in an image editor, rather than trying to define some sort of "global" editing adjustment that will be applied to batches of images while shooting.

However, if custom image processing parameters sound like a good solution to your photographic needs, then by all means, go further with these features. You should find detailed documentation included with your camera's software.

Exposure Strategy

We've spent a lot of time looking at theories and explanations of exposure and exposure controls, and when you set this book down and go shooting, all of that stuff needs to go with you. A lot of people think that when it comes to shooting, your process is all about feeling and expression. While this might be true when you first recognize an interesting subject, and while you might spend some time looking at that subject to determine how best to capture it, when it comes to the moment of actual shooting, your mind should be mostly technical. Remember: good photographs are *made* not *taken*, and to make a good one, you have a lot of purely technical decisions to make.

To help make better decisions, you should concoct an exposure strategy anytime you enter a situation where you think you're going to be shooting. This will give you a leg up on some of the decisions that you'll need to make, and will allow you to put your camera into a mode that provides control of the exposure parameters that you'll need quick access to.

For example, say you're walking down a street while on vacation and you come across some kids playing a pickup game of stickball. Before you even lift the camera to your face, you should think "Fast motion, I'll need control of shutter speed; it's dark in this alley, so I'll need to raise my ISO."

When you're just starting out, you'll probably need to make a conscious effort, anytime you encounter a new shooting or lighting situation, to think about what your exposure concerns will be. Will you need depth of field control? Motion-stopping control? Will low light levels be a problem? Are there windows or bright lights that might cause a bad backlighting situation? Are you in a situation where your camera's auto white balance usually fails? Are you facing a scene with a lot of dynamic range? Will your exposure vary wildly in the scene depending on where you're pointing? This list of questions goes on and on, and if you understand the effects of specific exposure controls—all that stuff we've been talking about throughout this book—then you'll be able to recognize potential exposure issues.

As you get more experienced, you'll find that this exposure strategy step happens without a lot of conscious thought. Before you realize it, you'll have changed modes, dialed in an exposure compensation, or popped up a fill flash.

In Chapter 11, "Raw Shooting," we'll discuss exposure strategies for specific situations. While I don't advocate a "recipe book" style of teaching—there's no recipe that will always work, so you need to understand how to concoct your own—these sections will hopefully give you an idea of how strategizing exposure works, and what you need to think about when you enter a new type of shooting situation.

Enough with the Button Pushing

So far, we've spent a lot of time learning a lot of theory and wading through lots of camera controls and features. While we still have a little more theory to cover, we're going to switch gears away from the craft side of things and move into more of the artistry of shooting.

You will need to continue to study the exposure concepts that we've covered—shutter speed, aperture, ISO, and their interrelationship need to be second nature to you. But the best way to learn these concepts is to practice, and when you're shooting, you'll want to think about more than just buttons and exposure settings. As I mentioned earlier, the art and craft of photography inform each other. As we move into the next chapter and explore the process of finding and capturing images, you'll get a different take on the theory that you've learned so far.

9

FINDING AND COMPOSING A PHOTO

Learning the Art of Photography

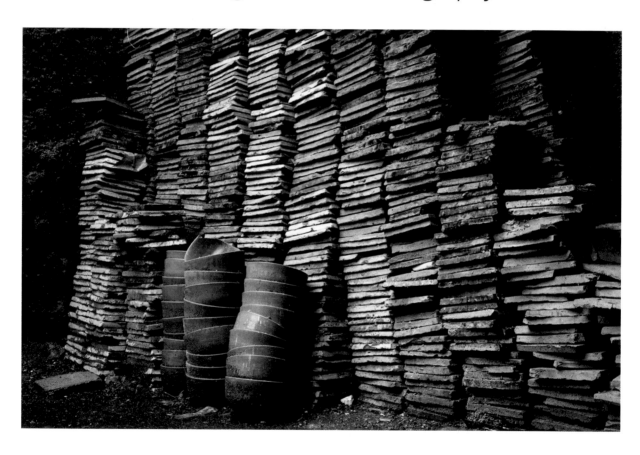

So far, in this book, we've been studying the theory behind all the different parameters that affect the creation of an image, as well as the controls that you have for manipulating those parameters. I have been calling this the *craft* of photography. Photographic *artistry* is the process of using these craft skills to represent a scene—whether it's a portrait, still life, event, landscape, or abstract—in a way that evokes some of what the subject makes you feel.

You can study theory and button pushing for the rest of your life, but if you don't know how to recognize a potential image and then how to compose it in a way that is compelling, your craft skills will have no purpose. Similarly, no matter how great an eye you have, if you don't understand how focal length, camera position, shutter speed, aperture, and overall exposure affect your image, then you will have a very limited photographic vocabulary. In this way, both art and craft are essential to good shooting. In this chapter, we're going to focus on the artistry side of things and explore how you find, visualize, and compose an image.

Looking Versus Seeing

Does this sound familiar? You're trying to get out of the house in a hurry, but you can't find your keys (or your sunglasses, your wallet, your goggles, riding crop, or whatever). You look on your desk, through the pockets of all of the coats you've worn recently, on the kitchen table, in the bathroom—then you start all over again. You try to retrace your steps to determine where you might have been when you last had the keys. Finally, after 20 minutes of increasingly maddening searching, you find them sitting in plain sight in the middle of your desk—in the very first place you looked.

This frustrating situation happens because, while it's very easy to look at the world, it's far more complicated to actually see it. While people generally use the words "look" and "see" synonymously, for a photographer there are very important differences between the two terms.

How is it that you can look at the desk where your keys are sitting but not see them? The answer has to do with what you learned in Chapter 1, "Eyes, Brains, Lights, and Images." Your eyes are far more than a simple optical instrument. While it's easy to think of the eyes as being just like a camera—they have a lens and an iris and a light-sensitive focal plane—they differ from a camera in one very important way: they're attached to a human brain. As you learned in Chapter 1, our brains dramatically alter our perception of what we're seeing, and not seeing the keys on the desk in front of you is a prime example of this phenomenon. Although it might be frustrating, there's a good reason why your brain evolved to work this way.

Consider the process of running a typical errand in town, either in a car or on foot. As you travel about, you will be acutely aware of dozens or even hundreds of cars, and possibly dozens or hundreds of people. Not to mention bicyclists, baby strollers, and many other things. If the day goes well, you will navigate successfully alongside, in-between, and past all these cars and people without ever colliding with one. Although you will engage in a complex choreography with these objects, when you get home you will most likely be hard-pressed to describe the details of the majority, if any, of these vehicles or people.

There might be one or two cars (or people) you took note of because they were particularly attractive or unusual looking, but you will have perceived most of the cars you looked at as simple generic objects. Upon returning home, you might not register any of them as specific types of vehicles, and instead report that "traffic was really heavy today." In a sense, you're not seeing the trees for the forest.

It takes an incredible amount of your neural bandwidth to process visual input—bandwidth that your brain needs for other things, such as keeping track of errands and so forth. To keep you from being overwhelmed with visual information, your brain tends to edit or abbreviate your visual experience. Consequently, when crossing the street, rather than seeing a large metal vehicle resting on four wheels, with a clear glass window on top, six dead grasshoppers stuck to the front grill, a license place that reads ILUVNY, and a middle-aged brunette woman in curlers behind the wheel, you very often just register *car*. By reducing the complexity of a big vehicle down to a simple concept and a simple iconic image, you don't have to spend so much time registering all of the details that you end up getting run over. Instead, your brain takes a shortcut that allows you to get on with your day, albeit in a way that possibly makes the world less visibly interesting.

Getting back to the lost keys. When you look at the desk, your brain might decide that it already knows what the desk looks like, so it won't bother to register details that it thinks it already knows. There normally aren't keys sitting there, so you don't see them. This is why someone who's not so familiar with your desk might walk into the room and see the keys immediately.

Little kids are different. Because the world is a new place for them, they notice far more detail. They have to see these details because they haven't yet learned to abbreviate the visual complexity of the world down to simple symbols like *desk*. Unfortunately, for a photographer, the visual complexity of the world is also the raw material for your images. So you don't want your brain to abbreviate your experience; you want it to see every detail. In other words, you want to learn to see again, as you did when you were a kid.

As you get older, you have more knowledge of the world, so your brain can abbreviate even more to further relieve you from the hassle of seeing. Consequently, one of your most difficult goals as a photographer is to learn to spend less time looking and more time seeing. As you learn to do this, your level of photographic artistry will increase, regardless of your current level of craftsmanship.

Fortunately, even though your brain frequently stands in the way of your ability to see accurately, there are still things you can do to try to open up your senses and learn to better spot the interesting visual matter around you. The more you do this, the more you will discover raw material that can be transformed into photos.

Seeing Exercises

Just as musicians can train their ears to recognize pitch, intervals, and chords, photographers can train their visual senses to be more open and receptive to the world. In other words, you can practice *seeing*.

One of the best ways to improve your seeing prowess is to remember what seeing feels like. However, if it's been a long time since your visual sense was really open, then it may be difficult to know what the difference is between seeing and not seeing. One of the easiest ways to get your visual sense going is to go somewhere new. Maybe you've noticed this when you travel or go on vacation. When you first get to some place very foreign or new, you often notice lots of different details. This is partly a survival mechanism—you're a little more wary than usual, a little more alert, so all of your senses are more active. But this also happens because there's lots of new stuff to see—stuff your brain isn't sure how to abbreviate yet.

This is often why a lot of people think they need to go somewhere when they want to practice their photography. They've recognized before that when they travel, they see more things. Next time you feel that charged visual sense, pay close attention to what it feels like. At those times, you're experiencing what it's like to really see, and once you've identified that feeling, it can be a little easier to find it again.

The other lesson to be learned from this is that it's not the place that matters—it's how you see. You should not have to travel to find interesting pictures, and you shouldn't count on traveling to activate your visual senses, because sometimes it won't happen. In fact, the odds are that if you can't shoot in your own backyard, then you're not going to do much better in an exotic location, because what makes good photography is a good visual sense.

Here are some exercises to get your sense of seeing going, without having to travel.

Warming Up

Don't assume that you can work at your job all day and then step out the door and suddenly be a photographer. You wouldn't expect to exercise or play a musical instrument without warming up, and your sense of sight can also benefit from some warm-up. While not tiring, the act of seeing is physical—it's something you have to feel. It can take some time to calm down from the everyday stresses of life and open yourself up to your visual sense.

When you first step out the door to go shoot, take a picture. It doesn't matter what it is—take a picture of your foot, the light pole across the street, a manhole cover, anything at all. Taking that first shot will remind you of the physicality of shooting. You'll feel the camera in your hands and remember the handling of it. Most importantly, you'll look through the viewfinder and be reminded of the frame shape and what the world looks like when it's cropped down to just what your camera shows. All of this will help you get out of the distractions of your everyday life and into seeing and thinking about images.

Make an Assignment

Photography takes practice, and you need to do that practice regularly. If you wait to shoot until you're on vacation, then you probably won't be doing a lot of shooting. As mentioned earlier, good pictures can happen anywhere, but only if you're open to them, and that openness comes with practice.

One way to make yourself practice, and to breathe new life into familiar locations, is to give yourself an assignment. You can choose a subject—old cars, doorways, local flowers—or maybe a phrase or a word—contentment; no pain, no gain; a penny saved. The subject matter or word doesn't have to mean anything to anyone else, and you can interpret it any way you want. The idea is simply to give yourself some way to frame your view of your location. Having a specific point-of-view or photographic goal will often make you see familiar ground in a new way.

I keep three ongoing projects: my street, my neighborhood, and San Francisco. Sometimes, when I have a moment to spare, I'll pick one of these projects and go shooting. Confining myself to just my street is the hardest project, while the neighborhood is easier, and having the whole city to work with is even easier. Trying to work on just my street can be the most interesting, though, because it makes me look for unusual lighting or composition among very familiar locales (see Figure 9.1).

A project can often be an inch wide and a mile deep. Set a limited goal to give yourself direction and then explore that goal in great detail.

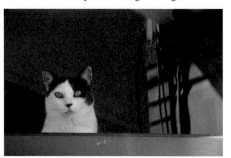 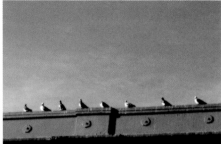

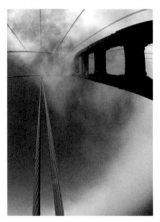

Figure 9.1

Images from my ongoing "My Street, My Neighborhood, and San Francisco projects," respectively. Choosing some projects can make it easier to find things to shoot.

Look at Other Photos

Lately, when teaching classes, I've noticed something strange: very few aspiring photographers know much about the history of their chosen form. While aspiring writers will be able to easily name their favorite writers and books, few photography students can name a favorite photographer or famous, important works of photography. Familiarity with great works, though, is an easy way to improve your own shots.

Fortunately, we live in an age where it's very easy to get access to the most famous, celebrated photos ever shot. Go to the library or bookstore, or do some Google searches, and find work by some of the great masters: Henri Cartier-Bresson, Paul Strand, Ansel Adams, Elliot Erwitt, Diane Arbus, Alfred Stieglitz, Walker Evans, and Dorothea Lange. Spend some time looking at their images with an eye toward seeing how they make you feel and also figuring out what was done technically to create the image. Pay attention to the composition of the images and try to think about what the photographer had to do (or wait for) to get the shot. Try to think about what the photographer might have done, exposure-wise, to achieve a given effect. See if you can figure out anything about the focal length they used. Does the image encompass a very wide field of view? If so, then you know they were using a wide-angle lens. If it's a narrow field of view, then you can assume a telephoto lens. Once you have an idea of the focal length, then you can start to figure out how close to their subject they were standing. If you find they had to stay far away from a portrait subject, you might then wonder about how they communicated with their subject and maintained a necessary rapport. By reverse-engineering their solutions, you'll learn a lot about how they saw a scene and what choices and decisions they had to make to turn that scene into a finished image.

Different types of photography present different problems. The photojournalist is usually operating on a specific assignment, while the landscape photographer is typically exploring a particular location. Street shooters, meanwhile, keep their eyes open for the characters or small dramas that cross their paths every day. Each of these requires a different type of attention and study, and each requires a particular skill set. They can all evince different types of feeling. Think about the reality that these photographers might have been facing, and what they had to do both artistically and creatively to translate those realities into photographic vocabulary.

Such study will help with your craft skills and your understanding of how other photographers work. But this type of study will also train your eye. You'll begin to develop a visual vocabulary for reinterpreting the world in ways that can be captured by a camera.

Sitting down with a book of photos is a great way to continue to practice, even when you can't get out to shoot.

Sketch and Draw

Sure, this is a photography book, but photography is a visual art form, and sketching and drawing can help a lot with getting your visual sense going. If you're like me, you probably insist that you can't draw. The goal, though, is not to produce a gallery-worthy masterpiece, but to become more attuned to your visual sense. Don't worry about drawing a perfect picture or even a good picture.

During the process of drawing something, you have to look at each shape and line that makes up that object. When you do this, you will cease to see it as an object and will begin to see it as lines and shapes. Whether or not you do a good job of recording those lines and shapes is irrelevant, because the process can activate your visual sense in a fairly profound way. Even just 10 or 15 minutes of concentrated effort can make you see the world in a fairly different way.

Pay Attention and Do What Works for You

Finally, one of the best ways to learn how to get warmed up and to get your visual sense going is to simply pay attention to what it feels like when you are seeing effectively. Once you're tuned in to how it feels, you might find your own process for getting into the zone. Don't be worried about what it takes to get you there—if it works for you, that's fine.

For example, sometimes when I go out shooting I get so focused on the idea of success that I pressure myself to a completely ineffectual place. Once I'm wrapped up in the idea that I have to get good shots, then I'm no longer present and seeing. So lately, I've been trying an exercise: I take the card out of my camera and go shooting. With no memory card, there is no going home with good shots. Instead, all I can do is find shots and visualize them in the camera. This often reminds me of what it feels like to simply be out seeing, without the pressure of what final images I might end up with.

And don't worry, even if you take a great picture without a card in your camera, that's fine. There will always be more great pictures.

Practice

Yes, I've been harping on practice a lot, but it's an important concept so I figure I'll mention it again: practice. Practice a lot. Not only will the craft and theory you've been studying become second nature, but you'll also get better at seeing and recognizing potential images. If you want to take it to the extreme, you can act like photographer Joe Buissink: If he doesn't have a camera but sees an image he would like to shoot, he says "click" or snaps his fingers. This "shooting without a camera" keeps him in the habit of seeing photographically, acknowledging when there's a shot he wants to take, and thinking about how he might compose it.

Practice is the key to all creative endeavors, and in the case of photography, practice is not just about memorizing what shutter speed and aperture do, but also about practicing composition, seeing, and interpretation.

Finding a Subject

A good photo requires a subject, of course. Sometimes a subject will be obvious, but more often, interesting photos are hidden from those who aren't necessarily looking for a picture. A photographer will often see an image in a location that otherwise appears mundane.

Developing your ability to see will help you recognize images and help you understand the best way to represent them. Employing your composition skills, understanding of exposure, and other aspects of your craft will help you capture the image you envision.

Beginning shooters often ask how to find things to shoot. They think that they must seek out interesting objects, landmark locations, or stunning vistas. The fact is that landmark locations and stunning vistas usually make fairly boring pictures because those places have already been photographed so much and in so many different ways.

Good pictures can happen anywhere, and they usually begin with a simple impulse based on something you've seen—a play of light, a beautiful color, an interesting piece of geometry. You might be walking down the street in late afternoon and find a weathered door that the setting sun is throwing into deep, textured relief. Or perhaps you come across an otherwise mundane object that's being lit brightly by the sunset. Or maybe you find a curious piece of repeating geometry, or some kids engaged in a serious game of tag.

All good photos begin with light. Very often, it is simply the light that compels you toward a scene, not the actual subject matter. For example, you may choose to shoot a landscape not because the landscape itself is particularly compelling, but because the light playing off it is. Good light can turn an otherwise pedestrian scene or subject into something interesting, as you can see in Figure 9.2.

Figure 9.2 is also an example of a subject that is not in itself interesting. It's the light that makes a compelling scene, which means good photo subjects can occur anywhere, not just in exotic locales or around big landmarks.

Conversely, a potentially good subject can be either boring or interesting, depending on the light you shoot it in (see Figure 9.3).

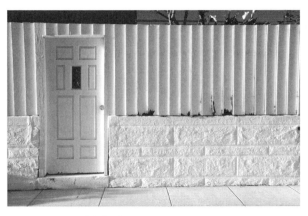
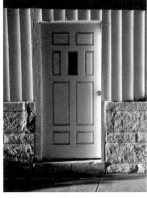

Figure 9.2

While the first shot in this figure is not especially interesting, as the light changed, the scene became increasingly dynamic. Quality of light is very often the defining characteristic of a scene.

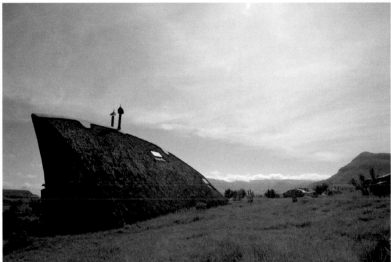

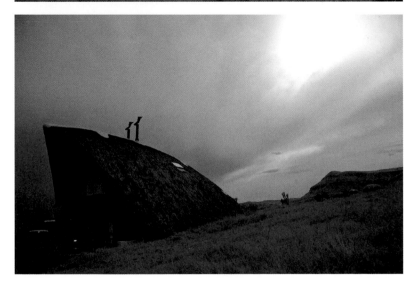

Figure 9.3

While this unusual architecture is good picture fodder, shooting it in boring light makes for a flat, uninteresting picture. Waiting for some color and contrast makes for a more compelling image.

As you learned earlier, your eye packs far more luminance-sensitive cells than it does color-sensitive cells. As such, it is much more sensitive to contrast than it is to color, so light with strong contrast is usually far more compelling than flat light.

Sunlight yields more contrast when it is shining from a low angle. So early morning and late afternoon light is far more interesting than the light of mid-day. Low-angle light casts longer shadows, which makes for surfaces that have more texture and visible detail. In the middle of the day, when the sun is shining straight down, there is very little shadowing, resulting in a flat, boring look.

You'll often work with existing light in two ways. When you find an area of particularly compelling light, stop to see if there's any type of picture to be had. As you explore the area, you might find a texture or subject that is worth shooting, since it is in good light, or you might find that a subject comes along if you wait long enough (see Figure 9.4). Conversely, if you're out and about and discover an interesting subject, try to assess if better light will fall onto it at some point. Perhaps the sun will pass out of shadow and illuminate your subject in a more interesting manner (Figure 9.5).

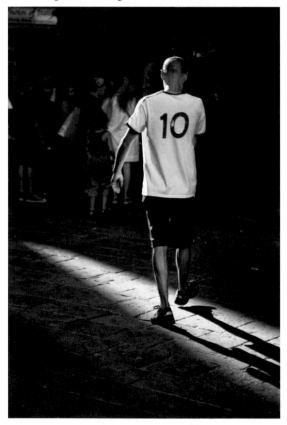

Figure 9.4

I came across this splash of light that I liked, both because it mixed nicely with the texture on the street, and because of the shadowy detail in the background. I waited until someone walked into the light, and then took this shot.

Early morning and late afternoon light have a very different color than mid-day light. While it will vary depending on atmospheric conditions, where you live, and the time of year, you'll generally find dusk and dawn to be warmer. Late afternoon light is especially warm and colorful, and can be ideal for landscapes and portraits (see Figure 9.6).

The light of the early morning and late afternoon changes *very* quickly, which can work both for you and against you. If you see something that isn't particularly well lit, it might change very soon. At the same time, when you see the image you want, you might have to work very quickly to capture it before you lose the light.

In the spring and fall, when the sun doesn't climb very high in the sky, you'll find good light during more of the day. The specific hours will vary, depending on your latitude.

All that said, just because it's raining or dingy doesn't mean there aren't still good photos to be had. Sometimes, too much contrast can be a bad thing, as it can serve to make your image harsh and complex. Also, shooting when there is less contrast affords you the opportunity of adding more contrast where you want it, later on (see Figure 9.7).

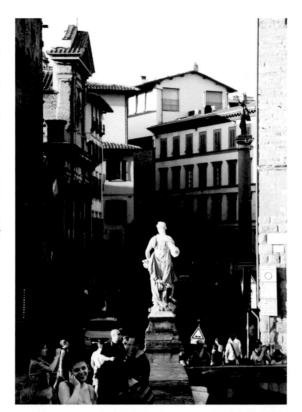

Figure 9.5

Normally, I wouldn't be interested in taking a picture of this statue, but the light was hitting it so that it lit up a bright white, against the darker background. I shot several shots until I found one that had people in the foreground in interesting positions, but it was the light that drove the shot.

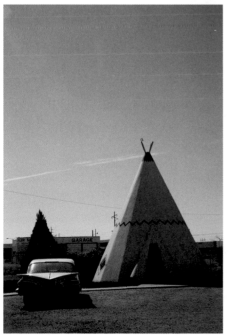
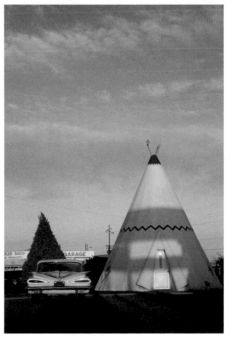

Figure 9.6

These images differ in terms of their shadows and the clouds in the sky, but note the difference between the morning light on the left and the warmer afternoon light on the right.

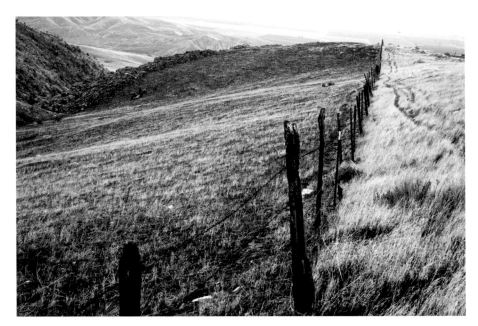

Figure 9.7

Just because it's overcast doesn't mean you can't get good shots. Many situations fare better without high contrast. This image was shot under completely overcast skies.

Look Through Your Camera

If you find you've been walking around for a while and you aren't seeing anything you want to shoot, even though the light is good, you might simply be in a location that isn't providing good subject matter. However, it might also be that your eyes and brain just aren't seeing things photographically. Sometimes you have to look through the camera before you begin to see potential photographs. If you're not seeing compelling subjects, lift the camera to your eye and look through it. The frame of your viewfinder often crops the world in ways that you can't visualize when you're walking around, and those crops often reveal interesting compositions.

Also, remember that you may have to shoot your way through some unusable, outright bad images before your photographic senses get working. If you suffer through this process, you may find yourself seeing more things to shoot.

If you try all this and still aren't finding images, then either there really isn't anything worth shooting, or your photographic juices just aren't flowing. Don't let this discourage you. Relax, give it a rest, and come back another day.

Photography as Abstraction

We've all probably experienced something like this: you're standing somewhere spectacular, like the edge of the Grand Canyon, and you think: *This is so amazing, I must take a picture of it!* You pull out your camera, hold it up to the scene, and capture a few images. Later, at home, you look at your prints, only to be disappointed. You think: *I dunno, somehow, I remember it being more…grand.*

The fact is: No one can take a photo that will make their viewers feel like they're standing on the edge of the Grand Canyon. It's simply not possible any more than it's possible for a dancer to choreograph a dance that will make someone feel like he or she is standing at the Grand Canyon. Although it appears that a photograph can capture an incredibly believable facsimile of a scene, you must remember that photography is a representational medium. Your live experience of the Grand Canyon involves much more than the visual stimulation you're receiving. First, it involves a very complex visual stimulus—a 3D panoramic stimulus with far more color and brightness information than your camera can capture. In addition, all of your other senses are mixed in as well, along with other emotions that you might experience for other reasons (happiness from being on vacation, the culmination of a dream to see the Grand Canyon, etc.).

However, although you may not be able to create a photograph that truly re-creates the *experience* of standing in a particular location, you can create a photo that evokes some of the *feeling* you had while you were there. Your job as a photographer is to determine what it is about a particular scene or moment that is compelling to you. In the case of the Grand Canyon, it might be the size or the colors. Perhaps it's the sense of geologic time that you can see in the layers of sediment. Or perhaps it's the people you're with, or simply something about the way the light is playing off a particular rock formation.

Rather than trying to capture the entire experience of where you're standing, you need to try to identify a more refined feeling of what it is about that moment that compels you. Then you can employ your craft skills to figure out how to represent that feeling as a flat, two-dimensional photo. Remember, photography is a representational medium, not a literal duplication of an experience.

Alfred Hitchcock once described drama as "life with all the boring parts removed." Dramatists very often take a normal, everyday event and blow it up into drama. They exaggerate some things, remove others, and make up entirely new things to create a representation that the audience will respond to. Photography is the same way.

For example, a few years ago I was in Death Valley. Because of the extreme geography of Death Valley (parts are below sea level), there is an interesting phenomenon where sand blows off the surrounding mountains, hits the weird air currents of the valleys that sit below sea level, and immediately falls to the ground, to form giant sand dunes. There are four such dune fields in the park, and when you see them from afar, they're quite striking. The dunes are huge, and when viewed from above, you get a tremendous sense of scale—you can imagine the sand flying off the mountain to be deposited on the valley floor.

One morning, I was driving out of the mountains and came across such a vista. I grabbed my camera and took the picture shown in Figure 9.8.

Because that image didn't really work out, I drove down to the valley floor to get closer to the dunes and took the picture shown in Figure 9.9.

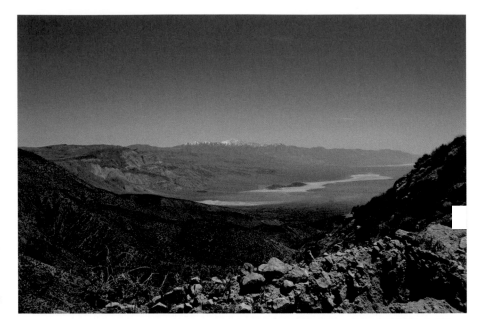

Figure 9.8

This isn't much of a picture. There's no real composition, and nothing for the eye to follow. What's more, the majestic dune field on the valley floor appears merely as a fairly boring, small patch of beige. The picture in no way captures what I was seeing and feeling.

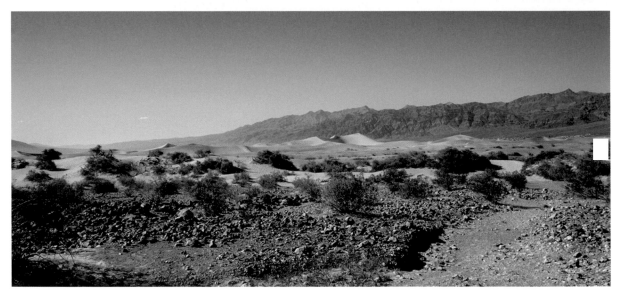

Figure 9.9 This isn't much better than Figure 9.8. There's no sense of scale and still no real composition to speak of. Your eye doesn't know how to read the image, and it's not particularly evocative of anything.

The next day, storm clouds blew in, and I hiked into the dunes themselves. Being in a dune field is a unique experience. The scenery is a constantly shifting play of geometry, and the mountains of sand are huge. All these factors add up to a profound sense of otherworldliness. I took my time, worked my subject, and shot the image shown in Figure 9.10.

I can say outright that it didn't look exactly like the image in Figure 9.10. However, it did *feel* like that image—mysterious, beautiful, and possessed of tremendous scale. So, although that photo is not a literal image of the sand dunes, it still effectively captures something about the truth of the experience I had there. This is your goal as a photographer.

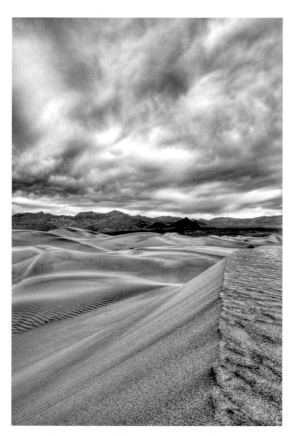

Figure 9.10

Finally, by getting into the dunes themselves, and working the shot, I came up with something that may not show a broad vista of scenery, but still captures the feeling of the place.

Know Your Audience

Photography is a strange medium in that it's used for so many things. Journalism, documenting everyday moments of your life, advertising, fine art, surveillance—photography is applied to all of these situations. Obviously, depending on what you'll be using your images for, you'll have different concerns. If you're a photojournalist, you'll probably need to get images of very specific things, whereas if you're a street shooter who's just trying to find some interesting pictures, then you most likely won't know what you want to shoot until you come across it.

You might be thinking: *I'm not interested in having a gallery opening, I just want to take better pictures of my kids.* Don't worry—the things that make a good photo, and the artistic and craft issues you face as a photographer are the same whether you're shooting your family or fine art shots.

Sometimes, of course, you just need to grab a quick shot to document something, and won't care too much about the "artistry" of the results. But with most any shot that you actually take time to work on, it's worth thinking about light, composition, and the other topics covered in this chapter.

Building a Shot

There are two different kinds of photographic subjects: those that you take, and those that you make. If you're standing near the Eiffel Tower just as the sun comes from behind a cloud to light up a beautiful supermodel who happens to be walking by, then there might be little that you have to do to get a good shot. That's simply a picture you can take.

Every so often, my grandmother goes to the portrait studio to, as she says, have her picture made. This idea of making a photo is kind of old-fashioned, but the concept of *making* an image is much closer to how good photographs often happen. No matter what the subject, effective photography involves making a lot of decisions and solving a lot of problems. You'll often have to shoot a lot of test frames as you experiment and try different ideas. Most of the time, good images are not taken; they are made from the raw material of your scene.

In the last section, we talked about how to recognize a shot. Shot recognition will happen in different ways, depending on the type of shooting you're doing. If you're working an event— a wedding or birthday party, for example—your recognition will probably come very quickly, as you move among the crowd looking for nice compositions, good moments, compelling expressions, and good light. If you're shooting on the street, you might happen upon split-second moments that require more reflex than thought.

But there might be other types of street shooting that require more consideration. Perhaps the light has fallen on a particular location in a beautiful way, and you want to try to take advantage of that light. Landscape shooting can be the same way: you spot the beautiful vista and then try to figure out what the picture is.

Depending on the pace and style of shooting, the way you decide to shoot will vary. Sometimes, you'll have to move quickly and shoot reflexively, while trying to keep one eye trained on your settings. At other times, you will have an impulse that a potential shot lies before you, but you'll have to spend time (and probably a lot of test shots) to work out what the image should be.

Often, I catch a glimpse of something out of the corner of my eye, and when I turn to look, I don't have the foggiest idea what it is that caught my attention. But once I raise the camera to my eye, I can see it. At other times, I'll shoot some frames and not feel like I got anything, but later when I'm back at my computer, I'll try some adjustments, and suddenly an idea for what the image is supposed to be will come to me. Your subconscious is often a good photographer in its own right, so when you get an impulse—any kind of impulse at all—you need to stop and examine it. The image won't always be obvious until you start trying to build a shot.

Learning to pay attention to these impulses takes practice because they don't always announce themselves very loudly. When you go out to shoot, you need to be present and you need to concentrate while you walk around, so that you can pick up on even the slightest photographic impulse. If you're talking to other people, or listening to music, or thinking that maybe you'll do a little window-shopping too, then you probably won't find many images. Photography is an active process.

Once you've identified a shot that you want to start building, you'll need to think about the following issues:

◆ **Shooting mode.** By now, you should be very comfortable with your camera's modes, and should have an understanding of what each one does. When you're ready to build a shot, you need to decide which mode is most appropriate. For many (or even most) shots, Program mode might be fine. Think about whether you'll want depth of field or motion-stopping control. If so, pick a mode that will facilitate the control you need. If your camera offers a Scene mode that's appropriate to your shot, you might want to try it.

Very often, the subject matter or style of shooting will dictate a mode immediately. For example, when shooting an event, you may walk into the room and realize the light is very low, and that you will need to choose a mode that allows you control of shutter speed, to guarantee sharper images. You'll probably stick with that mode for the duration of the shoot. Or perhaps you're off to shoot a social occasion with good lighting, and you decide to choose a mode that will allow control of aperture, so that you can opt to blur out the background behind people.

For some subjects, you may try several different modes as you work the shot and change your idea of what it should be. For example, you might start out in Program mode, and then realize later that to capture the image you want, you need more control.

◆ **White balance.** We've covered white balance extensively, so you should already know that when you move into any new lighting situation, you need to think about which white balance setting is required.

◆ **Metering.** While Matrix metering is good for most occasions, in some situations, you'll need to switch to a different meter to handle difficult lighting or to ensure that your subject is properly exposed. You may not know exactly what meter to use until you take a few shots.

Choosing a Camera Position and Focal Length

After you've spotted a scene and decided to try to make a photo out of it, you need to decide where to stand. You may think: *Where to stand? Don't I just shoot from where I spotted the scene? After all, that's where it came to my attention.* Most of the time, just because you were able to recognize a scene from a particular location doesn't mean you're standing in the best location to shoot that photo.

Obviously, standing closer or farther, or off to one side or the other, can make a big difference in your shot. But camera position also affects your choice of focal length, and focal length choice can have a huge impact on the sense of space in your scene.

Focal Length

The great thing about a zoom lens is that it provides tremendous flexibility when you frame a shot. Without changing your position, you can zoom in to a subject quickly to get a tighter view and a different framing. However, it's important to recognize that as you zoom, many things change in your image besides the field of view and magnification. A zoom lens is more than just a convenience. As you go from one focal length to another, you will alter the sense of space and depth in your composition, so focal length choice becomes another creative option at your disposal.

It's easy to think of your zoom lens as a big magnifying glass and, to a degree, it is. As you zoom in, your subject appears larger and larger. This is why digital camera manufacturers often label their lenses with a magnification factor 2×, 3×, and so forth. However, a few other things happen to your image when you zoom.

As you go to a longer focal length (zoom in), your field of view gets narrower. The human eye has a field of view of about 50° to 55°. This is considered a normal field of view, and any lens that produces a 50° to 55° viewing angle is said to be a normal lens.

More important, though, is to pay attention to the way your perception of the depth in your scene changes. Consider the images in Figure 9.11.

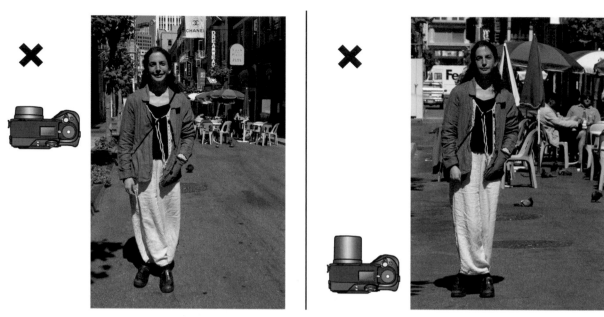

Figure 9.11 Although these two images are framed the same, notice how different the backgrounds are. In the left image, the camera was positioned close to the subject and zoomed out, whereas in the right image, the camera was pulled back and zoomed in. Note how much closer the background chairs appear in the telephoto (right) image. The sense of depth in the scene changes as you change camera position and corresponding focal length. In general, the entire sense of space differs in the two images, even though the subject didn't move.

In these two images, the subject remained in the same place, but I stood at different distances and used a different focal length to keep the images framed identically. Notice how much closer the tables and chairs look in the second image. As I moved back and zoomed in, the depth in the image became compressed, resulting in the background elements appearing closer. The result is an image that has a far more intimate sense of space than the first image, which has a very expansive sense of space.

As you can see, both field of view and the sense of space in an image are functions of the position of your camera and the focal length you choose to use. These two factors combine to create a very different sense of depth and space.

Controlling depth and perspective in your scene is yet another creative option you have available. Next time you're shooting a location, consider how you want to represent that space. Do you want it cramped and claustrophobic? Or deep and expansive? Choose your camera position and focal length accordingly.

Correcting a Mistaken Explanation

Photography textbooks for the last 150 years (including some previous editions of this book) have explained that as you change focal lengths, different parts of your image are magnified by different amounts. *This is not true!* For any given focal length, all elements of an image are magnified by the same amount. The change in perspective occurs because of your changing camera position and the field of view differences provided by different focal lengths. To see proof of this claim that all lenses magnify by equal amounts, take a look at the `Camera Position.pdf` movie, which you can download from the Chapter 9 section of the companion website at *www.completedigitalphotography.com/CDP8.*

Portrait Distortion

At some point, you've probably looked at a photograph of yourself and thought: *That doesn't really look like me.* One reason for the poor result might be that the photographer used a wide-angle lens. Shooting a portrait with a wide-angle lens can be problematic because of the weird perspective it provides. Check out the pictures in Figure 9.12. The image on the left was shot with a slightly telephoto lens and really does look like the actual person. The image on the right is not such a good likeness. The nose is too big, and the ears have been rendered too small. In addition, the distance between the nose and ears is too long. (Of course, although the picture on the right is less literally correct, it might be a better expression of the person's character. This is a creative, interpretive choice you get to make while shooting.)

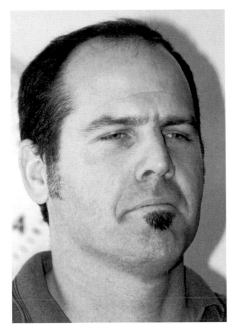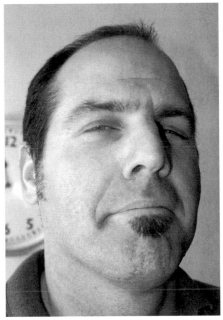

Figure 9.12

A change in focal length can make a huge difference in the appearance of your subject. The image on the left was shot with a long (telephoto) focal length. Next, I zoomed out to produce the oddly distorted image on the right. (As in the previous example, note how the depth in the telephoto image appears different. The clock over the man's shoulder appears much closer in the left image.)

Typically, portrait photographers use a slightly telephoto lens, which almost always yields a more flattering look. A slightly telephoto lens will guarantee that people's noses don't look too big, their faces aren't elongated, and their eyes won't bulge. Well, no more than normal.

Geometric Distortion

Most zoom lenses exhibit some form of barrel or pincushion distortion when zoomed to either of their extremes. With barrel distortion, horizontal and vertical images will bow outward. Pincushion distortion bows lines inward. These distortions will show up as curves and warps around the edges and corners of your image (see Figure 9.13).

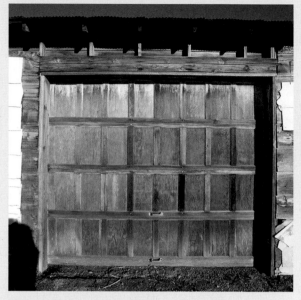

Figure 9.13

Wide-angle lenses often suffer from a bit of barrel distortion. Although it's slight in this image, note that the top of the garage door is curved, not perfectly straight.

When you find yourself at the limits of your zoom range, check the edges of your image to see if there's any distortion. If there is, and you can live with it, then by all means take the shot. If it bothers you, you might need to reposition your camera and select a new focal length. If the distortion isn't too bad, you might be able to remove it with your image editing software, as you'll see later.

Shooting Shallow Depth of Field

Making the decision to shoot with a shallow depth of field (to blur the background in your image) will dictate a few choices as you build up your shot.

The depth of field in your scene is dictated by three parameters: aperture size, the size of objects in the background of your image, and sensor size. Because larger apertures yield shallower depth of field, if you want to shoot with very shallow depth of field, you should choose a lower-numbered f-stop.

However, the only way that shallow depth of field is apparent is if there's something in the background that is noticeably soft and blurry. In other words, having larger, easier-to-see objects in the background will make your shallower depth of field more apparent. This means that you'll usually want to choose a longer focal length. As you've seen, shorter focal lengths make the background appear smaller and farther away (Figure 9.14).

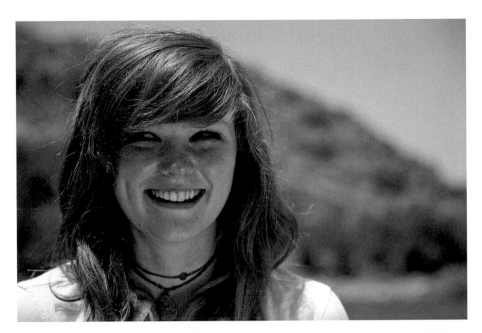

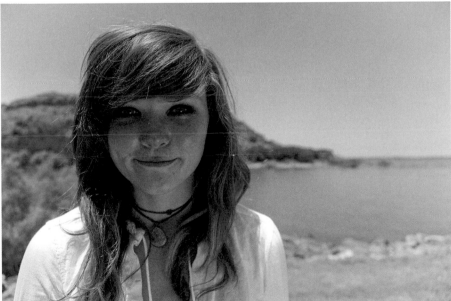

Figure 9.14

The depth of field in both of these images is exactly the same. However, the depth of field in the second image seems less shallow because of the wide-angle lens. The objects in the background are so small that you can't see that they're soft and blurry. So focal length choice and camera position are critical when trying to shoot shallow depth of field.

Depth of Field with Point-and-Shoot Cameras

If you have some experience with 35mm or larger formats, it is important to realize that because of the tiny sensors found on most point-and-shoot digital cameras (which are inherent to the small designs of those cameras), depth of field is much deeper than you might be used to. (Sensor size has a large bearing on depth of field, for optical reasons that are too complex to go into here.) On a typical point-and-shoot digital camera, the depth of field produced by an f5.6 aperture works out to be more like the depth of field produced by an f16 aperture on a 35mm camera. This is great news for users who want really deep depths of field. However, photographers who are used to being able to separate foregrounds from backgrounds using very shallow depths of field might be frustrated (see Figure 9.15).

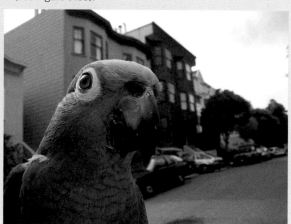

Figure 9.15

Most point-and-shoot digital cameras are not capable of capturing very shallow depth of field. Although this is great for maintaining sharp focus, you might be frustrated if you want to intentionally blur out the background. The slight blurring of the background in this image is about the most you can expect from a point-and-shoot digital camera.

Use an SLR for Very Shallow Depth of Field

If you want the option to shoot very shallow depth of field, then you'll want to shoot with an SLR. With their larger sensors, you can shoot shallower depth of field on an SLR than you can with a point-and-shoot, especially if you opt for a lens with a wide aperture and long focal length.

Focal Length Only Appears to Affect Depth of Field

There is a long-held, long-taught belief that longer focal lengths yield a shallower depth of field. This isn't true. Longer focal lengths yield an *apparently* shallower depth of field. You can learn more about this by reading `Focal Length and Depth of Field.pdf`, which you can download from the Chapter 9 section of the companion website, at *www.completedigitalphotography.com/CDP8* For all intents and purposes, though, when you want an image that appears to have shallower depth of field, use a longer focal length.

How Shallow Should You Go?

When you want to shoot with shallow depth of field, it's tempting to just crank your aperture open all the way, but this is not always the best choice. First, as depth of field gets shallower, your background becomes more blurred and abstract. You may not want to make your background completely unintelligible, so choose an aperture that gives you some blur, but not too much (see Figure 9.16).

Your other concern when shooting with shallow depth of field is focus. As depth of field gets shallower, focusing can become more difficult. For example, if you're shooting with a very wide aperture—1.8, for example—then your depth of field might be so shallow that if you focus on someone's nose, their eyes will be a little soft, as shown in Figure 9.17. When you shoot with extremely wide angles, know that accurate focusing becomes critical!

If you're in a situation and you need to shoot very quickly, you might not want to shoot with super shallow depth of field, simply because you'll have to take more time worrying about focus.

1.2

1.8

2.8

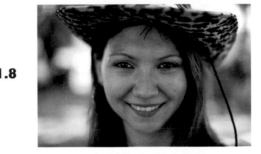
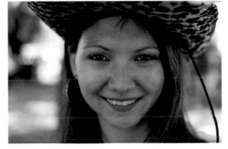

Figure 9.16

It's important to consider just how much you want to blur out the background when shooting with shallow depth of field. You may not want background details to go indistinguishably blurry. Note the difference in background blur with these three apertures.

It's a good idea to do some tests with your camera and shoot the same scene with different apertures, to get an idea of how much change happens from one aperture to another. At the wider end of your aperture range, you should see quite a change. Of course, if your lens doesn't offer a particularly wide aperture (f4, for example), then you won't be able to get super shallow depth of field. And, as mentioned earlier, if you're working with a point-and-shoot camera, you won't be able to attain very shallow depth of field because of the camera's small sensor size.

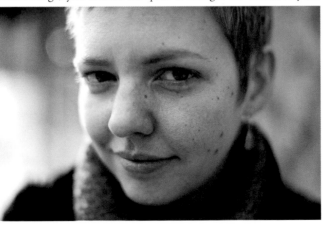

Figure 9.17

When shooting with extremely shallow depth of field, be very careful about focus. Here the subject's face was tilted slightly, leaving her right eye slightly farther away from the camera than her left.

Depth-of-Field Preview

If your SLR has a depth-of-field preview button (see Figure 9.18), you can use it to get an idea of the depth of field that will be provided by your current exposure settings. Until you press the shutter button, the iris in your lens is open as wide as it will go, regardless of the aperture choice you've made. This allows you to see a bright, clear view through the viewfinder, because as much light as possible can pass through the lens. When you press the shutter release to take a picture, the iris is closed down to your desired setting and then reopens to full wide after the picture is taken. Obviously, this all happens in a fraction of a second. This means that the viewfinder is always showing you the depth of field that you'll get with your lens' maximum aperture.

If you've chosen a small aperture, then the depth of field in your final image may be greater than what you see when you look through the viewfinder. If you press your depth-of-field preview button (after metering and setting your desired aperture), the aperture will close down and stay closed as long as you hold the button. This allows you to see the image through the actual aperture size that will be used when you take the shot. However, with the iris stopped down, your viewfinder will become much dimmer, which can make it hard to see your image at all, much less notice depth of field.

Give your eyes time to adjust to the dimmer viewfinder, and if need be, cover your other eye with your hand to give yourself as dark a viewing environment as possible. As your eyes adjust, you should be able to get a better sense of the depth of field in the image.

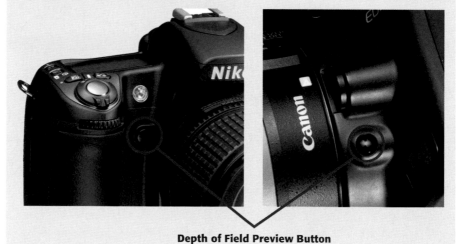

Depth of Field Preview Button

Figure 9.18 Most SLRs have a depth-of-field preview button, which shows the actual depth of field in your scene. Not all DOF preview controls are in these locations. Check your camera manual for details.

Composition

Just because something looks cool in real life, doesn't mean you can simply point a camera at it and get a good picture. Unlike the real world, a photograph is bounded by a frame. When looking at a photo, the viewer reads the contents of that frame to try to determine and understand what it is you're showing them. The simplest definition of composition is that it's the way you frame your scene, but good composition means much more than simply choosing a way to crop the world to fit into a rectangle.

Good composition is the process of arranging forms and tones in a way that is pleasing and guides the viewer's eye to bring attention to your subject. In a good composition, you will know precisely what the subject of the image is. In a bad composition, your eye will wander and search, and if pressed, you may not be able to identify the subject of the image. Good composition can also reveal things in the scene that viewers might not notice on their own— repetitive patterns, a play of light and shadow, or even a feeling about the particular moment you're photographing.

Earlier, you looked at some simple composition rules—fill the frame, lead your subject, and don't be afraid to get in tight. These guidelines can greatly improve your snapshots, and are relevant to all kinds of shooting. But composition is a complex topic that you will continue to study for the rest of your photographic career. It's also something that cannot be broken down into rules, or a recipe, or a step-by-step process. People with good composition skills can often feel their way through the process of composing a photo. At other times, they might need to start with one or two specific compositional ideas.

In this chapter, we're going to explore some of these compositional ideas. But to get your compositional skills to the point where you can "feel" your way through the process, you need to practice, so I'll also be outlining a specific practice regimen designed to get composition "into your bones."

Four Things All Good Compositions Have

Not every image will have all of the compositional ideas that we will discuss here. But all good compositions *will* have these four things: a subject and background, a sense of balance, a point of view, and simplicity.

A Subject and Background

This may sound simple, but it's one of the most oft-violated compositional rules. A photo needs a foreground and a background. Or, to put it another way, a subject and a background. What's more, the relationship between those two things is very important.

In Chapter 2, "Getting to Know Your Camera," you learned about the idea of filling the frame. Choosing what to fill the frame with is an important part of good composition. For example, Figure 9.19 shows a person standing in front of the Golden Gate Bridge.

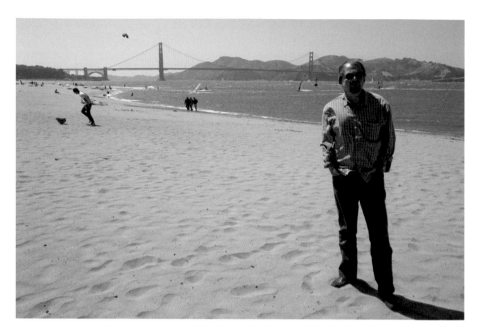

While I've filled the entire frame, and though you can see the bridge and the man's whole body, the image still doesn't really have a strong subject. In fact, the bridge is as much the subject as the guy, who serves little purpose other than to provide a sense of scale.

A better composition would be to go in tighter, as in Figure 9.20.

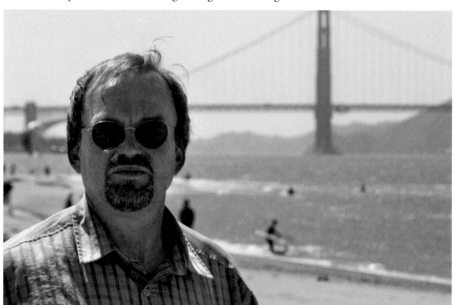

Here I've filled the frame with more of the person, and you know now that he is definitely the subject of the image. Yes, I've had to crop the bridge, but the image still plainly conveys the person in his environment. If you want a picture of the bridge, that's a different subject and a different photo, and you probably don't need a person at all.

In most cases, it's safe to say that you shouldn't try to take a single picture that encompasses everything in a scene. Sometimes, all you end up with is a picture with no discernible subject or purpose.

There will be times when you'll come across a beautiful or compelling vista that will be strong enough to stand on its own as a subject. You'll still need to think about framing and composition, and will want to go over the rules we've discussed, but you won't have a definite foreground and background (see Figure 9.21).

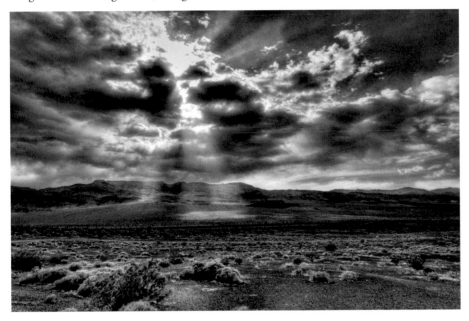

Figure 9.21

Sometimes, especially with landscapes, you won't have a definite foreground and background. In this image, the background itself is strong enough to act as a subject.

At other times, you might find a compelling vista, but not be able to find a composition that feels right. This might be because the scene lacks a subject, and your eye doesn't really know how to read the image. If you can find something to use as a subject, you'll probably find it's easier to compose a shot (see Figure 9.22).

Patience is often the most important photographic tool at your disposal. If you find a nice background, wait and see if someone walks into it to complete the composition or to serve as a subject.

If nothing in the scene changes, then change your vantage point to find something that can serve as a subject (see Figure 9.23).

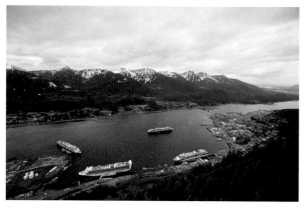
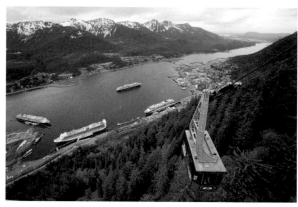

Figure 9.22 On the left is an interesting locale, but it's not an interesting picture because your eye doesn't really know what to do—there's no subject. But, after waiting a minute or so, the funicular came into view. It provides a subject, as well as some balance, and a sense of scale.

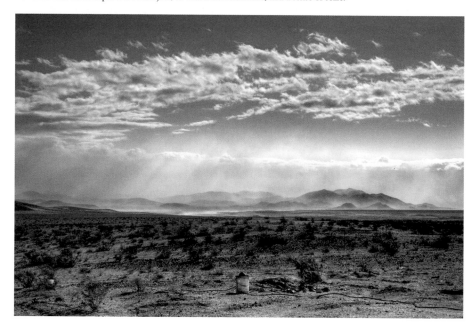

Figure 9.23

This sandstorm was interesting, but even finding a simple mundane subject, like this bucket that was sitting out in the desert, made for a more compelling image.

A Sense of Balance

Elements in your shot have different weights. A heavy element on one side of the frame might need to be balanced by an element on the opposite side of the frame. For example, in Figure 9.24, the two large birds on the left are balanced by the smaller bird on the right. The smaller bird manages to create balance because it is positioned in the lower-right corner. This shifts the center of balance to a different place in the image, just as a real weight would.

If I remove the right-hand bird from the image, as shown in Figure 9.25, the picture falls out of balance. Now the two left-hand birds are simply positioned oddly in the frame, flying out of the picture with a big empty space behind them.

Placing something in the dead center of the frame can also create a balance, as shown in Figure 9.26. In this case, center framing works fairly well because of the hills on either side that guide the viewer's attention to the middle of the frame.

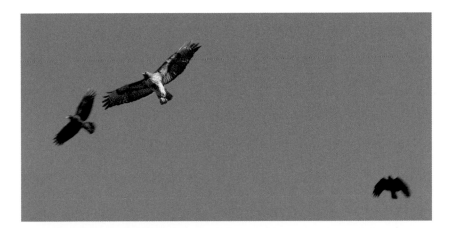

Figure 9.24

The elements in this image are positioned in a balanced way in the frame. Each has a weight that balances the other.

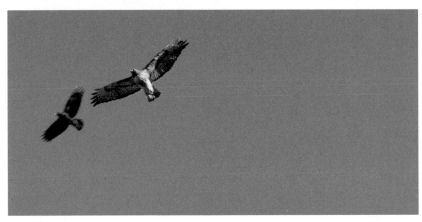

Figure 9.25

If I remove the bird on the right side, the image is no longer balanced—the left side is too heavy.

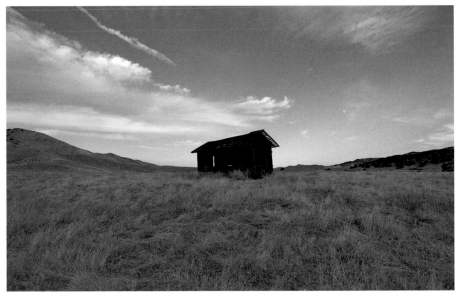

Figure 9.26

Balance can even be created by placing an element in the center of the image. Here the sloping hills on either side serve to create an even balance.

Compositional balance can be tricky because you don't have to have elements of equal size to create balance. Just as a small piece of lead on a scale can balance a tremendous number of marshmallows, some small graphic elements can balance elements that are much larger. This is almost always the case with people. We put a lot of import on people, and a single person in a frame can balance a huge amount of other compositional elements (see Figure 9.27).

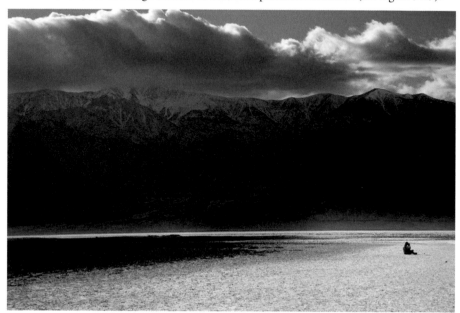

Figure 9.27

People carry a lot of compositional weight. Even a small person can balance a very large element.

Sometimes, empty space can create a balance, as in Figure 9.28.

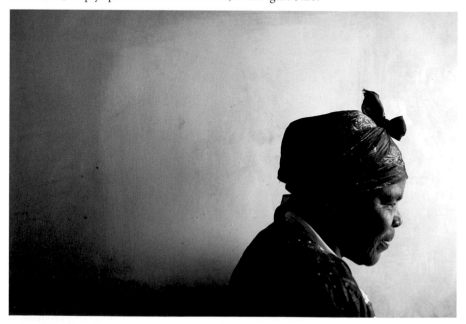

Figure 9.28

Empty space can sometimes be used as a balancing element.

Figure 9.28 is also a good example of breaking a rule, because I'm plainly ignoring the "lead your subject" rule that we talked about in Chapter 2. In this image, though, it works. The woman's pensive, reflective expression makes the empty space behind her more powerful. That space is evocative of emotional weight that is bearing down on her. It also might evoke the weight of her past. Graphically, the mostly empty space on the left balances out her presence on the right.

Finally, balance is not created just with geometry. You can also balance tones against each other. For example, in Figure 9.29, the dark tones on the left side of the image are balanced by the light tones on the right side. The bicyclist on the right side of the image also adds some additional weight.

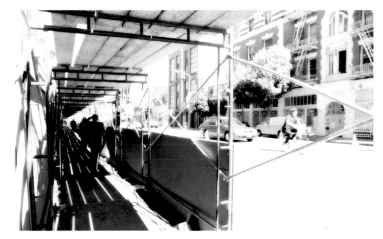

Figure 9.29

You can also create balance tonally by balancing light tones against dark tones. Here, the dark left of the frame is balanced by the lighter right half of the frame.

A Point of View

All images have to be shot from somewhere, and where you choose to shoot from determines the point of view of your final image. Unfortunately, it's very easy to shoot all of your images from the same point of view. That is, a point usually somewhere between 5 and 6 feet above the ground. But this default point of view—the one that you spend all day looking from—is not always the best point of view for creating a dramatic, compelling image.

Consider the light switch shown in Figure 9.30.

Because of my point of view choice, it's difficult to tell what the subject of this image is, and it's generally boring. But with a simple point-of-view change, I can create a much more interesting picture (Figure 9.31).

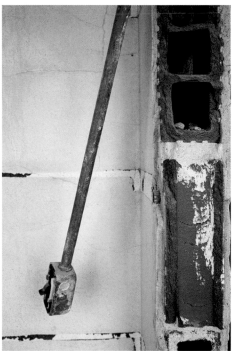

Figure 9.30

This bent light switch caught my attention, but shooting it from my normal point of view—which happens to be the exact point of view of how I saw it—doesn't produce a very compelling image.

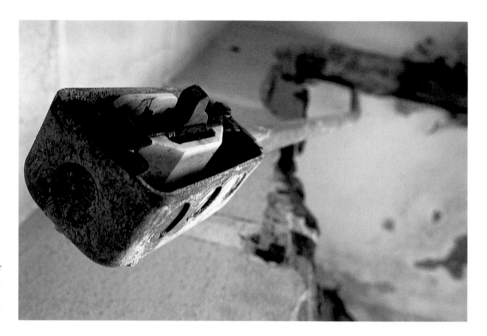

Figure 9.31

By changing my point of view and getting under the light switch and shooting up, I can create a much more interesting image.

Point of view changes don't always have to be as dramatic as this example. Sometimes, just taking a step or two in one direction or another can create a change in point of view that yields a better image. As you can see in Figure 9.31, I didn't just change location, I also changed altitude, bending down low and pointing upward.

In most circumstances, good shooting means lots of movement. After recognizing a subject, you should be moving around it, above it, below it, trying to find the point of view that yields the best image. This is something to check from time to time as you're shooting. If you realize that you're not moving very much, then you need to think more about point of view.

Simplicity

There are so many ways that the world can be annoying, but for photographers, one of the biggest is that there's just too much extra stuff in the world.

Painters have it easy because they start with nothing and add only the things they want in their scene. Photographers, though, have to figure out how to compose with (or in spite of) power lines, street signs, parked cars, people who walk into a shot, moving cars, trees that have one branch that's pointing in the wrong direction, and so on and so forth.

One of your most difficult compositional tasks is to reduce the clutter in a scene so that the viewer is not confused about what to look at, and so that his or her eye finds its way through the image to your subject.

If you work to fill the frame, you'll have a head start on reducing the clutter in your scene. One of the easiest things to try when you're looking for the right composition is simply to get in closer (Figure 9.32).

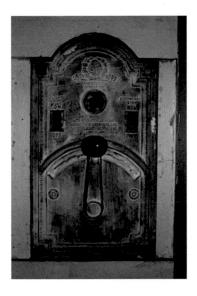

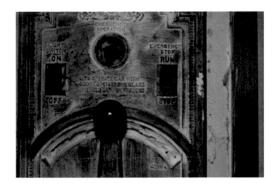

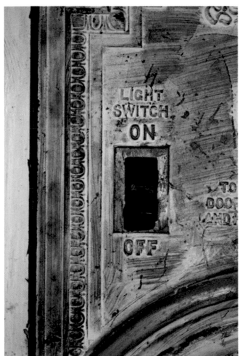

Figure 9.32

While the whole panel from this old elevator is interesting in person, the more interesting photo is to get in close and focus on a single detail.

It's very rare that you won't get a better picture by moving closer to your subject (see Figure 9.33). This is often the easiest way to simplify your composition and remove unwanted elements.

When you're in a crowded area, getting closer often means separating yourself from the crowd and moving toward a scene. This can make you feel like everyone is looking at you, but in reality, they probably aren't. These days, everyone is used to seeing people with cameras. More importantly, though, so what? They notice you for a few moments and then go on with their day, while you go home with an interesting photo.

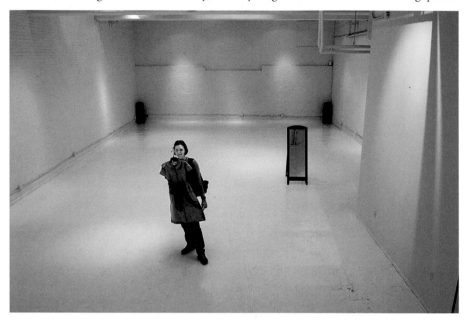

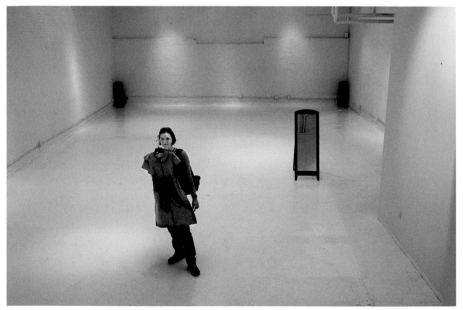

Figure 9.33

Even though the upper image looks very clean, there's still a lot of extra stuff in the scene. Cropping in tighter creates a simpler image that emphasizes the relationship of the elements in the composition.

Don't Be Afraid to Put Things in the Middle

A lot of people think that if they put their subject in the middle of the frame, they're shooting an uncreative, boring picture. While worrying about the rule of thirds, balance, and all of these other concepts, it's easy to forget that, sometimes, the best composition is to leave your subject in the dead center of the frame (Figure 9.34). It is possible to get too creative, so don't forget the value of simple composition.

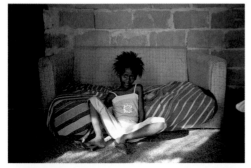

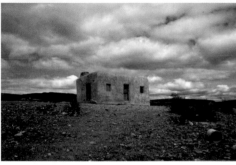

Figure 9.34

Often, the best composition is the simple composition place your subject in the middle and trust that they can carry the scene.

Examining Images for the Four Things

It's worth spending some time with images you've already shot, or images from your favorite photographers, and analyzing them for these four things. Look for balance, and take note of how it was created. Is the subject clearly defined? And if so, how did the photographer make you see the subject? Is there anything extra in the image? And is the point of view one you would have thought of? Looking at images this way can help you begin to develop the habit of looking at scenes in the real world this way, and that will translate into better compositions.

Point: A Compositional Exercise

To improve your composition skills, you need to expand your compositional vocabulary. The more compositional ideas that you have experience with, the more likely you'll be to be able to find a good composition for any particular scene. As you explore more compositional ideas, you'll possibly find more subject matter. Very often, an image begins, not because you've spotted something especially interesting, but because you've recognized the compositional potential of the scene.

Composition is often a very formal exercise: you simply arrange lines and shapes in a way that is simple, balanced, and pleasing. However, what the actual lines and shapes are made from—people, buildings, rocks—may not matter. In other words, good composition often stems entirely from geometry. Geometry, in turn, begins with a simple point. Go spend some time shooting, and build images around the simple geometric idea of the point (see Figure 9.35).

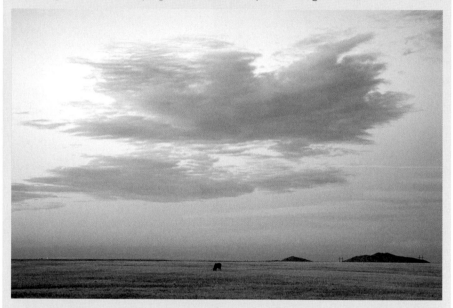

Figure 9.35 A point is simply a single, discrete object in your scene. It doesn't have to be round, and it doesn't even have to be especially small in the frame.

Other Compositional Ideas

There are many other compositional ideas that you can build images around. Here are examples of a few of them: repetition, rule of thirds, leading lines, and light and dark.

Repetition

Repeating patterns are often very interesting, like the repeating pattern of the fence you saw in Figure 9.2. Figure 9.36 shows another image with some simple repetition.

Repetition can create a sense of visual rhythm in a scene, and that rhythm can be satisfying and a way to guide the viewer's eye to your subject.

Related to repetition is the rule of threes. Obviously, a single object has no repetition, while two objects aren't enough to imply a repeating pattern. Four or more is sometimes too much complexity. (Remember, you want to keep your images simple.) Three, therefore, is often a good sweet spot for repetition. It's enough to establish a rhythm, but not so much that the image becomes complicated (see Figure 9.37).

Very often, if you find three things, you've got the makings of an image. Explore the scene and see what you can work up. Note that the rule of three is not to be confused with the rule of thirds.

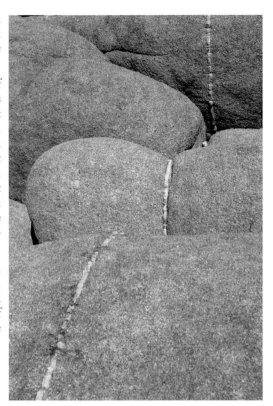

Figure 9.36

Repeating forms—geometric or tonal—are often interesting, and make for good composition.

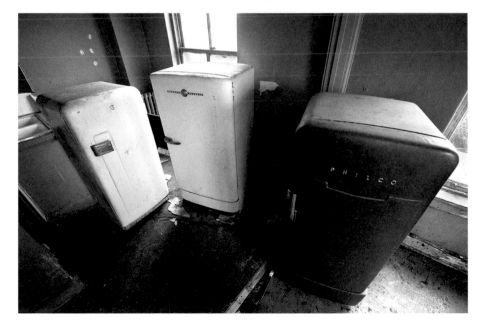

Figure 9.37

Most any group of three objects yields image potential. Three is a good number for establishing rhythm, without overcomplicating your image.

The Rule of Thirds

You can often achieve good composition by dividing your image into thirds and placing elements on your scene at the intersection of any of the grid lines. In Figure 9.38, the geometric components of the scene have been placed accordingly.

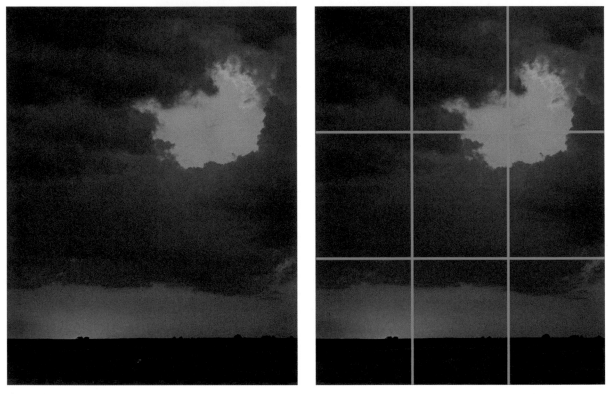

Figure 9.38 To employ the rule of thirds, you divide your image into equal thirds and try to place elements close to the intersections of the divisions.

Lines: A Compositional Exercise

String enough points together, and you have a line. Strong lines often make for good composition, especially strong diagonal lines. Figure 9.39 is a prime example of this, with the rock included to break up the repetition and to provide a focus for the eye. (Note too, that it's mostly placed according to the rule of thirds.)

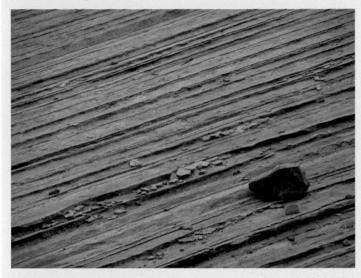

Figure 9.39

Strong lines make good compositional elements. This image obviously also has strong repetition.

It doesn't matter what creates the line. In the case of Figure 9.40, I have some lines created from pavement and other lines created from shadows (and on the pavement are lines created with paint).

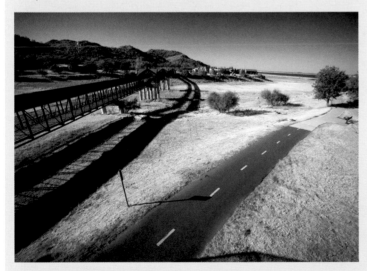

Figure 9.40

Line and geometric elements don't have to be overly pronounced or literal. This image has a strong sense of diagonal lines.

Curvy lines are often interesting, such as the path shown in Figure 9.41. This image also features a tonal balance. By placing the dark path more to the right, the darker tones of the path are balanced with the larger bright area to the left.

(continues)

Lines: A Compositional Exercise (continued)

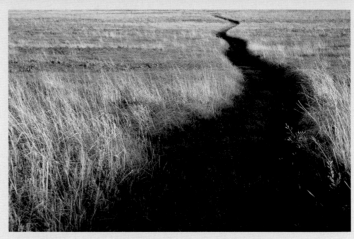

Figure 9.41

Strong curvy lines also make effective compositional images.

Take some time to go shoot with the idea of building compositions around lines.

Why Are So Many of These Examples in Black and White?

You may have noticed that a lot of these composition examples are in black and white. With color removed, pure composition becomes much easier to see and study. For your own composition exercises, you might consider working in black and white. Without the distraction of color, you might have an easier time focusing on pure geometry.

Leading Lines

Lines aren't just used as interesting subject matter; they can also serve to guide the viewer's eye around your frame. In Figure 9.42, the diagonal shadows along with the curving tire tracks serve to guide the eye directly into the trees.

Remember, the point of composition is to organize your frame in such a way that the viewer immediately understands what the subject is. Leading lines are a great way to make the organization of your image clearer.

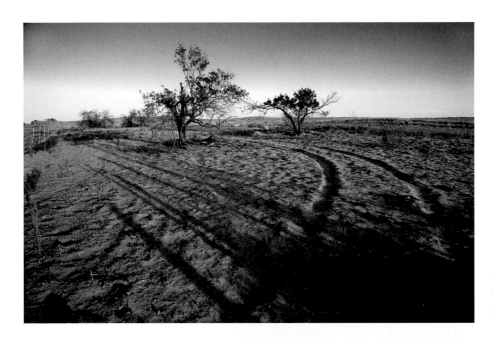

Figure 9.42

The strong lines in this image guide the viewer's eye directly into the trees.

Light and Dark

In Figure 9.29, you saw an example of an image that was balanced on one side by a dark area and on the right by a light area. You'll often build compositions out of light and dark, not just out of geometry.

Light is the raw material of photography, so pay attention to light and dark elements within an image, as they can make great compositional elements.

Remember, too, that a completely black shadow is sometimes just what an image needs. You don't always need to see detail everywhere in an image, and choosing what to show and what to hide is part of what makes a composition compelling and an image easier to read (see Figure 9.43).

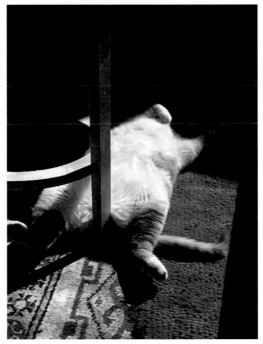

Figure 9.43

You don't have to see detail in every part of an image. Letting some parts go out to complete black often helps bring more attention to your subject.

Shapes: A Compositional Exercise

Points become lines, and lines can be built into shapes. Geometric patterns are also very compelling (and often include an element of repetition). Figure 9.44 is composed around a number of interlocking and overlapping triangles.

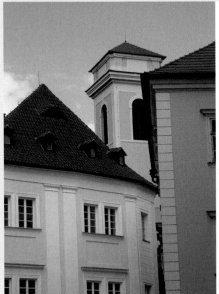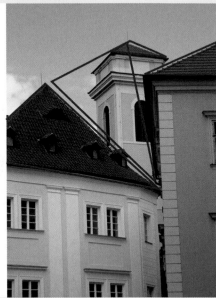

Figure 9.44 Geometric patterns, in this case triangles, are often compositionally interesting and usually have an element of repetition.

You don't have to have regular geometric shapes, as you can see in Figure 9.45. Neither do you have to have single, discreet shapes. You can combine elements in your scene to define entirely new shapes to compose around, as shown in Figure 9.45.

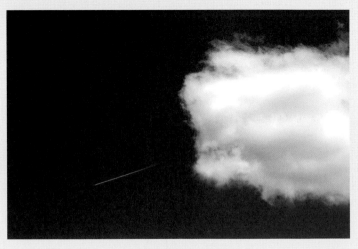

Figure 9.45

This big, puffy cloud is an easy shape to compose around, even though it's not a "regular" piece of geometry.

How a Good Composition Is Made

Typically, you'll craft an image in one of two ways: You'll see an interesting thing and figure out how to compose it, or you'll recognize a compositional idea—lines, points, repetition, etc.—and work to see if there's actually an interesting image that can be built around that idea.

Sometimes, as you look through the viewfinder, you'll simply feel the composition as you move around, change focal length, and consider depth of field. If you practice these ideas a lot, you'll find yourself able to "feel" your way through a composition more often.

At other times, you might not have any idea of how to compose your shot. In those instances, you might need to think your way through the composition. Start by thinking about camera position and focal length; then look through the lens to see how the sense of depth and space in the scene changes as you change position and focal length. Next start thinking about subject and background, and about geometry, pattern, repetition, and the rule of thirds. These can serve as guidelines as you explore the scene through your camera lens.

Exercise: Composition at Home

One of the great things about composition is that you can often correct it after the fact. The Crop tool in your image editor gives you the capability to recompose and change the balance of your images. Ideally, you want to get your composition as right as possible inside your camera, to save postproduction time and to maximize the use of your image sensor. But there will be times when cropping is the only way to get the shot you want.

Cropping is also a great way to practice composition. Print the `Cropping Tutorial.pdf` document, which you can find in the Chapter 9 section of the companion website at *www.completedigital photography.com/CDP8*. On it, you will find a collection of pictures shot by some vacationing tourists. With a pen, mark the image with a new crop. If you don't think it needs a crop, leave it alone. When you're finished, watch the `Cropping Tutorial.mov` to see how I recropped the images.

Four Practices for Better Shooting

While practicing how to see may seem abstract, it is something you can work at and improve. You will continue to explore and refine your composition skills for the rest of your life as a photographer. To help you along, there are some practices you can employ to improve the quality of your images.

Seeing *in* the Camera, Not *Through* the Camera

The brain has an amazing ability to focus your attention on something within your field of view. So much so, that it becomes very easy *not* to notice all the other things that are in your field of view.

For example, while walking downtown in San Francisco one day, I spotted the scene shown in Figure 9.46.

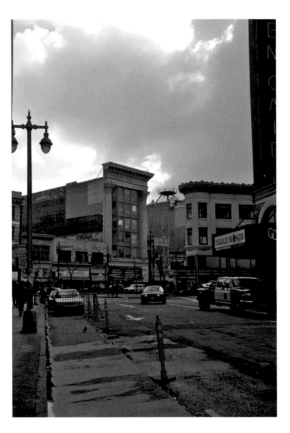

Figure 9.46

While walking down the street in San Francisco one day, I came across this scene.

It may not look like much in the picture because, well, it's not. There's no real composition, and no clear subject. Mostly, it looks like a photo of an empty parking space. Granted, this is often a pho-to-worthy event in San Francisco, but while standing at the scene, what struck me was the building with the tall facade in the distance. I found it compelling for some reason, and then noticed that the strong, rectangular shape of that building was balanced by the round turret of the building across the street.

In other words, my attention was focused on a very small part of my field of view, and I completely ignored all the clutter around it. Holding a camera up to my face didn't change this perception—my brain continued to focus my attention on one small part of what was in the frame, even though the framing included all that extra, un-necessary stuff. When shooting, it's very important to pay attention to the entire image that is being shown in the viewfinder, not just the small part that your brain might be paying attention to. This is a return to the idea of making an effort to fill the frame with your subject. Here, my frame is filled with far more than my subject.

The best way to guard against this is to trace your eyes around the edge of the frame before you press the shutter button. This will make you pay attention to other elements in your shot, and will also help you notice any strange intersections in your composition, such as telephone poles sticking out of people's heads and that sort of thing.

Work the Subject

Earlier, we discussed point of view, and how you need to move a lot to find the best point of view for a particular shot. Working the shot—shooting lots of coverage of a subject—is a critical part of getting a good image.

To carry on from the previous example, after coming across the scene I described earlier, I zoomed in and started to take some pictures of the two buildings I had spotted. I shot several different frames from slightly varying distance, some with cars passing in front and some without. You can see a few of the results in Figure 9.47.

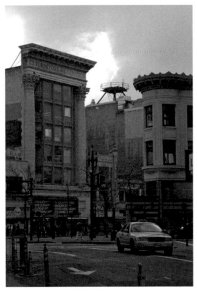 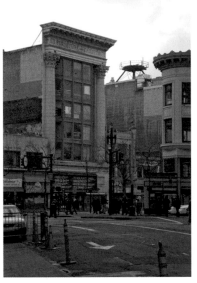 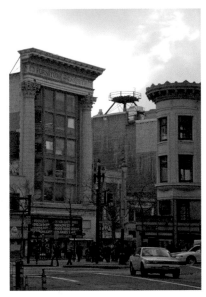

Figure 9.47 To attack this scene, I tried a number of different shots from slightly different positions, with slightly different framings, with and without cars.

One of the great advantages of digital photography, of course, is that you can see your compositions right away by looking at the LCD screen on the back of the camera. A quick check of my shot showed me something I was having trouble seeing through the viewfinder: The two buildings were too far apart to reveal the contrasting geometries that had struck me when I first saw the scene. This, again, is an example of my brain focusing my attention on something in the scene that wasn't actually being captured by my composition.

So I moved across the street and tried a few more frames, and finally ended up with a composition I liked, the one in Figure 9.48. I was visualizing the scene in black and white, so I chose an exposure that would allow me to render the final image in a particular way. We'll look at that process in Chapter 19, "Black-and-White Conversion."

It would have been easy to stop after the first few frames and conclude that there wasn't a good picture to be had there. I only came away with a keeper because I worked the shot. Move around, shoot from different angles, get closer, get farther, stand on your toes, get down on your knees, try different focal lengths.

Figure 9.49 shows another example, a series of images of the great jazz drummer Jack DeJohnette. This scene had to be worked for quite a while to find a combination of interesting composition, good facial expression, and dynamic movement. The smeary effect was creating using a Lensbaby, a cool SLR attachment you can learn more about at *www.lensbabies.com*.

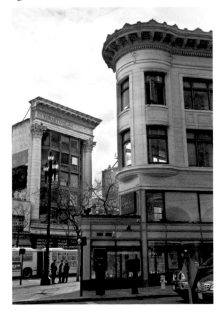

Figure 9.48

To get the scene I wanted, I finally had to move across the street and try a few more shots and angles.

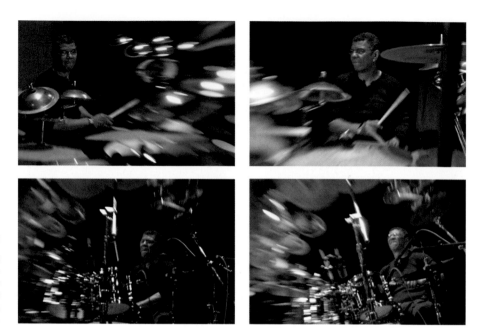

Figure 9.49

It took a number of experiments with composition and camera position, and a lot of frames containing different positions and facial expressions, to get a shot I liked.

Many people think that professional photographers go out, shoot 30 frames, and return home with 30 great shots. They don't. They work their shot, trying different angles, exposures, and ideas. Very often, they don't know which idea is best until they get home and look at their images. The more you work your shot, the more choices you'll have when you get to postproduction.

Find a Narrative

Narrative is the process of telling a story. Narrative is a fairly simple thing to understand when you're writing or shooting video because there's a temporal component that you can control. Consequently, it's possible to convey a series of events that have a beginning, middle, and end. In photography, narrative can be a little more ephemeral.

Obviously, you can shoot multiple images to create a diptych or triptych that tells a straight-forward story. But a single frame can also have a narrative. An image of a small child next to a broken vase tells a definite story of something that has just transpired. The image in Figure 9.50 also conveys a narrative, the promise of a big concert.

When trying to construct a photographic narrative, it's important to think about what information is required to tell your story. For example, this image in Figure 9.51 from the same shoot simply shows clarinet player Don Byron. Unlike the previous picture, this image doesn't have a lot of definite narrative. You don't know where he is, if he's playing with anyone else, whether he's preparing to play, or finishing.

As you've learned, the viewer will project a lot of information into a scene. An empty, lit concert hall implies rehearsal, which probably means daytime, which means there's going to be a show happening in the future. As a photographer, you can use the viewers' automatic projections to build a story, as long as you give them enough clues to point them in the right direction.

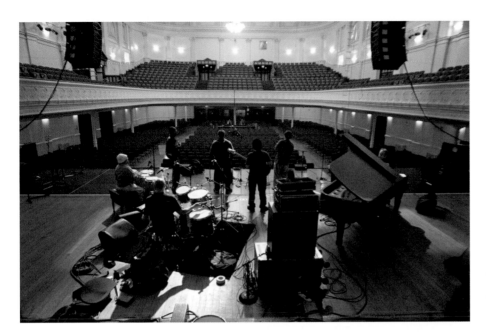

Figure 9.50

Although just a single frame, this image tells the story of an impending event.

However, don't expect that every single image can convey an entire narrative. If you try this, you'll be more prone to wide shots that lack an obvious subject. Sometimes, you can get a narrative shot, while at other times, you'll have to rely on good single images that build up to a narrative. At still other times, narrative is simply not an issue. Some scenes are purely attractive for their visual qualities, not their narrative ones.

Don't Be Afraid

It may sound strange to talk about fear when speaking of shooting photos. After all, unless you're shooting in particularly harrowing conditions, there's no real risk involved in photography. Nevertheless, most people still employ risk management behavior while shooting. To get good images, you

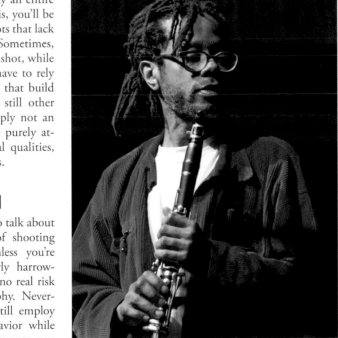

Figure 9.51

This figure doesn't convey quite as much narrative because you can't tell the location, the nature of the event, whether he's finished playing, or going to play, and so on.

have to have the courage to try something new, to experiment, and to consider compositions and ideas you might not have shot before.

Why are people afraid to try new shots? Sometimes, it's because they're in public and are afraid of looking stupid. Don't worry about this. Most people in public are so busy worrying about whether *they* look stupid that they don't have time to notice what you may or may not be doing with your camera.

More often, the fear of trying new shots is the fear of coming home to find that you shot bad photos. This is an awful feeling because it usually makes you question if you have any photographic skill. When you work a subject, as described in the previous section, you will get a lot of unusable images, possibly some stupid ones, and maybe even some bad ones. And none of that has any relationship to your skill as a photographer. Working a subject is just like sketching, and just as not every line in a sketch is the correct line, not every photo you take is the correct photo, but like the lines in a sketch, your incorrect photos serve to help you zone in on the keeper shot. Painters don't worry about what their sketches say about their painting skill. Similarly, you shouldn't worry about what your "sketch" photos say about your photography skill.

Of course, sometimes the idea that you're working simply doesn't yield a good photo, no matter how you shoot it. You simply have to accept that this is just how the creative process works: Sometimes you hit it, and sometimes you don't. The times you don't are no reflection on whether you're a good photographer or bad.

The fear of coming home with bad photos will often lead you to stay in a photographic comfort zone. When shooting in your comfort zone, you'll take the same kinds of shots that you've been pleased with in the past. The problem with staying in your comfort zone is that you'll eventually get bored with it and begin to feel like you can only shoot one type of photo. This will lead you right back to thinking you have no photographic skill.

If you find yourself shooting the same types of images, or always composing the same way, then make a deal with yourself: Go ahead and shoot that image that you're comfortable with, and then force yourself to try some different compositions. Get in closer, use a different focal length, try a different angle. This way, you'll still come home with an image that works, while your experimentation might teach you something new and help to expand your zone of comfort.

You won't get that keeper image if you don't have the nerve to try some new ideas. So shoot a little extra—shoot on impulse and take chances. After all, you can always delete them later.

Equipment Doesn't Matter (Usually)

Photography gear is so cool and so much fun that it can be very easy to think that buying more of it will make you a better photographer. It won't. Don't get me wrong: Some cameras take images that are much sharper and possess much more vibrant color than other cameras. For certain types of work, these technical specifications are imperative. But still, you can take a good picture with any camera. For example, Figure 9.52 shows a three-image panorama that was shot with an old 640×480, first-generation digital camera.

It was not possible to take a razor-sharp, finely detailed image with that camera, but that didn't mean it wasn't possible to shoot other types of images that worked fine. If your gear has weaknesses, it might be possible to exploit them.

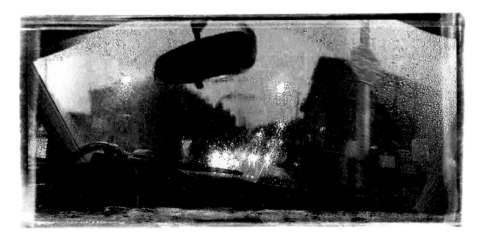

Figure 9.52

It's possible to take good images with any type of camera. Don't fall back on the excuse that you just need better gear to be a better photographer.

If you are editing an image and find a technical flaw you feel truly compromises the image—maybe the edges are soft, or the high-contrast areas suffer from distracting color fringes—and this flaw continues to plague you in more and more shots, then you might want to invest in some different gear. Or, if you find that what would have made the image great is if you'd been able to shoot with a wider angle or shallower depth of field, then expanding your toolbox might be a reasonable idea. But if you think that any one piece of gear is going to make you take more interesting photos, you're wrong. Henri Cartier-Bresson, arguably the most influential photographer of the 20th century, shot most of his images with a 35mm camera with a fixed 50mm lens. No autofocus, no auto metering, no auto winding, and only one focal length. The cheapest, decent digital point-and-shoot offers more features and flexibility, and often better image quality, than what he used.

If you want to take better pictures, spend your time worrying about light and seeing, not gear envy.

Combining Art and Craft

When you practice the creative process we've looked at in this chapter, you will employ the technical concepts that were covered in previous chapters.

For example, you might be working a scene—moving in, getting close, doing all that good stuff we've talked about—when you find a focal length and camera position that creates a wonderful sense of space, and that allows a composition that is balanced, with a nice subject/background relationship. At that point, you might realize that all it needs is a softer background to highlight the subject just a little more. So you might choose to go to a wider aperture using Program Shift. You'll look for an exposure combination that has a smaller aperture number, and then activate your camera's depth of field preview to check it out.

But maybe then you'll realize that your composition's balance is based on the left side of the frame being in shadow, and the shadow isn't quite dark enough. So you dial in a 1/3rd-stop underexposure using your Exposure Compensation control to darken the shadows.

You shoot the shot and then review the image to check out both the composition and the histogram, which will give you an idea of how well your exposure choice worked. In this way, your technical knowledge is combining with your artistic choices as you build your final shot.

10

LIGHTING

The Process of Controlling Light

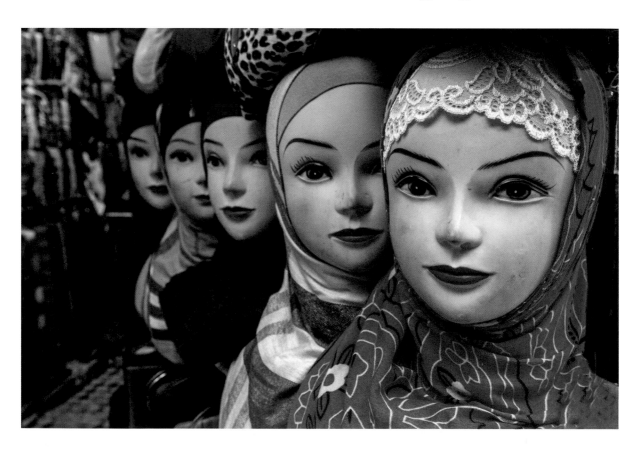

In an ideal world, the light would always be perfect. Shadows wouldn't be too harsh, but your subject would still have enough light on it to show contour and texture; your image would be filled with an appropriate warm (or cool, depending on your need) glow; and all of this light would be constant and last for hours, giving you plenty of time to get your shot.

Of course, it's not an ideal world, which means that very often you'll find wonderful subject matter, but it just won't be worth shooting due to bad, flat, or boring light. While there's not much you can do but wait and hope when you're shooting landscapes under bad lighting, if you're shooting portraits or still lifes, you have a tremendous number of options that allow you to craft the light exactly the way you want it.

In this chapter, we're going to look at a few different options for lighting portraits. If you think that lighting is beyond your skill, budget, or interest, take a look at some of these techniques. You may be surprised to find that with just a few dollars and some simple tools, you can greatly improve your portrait shots.

Controlling Available Light

Your camera might have a built-in flash or a hot shoe for connecting an external flash (or multiple flashes). Later in this chapter, we'll look closer at electronic flashes, but it's very important to understand that you can often achieve all of the lighting control you need by simply working with available light and simple reflectors and diffusers.

It's hard to beat the sun as a light source. It's bright, it's there half the time, it produces a strong even light, and it's a great color that both your eyes and camera are well adapted to. The problem with sunlight is that there are times when there's too much of it. When shooting in bright sunlight, one of your biggest problems will be to reduce the amount of light hitting your subject.

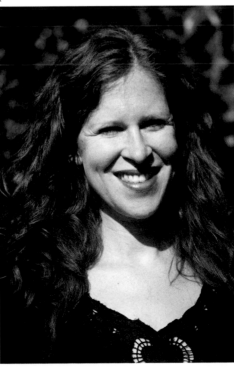

For portraits, too much contrast is not flattering. Strong light, like what you get from the sun on a clear day, produces dark shadows under eyes, makes lines and wrinkles more pronounced, and can cause skin texture to appear exaggerated.

Figure 10.1 shows a portrait shot in direct sunlight. Overall, the image is too "contrasty." Notice the strong shadow under the subject's chin and how her eye sockets are dropping into shadow (and the bright sun is making her squint). Her nose and cheekbones are also making harsh shadows.

Figure 10.1

This image, shot in direct sunlight, is too contrasty. The dark shadows created by the intense light are unflattering and distracting.

What we really needed (both to improve the lighting and because it was 103°F) was for a cloud to pass over the sun to cut the intensity of the light. Since no clouds were in sight, we employed a diffuser.

Diffusers are simply large pieces of white cloth that serve to diffuse light, casting a very soft shadow. Diffusers come in many varieties. The best diffusers are round ones that collapse easily to become portable. Photoflex (*www.photoflex.com*) makes diffusers in many different sizes and colors, but you can find similar reflectors from a number of other vendors, such as Calumet Photo (*www.calumetphoto.com*).

To use a diffuser to attack our high contrast problem, we simply held it above our subject to cast a shadow onto her face (see Figure 10.2).

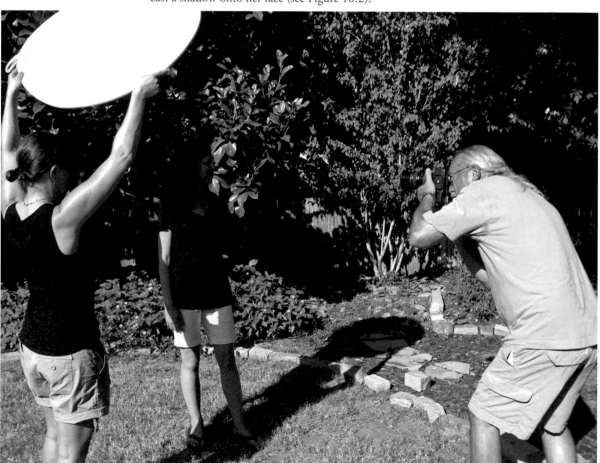

Figure 10.2 To reduce the contrast on our model, we held a diffuser above her to cast a soft shadow onto her face.

With our "cloud" in place, the harsh shadows on our model's face were greatly reduced, making for a more flattering light (see Figure 10.3).

Our work is not finished, though. While the shadows are softer, the left side of her face is a little darker than the right. We can eliminate these shadows by using a reflector to bounce some light up into her face, as shown in Figure 10.4.

When working with silver or gold reflectors, one of your biggest problems will be that the reflector will bounce *too much* light onto your subject. Fixing this is very easy: simply move the reflector farther away. This is true with any light source, be it a flash or a reflector (see Figure 10.5). As you move the light source farther away, the highlights it creates will become more diffuse.

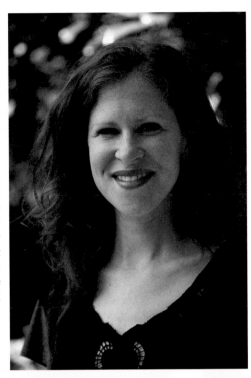

Figure 10.3

With the diffuser in place, the shadows on our model's face are now far less harsh.

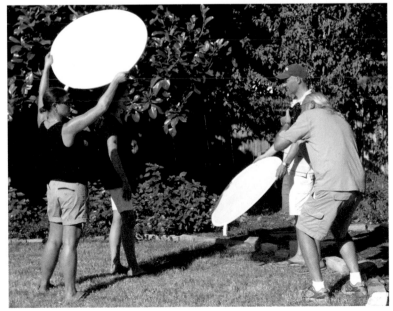

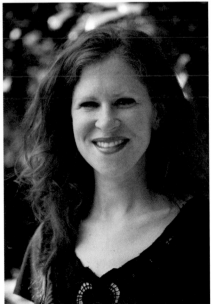

Figure 10.4 Here we're using a diffuser to soften the light striking the model and a reflector to bounce some light back onto her face from below. By controlling and redirecting the light, we can eliminate shadows to produce the portrait shown on the right.

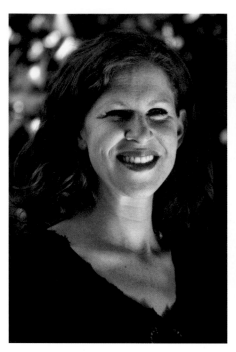 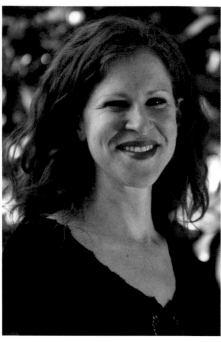

Figure 10.5

The gold reflector used in the left picture is throwing too much light into the scene. In the right picture, we moved the reflector farther back.

Collapsible reflectors are easy to carry, and they come in a variety of colors including white, silver, and gold. White reflectors create a very natural looking, even fill, while silver and gold reflectors move more light, with gold warming the light along the way. The Photoflex 5-in-1 includes zip-over covers that allow you to easily change the color of the reflector.

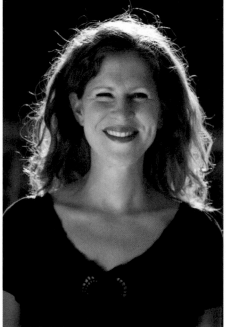

Although not as easy to carry, big pieces of white cardboard, paper, or foamcore will work just as well for creating a white fill.

Another way to handle harsh, contrasty lighting is to shoot *into* the sun. Position your subject with his or her back to the sun, and you will be shooting from within their shadow. This will serve to cut a lot of the harshness, *and* you'll get a nice rim light, or halo. If you add a reflector in front, you can have a rim light and even lighting on her face, as shown in Figure 10.6.

You can use these same techniques for shooting flowers and other still lifes, provided they're small enough to cover with a diffuser.

Figure 10.6

For this shot, we positioned the model with her back to the sun, to create a halo around her head, and then used a reflector to illuminate her face.

Broad and Narrow Lighting

Take a look at the two images in Figure 10.7. In both images the main light (sometimes called the *key light*) is to the model's right. In this case, the main light is simply the sun, and we're using a reflector to create a fill light that fills in the shadows on the right side. In the left image, because of the way her face is turned, most of her face is in the shadowy part of the light. This is called *narrow* lighting.

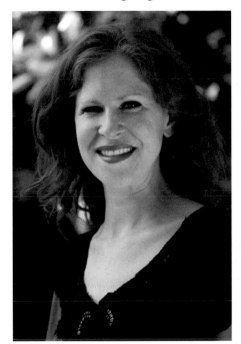 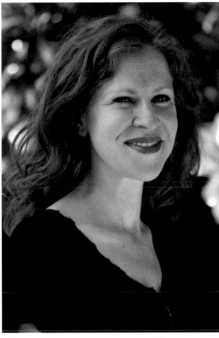

Figure 10.7

These two images are lit the same way, but as the model changes poses, very different effects are created.

In the right image, she has turned so that the broad part of her face is exposed to the light, and thus this type of light is called *broad* lighting. Narrow lighting tends to make a person's face look skinnier than broad lighting, while narrow lighting can sometimes be a little more dramatic than broad lighting.

When posing your models, pay attention to whether your lighting is more narrow or broad. On different shaped faces, some lighting approaches are more flattering than others. If you're not sure which will work best, shoot both.

Flash Photography

These days, most cameras—whether point-and-shoot or SLR—have a built-in flash. Like reflectors, a flash provides you with a way to control the light in your scene.

Using your camera's built-in flash is pretty simple: just turn it on and let the camera worry about when and how much to fire it. Using your camera's built-in flash well is a bit more difficult. In fact, most people have the mistaken idea that the flash is only used when it's dark, when in fact, it's most useful in bright daylight, as we'll see later.

Unfortunately, the small flash units provided by most cameras are low powered, and because of their positioning on the camera, they don't often produce very flattering light. However, your camera's built-in flash does have its uses, and with a little knowledge, you can get it to yield good results.

When you shoot a picture using your flash, many things happen in a short amount of time. First, the camera opens its shutter and begins exposing the image sensor according to the settings defined by you or your camera's light meter. Then the camera turns on the lamp in its flash unit. With the lamp on, the camera begins measuring the flash illumination that is bouncing off the subject and returning to the camera. In this way, the camera can meter the light of the flash while it is flashing. When it has decided that the flash has cast enough illumination, it shuts off the flash, finishes the exposure, and closes the shutter.

Flash Modes

Most digital cameras provide several different flash modes. If you're shooting in a fully automatic mode, your camera will try to determine, on the fly, whether the flash is needed. If it deems the flash necessary, it will fire it for the appropriate amount of time. In addition to this mode, your camera probably provides the following:

- ◆ **Fill.** This mode uses the flash to fill in shadows. It is typically used for backlit situations or other instances where you're shooting in bright light but your subject is in shadow. Usually, the camera uses a lower power flash setting so as not to overexpose the shadows in your image.

- ◆ **Red-Eye Reduction.** The "red-eye" effect (see Figure 10.8) occurs when the light from your flash bounces off the retinas of your subject's eyes as he or she looks into the lens. If the flash on your camera is placed close to the lens, there's a much better chance of getting red-eye, because it's easier for the light to bounce straight back into the lens. Red-Eye Reduction modes work by firing a flash, or the camera's autofocus-assist lamp, to close the subject's pupils. When you use these modes, be sure to inform your subject that there will be two flashes. Otherwise, your subject might move or close his or her eyes after the first firing. Whether you're shooting with or without a red-eye reduction flash, moving slightly to one side before you shoot can prevent your subjects from looking directly into the camera's lens. You can also try turning on all the lights in the room in an attempt to narrow everyone's pupils.

- ◆ **Cancel.** This feature simply deactivates the flash. This isn't exactly a mode, but it is important for times when you're shooting in an area where a flash is not appropriate or when you want to handle low light in a different way.

Spend some time using the different flash modes on your camera to learn their characteristics. In particular, determine if the flash consistently over- or underexposes, and if it tends to produce odd color casts. If so, you might want to adjust its settings as described in this section.

After the flash has fired, any leftover charge is saved for the next firing. Consequently, your flash's recycle time can vary depending on how much it had to fire. In other words, you'll get faster recycle times when you use your flash in brighter light, because the flash won't have to fire for as long and won't have to recharge as much.

One problem with on-board flashes is that they're really not positioned to provide flattering light. Our eyes are used to a strong overhead light source, so flashing a bright light directly in front of a subject usually produces a somewhat weird lighting perspective. In addition, a poor flash exposure can result in harsh lighting with overblown highlights and hard-edged black shadows if the flash fired too much, or an underexposed image if the flash fired too little (see Figure 10.9).

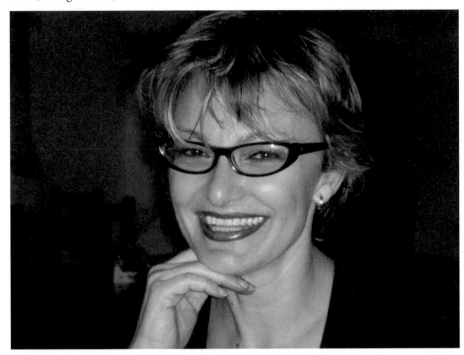

Figure 10.8

Red-eye is prevalent in small cameras because of the position of the flash. Fortunately, correcting the problem is fairly simple using tools found in most image editors.

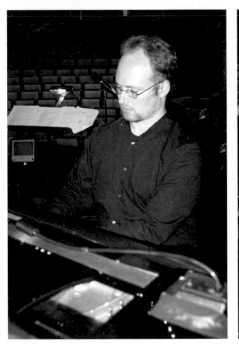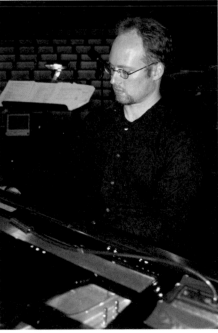

Figure 10.9

At times, you might find that your camera's on-board flash creates harshly lit scenes with blown-out highlights. Flash exposure compensation lets you dial down the power of the flash for better exposure.

Fortunately, many cameras offer flash power adjustment controls—sometimes called *flash exposure compensation*—that let you increase or decrease the power of the flash by one or two stops in either direction. After a test shot, you might find that your camera's flash is too strong. Dialing down the power by a stop or so might be enough to produce a much better exposure.

Remember that your camera's flash has a limited range, usually no more than 10 or 15 feet. Consequently, as your focal length increases, your flash's effectiveness decreases. That is, if you zoom in on an object 20 feet away, don't expect your flash to do a great job of illuminating it. Increasing the flash power by a couple of stops might improve your flash performance at these distances.

Flash White Balance

Your flash is usually not the only source of light in a room. In most cases, you'll be shooting flash photos in a room that also contains incandescent or fluorescent lights and maybe even sunlight. All of these light sources can serve to create a complex, mixed lighting situation that requires a special white balance.

Some cameras have a separate white balance setting for flash that can often correct color-cast problems, but on most cameras, manual or automatic white balance will yield the best results.

To get an idea of how your camera white balances when you use the flash, take some test flash pictures indoors under normal incandescent (tungsten) lighting using the camera's automatic white balance. If the images come out with a slightly blue cast or if the highlights are blue, the camera's white balance chose to favor the room's tungsten lighting. If the images come out a little yellow or have yellow highlights, the camera white balanced in favor of the flash.

There's little you can do about these color casts. Sometimes, dialing down the flash's power will reduce the effect, or you can try to filter your flash. If you find blue highlights in your flash pictures, buy some yellow filter material at your camera store and tape a piece of it over your flash. This will balance your flash for tungsten, making it match the indoor lighting better (which your camera is white balancing for anyway).

Using Flash in Low Light

When you shoot with a flash, your camera chooses an exposure that's appropriate for exposing the flash-illuminated area, which is usually a fairly small zone in front of the camera. However, if you're shooting in low light, everything outside of this zone will be underexposed, resulting in your background appearing as a dark limbo space.

If you're gunning for a quick snapshot in a dark situation, this may be your only option. But, if you have more time, you should consider two other possibilities: using a higher ISO or a slow sync flash.

High ISO Low-Light Shooting

As you've already learned, as you increase your camera's ISO, it becomes more sensitive to light, which means you can shoot in lower light. Shooting in low light without your flash will produce a more natural-looking scene, but you might have to shoot with a slower shutter speed, which means you'll run more risk of blurring due to camera shake and possible movement of your subject.

If your camera has a Shutter Priority mode, try locking the shutter speed on something that offers good motion-stopping power, for example, 1/30th or 1/45th. Your images might still come out too dark, but you'll be able to brighten them later.

If you have your camera stabilized, then you can use your camera's recommended shutter speed without fear of camera shake. This is true for static images or moving subjects (see Figure 10.10).

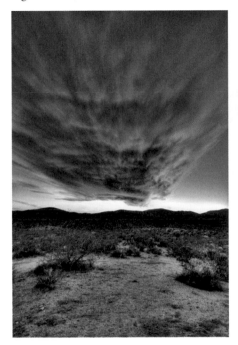 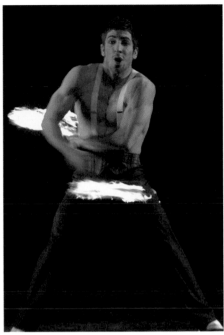

Figure 10.10

Raising your camera's ISO makes it possible to shoot in situations that would otherwise be impossible or inappropriate. For this sunset, I set the camera on ISO 1600, mounted it on a tripod, and used a long exposure. For this flame juggler, I set for ISO 1600, put the camera on aperture priority, and shot at a 50th of a second to ensure good motion stopping.

Anytime you switch to a higher ISO, you'll run the risk of increased noise in your images. In addition to producing noisier images, at longer shutter speeds, many of the individual pixels in the camera's sensor might begin to behave strangely, sometimes getting "stuck" so they appear bright white.

Some cameras employ special noise-reduction schemes when you shoot at speeds longer than one second. Most of these schemes employ some form of dark frame subtraction. When this feature is enabled, anytime you shoot an image with an exposure longer than one second, the camera automatically shoots a second frame, this time with the shutter closed. Because the exposure is the same, the pixels in the camera's sensor have time to malfunction exactly as they did in the first image. However, because the shutter is closed, the resulting black frame is essentially a photograph of only the stuck, noisy pixels from the first image. The camera then combines the images, essentially subtracting the second frame from the first. Because the second frame contains only the noise, the resulting image is much cleaner.

ISO choice when shooting long-exposure images can be a bit tricky. On the one hand, you might want to shoot with a higher ISO to reduce the shutter speed and avoid stuck pixels. On the other hand, shooting with a higher ISO introduces high ISO noise. So you might want to try both techniques and see which one ends up noisier.

Slow Sync Flash Mode

One problem with using flash in very low light is that, while the flash is capable of exposing your foreground properly, everything in the background lies out of range of the flash and ends up so underexposed as to be completely dark (see Figure 10.11).

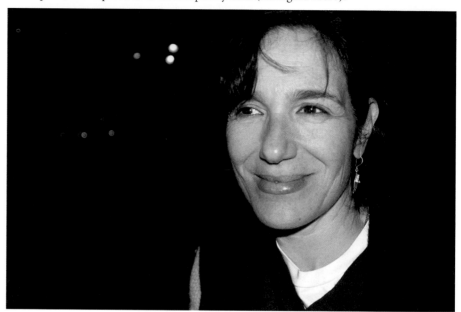

Figure 10.11

This exterior night shot was illuminated only by our flash. Although it did a good job of exposing our subject, nothing in the background is visible, because the camera chose a shutter speed that was appropriate only for the flash-illuminated woman.

Most cameras offer a special Slow Sync mode that uses a combination of a flash and a slow shutter speed to expose the foreground and background properly. The flash exposes the foreground, freezing any motion, while the slow shutter speed allows the camera to capture a good exposure of the background (see Figure 10.12).

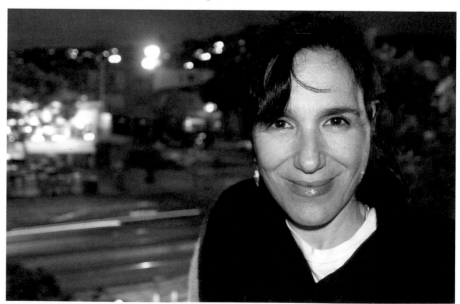

Figure 10.12

This image was shot a few seconds after Figure 10.11, using the camera's Slow Sync mode. The flash was fired to illuminate the subject and freeze her motion, but the shutter was left open for several seconds to capture the background, resulting in an image that reveals far more detail.

On many cameras, Slow Sync is a special Scene mode—just like Landscape or Portrait—that you select from the Scene Mode control.

On a higher-end camera that doesn't offer a Scene mode, or if you're using an external flash, you usually can achieve Slow Sync effects by putting the camera in Manual or Priority mode. Consult the documentation for your camera or flash for details.

When shooting people using Slow Sync mode, be sure to tell them to hold still *after* the flash fires. Many times, people will start moving after the flash has fired, while the long exposure is still going. This can result in weird blurs in your image.

Many Slow Sync modes offer the choice of first curtain or second curtain sync. This simply denotes whether the flash will fire before or after the long exposure, allowing you to control where you might want blur in your image.

Using Fill Flash in Bright Light

Most people assume that you use flash when it's dark and turn it off when you're back in bright light or daylight. While this is occasionally true, you can also argue that it's often the exact opposite of correct flash philosophy. As you saw in the last section, using a flash well in low light is very difficult, and doesn't often yield the best result—sometimes, shooting with no flash and a higher ISO is a better way to go. You'll probably find that your flash is *more* useful in the daytime than it is at night.

When shooting outside, you'll often find that the sky is much brighter than your subject. Most Matrix metering systems will favor the sky when metering, causing your subject to be rendered too darkly. If your camera has a Spot meter, you can work around this problem by Spot metering off your foreground subject, which will cause the background to overexpose and wash out completely.

A better solution is to activate your camera's fill flash. This will throw enough light on your foreground that the camera will expose both the foreground and background properly (assuming that your foreground is within range of your flash). See Figure 10.13.

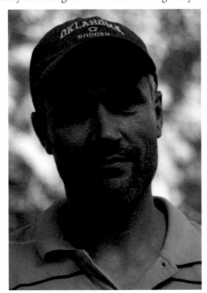 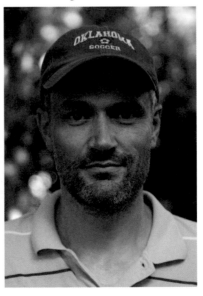

Figure 10.13

Your camera's flash is not just for shooting in dark, low-light situations. Even in bright sunlight, you might need to use your camera's flash to compensate for a bright background or for shadow-producing hats, trees, or buildings.

This is the same practice you'll use in a brightly lit room to counter any backlighting caused by bright windows. Fill flash is also great for subjects who are wearing hats or are shaded by overhanging trees or other foreground objects. Usually, the bright outdoor light will be so strong that your flash will provide a rather soft fill light, with none of the harsh shadows you might see indoors or in lower light.

Finally, in Figure 10.13, note that the flash has also resulted in a nice catch-light in the model's eyes. This simple highlight makes the eyes look much more alive. You can create catch-lights with flashes or reflectors.

External Flash

Although built-in flashes offer a measure of convenience, they also suffer from some significant liabilities:

◆ **Range.** Built-in flashes are usually very small, so they have very limited range. Once your subject goes beyond 10 feet, most built-in flashes are useless.

◆ **Propensity to red-eye.** Because they're positioned so close to the lens, most built-in flashes are very prone to producing red-eye effects.

◆ **Unflattering position.** Because light almost always comes from overhead, firing a flash directly into someone's face rarely looks natural. Shadows get cast in weird places, skin tones pick up unusual highlights, and dark shadows get thrown behind the person's head.

◆ **No creative control.** Since built-in flashes can't be moved, you have very little control over your lighting effects.

◆ **Slow recycle times.** Most built-in flashes take several seconds to recycle, which can often be long enough that you'll miss some shots.

With an external flash, you can eliminate all these concerns. Granted, you'll have to spend some money, and you'll have a little more gear to carry, but if you regularly shoot in situations that require a flash, you'll find an immediate improvement in your images if you use an external flash. To use an external flash, you must have a camera with a flash hot shoe.

What to Look for in an External Flash

Shopping for an external flash is pretty easy because there usually aren't too many options available for a specific camera model. While you can use almost any flash with almost any camera, you'll want to refine your selection immediately to flash units designed specifically for your camera. These models will integrate very tightly with the camera's metering system, which will make for much easier, better-quality flash exposure.

Once you've zeroed in on the models built for your camera, you'll want to consider the following criteria:

◆ **Power.** All flashes have a guide number that tells how much output they provide. Higher numbers will yield a longer range, but will also result in a physically larger flash unit. Think about the type of flash work you do and decide if you really need a flash with a huge reach or if you could get away with a smaller, less-expensive unit.

◆ **TTL metering.** If you're looking at a flash designed specifically for your camera, it will most likely have through-the-lens metering. If it doesn't, you'll want to consider going with a different unit.

◆ **Zoom.** If you're looking at a flash unit designed specifically for your camera, it should offer the capability to zoom automatically based on the focal length you've set your lens to. If you're shooting with an SLR, be aware that not all lenses transmit focal length information back to the camera. If some of your lenses don't, a flash zoom feature won't be of any use when you shoot with those lenses.

◆ **Tilt and swivel.** You want a flash head that can at least tilt, and ideally you want one that can swivel. As you'll see in the next section, the capability to tilt and swivel to bounce the flash off walls, ceilings, and reflectors allows you a tremendous amount of creative freedom (see Figure 10.14).

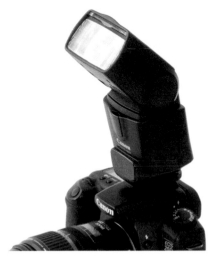 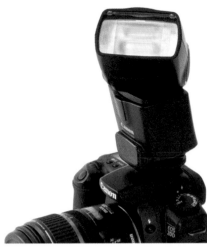

Figure 10.14

A flash unit that can tilt and swivel offers many more options for creating flash shots with natural-looking lighting.

◆ **Exposure compensation control.** While your camera probably provides an exposure compensation control that will work with an external flash system, having such a control onboard the flash is often a great convenience. Look for a control that's easy to access and use.

◆ **Slave control.** If you think you might want to eventually work into multiple-flash lighting setups, you'll want a flash system that allows one flash to trigger other, multiple slave flashes. This topic is beyond the scope of this book, but it's something to consider if you want to buy a flash that will grow with your shooting needs.

Fortunately, Canon, Nikon, Sony, Olympus, and Pentax all make very good flash systems, so you should be able to get a full-featured flash setup no matter what brand of camera you buy. Your main choice will simply be to decide about the level of flash power you want.

Shooting with External Flash

So now that you've bought the thing, what can you do with your external flash? Right off the bat, you'll probably notice that your external flash produces *much* more illumination than your camera's built-in flash. In fact, you may find that you regularly need to use flash exposure compensation to dial back the power a little bit. If your flash images look a little too "hot," you'll need to try lowering the flash exposure.

The most significant advantage of an external flash is its capability to bounce light off other surfaces. In general, the light sources we're used to seeing the world under are very large and diffuse. Your flash, by comparison, is a small, point light source, and it creates a very harsh light. However, if you tilt the flash so its light bounces off the ceiling, the ceiling becomes the source of illumination for your scene. Because the ceiling is very large, it creates a wide, diffuse, more natural light, as shown in Figure 10.15.

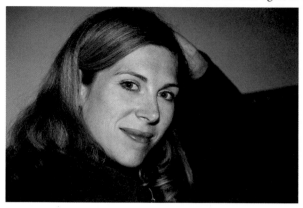 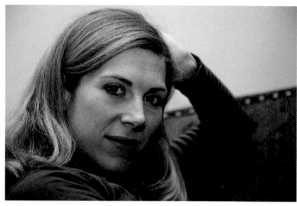

Figure 10.15 In the left image, we've fired the flash directly at our subject, resulting in a harsh front lighting. In the second image, we bounced the flash off the ceiling. In addition to being less harsh, we can see more contour on her face and the background gets illuminated.

On most flashes with tilt, the camera automatically adjusts its exposure to adjust for the amount of tilt you have on your flash. As long as you're using a flash with automatic TTL metering, the camera will be able to adjust flash exposure as you tilt and swivel the flash. Nevertheless, you'll want to keep an eye on your histogram and see if your flash exposure is correct. If it's not bright enough, use a positive flash exposure compensation. If it's too bright, set flash exposure compensation lower.

Direct flash has the advantage of "flattening" facial features. Notice in the direct flash image in Figure 10.15 that there are no shadows under her eyes or eyebrows. This can often be a good thing, as it affords you a way to, for example, reduce the apparent size of someone's nose. However, you'll run the risk of picking up dark shadows under the chin, as our model has in Figure 10.15.

If your flash can swivel and tilt, you can bounce the flash off walls or reflectors to create side lighting effects, which allow you more control over the shadows in your image.

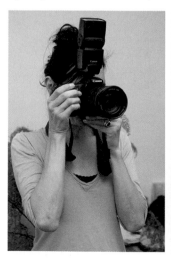 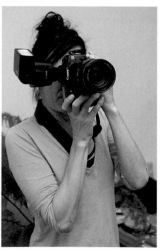

Tilting and swiveling also enables you to re-position the direction of the flash easily as you change from Portrait to Landscape mode (see Figure 10.16).

Figure 10.16

If your flash can tilt and swivel, it's easy to keep it pointed at the ceiling as you change from portrait to landscape orientation.

Getting Your Flash off the Camera

Like any light source, an external flash will cast a shadow behind your subject (assuming there's something there for the shadow to be cast onto). Perhaps you've noticed this before in flash pictures—a dark shadow behind your subject (see Figure 10.17).

In the case of a picture like Figure 10.17, you can try to get the person to move away from the wall, but this isn't always possible, especially when you're shooting candid shots.

Using an off-camera flash cable or a flash bracket, you can raise the flash up higher, so the person's shadow will be cast lower. This will often result in your subject's body hiding the shadow, as in Figure 10.18.

An off-camera flash cable simply provides an extension cord that allows you to hold the flash away from the camera, usually higher, although you can also position it from side to side to create different lighting effects. Off-camera flash is essential for creating flash shots that don't look like they were taken with a flash (see Figure 10.19).

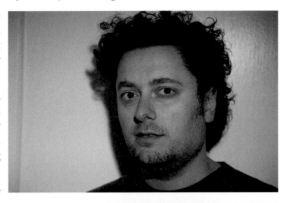

Figure 10.17

People in flash pictures often have annoying shadows behind them.

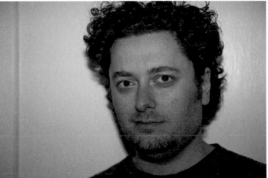

Figure 10.18

By raising the flash off the camera and using a bracket or off-camera cable, we can try to hide the shadow with the subject's body.

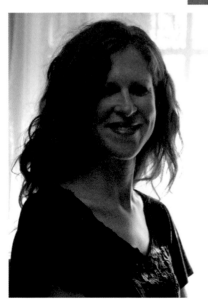

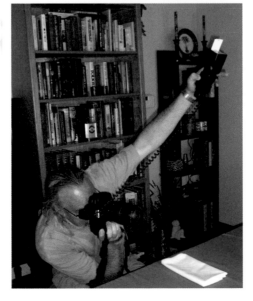

Figure 10.19

Here, the window is serving as a main light, and we're using a flash to fill in the darker side of the woman's face. Key to getting this effect is to use a flash cable to get the flash off the camera.

If we had left the flash on the camera, it would have fired directly at her face. By getting it away, it becomes an overhead light, which creates a fill light that's very natural.

Another option for getting your flash off-camera is to use a flash bracket, which allows you to continue shooting with both hands for greater stability and shooting flexibility (see Figure 10.20).

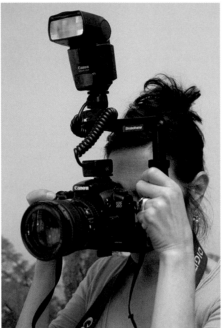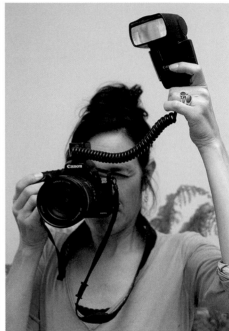

Figure 10.20

Off-camera flash brackets enable you to get your flash away from your camera and into a position that will allow you to reduce annoying shadows behind your subject. If you don't have a bracket, you can use an off-camera cable and simply hold the flash in a better position. (Note that, to use a flash bracket, you must have an off-camera flash cable.)

Slow Sync Flash

Earlier, we looked at special Slow Sync Flash modes that can be used with your camera's built-in flash. On many cameras, the same slow sync shooting mode you use with the built-in flash will work with your external flash. If it doesn't, or if your camera doesn't have such a mode, you'll need to use a Priority mode.

Set your camera on either Aperture or Shutter Priority mode. The camera will meter for the ambient light in the scene, and will choose an exposure that will properly expose your scene. But it will then fire the flash to illuminate the foreground in your scene. The result will be an image with a flash-illuminated foreground and a properly exposed background. (This is just like the Slow Sync Flash modes that we discussed earlier.)

Why Can't I Use a Fast Shutter Speed?

All cameras have a maximum shutter speed they can use with a flash. These typically vary from 1/90th of a second up to 1/250th of a second on higher-end cameras. This is sometimes referred to as *flash sync* or *x-sync speed*.

For many low-light situations, using manual exposure with your external flash is the best way to go. Put your camera in Manual mode, set your shutter speed to 1/30th of a second, and set your aperture to f5.6. Your flash will be used to illuminate your foreground elements and the longer shutter speed will help to expose your backgrounds better. If you're shooting scenes with a lot of motion, 1/30th of a second might result in your subjects being blurred. Consider switching to a higher ISO—say, 200—so you can change your shutter speed by one stop, to 1/60th of a second.

The flash-illuminated foreground in a slow sync image has a very different color temperature than the long-exposure background. If this bugs you, you can try placing a gel, or colored filter, over your flash to balance its output so that it's the same color temperature as the background.

Further Lighting Study

Lighting is a very complex discipline—one that you can spend a lifetime studying. This chapter is by no means a comprehensive look at lighting techniques and options. Practice with the techniques that you've learned here, and if you find you want to know more, you'll be ready to take a class or find a book on lighting. As you progress, you'll learn about multiple-flash units, studio lights, lighting modifiers like diffusers and reflectors, and many other important lighting techniques.

For now, we're going to move on to a discussion of raw format photography. Whether or not you have a camera that supports raw, you'll want to take a look at the next chapter in order to understand why this important shooting option might matter to you.

11

RAW SHOOTING

Gaining More Editing Power Through Raw Format

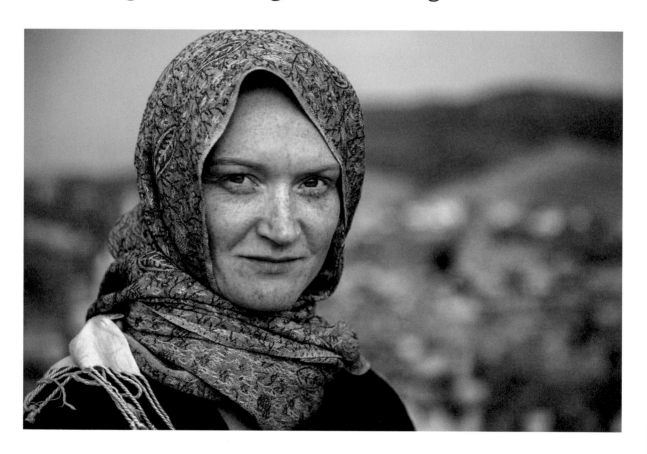

Many cameras these days (mostly SLRs and mirrorless, but also a few point-and-shoots) offer a raw format in addition to their various JPEG formats. You might have heard of raw as something that high-end photographers use, and therefore might have assumed that it's very complicated and requires vast technical knowledge and complex shooting theory. Fortunately, this isn't the case.

Shooting raw changes very little about the way you shoot your image, but offers great advantage over JPEG images once you start editing and adjusting your images. Raw files used to present a big workflow headache, but with modern image editing tools, working with raw files is not necessarily any more complicated than working with JPEG files. In this chapter, we're going to look at what raw is, and what its advantages and disadvantages are. By the time we're done, don't be surprised if you eschew JPEG shooting entirely.

What Raw Is

In Chapter 5, "Image Sensors," you learned how the image sensor in your camera detects light and turns it into a finished JPEG file. In that discussion, you saw how the camera takes the image sensor's captured data and performs a number of processes to it, from white balance adjustment to gamma correction, and how it also performs some of the same types of corrections and adjustments that you might apply in an image editor.

As you'll recall, one of the last things the camera does before saving a JPEG image is to throw out a lot of color data so that the 10 to 14 bits of data that your camera captures can be stored in the 8-bit space that the JPEG format specification dictates. (Different cameras capture different bit depths, but JPEG files are always limited to 8 bits.) You won't necessarily notice a lack of color in a JPEG file, but once you start editing and begin to brighten or darken areas, you might notice that gradient areas of your image—skies, shadows, or reflections on a curved surface, for example—start to look chunky as you push your edits farther. With only 8-bits of data per pixel in a JPEG file, the image editor simply doesn't have enough data to do a good job. In other words, because of that missing data, you won't be able to push your edits as far as you would have been able to do if all of the color had been preserved.

You've also learned that JPEG is a lossy compression scheme that can, when used aggressively, degrade your image. The high-quality JPEG compression on most cameras is very good, and you'll probably be hard-pressed to find evidence of compression artifacts in JPEGs shot with your camera's best setting. But, if you later perform a few edits in your image editor and save the file *again* as a JPEG—something you'll want to do if you're going to post the file to the Web—then you might start seeing some blocky patterns.

When you shoot raw, your camera does not perform any image processing steps. Instead, the raw data that is captured by the image sensor is read and saved. There's no bit depth conversion or JPEG compression, no demosaicing or color conversion is performed, no sharpening, no adjustment of contrast, saturation, or tone, no conversion down to 8 bits, and no JPEG compression. The data is saved, and *all* of the processing that the camera would normally perform is skipped entirely. Instead, you will use special software on your computer to perform the calculations that are necessary to turn the raw data into a usable image.

What Raw Is *Not*

The extra editing power that a raw file provides is significant, but it's important to understand that raw does *not* magically make your images sharper, or show more detail, or yield a wider range of colors. Actually, depending on how your camera settings are configured, it's possible that JPEG images might look better than raws when they come straight out of the camera. This is because your camera will have already applied some sharpening and other image editing functions.

Why Use Raw?

You've already learned two important reasons to shoot raw—the fact that the full bit depth of your image is preserved, and that there's no JPEG compression—but there are other reasons, which are even more compelling.

Editable White Balance

White balance is a function that is applied to your image data by the camera, after the data has been read off the sensor. This white balance adjustment alters the colors in your image so that they are properly calibrated for the type of light under which you were shooting.

As explained in the previous section, when you shoot raw, *no* adjustments are applied by the camera. Instead, they are performed later on your computer using special software. This means that you can set the white balance to anything you want *after you've shot the image!* For example, if you have images shot in an especially tricky white balance situation—perhaps a room with many different types of lights—then you can adjust the white balance to anything you want when you're back in your image editor. You can think of it as performing the equivalent of a manual white balance (see Figure 11.1). What's more, it's a "free" edit, in that it won't ever lead to the type of posterization artifacts that normal image editing can produce.

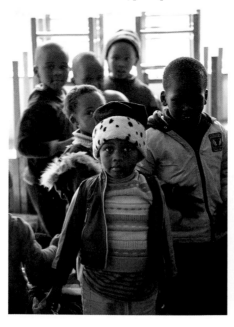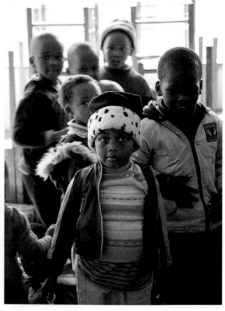

Figure 11.1

With a raw file, you can adjust the white balance of your image after you've shot it. In the left image, the camera chose a white balance that was a little warm. In the right image, a simple adjustment is made to make the colors more accurate.

Highlight Recovery

As you've learned in your study of exposure, when you overexpose highlights, they turn to complete white and lose all detail. If you're shooting JPEG, there's no way to restore that lost detail because it's simply gone. With a raw file, though, there's a good chance that you'll be able to recover the lost detail in your overexposed highlights and restore detail to areas that have gone to complete white (see Figure 11.2).

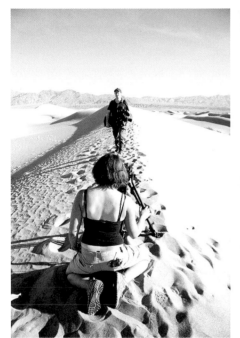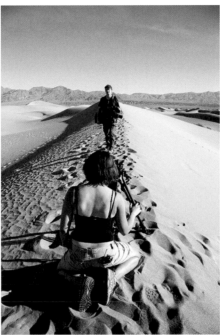

Figure 11.2

With raw files, you can often restore detail to highlight areas that have been overexposed to complete white. Note the restored detail in the sand and on the woman's shoulders.

While recovering image data from nothing might seem magical, the explanation is actually pretty simple. You've already learned that a pixel is composed of separate red, green, and blue elements. Sometimes when you overexpose an area in a scene, you don't overexpose all three color channels. Sometimes only one or two channels get overexposed, while another channel is properly exposed.

Your raw conversion software can often reconstruct the wrecked channels by analyzing the channel that's still intact and thus restore image data. This means that you can't recover *all* clipped highlights. Any highlight that is completely overexposed—for example, a highlight that has clipped all three channels—will be unrecoverable.

The ability to recover highlights doesn't mean that you can become careless about exposures, but it does give you a safety net for times when you, or your camera, choose an exposure that results in overexposed, blown-out highlights (see Figure 11.3).

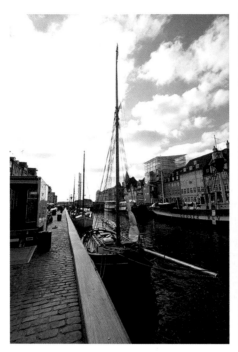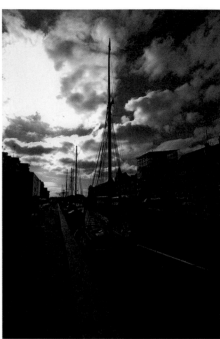

Figure 11.3

The highlights in this image are so overexposed that, while some areas are recoverable, others are not, and remain completely blown out to white.

More Editing Latitude

Shooting with raw is kind of like having a box of 64 crayons, rather than a wimpy box of 16 crayons. While both boxes might have white and black crayons, the box of 64 will have lots of other colors in between.

You'll be hard pressed to tell the difference between a 16-bit processed raw file and an 8-bit JPEG file that has come straight from the camera. But once you start editing, you'll find that raw files offer a lot more flexibility.

Smooth gradients and transitions are a critical component of quality color. For example, it's easy to think of the sky as simply "blue," but the sky is actually a huge range of colors from dark blue up high to light blue near the horizon. Later in the day, you might see it go from blue to purple to red, all in a perfectly smooth gradient.

Shadows often have a tremendous amount of gradient variation, as do reflective surfaces, shiny surfaces, and even skin tones. Because the visual world is made up of all these gradients and subtle variations of colors, it's essential that that your camera be able to capture a huge range of intermediate tones, if you want those gradients to render well in your final image. For a gradient to appear realistic and smooth, you want it to be composed of as many colors as possible. While an 8-bit JPEG file can render smooth gradients, when you begin to edit that file—brightening and darkening, or changing colors—the smooth color transitions in your image may start to suffer.

As you learned in Chapter 8, "Advanced Exposure," if you have only a few colors to work with, it can be hard to build a gradient that looks smooth and natural. While an 8-bit image includes enough tones to make nice gradients, once you start to edit them, things can fall apart quickly. For example, consider this nice smooth gradient that goes from dark gray to light gray in Figure 11.4.

Figure 11.4

This gradient shows a smooth ramp from dark gray to light white.

Let's say that you want to improve the contrast in this gradient, which is the type of edit that you'll commonly make to an image. To achieve this, you want to darken the dark tones and lighten the light tones so that the gradient stretches from full black to bright white. The problem with such an edit is that your image editing software cannot make up new, intermediate tones because it's simply not smart enough. Instead, it has to take the existing tones and brighten them or darken them. The result looks like the gradient shown in Figure 11.5.

Figure 11.5

After editing the gradient to improve the contrast, visible bands appear. The gradient has been posterized.

Those ugly banding patterns are the same posterization troubles that you saw in Chapter 8. Every edit that you make to an image "uses up" some of the editing latitude that's inherent in the file, because each edit—whether it's a change in brightness or a change in color—shifts some tones around and introduces the risk of posterization.

Because a raw file has so much more color data in it than what you have in a JPEG file (since it hasn't been reduced to 8-bit color), you have much more editing latitude. If you do a lot of adjustment and editing, this is a critical reason to use raw.

White Balance and Posterizing

Another great thing about raw files is that when you make a white balance adjustment, it doesn't use up any of your editing latitude, giving you a "free" way to make color adjustments. This is because rather than darkening or lightening tones in your image, like a normal edit does, when you change white balance in your raw converter, you're simply redefining what the converter thinks red, green, and blue are. All other colors are created by mixing those primaries.

Digital "Negative"

Remember that when you shoot a JPEG image, the computer in your camera takes care of all the processing that needs to happen to turn the raw sensor data that you've captured into a finished image. When you shoot raw, the camera does nothing to the raw sensor data but write it to the card. Later, you use software on your computer to perform all the processing that your camera would perform.

This computer-based raw processing has certain advantages. Because you're in control of the processing, you can tailor it exactly to your taste. So, if you want, you can choose to recover highlights, or render some areas brighter, or change the white balance.

During the conversion calculations, there's a good chance that your computer will do a better job than your camera will, simply because your camera is designed to perform as quickly as possible. Because it needs to be sure that it's always ready to shoot, your camera can't devote a lot of time to raw processing. Consequently, the processing employed inside the camera uses slightly less-sophisticated algorithms than what a desktop raw converter will use. This means that there's a chance that you'll get better color out of your desktop raw converter than you will out of a JPEG file that's been processed by the camera.

Because there are so many different ways to interpret raw data, your raw file is truly like a negative. Just as a film negative can be processed by using different techniques to achieve different results, the raw data in your camera can yield many different final results, depending on the software you use to process it. Raw conversion software is improving all the time as imaging engineers discover new algorithms and refine old ones. So years from now, you might be able to reprocess the same raw files in a newer raw converter and get better results.

But even if you never try a different raw converter, the fact that you can process the same raw file in different ways means that you can easily experiment with different looks and adjustments—all from the same original file. For example, you might process the image one way to produce a very warm result and another way to produce something much cooler (see Figure 11.6).

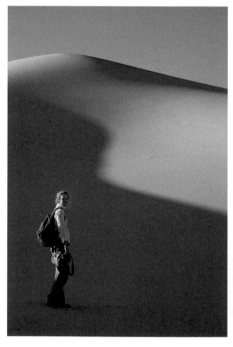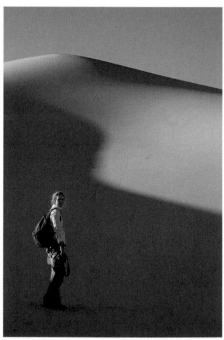

Figure 11.6

On the left is a fairly accurate representation of this scene, and on the right is one that has been warmed up. Both were processed from the same raw file.

Finally, as you learned in the last section, an image can only be edited so much before it begins to show visible degradation. If your camera has already performed some image edits before it writes out your JPEG file, then it has used up some of the image's editing latitude, meaning you'll have less room for making adjustments.

Batch Processing

When working with raw files, it's very easy to apply the same edits to multiple files. For example, if you come back from a shoot and find that the white balance is off on all of your images, and that they're all about a half-stop underexposed, you can easily apply a white balance change and exposure adjustment to the entire batch. In some image editing programs, trying to do the same thing with JPEG files is more complicated.

Nondestructive Editing

When you edit a raw file, the original file is never altered. In fact, it can't be because it doesn't contain any finished image data—your raw converter has to make that. Consequently, when you edit a raw file, you will always be working in a nondestructive editing environment. With a nondestructive editor, you can go back at any time and alter or remove any edit that you make. You'll learn more about nondestructive editing when we get to postproduction.

The Downsides of Raw

For all of the reasons listed above, I, personally, shoot exclusively in raw on all of the cameras that I have that support raw format. However, before you decide that you're going to change over to Raw mode, you should know that raw files can present some extra complications that you won't find when shooting JPEG images.

Raw Files Use More Storage

Because they're not compressed, and because they store more color data per pixel, raw files are larger than JPEG files. Sometimes a *lot* larger. JPEG compression is very effective at squeezing the size of an image. On a camera with 10–12 megapixels on the sensor, you'll typically find that shooting in raw adds about 10 megabytes to the size of *every image* you shoot.

For example, on a Canon Rebel XSi, you can fit about 174 JPEG files on a 1GB card, but only about 56 raw files. (These are approximate numbers because file size varies depending on the content of the image.)

Obviously, larger files mean you'll need more storage cards for your camera, more disk space for your postproduction work, and more long-term storage for archiving.

These days, storage of all kinds is cheap, so ramping up to a raw-worthy storage capacity is not expensive.

Other People May Not Be Able to Read Your Files

While there is a codified standard for JPEG and TIFF files, every camera maker uses a different raw format, and sometimes they even change formats from camera to camera. Because JPEGs are a standard, it's easy to hand other people images straight out of your camera and know that the files will be readable.

Your Software of Choice May Not Support Your Camera

Since there's no raw format standard, anyone who makes raw conversion software must build custom raw profiles for every camera that they want to support. When a new camera comes out, this often means you have to wait until your software of choice supports it. In some cases, your favorite camera may never be supported. For example, Nikon Capture NX, an excellent raw converter, only supports Nikon cameras.

Workflow Can Be a Bit More Complicated

Because JPEG files can be used with any program that can read JPEG files, workflow is pretty simple: take the images out of the camera and view them. There are lots of ways to view JPEG files. Your operating system probably shipped with a JPEG viewer; you can open them in any Web browser; you can open them in almost any image editing program; and your email program and cell phone can probably read them, so it's not too hard to build a workflow that you like.

Of course, a raw file has to be passed through a raw processor before you can even look at it. Windows 7 (and later) and the Mac OS both have raw converters built in, which means you should at least be able to see a preview of the raw file (assuming your camera is supported), but if you want to edit or create a file that you can give to someone else, then you'll have to run the images through a raw converter first.

In the early days of raw photography, this was a big hassle, but today it's very easy. Raw processing software has improved tremendously over the years, and raw workflow is now very smooth in programs like Adobe Photoshop Elements, Adobe Photoshop CS, Adobe Photoshop Lightroom, Apple iPhoto, and many others.

There might be one or two extra steps, but once you learn them, you'll probably find that raw workflow is no more difficult than shooting JPEG, and it's well worth the extra control.

Configuring Your Camera to Shoot Raw

Not all cameras provide raw capability. Today, most SLRs and mirrorless do, and a few high-end point-and-shoot cameras can shoot raw. Most point-and-shoots, though, are JPEG only. If you're not sure if your camera provides raw support, you can check the manual or just try the next step.

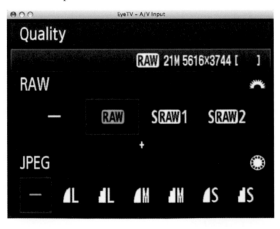

Configuring your camera to shoot raw is usually very easy, because you simply choose a raw option from the same menu where you select the JPEG option. There, if your camera provides raw support, you will see an entry for raw (Figure 11.7).

Figure 11.7

If your camera provides raw support, you'll find an entry for raw in the same menu where you select a JPEG format.

In addition to raw, you might find an entry, or several entries, for Raw + JPEG. In these modes, the camera will simultaneously record a raw file *and* a JPEG file. If the camera has multiple Raw + JPEG entries, then you can choose raw plus a specific level of JPEG quality.

Why would you choose both? The advantage of Raw + JPEG is that when you get home, you have a JPEG file that you can use right away without hassling with any raw processing.

If you're on a tight deadline, and your client only needs JPEG files, you can shoot Raw + JPEG and pull deliverable JPEGs right out of the camera. If any of the images have a bad white balance or clipped highlights, then you've got the raw file to use for correction. Later, you can write out a better JPEG from the raw file and send that off.

Shooting Raw + JPEG takes more space, and your camera will require more time to write out the files, so if you need to shoot sustained, speedy bursts, then Raw + JPEG is probably not a good idea, especially if you have a slower media card. But if you're not ready to commit completely to raw, then Raw + JPEG is a good intermediate step.

After you choose your raw format option of choice, you can start shooting.

12

SPECIAL SHOOTING

*Camera Features and Techniques
for Specific Situations*

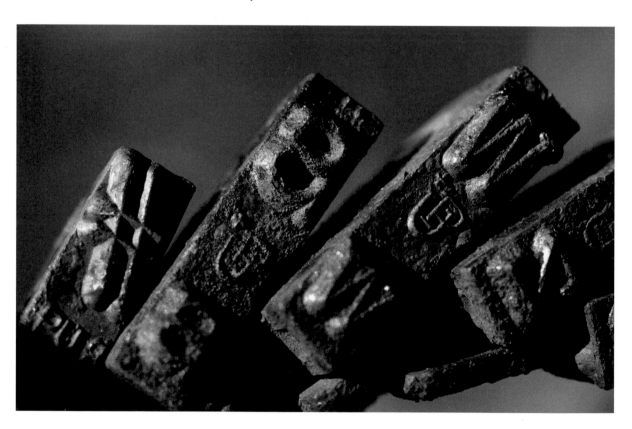

At the end of the Apollo 11 moon landing, Neil Armstrong and Buzz Aldrin blasted off from the moon in their tiny lunar module, aiming for a rendezvous with crewmate Michael Collins in the orbiting *Columbia* service module. As the tiny speck of a spaceship rose up from the moon, ground controllers recorded Collins saying, "I got the Earth coming up behind you—it's fantastic!" Back on Earth, after the rocks and spacesuits and Hasselblad cameras were all unloaded, and the film was developed, Armstrong and Aldrin were able to see what Collins had been so excited about: a photograph of the earth rising above the moon, with the lunar lander flying close by in the foreground. In other words, a single picture encompassing all of humanity except for one man: Mike Collins, the photographer.

Like all the astronauts, in addition to having the "right stuff," Collins had to have a comfortable knowledge of basic photographic principles. A quarter of a million miles from Earth, he still had to worry about f-stops, shutter speeds, and film stocks in addition to worrying about asphyxiation, burning up on reentry, and drowning in the ocean.

Hopefully, you won't ever have to face such photographic concerns. However, it is important to realize that certain types of photography require special equipment, techniques, and preparation. In the case of lunar photography, you would need a massive government-funded space program in addition to your digital camera and a decent computer. Web photography, on the other hand, requires a camera with appropriate resolution and a good understanding of how your images will be sized and compressed for delivery.

In this chapter, you'll learn about all types of special shooting considerations, ranging from shooting in black and white to shooting in extreme weather.

Black and White

Because digital cameras default to shooting in color, it's easy for the digital photographer to become something of a color chauvinist. While learning to use and manipulate color is an essential skill, it's important to remember that some of the most effective photos in history were shot in black and white.

Many of those photos, of course, were shot at a time when color film didn't exist and photographers had no choice. Given that we see the world in color, and that our digital cameras can capture exceptional color images, it may seem strange to consider shooting a color-free image. However, as you learned in Chapter 1, "Eyes, Brains, Lights, and Images," color is a very small part of our visual system. Most of your eye is black-and-white vision, with only a very small portion devoted to sensing color. As light levels dim, your color vision becomes less pronounced, and in the dark you can see very little color at all. So black-and-white images—images that record only luminance, or brightness—are not completely foreign to what your eye sees in the real world.

Black and white is also a form of abstraction, and as you make an image more abstract, you ask your viewers to do more work when they partake of your image. Very often, this results in the viewers becoming more engaged and involved with the image, since more of it will be created inside their heads.

The goal of any image edit or adjustment—whether it's a color or tonal adjustment, a crop, or the decision to convert to black and white—is to make your image easier to read. In a well-made photo, the viewer's eye is led through the image to provide a clear understanding of subject, background, and the relationships of the shapes and tones in the image. Black and white is another tool at your disposal to help guide the viewer's eye.

In many photos, color can be a distraction—it becomes another element that the viewer has to process and understand—and that distraction can make an image harder to read. For example, consider Figure 12.1.

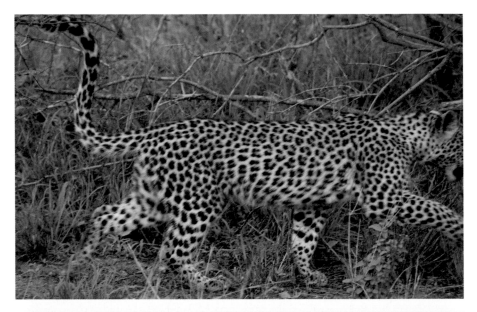

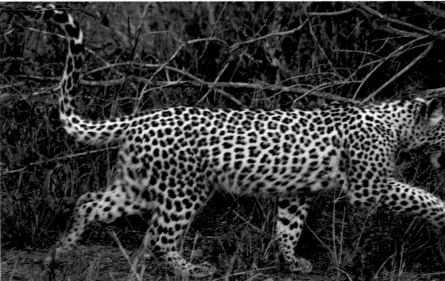

Figure 12.1

In color, this image is a little busy and hard to read. But if we remove the color, the subject becomes much clearer.

While the leopard is a pretty color, it doesn't really stand out against the background. Some of that is because of all of the lines created by the branches. But it's also because of the color. If we change the image to black and white, the leopard becomes more prominent, making for a better separation between the subject and the background.

Sometimes, an image will look *more* real in black and white. Stripped of their color, some images can achieve an immediacy that you can't get in color.

You Say Red, I Say Gray

Technically, when we speak of "black-and-white" images, what we really mean is "grayscale" because, as you learned in Chapter 5, "Image Sensors," an image that lacks color, still has far more than only black and white in it—it will have a full range of gray tones.

One thing that makes black-and-white photography compelling is that there's no quantifiable, absolute "correct" correspondence between a particular color and a specific shade of gray. A light blue sky, for example, can be represented reasonably by any shade of gray from dark to light.

In Figure 12.2, you can see two different black-and-white images created from the same original. In the first image, the sky is rendered with very dark tones, while in the second image, the sky is lighter. One image is not more "correct" than the other, but you might have a preference for one or the other, or a completely different approach.

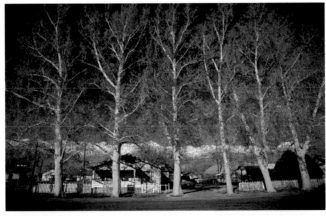

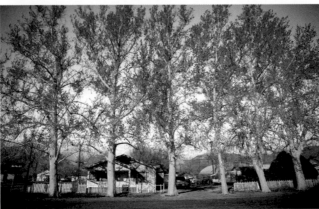

Figure 12.2

There's no "correct" gray tone that corresponds to a particular color value. As such, grayscale conversion can be very subjective. These two images were converted from the same color image, using different conversion settings in my image editor. Which one is "correct" depends entirely on your personal preference.

In the previous image, what struck me at the scene were the trees standing out against the sky. In color, this contrast was not apparent. At the time, I recognized this as a potentially good black-and-white image, because I knew I could render the sky so that the trees would really stand out.

Seeing in Color, Shooting in Black and White

Learning to recognize good black-and-white subject matter as you walk through a color world takes practice. The fact is, you might walk by scenes that don't catch your attention as a good picture, because they're not especially compelling in color. In black and white, though, the same scene might be great image fodder. As you've seen, color can be distracting in an image, so it can often keep you from seeing a potential black-and-white shot. Sometimes, you have to actively look for black-and-white images, or keep the idea of black and white in mind while you move about.

Beginning photographers often think that they have to be able to see or imagine the world in black and white, but they don't. Rather, they just need to learn to recognize the conditions that might lead to good black-and-white results. To find good black-and-white scenes, you want to keep your eyes peeled for contrast. Black-and-white images are all about luminance, or brightness. Anytime you see a particularly interesting play of light, or dramatically contrasty scene, you might be in the realm of a good black-and-white photo. Of course, with digital, if it turns out later that the image works better in color, then you still have the full-color image.

One day I was walking in downtown San Francisco and saw this building. It's not especially interesting as a color image, but what struck me was the brightness of it and how it looked like the prow of a ship. I was also intrigued by the contrast between the top and the bottom. With a little editing, it was easy to get a good conversion that turned this scene that I normally would have ignored, because it was boring, into a compelling black-and-white image (see Figure 12.3).

Figure 12.3

It would have been easy to walk by this building and not recognize that there was a potential black-and-white image there. Keeping an eye out for light-and-dark interplay helped me see the shot.

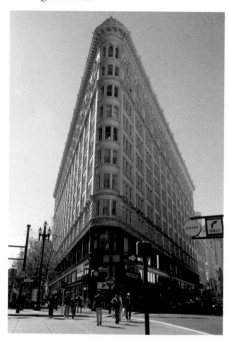 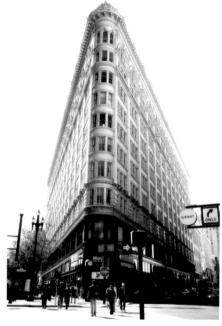

Since black-and-white images are often driven by form and tone, they become very good composition exercises. As you shoot more black and white, you may find your composition skills developing in new ways.

Black-and-White Exposure

When shooting black and white, your main concern will be to capture as much contrast as possible. Since black-and-white images are all about tone, you want to be sure you have as many shades of gray to work with as you can get. That means you'll want to see a histogram that's spread out as much as possible. (See the contrast histograms in Chapter 15, "Correcting Tone.")

If you come from a film background, then you might be familiar with the Zone System, a complex procedure for calculating exposure so that when you process your film a particular way, you can ensure that different elements in the image are targeted to specific tones. With digital black and white, the Zone System is not so critical, because you'll control the toning of specific elements using your image editor when you perform your black-and-white conversion.

This is why capturing as much contrast as possible is so important. You want plenty of image data to work with, so that when you start skewing tones around, you don't see the posterization and banding artifacts that we saw earlier.

Of course, in addition to keeping an eye on contrast range, you'll also want to ensure that you don't blow out your highlights. Even if you envision the final image as having overexposed highlights, it's still best to expose your shot to try to keep all of the tones well exposed, because you can create your blown-out effect later in your image editor.

Don't Use Your Camera's Grayscale Mode

Some cameras have a special mode or setting for shooting grayscale images. With this feature, your camera still shoots a color image, but it then does a grayscale conversion for you, in-camera.

As you saw earlier, the great power of black and white is that you get to choose what gray tones correspond to what color. The camera will use a stock recipe for conversion, and its idea about what tones should be used may not be what you had in mind. Therefore, it's better to stay away from these modes and perform your grayscale conversion by hand.

Use Raw + JPEG for Black-and-White Shooting

If your camera has the capability to shoot raw and JPEG files simultaneously, consider using this mode and configuring the JPEG image to be black and white. When you shoot, your camera will show the black-and-white JPEG on its screen, so you can see the image in black and white immediately, but you'll still have the raw file for performing your own custom black-and-white conversion later. If you're not comfortable visualizing in black and white, this feature can provide you with immediate feedback. Not all cameras have both of these features—check your camera manual for details.

Infrared Photography

Infrared light is not visible to the human eye. However, special infrared-sensitive films can be used to capture infrared light, allowing you to record scenes in a very different…er, light (see Figure 12.4). Skies and foliage are particularly well suited to infrared photography—leafy greens will appear white and skies will be rendered with much more contrast.

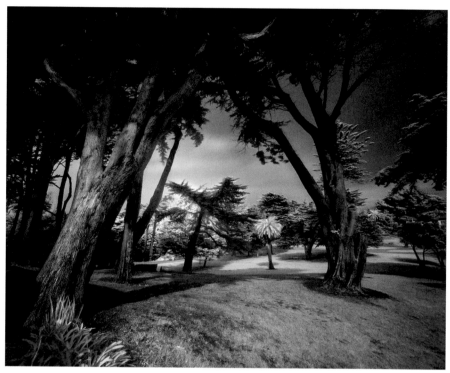

Figure 12.4

With an infrared filter, you can capture just the near-infrared spectrum of light. In infrared, vegetation appears very bright whereas skies turn very dark.

Your digital camera might be capable of infrared shooting, and you can learn the entire process of IR photography by checking out the `Infrared.pdf` document located in the Chapter 12 section of the companion website, at *www.completedigitalphotography.com/CDP8*.

Stable Shooting

No matter what your shooting conditions are, from simple street or event shooting to more complex shooting in harsh environments, keeping your camera stable is an essential part of getting sharp images and having maximum creative control.

Many people believe that if you're shooting with a fast shutter speed, you don't have to worry about camera stability, but camera shake can impact your images at even very fast shutter speeds. What's more, camera stability becomes more important if you're shooting with a camera that has a very high pixel count. A camera with 10 or 12 megapixels is capable of revealing the softness that can be caused by very fine camera shake and vibration.

First and foremost, you'll want to remember the camera holding tips that were covered earlier. For maximum stability, you should shoot with a tripod. Once you have a tripod, there are a few things to keep in mind when using it.

◆ **Use a remote control or self-timer.** As long as your camera is on a tripod, you might as well get your potentially shaky hands completely off the camera by using a remote control or the camera's built-in self-timer.

◆ **Don't use the center column if you don't have to.** If you can get your camera to the height you want using the legs, do that rather than using the center column. With the center column extended, your camera is not as stable as when it's resting directly on top of the main platform.

◆ **When in muddy, dirty terrain, extend the tripod legs from the lowest segment first.** This will ensure that the majority of the leg latches are lifted off the ground, away from the mud and dirt that could gum up the latch workings.

◆ **Make sure the tripod is level.** Some tripods have a built-in level (as do some cameras). If yours doesn't, you need to pay particular attention to horizontal lines in your image to ensure that they are level. Yes, you can straighten an image in postproduction, but straightening requires a crop. If you're shooting with a ball head, remember that just because the tripod is level, the head may be askew.

◆ **Pay attention to wind.** Wind can cause vibration in even the heaviest tripod. If you're shooting in a very windy environment, you will most likely not want to use the center column.

◆ **Use the weight hook.** Hang your camera bag or a sandbag from the weight hook at the bottom of the center column (if there is one) for additional stability (see Figure 12.5).

◆ **Make sure the camera is not front-heavy.** If you have an especially big lens on the camera, and the tripod is on uneven terrain, be sure the tripod is stable before taking your hands off the camera. You don't want a heavy lens to tip the entire apparatus forward, so make sure that one leg is extending under the lens. Also, be sure the tripod is not in danger of tipping or being blown over if you leave it unattended.

◆ **When appropriate, use mirror lockup.** If you're shooting a fast exposure using a digital SLR (say, exposures you've calculated with the handheld shutter rule), then you might want to activate the camera's mirror lockup feature, if it has one. This feature can prevent small extra vibrations caused by the mirror flipping up and down.

◆ **Finally, the best advice for shooting with a tripod is to remember to take the tripod.** If your tripod is so big, heavy, or unwieldy that you don't ever take it shooting, maybe you should consider getting a smaller, lighter tripod. Even though a smaller tripod offers less height and stability than a larger tripod, if it means you'll carry it more often, it's a more useful piece of gear.

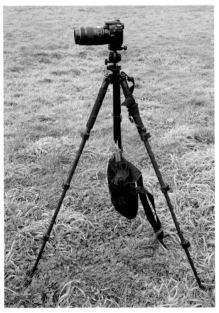

Figure 12.5

For extra stability in this shot, I attached the weight hook to the bottom of the tripod and hung my camera bag from the hook. Note, too, that I have not elevated the center column.

Monopods

A monopod is basically a pole with tripod head at the top. They won't provide as much stability as a tripod, but they're usually lighter and easier to carry, so there's often a better chance that you'll take a monopod with you. Monopods are also ideal in situations where you need stability but don't have the time or space to set up and move a tripod from place to place. Sporting events and theater performances are ideal situations for monopod use. Monopods are also extremely handy if you're shooting with a heavy lens. In addition to providing more stability, the monopod will give your arms and hands a break when you're shooting.

Landscape Photography

While landscape photography is not significantly different from any other type of shooting—you still have to find your subject, calculate an exposure, and work the scene to find the shot that's right—there are a few things to keep in mind when shooting landscapes.

While it might be tempting to just use the widest angle you can, to capture as broad a vista as possible, bear in mind that as you go wider, the objects in your scene will become smaller and less distinct. You're not going to be able to take a single image that encompasses your entire field of view, so try to find a slice of that vista that is compelling. You'll need to employ all the same compositional ideas we discussed in Chapter 9, "Finding and Composing a Photo," as you strive to create a landscape image that works. Your landscape shots still need to have a subject, and you'll look for balance, repetition, good light, and all of the other usual compositional elements when working on landscapes.

One of the most difficult things about landscapes is trying to choose one frame's worth of imagery out of the entire 360° that you can see. If you're looking at a forest, a huge canyon, a massive valley, or endless prairie, there might not be obvious "boundaries" that mark the beginning and end of your picture. Again, finding a subject will provide a point of focus around which you can compose additional elements (see Figure 12.6).

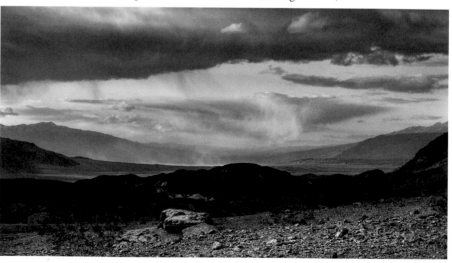

Figure 12.6

This entire valley was filled with incredible sky, as a series of storms blew through, kicking up sandstorms all around in the distance. I knew I wanted to shoot the sky so I walked around until I found something I could use as a subject, to anchor my shot. In this case, it was this rock that was being slightly illuminated by a break in the clouds.

While you might find occasions to shoot with shallow depth of field, in most landscape shots you'll want to ensure that everything in the shot is in focus. The great landscape works of Ansel Adams and others are notable partly because of the photographer's attention to focus. With great detail throughout the image, you really feel like you can walk right into the picture.

Keep an Eye Out for Flare

When shooting landscape images, especially with a wide lens, you'll want to be very careful to avoid flare. Any time your camera is pointed toward the sun, you'll run the risk of lens flares.

Sometimes flares are very obvious because they'll appear as bright circles. At other times, you may not notice a flare problem, because it might manifest as a broad reduction in contrast across a big part of your image.

If you're shooting with an SLR, then your lens might have come with a lens shade. These can often reduce or eliminate flare. If you're using a point-and-shoot or a lens that doesn't have a lens shade, then try holding your hand up to shield the lens (see Figure 12.7). This will often eliminate flare.

The closer you get to shooting directly into the sun, the more difficult it will be to shield flare without getting your hand in the frame, but you'll usually only encounter this trouble when shooting close to sunset.

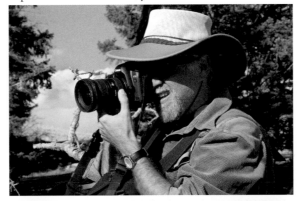

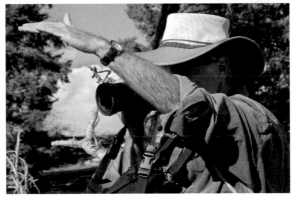

Figure 12.7

In the upper picture, you can see glare on the end of the lens. This is manifesting inside the lens as bad flares. By holding my hand up to shade the lens, I eliminate the flare.

Exposing for Extreme Depth of Field

Obviously, to get a deeper depth of field, you'll want to use a smaller aperture (high f-stop number). This will require a longer shutter speed, so you might need to use a tripod.

However, even with the deeper depth of field provided by a smaller aperture, it's still possible for your image to have focus problems. Remember, depth of field is centered on the point you focus on, and when shooting landscapes, there's usually less depth of field in *front* of that point and much more *behind*. When you shoot a landscape and focus on distant mountains (which usually means that you're focusing on infinity), there's a chance that your foreground will be out of focus because there's not enough depth of field in front of your focus point to render near details in sharp focus. Plus, all that potential depth of field behind your focus point will be wasted.

Every lens has a hyperfocal distance. When you focus your lens on infinity, the nearest point that is also "acceptably sharp" is the hyperfocal distance, and this distance changes with your aperture setting (see Figure 12.8).

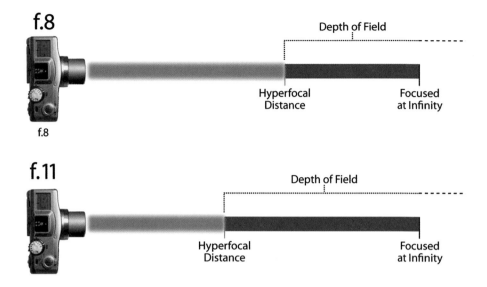

Figure 12.8

When focused on infinity at a given aperture, the hyperfocal distance is the nearest point that is acceptably sharp.

"Acceptably sharp" is a purely subjective measure, and varies depending on how big an image you want to output. When focused on infinity, your depth of field extends from the hyperfocal distance to infinity and possibly beyond. This "beyond" distance can be considered wasted depth of field because, obviously, there's nothing beyond infinity, and there might be a considerable amount of foreground that's not within your depth of field.

If you set the camera's focus to the hyperfocal distance, your depth of field will extend from half of the hyperfocal distance to infinity—a much deeper depth of field (see Figure 12.9).

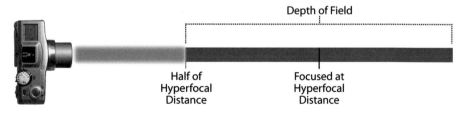

Figure 12.9

You'll get deeper depth of field by focusing at the hyperfocal distance from the camera. This will keep you from "wasting" depth of field behind infinity.

In the old days, lenses included markings that let you identify the depth of field range for any aperture/focus combination. Today, zoom lenses for SLRs and the lenses on point-and-shoot cameras lack these markings, as do many SLR prime lenses, meaning it's much more difficult to make these kinds of depth-of-field calculations. Even if your lens has these markings, making depth of field calculations can be somewhat difficult, as it requires an accurate facility for estimating distance.

Whether you have lens markings or not (or understand any of the theory), there are some simple rules you can follow to ensure deeper depth of field in your landscape images.

◆ **Think about where you're focusing.** When you focus on the horizon or another point in the very far distance, there's a good chance that you'll lose depth of field in the near foreground. If you are unable to calculate the exact hyperfocal distance for your lens, focus on a point halfway to two-thirds of the distance to the farthest point in the scene. You can do this by selecting a different focus point or by using the focus and reframe technique we discussed earlier. If you're working on a tripod, then choosing a different focus point might be the easiest method. Some SLRs that offer Live View let you move a cursor to any point on the screen and use that as your focus point.

◆ **Remember the 1/3rd 2/3rds rule.** In typical landscape situations, one-third of your range of depth of field falls in front of your point of focus and two-thirds falls behind.

◆ **Bracket your apertures.** As you already know, smaller apertures yield deeper depth of field. However, if you simply set your camera on the smallest aperture, you'll run the risk of incurring diffraction artifacts, which can result in a softening of your image. So when closing down your aperture, you may find that you lose as much sharpness from diffraction artifacts as you were hoping to gain from depth-of-field control. To be safe, take several shots with different-sized apertures.

◆ **Bracket your focus.** As you can see, your choice of focus point is critical to getting the deepest possible depth of field. To be safe, take a few shots with the same aperture at varying focal distances. This will improve your chances that one of them will have very deep focus.

If you're shooting with a point-and-shoot camera, you will inherently have deeper depth of field than you will on a camera that uses a bigger sensor. Consequently, these issues might not be as critical.

Depth of Field and Subject Size

It's not always possible to achieve the deep depth of field that you want, but depending on your composition, this may not be a deal-breaker (see Figure 12.10). You will sometimes struggle if you're trying to keep an element in the foreground in focus while also capturing sharp focus of distant background objects—say, a distant horizon. At these times, remember that those background details are going to be very small in the final image—so small that any softness may not be immediately apparent. If your foreground elements are in focus and your background elements are close enough to good focus, then you'll probably be fine. The viewer's attention will be held by the foreground element, meaning their overall impression of the scene will be one with extremely deep depth of field.

Portable Depth of Field Calculators

There are many smart phone apps that will perform depth-of-field calculations for you. Enter your current focus distance and aperture, and these apps will yield depth of field and hyperfocal distance. However, for accurate results, you need to be able to calculate the distance to your subject. If your lens has focus markings on it, you can get a rough idea of focus distance by looking at the lens after the camera autofocuses. If you're really serious, you can carry some kind of laser range-finding device. In general, it's easier to just bracket your focus—shoot multiple images while focused to slightly different distances.

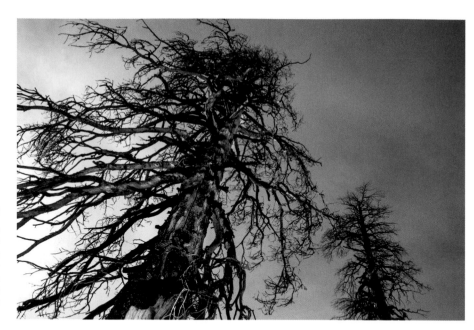

Figure 12.10

When examined up close, the tops of these trees are not actually in perfect focus. I couldn't get enough depth of field to render them sharp. However, because the foreground *is* in focus, the overall impression is of an image that is sharp and well-focused.

If you're shooting in low light, shooting with deep depth of field becomes more complicated. The small apertures will require longer shutter speeds and higher ISO settings, both of which will lead to increased noise.

Using A-DEP on Canon SLRs

Some Canon digital SLRs include a special shooting mode called *A-DEP*, which can automatically calculate an exposure that will yield the deepest depth of field. You'll find A-DEP alongside the camera's other shooting modes. You should frame and focus just as you normally would. The camera will measure the distance to the nearest and farthest points automatically, and it will select a focus distance and aperture that will yield the deepest depth of field. After prefocusing, you can use the Depth of Field Preview button to see how much depth of field you have.

A-DEP can work well, but you might want to experiment with it to get an idea of its effectiveness.

Depth of Field and Focal Length

While the "one-third/two-thirds" rule discussed earlier will get you through most landscape situations, the fact is that depth of field doesn't always distribute this way. As the distance to your subject increases, depth of field increases, but it increases more rapidly *behind* the focus point. When the focus point is roughly one-third of the hyperfocal distance, the one-third/two-third rule applies. When you're focused at the hyperfocal distance, the depth of field extends to half the hyperfocal distance in *front* of the focus point and to everything behind.

Tilt-and-Shift Lenses and Depth of Field

If you're using an SLR, you have another option for capturing deep focus, which is to use a tilt-and-shift lens. These lenses allow you to shift the front and back planes of the lens in different ways to correct for perspective distortion and to ensure that things both near the lens and far away are in focus. Shooting with tilt-and-shift lenses takes more time, as you can't autofocus, and metering can sometimes be a little complicated. In addition, these types of lenses are usually pricey and heavy. If you're interested in experimenting with one, you might try a rental. Websites such as *www.rentglass.com* offer inexpensive lens rental by mail.

Tilt-and-shift lenses are also commonly used in architecture and product photography, because they allow you to reduce or eliminate perspective distortion (see Figure 12.11).

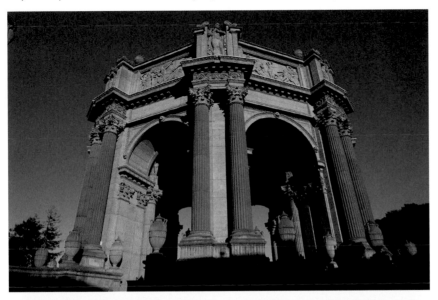

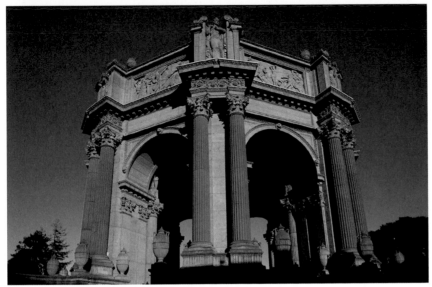

Figure 12.11

In addition to controlling depth of field, you can use a tilt-and-shift lens to adjust perspective, allowing you to straighten horizontal or vertical lines.

Shooting Panoramas

No matter how wide your lens, there will be times when you want to shoot a vista that simply can't be captured with a single image. However, by shooting a series of images that overlap, and then using special panoramic stitching software, you can create panoramic images that encompass a much wider field of view than you can capture within a single shot (see Figure 12.12).

Panoramic software can take a series of overlapping images and stitch them together to create a single image (see Figure 12.13).

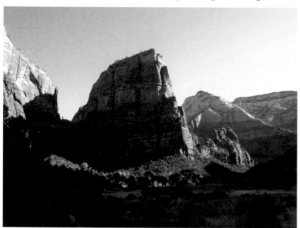 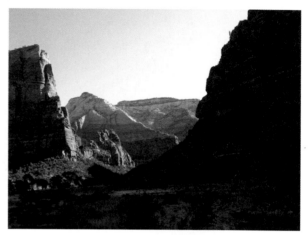

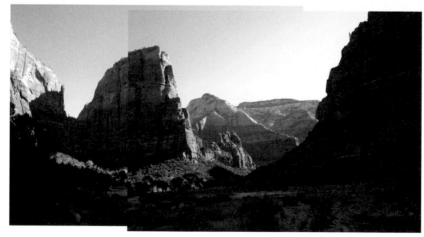

Figure 12.12 These two images were shot separately with the idea that they would be stitched into a panorama. Panoramic images can be stitched together from any number of overlapping images.

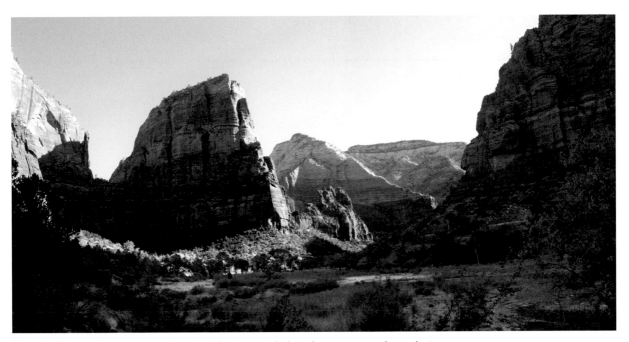

Figure 12.13 Here, the two images in Figure 12.12 have been stitched together to create a single, seamless image.

Besides blending the seams of an image, panoramic software corrects the perspective of each original image by essentially mapping the images onto the inside of a giant virtual cylinder. The curvature of the imaginary cylinder corrects the perspective troubles in your image.

In addition to printing wide panoramic prints of your images, you can deliver your panoramas as virtual reality (VR) movies that present a window onto your panoramic scene and allow users to "navigate" the scene by pivoting and tilting their view (see Figure 12.14).

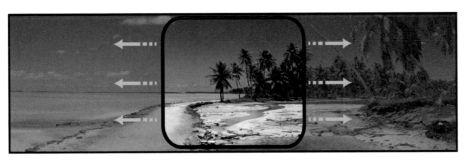

Figure 12.14

If you store your images as VR movies, users can use special viewing software to pan and tilt around your scene. With more advanced authoring tools, you can build fully navigable VR environments.

You'll learn all about stitching later, but getting a good-looking panorama begins with your shoot.

Preparing Your Camera for Panoramic Shooting

You can use any focal length to shoot a panorama; however, your focal length choice *will* affect your final image. With a longer focal length, objects that are more distant will appear larger in your final image, but you'll see less foreground. With a shorter focal length, you'll see more foreground, but distant objects might be very tiny (see Figure 12.15). As your focal length increases, the number of shots required to shoot your panorama will increase. If you need to shoot in a hurry because of changing weather or moving subject matter, you may be better off with a wider angle that will allow you to shoot fewer frames.

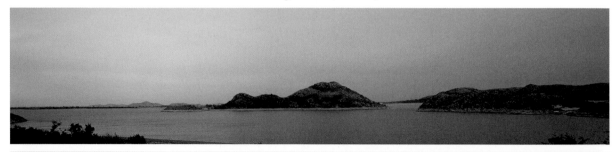

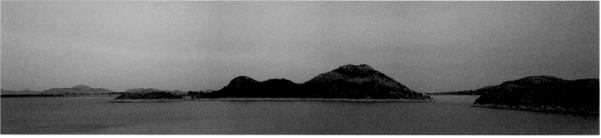

Figure 12.15 Your choice of focal length has a big impact on your final panorama. In the upper image, I used a shorter focal length, which allowed me to shoot a wider panorama with fewer shots, but left the mountains a little small. In the lower image, I used a longer focal length, which obscured much of the foreground, but rendered the landscape larger.

Note that shorter focal lengths (wider angle) are more prone to vignetting, which can lead to visible seams in the final panorama. Also, wider angles are more prone to flares, which can be difficult to manage when panning across a wide range of brightness values.

Panoramas can be shot in either Portrait or Landscape mode. Portrait mode will allow you to capture more vertical details (such as sky or foreground), but will also require more shots, because a portrait image is not as wide as a landscape image.

One disadvantage of having to shoot *more* frames is that more frames mean more opportunities for mistakes in your final image. Each time you shoot an additional frame, you create at least one additional seam, and seams are where artifacts and troubles can develop.

There are two ways to shoot panoramas: the correct way, which involves a lot of special equipment but produces very precise, accurate images for stitching; and the sloppy way, which can be more prone to error, but is far easier and usually produces perfectly usable results.

Proper Panoramic Panning

The most critical steps of shooting a panorama are panning the camera properly and overlapping your separate frames.

For best results, mount your camera on a tripod and set the tripod to be level. Note that if your camera's tripod mount is positioned off-axis (see Figure 12.16) from your lens, you're not going to be able to use your tripod for shooting full 360° panoramas, and you might even have trouble with landscape panoramas comprised of three or four frames. Because of the off-axis rotation, the ends of your panoramas won't necessarily fit together. For smaller panoramas, you should be fine no matter how your tripod mount is positioned, although your final panorama will need more of a crop if your tripod mount is off-axis.

While a tripod is the best guarantee of good results, to be honest I almost always shoot panoramas handheld. With a little practice, you can get very good results.

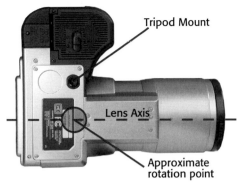

Figure 12.16

If your camera's tripod mount is off-axis from the rotational center of the lens, you'll have a hard time shooting full 360° panoramas from a tripod.

When you shoot handheld panoramas, remember to pivot the *camera*, not your head or body. Your eyes are a few inches in front of the center of rotation of your neck, and your camera's image sensor will be even further removed from your neck or body's rotation, meaning that if you simply turn your head or body, you'll actually be rotating around a point several inches *behind* the camera. Therefore, between shots, rotate the *camera* properly and then—if necessary—reposition your body behind the camera's new position. Your main concern when you rotate the camera is to keep its bottom parallel to the ground. If you tilt the camera in addition to rotating it, you'll run into some problems when you are stitching (see Figure 12.17).

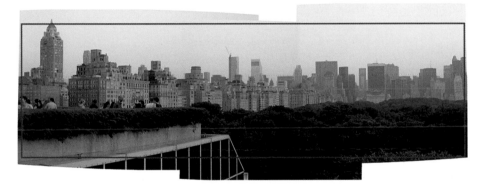

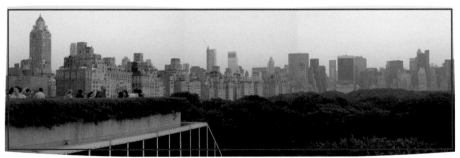

Figure 12.17

If you don't keep the bottom of the camera level as you rotate it, you'll end up with lots of unusable, wasted content in your final panorama that will have to be cropped. When your camera is level, you end up with more usable image for your final crop.

When you pivot the camera, remember that your images must *overlap*, not sit adjacent to each other. Most stitching software recommends a 15 to 30 percent overlap between images, and some vendors recommend a 50 percent overlap. Many cameras feature panoramic assist modes that offer on-screen cues as to how much you need to overlap. If your camera has such a feature, it's definitely worth using. A little experience with your stitching program will give you a better idea of how images need to overlap.

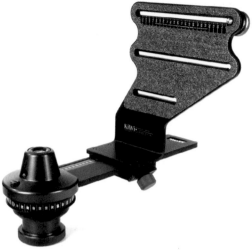

If you're a stickler for extreme precision, or if you're shooting full 360° panoramas for use as VR movies, you're going to have to do a little more work when you shoot to ensure that your source images are accurate enough to yield the results you want. You will absolutely need a tripod (preferably one with a built-in level), and you'll probably want to invest in a panoramic tripod head. A panoramic head is a special mount that attaches to your tripod and includes preset rotation controls that allow you to rotate your camera quickly by a specified amount. Such heads typically sell for $100 to $300 (depending on the size of the camera they must support), and are worth the money if you do a lot of panoramas (see Figure 12.18). Check out *www.kaidan.com* for a range of panoramic options.

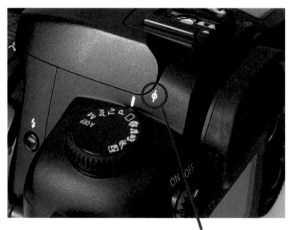

Nodal Point Marker

To ensure that you're rotating your camera precisely around its focal plane, you'll want to identify the camera's nodal point, the optical center of the camera's lens (see Figure 12.19). Most panoramic mounts include special adjustments for ensuring that the camera's nodal point is positioned directly above the tripod's axis of rotation, even if the camera's tripod mount is off-center. If your camera's nodal point is not marked, you might have to do a little experimentation to determine the best axis around which to rotate the camera.

Panoramic Exposure

Because you will be pointing your camera in many different directions as you shoot a panorama, it's important to plan your exposure ahead of time. Your goal is to have an even exposure across all the images in your panorama so that seams are not visible.

In general, if you have more than a one- or two-stop difference in exposure between two adjacent images, you're going to see a band along the seam when the panorama is stitched.

If your camera provides an exposure lock feature, you can lock your exposure after the first frame to ensure that the second frame is exposed with the same values. Or you can meter off a more intermediate part of the image, lock that exposure, and then shoot each frame with that metering. If your camera includes a panoramic assist mode of some kind, it will lock the exposure automatically after each frame.

If you're shooting a scene that encompasses a bright light on one end (say, the sun or the lamp in a room) and ambient light or dark shadow on the other end, things are going to be a bit more complicated. The simplest way to handle this situation is to shoot the same way you would shoot an evenly lit scene: choose an intermediate exposure, lock your camera's exposure settings, and then shoot your panorama. (You can lock exposure by using an Exposure Lock button or by switching to Manual mode and dialing in the specific exposure settings that you want.) Your bright light source will be overexposed, but your midtones and shadows will probably be okay (unless you have some exceptionally dark areas). Despite these potential issues, your finished panorama will be evenly exposed and free of banding.

If you're willing to do a little more work, set your camera to Aperture Priority and pick an aperture that will give you the depth of field that you want. Then take an initial, intermediate exposure reading and lock it into your camera. For frames that are significantly brighter or darker, use your camera's exposure compensation control to over- or underexpose on particularly bright or dark frames. To prevent banding, keep your compensations to within 1/2 to 1 1/2 stops. Because you're in Aperture Priority mode, your camera will only alter shutter speed, so your depth of field will not change.

If you're using a point-and-shoot camera that lacks Aperture Priority, then you can do this same trick in Program mode. Your camera's small sensor probably gives it very deep depth of field anyway, so slight aperture shifts shouldn't be an issue.

Shoot with Care

When you shoot around people, animals, or other moving objects, pay attention to where you position the seams of your image. A vehicle that is present in one image and gone in the next might turn partially transparent if it falls on a seam in the final panorama (see Figure 12.20).

If the objects in your panorama are moving in a particular direction, shoot in the opposite direction. That is, if a person is walking across your scene from right to left, shoot your images from left to right. This is assuming that you don't *want* to see multiple copies of the person across your panoramic field of view. If you *do*, then by all means, shoot from right to left, in the direction of the movement, and ensure that the person is in the middle of each shot when you shoot (see Figure 12.21).

Finally, learn to think of the panoramic process as a complex (but free) super-wide-angle lens. Don't just use panoramas for capturing wide vistas; use them for any occasion when you'd like to have a wide-angle or fisheye lens (see Figure 12.22).

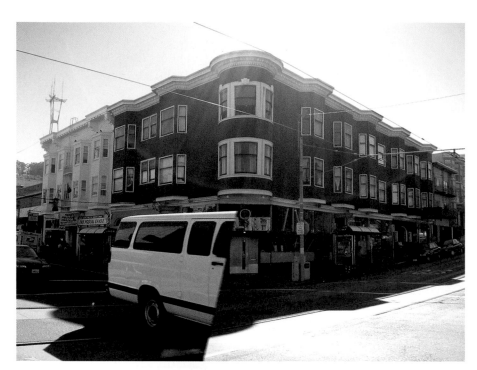

Figure 12.20

When shooting a panorama, be certain that moving images do not fall on a seam, or you'll end up with weird, split objects in your final panorama.

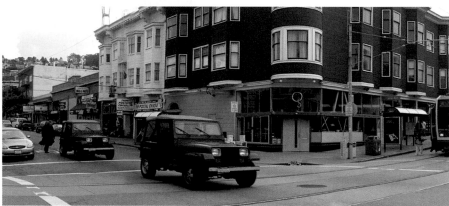

Figure 12.21

Because I was shooting my panorama images from left to right, I shot the Jeep twice. Consequently, when stitched, there are two identical Jeeps in the shot. If I had panned in the opposite direction, I most likely would have had only one Jeep.

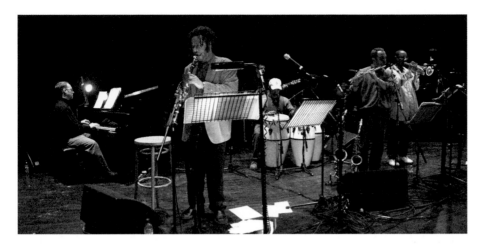

Figure 12.22

Panoramas aren't just for land-scapes. Think about shooting them any time you would normally opt for a wide-angle—or even fisheye—lens.

Also, remember that you *can* shoot panoramas vertically. Just as with a horizontal panorama, shoot a frame, then rotate the camera upward (or downward if you started at the top of the scene), and shoot additional frames (see Figure 12.23). You'll need to consider the same exposure issues you face with a horizontal panorama. We'll discuss vertical stitching in Chapter 21, "Panoramic Stitching and HDR Merging."

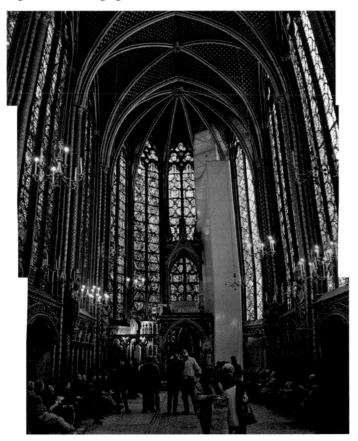

Figure 12.23

Panoramas can also be shot vertically. This three-shot panorama was shot from bottom to top and then stitched using normal panoramic stitching software.

Special Panorama Attachments

If you regularly need to shoot panoramic images, you might want to invest in a special, single-shot panoramic attachment. Products such as the Kaidan 360 One VR adapter allow you to shoot full 360° panoramic images with a single shot from your digital camera.

These contraptions work by positioning a parabolic mirror in front of the lens. When the camera—with the device—is pointed straight up, the mirror reflects a full 360° down into your camera lens. The resulting image requires special "dewarping" software (included with the device) to dewarp the image into a normal panoramic picture. As with any other 360° panorama, these files can be used to create a QuickTime VR movie in addition to simple panoramic images.

If you need to shoot a panorama of a dynamic location—such as a plaza full of people or a landscape with waving trees—or of a dynamic event such as fireworks, then a single-shot panoramic attachment is really your only option.

Collaging

While panoramic stitching software is a great way to shoot wide panoramic vistas, that doesn't mean you shouldn't forget about the old techniques people used to use to create panoramas and collages. Layering overlapping images on top of one another *without* stitching allows you to create stylized representations of a scene without the seamless perfection of a computer-stitched panorama.

Figure 12.24 shows a collage of a Roman amphitheater created by graphic designer Kalonica McQuesten.

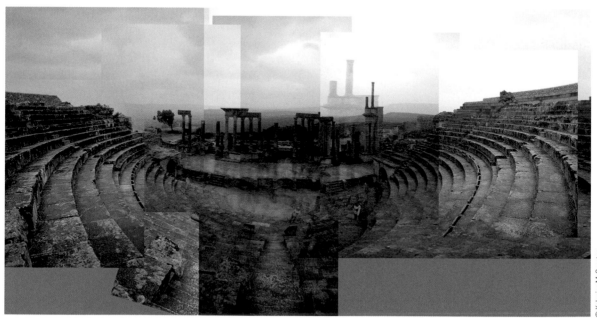

Figure 12.24 While not seamless or optically correct, collaging sometimes yields more evocative effects than does panoramic stitching.

She shot "coverage" of the scene by shooting many overlapping images of the entire scene, not just of a single panoramic swath. These were layered on top of each other in Photoshop, and special selection masks were used to alter the transparency in different places within the image. You'll learn about this type of masking in Chapter 21.

Collaging is also a great way to salvage panoramas that don't stitch properly.

Macro Photography

Although the term *macro photography* would seem to describe a process of photographing very large objects, it's actually the opposite. With your digital camera's macro feature, you can take high-quality images of extremely small things. Technically, what makes a macro photo "macro" is that the image projected onto the sensor is the actual size. Another way to say it is that there's a 1:1 size relationship between the object and the image of the object on your camera's sensor.

What's Different About a Macro Lens

All lenses have a minimum focusing distance. You will not be able to achieve focus—either manually or with autofocus—if you get closer to your subject than the minimum focusing distance of your lens. On a typical SLR lens, minimum focusing distance is somewhere between 12 to 18 inches. A macro lens is simply a lens that has been engineered to have a very short minimum focusing distance. With a macro lens, you can focus at extremely short distances, which allows you to get your lens extremely close to your subject (see Figure 12.25).

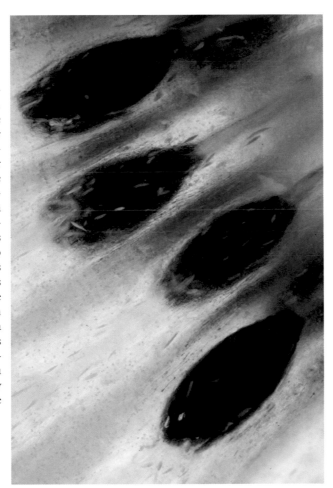

Figure 12.25

A macro lens lets you focus at extremely close distances. Ordinary objects, such as this kiwi fruit, can reveal fascinating textures and contours when viewed this way.

Macro lenses for SLRs come in different focal lengths (see Figure 12.26). For example, you might have a 50mm macro, a 100mm macro, or a 180mm macro. These lenses work just like a normal 50, 100, or 180mm lens, but also offer the ability to focus extremely closely. Because of its longer reach, a more telephoto macro lens will allow you to shoot macro shots from farther away. For shooting insects or other subjects that can be difficult to approach, this can be a great advantage. However, a longer macro lens will also be bigger and heavier than a shorter lens.

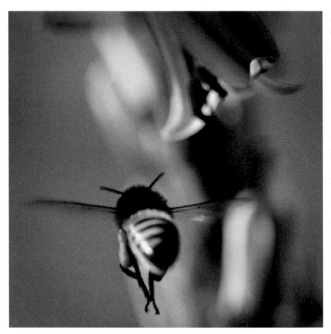

Figure 12.26

I normally shoot with a 65 or 100mm macro. A 180mm made it possible to shoot this bee, which was moving so quickly that getting in close with a shorter lens would have been very difficult.

Macro photos often require a lot of light. The nature of small things is that they're often in dark places, but sometimes the macro light requirement comes from the fact that you have to get so close to your subject that your body and lens will block the light striking your subject. For this reason, it's helpful to have a macro lens that's very fast (that is, that can open to a wide aperture). Holding the camera steady at extremely close distances can also be difficult, so stabilization is also a great feature to look for in a macro lens.

An alternative to a macro lens is to buy a point-and-shoot camera with a good macro feature. These are often less expensive than a macro lens and usually easier to work with because they can be positioned in strange locations more easily. A good point-and-shoot will often have a macro capability that allows you to shoot as close as a single centimeter! A point-and-shoot with good optics and good low-light performance can be a great macro tool. With their small size, they're often easier to work with than an SLR.

Smart Phone Macros

A good cell phone camera can make a very good macro tool. However, you'll need a special lens attachment for your phone if you want to use it for macro work. There are a number of clip-on macro lenses that are very good, but the cheapest—yet still very effective—solution is the Cel Lens available from *photojojo.com*.

Macro Focusing

Your camera's autofocus mechanism should work normally when you shoot in Macro mode. However, be aware that at very close distances, even slight, subtle changes in camera position can ruin your focus.

The best approach for focusing on macro subjects is to use your camera's autofocus to get an initial focus and then refine and adjust focus simply by moving the camera forward and backward. Note that, at macro distances, depth of field is so shallow that even a tiny camera movement will throw part of the image out of focus.

When shooting macro photographs, your camera must be extremely close to your subject, which means there's a good chance that you and your camera will block out much of the light in your scene. If light levels drop, you'll have to use a slower shutter speed, so you'll need to increase ISO to get the shutter speed back up. Often, a tripod is essential when shooting macro. If you do a lot of macro shooting, you might want to consider getting a small tabletop tripod.

The best macro rule of thumb is simply to work quickly. Get the image framed, prefocus, and then shoot right away before your focus drifts. Finally, just to be safe, shoot a few frames. If your first is out of focus, perhaps the second or third will be okay. If you're facing a difficult macro shot, shooting a burst of images as you push forward toward your subject will improve your chances of getting a good shot.

Macro Depth of Field

Be warned that when you are in Macro mode, your camera will have a *very* shallow depth of field. At some macro distances, depth of field will fall to only a few millimeters or even *fractions* of a millimeter.

Consider the image in Figure 12.27.

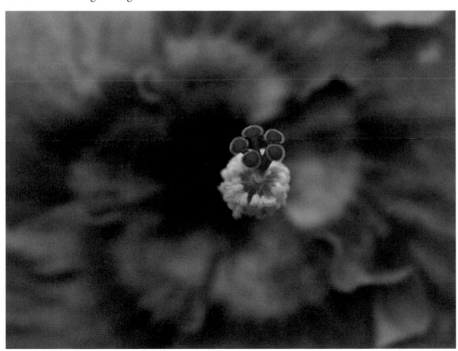

Figure 12.27

This flower was shot with the camera's Macro mode. Although it's not a particularly large flower, it is deep enough that, at macro photography distances, the image has a depth-of-field problem. The flower's stamen is in focus, but the petals are blurry.

The depth of field in this image is so shallow that the flower's petals are out of focus. In fact, the depth of field is short enough that this image might have been better served by switching out of Macro mode, pulling the camera back, zooming in, and shooting the image normally.

Another option would have been to autofocus on the petals and reframe the shot; however, the stamen in the center of the flower would have been out of focus.

If you're shooting a flat subject, depth of field won't be a problem. If you're shooting something that's even a few inches deep, though, you need to think about which parts will be in focus. Judging depth of field on your camera's LCD can be very difficult because the screen is simply too small to reveal which parts of your subject are in focus. Sometimes, you can use your camera's playback zoom feature to examine different parts of your image up close. Even with a 4× magnification, you probably won't be able to see subtle changes in focus. If you're concerned about depth of field, your best option is to protect yourself by shooting multiple shots with a number of different focal lengths—including some non-macro shots.

If you're shooting a flat subject, try to keep the camera parallel to the plane of your subject. Any tilt will introduce extra depth into your image. Those areas of depth might be rendered blurry by your camera's shallow depth of field.

Improving Macro Depth of Field

The easiest way to get deeper depth of field in your macro shots is to mount your camera on a tripod and dial in a smaller aperture. This will lengthen your shutter speed, of course, but will deepen your focus. However, even a small aperture at macro distance might still only yield depth of field of a few millimeters.

If you're serious about macro shooting, then you'll want to look into a technique called *focus stacking*, which is the process of shooting a batch of images, each with a slightly different focus. The goal is to start with focus on the nearest part of your macro subject and then push forward shooting "slices" of focus until you get to the farthest part of your subject that you want sharp.

With these images secured, you then can use special software (Photoshop CS4 or later, or an application called *Helicon Focus*) to merge the group of images into a final, sharp image (see Figure 12.28).

Unfortunately, to shoot each "slice" of focus, you can't zoom your lens because different focal lengths and camera positions yield a different field of view. So, after shooting the first slice of your subject, you need to move the camera forward and then shoot the next slice, and so on. Because of the huge quantity of slices that you might need, as well as because of the tiny distances that you need to move the camera, you'll need an automated focus stacking rig. I use the StackShot from CogniSys, Inc. The StackShot is a simple robot that can move your camera forward and backward with great precision, and fire a shot between each movement.

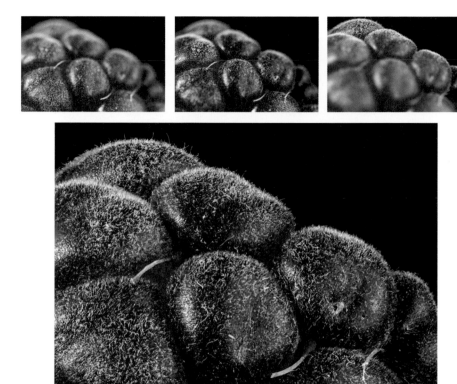

Figure 12.28

To get deep depth of field on this macro shot of a raspberry, I shot 84 separate images. Between each shot, I moved the camera forward by about a millimeter.

Finding the Optimal Macro Focal Length on a Point-and-Shoot Camera

The macro features on most point and shoot cameras are optimized for a particular range of focal lengths. Although most cameras will let you shoot macro pictures with your lens zoomed to any point, you'll get much better results if you put your camera in the macro "sweet spot." For some cameras, this is full wide, while for others it's somewhere else in the zoom range. Some cameras won't focus at all in Macro mode unless they are set within a particular focal range. Cameras that usually require you to be in a specific zoom range will have some kind of indicator in the viewfinder that will indicate when you're in the optimal macro focus range.

Some cameras include a "Best Shot Selection" feature that is ideal for macro photography. This feature shoots a burst of images and tries to identify the one that is in sharpest focus. The others are automatically discarded.

Finally, it's usually easier to hold the camera steady if you *don't* try to press the camera's zoom buttons. Instead of using the camera's zoom controls to frame your shot, simply move the camera in and out. At macro distances, you won't have to move it very far to get a reframing.

Lens Reversal

A nice macro lens can be an expensive piece of gear. If you're curious about macro shooting or don't want an extra lens in your bag, then you might consider *lens reversal*. If you simply take your current lens off the camera and flip it around so that the camera end is pointing

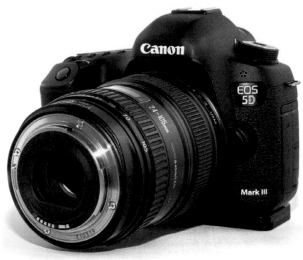

Figure 12.29

Using a reversal ring, I've reverse-mounted this lens to my camera, turning it into a macro lens.

outward, you'll have a very effective macro lens. Obviously, shooting while having to hold the lens against the camera is a little cumbersome. Fortunately, you can get inexpensive reversal rings that screw on to the filter threads on the end of your lens, which allow you to attach your lens to your camera backward (see Figure 12.29).

While this is an easy way to get high-quality macro shots, there are a few caveats:

◆ You will only be able to focus by moving the camera forward and backward. However, this is usually how you refine focus with a real macro lens.

◆ If you're using a zoom lens, then zooming the lens to its shortest focal length will give you the *most* magnification.

◆ By default, the aperture on your lens will be wide open, leaving you with very shallow depth of field. On some lenses, it's possible to force a smaller aperture. Mount the lens normally and use Manual mode to dial in an aperture that you want. Press the camera's depth of field preview to close the lens down to that aperture and then shut off the camera. The aperture might stay in its closed state, letting you reverse the lens while maintaining the small aperture.

High-Dynamic Range (HDR) Imaging

As already discussed, your eye can perceive a much greater dynamic range than your camera can. If you find yourself in a scene with a very extreme dynamic range, you have a few options. First, you can elect to capture just one part of the scene—either light or dark—and let the other part of the scene plunge into shadow or blow out to complete white.

If you want to hold detail in both the light and dark areas of the scene, you can shoot two images—one exposed to capture the lighter parts of the image, and the other exposed to capture the darker parts, and then composite these two images using your image editor. This type of compositing can vary in difficulty, depending on the content of your scene. Fine details such as leaves or complex transparent textures can be extremely difficult and time-consuming to composite. In some cases, getting a good composite might be impossible.

A better option is to use a special postprocessing technique that allows you to represent the full dynamic range of a scene by shooting multiple images, which are then combined using special software to create a high-dynamic range (HDR) image (see Figure 12.30).

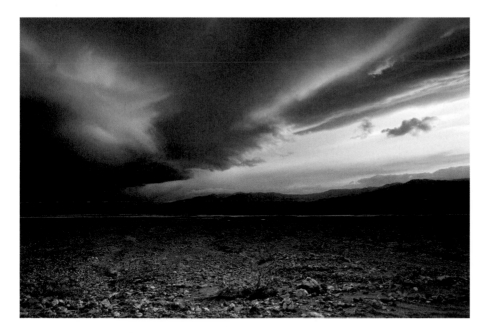

Figure 12.30

In a scene like this, you can choose to expose either for the bright part of the sky or for the dark ground. If you use HDR techniques, though, you can create an image that has good exposure throughout the entire tonal range.

In an HDR image, different tones are selected automatically from each of your source images to produce a final image with a full range of tones. HDR images can have dark shadows *and* bright highlights, each culled from a different source image. Notice in Figure 12.30 that the clouds and background have tremendous amounts of detail.

Shooting and processing HDR images is not difficult, but there are a few caveats to accept before you begin:

◆ Because HDR images require multiple source images, each shot with a different exposure, shooting HDR imagery of moving subjects is very difficult. In fact, it's often impossible to get usable results if there's a moving object in your image, such as blowing trees or moving people. With some work, you can often save these images in postproduction, but you shouldn't count on it.

◆ A little bit of HDR goes a long way. Sometimes, HDR images end up looking very stylized, and many people do not like the "hyper-real" look of HDR. We'll discuss HDR processing in detail later.

◆ HDR requires a camera with an Aperture Priority mode.

◆ Because you must shoot multiple images with identical framing, HDR usually requires a tripod. I say *usually* because some HDR processing programs can align images automatically. If your software is good enough and your hand is not too shaky, then you might be able to get away without using a tripod.

Shooting HDR

Your goal when shooting HDR is to shoot a series of identically framed images, each exposed one stop apart. Because you don't want any change in depth of field between the images, you'll need to shoot in Aperture Priority mode to ensure that your aperture doesn't change from one shot to the next, since a change in aperture could result in a variation in depth of field.

To shoot an HDR image:

1. Mount your camera on your tripod and frame your shot.

2. Set your camera to shoot in Raw mode. HDR can work with JPEG files, but raw preserves more color information, which can make for better merging later.

3. Set your camera to Aperture Priority and dial in an exposure compensation of –1.

4. Shoot the first image and then change exposure compensation to 0. Shoot the next image and then shoot an image at +1 (see Figure 12.31).

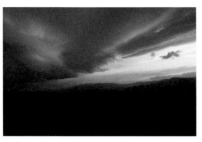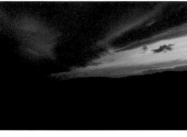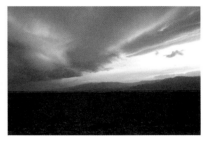

Figure 12.31 These source images were used to create the HDR image in Figure 12.30.

If you're shooting a scene with clouds, bear in mind that if it's windy, the clouds might move between shots, resulting in blurry skies. Also, wind might cause vegetation to wave and move. In these situations, you'll need to work as quickly as possible. To speed things up, you can consider using your camera's autobracketing features with Drive mode. This will allow you to rattle off an auto-bracketed set quickly.

Some people prefer a wider bracket of five or six shots. In other words, they shoot at –2, –1, 0, +1, +2. This larger bracket gives your HDR merging software more to work with, and can result in finer details and better gradients.

If your camera only allows a three-stop bracket, and you want to shoot more than three frames, you'll need to do two different bursts, one at –2, –1, and 0, and another at 0, +1, and +2. Obviously, you'll discard one of the images shot with 0 exposure compensation.

Personally, I've never found that shooting more steps yields any advantage over shooting three. Occasionally, you might find that you get a slight increase in editing latitude, but mostly the only difference is more complex postproduction. If you're shooting landscapes on a windy day, then shooting more steps simply means more blur as clouds and vegetation move between shots.

In Chapter 21, we'll look at how to process HDR images.

Are HDR Images Really Higher Dynamic Range?

The term "high dynamic range imaging" is actually a little misleading. The HDR process does not actually yield any more dynamic range in the final image. In fact, if you were to look at the histograms of the three source images I showed earlier, you'd find there is perhaps more dynamic range in a couple of the original images than there is in the final HDR. (Examine the histograms of some of your own HDR images, and you'll probably find similar results.)

Are HDR Images Really Higher Dynamic Range? (continued)

The HDR process does two things. First, it compresses the extremes of your exposures—the highlights and shadows—into the available dynamic range space. (In the previous example, this would be the almost blown-out sky and the almost totally dark mountains just below.) Second, it changes the exposure selectively throughout the image so that more detail is seen (the desert floor and clouds).

So your final image has a selection of stops that have been cherry-picked from your source images (this process is called *tone mapping*), but the total range is not necessarily expanded.

Shooting Concerts and Performances

Thanks to their exceptional low-light performance, digital cameras are ideal for shooting concerts and performances. In general, the problem with concerts and performances is that your subject is usually moving and the lighting conditions are generally dim. The moving subject will require you to use a faster shutter speed, but because of the low light conditions, you'll have to increase your ISO to afford the faster shutter. Depending on your camera, this ISO increase might lead to more noise in your final images.

Obviously, if you're shooting outdoors on a bright sunny day, you won't have these issues, so you can focus more on composition and content.

For shooting in an auditorium, though, battling the lighting conditions will be an extra chore that you'll have to address. You'll need to consider the following concerns:

◆ **ISO.** First, you need to know what the noise penalty is on your camera as you shift to a higher ISO. Before you head into a concert or performance-shooting scenario, spend some time working with your camera in low light at various ISO speeds. Process your images, and if your ultimate goal is print, then print out some tests. Use these to determine how high you can crank your ISO before the images become unacceptably noisy. Once you know your highest acceptable ISO, you'll be able to make some informed decisions after doing some metering tests at the venue.

◆ **White Balance.** The point of white balance is to calibrate your camera for the inherent color of different types of light, but stage lighting is almost always *intentionally* colored. This presents an interesting white balance quandary. You don't *want* to correct away the color that the performers have intentionally added, but that color could confuse your camera's automatic white balance to the point where it gets *all* the color wrong. Unfortunately, in most cases there's no way to white balance manually, because there's simply no place to take a white balance reading off of—one part of the stage might be lit with red lights, and another blue, and those lights may change during the show.

Your best bet is to stick with auto white balance and hope your camera is good enough. If your camera can shoot in raw format, then *definitely* opt for that. With raw files, you'll be able to correct your color later. If you can't shoot raw, then you'll have to hope that your auto white balance is up to the task, and if it's not, that you can perform some correction later.

Setup

When you get to the venue, try to determine a location where you can get a good angle on where you think the performers will be, but one that doesn't interfere with any audience member's line of sight. If you don't have open access to the venue and will only be able to shoot from a specific seat, then you'll just have to do the best you can.

Be Sure You Have Permission

Many performers do not like to have their shows photographed, both for copyright reasons and because it's distracting. If they've paid a license for the right to perform a particular piece of music or theater, that license may not include any electronic reproduction, so follow their wishes and don't shoot. If you've been asked to shoot a performance, contact the venue and make certain that shooting is allowed. In some venues, union rules may prohibit nonunion shooters.

If you're allowed to move around the hall, try to assess the best angles before the performance starts and identify the easiest, least intrusive way to move between those locations.

If you're shooting a musical event, be aware that some bands may allow you to shoot from directly in front of the stage, but only for the first song or two. The songs might be short, so you'll need to work quickly to take advantage of your position.

Turn the beep on your camera off. If you're shooting with a point-and-shoot camera that has an LCD viewfinder, turn the brightness down as far as possible (assuming your camera has a brightness control). If you're shooting with an SLR, turn the image review feature off. Bright LCD displays can annoy audience members, and can wreck your low light vision, which can slow down your shooting. Some SLRs also offer special quiet shutter modes, which slow down the process of re-cocking the shutter and lower the mirror more slowly to reduce noise. The downside is that you'll have a slower burst rate.

Obviously, with most performances, a long telephoto lens will be the order of the day so that you can get close-ups of performers and action. However, if your goal is to document the event, you might also want to have a wide-angle lens for capturing a few shots of the entire stage. If you're shooting in an auditorium, you'll want the fastest lenses you can lay your hands on. A faster lens can have a wider maximum aperture, which means you can use faster shutter speeds. Finally, be *absolutely certain* that your flash is off. Flash photography can be distracting to performers (or even dangerous, if they're engaged in a physical activity), and it is definitely annoying to the rest of the audience. Besides it doesn't do anything to improve your pictures. So turn your flash off and leave it off!

Exposure Strategy

Your first few shots will most likely be experimental as you work to determine the best exposure. Again, your main concern will be motion stopping. However, if the stage is too dark, you may have to accept that it's not possible to get a good exposure in-camera, and you will need to do some brightening later. Work through the following steps to find a good exposure:

1. Put your camera in Shutter Priority mode. Since shutter speed will be your main concern, you'll want control over it during your entire shoot.

2. Start at your slowest ISO.

3. Using the handheld shutter speed rule, shoot some shots with the "correct" shutter speed.

4. Discretely review your image's histogram. (You don't want the screen disturbing other patrons.) If the image is grossly underexposed, raise the ISO until you get a good image. If you have to go into an ISO that you've already deemed too noisy, then stop at your maximum acceptable ISO.

5. Now try lowering the shutter speed to brighten your image. Review your image to determine if the slower speed results in motion blur. If it doesn't, then you're good. If it *does*, then you'll have to go back to a faster shutter speed and accept underexposed images. Fortunately, you can probably brighten these back up later (see Figure 12.32).

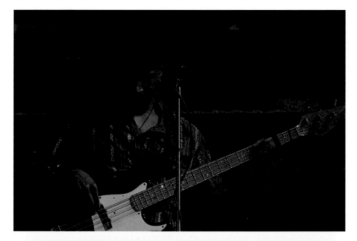

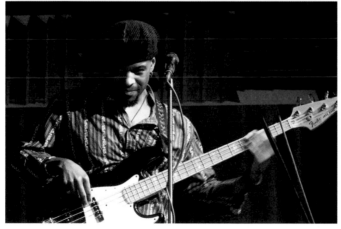

Figure 12.32

The only way to get a sharp shot of this moving musician was to use a fast shutter speed that resulted in an underexposed image. Fortunately, it was no trouble to brighten the picture back up to something usable.

After you've identified a workable shutter speed, you can probably shoot with it for the entire show. If the lighting changes dramatically or the action speeds up, you may need to perform more experiments. Motion stopping is your primary concern, so you might have to settle for images that need brightening later.

Bear in mind that when shooting in low light with a fast shutter speed, your camera will open its aperture all the way, which means depth of field will go down. Any time depth of field is shallow, you must be extra careful to ensure that you're focusing correctly. If you're autofocusing, make sure that your camera is selecting the right points.

If the venue is dark enough that your camera has trouble locking focus, you'll need to employ some of the low light focusing tips we discussed earlier.

If performers are wearing white shirts, bear in mind that these can easily overexpose, so take some test shots and check your histogram to ensure that white clothing isn't overexposing. If it is, then you'll need to adjust your exposure accordingly.

Shoot Sound Checks and Rehearsals

An easy way to get better shots is to try to get permission to shoot rehearsals. If it's a musical performance, find out if you can shoot the sound check. With sound checks and rehearsals, you don't have to worry about disturbing other audience members, the lighting is often better, and you might even be allowed on stage, where you can get close-ups. Even if the performers say that what they want are shots from an actual performance, remind them you'll shoot those also, but that a rehearsal or sound check is a nice place to get close-ups that aren't possible during a performance.

Performance Composition

Composing during a concert or performance can be tricky because the scene is constantly changing. You'll have to work quickly and be ready to adapt and adjust as the performers move and the lighting changes. Keep the following tips in mind:

♦ **If you're shooting a play or musical, don't try to tell the story that's being presented.** You don't have to worry about showing the relationship between characters or shooting sequences that convey what's going on.

♦ **Less is more.** Generally, nice close-ups of performers are going to be the most successful shots. Shooting close-ups will also make you less inclined to try to tell the story. If multiple performers are having a very compelling interaction, then go for wider two- and three-shots.

♦ **Be careful of mouths.** It's easy to take an unflattering shot of an actor or singer if you catch them speaking or singing, simply because their mouth might be in a weird position. While it's important to try to get good shots of these actions, it's also good to get shots of performers when their mouths are closed. Sometimes the best shots will be shots of a performer listening to other performers. Similarly, musicians who play wind instruments often have to hold their mouths in unflattering positions. Shots of them not playing, but reacting to other musicians, are often the most successful.

♦ **Keep your non-viewfinder eye open.** Because your attention will usually be drawn to whomever is currently speaking or playing, it can be easy to miss a nice reaction shot somewhere else on stage. Similarly, because action can change quickly, you want to be sure you can see the rest of the stage. Keeping your other eye open, and observing the whole stage as you shoot can help you spot the less obvious shot.

♦ **Look for the interesting angle.** A few shots of an actor speaking, or a trumpet player blowing, go a long way. If you're free to move around, then bring all of your composition skills to bear and look for interesting ways to compose shots of the performer with other elements on the stage. Also, remember that often the most interesting compositions are created from light and dark, which can be easy to find on a lit stage.

♦ **If you're shooting musicians, be ready to work around microphones and music stands.** You'll probably quickly learn to hate all of the hardware—amplifiers, stands, microphones, cords, and more—that accompanies a group of musicians. These will block mouths, faces, and hands; will interfere with your compositions; and will generally look ugly. Usually, your only recourse when confounded by an ugly stage implement is to move. If you aren't allowed to move, then you'll just have to suffer the extra visual element. When microphones are unavoidable, try to frame in a way that will make it easy to remove the microphones in post (see Figure 12.33).

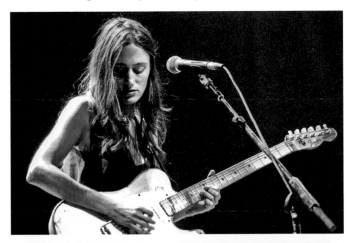

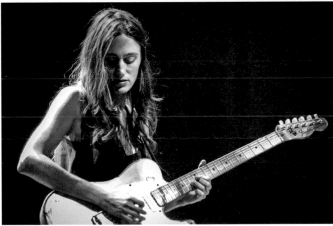

Figure 12.33

I was careful to frame this shot so that the microphone didn't overlap with the singer. This made for easy retouching later.

Finally, give some thought to battery and storage. If you're going to spend a few hours continuously shooting, you'll want a fully charged battery. You'll also need to think about how much storage you need. When shooting a long-duration show, I opt for larger cards so that I don't have to perform a card switch in the middle of a performance. Having to swap cards can disturb other audience members, and can lead to missed shots.

Shooting Events

Event shooting—be it a wedding, conference, or party—presents a tricky balance. On the one hand, you need to be non-obtrusive, but on the other hand you've got to get where the action is and get the good shots.

It's easy to be shy during an event shoot, and a lot of beginning shooters will make the mistake of erring too much on the side of being unobtrusive. They'll hang back and shoot lots of wide shots of groups of people. The results will be pictures of the sides and backs of people's heads, with the occasional shot of someone who happened to have turned toward the photographer.

To be a good event shooter, you have to be willing to engage with people and get into the action. Most people at an event—especially at a wedding—aren't surprised to see a photographer, and won't feel resentful if you take their picture. You don't want to interrupt the proceedings, or get in the way of people conversing, but it's okay to move about, get in front of people, and even talk to them. Turn on some charm, and you'll stand a better chance of getting good smiles and expressions.

For many events, there will even be a photographic agenda for you to follow. At a wedding, for example, you will most likely be expected to shoot the bride and groom preparing, the cutting of the cake, the kiss, the toast, and so on. What's more, you will be expected to get good shots of these moments, which often means being right in the thick of the action.

Similarly, at a corporate event of some kind, there might be specific moments you're expected to capture—two CEOs shaking hands after signing a deal, and so on. Such occasions usually demand close-ups.

To that end, talk to the client ahead of time and find out if there are specific shots that he or she is expecting. Be clear on what your deliverables are and try to get a sense of whether the client has specific needs for the final output.

Event shoots are usually fast-paced, and you'll often have to move, compose, and expose one shot after another. To facilitate this, choose a lens with a versatile focal length range, from fairly wide to somewhat telephoto. A 35–135mm range is ideal. Sure, you can carry shorter or longer focal lengths, but you probably won't have time to do a lot of lens changing, so take a good all-rounder with you.

Similarly, plan your storage strategy carefully, as discussed in the last section.

As always, look for the interesting angle when you can find it. Don't get too creative—the goal is to cover the people who attended the event, so follow the basic people composition rules presented in Chapter 2, "Getting to Know Your Camera." As with performance shooting, you don't have to get images that tell grand stories or complex relationships. You're just looking to document attendees and simple moments.

Exposure Strategy

Your exposure strategy will vary depending on the type of event you're shooting. If you're indoors shooting people at a conference, party, or meeting, then your main concern will probably be depth of field, since you'll want the option to blur out backgrounds. In these instances, stick with Aperture Priority mode, or if you think depth of field control won't be especially critical, then stay in Program mode and ride your camera's Program Shift feature. As always, keep an eye on your shutter speed and get ready to raise the ISO if light levels get too low.

If you're shooting an outdoor event such as a fair or music festival, then you might have either aperture or shutter speed concerns. If it's an event with fast-moving people or activities, switch to Shutter Priority to give yourself some control of motion stopping. If you're just walking around shooting candids of people, then you'll probably be more concerned about depth of field, so switch to Aperture Priority. Program mode with Program Shift is a good way to have access to both of these options.

In either event, be aware of backlighting and stay ready to use your camera's exposure compensation feature or fill flash.

Shooting Sports

As a sports shooter, one of your biggest assets is an understanding of the game that you're shooting. It's usually pretty easy to go out and compose nice shots, but what you want are nice shots of critical moments or especially impressive achievements. The more you understand the sport you're shooting, the better your chances of anticipating and capturing key moments. As in performance shooting, keep your non-viewfinder eye open and track your entire field of view. Keeping your off-eye open can also let you see what's about to move into the frame, making it easier to know when to fire.

In general, long, fast lenses are the lenses of choice for sports shooting. In addition to giving you the ability to get close-ups and to work in low light, a long, fast lens lets you shoot shallow depth of field that will let you separate your subject from what is usually a very complicated background. Note that if you're going to a game as a spectator, the venue may not allow you to carry a long lens. In general, a point-and-shoot camera is a safer way to go if you're going to a commercial event and don't have a press credential.

It's often said that sports writing is the hardest type of writing, because you have to find a new way of writing the same story over and over. Sports shooting can be the same way.

To avoid shooting the same shots over and over (and the same shots that everyone else is shooting), try to find a different angle. This often means getting in close and finding vantage points that are a little unusual, as you can see in Figure 12.34.

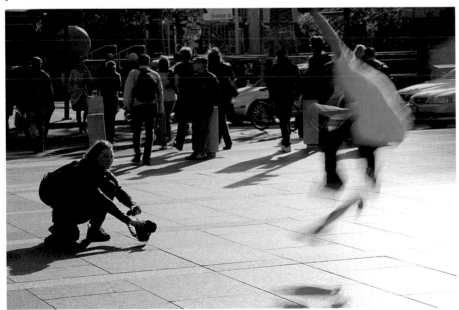

Figure 12.34

To get the shot in Figure 12.35, photographer Janine Lessing had to get in close and find an unusual angle. With her camera in Burst mode, she didn't even look through the viewfinder, but simply tried to imagine a dramatic vantage point for her camera.

Exposure Strategy

When shooting sports, your main concern is shutter speed. If you're shooting a day game in bright daylight, then your shutter speed choice will largely be about how much motion stopping you want (see Figure 12.35). In most cases, you'll want all the motion-stopping power you can get, so you'll opt for fast shutter speeds that go well beyond the handheld shutter speed rule. To achieve these, you might need to go to a faster ISO.

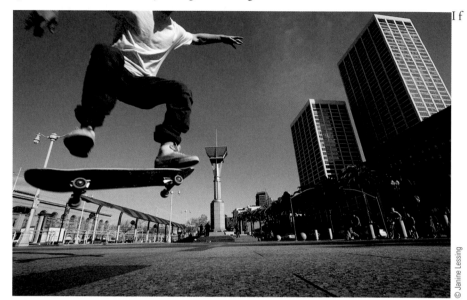

Figure 12.35

In general, your main concern when shooting any kind of sports or action is to decide how much motion stopping you want. Do you want a blurry action shot, a razor sharp freeze, or something in between?

If you're shooting a night game under more limited lighting, then your shutter speed options will be a little more limited. While most arenas and fields will be lit well enough for the players to see, they might not be bright enough for a super-fast, motion-stopping shutter speed. Again, you'll need to crank up your ISO. Note also that some parts of the field may be brighter than others, so you might need to adjust ISO as you shoot into different parts of the venue. As with concert shooting, you may have to shoot some underexposed images with the idea of brightening the images later.

Bright lights can wreak havoc with white uniforms, causing them to overexpose, so keep an eye on your histogram until you determine if you need to dial in some negative exposure compensation to get detail back in overexposed uniforms.

If you're shooting in an indoor arena, then white balance will be an issue, due to the colored lights used in most arenas. Shooting in raw format is your best bet here, as you'll be able to adjust white balance later. Try to find something gray on the floor of the stadium and take a shot of it. This will give you a white balance reference for postproduction correction.

If you must shoot JPEG, then see if you can get to the floor of the stadium and perform a manual white balance.

Street Shooting

Earlier, I mentioned that you shouldn't have to go to an exotic location to find good subject matter. No matter where you live, shooting on the street will often yield great subject matter.

By "street shooting," I'm talking about getting outside in your neighborhood or town and shooting the people and situations that you find there. Some of the most famous photographic images in history are candid street shots, and you'll often find that your most interesting, dramatic, and often pretty shots occur on the street.

Street shooting is also the scariest type of shooting for most people. Approaching strangers and taking their picture can be terrifying. Unfortunately, there's no way around the fear problem, other than to face it and dive in. It *will* be scary, and it will continue to be scary for quite a while. However, this doesn't mean you shouldn't do it, and more importantly, just because it *feels* scary doesn't mean there's any actual risk.

Street shooting is something you can practice, and there are some guidelines you can follow that will help mitigate some of the fear.

For the most part, approaching strangers involves common sense. While you can choose to skulk around with a long, telephoto lens, so that you don't have to confront people, this is not really "street shooting" but is more akin to "surveillance," and it's a sure way to make people angry with you.

The best way to shoot candids on the street is to engage with people and establish a dialogue with them. When you find someone doing something interesting, talk to them about it. Discuss what they're doing and why. At some point, if you're still interested, and you feel the person is open, then ask if you can take their picture. Most of the time, you'll find that people will say yes. If they don't, then you can simply thank them and move on.

Obviously, this approach doesn't work if you see someone involved in an activity that is fleeting because engaging with the person will destroy the very moment you want to capture. If that's the case, get the shot, and then consider talking to the person and establishing some kind of rapport. This is the "shoot first, ask questions later" approach. At the least, you'll establish good will and leave the scene without worrying that you've invaded someone's space. In many cases, though, if you engage with the person they may lead you to more shots.

When grabbing shots like this, you don't have to have a conversation with your subject, but after taking the shot, you should at least try making eye contact with them and giving them a nod of thanks.

If, at any time, you get the feeling that someone doesn't want to have his picture taken, or that you're invading someone's privacy, then don't take the shot. There are plenty of pictures in the world, and there's no need to make someone angry. By being polite, you make the world a better place for other photographers.

Technically, when you're in a public space, you're allowed to take pictures of people, buildings—anything you want. If someone tells you you're not allowed to take a picture of their house or storefront, or whatever, they're not actually correct. But this is rarely a fight that's worth having. In most cases, it's easier—and less stressful—to simply move on and find something else to shoot.

Sometimes, you'll find that people might give you a puzzled, "Did you just take my picture?" look. In these cases, take the time to say, "I'm just out shooting some pictures, and I got a nice shot of you doing [whatever.]" Once you speak, you become more of a normal human to them and less threatening. But you might also consider offering a little bit more.

Offering Something in Return

One of the great things about street shooting in the digital era is that you can show your final work to the people you shoot on the street. If you engage with your subject before or after a shot, ask them if they have an email address. You can then email them pictures or a link to a photo-sharing site. Or you can simply tell them your Web address and let them know that the pictures might be appearing there within a certain time frame.

A lot of photographers have business cards made that includes their photo sharing address. There are lots of free, online business card printing services, so it's easy to have cards made that you can hand out to people who might be interested in seeing what you're doing. This is a great way to give something back to your subject.

You can also choose to show them the image right then and there on the back of your camera. However, it's usually best to wait and let them see the finished work. There's no guarantee that you won't hold up your camera, only to find that the shot was somehow unflattering. When shooting kids on the street, you want to be particularly careful about showing the results. Kids will often become so interested in seeing the back of the camera that they'll simply start mugging and performing rather than being natural.

When shooting people in other countries, especially those who don't have much, you will often find yourself facing a subject who wants money. Whether you choose to pay or not, is up to you—there's no right or wrong answer. There's some compelling data that shows that, if you're shooting in a heavily trafficked tourist spot, then giving away money for shots is not great for the locals. Kids, especially, will learn that they can go hang around and get their picture taken for money, rather than trying to find more gainful employment.

Nevertheless, when faced with extreme poverty, it's very hard not to want to help the people you're shooting. When I spend time with someone in a poor, remote village, I give them money afterward. (They invariably ask, so it's not a difficult situation to broach.)

For kids, consider carrying pencils, nuts, balloons, or stickers. What they really want is sugary candy, and you can always indulge that, but it's not necessarily in their best interest.

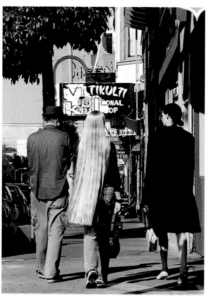

Figure 12.36

You must be careful to have proper permissions when using images for any for-profit venture, such as book use or fine art printing.

Using Street Shots

Now the bad news: It's hard to do much legally with images you shoot on the street. Images shot in public can be used for journalistic purposes, and you're free to upload them to a photo-sharing site or post them on a Web page. But if you want to use them for any purpose that generates a profit for you—selling fine art prints or including them in a book, for example—then you can't legally use the image without a signed release form from the subject. If this is your goal, then you need to either carry release forms with you (you can find generic ones online) or get an email address or phone number of anyone whose image you think you might want to use. Or you can simply choose to risk it and hope that you won't be discovered using the image, or you can choose images that aren't recognizable (see Figure 12.36).

Release Form for Your Smart Phone

There are a number of model release applications for smartphones. These provide an electronic model release form that a subject can sign directly on the phone. These applications often also have location release forms, which can be necessary if you're shooting inside a location such as a restaurant or store.

Exposure Strategy

Depth of field is usually your main concern with street shooting. In a rapidly changing street environment, you might opt for deeper depth of field to improve your chances of getting images in focus. This is especially true if you're shooting "from the hip" and can't be sure about focus. The deeper depth of field will help ensure that your images are sharp.

Street scenes often have very busy backgrounds, so there will be times when you'll prefer a shallower depth of field to create separation between your subject and background.

Shooting at Night

We've spent a lot of time in this book talking about light and what makes good light, but often dark is just as compelling as light. Digital image sensors are incredibly sensitive to light, and at the time of this writing, cameras with ISO settings as high as 25,000 are commonplace and yield very good images.

At night, the world is lit up in a very different way. Street lighting illuminates things from different angles and at different intensities than what you're used to during the day. The upshot is that at night you might find subject matter in places that are featureless and boring during the day (see Figure 12.37).

Low-light images are largely about luminance. We don't perceive a lot of color at night, so you'll often find yourself working in black and white when shooting at night. Whether working in color or black and white, here are some things to consider:

◆ When working in color, be careful about white balance. You'll probably want to manually white balance off a gray white balance card, or you'll want to shoot in raw mode and shoot a white balance reference shot, as shown in Chapter 7, "Program Mode."

◆ You'll typically be shooting at higher ISO, so be aware of how high your camera can go, ISO-wise, before its images get too noisy.

◆ In low light, you'll usually shoot with longer exposures, so be careful about stabilizing the camera and about shooting subjects that move. You might also want to use faster lenses, which will mean shallower depth of field, which will require you to be very careful about focus.

◆ One of the trickiest things about shooting in low light is that, when it's very dark, you won't be able to see your subject through the viewfinder. This can make composition more difficult. If you're working on a tripod, take a shot, then review the image to test composition, and reframe accordingly.

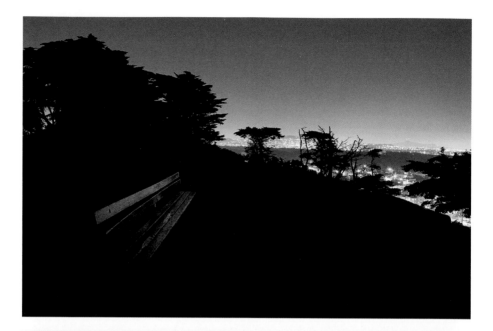

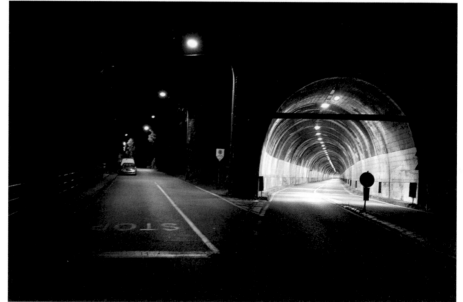

Figure 12.37

The world lights up in a very different way at night and reveals an entirely new range of subject matter. Digital cameras are ideally suited to capturing low-light imagery.

Low Light Focus

Because your camera's autofocus requires a fair amount of light to be able to achieve focus, low light can render it useless. You can try manually focusing, but if it's dark enough to trip up your camera's autofocus, then your eyes might not be able to do much better.

Try to find something bright that's at the same distance as your subject and focus on that; then reframe and take your shot. If you're trying to shoot a person, ask him to turn on his cell phone and hold it up where you can see it. Your camera can probably focus on that light.

If you have a really bright flashlight, you can try shining it into your scene to create a spot that's bright enough to focus on. Then shut the flashlight off and shoot.

If you're going to take multiple shots of the scene, and you're working with an SLR, then switch your lens to Manual focus after you've achieved focus. As long as you don't turn the focus ring, this will lock in the correct focus.

Real-World Low Light Shooting

Consider Figure 12.38, a 25-second exposure shot in Monument Valley. The only light in this scene was the full moon, which was shining brightly enough to cast hard-edged shadows. Still, when looking through the viewfinder, it was hard to see the edges of the frame, so composing was difficult.

To get the shot, I mounted the camera—a Canon EOS 5D Mark II—on my tripod and tried my best to get a rough composition. I had to look through the viewfinder for a long time before my eyes adjusted, and even then I could only see vague forms.

I put the camera in Aperture Priority mode because I was concerned about depth of field. I didn't want to use any mode that would let the camera choose the aperture, because I figured it would choose a wide-open setting (to help reduce shutter speed), which would wreck my depth of field.

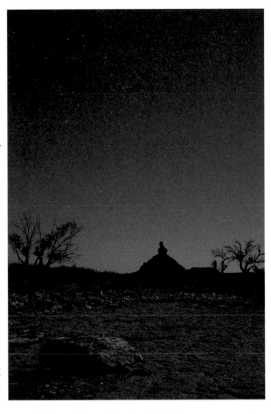

Figure 12.38

This image was illuminated solely by the full moon. Capturing this image required some very specific techniques.

I chose an aperture of f5.6. In daylight I would have chosen f11, but I didn't want to go that small, because I didn't want a very long shutter speed. When shooting low-light landscapes, shutter speed choice is tricky. With an aperture of f11, I would have been looking at an exposure of around a minute-and-a-half. At that length, the stars would begin to leave trails. While star trails are often a nice effect, for this image, I wanted pinpoint stars, so I had to do whatever I could to shorten exposure time.

Note too, that with a longer exposure time, you stand the chance of getting a noisier image. As exposure time lengthens, some pixels on the sensor can get stuck in the On position. They'll appear in your final image as yet another type of noise.

The 5D Mark II can't shoot with shutter speeds over 30 seconds. For longer shutter speeds, you have to put the camera in Bulb mode and time the exposures yourself, so that was another reason I wanted to keep the exposure under 30 seconds.

I figured, though, that at f5.6, I could get the depth of field that I needed for the shot.

The next issue was focus. It was too dark for autofocus to work, but also too dark for me to see well enough to manually focus. Instead, I had to go by the numbers.

For a landscape shot, it's tempting to simply turn the manual focus ring to infinity. But as you've already learned, if you focus on infinity, you'll be wasting a lot of depth of field, because it will fall *behind* the infinity point. Instead, you'll want to focus just a little short of infinity. Note that on most lenses, as you approach infinity, a tiny turn of the lens ring can equate to a big change in focus, so make only very small moves when you pull back from the infinity mark.

Figure 12.39

On some lenses, infinity is indicated by an L-shape. The vertical mark represents infinity at normal temperatures, with infinity moving to the right as temperatures rise.

On the focus readout of some lenses, such as most lenses from Canon and Sigma, infinity is denoted by an L-shaped mark. The vertical mark represents infinity at normal temperatures.

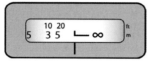

As temperatures rise, infinity moves more to the right. Most of the time, the normal infinity mark will be your reference point (see Figure 12.39). For this type of shooting, you'll want to focus just a little bit short of that mark.

With an initial stab at framing and focusing, I was ready to take a test shot. As already mentioned, exposure time on a shot like this is really long for my test shot. I'm only interested in getting a better view of my composition and checking my focus. So I set ISO up very high—in this case, 6400. This setting produced an image that was noisier than I wanted, but I didn't care, because I was just after a quick reference shot. With the reference taken, I could adjust my composition as necessary, zoom in to the playback display to examine focus (not the ideal way to check focus, but the only option in these circumstances), and adjust accordingly. If need be, I could take another reference shot.

When I was ready for a final image, I turned my ISO back down to what I wanted to use for my final shot—in this case, 1600, which provided a clean image without lengthening my exposure time so much that I lost sharpness in the stars—and I took the shot.

On long-exposure shots, you'll either want to use the self-timer or a remote control to help reduce camera shake. With an SLR, the movement of the camera's mirror can also cause camera shake, so if your camera has a mirror lock-up feature, you might want to activate that as well. With mirror lock-up, the camera flips up the mirror when you press the shutter button, but doesn't trip the shutter until you press the button a second time. So you can flip the mirror up, wait a moment for any vibration to die down, and then trip the shutter. Because the mirror isn't clacking around before the shot, chances are better that the camera will be more stable. This is really only a concern on exposures of a second or two—longer exposures won't suffer from mirror-generated shake.

As you can see, this type of shooting is a process of balancing noise with motion, and all while trying to compose and focus in the dark. If your camera can display a status display on the rear LCD, activate this feature, as it will make it much easier to check your current settings. The 5D Mark II even lets you change settings using this screen. With the camera mounted on a tripod and light levels low, this is usually the easiest way to change settings.

Long Exposure Noise Reduction

Some cameras have a noise reduction feature that's tailored specifically to long exposures; however, sometimes, these features require processing time that's equivalent to your exposure time. For example, if you shoot a minute-long exposure, then the camera will be unusable for another minute and process after the shot. Other cameras can perform the reduction in real time, while the shot is being taken. Either way, it's almost always worth using this feature, but you'll want to check your camera ahead of time to find out how it processes.

Calculating Exposure Time for Star Trails

You can easily calculate the longest shutter time that will give you sharp stars in a long exposure. Simply divide 500 by your focal length (in 35mm equivalence) to get the longest shutter speed that will still give you sharp stars. Anything longer will begin to produce trails.

Underwater Photography

Thanks to their small size and excellent low-light capabilities, digital cameras make for excellent underwater photography. To shoot underwater, you'll first need an enclosure for your camera. Some camera vendors make their own underwater housing, but if yours doesn't, you can probably find a third-party housing. Be sure to get a housing designed for your specific model of camera. An ill-fitting housing might leak, which would, obviously, be very bad. A good housing will provide access to all of the camera's menus and controls, and if you plan to do a lot of underwater photography, you should consider the availability of underwater housings when shopping for a camera.

Once you have a housing, your next step will be to get underwater. Each type of housing will be rated to be safe to a specific depth, so make sure you don't exceed the capabilities of your housing.

Today, many point-and-shoot cameras have special white balance settings for shooting underwater. If yours has one, give it a try. It can be dim and murky underwater, so you may need to switch to a higher ISO. In many cases, you'll be using the camera's flash, which means you can stick to a lower ISO setting. Depending on your subject matter, you might need to use your macro setting (see Figure 12.40).

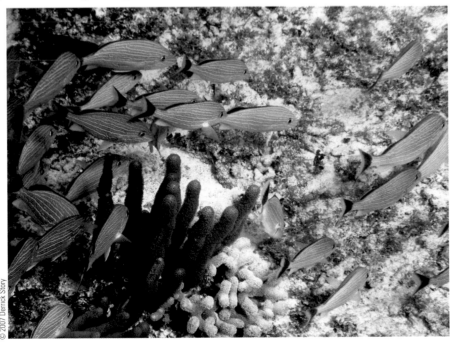

© 2007 Derrick Story

Figure 12.40

Thanks to their low-light sensitivity, digital cameras allow for excellent underwater photography. You'll need a special housing designed for your specific camera.

Vacation Shooting

When shooting on your vacation, you'll have all of the same photographic concerns that you do with any other kind of shooting—shutter speed, aperture, ISO, finding a good place for lunch. In the face of exciting new vistas and venues, though, it's easy to fall back into bad habits as you find yourself overwhelmed by new imagery. To come home with good results, you'll want to avoid certain common pitfalls.

◆ **Get closer.** Remember that, just because a big wide vista is beautiful, you don't need to try to capture all of it—in fact, you probably can't. Rather than zooming out to your widest angle and coming home with shots of a distant, small horizon, zoom in and work the details of the scene. Sure, you won't be able to show your friends the huge view that you saw, but sometimes that's just how it is—a photograph is no substitute for being there.

◆ **Balance your sunsets.** Remember that shooting someone in front of a sunset is a bad backlighting situation. The sun is going to cause your camera to err on the side of underexposure, so you'll lose all details in your subject. Use your camera's fill flash to illuminate them.

◆ **Be selective in your presentation.** When you get back home, keep in mind that a few, really good photos will deliver more impact than a never-ending stream of every detail of your trip. When it comes to looking at someone's vacation pictures, less is *always* more, so give careful consideration to the images you choose to show.

◆ **Put down your camera.** Remember: you went on vacation to vacate. Leave your camera in your room from time to time. If you're worried that you'll miss some kind of "once-in-a-lifetime" photo, don't. There will always be another, and having actual memories of your trip might be more valuable than only having memories of taking photos.

Product Shots

Product photography is a very specialized skill, and good product photographers command very high fees. There's a reason for this—quality product photography is hard.

Normally, I wouldn't cover such a specialized form of photography, mostly because, in the past, few people have had a need for product photography. But with eBay, Craigslist, Amazon, and other online sales venues, more people need to take quality photos of objects.

At the most basic level, lighting a product is just like lighting a person, and you can start with the same two- or three-point lighting schemes that we looked at in Chapter 10, "Lighting." The easiest solution for the simple product shots that you need when posting items online is to invest in a light tent. Available at most chain photo stores and easily found online, these tents are composed of light diffusing material. Put the object you want to photograph inside the tent and point your camera through the door. Place any kind of lights outside the tent and shine them through the walls, and you'll get nice, even lighting. The resulting shots will have a white, limbo background that is ideal for showing off products.

When shooting close-ups of a product, depth of field becomes critical. Your camera's auto settings will probably err on the side of shallower depth of field, which will leave details on your object out of focus. To get deeper depth of field, change to Aperture Priority and dial in a smaller aperture. Because this will lower your shutter speed, you might need to increase your ISO or place your camera on a tripod.

Tethered Shooting

Tethered shooting is the process of connecting your camera to your computer so that as soon as you shoot, the image is transferred to the computer and becomes immediately viewable. For product photography, tethered shooting is a great convenience because you can review your shots immediately on a nice, large monitor, and even try some edits and adjustments.

Most cameras these days tether through a USB connection. Your camera might have shipped with tethering software. If it didn't, there are third-party options, including Adobe Lightroom. Unfortunately, there's no standard for camera-to-computer communication protocol, so it's difficult for third-parties to support particular cameras. So third-party apps may not work with your specific camera, and if they do, they may not provide all the functionality that you get from the software made by your camera vendor.

Another option to tethering into your computer is to simply take the video out from your camera and plug it into a large TV. Most cameras provide either composite S-video connections or HDMI HD connections. When working this way, you can shoot normally and then put your camera into Playback mode to review your images on the big screen or shoot in Live View mode and use the big monitor as a viewfinder.

Finally, consider an Eye-Fi card. These special SD cards include a WiFi transmitter and now can transmit images directly to a computer, smart phone, or cloud service. You won't need any additional software on your computer, and you won't have to hassle with a cable. Transfer times will be a little slower, but this might be the easiest way to arrange a tethered shoot.

Using Filters

Lens filters can be used for everything from creating special effects to correcting image problems, but before you can start using a filter, you have to figure out how to get it onto your camera.

First, check the lens on your camera for lens threads. If the front of the lens is too curved, you may not be able to attach any filters, unless the camera provides some kind of filter adapter that attaches by using some other kind of mount. The filter size for your lens is probably written on the end of the lens (see Figure 12.41). If not, check your manual.

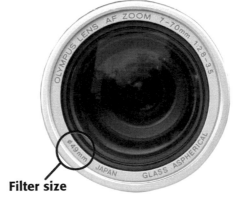

When you buy filters, be sure to get filters that have the same thread size as your lens. Most filters will have threads of their own, which will allow you to stack filters.

Filter size

Figure 12.41

If your lens has threads, you can find out what size filters you need by looking for a thread-size marking on the end of your lens. The lens shown here needs 49mm filters.

Other filters might not be available in the right size for your lens, and they might require the use of a step-up ring, a simple adapter that screws onto the front of your lens and provides a bigger (or sometimes smaller) set of threads for accepting filters with different thread sizes. Be careful with step-up rings because if they're too big, they might block your camera's metering sensors, flash, or optical viewfinder.

Lens filters are completely flat, meaning they don't add any magnification power to your lens. Although optically they are simpler than a lens, you still want to be careful about your choice of filter. There *is* a difference between a $100 ultraviolet filter and a $35 ultraviolet filter. A more expensive filter will be flatter and will have higher-quality glare-reducing coatings on it. Just as an element in your lens can introduce aberrations, a poorly made filter can introduce flares and color shifts. Although it can be tempting to go for the less-expensive filter, spend a little time researching the more costly competition. You might find there is a big difference in image quality.

Types of Filters

There are many types of filters—too many to cover here. However, if there were a group of "essential" filters, it would probably include the following.

- **Polarizers.** Polarizers will pass only light that is polarized in a particular direction. The practical upshot is that polarizers can completely remove distracting reflections from water, glass, or other shiny surfaces. To use a polarizer, you attach it to the end of your lens and rotate it until the reflections are gone. Polarizers can also be used to increase the contrast in skies and clouds (see Figure 12.42).

- **Ultraviolet filters.** Ultraviolet filters are used to cut down on haze and other atmospheric conditions that can sometimes result in color shifts in your image.

- **Neutral Density filters.** These cut down the amount of light entering your lens, without altering the light's color. By cutting down the light, you might find that you have some extra flexibility with regard to exposure.

  Neutral density filters are usually rated using an ND scale, where .1ND equals 1/3 stop. Therefore, a .3ND filter will reduce the incoming light by one full stop. Neutral density filters can be stacked on top of one another to add or subtract more stops selectively. However, even the best filters are not optically perfect, so it's better to use as few as possible to reduce the chance of introducing optical aberrations into your lens system. In other words, if you want a one-stop filter, use a single .3ND filter instead of three .1ND filters.

  You can also get variable neutral density filters. As you turn them on the lens, you'll get more or less ND strength. While convenient, these filters often suffer from bad moiré patterns when turned to their extremes, giving them much less ND range than advertised.

A Great Neutral-Density Filtering Trick

Say you want to photograph a building on a busy street corner at noon, but you don't want to include any of the people who are pouring into and out of the building. Stack up a few neutral density filters until you have an 8- to 10-stop filter. This will increase your exposure time to 10 or 15 minutes, meaning that anything that's not stationary for at least that long won't be included in the shot. Obviously, you'll need a camera that provides a manual shutter speed control and allows for such long exposures. When the exposure is finished, you'll have an image of just the building.

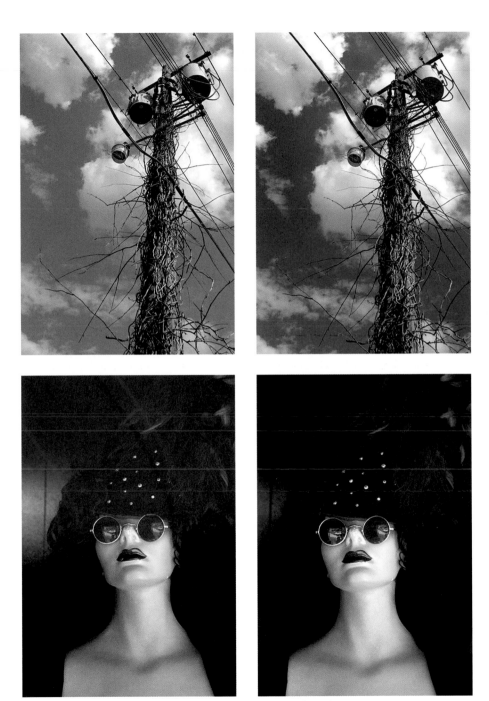

Figure 12.42

These images show the difference in shooting with and without a circular polarizing filter. In the top images, you can see how a polarizer lets you control the color and contrast of skies and clouds, whereas the bottom images show how you can use a polarizer to eliminate reflections. No postprocessing was applied to any of these images.

- **Graduated Neutral Density filters.** These filters cut the light from one-half of the lens while leaving the other half untouched. A graduated filter provides another way to shoot high dynamic range landscape scenes. With the graduated filter, you can reduce the exposure of the sky, allowing you to get a more even exposure in the sky and foreground.

- **Effects filters.** There are any number of effects filters, ranging from filters that will render bright lights as starbursts to filters that will soften, or haze, an image. Major filter manufacturers such as Tiffen, B+W, and Hoya publish complete, detailed catalogs of all their filter options.

- **UV filters.** Ultraviolet filters cut out the little bit of ultraviolet light that makes it through the atmosphere. UV filters can provide valuable protection for your lens. If you smash the lens into something, a filter can bear the brunt of the damage, usually leaving the lens unharmed. UV filters also offer great protection in harsh environments, such as beaches or wet environments where you need to be able to wipe off the lens quickly without worrying about scratching the front element. When shopping for a UV filter (or Skylight filter, a variant of the normal UV filter), don't settle for anything but a multicoated filter, which helps reduce glare, and helps with light transmission, resulting in a brighter image.

- **Clear filters.** If you're only interested in protecting your lens, then you might want to consider a clear filter, which serves no function except to shield the front element of your lens. In addition to protecting it from scratches, a filter can also prevent dust from getting inside the lens.

If your camera does not have a TTL light meter, you'll have to do some manual compensating when you use a filter. Because the metered light is not passing through the filter, the meter will lead you to underexpose. Most filters will have a documented filter factor, which will inform you of the exposure compensation (in stops) required when you use that filter.

Similarly, if your camera does not use a TTL white balance system, your white balance might not be adjusted properly for the filter's effect. The only way to find out for sure is to do a little experimenting.

These days, it's very rare for a meter or white balance system not to be TTL.

Obviously, if your camera is not an SLR, you won't see the effects of the filter when you look through the camera's optical viewfinder. Switch to the camera's LCD.

In general, except for polarizing filters and possibly neutral density filters, you can use your image editor to achieve all the effects that can be created with lens filters. Lens filters have the great advantage of not requiring additional edits, so if you know you need an effect, and can achieve it with filters, this will greatly speed your workflow. However, if you shoot "clean" images and add filter effects later, you'll also have the option of repurposing that image for nonfiltered uses.

Lens Extensions for Point-and-Shoot Cameras

Some point-and-shoot cameras support screw-on lens extensions that attach to your camera's filter threads, or to a special bayonet mount on the front of the camera, to create a more telephoto or wide-angle lens. As with filters, these extensions might require a step-up ring. Also note that some cameras require you to choose special settings—usually accessed through a menu option—when using a lens extension. If you don't let the camera know that an extension is attached, its focus and metering operations can become confused.

Spend some time experimenting with your camera's extensions to determine their idiosyncrasies. For example, some lenses might have bad barrel or pincushion distortion or vignetting problems.

Finally, if the extension or step-up ring is very large, it might obscure the camera's optical viewfinder or on-board flash. If the extension protrudes too far in front of the flash, it will cast a shadow when you take the shot. Usually, the only solution is to use an external flash.

Exploring on Your Own

There are many specialized forms of photography, and the topics we've discussed in this chapter can be explored in much greater depth. Hopefully, you've gotten an idea of the types of issues you'll face and how to think about solving them. To get good at any of these types of shooting, you'll need to practice. But perhaps the most important thing to remember is that there are many different solutions to the problems that you'll encounter when shooting in any of the situations described in this chapter. Don't hesitate to improvise and try to find your own solutions.

13

WORKFLOW
Managing Your Images and Starting Postproduction

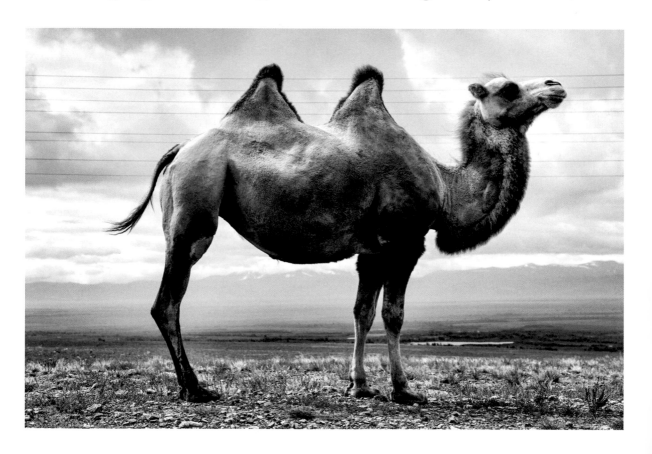

In the rest of this book, you will learn about what happens after you've finished shooting. From color correcting to editing to printing, the following chapters will cover the processes that have traditionally happened in the darkroom but that now happen inside your computer.

Workflow is the process of managing this whole business. The workflow you choose will govern how you import images, keep them organized, edit and correct them, tag them with searchable metadata, output them, and archive them for safekeeping. As discussed in Chapter 4, "Image Transfer," there are several approaches to workflow. You can find a single application that can manage all of the steps of your workflow or gather a collection of applications, each aimed at a specific part of your workflow needs.

If you're in a hurry to get to the image editing chapters of this book, you might be thinking "Workflow, right…I'll figure that out later, when I get more serious. Right now I just want to correct my images." Bear in mind, though, that image editing takes time, and you don't want to waste time editing an image only to discover later that there's another shot of the same subject that you like even more. Also, remember that those hundreds of images that you've imported have arcane file names, and are not organized into any particular file structure. As your image library grows, it can become harder and harder to find images and to keep track of different versions you may have created. (Perhaps you've got color *and* black-and-white versions of some images, or different versions edited in different ways.) If you're not careful, you can easily end up accidentally deleting images or saving over older versions with newer files, all while getting frustrated with the difficulty of finding particular images.

Defining a good workflow process will not only help you stay organized in the long run, but it will also help your short-term image editing goals by forcing you to evaluate intelligently which images are worth editing and which are not.

No matter what software you use, your workflow will probably follow roughly the same steps. So before we consider specific software applications, I'm going to define exactly what needs to happen in a typical workflow.

Postproduction Workflow

If you're coming from a wet darkroom background, this whole "workflow" discussion may seem a little strange. But even in a traditional darkroom, you have a workflow, a method for keeping track of your negatives and prints, and the custom instructions you might come up with for printing each image. As much as anything else, defining a workflow is a process of figuring out how to stay organized, both in your current project and as your library of archived images grows.

Whether you choose to handle your workflow using a dedicated workflow application or a combination of applications (we discussed various software options in Chapter 4), you can break down the most complex postproduction workflow into eight steps:

◆ **Import.** Before you can do anything else, you need to get your images off your camera's media card. It doesn't really matter if you choose to import your images directly from your camera using a cable or from a storage card using a media card reader. However, importing directly from your camera will drain your camera battery.

- ◆ **Organize and rename.** If you use multiple applications for managing your workflow, you probably use your operating system's file manager to organize your image files into folders and possibly to rename them. There's no right or wrong way to name and organize your files, so do whatever makes the most sense to you and feel free to experiment with different schemes.

- ◆ **Add metadata and keywords.** Metadata tags are simple bits of text that can be stored in your image file. There are several different kinds of metadata tags. As you've already learned, your camera stores EXIF metadata tags to record the parameters that were used for shooting. IPTC metadata is a standard set of metadata tags that lets you record copyright information, keywords, location, and many other pieces of standardized information. Metadata tagging and keywording can be an essential step for the long-term organization of your image archive. For example, with categorical keywords assigned to your images, you'll be able to search easily for images later that fit a particular description. With metadata and keywords stored in your image, you aren't limited to organizing only by file name. This is also probably the stage where you'll geotag your images—encode them with location information.

- ◆ **Select your pick images.** You'll typically shoot far more images than you will actually deliver or use. There's no reason to spend time correcting and editing images that aren't going to make the cut for final delivery, so once you've tagged and keyworded your images, you're ready to start selecting your *pick* images—the "keeper" or "hero" images that you'll pass on to the rest of your workflow. Note that some people swap this step with the last one, figuring they'll delete any images that don't get selected as picks, so there's no reason to waste time keywording and tagging nonpick images. Other people feel it's a mistake to delete any images, as you never know what you might need later. Storage is cheap these days, and workflow tools make it easier to manage large numbers of images, so there's little reason not to keep your secondary images, at least for a while.

- ◆ **Correct and edit.** Now you're ready to perform any corrections, edits, or special effects you have in mind. This stage can involve anything from the simplest contrast and tone adjustments to complex compositing and filtering operations. If speedy workflow is a must, you'll try to minimize this step by shooting your images so they're as correct as possible when they come out of the camera.

- ◆ **Output.** With your images edited, you're ready to output to your final media. This step often involves sharpening and resizing operations. You'll then print your images or save them as files for electronic delivery via email, the Web, or disk.

- ◆ **Archive and backing up.** Accidents happen, and you don't want to lose images in a disk crash. Be sure to archive your project once you've finished your final images. Archiving can be achieved by copying images to a second hard drive, burning them to optical media, or uploading them to a server.

- ◆ **Catalog.** As you amass more images, you'll want a way to browse and search your ever-growing library, so you'll need to catalog the archived volumes you create in order to find your images later.

These are the steps you'll take with just about any type of photo work you do. Obviously, there will be times when you might grab a shot or two and move them into your computer to edit and output quickly without going through the rigmarole of an entire workflow. However, for most shoots, you'll perform some variation of the workflow just described. Depending on the software you use, you might perform those first three steps simultaneously, since some programs allow you to add metadata and perform rudimentary organization upon import (see Figure 13.1).

If you're working with a client, you may find yourself performing the last part of the workflow a little bit differently. For example, you might have a quick output step before the correct and edit step, so you can post your pick images to the Web for client approval. If they don't like some images, you'll want to select alternates and output them again. When they sign off on the images, *then* you can start the correction stage and ultimately post a final Web gallery of edited images for approval. If they like those, you'll do your final output to electronic files, print, or whatever your client may need (see Figure 13.2).

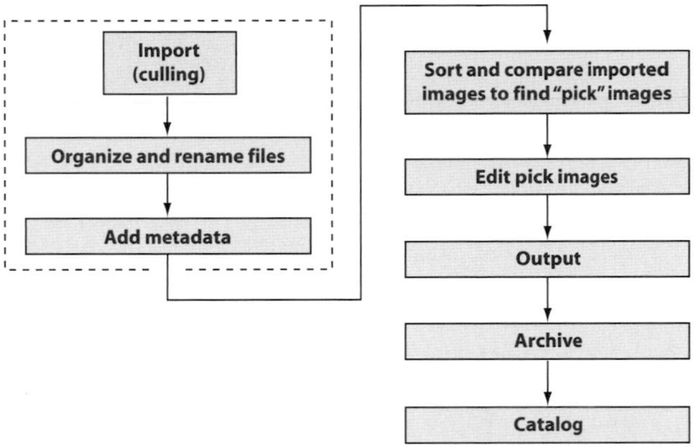

If you're delivering electronic files (for, say, publishing in a magazine), you may have to use particular naming conventions. You'll have a specific naming step at some part of your workflow to get your files renamed properly. You also might have very specific output requirements, and might possibly need to output the same image in different sizes and formats.

Figure 13.1

Most workflows can be broken down into eight steps. Depending on the software you use, you might perform those first three steps simultaneously.

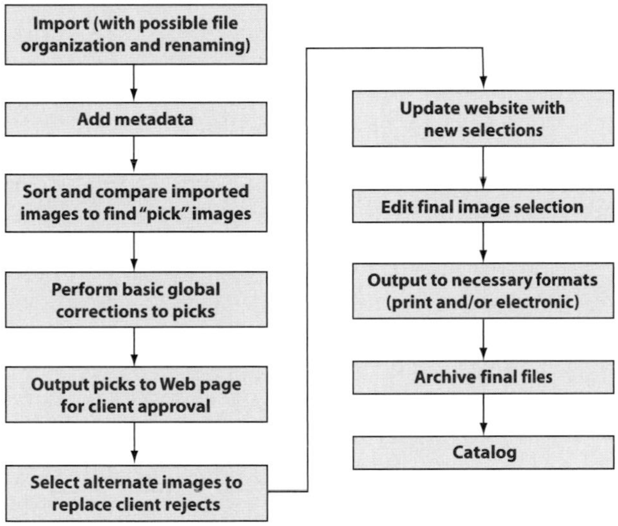

Figure 13.2

More advanced workflows allow for client approval before your final edit step.

Some people like to do an initial archive immediately after they import images into their computer, which gives them a backup copy of all their original files. In addition to security in the event of drive trouble, this process also provides a fallback plan should they end up creating edits they don't like.

Different types of images and different types of jobs might require slightly different variations of the workflow described here. Consequently, you'll probably find yourself regularly making little tweaks and adjustments to the way you do things, both because you'll need to experiment to work out the best workflow for you and to tailor your workflow to your current needs.

You'll follow these steps with any type of workflow software and in the rest of this chapter we're going to look in depth at each step. I'll be using Photoshop Lightroom for these tutorials. If you prefer a different workflow application or combination of applications, that's okay. You'll still need to go through the steps that we'll be exploring here, and any worthwhile workflow tool will have analogous features to the ones you'll see here. So you can either follow along in Lightroom or try to translate what we do here to your own tools.

Getting Started with Adobe Photoshop Lightroom

Lightroom is a single application that can handle all of the workflow steps that we looked at in the previous section. In addition to its own editing tools, Lightroom also provides excellent integration with Photoshop, so when you need to perform an edit that Lightroom can't handle, you have an easy path to full editing in Photoshop.

At the time of this writing, you can get a subscription to Adobe Photoshop, Lightroom, and Adobe's mobile version of Lightroom, and all for $9.99 a month. This is a fantastic deal on a toolset that will truly give you 99 percent of what you need for your image editing chores.

If you don't already have Lightroom, you can download a trial version from *www.adobe.com/ lightroom.*

Bridge-based Workflow

Previous versions of this book taught an Adobe Bridge-based workflow. Bridge is an excellent image browser that is bundled with Photoshop. Unfortunately, Adobe has stopped development on Bridge. Because of that—and because Lightroom 5 is such a good tool—I have switched my regular workflow away from Bridge. If you still want to use a Bridge/Photoshop/Camera Raw workflow, you can download the Bridge-based tutorial from the Chapter 13 folder at *www.completedigitalphotography. com/CDP8.*

Understanding Lightroom and Its Catalog

For those of you who have been using Photoshop since version 1, it's hard to believe that the program is nearly 25 years old. When Photoshop was first created, there were no digital still cameras. Photographers using Photoshop typically worked on a small handful of images, scanning and correcting them one-at-a-time. A digital photographer works with much greater volume and now faces organization and image management tasks that didn't exist when Photoshop was originally designed. Since then, the program has grown into an indispensable tool for photographers, but it's also become a critical tool for graphic designers, print professionals, animators, visual effects and motion graphics artists, and more.

Recognizing that Photoshop's design couldn't be radically altered to facilitate modern photo workflow, Adobe started mostly from scratch and created Lightroom, a single tool that provides a smooth path through an entire photo postproduction workflow.

I say "mostly from scratch" because Lightroom is built on top of Adobe Camera Raw, the raw processing engine that's included with Photoshop. Camera Raw is a fantastic tool for processing raw images, and it sports an excellent interface. It allows you to perform most of the edits that you'll ever need to make to an image, so Adobe retooled Camera Raw to work with non-raw images as well as raws, and then used that as the foundation for Lightroom. If you've used Camera Raw in Photoshop, then you'll have no trouble adjusting to editing within Lightroom.

But Lightroom is more than just an image editor. Adobe wrapped a database-driven cataloging system around the Camera Raw core. With its database back-end, you can quickly search even a huge archive for specific keywords or metadata. This "managed" system offers other advantages, though. You don't ever have to explicitly open or save an image in Lightroom, which makes it easy to move very quickly through a large batch of edits. You also get a completely nondestructive image editing environment with a simple mechanism for creating multiple versions of the same image. And finally, Adobe added excellent geotagging, Web output, and slideshow capabilities.

The Lightroom Catalog

While Lightroom socks a lot of data away inside its own database, your images are still stored as normal files on your hard drive in regular folders. This means you can still access them from other applications, though you may or may not see your Lightroom-based edits in the image if you view the image somewhere else.

The catalog file itself is where Lightroom stores the metadata for your images, the edits that you make to your images. Collections—the digital equivalent of photo albums—are also stored in the Library along with preview images, which are used for a number of different purposes.

You can have as many catalogs as you want, but Lightroom can only open one catalog file at a time. In general, you'll probably find that you can get away with a single, well-organized catalog. Personally, I keep two catalogs, one for certain types of work-related images, and the other for all my other images.

For these tutorials, I'm going to ask you to create a new catalog specifically for the images you'll be working with in the remaining tutorials.

You'll want to give some thought to the location of your main everyday catalog. First, you want a location with a good amount of space. My catalog currently has roughly 77,000 images in it, and the catalog file itself takes up around 107 gigabytes. For the best performance in Lightroom, you'll want your catalog stored on a speedy drive—either an internal or external one that uses a speedy interface, like USB-3 or Thunderbolt. A solid state drive is also a good option for your catalog.

I keep my main Lightroom catalog on a 2-terabyte, external USB-3 drive. I chose an external because I travel a lot. At any time, I can unplug it from my desktop machine and plug it into my laptop and have my regular Lightroom catalog and environment with me.

 Creating a New Catalog

If you don't already have Lightroom installed, download the demo version from *www.adobe. com/lightroom*. Installation on a Mac or Windows is very straightforward. By default, Lightroom will create an empty catalog. Just to ensure that your experience matches what's in this tutorial, you're going to create a new catalog for the images in this book.

STEP 1: LAUNCH LIGHTROOM
If you're not already in Lightroom, launch it now.

STEP 2: CREATE A NEW CATALOG
Choose File > New Catalog. In the resulting dialog box, navigate to the location where you want to store the catalog and enter the name CDPCatalog. Lightroom will quit and restart with your new catalog selected.

STEP 3: DOWNLOAD THE CHAPTER 13 IMAGES
Download LightroomIntroTutorial.zip from the Chapter 13 folder of the companion website at *www.completedigitalphotography.com/CDP8*. Unzip the file. You can put the resulting image

folder anywhere on your drive, but just be sure you know where it ends up. In the next section, you'll import these into your new Lightroom catalog. ◄▮

Importing

Importing is the first part of any workflow, and as you saw in Chapter 4, there are many tools available to tackle your importing and organizing chores. Some systems, like iPhoto, import your images into an internal file structure that you can't see or access. With most workflow tools, though, you'll simply import your images into the normal directory structure of your operating system, which means you'll organize them into a folder structure that makes sense to you.

Image Folders

There's no right or wrong way to organize your images on a drive, but there are advantages to certain approaches. First, you need a drive to store them on, ideally a large, fast drive. I currently use a Drobo as my main image storage medium because it's easily expandable. Of course, it's possible to add additional drives to your system as your image requirements grow, but there are advantages to having a single, large volume.

On my designated image drive, I have a single folder called "Images." Every image I import goes into a subfolder inside the Images folder. Later, you'll see how this scheme makes it easy for me to take my library and a selection of images on the road when I travel.

As for the subfolders, how you choose to organize your collection is up to you. Some people create subfolders by date, so they'll have a subfolder for the year, and then within that a subfolder for each month, and within that they'll have subfolders for each date on which they shot.

I don't tend to think of photos in terms of when they were shot, so instead of dates I usually create subfolders based on location or events. For example, I have a "California" subfolder. Within that, I have "San Francisco," "Los Angeles," and "Death Valley."

Sometimes I mix and match, adding date-based subfolders to my location-named subfolders. For example, in my Death Valley folder, I might have an "April, 2012" subfolder and within that I'll have subfolders for each day of my trip at that time.

Lightroom and other workflow applications can take care of automatically creating date-based subfolders and sticking the appropriate images in each one. But they can also work with subfolder hierarchies that you create on your own.

What Happens When You Import into Lightroom?

Before you can use an image in Lightroom, it must be imported. Lightroom contains an Import command that can handle every step of your import process, but before we look at it, let's examine what happens when you import.

Most often, you will import directly from a media card. Using a card reader or USB camera connection, you'll copy the images from your media card to a folder on your drive. You can perform that copy manually, using one of the methods discussed in Chapter 4, or you can ask Lightroom to do this step for you. If you copy the images yourself, you'll still need to import them into Lightroom, but there just won't be a copying step in that import process.

Upon import, Lightroom applies any metadata that you specified in the Import dialog box. This makes it easy to automatically add copyright info and appropriate keywords anytime you add images to a Lightroom catalog (see Figure 13.3). You can even have Lightroom perform a set of image edits to each image as it's being imported. Finally, you can also tell Lightroom to automatically back up the images to a separate location.

Once the images are copied, Lightroom puts a reference to each image into the current catalog. The reference is simply a small link that lets Lightroom know where the file is. If you use your file manager to move the file, Lightroom will no longer be able to find it and will ask you to locate the file.

Next, Lightroom builds a JPEG file for each image and stores those in the catalog. By default, those preview files are half the size of the original image, but you can use Lightroom's preferences to change this to a full-size image. This JPEG is what you see when you're viewing thumbnails in Lightroom's browser.

Finally, if you have told it to do so, Lightroom also builds a *Smart Preview*. This is a custom Adobe format (it's a variant of Adobe's DNG format, which you'll learn more about later), and these Smart Previews enable a lot of cool mobile functionality, which you'll see later.

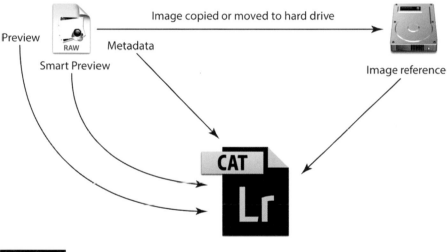

Figure 13.3

When you import into Lightroom, a lot of critical data is generated and placed in the Lightroom catalog file. Your actual image file is copied or moved to a final destination of your choosing.

Tutorial Importing into Lightroom

If you've downloaded the tutorial images from the companion website, then you've essentially done the same thing as copying images from a media card to your computer. The images should all be inside a folder somewhere on your hard drive. You'll now use Lightroom's Import command to load them into a Lightroom catalog.

STEP 1: OPEN THE IMPORT DIALOG

Click the Import button that sits at the bottom of the left-hand panel in Lightroom. Alternately, you can choose File > Import Photos and Video. The Import dialog should appear (see Figure 13.4).

On the left side of the dialog is a navigation panel that lets you select the location that you want to import from. This can be any volume that's attached to your computer—a hard

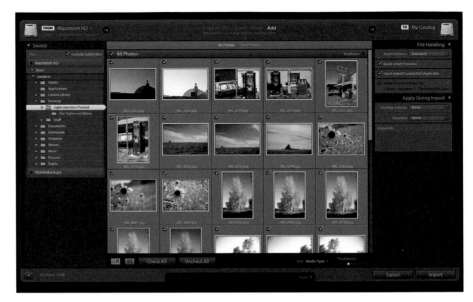

Copy as DNG   Copy   Move   Add

Figure 13.4

Lightroom's Import dialog box lets you select whether you want to move, copy, or add media to the catalog. You'll also choose a destination and add metadata and possibly edits.

drive, a media card reader, or a file server. In the middle, you'll see thumbnails of all of the images that sit in the directory that you've selected with the navigation panel. On the right side is a panel with a number of extra import options.

STEP 2: NAVIGATE TO THE TUTORIAL IMAGE FOLDER

Using the navigation panel on the left side, navigate to the folder full of sample images that you downloaded from the companion website. Note that you can click on the arrows to open each level of your directory structure, or you can double-click on the name of each level to hide all previous levels. This makes for a tidier view of your directory.

Click on the Lightroom Intro Tutorial and thumbnails should appear in the middle window. You should see the same selection of images that were shown in Figure 13.4.

STEP 3: SPECIFY HOW YOU WANT TO IMPORT

Each thumbnail should have a check next to it. This indicates that each image will be imported. There are four options for how to manage each of those files. Along the top of the Import dialog, you should see the options shown in Figure 13.5.

Figure 13.5

You can choose to move the imported files, copy them, or leave them where they are and simply add the relevant data to the Lightroom catalog.

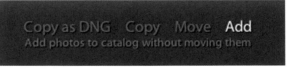

Depending on which option you click, Lightroom will do very different things with the checked files.

◆ **Copy as DNG** will convert the images to DNG files, copy them to a new location, and add the results to the catalog.

◆ **Copy** will copy the images as they are to a new location and then add them to the catalog.

◆ **Move** will move the images as they are to a new location and then add them to the catalog. It's just like Copy, but they will not be left in the original location.

◆ **Add** leaves the images in their current location and adds them to the catalog. Click the Copy option.

STEP 4: EXPLORE THE DESTINATION OPTIONS

Once you click on Copy, you should see a Destination option pane in the right-hand panel of the Import dialog. You're not actually going to perform a copy right now, but it's important to understand how it works. If you were importing from a media card, this is the option you would use.

The Destination pane includes a navigator for selecting a destination to copy into. Note that it also includes an "Into Subfolder" option. Check this box and then pick an organization option from the Organize pop-up menu. By default, Lightroom will automatically create subfolders for the dates of each image that is imported.

These same destination options appear when you choose Move or Copy as DNG.

STEP 5: CHOOSE ADD

Click the Add button at the top of the window. The Destination panel should disappear because your images are already in the correct destination. This is the option you'll use if you prefer to import images into your computer manually. You'll also probably use this for times when someone has sent you images electronically. You'll download the images to the correct location and then add them to the catalog.

STEP 6: CONFIGURE THE FILE HANDLING OPTIONS

Finally, there are a few options to configure before you perform the actual import. At the top of the right-hand panel is a File Handling pane, which lets you configure a few important options.

Under the Build Previews pop-up menu are options for controlling the size of the preview images that Lightroom creates. The default "Standard" option stores half-sized previews. If you like, you can change this to 1:1 to store a full-size preview. Standard size are big enough for everyday use and don't take up as much room. As we dig more into Lightroom's browser, you'll get a better sense of whether you want standard or 1:1 images.

Build Smart Previews tells Lightroom to build Smart Preview images in addition to regular preview files. If you would like the option of working with images that are offline, or for working with the mobile version of Lightroom, then you'll want to check this.

"Don't Import Suspected Duplicates" does a great job of ensuring that you don't accidentally import the same image more than once.

Finally, you can check the "Make a Second Copy To" checkbox to automatically make a second copy of your images in a separate location.

STEP 7: CONFIGURE APPLY DURING IMPORT

Lightroom can automatically add metadata and image edits, and you can easily configure these with the options in the Apply During Import panel. Open the Develop Settings pop-up menu, and you'll see a batch of presets that perform everything from black-and-white conversion to stylized color treatments. You can, of course, make your own presets. If you regularly shoot similar subjects and find yourself routinely performing the same adjustments, you can create a preset and automatically apply it each time you import appropriate subject matter.

Similarly, you can use the Metadata pop-up to create a metadata template that will automatically be applied to every image that you import. Using the New and Edit commands under the Metadata pop-up is very simple. You should consider creating a basic ownership template that includes your name and copyright info.

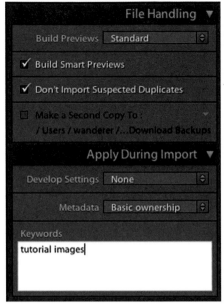

Figure 13.6

You can tell Lightroom to add specific keywords to each image that it imports.

Finally, you can specify keywords that you would like applied to each image. Enter "tutorial images" into the Keywords box.

When you're done, you should see something like Figure 13.6.

STEP 8: CLICK IMPORT

Click the Import button, and Lightroom will perform the import. A progress bar in the upper-left corner will track the process. These images are all fairly small, so importing should go pretty quickly. Note that Lightroom will return control of your computer almost immediately and then begin the process of building previews and Smart Previews. You can continue to work with the program while these previews are being constructed.

The left panel will now show the Lightroom Intro Tutorial. As you continue to import folders into Lightroom, they will show up in this navigation panel. Currently, Previous Import should be selected, and thumbnails of all of the images from the previous import are shown. Note that you can also click on All Photographs to see every image in your catalog. Right now, clicking All Photographs, Previous Import, or Lightroom Intro Tutorial will show the same images.

This is the panel that you'll use to navigate your catalog. Note that once you've selected the directory that you want to view, you can click the reveal arrow on the far left side of the screen to hide the left-hand panel. On a small laptop screen, this can regain you some important real estate.

These are the basics of importing, a process you'll use with every shoot, so take some time to explore the options and try to get familiar with them. ◢◣

Exploring the Lightroom Interface

With images imported into Lightroom, you can now take a quick look at its interface. Lightroom is a deep program, and full coverage of it is beyond the scope of this book, but we'll be hitting most of the everyday features that you'll regularly use.

STEP 1: IDENTIFY THE DIFFERENT PANES

Lightroom's interface is contained within a single window, and you've already seen how the window is divided into different panes. In the Import tutorial, you worked with the leftmost pane, which lets you navigate the different folders in your catalog. In that pane, you'll also find tools for creating *Collections*, which are the digital equivalent of photo albums, and for posting images to various photo sharing and social media services.

The middle of Lightroom's interface is dominated by the image pane, which shows thumbnails of the images in the currently selected folder. The rightmost pane shows a histogram, EXIF data, some simple adjustment tools, and lots of keyword and metadata controls.

At the bottom of the window is a horizontal filmstrip. At first glance, this may seem redundant, given the big thumbnail display that sits just above it, but when you move into different Lightroom modules, this filmstrip will become more useful.

STEP 2: WINDOW CONTROLS

Next to the panes on the edge of the Lightroom window are small arrows. If you click these, the panes will hide. Simply mouse to the edge of the screen, and the panes will reappear. The filmstrip display at the bottom of the window has a similar hide/reveal arrow (see Figure 13.7).

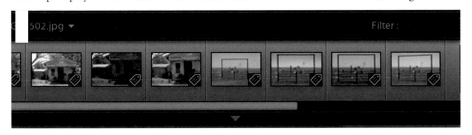

Figure 13.7

On each edge of the Lightroom window is a reveal arrow that hides the associated pane to afford you more usable space on your screen. Mousing over a hidden pane will cause it to reveal.

STEP 3: CHANGE THE SCREEN MODE

By default, Lightroom shows a window title bar and normal OS menu bar. These things take up a fair amount of space on the screen, though, so Lightroom allows you to deactivate them. Choose Window > Screen Mode > Full Screen, and Lightroom will hide these interface elements to buy you more screen space. Mousing to the top of the screen will reveal the menu bar.

STEP 4: CHANGE MODULES

Finally, Lightroom has one other major interface element. At the top of its interface are simple controls for changing between Lightroom's different modules (see Figure 13.8).

Figure 13.8

You can switch between Lightroom's different modules using these buttons at the top of the screen or keyboard shortcuts.

By default, the program first opens in the Library module, where you can see image thumbnails, add metadata, and organize your library. The Develop module is where you'll perform image edits and adjustments. The Map module offers a robust geotagging interface, while Book, Slideshow, Print, and Web give you tools for outputting to these different media.

While you can click the mouse on these names to change modules, it's much better to learn the keyboard equivalents. G will always return you to the Library module (think "G for Grid"), while D will take you to the Develop module. Alternately, on Windows, you can press Control+Alt-1 through 7 to switch between the various modules (Command/Option-1 through 7 on the Mac). Learning these keyboard shortcuts will greatly speed up your Lightroom work.

Obviously, there are lots of other interface widgets and controls, and we'll work through them as we explore more of Lightroom's features. ◣

Selecting Your Pick Images

As mentioned earlier, you won't want to edit and adjust *every* image you shoot. Instead, before you start editing, you'll identify the "keeper" images that should be passed on to the rest of your workflow. Selecting your picks is usually a simple process of browsing through thumbnails or preview images to find the ones you like best. Usually, you give the pick images some kind of rating that indicates they are the best image (five stars, or something like that, depending on the browser you're using).

While searching for the best images, you'll apply ratings to alternate images—four stars to the second best, for example—so you can find alternative images easily when you need them.

Picking your selects is sometimes easier if you're using an application that provides a compare feature; that is, some way to view images side by side. Ideally, you also want a zoom or magnifying tool to view the images at 100 percent to check sharpness and detail. Lightroom provides excellent comparison tools, as does Adobe Bridge. Other image browsers, such as iPhoto and PhotoMechanic, also include good tools for picking your select images.

When making selects, good composition and subject matter will probably be the first characteristics that attract your attention. In addition, assess the following:

- **Sharpness.** Is the image in focus?

- **Exposure.** Is the image well exposed? Are the highlights blown out? Are the shadows too dark? Does the image have the detail, color, and tonal qualities that you want?

- **Noise.** Does the image suffer from noise problems or other lens or camera artifacts? Bear in mind that just because an image looks noisy on-screen, it might still print okay. With more experience, you'll get a better eye for how much noise is acceptable.

- **The data in the image.** Does the image provide the data that you need for the types of edits that you want to perform? This is especially true when evaluating raw images. You'll learn more about how to recognize good image data when you start editing.

Tutorial — Making Selects and Rating Images in Lightroom

STEP 1: NAVIGATE TO THE TUTORIAL FOLDER
If you worked through the last tutorial, then you should already have the tutorial images imported into Lightroom. Make sure you're in the Library module and navigate to the image folder in Lightroom.

STEP 2: SELECT THE FIRST IMAGE
Click on the first image in the thumbnail display. Below the thumbnail, Lightroom shows you a readout of how many images you're currently viewing, how many are selected, and the name of the currently selected image (see Figure 13.9). We'll use this readout in these tutorials to refer to specific images.

Figure 13.9

When you select an image, Lightroom displays its title beneath the thumbnail display.

36 photos / **1 selected** / _MG_5502.jpg ▾

STEP 3: CHANGE THE SORT ORDER
Just above the image name, at the bottom of the thumbnail panel, is another readout that shows the current Sort Method. This is a pop-up menu that lets you control how Lightroom should sort the current images. Open this menu and change the setting to File Name (see Figure 13.10).

This will sort all of the images in ascending order, by name.

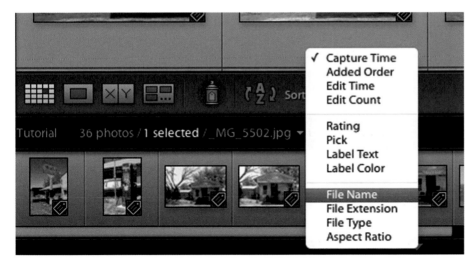

Figure 13.10

The Sort pop-up lets you control how the current images are sorted.

STEP 4: SELECT THE FIRST SHIPROCK IMAGE

Select image 6532, which should be the seventh image. It's a photo of Shiprock in northern New Mexico.

STEP 5: EXAMINE THE METADATA

When you click an image to select it, the right-hand pane fills with a lot of data. You get a histogram, which shows important exposure information. Directly beneath that is the critical exposure data—ISO, focal length, aperture, and shutter speed. Scroll down and you'll find keywords and then a Metadata section, which offers additional camera metadata (known as *EXIF data*), as well as IPTC metadata.

EXIF metadata can be handy for answering questions you might have about your image. For example, if an image appears out of focus, you might look at the metadata and see that the shutter speed was 1/50th. Digging farther, you might see that you were using your 300mm lens, and that it was focused at a distance of 180 feet. Note that not all cameras record all of these specifics.

From this data, it's obvious that, according to the handheld shutter rule, your shutter speed was too low. So you can rest assured that the camera did not misfocus. Similarly, you can use EXIF metadata to answer other questions: Was that a flash shot? Why is there bad backlighting? What meter was I using? Is this image part of a bracketed set?

Not all cameras store the same metadata. For example, you might not always find the exact focal length that was used.

You'll use IPTC metadata to keep your images organized and to search for particular images.

STEP 6: VIEW THE IMAGE LARGER

Press the spacebar. The image should now fill Lightroom's entire middle pane. If you haven't done so already, click the arrow to the left of the Library pane to hide it. This will give you an even larger image (see Figure 13.11).

If you'd like an even larger view, press F to view the image in full screen mode. This completely hides the Lightroom interface to give you an unadulterated view. Press F again to return to the normal Lightroom interface.

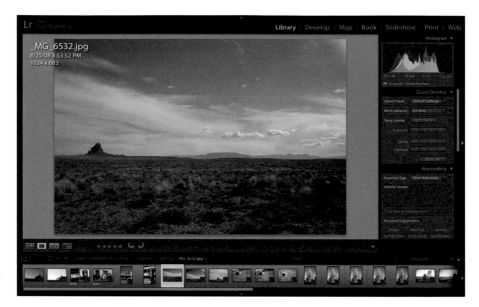

Figure 13.11

A simple tap of the spacebar will give you a much larger view of the current image.

STEP 7: VIEW THE NEXT TWO IMAGES

It should now be obvious why Lightroom offers the thumbnail filmstrip at the bottom of the screen. When you're viewing an enlarged image, you can still use the filmstrip to see other shots in the current folder. After this image are two more images of Shiprock. You want to find out if any or all of these image are worth keeping. They might all be good, but often you'll find that you only need one shot of a particular subject. In a case like this, before deciding if the current image is a keeper, it's worth taking a quick look at the other two images. Using the right and left arrow keys, navigate between the three Shiprock images to get a better idea of what they are.

STEP 8: CHOOSE A PICK

While the first and second images have some nice clouds in them, and could possibly be cropped to a more interesting composition, I think I like the third one the best (number 6544).

Lightroom lets you assign a rating of zero to five stars to any image. Select the third image (number 6544) and press 3. Both the thumbnail image in the filmstrip and the large image in the Preview pane should now have three stars underneath them (see Figure 13.12).

Typically, I choose three stars to mark my pick images because this gives me a little extra rating "headroom." Image 6544 is strong, but as we go along, you might find other images that are stronger, which you'll want to rate as such. Having the possibility for four and five stars gives you options later.

STEP 9: RATE A SECOND IMAGE

I like the idea of trying to crop one of those other images later, so let's give it a two-star rating. It's not a strong contender, but something you might want to play with. Select image 6535 and press 2 to give the image a 2-star rating.

I chose this one rather than the first image because I preferred the position of Shiprock, and I liked the option of having more sky, if I wanted it.

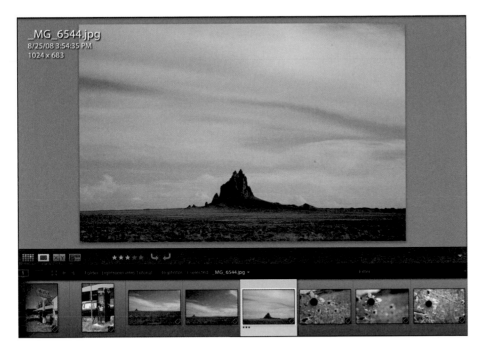

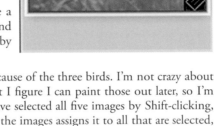

Figure 13.12

Ratings are displayed beneath image thumbnails and previews.

STEP 10: CONTINUE RATING

Move on to the next images, the flowers. A quick look at them makes me think that 6660 is the best one. Give it three stars. Image 6661 is okay, but not great. As you've seen, you don't have to give every image a rating. Let's leave this one as-is.

STEP 11: REJECT AN IMAGE

Image 6662 is definitely not a keeper. The stick above the flower messes up the composition, and the image is not as interesting as the ones that have a bit of horizon in the background. Let's mark this image as a reject. You can either choose Photo > Set Flag > Rejected or simply press X (see Figure 13.13).

Later, you'll see how the reject label can be useful.

STEP 12: MOVE ON TO THE NEXT BATCH

Next are a series of shots of a tree. Again, take a quick pass through all of them to see if any stand out. You can also line them up side-by-side by Shift-clicking each of them.

Figure 13.13

You can also label images as rejects.

Personally, I'm partial to the first image, just because of the three birds. I'm not crazy about the branches on the right side of the image, but I figure I can paint those out later, so I'm going to give image 6741 three stars. (If you have selected all five images by Shift-clicking, you will notice that assigning a rating to one of the images assigns it to all that are selected, so you should deselect all images except the one you want to rate.)

The rest of the tree images are pretty redundant, and there's not really any need to keep them. Sometimes, you keep alternates because you never know if you might need additional coverage of a subject. At other times, it's worth having additional shots because you might be able to use data from one to repair troubles in another. In this case, I'm going to delete all of the tree images except for the pick, 6741.

STEP 13: RETURN TO GRID VIEW
Anytime you want to go back to the thumbnail view of your images, press the G key. This is a little unintuitive—you use the spacebar to go into the large view of the image, and G to go back out. If you press the spacebar while looking at the large view, Lightroom will zoom you all the way in to a 1:1 view of your image. Obviously, this is handy for assessing focus and fine detail.

This is the basic process of making selections. Before you work through the rest of the images, though, let's take a look at some extra Lightroom features that can make it easier to compare similar images. ◼◀

Deleting Rejected Images

If you press Command/Control-Delete while in the Library module, Lightroom will show you all of the currently rejected images and give you the option to either remove them from the catalog or remove them and delete the original files.

 ## Viewing Multiple Images with Survey Mode

STEP 1: COMPARE TREE IMAGES
After the yellow flower images that you just looked at are a series of five pictures of a tree. As before, you can press the spacebar to get a bigger view and then use the arrow keys to move from one to another. But I can also compare them side by side.

STEP 2: SELECT MULTIPLE IMAGES
Click on the first tree image to select it (6741) and then hold down the Shift key and click on the last tree image. Lightroom will select all five of the tree images. Note that the first image is a slightly brighter selection. This "primary" selection is the only image of the five that will receive certain edits and adjustments.

STEP 3: ACTIVATE SURVEY VIEW
Press the N key or choose View > Survey. Lightroom will display all five images side by side (see Figure 13.14).

STEP 4: EXPLORE THE CONTROLS
If you hover the mouse over each image in the main window, you'll see some additional controls appear. Beneath each image will be icons for setting a flag or rejecting, as well as small dots that you can click on to assign ratings.

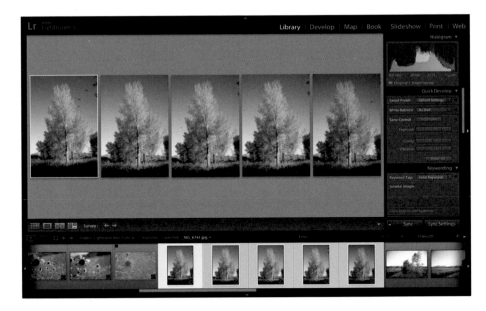

Figure 13.14

Survey mode lets you view multiple images simultaneously.

STEP 5: REMOVE AN IMAGE FROM THE SURVEY

In the Filmstrip, Command/Control-click on the middle image. This will deselect it, and it will disappear from the main window. In this way, you can remove images from the survey as you rule them out. In Lightroom, Shift-click selects a contiguous range of images, while Command or control-clicking lets you select and deselect noncontiguously.

STEP 6: DESELECT

Survey mode is an easy way to see images side by side, but as you throw more images into the selection, each image will get smaller, making it harder to assess image quality. Fortunately, Lightroom has another tool for performing image comparisons. Before we explore it, press Command/Control-D to deselect the current images. ◢◣

Using Compare Mode

Comparing five images against each other can feel complicated, but really you only need to compare two images at a time. Take the first two, decide which you like better, and compare that to the third. Then take the best of those and compare to the fourth, and so on. Lightroom includes a special Compare mode to facilitate just such a process.

STEP 1: ENTER COMPARE MODE

Select the first of the tree images and press C to enter Compare mode. Lightroom will automatically show the image you selected and the next image side by side.

STEP 2: USE THE LOUPE

If you mouse over either of the images, your cursor will turn into a magnifying glass. Click on the trunk of the tree to zoom in, and both images will zoom. This makes it easy to assess the same point of detail in both images. Click anywhere in either image to zoom back out (see Figure 13.15).

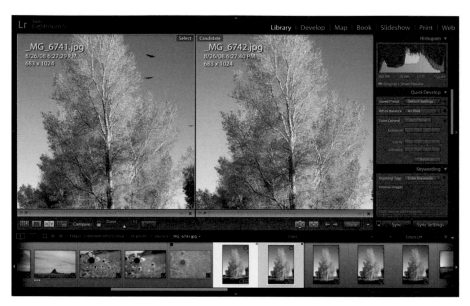

Figure 13.15

In Compare mode you can click on any image to zoom into that location on all images, making for a quick way to assess sharpness across multiple images.

STEP 3: MAKE A CHOICE

I like the first image better than the second image, so I'm now ready to compare it to the third. Press the right arrow key to select the next image. The left image—my current favorite—stays where it is, but the right image changes.

STEP 4: MAKE ANOTHER CHOICE

In the Filmstrip panel, I can see that I'm now comparing the first and third images. I can tell because those are the images that are highlighted. I like the comparison image better (the one on the right), so I would like to make it my new choice. If you press the Up arrow key, the third image will now become the choice. Lightroom will automatically move it to the left position and then select the fourth image and place it on the left.

STEP 5: LOOK AT THE LAST IMAGE

Press the right arrow key one more time to select the last image. I like the bird in that image, so I would like to make it the pick. Press the up arrow key. Lightroom moves it to the pick position and then picks the next image, which is not actually a part of this sequence.

STEP 6: REASSESS

The bird in my pick image really does make for a better image, but the first image had birds as well, so I'd like to compare the last and first. Press the left arrow key four times to select the first image. Now you can compare both (see Figure 13.16).

After all that, I think I ultimately prefer the first image. Press the up arrow to make it the new pick image.

STEP 7: ASSIGN A RATING

I want to rate my pick image. Press 3 to assign a rating of three stars to the left-hand image. In Compare mode, there's no way to assign a rating to the right-hand image.

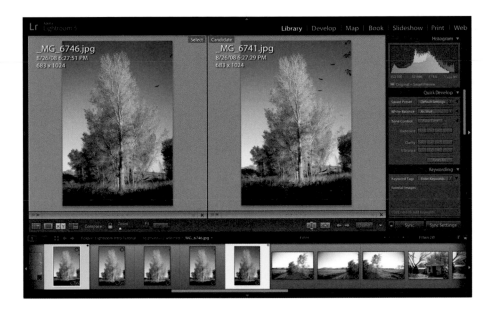

Figure 13.16

Here I'm comparing the first and last images in the batch. The left image is always the current favorite; the right image changes as you press the arrow keys.

STEP 8: EXIT COMPARE MODE

Press G to leave Compare mode and return to regular Grid view.

As you can see, Compare mode can be driven entirely from the keyboard. Once you learn the shortcuts, you should be able to move quickly through a large batch of images, comparing and rating from the keyboard with considerable ease.

STEP 9: RATE THE REST OF THE IMAGES

You've seen the basics of rating images. Work through the rest of the pictures in the Tutorial folder and rate them as you see fit. In the next tutorial, you'll see what you can do with these ratings. Note that images 6764 through 6766 are intended to be part of a panorama. Give them each three stars, and you'll get back to them later. Remember, not every image has to have a rating. ⬛

Filtering Images

After you've made your picks, you're ready to start editing your images. However, as you continue to work with the folder full of images, it's best if you don't have to look at the images that you have *not* picked as selects. Fortunately, once you have rated your images, Lightroom provides some handy functions for filtering and sorting the images in a folder.

STEP 1: SWITCH TO GRID VIEW

If you're not already in the Library module in Lightroom, switch to it now by clicking on Library at the top of the window, or by pressing G. You should see all of the tutorial images. Any images you've rated should show their ratings as a series of stars beneath the image thumbnail.

STEP 2: CONFIGURE THE FILTER

Beneath the main thumbnail display, you should see a row of icons labeled "Filter." With these icons, you can choose to filter by rating, label, or flag. (We'll discuss labels and flags shortly.) Click twice on the middle star to define a filter that shows only images with a rating greater than or equal to three stars (see Figure 3.17).

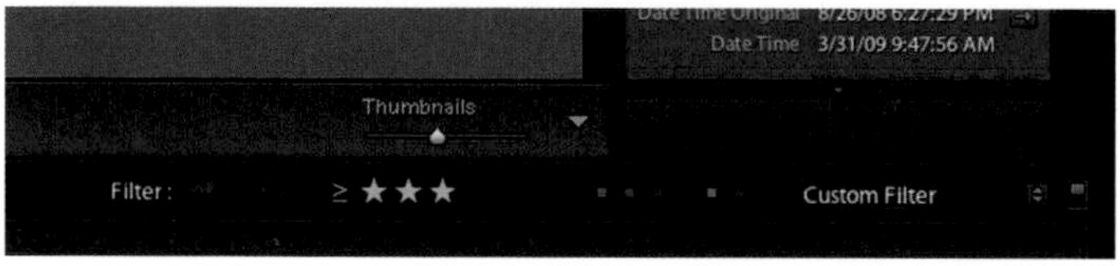

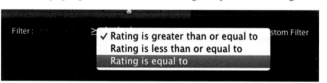

Figure 13.17

I'm defining a filter that will select only images with a rating greater than or equal to three stars.

All thumbnails with a rating lower than three stars (including no rating at all) should vanish. Don't worry, the images are still there, you're just not seeing them.

STEP 3: NOTE THE ATTRIBUTES TOOLBAR

When you click to define a filter, the Attributes toolbar will open, above the thumbnail display. This is simply a duplicate set of filtering controls.

STEP 4: SHOW ONLY THREE STARS

You're looking at any image with a rating greater than or equal to three stars. If you have any four or five star images, they will be shown as well. If you want to view only images with a three-star rating, click the Compare switch next to the leftmost star in the Filter controls. From the pop-up menu, choose "Rating is equal to" (see Figure 13.18).

Figure 13.18

You can configure whether Lightroom should select images equal to or greater or less than the selected star rating.

You should now see only thumbnails of images with a three-star rating.

STEP 5: DEACTIVATE THE FILTER

To deactivate the filter, either click on the middle star in the filter controls or click None in the Attributes toolbar. Your display will again show all of the images in the folder, regardless of their rating. ◪

What Are Labels and Flags?

In addition to ratings, Lightroom lets you assign color labels to an image or to simply flag an image. To assign either, select a thumbnail (or thumbnails) and choose Photo > Set Flag or Photo > Set Color Label. In these menus, you can also see the keyboard shortcuts for each command. Flags give you a quick way to simply tag an image for later filtering, while labels give you an additional set of criteria by which to organize and filter the images in a folder.

Stacking Images

As we discussed in Chapter 4, you can organize your images into folders, using whatever organizational scheme you want. Within a folder, Lightroom provides an additional organizational scheme, called a *Stack*.

STEP 1: NAVIGATE TO THE LIGHTROOM INTRO TUTORIAL FOLDER ON YOUR DRIVE

STEP 2: TURN OFF ALL FILTERS

If you still have any filters activated from the previous tutorial, turn them all off so that you're viewing all of the images.

STEP 3: SELECT IMAGES 6764, 6765, AND 6766

I shot these three images with the idea of stitching them into a panorama later. There's no reason for your view of the images to be cluttered with all three.

STEP 4: CREATE A STACK

With the images selected, choose Photo > Stacking > Group into Stack or press Ctrl/Cmd-G. The images will "collapse" into a single image that looks like the one in Figure 13.19.

The number "three" in the upper-left corner indicates that there are three images in the stack.

STEP 5: OPEN THE STACK

Click the three to open the stack and see all of the images contained within (see Figure 13.20).

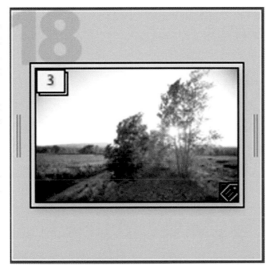

Figure 13.19

You can group a collection of images into a stack. The number in the upper-left corner shows how many images the stack contains.

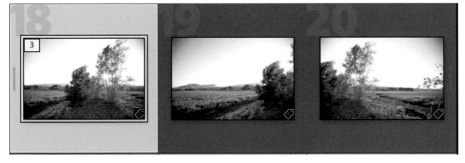

Figure 13.20

When a stack is opened, you can see all of the images contained within.

You can open and close the stack by clicking its number. You can rearrange the items within the stack by dragging them into a new position within the stack. You can also assign ratings just as you would to any unstacked images. Note that, by default, all of the images are selected when you open a stack, so if you open a stack and choose a rating, all of the images will receive that rating.

Stacks and Filtering

It's very important to understand that only the first image in a stack—the one that's shown when the stack is closed—is found by filtering operations. For example, five-star images that are not the first image in a stack will *not* be shown if you elect to filter for images with five stars. If you have more than one image in a stack that you want to be able to see with a filter, then you need to make multiple stacks or pull that second image out of the stack. If the stack is open, you will see the image.

STEP 6: REMOVE AN IMAGE FROM THE STACK

Click the middle image in the stack and drag it to a location outside of the stack. It will now be an individual image again.

STEP 7: ADD AN IMAGE TO A STACK

Now drag the image that you removed in Step 8 back into the stack. You can easily add and remove images by simply dragging them in and out of a stack.

STEP 8: MOVE A NEW IMAGE TO THE TOP OF THE STACK

Click the middle image in the stack to select it, then choose Photo > Stacking > Move to Top of Stack, or press Shift-S.

You can choose to group any type of image that you want. For example, the shots of the snack bar could all be grouped into a stack because they're all shots of the same subject, and you probably only need one of them. I use stacks to group panorama shots with their resulting, stitched panoramas, related subject matter, groups of shots where I've bracketed exposure, and so on. ◢◥

Autostacking in Lightroom

In the Stacks menu, you'll find a command called *Auto-Stack by Capture Time*. This automatically stacks images that were shot within a specific interval.

Sorting Images

You've seen that you can filter images by different criteria, but you can also sort images. The easiest way to sort images is to simply drag them into the order that you want them. This creates a custom sort, and you'll perform this type of sort if you use Lightroom's Web output features or slideshow and want your images in a particular order.

As you've already seen, you can automatically sort by different criteria by choosing an option from the Sort menu beneath the thumbnail display.

IPTC Metadata

By now, you should be fairly familiar with EXIF metadata, the exposure and shooting information that your camera embeds in your images. Lightroom shows some of this information beneath its Histogram display and the rest in the Metadata panel.

If you open the pop-up menu at the top of the Metadata panel, you'll find a selection of different Metadata categories (see Figure 13.21).

Most of these categories should be pretty self-explanatory. One of the most important categories is IPTC, which stands for International Press Telegraph Committee, the organization that defined a metadata standard for ownership metadata. In this category, you'll find metadata fields for creator, your address, your website, and more.

If you use nothing else, you'll want to fill in the Creator field and Copyright Notice fields. This information will travel with the image even if you post it to the Web.

To apply metadata to an image, simply select the image(s) you want to add metadata to and fill in the appropriate fields in the metadata panel. To ease the process of adding metadata to images, Lightroom lets you create metadata templates.

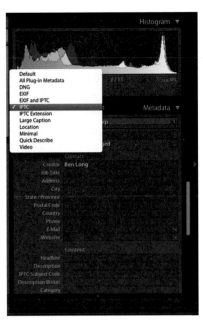

Figure 13.21

In the Metadata panel, you can select which metadata fields you would like access to.

Create and Use a Metadata Template

Because you'll often want to apply the same metadata to many images, and usually want to apply at least your name and copyright to every image you shoot, Lightroom allows you to create a metadata template to speed the application of metadata.

STEP 1: CREATE A NEW TEMPLATE
At the top of the Metadata panel is a Preset pop-up menu. Open it now and choose Edit Presets (see Figure 13.22).

STEP 2: DEFINE YOUR PRESET
Lightroom will present the Edit Metadata Presets dialog box. Fill out the fields any way you want. For a template, you typically want to keep the entries general, so you should only fill in fields that you want to apply to groups of images. However, if you

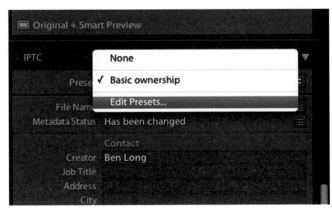

Figure 13.22

A metadata template will let you quickly add predefined metadata to a batch of images.

regularly shoot specific events—weddings, for example—then you might want to get more specific. We're going to make a template just for copyright and ownership information.

STEP 3: FILL IN THE CREATOR AND COPYRIGHT FIELDS

Enter your copyright information, as shown in Figure 13.23. To type a © in Windows, press Alt-0169. On the Mac, press Option-G.

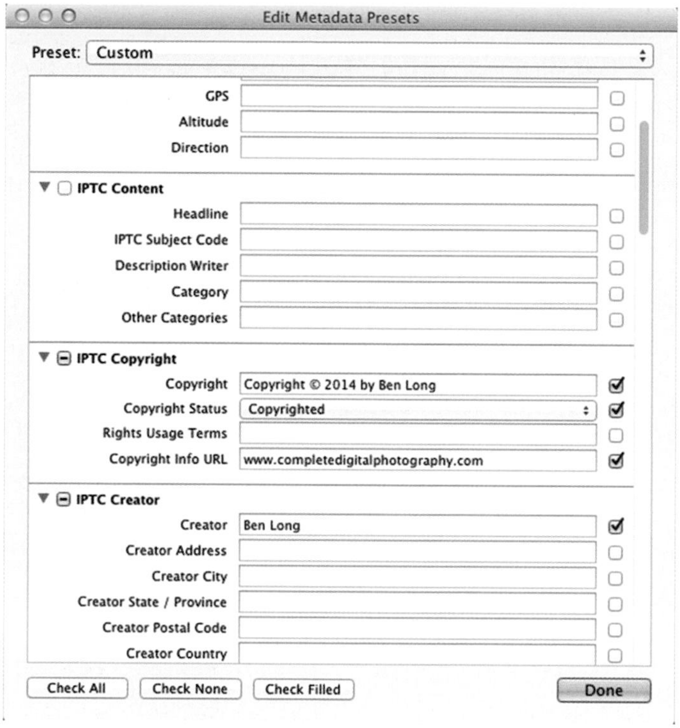

Figure 13.23

When defining your preset, you'll want to fill in at least the Creator and Copyright fields. You might need to scroll the dialog box to find them.

STEP 4: GIVE THE TEMPLATE A NAME

From the Preset menu at the top of the dialog box choose Save Current Setting as New Preset and then enter a name. I called mine *Basic Ownership*.

To apply the metadata preset to an image or group of images, simply select them and then choose Basic Ownership (or whatever you called your Preset) from the Preset pop-up menu at the top of the Metadata panel.

IPTC metadata is searchable in Lightroom and many other programs. Later, you'll see how you can filter your images by IPTC metadata. ◀▮

Keywording

Good metadata means you're not constrained to one particular organizational strategy; you can view your image library by any criteria that you want and change that criteria at any time. Lightroom—and most other image browsers and managers—lets you search images based on metadata. So you can search for images shot on a particular date, or images in a particular location, or with a particular lens. Each of these properties is stored in a specific metadata field. If you haven't noticed already, one of the IPTC metadata fields is Keywords. You can place any words that you want in here, with specific entries separated by commas. If you've added good keywords to your images, your search power grows tremendously.

Keywording takes a little bit of time, but if you get into the habit of adding keywords to your images, you shouldn't find it to be a drag on your workflow. With keywording, it's best to start with broad categories and then add more specific categories for specific shoots. For example, you might apply very general keywords such as "Interior," "Exterior," "Travel," "Landscapes," "Family," and "Candids." If you're on vacation and you take a nice candid shot inside a museum, you could tag that image with "Travel, Candids, Interior, Museum." As you shoot images of specific family members, you might want to create keywords with those people's names. Similarly, you might want to create specific keywords for subject matter: "Animals, Architecture, Forest, Desert, Dessert, Entrees," and so on. There's no right or wrong to keywording, but it is of little value if you don't keep a consistent set of keywords, and you don't tag your images.

You might think "But I don't do a lot of shooting in museums so that's not going to be a regular category." Remember, though, that the goal of keywording is to help you find images later. A year from now, you may think "I had that great shot that I took in that museum." Though "museum" may not be something you regularly shoot, in this instance, it is your primary description of the image so that keyword becomes very useful. Keywords don't take up much space and having lots of them won't bog down your workflow, either in terms of computing power or mindshare.

To add keywords to an image in Lightroom, simply select the image or images that you want to use and then type the keywords that you want into the Keywords box located in the Keywords panel (see Figure 13.24). Put commas between separate entries and press Return when you're finished.

When you select an image, any keywords that have been assigned to that image will appear in the Keywords box.

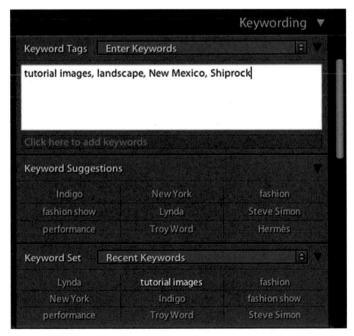

Figure 13.24

Using the keywording controls, you can easily add keywords to individual or batches of images.

Keywords with Asterisks

Sometimes you will select a group of images that don't all have the same keywords. The keywords box will show an * next to keywords that are only present in some of the selected images.

Pushbutton Keywording in Lightroom

Just below the Keywords box are two panels of buttons. The Keywords Suggestions box contains buttons for the nine keywords that Lightroom thinks might be relevant. The program does a pretty good job of guessing at what keywords might be handy, but I get frustrated by how the keywords move around as I click on them. Far more useful to me is the Keyword Set panel, which defaults to providing buttons for the nine most recently used keywords.

At the top of the Keyword Set panel is a pop-up menu that lets you choose a different set of keywords and offers controls for defining your own sets. Between all of these controls, you should find that keywording in Lightroom is quick and easy.

Editing Keywords in Lightroom

If you want to delete a keyword from an image or group of images, simply click the appropriate button in either the Keyword Suggestions or Keyword Set panels. Alternately, you can edit the text of the Keyword box itself.

Why Keywords and Metadata Matter

Perhaps it's obvious to you now, but if not, I'm going to say it again: It's worth taking the time to keyword your images. Even though Lightroom, iPhoto, and many other applications offer excellent organization tools, as your image library grows, it's going to become more time-consuming to find specific images. If you've got good keywords on your images, searching for specific subject matter will become much easier.

Because of metadata and the ability to search metadata, the names of your image files become less important. Even the folder structure of your library becomes less critical because you can simply search for images based on date, keyword, location, or other criteria.

 ## Filtering by Metadata in Lightroom

You've already seen how you can filter the current folder by ratings and labels, but it's also easy to filter by any type of metadata.

STEP 1: OPEN THE METADATA FILTER

At the top of the thumbnail display in the Library module, click on Metadata to reveal the Metadata filter (see Figure 13.25).

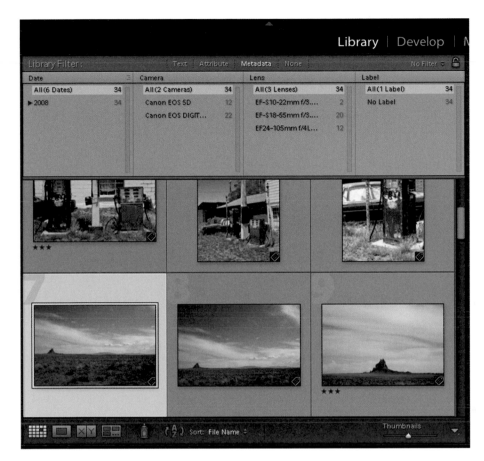

Figure 13.25

Building a complex metadata filter is easy in Lightroom.

STEP 2: DEFINE A METADATA FILTER

By default, you'll see columns for Date, Camera, Lens, and Label. Lightroom automatically fills in each of these columns with all of the dates, cameras, lenses, and label metadata tags that are assigned to the images in the current folder (see Figure 13.26). Click on any entry in any of these columns and the current images will be filtered accordingly. Click on the word Camera at the top of the Camera column and choose Keywords from the resulting pop-up menu.

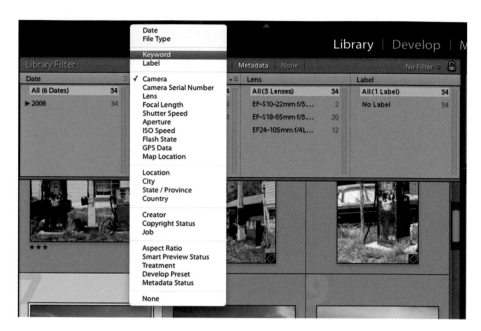

Figure 13.26

Each column can be changed to show a different metadata field.

STEP 3: FILTER BY KEYWORD

The Camera column should now be a Keyword column, which should contain all of the keywords attached to the currently visible images. Click on any keyword to filter by that keyword. Use Control/Command-click to select multiple keywords.

STEP 4: ADD A RATING FILTER

Click on the Attribute button on the Library Filter toolbar. The Metadata filter should remain open, and the Attributes filter should appear above it. You can now add a rating or label filter in addition to the metadata filter that you already defined. In this way, it's easy to create complex searches, such as "3-star images shot on a particular date that have keywords for cat, dog, and mouse."

STEP 5: CANCEL THE FILTER

To remove the filter and return to a view of all of your images, click the None button in the Library Filter toolbar. ◢◣

Searching by Text

The Library Filter toolbar also includes an entry for Text. Enter text into this field and configure the pop-up menus appropriately, and you can search specific metadata fields for specific text. Note that you can also search all metadata fields at once. This is sometimes a faster way to create a filter than hassling with the various columns and filter browsers.

Collections

Lightroom lets you create collections of images. Collections are the digital equivalent of photo albums. When you place an image into a collection, the original file is not moved. Rather, a reference to the image is placed in the collection. This means the same image can be placed in multiple collections. Collections give you another organization level within your Catalog. Smart Collections are simply collections that have a search attached to them. Any images that match the search criteria of the Smart Collection are automatically added. I don't have enough space to cover the use of Collections, but Lightroom's collections interface is easy enough that you should be able to figure it out on your own.

Image Forensics

There's a lot you can learn about exposure and shooting once you get into postproduction. Paying close attention to the metadata for your image can help you understand why certain problems may have occurred. For example, if an image appears out of focus and the shutter speed metadata shows a quarter of a second, it's probably safe to assume that focus was not the problem—rather, handheld camera shake was the problem.

Or maybe your image was too dark. Looking at the metadata might reveal that you had some negative exposure compensation dialed in—an easy mistake to make if you'd used it in for a previous image and then forgotten to reset it.

Conversely, maybe an image has a lot of harsh highlights. A quick look at the metadata might tell you if the flash fired, or not, which might explain some of the overly bright spots in your image.

If your images appear excessively noisy, double-checking the ISO readout can tell you if the problem was an excessively high ISO setting.

Checking in on the metering mode can often be a clue to problems. If bright parts on the edges or in the background of your image are overexposed, check the metering mode to see if your meter was in a Spot, or Center-weight, mode. If it was, then it's safe to assume that this is what caused the peripheral elements to be improperly exposed.

When combined with a little deduction, the Metadata panel makes a great forensics tool for identifying shooting mistakes, and this can help you prevent those mistakes from happening again.

Geotagging

Geotagging is the process of adding latitude and longitude metadata to your images so that you will have a record of where they were shot. Some cameras have built-in GPS units that automatically store your latitude and longitude coordinates every time you shoot. If your camera doesn't have a built-in GPS, there are still many options for geotagging.

Manual Geotagging in Lightroom

Lightroom includes a robust geotagging module that makes it simple to manually or automatically add location data to your images. Note that you must have an active Internet connection to use the Map module. In this tutorial, you'll see how to manually geotag your images.

STEP 1: SELECT THE MAP MODULE
Click on Map at the top of the Lightroom window to switch to the Map module.

STEP 2: SELECT THE SHIPROCK IMAGES
Using the Filmstrip panel at the bottom of the Lightroom window, select the three images of Shiprock. Click on the first image to select it and then Shift-click on the third to select all three. These images have no location data, so you won't see anything appear on the map.

STEP 3: SEARCH THE MAP FOR SHIPROCK
At the top of the mapping window is a Location Filter toolbar that includes a search field. Enter "shiprock new mexico" in the search field and press Return. Lightroom should update its map accordingly (see Figure 13.27).

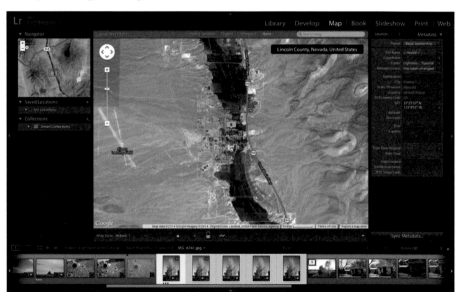

Figure 13.27

Lightroom's Map module makes it simple to geotag your images with very precise location data.

STEP 4: GEOTAG THE SHIPROCK IMAGES
Drag the three Shiprock images from the filmstrip pane to Shiprock on the map and release the mouse. Lightroom will tag the images, and you should see the Latitude and Longitude fields populate with data in the Metadata pane.

Anytime you enter the map module, map pins will appear to show the locations of the images you are currently viewing.

STEP 5: LOCATE ALAMO, NEVADA
Enter "Alamo, Nevada" in the search field in the Location Filter.

STEP 6: GEOTAG THE TREE IMAGES

Drag the five tree images to Alamo, Nevada. These images were not actually shot in Alamo, but in a bird sanctuary just south of town. Still, Alamo is close enough for me to remember where the images were shot.

STEP 7: NOTE THE UPDATED LOCATION DATA

With the tree images still selected, note the location data that now appears in the Metadata panel. In addition to Latitude and Longitude, City, State/Province, Country, and Country Code are also now filled in. Lightroom has automatically performed "reverse geocoding," which means it has used the latitude/longitude data to look up additional metadata fields (see Figure 13.28). ◤

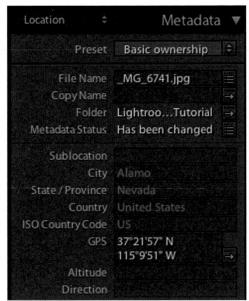

Figure 13.28

Once Lightroom knows the latitude and longitude of an image, it can look up data for the other location fields.

Automatic Geotagging

If your camera doesn't have a built-in GPS, there are other ways you can collect geo data. If you have a GPS device in your car or a hand-held GPS that you use for hiking, then it most likely stores a data file that lists your location at any given time. These files can be stored in a number of different formats, but GPX is the most common. Lightroom can use this GPX file to automatically tag your images. If your camera was set to the same time as your GPS device, Lightroom can simply look up the location that matches the time stamp in your image and automatically add that location data to the image.

If you don't have a GPS device, then you might want to consider buying a geologger. These are small GPS receivers that don't have a screen or provide any kind of map view. They do nothing but store a GPX file that can be used for automatic geotagging.

If you have a smart phone, you might be able to find an app that will turn your phone into a geologger. On the iPhone, I use GeotagPhotos, which generates a GPX file that can be emailed or uploaded to a cloud service directly from the phone. The downside to using your phone as a geologger is battery drain, but it's hard to beat the convenience.

Why Geotag Your Images?

At the simplest level, geotagging your photos means that you'll always have a record of where they were shot. On long vacations or journeys, this can be a real boon, especially if you were shooting in several similar locations. Once your images are geotagged, it becomes possible to search your library for specific locations, which can be handy if you haven't added keywords to an image, but remember where it was shot.

Lightroom, iPhoto, and other applications can show you your photos on a map, as can Google Earth. Many photo sharing sites provide a similar service. Journaling applications and page layout applications can often access geotags to caption your images automatically.

With the ease with which Lightroom and other applications let you geotag your images, there's really no reason not to, and plenty of benefit to be had as your library grows.

Additional Workflow Steps

Once you've organized your images and identified your pick images, you'll be ready to pass those through to the rest of your workflow. Those steps are what the remainder of this book will detail. Here's a quick overview of the steps that would follow in a typical workflow.

Correcting and Editing

After selecting your pick images, you're ready to start editing and correcting. Which software to choose for this depends on the amount of work your images will need. If your workflow tool of choice provides all the tools you need for the types of edits you typically make, then you may not need to add any additional software to your workflow. If you need to make more complex edits, you may need to go to a more advanced image editor. In the editing chapters that follow, we will be using a combination of Lightroom and Photoshop tools.

Don't Forget Photoshop Elements

When I mention Photoshop in these descriptions, I mean either the Creative Cloud version of Photoshop or the much more affordable Photoshop Elements, which offers all the Photoshop features most users need.

Output

Output covers everything from printing your images to posting Web pages to emailing pictures to creating files that can be given to a friend, publisher, or printer. Depending on the editing you've been doing, you'll probably output your images using your image editor or your workflow application. If you're using your image editor, you'll have to take care of resizing and saving in the appropriate format. If you're using a workflow management tool or file browser, you might have options for automatically outputting Web galleries and email, complete with automatic resizing.

Output will be discussed in detail in Chapter 22, "Output."

Archiving and Backup

With your work complete, you should make backup copies of your edited images and your original files (if you haven't already). You can create backups by simply copying images to another drive or by burning them onto optical media such as recordable DVDs. When a project is completely finished, you might want to back up all the images and remove them from your main drive to free up space.

When backing up your images, you should exercise all of the same concerns as when backing up any kind of digital data. For extra safety, use multiple backups and check your backup media from time to time to ensure that it's still readable. Some people have expressed concern over the longevity of optical media, such as recordable CDs and DVDs, so you might want to recopy your backup disks periodically onto new media.

To perform your backups, you can use the file manager in your OS, CD burning software, or backup software.

When considering backup or file synchronizing software, look for a package that allows you to do a progressive backup. In a progressive backup, only files that are new or changed (since the last backup) are copied. This makes for a much speedier process than recopying all of the files you want to back up.

The capability to create a perfect duplicate of your images is yet another digital advantage over film. For extra safety, you can create a copy of your images to store off-site, allowing you to ensure that your images will remain secure even in the face of property damage.

Cloud Backup

There are a lot of services that allow you to back up your data to a cloud-based server. These services are very convenient and offer the advantage of offsite backup. Whether they're right for you depends on how much you shoot. If you work in raw format then you probably routinely come back from a shoot with many gigabytes worth of images, which makes cloud backup impractical. If you're a JPEG shooter and tend to produce smaller batches of data that can be uploaded at a reasonable speed, then cloud backup might be a good solution.

Cataloging

If you've archived any images to offline volumes, or if you're not using a workflow tool that maintains a catalog (like Lightroom or iPhoto), then you'll want to use some kind of software for keeping track of your archived images. A cataloging program such as Extensis Portfolio or Phase One MediaPro is the easiest way to do this.

Mobile Workflow

Whether it's editing on your tablet or cell phone or taking your laptop computer into the field, there will be times when you need to include a mobile component in your postproduction workflow. In this section, we're going to look at some of the issues and options you'll face when you decide to take your workflow into the field.

Taking Your Images on the Road

If you travel a lot, there might be times when you want to take your image library on the road. This can present a problem if your library is too big to easily fit on a portable drive. If you normally keep multiple terabytes of images on a large drive or server at home, moving those to a portable drive or drives may not be possible. Fortunately, Lightroom and some other applications make it possible to take "offline" versions of your images.

Traveling with Your Lightroom Catalog

As I explained earlier, I keep my Lightroom catalog on an external USB-3 hard drive that I keep attached to my desktop computer. When I want to go portable, I simply detach the drive and connect it to my laptop. When I launch Lightroom, I see my normal catalog, just as if I were still at home.

However, because I keep all my images on a separate drive, Lightroom won't be able to find my original image data. These "offline" directories are shown in Lightroom with a question mark badge (see Figure 13.29).

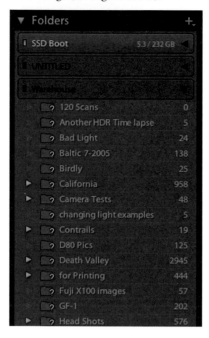

The question mark indicates that the original files cannot be found. Lightroom doesn't do anything to the original links, though, so as soon as the original volumes come back online, the question marks will vanish. However, because Lightroom builds previews and Smart Previews for all of your images, you'll still be able to view all of your images, add keywords and metadata, and even perform image edits. In addition, you can export images up to the maximum preview size that you built. This gives you a tremendous amount of flexibility on the road.

There will be some image editing operations that you won't be able to perform, and you won't necessarily have access to the full pixel count of your images. When I'm traveling on the road and know that I'll need certain images, I take an additional external hard drive and load it up with the images that I think I'll need. I name it the same as the image drive that I use at home and make certain to keep the same directory structure. When it's plugged into my laptop, Lightroom only shows question marks on the missing directories; the ones I've brought with me appear and work as normal.

Figure 13.29

When Lightroom can't find an image, it displays a question mark badge over the directory entry. The original link is not broken.

At the bottom of the Histogram panel in the Library module, Lightroom provides a readout showing what data is currently available for the selected image. In Figure 13.30, you can see that I currently have access to both the original data and the Smart Preview data.

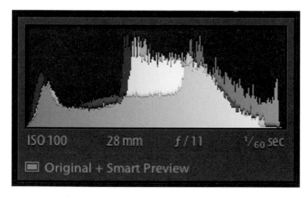

Using this multiple drive scheme, I can easily take a subset of my image library on the road while maintaining editing and preview access to the entire catalog.

Figure 13.30

From this readout, I can see that the current image has original data and a smart preview.

Why Do I Need Both Previews and Smart Previews?

In Lightroom, regular previews are used by the Library module for thumbnail display and to show a 1:1 enlargement of your images. (Assuming you've told Lightroom to build 1:1 previews, you can configure the preview size in Lightroom's preferences.) Smart Previews are used by the Develop module for times when the original image data is not available. Both are stored inside the Lightroom Catalog file.

Lightroom Mobile

At the time of this writing iPad users have access to the first version of Lightroom Mobile. Depending on the plan that you have, Lightroom Mobile might already be included in your Creative Cloud subscription.

Your Lightroom Mobile work begins on your desktop where you select Collections within your Lightroom catalog that you would like to take on the road. The Smart Previews for the images in these collections will be uploaded to Adobe's cloud service. On your iPad, Lightroom Mobile will download these Collections and allow you to perform a limited set of editing and tagging operations.

With the version 1.0 release you can perform almost all of the image editing tasks that you would perform in the full desktop version of Lightroom but you can't currently add keywords or other metadata. Any edits or added images will get synced back to your desktop automatically.

Though currently limited, Lightroom Mobile is a very good first release and will most certainly grow into a great mobile workflow solution. Presumably it will also grow an Android version at some point.

Integrating Cell Phone Pictures into Your Workflow

The workflow that I've defined so far begins with importing data from your camera's media card. If you also shoot images with your cell phone, you might find yourself wanting to integrate those images into your normal workflow. If your cell phone has a media card, you can simply follow the workflow that I've already defined here.

If you use an iPhone, then you have the option of syncing photos using iPhoto or simply connecting your iPhone to your Mac via a USB cable and using Image Capture to copy images over. Personally, I prefer to use a simple app called *Photo Transfer*. With Photo Transfer, I can easily copy images wirelessly to and from the phone using either a Web browser or a companion app on my Mac. Once I've moved the images, I simply integrate them into my normal workflow.

No Right or Wrong Approach to Workflow

There's no right or wrong approach to postproduction workflow. If you can find a system that makes sense to you, allows you to identify selects quickly, perform edits, output files, and offers a long-term mechanism for managing your image archive, then you've got a good workflow.

Bear in mind that your workflow methodology might change many times before you settle on something that you like. As you refine your organizational ideas or try new or different pieces of software, you might rethink how your workflow process will go.

When altering your workflow process, there are some concerns to bear in mind:

- **Be very careful when moving your images.** If you implement a workflow change that requires a reordering of your files—maybe to new folders or to a different drive—then you'll want to be very careful about moving your files. You don't want to misplace or forget to copy any images.

- **Ratings aren't universal.** Unfortunately, there is currently no standard for how to store the rating of an image. If you rate a bunch of images in Lightroom and then decide you want to try iPhoto, those ratings will not transfer. You can work around this by storing ratings in a metadata field that *is* common—maybe in a field you're not using, like Headline—but this is a lot of work.

- **Edits don't necessarily travel.** If you've made lots of edits to an image in a program like iPhoto or Adobe Lightroom, you might lose these edits when you switch to a new system. You'll be able to "bake" the edits into a finished image, but you won't be able to go back and alter them again later. Note that when moving from Bridge/Photoshop to Lightroom or vice versa, you won't have this problem.

- **Some operations may require specialized workflows.** Panoramic stitching and HDR merging are two operations that can throw a wrench into your normal workflow. If you're a Bridge user, you can launch images directly into the stitching and merging features of Photoshop. If you use another tool, then you may need to come up with a different workflow. I'll discuss this in more detail when we cover stitching and merging.

Making minor changes to your workflow—adjusting the order you do things, adding an additional backup step, and so on—shouldn't create any additional headaches or troubles.

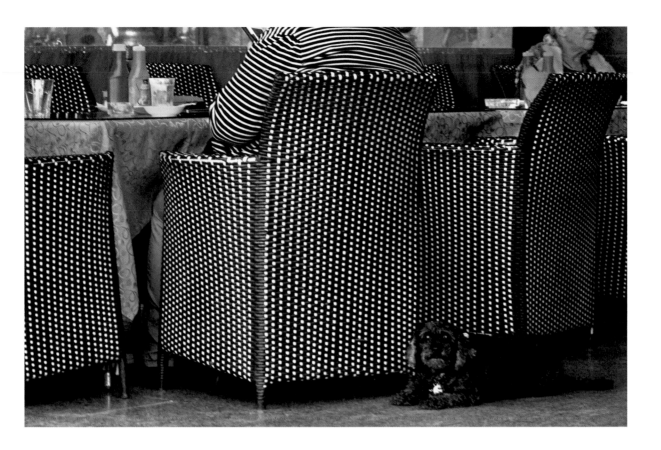

14

EDITING WORKFLOWS AND FIRST STEPS

Understanding the Order of Edits and Making Your First Adjustments

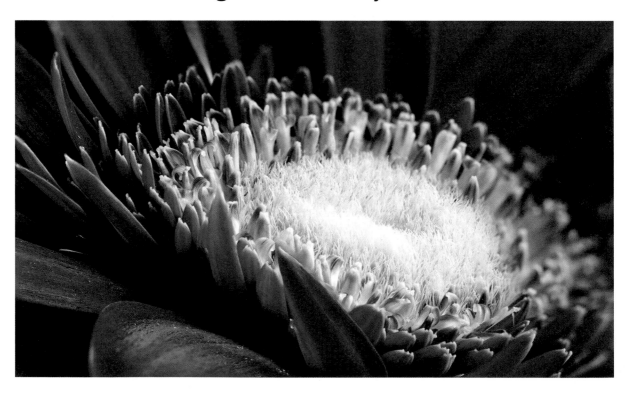

After the last chapter, you may find yourself a little weary of "workflow," but the work flow we're going to talk about in this chapter is not the organizational workflow that we discussed in Chapter 13, "Workflow." Rather, we're simply going to take a quick look at the order in which you need to perform specific edits.

When working on an image, in addition to making it look better, you want to make sure that you preserve as much quality as possible. As you've learned, it is possible to degrade an image by introducing posterization—banding artifacts that can occur when you push certain edits too far. In addition to these concerns, you want to be sure that you don't perform certain operations, especially sharpening, at the wrong time.

In this chapter, we'll look at an ideal order for performing edits, and we'll get started editing.

Editing Order

For maximum flexibility and to preserve image quality, you'll usually want to perform your edits in a particular order. For example, you almost always want to apply any sharpening operations *after* you've performed all of your other corrections and edits. Because sharpening can be a very destructive operation, you want to do it only once, after you're sure nothing else in your image will change.

There are some edits that you need to get out of the way early, such as cropping and spot removal, while many of the operations in the middle of your editing cycle can be performed in any order.

You'll typically perform your edits in this order:

◆ **Geometric corrections.** Cropping, straightening, perspective distortion—all of these edits can result in a crop of your image. You want to perform these functions first, so your histogram (which you'll use heavily when adjusting tone and color) doesn't include irrelevant data. Often, a big crop is required to achieve the composition you originally envisioned, so cropping first is necessary simply to find out if the image is one that you like. If cropping doesn't achieve the composition you thought it would, you might want to abandon the image. Discovering this early will save you from wasting time with additional edits.

◆ **Dust and spot removal.** If you shot with an interchangeable lens camera, and your image has sensor dust issues, or if your image has lens flare troubles (which can happen with all cameras), then you want to address those early. If you can't adequately address spot concerns, you might need to give up on the image.

◆ **Tonal adjustment.** Because good contrast is essential to a good image, your first major adjustment after cropping and spotting will be to correct the tone in your image. In this step, you'll adjust the black-and-white values in the image to correct any contrast troubles. Often, these will be the only adjustments your image needs because correcting contrast sometimes fixes color problems as well.

◆ **Color correction.** After handling the contrast in your image, you'll move on to adjusting color. Color adjustments can include everything from changes in saturation to removing a color cast to radically altering a particular color in the image.

◆ **Grayscale conversion.** If you ultimately plan to convert your image to grayscale, that adjustment will happen during your tone correction stage.

◆ **Retouching.** If you need to remove bags from beneath a model's eyes, improve skin tones, take out ugly telephone wires, or perform any other type of retouching, you'll do that now. Retouching comes after tone and color correction, because retouching operations often involve copying data from one part of the image to another. To ensure that you're copying good data, you want the tone and color in your image correct before you start retouching. Also, because tone adjustments can reveal or hide detail in your image, you should perform those operations before retouching, so that you don't waste time retouching something that then gets hidden by a tonal adjustment.

◆ **Additional color and tonal corrections, special effects, compositing.** Any additional edits come next.

◆ **Noise reduction.** If your image has any noise problems, you'll attack them now. Tone and color corrections can often exaggerate noise troubles, so you want to have all your other edits out of the way before you take the time to address noise. There's another school of thought that says you should address the noise *first* before you do anything that might exaggerate it. On a particularly troublesome image, you might want to try it both ways.

◆ **Sizing, sharpening, and output.** Your very last step is to resize and sharpen your image in preparation for output.

Obviously, this workflow is not carved in stone, and you'll often move back and forth between different steps, as some edits and adjustments will predicate a change or alteration in other edits and adjustments.

Also, just as you crop first to determine if your image is worth editing further, if an image has a very bad color problem, you might need to perform an initial color adjustment early on, simply to find out if the image can be saved.

For example, if you shoot at night or in a dark theater, you'll probably have a white balance problem. Before you go too far into editing one of those images, you'll want to ensure that you can get the white balance back to something close to normal. Similarly, if your night shots are very dark, you might want to perform a quick brightening, simply to find out if you can see anything at all in the images. These types of adjustments can be rough initial adjustments that get refined in the normal tone and color correction parts of your workflow.

If you're working on a panoramic shot or a high-dynamic range image—images that require a preliminary process of stitching or merging—then you'll have to perform those steps *before* any of the steps mentioned here.

The ultimate goals of the workflow presented here are to preserve the highest-quality image data throughout your editing cycle and to ensure that you don't get too far into the work on an image before you discover that it's not a keeper. A slight variation is not going to destroy your image. In fact, you might do things very much out of order and still not see a difference. However, if you want to make more edits later, or different edits, you might wish you'd been a little more careful with your data.

Editing Order in a Nondestructive Editor

We're going to be working in Lightroom, which like iPhoto and some other editors is nondestructive. In a nondestructive system, the order of edits is less important because your edits will be applied in the correct order by the program at the time of output. However, it's still a good idea to work in the order described here. You'll want to crop before making tonal adjustments to ensure a more relevant histogram, and you'll want to perform any geometric corrections and grayscale adjustments before you start editing in earnest, so you're editing on something closer to your final composition. If you're using Photoshop nondestructively (as you'll learn to do in this book), you'll find similar flexibility, but again you'll be best served by following this order.

About the Tutorials in This Book

The tutorials in this chapter are all built around Lightroom and Photoshop CC. The tools and interfaces in these programs have been widely imitated in other applications (and, in some cases, improved upon), so you shouldn't have any trouble following along in your image editor of choice. If you're using an earlier version of either application, you might see some differences in the interface, but the controls and steps described here should still work.

You can download a 30-day, full-featured trial version of both applications from *www.adobe.com/ downloads*. These will provide everything you need to perform the tutorials..

Histograms Revisited

In Chapter 8, "Advanced Exposure," you learned about histograms, which are graphical representations of the tonal values within an image. As you saw, a histogram is a bar chart of the distribution of different tones in a picture, with black on the left and white on the right. Most cameras can produce histograms of images you've shot, making it easier to determine if you have over- or underexposed an image while you're in the field.

Your image editor can also produce a histogram of an image. Consider Figure 14.1.

Figure 14.1 is a simple gradient from black to white, created using the Photoshop Gradient tool. The histogram confirms that the image goes from complete black to complete white with most of the tones distributed at either end of the spectrum. You can also see from the histogram that there is a lot of contrast in this image—that is, the range of black to white covers the entire spectrum of the histogram.

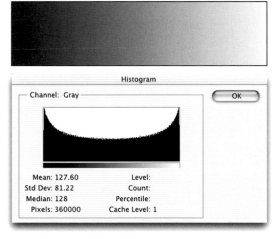

Figure 14.1

This gradient from black to white yields a simple histogram.

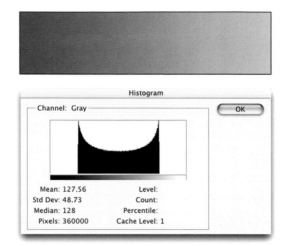

Now look at Figure 14.2.

Also created in Photoshop, this gradient was specified as having a range from 80 percent black to 20 percent black instead of pure black to pure white. If you look at the histogram, you can see that the tones in the image fall in the middle of the graph. There are no dark or completely black tones, nor are there any light or completely white tones. In other words, there's not much contrast in this gradient—the range from lightest to darkest is very small.

The histogram is an essential tool for image editing, so it's very important that you understand how to read it. We'll be relying on it extensively through the rest of these tutorials.

Figure 14.2

This grayscale ramp from 80 percent black to 20 percent black yields a histogram similar to the one shown in Figure 14.1, but the tones are centered in the middle of the spectrum.

Why Is the Histogram of a Gray Ramp Curved?

If a grayscale ramp is just a progression from black to white, why does the histogram show more data at the dark and light end of the scale? Remember, your eyes don't see things in a linear fashion; they expand highlights and shadows to reveal more tones and details in bright and dark areas, so the edges of the histogram accurately show more tonal information there.

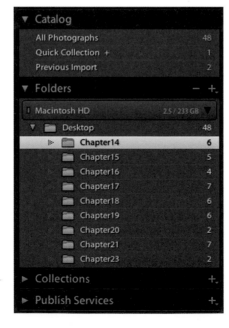

Figure 14.3

Here I've imported all of the tutorial folders for the rest of this book. Now I can easily move from chapter to chapter. Obviously, your directory structure will look different than mine, depending on where you choose to store the downloaded folders.

Preparing Lightroom

On the companion website, at *www.complete digitalphotography.com/CDP8*, there is a folder full of tutorial images for this chapter. Download it now and import the folder into Lightroom. If you want, you can download all of the remaining chapters and import them. If you do, your Lightroom catalog should look something like the one in Figure 14.3.

Note that some chapters contain tutorial videos. Uncheck these when importing as there's no reason to take up space in your catalog with these files.

The Lightroom Develop Module

Lightroom's editing tools are kept in the Develop module, which you can access by clicking Develop on the toolbar at the top of the screen, or by pressing D (Figure 14.4). Note that if you're working with raw files and they're not showing up properly in Lightroom, then you're probably using a raw format that Lightroom doesn't yet support. As mentioned earlier, there's no standard for raw format, so Adobe has to update Lightroom and Camera Raw any time a new camera is released. To find out if you're using the latest Camera Raw, choose the Check for Updates item from the Help menu in Photoshop.

Note that older versions of Lightroom won't necessarily run the latest Camera Raw. So, if you're using a recently released camera and an older version of Lightroom, then you may have no option but to upgrade Lightroom if you want to process the raw files from your camera.

| Library | **Develop** | Map | Book | Slideshow | Print | Web |

Figure 14.4 At the top of the Lightroom window are controls for moving among its different modules. To move to the Develop module, either click on the Develop button at the top of the screen or press D.

Cropping

It may not be the most technically impressive tool in your digital toolbox, but over time, you'll probably find that your image editor's Crop tool is one of the most powerful editing features at your disposal. With it, you can change the composition of your image after you've shot it.

Cropping is a very important first step because, in addition to changing the composition of your image, when you crop you will also remove tones from your image, and this will affect your final histogram. For example, you might crop out areas of overexposed highlights, which will greatly change the appearance of your histogram. As you'll see later, this will ease your editing process.

In Chapter 9, "Finding and Composing a Photo," you performed a cropping exercise on paper as a way of exploring composition. You'll apply those same ideas when you use the Crop tool in your image editor. In this section, we're going to look at the Crop tool in Lightroom, but you'll find the same features described here in the Crop tools provided by Photoshop, iPhoto, and most other image editors.

 Cropping an Image

The hardest part of cropping is simply to decide what kind of crop you want. Using an actual Crop tool is fairly simple. Fortunately, most Crop tools make it easy to explore different crops. We'll be using Lightroom for this tutorial, but you should be able to follow along in any editing program that has a Crop tool. Photoshop offers a similar crop tool.

Cropping in Previous Editions of Photoshop

Versions of Photoshop prior to Photoshop CS6 used a very different type of cropping tool than what you'll see in Lightroom or Photoshop CC. If you're working with an earlier version, check out the Pre-CS6 Straightening tutorial located at *www.completedigitalphotography.com/CDP8*.

STEP 1: SELECT THE IMAGE

In Lightroom, navigate to the Chapter 14 folder that you imported and select the image `crop me.CR2.jpg`. This is an image of birds on a telephone wire (see Figure 14.5). Note that, just above the filmstrip panel, Lightroom displays the file name of the currently selected image.

The subject of this image should be the birds on the telephone wire, which, with the telephone pole, look sort of like musical notes. Because I didn't have a long enough lens, I shot this image with the intention of cropping it later. I tilted the camera to straighten out the telephone wires, but now you need to crop out a lot of extraneous detail.

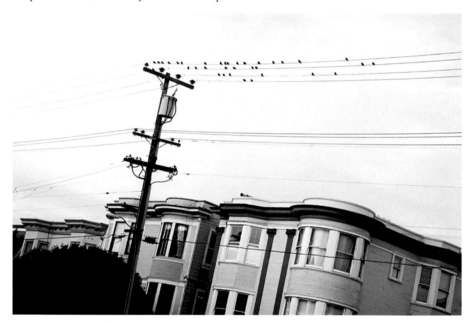

Figure 14.5

I didn't have a long enough lens to get this shot framed the way I wanted, so you can use the Crop tool to recompose it.

STEP 2: SWITCH TO THE DEVELOP MODULE

If you're not already in the Develop module, switch to it now by pressing D. As you can see, this image is a little bit crooked.

STEP 3: FIND THE CROP TOOL

Just below the Histogram display is a toolbar (Figure 14.6). Here you'll find tools for cropping, spot removal, red eye correction, and selective editing. Click on the Crop tool (or press R) and a selection of Cropping options will appear.

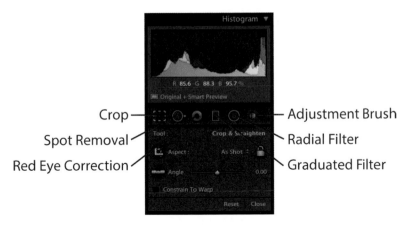

Crop

Spot Removal

Red Eye Correction

Adjustment Brush

Radial Filter

Graduated Filter

Figure 14.6

Lightroom provides a simple toolbar for some basic correction tools, including Crop and Straighten.

STEP 4: DRAG OUT A CROP

When you select the Crop tool, you'll see a grid appear over the image. This allows you to see the thirds of your image easily. Around the edges and in the corners of the image, you'll see handles that you can drag to define the crop. Drag to move the lower-left corner in. The crop rectangle will remain centered as you drag (see Figure 14.7).

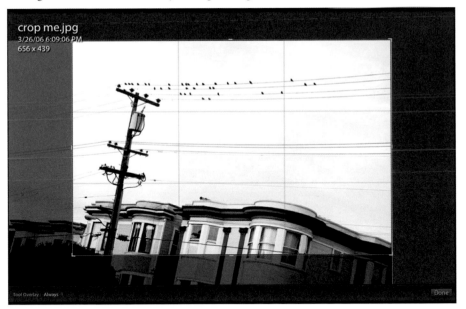

Figure 14.7

Using the Crop tool, drag out an initial crop. It doesn't matter if you don't get it correct right away, as you can fix it later.

STEP 5: ADJUST THE CROP

If you find the thirds grid annoying, open the Tool Overlay pop-up menu that sits beneath the image. There you can deactivate the grid.

The crop rectangle provides control handles at the corners and in the middle of each edge. You can drag these to reshape the crop. You can also click and drag within the crop area to shift the crop horizontally and vertically (see Figure 14.8).

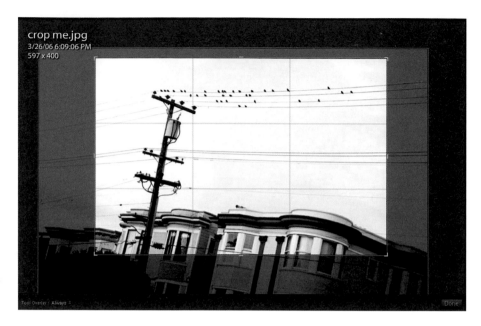

Figure 14.8

Using the handles on the cropping rectangle, and the ability to pan the crop about, you can resize your crop.

STEP 6: MAKE THE CROP

Press Return or double-click within the crop rectangle to accept the crop. Your image will be cropped, and the Crop tool will deselect (its controls will disappear).

STEP 7: CROP NONDESTRUCTIVELY

Press R to select the Crop tool again. Your entire image will reappear, with the Crop handles where you left them before. You can now adjust your crop. Because Lightroom is nondestructive in its edits, you can always adjust your crop at any time.

In this example, you performed a locked aspect ratio crop. That is, your final image has the same aspect ratio as the original. There will be times, though, when you'll want to crop free-form.

STEP 8: UNLOCK THE ASPECT RATIO

On the right side of the Crop & Straighten toolbox is a small padlock next to a menu that says "As Shot." Click on "As Shot" to pop open a menu of additional cropping options (Figure 14.9).

You've already used the "As Shot" option, which constrains the crop rectangle to the same aspect ratio as the original image. Custom allows you to crop freely, with no constraints on proportions, while the rest of the options let you lock the Crop tool so that you can only define crops with specific proportions. This is ideal for cropping to fit a particular size frame.

Figure 14.9

This menu allows you to specify an aspect ratio for your crop.

When the Crop tool is locked, you'll still use the handles and panning ability just as you saw in the last section. The only difference is that the crop rectangle will be constrained. Experiment now with some of the aspect ratio choices.

Remember that you don't *have* to crop to the same aspect ratio your camera shoots or to any of the preset aspect ratios in your image editor. Very often, the best crop for an image has an unusual aspect ratio. Landscapes often look better with a long, skinny, panoramic crop, while other situations might call for a narrow, vertical crop.

Don't hesitate to play around with different crops. The capability to drag and reshape a crop on the fly makes it possible to see the possibilities of different croppings easily. ◄▪

Nondestructive Editing

In the previous tutorial, you saw how Lightroom's Crop tool does not actually delete any of the pixels in your image. Because of this, you can go back at any time and adjust the crop of your image. This is possible because every edit you make in Lightroom is stored separately from the original file. Anytime you view an image, Lightroom consults the corresponding edit list for that image to find the edits you've specified. It then applies them to that original image data. If this is confusing, take a look at the nondestructive editing section of Chapter 4, "Image Transfer."

Because edits are kept separate from the original image data, you can go back and change them at any time. Once you're used to the flexibility of nondestructive editing, it's hard to go back to normal destructive editing.

As explained earlier, Lightroom is built on top of the Photoshop Camera Raw engine. Camera Raw, which is built into Photoshop is also completely nondestructive. In fact, all raw converters are nondestructive because raw files don't contain usable image data. There's no way for you to apply an edit that increases the contrast in a raw file, say, because the raw file doesn't have any finished image data. Consequently, a raw converter always has to create an editable image that's separate from the original raw file.

Lightroom is not just a raw converter, though. It applies this same nondestructive approach to JPEGs, TIFFs, and other non-raw formats. This means that, with Lightroom, you have a single set of tools for all image formats. Apple's iPhoto works this way as well.

Saving Your Image

Because of Lightroom's nondestructive nature, you never have to execute a Save command. In fact, if you look in Lightroom's File menu, you'll see no Save or Save As commands. This is because every time you make an edit, Lightroom adds it to the list of edits that's associated with that image. (The list itself is kept inside Lightroom's catalog file.)

If you edit an image in Lightroom and then open up the original image file in another image editor, you won't see any of the adjustments you've made. You can only see those in Lightroom. If you want to have a new file that contains your Lightroom edits, then you'll need to perform an Export command.

Lightroom also lets you write out a copy of an image's edit list in XMP format, a standard format created by Adobe. This is particularly handy if you want to give someone an original raw file as well as your edits. With both documents, anyone can continue to refine the image and make changes to white balance and highlight recovery, two things that you can't do if you save the image in a non-raw format.

For now, know that you can freely click on an image at any time to open it. If you already had an image open, there's no need to save. Lightroom has already stored away all your edits while you worked.

Straightening

No matter how careful you are when you shoot, your images won't always be perfectly level. Determining what's straight when you're shooting can be difficult, especially if you're shooting on unlevel, hilly terrain. A tripod with a level can help, but this isn't always an option. Straightening is an edit you should perform early in your editing pipeline because it requires a crop.

Straightening an Image

Photoshop and Lightroom all have very good straightening tools, as does Photoshop Elements.

STEP 1: SELECT THE IMAGE

In Lightroom, select the image `Straighten Me.jpg` in the Chapter 14 folder. Remember, you can use G to switch back to Grid view, where you can navigate your images. With the image selected, switch to the Develop module, if you're not already there. (see Figure 14.10).

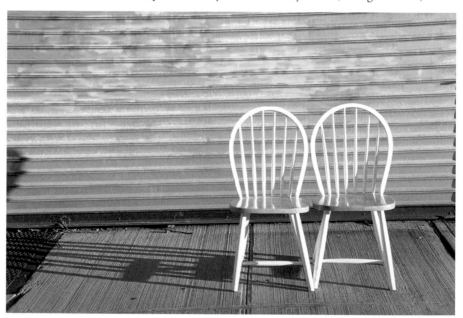

Figure 14.10

This image needs to be straightened, an easy task for Lightroom's Straighten feature.

STEP 2: SELECT THE CROP TOOL

Press R to select the Crop tool. Click the level icon labeled "Angle" to select Lightroom's Straighten tool.

STEP 3: STRAIGHTEN THE IMAGE

With the Level tool selected, click and drag across one of the lines on the garage door. These are lines in the image that should be horizontal but aren't. By clicking and dragging across one of them with the Level tool, you're telling Lightroom to rotate the image until that line is truly horizontal.

When you release the mouse button, Lightroom will show you a rotated crop box that indicates how your image will be rotated and cropped (Figure 14.11).

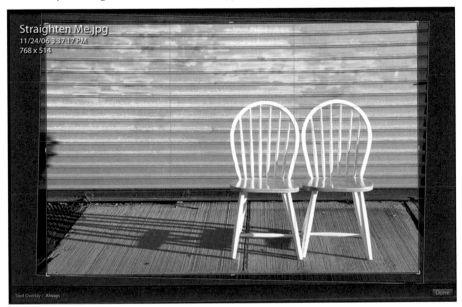

Figure 14.11

Using the Straighten tool, you can straighten an image by dragging across something that is supposed to be horizontal.

STEP 4: REFINE STRAIGHTEN AND CROP

If you don't like the crop that the straighten operation chose, you can refine it by dragging the crop handles, just as you would with any other crop. You can also refine the rotation. Hover the mouse around any of the corner handles, and you'll see a curved arrow appear. Click and drag, and the image will rotate. This allows you to refine the straightening.

When you're done, double-click within the crop rectangle, or press Return to accept the straightened and cropped image. ◄◣

Correcting Geometric Distortion

As with straightening, there are certain types of geometric distortions you need to correct early in your workflow because they will also require a crop. If you're a stickler for geometric accuracy, you may want to try your geometric corrections right away because if it turns out that you *can't* correct your image to your liking, you'll want to know that early so you won't waste time on other edits.

Barrel and pincushion distortions are simple geometric distortions that occur in images shot with extreme wide-angle or telephoto lenses. If you had to zoom way out when you were shooting your image, there's a good chance the vertical and horizontal lines in your picture got bowed outward. Conversely, if your lens was zoomed in all the way, there's a chance that straight lines in your scene are bowed inward. If you're using a wide-angle or fisheye attachment on your lens, your images will almost certainly be distorted (unless you're using a rectilinear wide-angle lens on a digital SLR).

These distortions don't occur in all lenses. In fact, the lack of them is the mark of a very good lens, and even lenses that *do* have trouble with geometric distortion probably exhibit these issues only in specific, somewhat rare circumstances. If you find yourself facing distortion problems, you can correct them easily using Lightroom.

Tutorial Correcting Barrel and Pincushion Distortion in Lightroom

Lightroom provides excellent tools for correcting all kinds of lens distortions.

STEP 1: SELECT THE IMAGE

In Lightroom, select the graphwall.tif image (see Figure 14.12). Switch to the Develop module by pressing D.

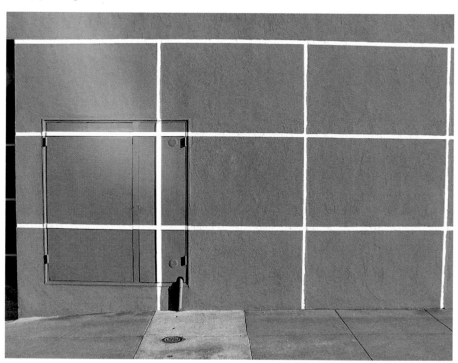

Figure 14.12

This image suffers from barrel distortion, a problem you can correct easily in Lightroom.

STEP 2: FIND THE LENS CORRECTION CONTROLS

In the right-hand pane, scroll down until you see the Lens Correction controls (Figure 14.13). At the top of the Lens Control toolbox is a small toolbar. Click on Manual to select the manual correction controls.

STEP 3: REMOVE THE BARREL DISTORTION

The Distortion slider allows you to easily correct either barrel or pincushion distortion. Slide it to the right to correct the barrel distortion. A value of +9 should do it (see Figure 14.14).

That's all there is to it. As you can see, after correction your image will need a crop, which you can perform easily using the Crop tool. ◢◣

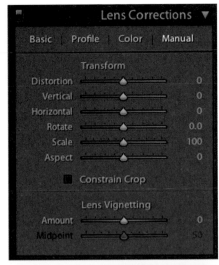

Figure 14.13

Use the Lens Correction tools to eliminate the barrel distortion in the image.

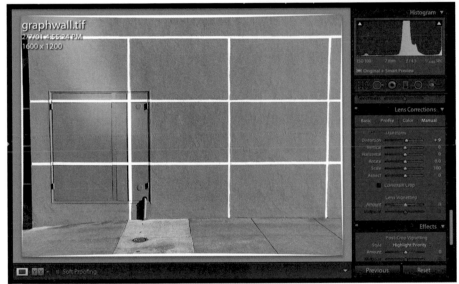

Figure 14.14

By simply sliding the Distortion slider to the right, you can remove the barrel distortion from this image. To correct pincushion distortion, slide to the left.

Auto Lens Correction

While Lightroom's manual lens correction features are very effective, you can also ask Lightroom to correct your images automatically.

STEP 1: SELECT THE IMAGE

In Lightroom, select the Lake Tahoe.CR2 image and then press D to switch to the Develop module.

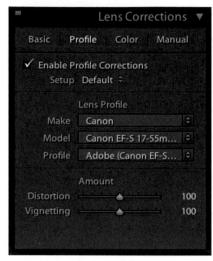

Figure 14.15

Using Profile Correction, you can ask Lightroom to automatically correct the image based on its understanding of the lens that you used to shoot the image. Here you can see that Lightroom has identified the lens that I used to shoot the image.

STEP 2: CONFIGURE THE TOOLS

In the Develop Module, find the Lens Correction tools that you used in the last tutorial and click on the Profile tab. You should see a checkbox labeled Enable Profile Correction. Check this now (Figure 14.15).

When you allow Profile Corrections, Lightroom reads the EXIF information to determine what type of lens and camera you're using. If a profile is available for that lens/camera combination, then Lens Correction will automatically correct geometric distortion, chromatic aberration, and vignetting.

If Lens Correction doesn't find a profile, you can help it out by telling it specifically what camera and lens you have.

Note that, if you choose to use automatic correction, the Custom parameters still work, so you can refine your correction further.

STEP 3: VIEW BEFORE AND AFTER

Press the \ key to see the image before the profile correction. Press \ to switch back to the After view. The \ key will always show you the original image file, providing you with an easy way to see the effects of your adjustments. ◄▌

Correcting Perspective

There might be times when you want to adjust the perspective in an image, most commonly if you're shooting architecture. For example, when you're standing at street level shooting up at a building, the top of the building will be narrower than the bottom. Perspective correction is another edit you want to perform early in your workflow because it requires cropping.

Correcting Perspective in Lightroom

Using the Lens Correction tools, let's correct the perspective in a simple architectural snapshot.

STEP 1: SELECT THE IMAGE

Select the image `Perspective Correx.CR2` from the Chapter 14 folder (see Figure 14.16), and if you're not already in it, switch to the Develop module by pressing D. Shot from ground level, this image has a perspective "distortion" that results in the top of the building appearing smaller than the bottom. Using the Lens Correction tools, you can adjust the image to reduce the perspective and restore the building to a stronger rectangular shape.

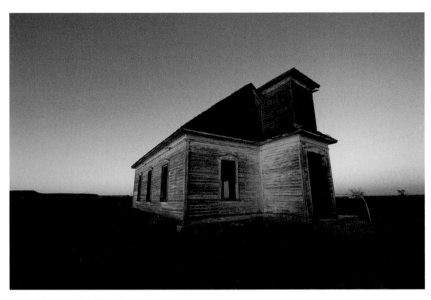

Figure 14.16

You can correct this image to adjust the perspective distortion so that it looks more rectangular.

STEP 2: ADD PROFILE CORRECTION

In the Develop module, scroll down the right-hand pane until you get to the Lens Correction tools. Make sure the Basic tab is selected and then click Enable Profile Corrections. You should see some vignetting and a bit of barrel distortion disappear. If you don't see the difference, toggle the Enable Profile Corrections checkbox a few times and watch the difference.

This image was shot with a Canon 10–22mm lens on a Rebel SL1. This is an ultrawide lens, so vignetting and distortion are not surprising. Fortunately, Adobe's profile for this lens does a great job of correcting those problems automatically.

STEP 3: ADD UPRIGHT CORRECTION

At the bottom of the Lens Correction tools are the Upright tools. By default, Upright should be highlighted, and the Off button should be selected. Click the Auto button, and you should see something like the results in Figure 14.17.

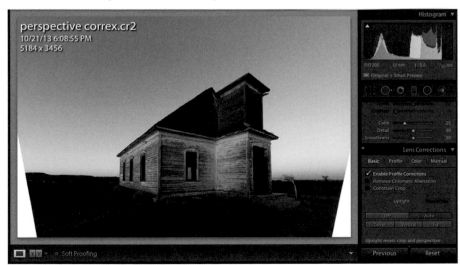

Figure 14.17

After activating automatic Upright correction, Lightroom tilts the image so that lines in the image that should be vertical are actually vertical.

At first, it may look like the only thing that Lightroom has done is chop off the corners of your image. But take a look at the vertical lines on the corner of the building. Press the \ key to view your original image and note how the lines are tilted inward before the correction. With the vertical correction applied, they're more upright. Yes, this comes at a cost—you'll have to crop the image—but the perspective on the building looks more correct.

STEP 4: EXPERIMENT WITH THE OTHER CORRECTIONS

In addition to Off and Auto, there are three other options for vertical correction: Level, Vertical, and Full. Hover the mouse over each button to see a description of what each one does. The Auto button applies a mix of each of these, but there might be times when one of the other modes works better. As you try each button, keep an eye on the vertical and horizontal lines; they will be your guide as to which choice is best. You'll be balancing this correction against how much cropping the image will need and how much additional distortion gets introduced.

STEP 5: CROP THE IMAGE

After you've chosen the correction that you like, use the Crop tool to crop the image. Ultimately, I decided to stick with Auto correction. While Vertical straightened out the vertical lines a little bit more than Auto does, it also stretched the top of the building a little too much for my taste. The final adjustment and crop is shown in Figure 14.18. ◥

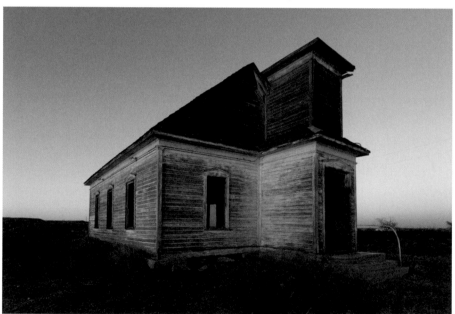

Figure 14.18

After perspective correction, the image requires a crop. The result is a building with truly vertical lines.

Correcting Chromatic Aberrations

Chromatic aberrations are colored fringes that can appear along high contrast lines, usually at the edges of your images. They are caused by lens distortions that prevent all wavelengths of light from being focused equally. Correcting chromatic aberrations doesn't require a crop, but it is something you might want to do early on, because if you *can't* correct these troubles, you may decide the image isn't worth further edits.

Lightroom's Lens Correction tools provide an easy way to fix this problem.

Figure 14.19 shows an image with some chromatic aberration troubles. While they may not appear obvious at the print size used in this book, when printed out at 8" × 10", the pink fringe along the edges of the canyons is very annoying.

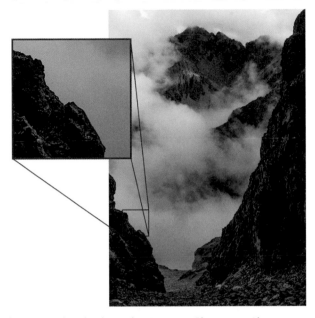

Figure 14.19

This image suffers from some chromatic aberration troubles.

You can easily fix chromatic aberrations by checking the Remove Chromatic Aberrations checkbox in the Lens Correction toolbox of the Develop module. Lightroom will simply remove the fringes (Figure 14.20).

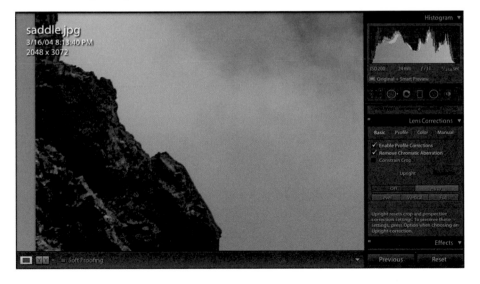

Figure 14.20

Lightroom's Remove Chromatic Aberrations tool makes short work of correcting annoying fringes.

This image, saddle.jpg, is included in the tutorial files so you can easily try this fix on your own.

Correcting Vignetting

The Lens Corrections toolbox offers one more feature, which is the capability to correct vignetting, the darkening of corners that can occur sometimes with wide-angle lenses. In the Manual tab, you'll find two sliders under Lens Vignetting. Use the Amount slider to control how much lighter or darker to make the corners, and use the Midpoint slider to control the size of the area that is altered. We'll explore these controls later to see how you can add a vignette for creative effect.

Dust and Spot Removal

If you shoot with an interchangeable lens camera, then there's a chance that you will occasionally get dust on your sensor. As with geometric corrections, you'll want to get your dust correction out of the way early, since if you can't fix it to your satisfaction, you might want to abandon the image. However, you might perform additional dust removal after you make your tonal adjustments, since tonal corrections might reveal more dust.

Almost all image editors have a tool that's suitable for dust removal. In Lightroom, we're going to use the Spot Removal tool. If your image editor has a Clone or Rubber Stamp tool, that will work well too, and we'll discuss these tools in Chapter 20, "Layers, Retouching, and Special Effects."

Tutorial: Correcting Dust Problems

In this tutorial, we're going to use Lightroom's Spot Removal tool to take some dust off an image.

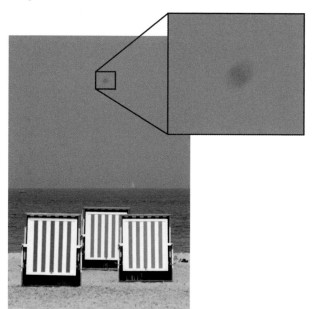

Figure 14.21

This image has a problem with some dust spots. Here, I remove them with a very easy-to-use tool.

STEP 1: SELECT THE IMAGE

Select the image `sensor dust.tif` in the Chapter 14 folder in Lightroom. The sensor dust should be pretty obvious—it's that big black smudge in the sky, as shown in Figure 14.21. If you look closely, you'll see some additional, smaller dust problems along the edge of the image. One of the lessons to learn from this image is that shooting on a sandy beach can lead to sensor dust problems.

STEP 2: SELECT THE SPOT REMOVAL TOOL

Select the Spot Removal tool from Lightroom's tool palette or press Q (see Figure 14.6).

STEP 3: ASSESS THE BRUSH SIZE

When you hold the mouse over your image with the Spot Removal tool selected, you'll see a circle that represents the current brush size. Place the brush over the big dust spot in the sky (see Figure 14.22).

STEP 4: SET THE BRUSH SIZE

You can change the size of any of Lightroom's brushes by using the [and] keys. The left bracket makes the brush smaller, and the right bracket makes it bigger. Adjust the brush size until the brush covers the dust spot.

STEP 5: CLICK TO ERASE THE SPOT

A single click is all it takes to remove the dust spot. The Spot Removal tool copies the pixels from a similar part of the image *into* the area you click on. It then performs some additional blurring and adjustment to create a smooth patch over the affected area. After you click, Lightroom will show you the source and target areas (Figure 14.23).

You can click and drag on the source circle to move it around. Sometimes, Lightroom will guess wrong at the best source for covering your spot. In these instances, dragging the source circle gives you an easy way to improve the quality of the spot removal.

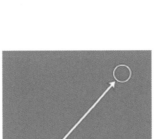

Figure 14.22

You want to ensure that the current brush size is big enough to cover the dust spot you want to remove.

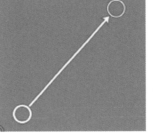

Figure 14.23

Here you can see precisely where Lightroom is copying from to repair the area that I clicked on.

Next, adjust the size accordingly and take out the rest of the dust in the image. After all of the dust is removed, press Q to close the spot remover tool. Note that if the dust is sitting on an area that's not an even color, the Spot Removal tool might not work very well. In these cases, the data that it copies won't necessarily merge well into the affected area. For times when the Spot Removal tool doesn't work, you'll need to resort to Photoshop's tools, which we'll get to later. ◤

Red Eye

Because of their small size, many digital cameras are particularly prone to red eye, that demonic look that can appear in your subjects' eyes when the flash from your camera has bounced off their retinas and back into the camera's lens. Although there are ways to avoid red eye when you shoot (see Chapter 10, "Lighting"), there will still be times when you will face this problem in an image and need to remove it. Pet eye is a variation of this that can cause dog and cat eyes to appear blue or other incorrect colors. Some cameras now include built-in red-eye and pet-eye removal.

There are several effective methods for removing red eye in your image editor. Which one you use depends mainly on the capabilities of your image editing software.

- ◆ **Use a red-eye removal filter or tool.** Many editing programs include special tools and filters for automatically removing red eye. Lightroom has a simple red-eye reduction tool, located next to the Spot Removal tool that you just used.

- ◆ **Desaturate the red area.** Because the pupil turns red, and pupils are usually black or very dark brown, simply desaturating the red area will drain it of color and restore it to its normal dark tone. Select the affected area (you'll probably want to feather the edge of the selection by a pixel or two) and then use your desaturation method of choice. In Photoshop, you can use the Sponge tool or the Hue/Saturation dialog box. You'll learn about all these tools later.

◆ **Repaint the area by hand.** If there's any natural color visible in your subject's eyes, you can try to sample it with the Eyedropper tool and repaint the rest of the area with a Paintbrush or Pencil tool. This is probably the most difficult technique because you will need to be careful to preserve any highlights or catchlights in the subject's eyes. An eye without a glint of light does not look natural. Examine some non–red-eye flash photos to see what this highlight should look like.

With your geometric corrections out of the way, your image should now be at its final crop. This means that you're ready to move on to the next stage of your image editing process, tonal corrections, which we'll cover in detail in the next chapter.

Undo and History

A standard feature of both the Mac and Windows operating systems is Undo. After you perform an action in just about any program, if you want to undo that action you can simply choose Edit > Undo or press Cmd/Ctrl-Z. If you decide that you want to restore the edit, choose Edit > Redo or press Shift-Cmd/Ctrl-Z. Lightroom provides up to 32 levels of Undo.

Of course, sometimes you don't realize that you'd like to undo a particular edit until you've performed some other edits, at which point, the offending edit may be too far back in the editing stream. For these instances, you can use Lightroom's History palette, which appears in the left-hand panel when you switch to the Develop module.

With the History palette, you can step forward and backward through edits (see Figure 14.24). Click on any edit, and your document will revert to that state.

Note that you cannot go nonlinearly. That is, you can't pick and choose a few different steps

Figure 14.24

The History palette makes it easy to step back through any of the previous states of your document.

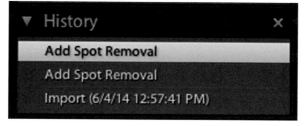

to activate. The History palette simply gives you a visual way to work back through the cached history states.

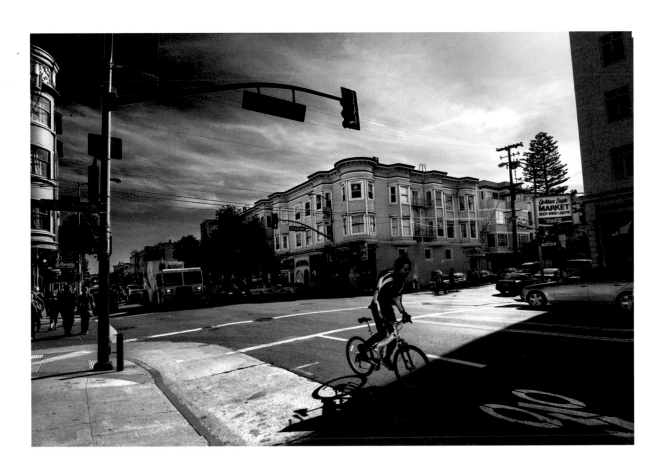

15

CORRECTING TONE

Ensuring That White, Black, and Overall Contrast Are Correct

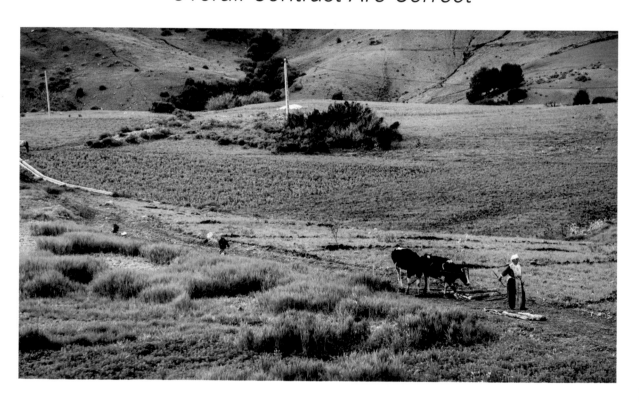

In general, when shooting you'll want to try to calculate exposures that will allow you to capture "finished" images directly in your camera. It's very easy to get into the mindset of "I can fix it later in my image editor," and you often *can* fix it later in your image editor, but this is not a good habit to get into. First of all, if you're shooting a lot of images, this approach can mean a *lot* of image editing work. Second, using your image editor to restore proper exposure might result in an image with more noise or posterization than if you had simply shot it correctly in the first place.

However, there will be times when conditions don't allow for an ideal exposure, and other times when the image you see in your head is impossible to produce without additional editing. Finally, sometimes you simply mess up and don't choose the right exposure, or a moment passes so quickly that you don't have time to adjust exposure to the ideal. For all of these occasions, you'll want to turn to your image editor.

With your image editing software, you can perform some amazing manipulations (some would say "deceptions") of your images. It's easy to be wowed by image editing tools that allow you to wildly alter the content of your image. But while creating extreme special effects and dramatic changes to an image are very technically impressive, the most useful features of your image editor are its capabilities to alter the tone and color so that the image—no matter what its content—looks better in final output. Sometimes, you'll use tone and color adjustments to correct the exposure you initially shot, and at other times, you'll use these features to *finish* the image you originally shot.

In terms of fundamental image editing, little has changed since the first edition of this book. The main tools you'll use to achieve your adjustments are Levels and Curves controls, which provide very similar functionality using two different interfaces. Most image editing programs include a Levels adjustment, and higher-end applications include both Levels and Curves. For the purposes of these tutorials, you can use any application that provides Levels and Curves. These tutorials are built around Lightroom, and while all image editors these days have Lightroom-like Levels controls, they don't all offer Curves. Even if you won't be using a Curves-equipped image editor regularly, it's worth going through the Curves tutorials simply for the theory that is explained.

Be Sure You Know What a Histogram Is

In this chapter, we're going to be spending a *lot* of time looking at histograms. If you aren't clear on what a histogram is, reread the histogram discussion in Chapter 8, "Advanced Exposure," and the recap in Chapter 14, "Editing Workflow and First Steps."

Correcting Tone

Tonal correction is simply the process of ensuring that the contrast in your image is good. You correct tone to ensure that the blacks, whites, and gray levels look the way you want them to look. Very often, tonal corrections are the only adjustments your image will need. With a simple tonal change, you can take an otherwise dull, hazy image and turn it into a scene that pops off the page.

Because colors also have a tone, many of your color problems will disappear with tonal correction. There are many tonal correction tools, and different ones are used to solve different problems. However, the tool you will probably find yourself using most often is a Levels adjustment, which can be found in all major image editors.

Basic Edits

In Chapters 8 and 14, you spent some time reading histograms. From the histogram, you saw that you could easily determine when an image was too dark, too bright, or lacked contrast. What you cannot do with a histogram is correct these problems. Lightroom's Basic editing tools provide very powerful controls for altering the tone and color in an image.

What makes the Basic editing tools so useful is that they let you edit different parts of the tonal range independently. So you can brighten the dark parts of your image without blowing out the highlights or alter highlights without worrying about washing out the dark tones in your image.

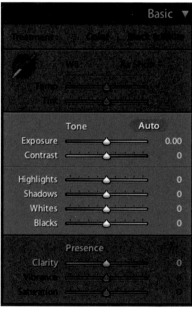

The Basic section of the Develop module contains six sliders for adjusting tone: Exposure, Contrast, Highlights, Shadows, Whites, and Blacks (see Figure 15.1). Except for Contrast, they all work the same way: drag to the left to darken, drag to the right to lighten. With Contrast, you drag to the left to lower contrast and to the right to increase contrast.

Each slider affects a different part of the tonal range. Shadows and Blacks obviously affect the lower part of the range, while Highlights and Whites impact the upper part, and Exposure hits a broad swath in the middle (see Figure 15.2).

While Adobe recommends that you work through the sliders from the top down, I find it's usually better to get your whites and blacks set properly, simply because those are quantifiable. From there, you can begin to assess midtones and overall contrast.

Figure 15.1

They may not look like much, but the six highlighted sliders shown here are powerful tone correction tools that you'll likely use on every image that you process in Lightroom.

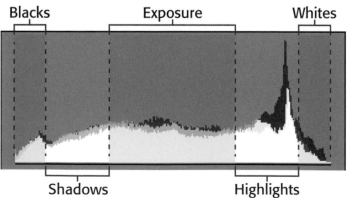

Figure 15.2

Each tone slider in Lightroom affects a different tonal range, as shown here.

In this tutorial, we're going to correct the tone in an image.

We're going to begin our tone adjustment work by correcting the grayscale ramp shown in Figure 14.2. As you'll recall, this image suffers from low contrast. The brightest areas aren't white, and the darkest areas aren't black, which means that, overall, there's not much range from the darkest tone to the lightest. In other words, the darkest and lightest tones don't contrast very much.

Fortunately, if your image editor has a Levels or Curves control, or a tonal adjustment like you'll find in Lightroom, you have a solution to these problems.

Using the Basic Edit Sliders

Your goal is to correct the grayscale ramp that you saw earlier in Figure 14.2 so that it has better black-and-white values and improved overall contrast. You want it to look like the smooth gradient that was shown in Figure 14.1.

STEP 1: SELECT THE IMAGE

Select the image `grayramp.tif`, which should be in the Chapter 15 folder of your Lightroom catalog. (If you skipped Chapter 14, you'll need to go back and follow the "Preparing Lightroom" section to ensure that you have access to the images that you'll need in the rest of these tutorials.)

STEP 2: EVALUATE THE IMAGE

With the image selected, switch to the Develop module, if you're not there already. From the histogram, you can see that the majority of the tones are gathered in the center of the tonal range. There's no black in the image, nor is there any white (Figure 15.3).

Tones in an image that are clustered in the center are the hallmark of a low-contrast image.

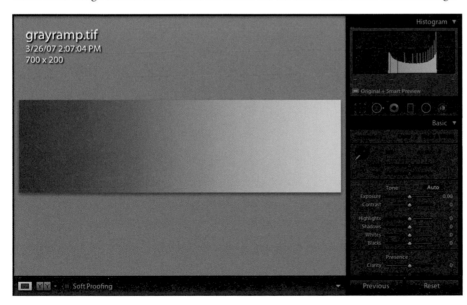

Figure 15.3

The gray ramp has no black, no white, and all of its tones are clustered in the center of the image.

STEP 3: ADJUST THE CONTRAST

Since this image is low-contrast, it seems like a good initial edit would be to simply increase the contrast slider. Drag it all the way to the right, and you'll see that the image does, in fact, gain contrast. However, the Contrast slider doesn't have enough latitude to get the darkest tones all the way to black or the brightest tones all the way to white.

STEP 4: ADJUST THE BLACKS

While watching the histogram, slide the Blacks slider to the left until the leftmost tone in the histogram touches the left edge. This indicates that you've now darkened the lowest tones in the image until the darkest of them is completely black (see Figure 15.4).

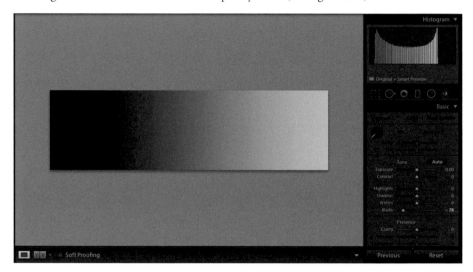

Figure 15.4

Moving the Blacks slider to –78 put the darkest tones in the image back to black.

Note that the lightest part of the histogram remained stationary. As mentioned before, you can edit each part of the tonal range independently.

STEP 5: ADJUST WHITES

Now move the Whites slider until the rightmost tone in the image touches the right edge of the histogram. You should end up around +74. Note that I'm not paying attention to the actual image at all. Because I can't trust my monitor to indicate true black and true white, I'm working strictly by the histogram for these edits.

STEP 6: ASSESS YOUR PROGRESS

The image does have more contrast now, but it's hardly a smooth gray ramp. Almost the entire left third of the histogram looks black while at least that much of the right side looks completely white (see Figure 15.5). Note how much data there is on both ends of the histogram, and how little there is in the middle. (Remember, higher spikes mean more data in a given area.)

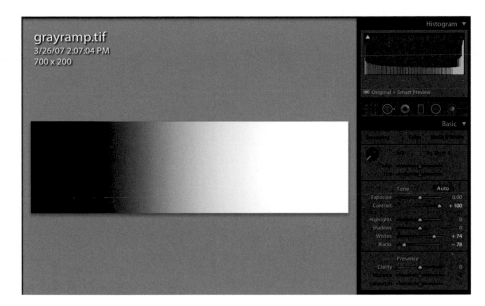

Figure 15.5

The image has more contrast, but now it has too much. The majority of the data is piled up on the left and right sides of the histogram. This is why the image looks predominantly black and white on the edges, with few variations of grays in the middle.

STEP 7: ADJUST SHADOWS

Look back at Figure 15.2. Although the histogram in that image is not accurate for the editing that you're doing, you can still see from the diagram that the Shadows slider alters darker tones in your image, but not the very dark tones that are targeted by the Blacks slider. That area that the Shadows slider targets is an area where you need some more data—right now there's not much in that part of your histogram.

Watch the image while you drag the Shadows slider all the way to the right. You should see the black region on the left side of the histogram begin to lighten. As you drag, it will look as if gray is "invading" that part of the tonal range.

Put the Shadows slider back to zero and perform the same adjustment while watching the histogram. You should see tones in the shadows part of the histogram changing and moving. Note, too, that Lightroom highlights the part of the histogram that is the primary target of the slider that you're dragging.

Leave the Shadows slider set to +100. In both the image and the histogram, you can see that there's a very sudden transition from dark gray to light gray. Don't worry, that problem might resolve itself as you continue your edits.

STEP 8: ADJUST HIGHLIGHTS

From Figure 15.2, you can see that the Highlights slider targets a brighter part of the tonal range that roughly corresponds to the Shadows slider. Drag it all the way to the left while watching the image, and then again while watching the histogram, just as you did with the Shadows slider (see Figure 15.6).

Notice that, as you darkened highlights, you smoothed out the transition into the shadows. Note, too, that you no longer have true white and true black in the image. The Shadows and Highlights adjustments slightly dimmed the brightest tones and lightened the darkest. Adjust the Whites slider to +81 and the Blacks slider to −83, and you should end up with an image that goes from complete black to complete white.

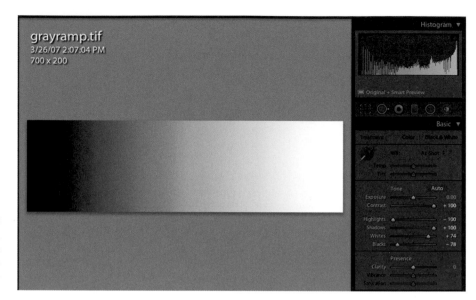

Figure 15.6

With the Shadows and Highlights slider, you've managed to redistribute the extreme light and dark tones to create a smooth range of midtones.

STEP 9: LOOK CLOSER

If you mouse over the image in the Develop module, your cursor should change to a magnifying glass. Click on an area, and Lightroom will zoom in to a 1:1 view of that location. When zoomed in, if you mouse over your image, the cursor will change to a grabber hand, which lets you pan about the image. As you look up close, you should notice two things: There are places where the gradient isn't perfectly smooth, and in the darker areas there is noise.

Neither of these artifacts are necessarily so bad that the image won't print well, but they are a direct result of pushing a small amount of data to cover a large tonal range. That is why it's important to capture the best exposure that you can. While it's possible to radically alter tone, altered tones won't necessarily look as good as well-captured tones. What's more, if you wanted to do more to this image, you would only increase the noise and tone breaks.

Adjusting a Real-World Image

Using the Basic sliders on a real image is no different from the process you just performed on the grayscale ramp. In this tutorial, you're going to correct the image shown in Figure 15.7.

STEP 1: SELECT THE IMAGE

Select the image `Real World adjustment.jpg`, which is located in the Chapter 15 folder.

STEP 2: EXAMINE THE HISTOGRAM

Before you can begin making any corrections or adjustments, you need to devise a plan of attack, and the easiest way to do that is to examine your image's histogram. The histogram will help you determine what adjustments will be necessary and in what order. This is why you should perform any necessary cropping operations right away. You need to be sure that your histogram contains only relevant data.

As you can see from the histogram, this image has some contrast problems. There's no black or white in the image, and this lack of contrast is giving it an overall dull appearance.

STEP 3: SET THE BLACKS

You're first going to set the black point in the image to restore the

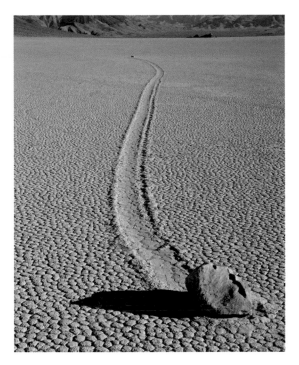

Figure 15.7

We didn't do a very good job with the exposure of this image when we shot it. It has a murky quality that stems from a lack of contrast.

dark tones to their proper values. There's no objectively correct black point; you can set it to wherever you want, depending on how much contrast you want to have in the image and how worried you are about shadow detail. (As you darken shadows, they'll lose detail.) Lightroom provides a handy utility for determining exactly which tones are clipped by your black point adjustment.

Hold down the Option/Alt key while you drag the Blacks slider to the left. As soon as you begin to drag, your image will turn completely white. Don't worry—your picture hasn't been erased. As you continue to drag, any pixels that are getting clipped (pushed to completely black) by your adjustment will be highlighted. This is referred to as a *threshold view* (see Figure 15.8).

In Figure 15.8, some of the clipped pixels are colored. This indicates pixels that are being clipped in only one channel. For example, blue pixels are pixels that have been clipped only in the Blue channel.

We aren't as concerned about these as we are about the black pixels, which indicate clipping in all three channels. The first pixels to appear black are the dark shadows directly beneath the rock. If you want, you can back off until these pixels return to white, to guarantee that you don't clip any tones. However, it doesn't really matter if some of the shadows underneath the rock turn completely black since there's no meaningful detail in that part of the image anyway.

You can freely release and press the Option/Alt key to toggle in and out of threshold view, allowing you to easily determine the effects of your black point adjustment.

Here, I went for a fairly aggressive black point change to produce stronger contrast in the image, and I set the Blacks slider to –60. Note, though, that I didn't go so far that all the detail in the rock's shadow has gone to black (see Figure 15.9).

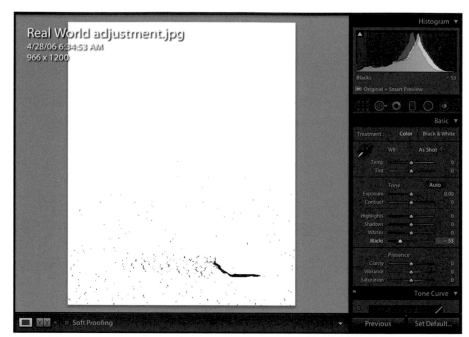

Figure 15.8

The threshold view in Lightroom makes it easy to see exactly which pixels are being clipped by your black point adjustment.

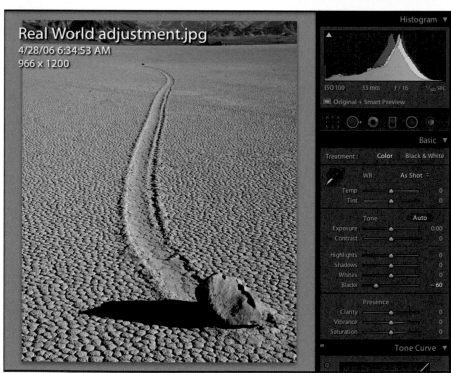

Figure 15.9

I settled on a Blacks slider adjustment of −60. While this clips some tones, they're not areas that contain important detail, and I wanted the stronger contrast.

STEP 4: SET THE WHITE POINT

You can use the same threshold view when setting the white point—just hold down Option/ Alt while dragging the Whites slider to see a threshold view. In general, you can't push a white point adjustment as much as you can a black point adjustment because clipped highlights are much more noticeable than clipped shadows. So I set the white point to around +45 (see Figure 15.10). I chose this amount simply by looking at the histogram and aiming for an adjustment that didn't cause a spike on the right side.

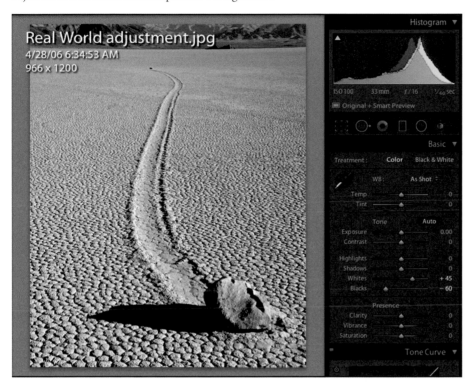

Figure 15.10

A Whites adjustment of +45 brightens the image, removing some of the dullness, without blowing out any important details.

Turn Off the Info Overlay

By default, Lightroom overlays the file name and dimensions when you view an image in the Develop module. You can toggle this overlay on and off by pressing Command/Control-I. You can change what is displayed in the Overlay by choosing View > View Options.

STEP 5: ADJUST THE MIDPOINT

My image already looks much better. The dull cast is gone, and there is a "punchier" level of contrast. However, you can improve the image a little more with a Contrast adjustment.

This is a bright image so the majority of the tones are piled up just above the midpoint in the histogram. The Contrast slider targets the midtones in an image and attempts to leave black and white alone, so it's a good tool for expanding that big pile of bright tones.

Move the Contrast slider to +61. Again, I arrived at this number by looking at the histogram. I watched how the tones spread, and made certain not to make an adjustment that yielded spikes on either end of the histogram.

STEP 6: EVALUATE

Press the \ key to see a before view of your image; then press again to toggle back to the edited view. While the before image looks okay, the after image has a lot more punch to it (see Figure 15.11). It's as if a dull sheen has been lifted from the image. This is what a proper level of contrast can do to an image. ◢◣

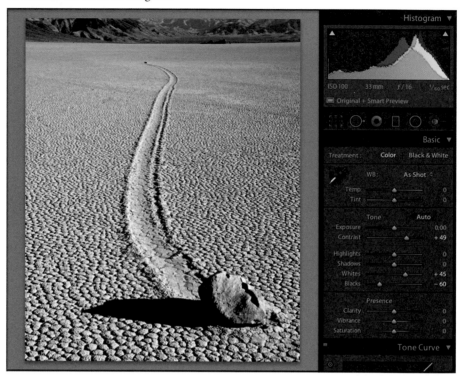

Figure 15.11

After a Contrast adjustment, my image has more punch.

Another Way to Think About Edits

All of the tonal correction tools that you'll use perform slight variations of the same function: They allow you to selectively brighten or darken specific pixels in an image. Some also allow you to brighten or darken only the red, green, or blue component of a color. But, ultimately, they all perform a controlled increasing or decreasing of pixel values.

When you adjusted the black point in the grayscale ramp, you told Lightroom to darken a specific set of tones in the image. Lightroom was smart enough to darken the tones by varying amounts to try to create a smooth transition from the adjusted to nonadjusted tones.

The histogram provides a great visual aid for this lightening and darkening—it allows you to think of the tones in your image as a quantity that can be pushed around to different parts of the tonal range. When you darken an image with Lightroom, it looks like you're pushing tones down to fill in empty regions in the shadows. Really, you're simply darkening tones that are already in the image. As they darken, they fall onto a different place in the histogram.

Auto Adjustment

Clicking the Auto button in the Basic toolbox automatically adjusts the black-and-white points on your image. How it makes these adjustments varies from image to image. Sometimes, it will move some of the tone sliders but not others. Also, it may not get things exactly to your taste, so you might find you need further adjustment.

Whether you're using Auto or not, it's important to consider which data in the histogram is relevant. Sometimes, determining what should be white can be complicated—more complicated than the Auto algorithms can figure out. For example, the rightmost point in the histogram might be a specular highlight (the type of highlight that you might see on a rippling lake in bright sunlight) or a bright flare, whereas true white is farther to the left. You might also find that, for printing purposes, you want to leave a little "headroom" above and below your tonal range.

Look at Figure 15.12. On the left, you can see an original image, with its corresponding histogram.

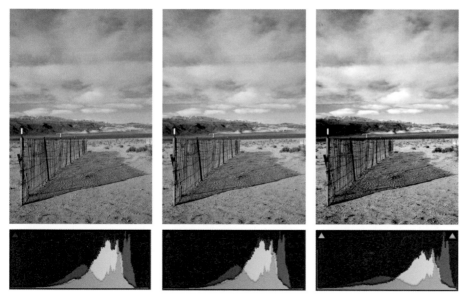

Figure 15.12

Simply adjusting the black and white so that they hit the edges of the histogram isn't enough to make this image look its best. Instead, you need to identify the darkest and lightest relevant data.

In the second image, I adjusted the image so that black and white touched the edges of the histogram. The image is a little better, but it still lacks punch. The blackest parts of the image are probably those shadows up there in the mountains, while the very brightest parts are probably a very few pixels scattered about the snow on the top of the mountains. While those little bits are now properly exposed, the bulk of the tones in the image still lack proper contrast.

In the third image, I adjusted it to ensure that some of the darker tones in the foreground of the image were deepened. Next, I slid the Whites slider farther to the right so that it was impacting the sky.

Very often, Auto will figure out these same sort of "relevant data" issues, and if you're trying to automate your postproduction, Auto can be a real time-saver. But it doesn't take that long to position the white and black points yourself, and learning to recognize which tones are more relevant in your image is a valuable skill.

More Editing Practice

Lightroom's Basic sliders work best when used in concert with each other. To help you understand how they interact, you're going to spend some more time performing basic tonal adjustments. While Adobe recommends that you work through the sliders from the top down, I find it's usually better to get your whites and blacks set properly, simply because those are quantifiable. From there, you can begin to assess midtones and overall contrast.

STEP 1: SELECT THE IMAGE
Click on `self-portrait.CR2` and enter the Develop module, if you're not already there.

STEP 2: ADJUST THE BLACKS
As mentioned earlier, if you start by correcting black and white in your image, then you'll have an easier time assessing overall contrast. From the histogram, you can see that there are no overexposed highlights or underexposed blacks. In fact, there's very little dark data at all. I'm going to set blacks first, because they're going to require a fairly large adjustment, and that could change a lot of other things.

You've seen that the Blacks slider affects the very darkest tones in the histogram, so let's start with it. Drag the Blacks slider to the left until you see black appear in the histogram (see Figure 15.13).

I set Blacks to –58, because if I go any farther, I start seeing a lot of shadow clipping in the Histogram.

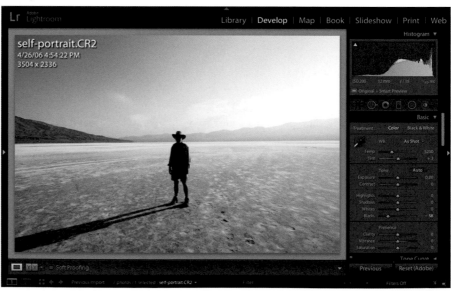

Figure 15.13

I'll start my tonal adjustments by setting the Black point.

STEP 3: ADJUST SHADOWS

The ground now has more contrast in it, thanks to the black point adjustment, and the shadow on the ground looks nicer. The shadows on the hills in the background aren't true black, but that's okay because they're being viewed through hazy air, so they shouldn't be black.

Obviously, the problem with the dark tones in the image is that there are too many of them on my face. Because this was a backlighting situation, the camera underexposed me.

The shadows on my face fall into the target range of the Shadows slider. What's more, the Shadows slider performs some adaptive calculations to try to target, identify, and lighten shadows, rather than simply things that are dark, which may not need lightening.

Drag the Shadows slider to the right to brighten up the shadows on my face. A value around +75 should be about right (see Figure 15.14).

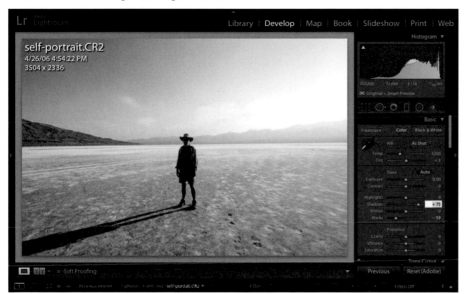

Figure 15.14

With the Shadows slider, you can easily lighten the shadows on the figure.

Now check out the histogram: Your Shadows adjustment lightened up some of the blacks. Drag the Blacks slider farther to the left to restore true blacks. I set it at –76. This, in turn, darkens the shadows that were just brightened! Kick the Shadows slider up to +85.

As mentioned before, trying to balance multiple sliders like this is a normal part of image editing. You'll often work multiple sliders simultaneously to find the combination that gets you what you want.

STEP 4: ADJUST THE BRIGHTER TONES

The histogram shows that the majority of the tones are still piled up above the midpoint. This indicates that maybe we don't have as much midtone contrast as we could have. More contrast might make the texture on the ground look nicer and create an image that isn't so generally bright.

The Exposure slider targets the midtones in the image, so let's use it to darken the mids. Drag it to the left to about –.40. Right away, you should be able to see that it's a very "strong" tool. A slight adjustment moves a lot of tones.

Now the image lacks true white, and has lost some brighter tones. Drag the Whites slider to the right to +36. I chose 36 because any farther will push the right end of the histogram into clipping.

With these two edits, we've greatly expanded the contrast in the midtones. You can see that both from the histogram and by looking at the ground, which now has more detail. The Contrast slider might have done the same thing, and it's worth giving it a try. You'll often find that you need more control than the Contrast slider provides. Working with the individual sliders like this enables you to expand contrast in specific parts of the tonal range.

STEP 5: ADJUST SHADOWS—AGAIN

As you might have noticed, all this darkening has darkened up the shadows on the face again. So return to the Shadows slider and drag it to the right, all the way to 100 (see Figure 15.15).

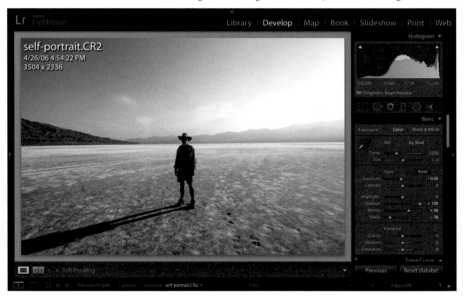

Figure 15.15

With one more Shadows adjustment, my tone is fixed.

Working effectively with these tools takes practice. The process is pretty simple, though. Identify the slider that targets the tonal range you need to correct and use it to brighten or darken those specific tones. Perhaps the most important lesson here, is to recognize that a single slider usually won't fix a problem. You'll get still more practice in the next tutorial.

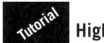 **Highlight Recovery**

One of the best reasons for shooting in raw format is that raw often allows you to recover overexposed highlights. As we've discussed, an overexposed highlight appears in your image as an area of complete white. Totally devoid of texture, an overexposed area can disrupt your composition and create an unwanted distraction.

Very often, though, an overexposed area is not overexposed in all three color channels. Remember, color in your image is composed of separate channels of red, green, and blue information. If only one or two channels overexpose, but the third is intact, Lightroom can use that intact information to try to reconstruct what's missing from the other two. In this next tutorial, you'll see this in action.

STEP 1: SELECT THE IMAGE
Select the `teakettle.CR2` document and switch to the Develop module.

STEP 2: ANALYZE THE HISTOGRAM
Right away, you might notice the overexposed white areas in the sky. Because clouds can often look like wispy fields of white, it's difficult to tell if whiteness is overexposure or just a sky that's soft and white. The histogram provides the answer.

There's a huge pile of data on the extreme right side of the histogram, indicating that the highlights are overexposed. Clicking the Highlight Warning button in the upper-right corner will show you where the overexposed parts are located (see Figure 15.16).

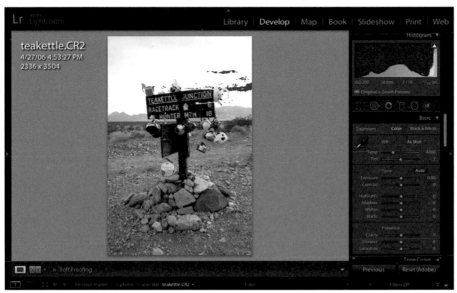

Figure 15.16

This image is suffering from overexposure in the sky, as indicated by Lightroom's Highlight Clipping Warning.

In addition to the areas that are overexposed, there are other tones that are simply brighter than they should be; those areas have also lost detail.

Click on the Highlight Clipping Warning triangle to deactivate it.

STEP 3: RECOVER THE HIGHLIGHTS
The Highlights slider controls the very brightest tones in the image, and it also has the ability to reconstruct tones that have been overexposed to complete white. Drag the Highlights slider to the left while watching the histogram. You should see the spike on the right side get smaller and smaller, and eventually disappear. I stopped at around –90. If you want, you can activate the Highlight Clipping Warning and drag until you see all the red bits disappear.

STEP 4: COMPARE TO BEFORE
Press and hold the \ key on your keyboard to see the original raw file. Notice how much detail was hidden in that white sky. There are actual clouds with structure in there, which can be revealed by taking what appears to be a big mush of white data in the histogram and spreading it out into its constituent tones.

STEP 5: ADJUST WHITES

Highlights affects only the very brightest tones in the histogram. There are a lot of other tones over there on the right side that fall more under the influence of the Whites slider. Drag it to the left to darken those tones. Using the clouds on the left side as a guide, I moved the Whites to about –38.

STEP 6: ADJUST BLACKS

It's usually best to begin editing by getting your white-and-black points set properly, especially when there's an overexposure problem. If it had turned out to be impossible to recover the overexposed areas, I probably would have abandoned this image, so it didn't make sense to waste time with any other edits first. With the whites looking good, let's now set the blacks, to get a sense of the overall contrast in the image.

Drag the Blacks until you've got data at the left edge of the histogram. I set it to –58.

STEP 7: ADJUST EXPOSURE

The majority of the tones are still shifted to the right of the histogram, but this image is not necessarily supposed to be a bright image, so you need to darken it. The Exposure slider controls the biggest expanse of tonal information in the image, so let's slide it to the left to shift the midtones into darker areas. I set mine to –.4 (see Figure 15.17).

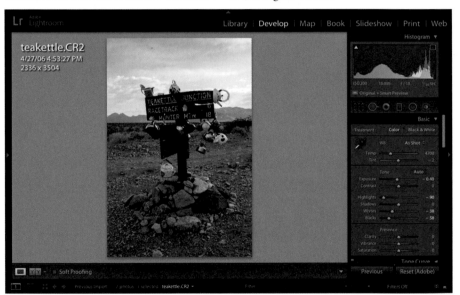

Figure 15.17

A negative Exposure adjustment brings out more details in the bright areas, but overall leaves things a little too dark.

This revealed even more detail in the sky, but now the foreground is looking a little dark. Also, you still don't have really strong shadows, and your brightest areas aren't extending all the way to the right of the histogram. The majority of the tones are gathered in the middle. It would be nice if you could spread them out.

STEP 8: ADJUST CONTRAST

Drag the Contrast slider to the right, to about +44. This will increase the contrast in the image, spreading the tones across more of the middle of the histogram. You'll lose some blacks, but you won't see a terrible change in the white point.

STEP 9: ADJUST SHADOWS

Now let's use the Shadows slider to brighten the dark areas on the sign. Slide it to the right to about +58.

STEP 10: FINAL TWEAKS

The image is looking pretty good, but you need to balance a few things. The Shadows adjustment you made brightened your blacks. To darken the blacks, move the Blacks slider to the left a little, to about –69. Notice that you won't lose detail on the sign.

Finally, let's add some clarity to the image. The Clarity slider makes very slight expansions to the contrast of the middle tones in the image, to help improve the detail along edges. I set mine to +25, and now the rocks and other details have better definition (see Figure 15.18).

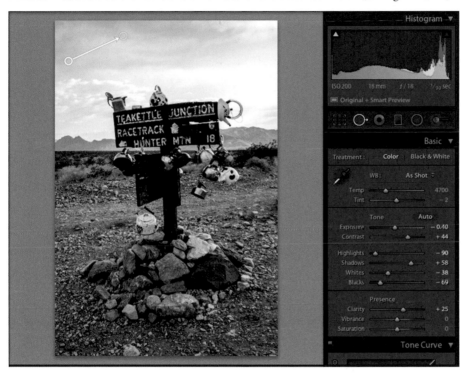

Figure 15.18

My final tone adjustments.

By now, you've probably noticed the sensor dust problems in the sky. You can easily handle these with the Spot Removal tool. ◥

 Highlight Recovery and Detail

It's easy to spot overexposure in a bright feature like clouds. But overexposure can also cost you detail in colored objects, and it may not be obvious that there's more detail to be had in some areas until you perform your recovery. This is another reason that it's critical to pay attention to the histogram, and when you see that there's overexposure, attempt a recovery. You may be surprised at how much new detail comes into your image.

STEP 1: SELECT THE IMAGE

Select the image sunflowers.CR2 and switch to Lightroom's Develop module.

STEP 2: ASSESS THE IMAGE

These sunflowers were heavily backlit, so they don't look obviously overexposed; they simply look like flowers with sun behind them. The image is a little low in contrast, but otherwise looks mostly okay (see Figure 15.19). However, the histogram shows a spike on the right side. It's not a white spike, which means not all three-color channels have been clipped. Rather, it's a red spike with a tiny bit of yellow at the bottom, which means that the Red and Green channels have been clipped (red and green make yellow).

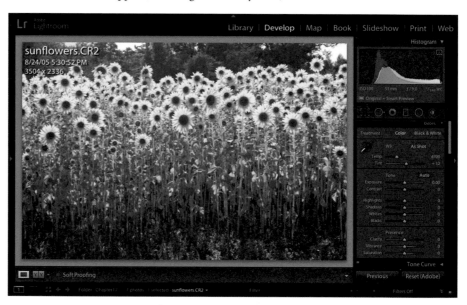

Figure 15.19

While it's not necessarily obvious from looking at the image, the histogram shows that this image has some overexposure.

STEP 3: RECOVER HIGHLIGHTS

As always, we begin with highlight recovery. Slide the Highlights slider to the left. You should find that, even all the way at −100, you couldn't entirely get rid of the spike. Switch to the Whites slider and drag it to the left until the spike is gone—around −34. The Whites slider can also be used to recover highlights.

STEP 4: ADJUST BLACKS

The image is sorely lacking in contrast, so before we spend too much time assessing our highlight recovery, let's get the Black point where it needs to be, to give our image a more reasonable amount of contrast (see Figure 15.20).

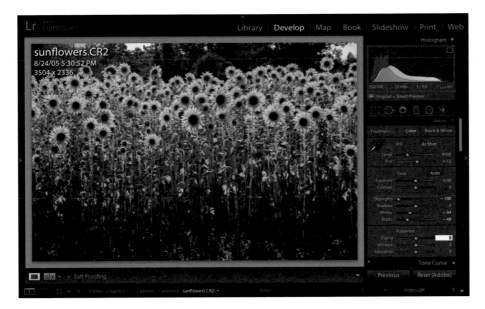

Figure 15.20

After moving the Highlights slider all the way to the left, the big pile of data on the right side of the histogram has spread out.

STEP 5: COMPARE TO ORIGINAL

Use the \ key to view the original image versus your adjusted version.

Note the overall improvement in detail on the petals of the flowers. Also, notice that, with the adjustment, there's been a color shift—the flowers are now more orange than they were before.

At this point, you might decide that you like the extreme backlit flowers better. That's fine, but the point of this exercise was to demonstrate that lost detail from overexposure is not always obvious. ▸◀

Expanding Dynamic Range with Whites, Highlights, Shadows, and Blacks

If you've used previous versions of Lightroom, you might have found yourself facing different sliders. Prior Lightroom versions used sliders with different names and very different functionality. As Adobe comes up with better algorithms for adjusting tone, they sometimes make radical changes to the controls in the Develop module. In my opinion, the Whites, Highlights, Shadows, and Blacks sliders in the current Lightroom offer the very best tools yet designed for manipulating tone. With them, you have a fantastic facility for expanding dynamic range in your image, while maintaining a tremendous degree of control. To make the best use of these sliders, you need to think of them as related pairs. You'll typically use Highlights and Whites together to alter the bright tones in your image and then use Shadows and Blacks together. You've seen some of this already, but let's take another look at the best approach to using these tools.

STEP 1: SELECT THE IMAGE

Select the Lake Tahoe.CR2 image and switch to the Develop module. Overall, this image is well-exposed. There are no overexposed highlights or underexposed shadows. In fact, there are no strong whites or blacks at all, so you'll have to fix that. But note, too, that there's a big pile of data on both ends of the histogram. There's a lot of shadow data piled up, but without underexposing, and a lot of highlight data piled up. If you could expand those piles to cover a broader area, you'd have an image with more detail (see Figure 15.21).

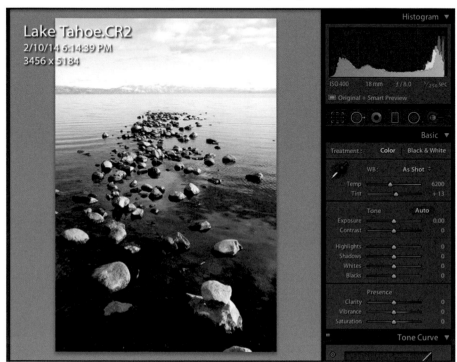

Figure 15.21

This image is generally well-exposed, but it's not making the best use of the data. If you could spread out all of that highlight and shadow data that's heaped up on the ends of the histogram, you'd end up with an image with more tonality and contrast.

STEP 2: ADJUST THE HIGHLIGHTS

Let's begin by fixing the highlights in the image. I'm choosing these simply because the sky is the most interesting part of the image, and I'm curious to see what I can make it look like.

The Highlights slider happens to target the lower range of the big pile of highlight data that sits on the right side of the histogram. Meanwhile, the Whites slider targets the upper part. That means that you can use the two sliders in concert to expand the contrast of that area.

While keeping your eyes on the histogram, drag the Highlights slider all the way to the left. You should see the big pile of highlight data spread out (see Figure 15.22).

Use the \ key to see before and after views of your image.

STEP 3: SET WHITE

You still don't have any actual white in the image, which it needs since the snow and clouds should have some points that are pure white.

Move the Whites slider to the right until the Histogram shows that you have achieved true white in your image. You should find that around +28.

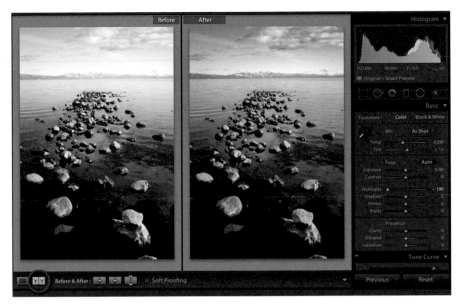

Figure 15.22

By using the Before/After controls (the circled widget in the lower-left corner), you can easily see how the Highlights slider was used to darken the lower part of the brightest highlights.

STEP 4: ADJUST THE BLACKS

The Shadows and Blacks sliders have a similar relationship. Drag the Shadows slider to the right to brighten the shadow areas and then move the Blacks slider to the left to set pure black. I ended up setting Shadows at +51 and Blacks at −57.

STEP 5: ADD SOME CLARITY

Finally, slide the Clarity slider to the right to add a little edge definition to the rocks. The Clarity slider will always add contrast to your image so it's important to set it while adjusting your other tonal controls (see Figure 15.23).

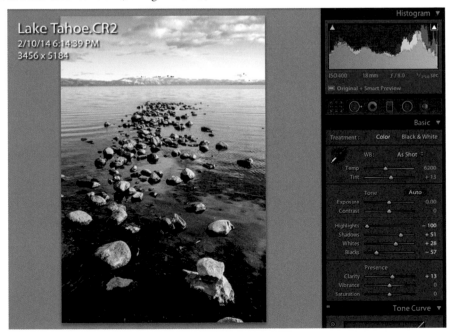

Figure 15.23

The final image. I easily expanded the dynamic range in the highlights and shadows while maintaining full control over white and black.

Obviously, you won't always need as aggressive a Highlights adjustment as I made here. In the case of all of these sliders, the histogram should serve as your guide while adjusting. The important thing to remember is that each pair of sliders works together. With them, you have a tremendous level of control over the brightest and darkest tones in your image.

Curves

The Basic controls provide the simplest way to perform the basic tonal adjustments you will need to make regularly, but it's not the answer for all corrections. You might find yourself occasionally frustrated when one of the Basic sliders doesn't target the precise tonal range that you need. For these instances, the Lightroom Tone Curve might prove a better tool.

A typical curves interface (see Figure 15.24) is really just a different interface to the same adjustments you were making before.

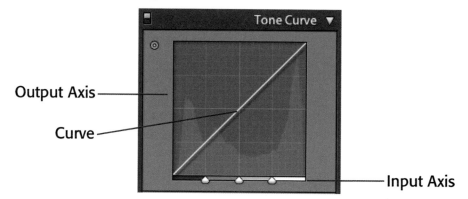

Figure 15.24

The Lightroom Tone Curve is typical of most Curves tools, offering a simple graph of input (the tonal values before the edit is applied) values to output (after the edit is applied) values.

Notice the gray ramp that runs underneath the Tone Curve interface. It goes from black on the left to white on the right. If you imagine a similar gray ramp running up the left side of the interface, then the tone curve will make more sense. The horizontal gray ramp represents the tones in your image *before* they are altered by the tone curve. The vertical axis represents the tones in your image *after* they are altered.

By default, the Tone Curve shows a 45° line from black to white, indicating that the input tones (the ones along the bottom) are identical to the output tones (the ones along the side). If you change the shape of the line, you change the correspondence of the input tones to the output tones (see Figure 15.25).

Figure 15.25

In the left diagram, before editing, each point on the input axis corresponds to the same spot on the output axis. After adding a point, the corresponding spot on the input axis in the right diagram is equal to a lighter spot on the output axis. What's more, all of the surrounding points have been altered along a smooth curve.

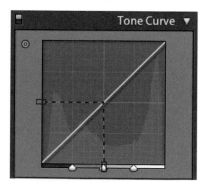

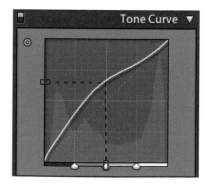

When you used the Blacks slider earlier, you told Lightroom that there was a new value it should consider to be black. The image editor then stretched and squeezed the values in your image to make your desired adjustment. The curve in the Curves dialog box, which starts out as a straight line, lets you see clearly how all the tones in your image are being stretched and squeezed.

The main advantage of Lightroom's Tone Curve is that it lets you specify more exactly which part of the tonal range you want to work with.

Correcting Tone with Curves

In this tutorial, we're going to use the Tone Curve tool to color-correct the fence image that you saw earlier.

STEP 1: SELECT THE IMAGE
In Lightroom, select the image fence.jpg, which should be located in your Chapter 15 folder (see Figure 15.26).

As you can see from the histogram, the image has a good amount of dynamic range. However, as is obvious from both the image and the histogram, the picture lacks contrast, so we need to reset the white-and-black points.

STEP 2: SET THE BLACK POINT
The Tone Curve itself is superimposed over a histogram of your image. This makes it easier to see which parts of the curve correspond to which tones in your image. Directly beneath the Tone Curve itself are four sliders. Like the Basic sliders, each one of these targets a different part of the tonal range. If you mouse over the name of each slider, you can see exactly which part of the curve it will affect.

We need more black in the image. Mousing over the sliders reveals that the Darks control will affect most of the darker data in the image. Slide it to the left, and you'll see the curve change and the image darken (see Figure 15.27).

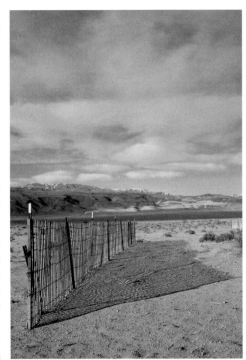

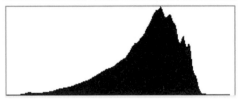

Figure 15.26

The histogram confirms what your eyes will tell you: This image lacks true black and true white—it needs more contrast.

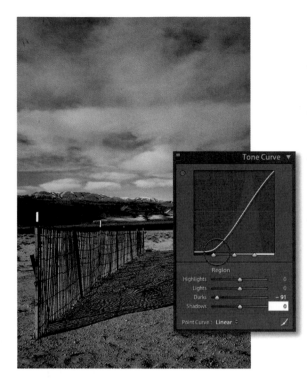

Figure 15.27

By sliding the Darks slider to the left, I push the darker tones in the image down to black.

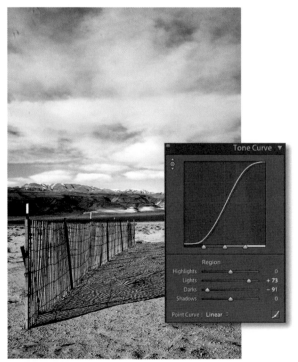

Figure 15.28

Adjusting the Lights slider lets you brighten the upper tonal range.

I moved the slider to –91. I chose this point because by dragging to here, I push lower the point on the curve that corresponds to the leftmost significant data on the histogram. The curve now shows that the leftmost data is pushed down to true black.

STEP 3: SET THE WHITE POINT

The Lights slider corresponds to the area of the histogram that has the most highlight data. Drag it to the right to around +73. This will raise the point on the curve that corresponds to the brightest significant data in the histogram (see Figure 15.28).

The image is brighter now, but something's not right. The brighter midtones are too bright, and the clouds are beginning to overexpose. The Lights slider did not adjust the right part of the tonal range. Press Command/Control-Z to Undo, and let's take a different approach.

STEP 4: DIRECTLY ADJUST THE TONE CURVE

In the upper-left corner of the Tone Curve panel is a small circle with a dot in it. Click on this circle to activate direct adjustment. Now click on the brightest part of the cloud that sits in the middle of the image and drag upward. As you drag, you should see the Tone Curve change. Based on where you clicked, Lightroom has identified the corresponding part of the curve and adjusted it for you (see Figure 15.29).

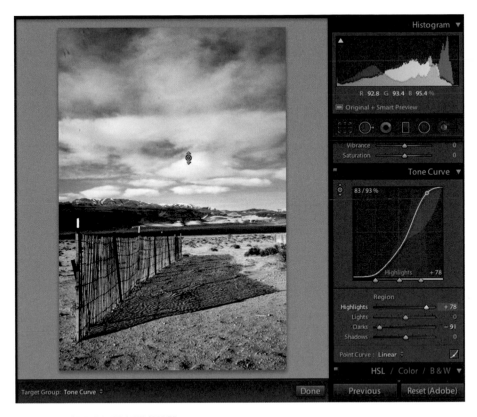

Figure 15.29

You can also adjust the Tone Curve by dragging directly in the image.

STEP 5: ADJUST THE MIDPOINT SLIDER

Finally, you can also adjust the curve by moving the sliders that sit below the Tone Curve itself. Click on the middle slider and drag it to the left to lighten the midtones in the image.

By using all of these controls, you can reshape the curve. In certain instances, you'll find that this gives you a finer level of control than the Basic sliders alone. ◣

Learning to See Black as Black

One of the most important senses you'll develop as you grow as a photographer is the ability to recognize black and white. This may not sound especially difficult, but it is important to understand that "black" is not a subjective term. While an image may have some very dark tones that you recognize as representing black, they may not really be black.

For example, consider Figure 15.30, which has shadow tones that look very dark.

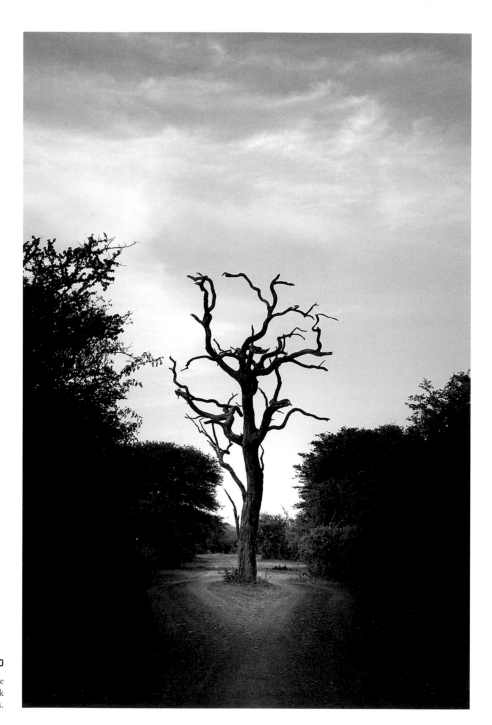

Figure 15.30

This image has a wide tonal range with bright highlights and dark shadows.

But the dark shadows aren't actually black, and this is something you need to be able to recognize. On the next page, look at Figure 15.31, which has shadows that are truly black.

In this case, it doesn't matter if you think one image looks better or not. The point is simply to recognize that there can be a subtle, but very important difference between very, very dark gray and black. In most cases, very, very dark gray will not yield as good a print as true black.

Mobile Tone Correction

When considering tonal correction on a smartphone, you'll look for the same features that you look for in a desktop—the ability to adjust separate parts of the tonal range independently, and ideally a histogram so that you can determine whether you have full contrast. However, the small screens of mobile devices add an extra wrinkle: You want an interface that's easy to use with a finger. Manipulating small sliders with your finger can be tricky.

Whether you use an iPhone or Android phone, you'll want to check out Google Snapseed. Its interface is ideally suited to touch devices, it offers the best localized editing tools of any mobile app, and it includes a wide range of features from basic tone and color adjustments to cool effects and treatments. The only downside is that it lacks a histogram, so getting accurate edits can be difficult.

For that reason, you might want an additional editing application that provides a histogram and basic Levels control. On the iPhone, consider Filterstorm. If you use Android, then you'll want to take a look at PicsPlay.

Next Steps

You will not necessarily be able to get the tone in your image adjusted completely with the tools you've just seen. There might be isolated shadows that need to be brightened or midtones that have gone a little dark. For these troubles, there are specialized tools, which you'll learn about later.

But before you address specific areas, you should ensure that the baseline tone in your image is good. Along with the Crop tool, the tools you learned in this chapter are the ones you'll use most often.

While we'll continue to work with these tools, if you're not feeling confident with them, try doing some experimentation on your own. Competency with tonal adjustments is essential to getting good results from your postproduction process, and like many tools, the ones you've learned here will get easier with practice, as you begin to develop a sense of how a particular adjustment will work.

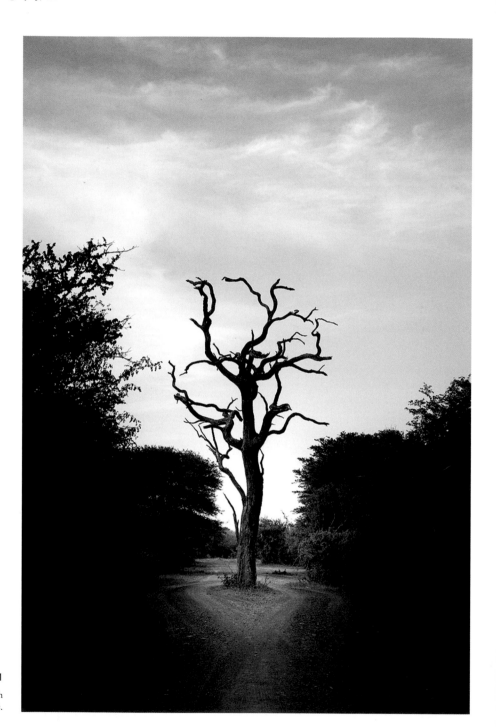

Figure 15.31

This image has true blacks, which
Figure 15.30 lacks.

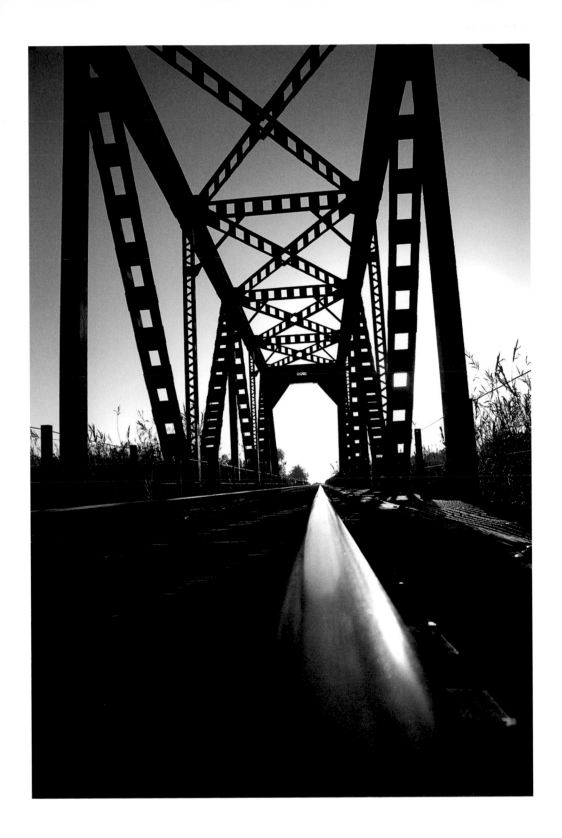

16

CORRECTING COLOR

Repairing, Improving, and Changing Color

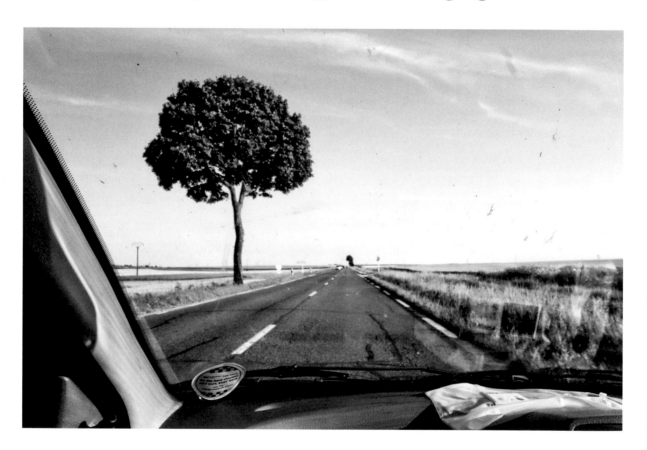

Digital cameras have a lot of advantages over film, but it can actually be a little harder to learn photography with a digital camera for one reason: They shoot in color. In the film days, you typically learned to shoot exclusively in black and white, for the simple reason that a color darkroom was very expensive. The upside to this was that working in black and white meant you only needed to concern yourself with tone and luminance. As a digital photographer, it's every bit as important to concern yourself with tone and luminance, but because we all shoot in color with our digital cameras, we have to learn luminance and color simultaneously—both how to capture them and how to use them creatively.

You might think "but color's easier, because it's how I see the world." But as we've already discussed, a photo is not a perfect recording of your experience of the world. It's a flat, small sample of the world, represented with far less color than what your eye can perceive. So color and tone have to be used very skillfully to create a resonant image, and trying to learn them both at the same time can be difficult.

Fortunately, most cameras today are very good at capturing accurate color, and most image editors have very sophisticated tools for manipulating and altering color, and this can make your color explorations much easier.

You'll perform your color correction after your tonal adjustments for the simple reason that, once you've corrected the tone in your image, you may no longer have any color problems. (Bear in mind, that on many images, you'll make initial tonal corrections, then initial color corrections, and then possibly continue to tweak both through the rest of your editing work-flow, as you refine your sense of how the image should look. If you haven't read the tonal correction lessons in the previous chapter, you need to do so before proceeding.)

You'll adjust color to make it more accurate, to make it more aesthetically pleasing, or because you want to change the color of a specific feature to make it more or less visible, or more stylized.

In this chapter, we'll look at a number of tools for editing color. As with the tonal correction tools we explored in the last chapter, most image editors will have similar features to the Photoshop tools we'll look at here. Like the tonal corrections you've learned, the color correction tools you'll see here are global tools. That is, they'll affect your entire image. Later, you'll learn how to constrain the effects of your color correction tools to specific parts of your image. But, as with tone, it's important to have the color correct in your image before you begin working on localized problems or manipulating the color in more "creative" ways.

Color Channels

So far, you've seen how Lightroom's Basic controls can be used to adjust tone and contrast. You've only worked with them on color images, but they work just as well on grayscale images. These tools, however, can also be used to adjust, correct, and change color. In previous chapters, you read about many ways in which color could go wrong when you shoot. The Basic controls allow you to fix color problems that arise from bad white balance or improper exposure.

To understand how these tools affect color, you have to understand how color is stored in an image. In Chapter 1, "Eyes, Brains, Lights, and Images," you learned that digital cameras make color by combining red, green, and blue information. These separate red, green, and blue components are referred to as *color channels*, or just *channels*, and many image editors allow you to perform corrections and adjustments on these individual channels.

Figure 16.1 shows how an image is composed of three separate channels, one each for red, green, and blue (see Figure 16.1).

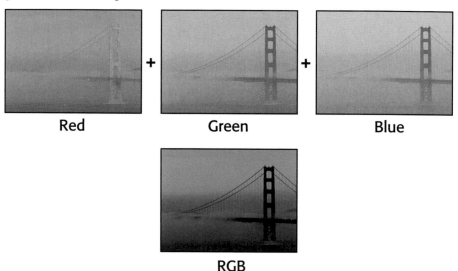

Figure 16.1

All color images are composed of three channels, one each for red, green, and blue. Together they create a full-color image.

Individual color channels are grayscale because they simply record how much of that component (red, green, or blue) is included in each pixel. A bright white pixel in a Red channel equates to full red in your final image. A black pixel indicates no red at all. The Blue and Green channels work the same way (see Figure 16.2).

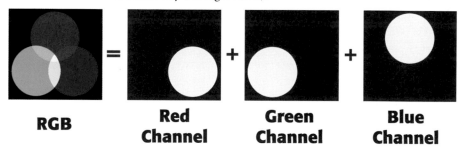

Figure 16.2

Individual channels are displayed as grayscale images. White indicates the full amount of that channel. Here, you can see the individual color channels that add up to create a finished color image.

Combine a bright red pixel in a Red channel with identical pixels in the Green and Blue channels and you'll have a white pixel in your final image, because full red, plus full green, plus full blue equals white. In other words, what you see in individual channels is a representation of the quantity of that particular component color.

For example, Figure 16.1 is a picture of the Golden Gate Bridge against a blue sky. The bridge, of course, is a deep reddish orange. If you look at the Red channel, you'll see that the bridge appears white. This is because it has a lot of red in it, and lighter pixels in the red channel mean more red in those pixels in the final image.

Now look at the Green channel. The bridge is very dark because the particular reddish-orange color of the bridge contains very little green. Same with the Blue channel. The sky in the Blue channel is pretty light, because the sky is blue and contains a lot of blue image data. So, a color channel is simply a map of each of the three color components in your image, showing how much of each color occurs at each pixel in the final image.

On average, the green channel impacts about 60 percent of what's in your image, red is about 30 percent, and blue is the rest. In other words, the blue channel very rarely has much significance to your image.

In Photoshop, it's possible to edit the color channels directly, and there are a number of editing tricks you can employ that rely on individual channel edits. For example, some cameras produce more noise in one channel than another. With Photoshop, you can try to attack the noise in an individual channel by applying noise-reducing filters or blurs—or even painting by hand—directly into that channel.

Depending on how you like to perform your edits, you may not find that you ever need to edit an individual channel directly. However, an understanding of separate channels is necessary to understand how certain color correction operations work, such as the one you'll see in the next tutorial.

White Balance

The first, and sometimes only, color correction that you should perform is white balance correction. Not every image will need it, and white balance adjustment might not get your image to precisely where you want it to be, color-wise. What white balance will do is let you get your color to be accurate. From there, if you decide that you want a different color treatment for creative purposes, you can continue with other color adjustments.

In this tutorial, we'll look at the basics of white balance adjustment on a non-raw image.

 Correcting White Balance

STEP 1: SELECT THE IMAGE
In Lightroom, select the image tumbleweed.jpg, which should be located in the Chapter 16 folder.

This image needs a contrast adjustment, but it also has a reddish color cast that should be corrected (see Figure 16.3).

STEP 2: SET THE WHITE POINT
Using the Basic controls, adjust the white point of the image. I set the Whites slider to +82 to get the brightest data pressed to the right of the histogram. To spread out the highlight contrast some, I then lowered the Highlights slider to −100 (see Figure 16.4).

STEP 3: SET THE BLACK POINT
There's still more contrast to be had, and it will come from setting the blacks properly. In this image, this is a little tricky because there's nothing in the image that should be completely black. Therefore, you don't want to push the black data too far. Because you want improved shadow detail but not necessarily strong blacks, start by dragging the Shadows slider to the left to −100. That will spread out some of the shadow detail and darken the image overall.

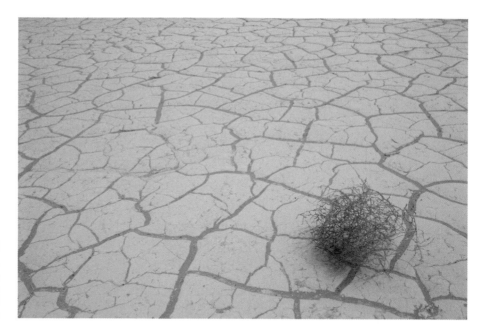

Figure 16.3

This image needs a contrast adjustment to correct contrast, but it also has a reddish cast. That sand on the ground should be white.

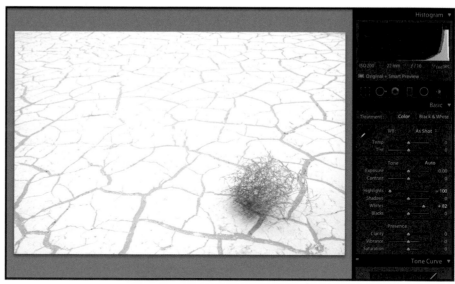

Figure 16.4

With simple Whites and Highlights adjustments, you can greatly improve the whites in the image.

From the histogram, you can see that I still don't have data down into the darkest parts of the image, and maybe that's okay. It's still worth performing a Blacks adjustment, though. This will push some data down into those dark parts and give me a more contrasted look. I set Blacks to –52 (see Figure 16.5).

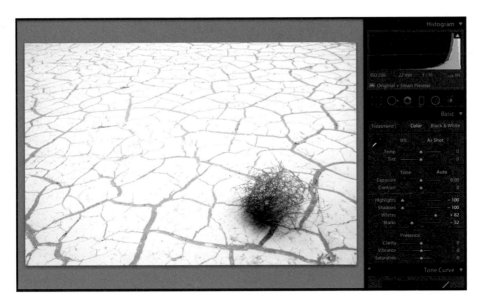

Figure 16.5

As you can see in the histogram, there's no actual black in this image. Obviously, this image doesn't have a lot of dark tones, but you still need to darken the blacks.

I judged the extent of this adjustment both by looking at the histogram and by looking at the darkest part of the image—the shadow underneath the tumbleweed. That shadow should not go to complete black, but it can withstand some darkening.

STEP 4: CORRECT THE WHITE BALANCE

At the top of the Basic toolbox are the white balance controls. You should see a slider for Temperature, a slider for Tint, and a large eyedropper. Click on the eyedropper to select it. Ideally, you want to click with this dropper on something that should be neutral gray. If you can't find anything in your image that should be gray, then something that should be white will do. Fortunately, this image has some gray in it—the "grout-like" areas beneath the areas of white sand. Click once with the dropper on one of these areas, and your color should improve dramatically (see Figure 16.6).

A few things happen when you click with the dropper. First, the dropper goes away; second, the color in your image changes. The white sand should look much whiter. Third, the Temperature and Tint sliders should change value (see Figure 16.7).

If the whites and grays in your image don't look correct, then you probably didn't click on a gray or white pixel. Undo, re-grab the dropper, and try again.

When you click with the White Balance eyedropper tool, Lightroom analyzes the color at the location you clicked and calculates a white balance adjustment that will render that tone neutral. So, while it might look like you should click on something white, the White Balance eyedropper actually works best when used on something gray. But again, if there is nothing gray in your image, white will usually work.

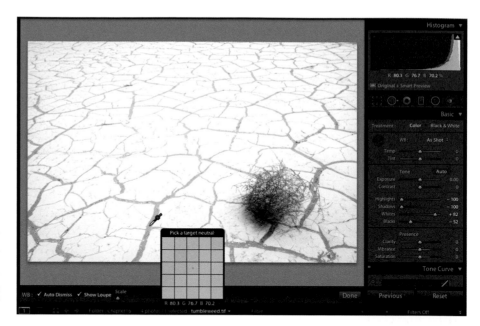

Figure 16.6

When you move the White Balance dropper over your image, Lightroom will show you a magnified view of the surrounding area, allowing you to click on the precise target pixel.

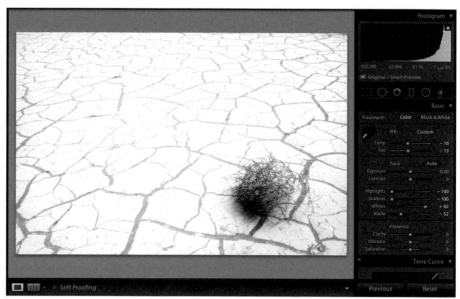

Figure 16.7

My image has lost its red cast. This is reflected in the histogram, and the exact adjustment is shown in the Temperature and Tint sliders.

STEP 5: EXPLORE THE TEMPERATURE AND TINT SLIDERS

Slide the Temperature slider back and forth and notice how the white balance changes. Moving the slider to the left makes for a cooler white balance, while sliding to the right warms the image.

Because it's impossible to build a light source out of completely pure, refined substances, most man-made light sources have a little bit of a tint to them, which can often introduce slight color casts that can't be corrected with a simple temperature adjustment. The Tint slider in Lightroom (most other converters also have a Tint slider) lets you adjust the color in your image from green to magenta, and is intended to correct any extra tint introduced by impurities in your light source.

Above the Temperature slider is a WB pop-up menu that lets you choose a white balance preset, just like you would on your camera. Presets are provided for all the usual light sources. "As Shot" selects the white balance settings that your camera stored with the image when you shot. ◀◀

If you simply follow the order of the sliders in the Basic tab, then you will adjust white balance before performing any tonal corrections, and there's nothing wrong with doing that. In this case, I wanted to adjust contrast first to get a better sense of whether the image was good enough to continue working with. Also, I wanted you to be able to see just how far off the color cast was once contrast was adjusted properly. As I increased contrast, the red cast worsened. What you'll find, though, is that white balance correction is often so easy that there's no reason not to do it right away.

Adjusting White Balance in a Raw File

In the previous tutorial, you corrected the white balance of a JPEG file. As you dragged the Temperature and Tint sliders, Lightroom altered the color of your image. It did this by very intelligently manipulating the individual color channels in the image so that red, green, and blue mixed properly to create white or gray. As you saw before, because white contains every other color, if you properly represent gray or white, then other colors should fall into place correctly. I say "should" because sometimes an improper white balance does not alter all colors equally. So, while the white balance tools in Lightroom are very powerful, be aware that bad JPEG in a non-raw file (JPEG, TIFF, Photoshop, and so on) can be a very difficult thing to correct.

Things are different when you shoot with raw. As you've learned, a raw file undergoes no processing in-camera. Instead, all of the processing required to go from raw data to a finished image happens in your raw converter. In the case of these tutorials, that converter is Lightroom, but it could just as easily be another piece of software. One of the raw conversion parameters that you get control of is White Balance. The white balance controls in Lightroom work the same whether you're working with raw or non-raw files, but as you'll see in the next tutorial, they have a lot more latitude when you work with a raw file.

 Fixing White Balance in a Raw File

STEP 1: SELECT THE IMAGE
If you didn't do the previous straightening exercise, then you should now select the image basic raw adjustments.cr2, the image of a gas pump.

STEP 2: ADJUST WHITE BALANCE
The white balance in this image is not terribly wrong, but the shady areas make for an image that is a little cool.

As before, slide the Temperature slider back and forth and notice how the white balance changes. Because this is a raw file, you should find that you get a lot more color shift as you move to the extremes of the range. You should also find that all the colors in the image shift uniformly. When adjusting white balance in a non-raw image, you might find that you don't get as dramatic a change in the shadowy tones as you do in the highlights or vice versa.

STEP 3: USE THE WHITE BALANCE DROPPER

As before, the white balance dropper will be the easiest way to set white balance. Use it now (see Figure 16.8).

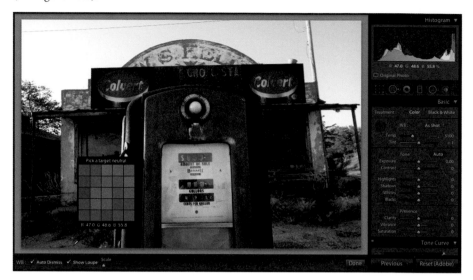

Figure 16.8

The stones on the ground are obviously supposed to be gray, so they make a perfect white balance target.

The goal of white balance adjustment is to get the color in your image correct. Even if your ultimate goal with your image is color that is somewhat stylized or altered, it's almost always best to start with correct color, and white balance is usually the key to precise color. ◤◥

More About White Balance

You've already learned how data can be lost as you brighten and darken the tones in your image, pushing them from one part of the histogram to another. As you saw, if you stretch the tones in your image too much, you begin to see tone breaks and other visible artifacts in your image. One of the great things about the white balance control in your raw converter is that it's a completely "free" edit. No tones are used up as you make white balance adjustments, because the raw converter simply changes its fundamental assumptions about what red, green, and blue are, and, as you've learned, all other colors are made from these primaries. Therefore, if possible, you should make your color adjustments using the white balance adjustment.

White balance adjustments can sometimes yield a change in contrast, so it's not a bad idea to perform your white balance adjustment first, to get a better sense of the actual tone in your image. You can then move on to your tonal adjustments.

When you first open a raw file, Lightroom (and most other converters) reads the white balance setting that the camera stored. For example, if your camera was set on Auto White Balance, and it determined that 4800° was a proper white balance, then this is where Camera Raw's Temperature slider will be set. The White Balance pop-up menu, located directly above the Temperature slider, allows you to change from the camera's specified white balance (which is listed as "As Shot" in the menu) to a preset white balance. You can also choose Auto, which tells Lightroom to perform its own auto white balance process on your image.

If you've been careful to set white balance while shooting, then As Shot might be a perfect white balance setting. If your white balance is off, then Lightroom's preset white balance options might fix your image.

Manual White Balance

As you've seen, you can use the White Balance eyedropper to set the white balance in your image. The trouble with the dropper is that there's not always something gray in your picture, and if you're shooting in low light or under mixed lighting, it can be difficult to find something that you can plainly identify as gray.

For these situations, you might want to use a White Balance card like the one discussed in Chapter 7, "Program Mode" (see Figure 7.17). In that mixed-lighting night shot, I shot a second frame that included my WhiBal White Balance card. Because I know the WhiBal card is neutral, I can click it with the White Balance dropper in my raw converter to calculate an accurate white balance (see Figure 16.9).

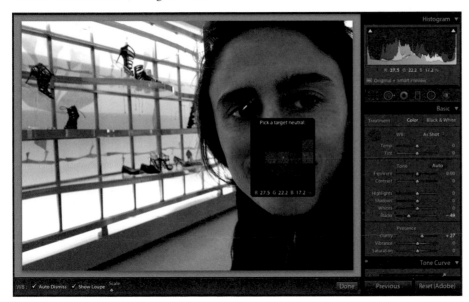

Figure 16.9

I'm using Lightroom's White Balance dropper to sample my gray card. This will give me an accurate white balance, like you saw in Figure 7.17.

After clicking on the gray card, your white balance will be set properly, and the Temperature and Tint sliders will have new values. However, so far all you've done is correct the white balance in the shot of your White Balance card—you also want to correct white balance in your original shot. You can take note of the new Temperature and Tint values and manually change them in your original image, or you can copy them into your original image, a process we'll explore later in this chapter.

Correcting White Balance When There's No Gray to Sample

There will be times when it's hard to find an obvious area in your image from which to sample white balance. For example, Figure 16.10 shows an image with a white balance that's plainly wrong.

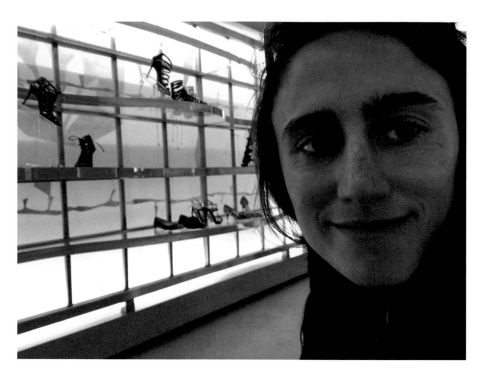

Figure 16.10

This image was shot in a store with a difficult mixed lighting situation, which threw off the auto white balance system of the camera. What's more, it's a JPEG file so I have limited white balance latitude!

There's a bright white light on the lower part of the shelving to her left, but when I click in that area, Lightroom puts up an error message that says "Cannot set the white balance. Please click on a darker neutral area." The problem is that that white area is an area of complete overexposure. Completely overexposed white in an image is actually an area of the image that is completely devoid of data. Consequently, Lightroom has no data that it can analyze to calculate white balance.

There's some shelving that looks silver, which is really just gray, and that might be a good choice. However, this image also has a pair of eyes in it, and eyes almost always have some white catchlights in them, and those lights almost always work well as white balance samples.

Ideally, I would have had a bright white catchlight, but in this case even the slightly faded highlight contains a pure enough white that I can get an accurate white balance adjustment. A single click on the location shown in Figure 16.9 yields the corrected color shown in Figure 16.11.

Note that the white of an eye or very white teeth will sometimes also work.

Finally, there will be times when you can't find something white or gray, so you will have to move the Temperature and Tint sliders by hand as you did earlier.

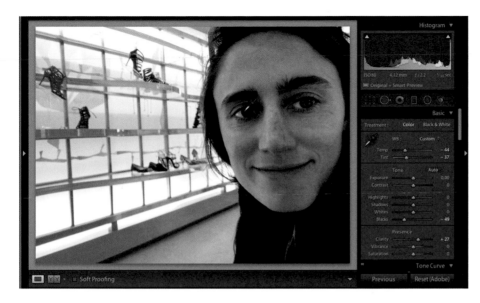

Figure 16.11

With a single click on the catchlight of the woman's eye, the white balance is set properly, and the color is corrected.

White Balance and Posterizing

Be aware that a wildly incorrect white balance can make an image appear to be posterized. Notice that in Figure 16.12, the tones on his forehead appear to be flat and posterized. They're not, actually, and if I correct the white balance, you can see that there's a full tonal range in the image (see Figure 16.12).

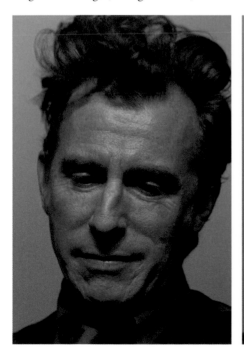 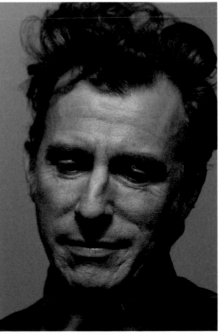

Figure 16.12

The uncorrected image on the left looks like it suffers from posterized color, but there's actually plenty of data in there, which you see as soon as I perform a white balance adjustment.

The lesson here is that if you have an image that appears to lack detail, but that also has a bad white balance, don't discard the image until you try a white balance correction. The image might turn out to be more usable than you initially thought.

When "Correct" White Balance Isn't the Best Choice

Some images look better when they're a little warmer or cooler than normal, and the ability to manipulate the overall color tone of an image is part of your creative palette. However, before taking artistic license, it's best to get the white balance as accurate as possible, and then decide from there how interpretive you want to go. This is especially true with skin tones because even subtle variations in skin tone can have a profound impact on an image. Though not always voluntary, skin tone is part of the way we express ourselves ("feeling blue," or being "red with anger" are just two examples), so you want to be careful about the emotional impact of warming or cooling people's faces.

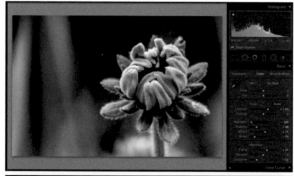

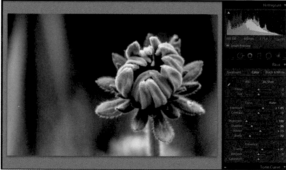

Saturation and Vibrance

The Basic controls in Lightroom have two controls for adjusting color: Saturation and Vibrance. You'll find similar tools in most other image editors. Saturation should be familiar to you already; it simply increases or decreases the richness or depth of the color in your image. Figure 16.13 shows the same image with a lessening of saturation, no saturation adjustment, and an increase in saturation.

Figure 16.13

Here you can see how a saturation adjustment affects the color in an image. These adjustments were made simply by moving the Saturation slider in the Basic controls.

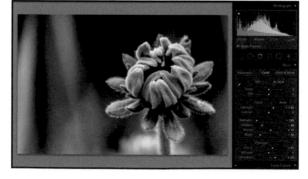

Vibrance

It's very easy to be taken in by the Saturation slider. Saturation often seems to make an image look better immediately; however, it's usually best to use Saturation sparingly. While the image might look better at first, as you look at it further, you might find posterized colors (areas where fields of color have lost all gradation and transition from one color to the next), and you might start realizing that the color looks completely unnatural. More is not always better; sometimes, it's just more.

You must be particularly careful with saturation when working on shots of people. Skin tones very rarely respond well to a saturation adjustment. In addition to appearing too red, a saturation adjustment can reveal ugly patterns and mottling.

Lightroom's Vibrance slider works much like you'd expect a saturation control to work, but it protects skin tones. In general, you'll find that when you use Vibrance, saturation increases, but skin tones don't see much of a change (see Figure 16.14).

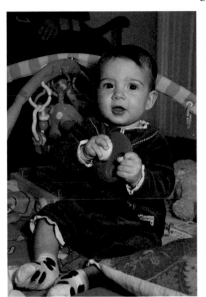 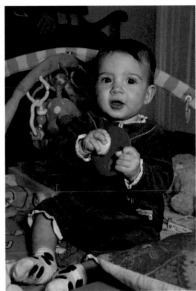 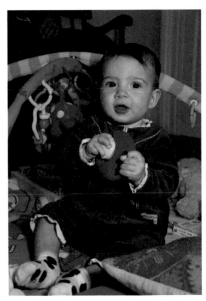

Figure 16.14 On the left is the original image. The center has seen a saturation increase, which has yielded stronger colors, but produced harsh flesh tones. The right image has had a strong Vibrance increase, which has boosted saturation while protecting the flesh tones.

Obviously, your results will vary depending on your image and the specific flesh tones you're working with.

Both of these tools provide a simple way to alter the color in your image. However, they're somewhat blunt in their application because they affect all colors equally. Sometimes, you want to alter or correct only some of the colors in your image. Fortunately, Lightroom has a simple control for doing that.

Mobile Color Correction

The same applications that you use for tone correction probably have color controls as well. In fact, the same recommendations that you saw for tonal correction in the previous chapter are also ideal for color correction. Because phone screens are even less predictable than a computer screen, making accurate color adjustments can be tricky. A histogram is imperative if you want predictable output. If you're just making images for online viewing, then you probably don't have to be too finicky about color accuracy.

Hue/Saturation

Hopefully, as you've been working with the Basic controls to alter tone you've been noticing how tonal adjustments can impact color. As you strengthen the blacks in an image, you'll often see a boost in color saturation. As you improve the whites, the colors in your image will brighten. Very often, simply by fixing the contrast, you'll fix your color, assuming your image has a correct white balance.

There are times, though, when contrast adjustment won't get your color exactly right, and other times when you might simply have other creative ideas about the color in your image. For these occasions, you'll want to turn to specialized color correction tools in your image editor. In Lightroom, these tools sit in the HSL/Color/B&W section of the right-side pane.

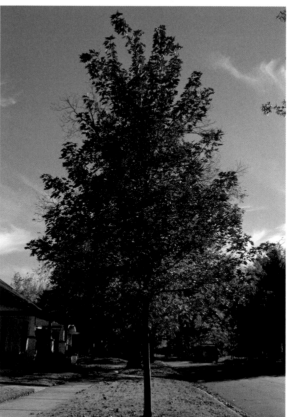

The HSL, Color, and B&W tabs give you three different sets of controls for altering color. Obviously, the B&W section is for removing color altogether. Let's begin by looking at the HSL tab.

The goal of this tutorial is to fix up the image shown in Figure 16.15. While the image looks okay as-is, it's a little bit flat. I'm going to use a saturation adjustment to give it more punch.

Figure 16.15

The red in this tree is beautiful but the composition is cluttered by all that stuff in the background. With some targeted saturation adjustments, I might be able to bring more attention to the tree.

Adjusting Saturation

STEP 1: SELECT THE IMAGE
In Lightroom, select the image `fall tree.tif` located in the Chapter 16 folder.

STEP 2: SELECT THE HSL CONTROLS
Scroll down the right-hand panel until you see HSL/Color/B&W. By default, the HSL tab should be selected; if it's not, click on it now. HSL stands for Hue, Saturation, Luminance, and when you select the HSL tab, you'll see three subtabs, one for each of these parameters (Figure 16.16).

Earlier, you learned that any color could be represented as a mix of red, green, and blue values. This is known as *RGB Color*, and it's just one color model that you can use to represent color. HSL is another color model, and as you might expect, it represents colors using separate values for hue, saturation, and luminance.

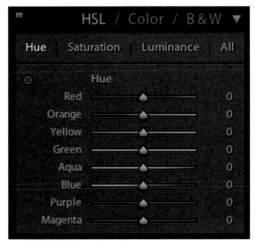

Figure 16.16

The HSL tab gives you separate controls for adjusting the hue, saturation, and luminance values of your image. As you'll see, this gives you a way to target specific colors in an image.

The standard Apple color picker, which you'll find in a number of different Macintosh applications, offers an easy way to understand HSL color. As you move your selection around the color wheel, the selected hue changes. You're essentially denoting hue by choosing an amount of rotation on the wheel that gives you the hue that you want. Moving from the center of the wheel to the edge selects a different level of saturation. Finally, moving the slider up and down changes the overall lightness of the wheel. These three values—the hue, how saturated it is, and how much luminance there is on the wheel—give you a simple set of numbers for describing a color (see Figure 16.17).

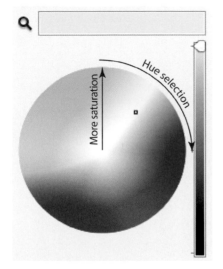

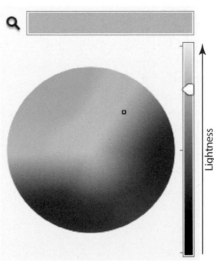

Figure 16.17

In an HSL model, a specific color is described with a hue value, a saturation value, and a luminance value.

The Lightroom HSL controls let you alter the hue, saturation, or lightness values of eight different color ranges. In each tab, a simple slider is provided for each color range that can be altered.

STEP 3: ADJUST THE SATURATION OF THE SKY

With the Saturation tab selected in the HSL controls, drag the Blue slider to the left to about –40. This will lower the saturation of the blues in the image. This tones down the sky some, letting the tree "pop" off the image a little more. I chose the Blue slider simply because the sky is blue, so I figured it would target the color I wanted (Figure 16.18).

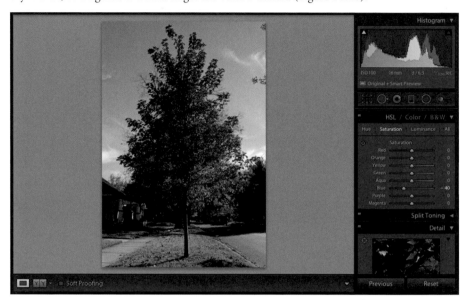

Figure 16.18

By dragging the Blue slider to the left, I pulled some saturation from the sky, making the red tree more pronounced.

Note that if there were blue anywhere else in the image it would also receive the desaturation effect. This is a "global" edit, meaning it impacts the entire image. All blue areas in the image, whether contiguous or not, will be equally altered.

This edit has helped the image a lot. Remember, as a photographer, your job is to find choices that you can make that will help the viewer understand where the subject of your image is. By pulling some color out of the sky, you've decluttered the background, making the foreground have more compositional weight. But there's more that you can do.

STEP 4: ADJUST THE SATURATION OF THE GROUND

There are yellow and green tones on the ground that you can adjust, but how do you know which slider to use? Fortunately, you can have Lightroom figure that out for you.

Click on the small circle in the HSL controls, just to the left of the word Saturation. Next, click on the grass and drag down. You should see both the Yellow and Green sliders move to the left (Figure 16.19).

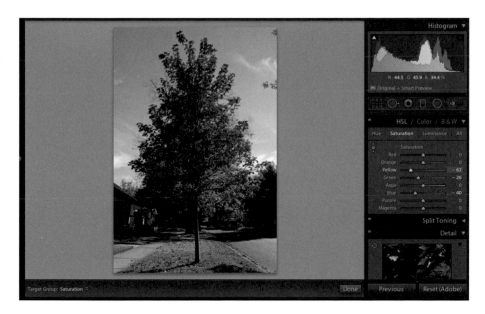

Figure 16.19

Lightroom's targeted adjustment tool lets you simply click and drag in the image to alter the saturation.

When you use this tool, Lightroom analyzes the color you click on and automatically determines which sliders to alter. This provides you with an easy way to quickly control the saturation of specific colors in your image. ▨

 ## Adjusting Hue and Lightness

STEP 1: SELECT THE IMAGE
In Lightroom, select the image scarves.cr2 located in the Chapter 16 folder. As with the picture of the tree in the previous tutorial, this image suffers from a background that's a little too strong. Switch to the Develop module, if you're not already there.

STEP 2: DESATURATE THE WALL
Using the Saturation controls in the HSL box, pull some saturation from the wall. You should end up with something like Figure 16.20.

STEP 3: EXPLORE THE HUE TAB
Click on the Hue tab in the HSL box, and you'll see a set of sliders identical to what you were working with in the Saturation tab. There's a difference, though. Click on the red tab and drag it to the right. You should see the reds in your image become more orange. Drag it to the left, and they will turn pinker.

This control does not make huge adjustments, and you may have to drag the slider a long way before you see a change. This control is intended to let you correct slight color casts in particular color ranges. I felt that the wall was a little too pink for my taste, so I dragged the reds to +59 to add some orange.

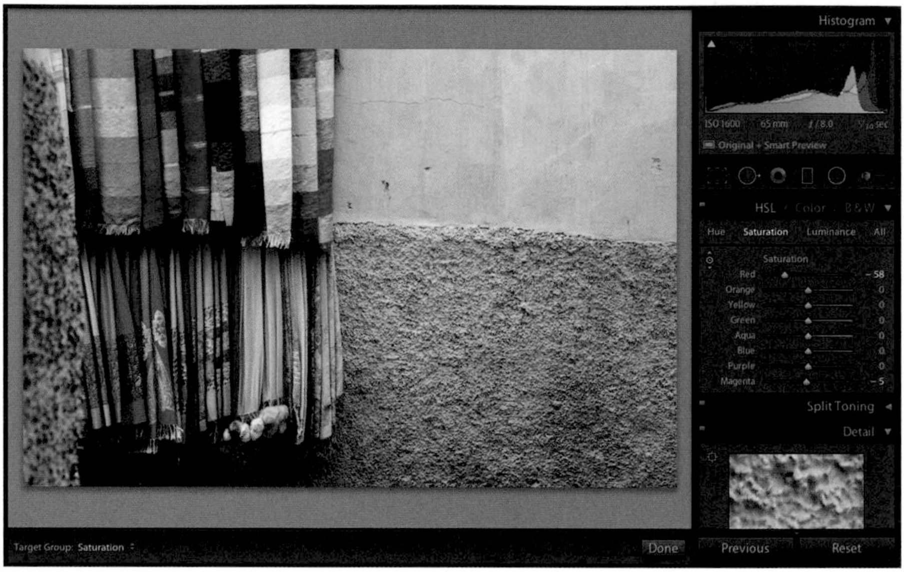

Figure 16.20

Start your correction of this image by desaturating the wall. You can do this by manually dragging the HSL sliders or by using the targeted saturation tool.

STEP 4: EXPLORE THE LUMINANCE TAB

Now click on the Luminance tab where you will see another set of sliders. These change the luminance or brightness of each color range. Drag the Red slider to the right, and you'll see many of the tones on the wall brighten. Not every tone on the wall falls into the scope of the Red slider.

Now drag the Red slider to the left to about –49. Many of the tones on the wall will darken, and this proves to be a nice way to add some extra texture to the wall (see Figure 16.21).

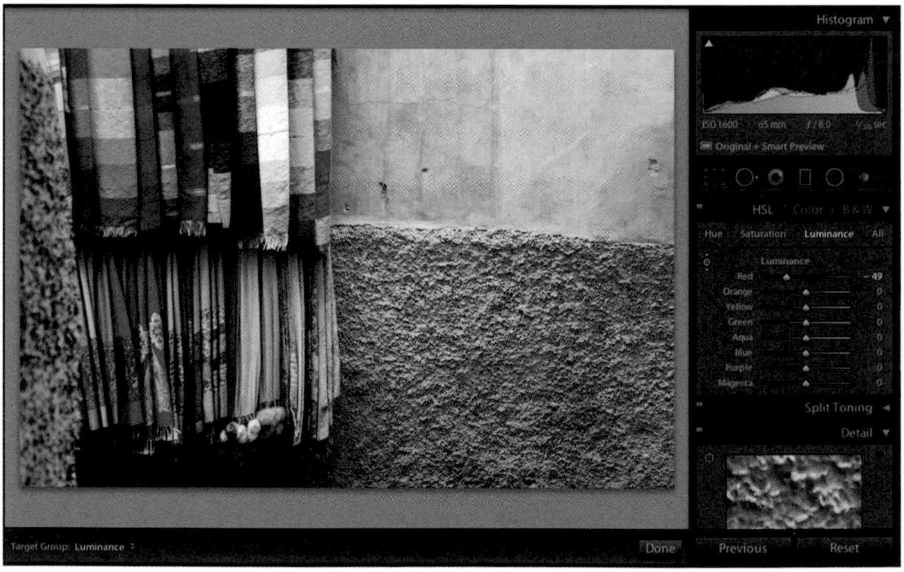

Figure 16.21

By darkening the reds in the Luminance tab, you add more contrast to the wall.

The Luminance tab makes larger edits than the Hue tab. A small adjustment will yield a pretty big effect, but as with the other controls in the HSL box, this one is meant to help you make slight corrections to colors that might be a little bit out-of-whack.

STEP 5: EXPLORE THE COLOR TAB

Click on the Color tab at the top of the HSL box. This will change you from the HSL view that you've been looking at to a different set of controls. Along the top, you'll see color swatches for each of the color ranges you've been editing. Below them are sliders for Hue, Saturation, and Luminance. These afford you all the same capabilities that you've already seen but collected into a single interface (see Figure 16.22).

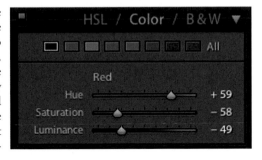

Figure 16.22

The Color tab gives you simultaneous access to the Hue, Saturation, and Luminance controls for each color range.

If you know that you need to alter the reds, and you plan on altering all three parameters, the Color tab will save you the hassle of clicking between the different HSL tabs. This is just a measure of convenience, though—you don't gain any functionality. ◄¶

Deactivating a Single Edit

Each of Lightroom's tool sections can be individually deactivated. In Figure 16.22, you can see that there's a small switch in the upper-left corner of the HSL toolbox. If you switch it off, the HSL effect will be removed from your image. However, the HSL settings will not be reset, so this gives you an easy way to preview the effects of an individual edit.

The HSL / Color controls can be real lifesavers for times when white balance doesn't give you precisely the color you want in your image. With these controls, you can tweak separate colors individually. However, these edits are global, which means that you might alter things in an image that you don't want to change. For example, when you changed the color of the wall, you probably noticed that the color on some of the hanging scarves altered also. With this tool, there's nothing you can do about that, but in the later chapters you'll learn several other methods for making selective adjustments.

Copying Your Edits from One Image to Another

Because Lightroom is a nondestructive editor—that is, because your edits are kept separate from your image data—you can copy edits that you've specified for one image to a bunch of other images. Every edit and adjustment that you make to an image can be copied and pasted onto any other image. Since images shot under the same lighting conditions often need the same edits, you might be able to quickly process an entire batch of images by editing the first image and then copying those settings to the other images in the batch.

To copy edits from one image to another in Lightroom:

◆ Switch to the Library module.

◆ Select the image that contains the edits you want to copy.

◆ Choose Photo > Develop Settings > Copy Settings.

◆ The Copy Settings dialog box will appear (see Figure 16.23). Here you can specify exactly which edits you want to copy.

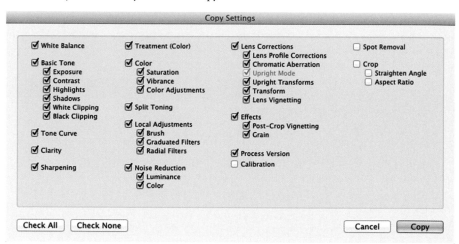

Figure 16.23

Using the Copy Settings dialog box, you can copy settings from one image and then paste them onto another.

◆ Select the image or images that you want to copy images to.

◆ Choose Photo > Develop Settings > Paste Settings. The adjustments should appear on the new image.

Note that you can also copy and paste settings using the Filmstrip panel; however, you won't be able to paste settings onto multiple images simultaneously. You can also use Command/Control-Shift-C and Command/Control-Shift-V to copy and paste settings in either the Library or Develop modules.

Exporting Lightroom Edits

When you selected the `scarves.cr2` image in the last tutorial, you might have noticed that the image already had some adjustments set in its Basic controls. If you look in the Chapter 16 folder that you downloaded, you'll see a document called `scarves.xmp`. XMP files are simple text files that store the specifics of edits made in Lightroom or Photoshop Camera Raw. Earlier, you learned that when you make an edit it's stored in the Lightroom database. You can tell Lightroom to export these edits to an XMP file by simply pressing Command/Control-S.

The resulting XMP file will have the same base name as the original image file. Every time Lightroom imports an image it looks for an associated XMP file. If it finds one, it copies the edits to its database.

XMP files are small making them an easy way to pass your edits along with your original files to someone else.

The Story So Far

At this point, you should feel very comfortable reading histograms to assess what corrections are necessary in your image. You should also know how to perform basic contrast and tone corrections using the Basic controls, the HSL tab, and possibly the Tone Curve, and you should have spent some time adjusting some of your own images.

After the last lesson, you should be comfortable with using the white balance and HSL tools to adjust the color in your image. As you've seen, though, constraining these tools to one part of an image is not possible. In the next chapter, we're going to begin to learn how to edit your images selectively.

17

SELECTIVE EDITING AND MASKS

Making Edits to Specific Parts of an Image

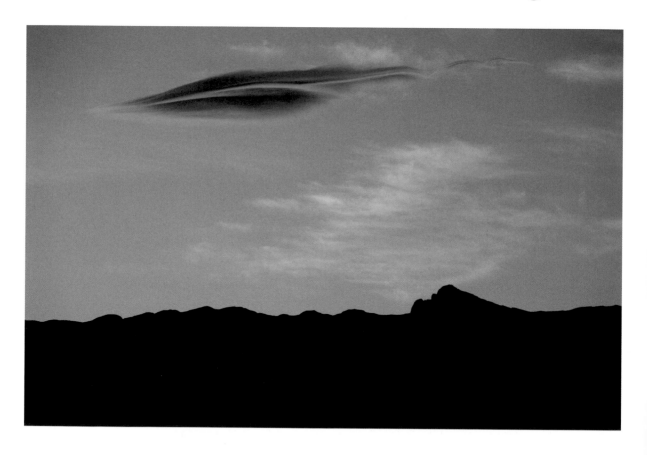

In the last few chapters, you've learned how to use some very important, very powerful adjustment tools. However, they have all been global tools, meaning the adjustments they make affect the entire image. Unfortunately, you'll often encounter tone and color problems that are isolated to one part of your image. For these instances, you'll need to employ selective editing tools. In this chapter, we're going to look at the selective tools provided in Lightroom and then take our first foray into Photoshop to explore its masking tools. While Lightroom's selective tools are good enough for most everyday selective editing chores, Photoshop's more powerful options are necessary for certain complex edits.

Selective Editing in Lightroom

The controls that you've looked at over the last two chapters provide you with the ability to edit specific tones and colors in your image, but not specific tone and colors in specific *parts* of your image. Lightroom includes two controls that allow you to do just that.

Using the Lightroom Adjustment Brush

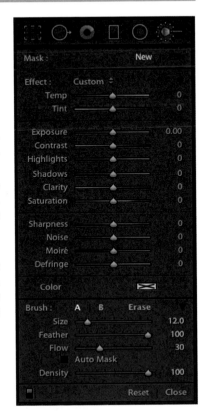

Lightroom's Adjustment Brush lets you paint many of Lightroom's adjustments onto any part of your image.

STEP 1: SELECT THE IMAGE
In Lightroom, select the heather.jpg image that should be in your Chapter 17 folder and then switch to the Develop module.

Shot at an aperture of f1.2, this image has extremely shallow depth of field. This gives it a nice dreamy quality and lends a lot of focus to the woman's eyes. However, her coloring so closely matches that of the mural on the wall behind her that she's a little lost in a field of pink and red tones. You want to desaturate the background to bring more focus to her.

STEP 2: SELECT THE ADJUSTMENT BRUSH
Click the Adjustment Brush on the toolbar, to select it. When you do, a new panel of controls will open directly beneath the Lightroom toolbar (see Figure 17.1). You use these tools to configure the effect that will be applied by the Adjustment Brush.

Figure 17.1

The Adjustment Brush controls let you dial in precisely what tone, color, and sharpness adjustments you want to brush into the image.

STEP 3: CONFIGURE THE ADJUSTMENT BRUSH

Dial the Saturation control down a bit. Without strokes in place, it's impossible to know how much adjustment is correct, but you can always refine your setting later. I chose –41. Note that the Selection Brush settings always default to the last settings that you used.

The Flow slider determines how much effect is applied to your image with each brush stroke. By default, Flow is set to 30, which is pretty light. This means you'll need a lot of strokes to see any effect. Set Flow to 80 so that the brush will be more "dense."

STEP 4: BRUSH INTO THE IMAGE

Starting at the edges, brush into the image to desaturate the background. Don't get too close to the woman's face yet. Your goal right now is to get some strokes onto the image to assess the strength of your Saturation setting. You'll probably find that it looks okay, but that the background is still a little orange.

Dial the Saturation down to –80, and the background will go a little more monochrome (see Figure 17.2).

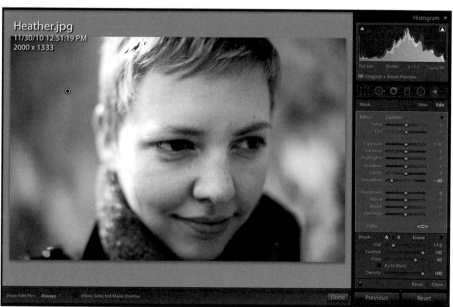

Figure 17.2

I brushed around the edges of the image to judge my Saturation adjustment and then altered it until I got the level of desaturation that I wanted.

With the Saturation dialed down, you can now more easily see the areas that you haven't hit with the brush yet. The background around her face is still too saturated.

STEP 5: ADJUST THE BRUSH SIZE AND CONTINUE

You can alter the size of the Adjustment Brush by pressing [and]. Press [a few times to make a smaller brush and then brush around the woman's face (see Figure 17.3).

The brush icon itself consists of two circles. The inner circle receives the full strength of the adjustment, while the outer circle is a feather radius. The effect is ramped off through this outer circle. You can change the size of the feather radius by adjusting the Feather slider in the Adjustment Brush controls.

Obviously, this tool is something of a "blunt instrument." It's difficult to get fine control with it. However, it is possible to get away with a lot of sloppy painting with the Selection Brush. Because the edge has a big feather on it (mine is set to 100), I can brush very close to the woman's face with a small brush and do a reasonable job of desaturating the background. Technically, I will also be applying a little desaturation to her face, but because it's such a slight amount, it's not noticeable.

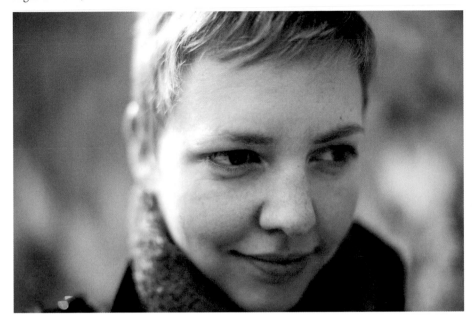

Figure 17.3

After fine-tuning with a small brush around her face, you have a nicely desaturated background. Now it's time to add a few final adjustments.

STEP 6: BRIGHTEN HER EYES

I would like to brighten her eyes and add a little more sharpness to them. To do that, I'm going to make an additional brush stroke. Click New at the top of the Adjustment Brush controls. You won't see anything happen except that the word *New* will be highlighted. The controls will remain at their previous settings.

STEP 7: CONFIGURE AND USE THE BRUSH

Set Saturation to 0, Exposure to 1, and Clarity to 40. Again, I'm just guessing at these initial adjustments. Next, set the brush size to something appropriate for her eyes and begin painting.

As soon as you paint, a black circle will appear somewhere in the image. You might have noticed this with your previous edit. This circle represents the new brush stroke you're making. The other black circle should have turned gray. Black indicates which stroke is selected. If you want to go back and edit the other brush stroke, you simply click on its circle to select it and then make your changes, either by rebrushing or altering its parameters. You can also delete a brush stroke altogether by clicking on its circle and then pressing the Delete key.

If you make a mistake in your brushing, click on the word Erase near the bottom of the Adjustment Brush controls. This changes the brush from a brush to an eraser, allowing you to refine your painting.

For my final image, I added two additional strokes. On her eyebrows, I painted in some Clarity to make them sharper. Clarity increases contrast, though, and her eyebrows ended up a little too dark, so I increased the Shadows slider on that stroke.

Finally, I added a stroke that lightened shadows and painted into her eyelashes and the darker parts of her eyeballs. The finished image can be seen in Figure 17.4. ◤◢

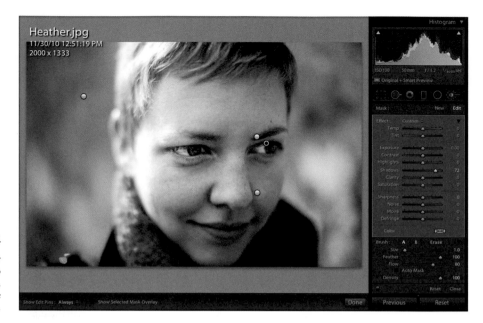

Figure 17.4

My final image contains four brush strokes that serve to desaturate the background, brighten her eyes, and improve the detail on her eyebrows.

Using the Graduated Filter

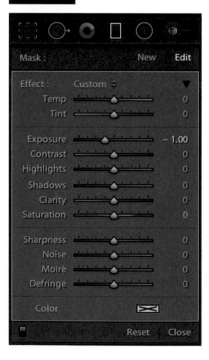

Figure 17.5

The Graduated Filter controls are similar to the Adjustment Brush controls that you already used.

While the Adjustment Brush gives you a lot of selective editing power, it can be difficult to control. There will be times when you need to make an adjustment that ramps off from one part of your image to another. For those times, you'll use the Graduated Filter tool.

STEP 1: SELECT THE IMAGE

In Lightroom, select the `Lake Tahoe.CR2` image in the Chapter 14 folder. While this image looks okay, it would be nice if the sky had a little more contrast in it.

STEP 2: CONFIGURE THE GRADUATED FILTER TOOL

Select the Graduated Filter tool from the Lightroom toolbar and dial the Exposure slider down to –1. As with the Adjustment Brush, you don't really know if this is the correct setting, but you can always refine it later (see Figure 17.5).

STEP 3: APPLY THE GRADUATED FILTER

Click in the sky and drag down to define the graduated filter effect. I released the mouse just below the horizon. You'll see three lines as you drag. Everything in the image above the first line will get the full strength of the edit. Everything below the bottom line will get no effect at all. The middle line represents the midpoint of the adjustment. Note that you can drag at any angle that you want. Figure 17.6 shows you where I placed the filter.

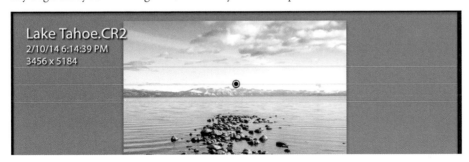

Figure 17.6

Everything above the top line (where I originally clicked) gets the full adjustment. Everything below the bottom line (where I released the mouse button) gets no adjustment. The middle line shows the halfway point.

STEP 4: ADJUST THE EDIT

The Exposure adjustment has added some saturation, so drag the Saturation slider down to around –23 (see Figure 17.7). You don't want the sky to look artificially saturated. It should have about the same level of saturation as the water. Use the \ key to see a before/after view of your effect.

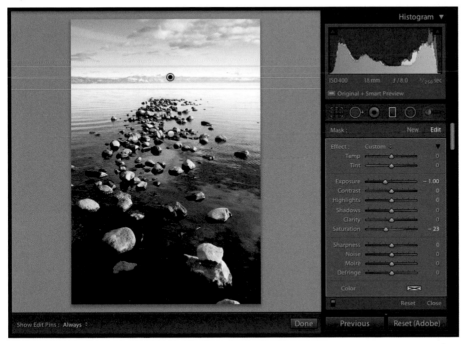

Figure 17.7

My final gradient adds a subtle contrast boost to the sky. Thanks to the Graduated Filter tool, the adjustment is smoothly ramped off to the foreground.

As with the Adjustment Brush tool, you can create multiple graduated filters in an image. However, you can't erase any part of the effect, as you can with the Adjustment Brush. This means that if there's something poking up above the horizon, your graduated filter will affect it as well.

Lightroom's selective editing tools are very good for many selective adjustment chores. However, they're no substitute for the full power of Photoshop's selective editing features, so it's important to be competent with both sets of tools. ◀

Masking in Photoshop

Photoshop has a large suite of tools for making selective adjustments in an image, and you'll turn to these when Lightroom's Adjustment Brush and Graduated Filter tool aren't up to the task. With Photoshop's tools, you can create complex selective edits that can handle such tricky situations as wispy hair and soft edges.

The key to selective editing in Photoshop is the mask. A mask is really nothing more than the digital equivalent of a stencil. With it, you can constrain an edit to a particular spot in your image, just the way a stencil constrains paint to one place on a canvas.

Masking can be an essential color-correction tool, allowing you to create adjustments and corrections that would otherwise be impossible. For example, if you want to color-correct only the foreground of an image, you might build a mask over the background elements (see Figure 17.8).

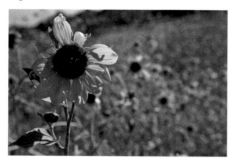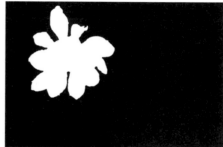
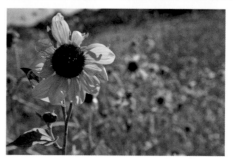

Figure 17.8

To adjust the saturation of only the flower without altering the sky, I created a mask that protects the sky during the Hue/Saturation adjustment that alters the flower.

Masks are also necessary when you want to superimpose a new element into an image or replace a background image (see Figure 17.9). A digital mask sits between two different elements in an image and controls which parts of each image are visible. Masks are like stencils in the real world, but with the advantage of allowing for varying degrees of transparency.

Like many editing tasks, knowing how and when to use a mask is a skill. And learning the basics of your masking tools is pretty easy once you understand a few simple concepts. Before you get started, you need to configure Lightroom to run smoothly with Photoshop.

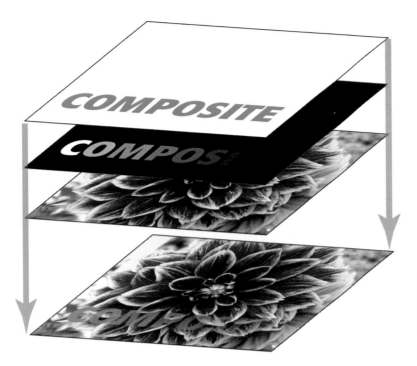

Figure 17.9

Here, the top layer is being composited with the bottom layer, with a mask knocking out the background of the top layer so that only the blue text gets combined with the flower.

Launching an Image from Lightroom to Photoshop

While Lightroom provides an incredible amount of image editing power, there are still things that it can't do that Photoshop can, such as the masking chores that we're going to look at next.

Fortunately, Lightroom and Photoshop are very good at passing images back and forth. By default, Lightroom should be configured to allow you to automatically move an image into Photoshop, assuming you have Photoshop installed.

To edit an image in Photoshop:

◆ Select the image you want to edit.

◆ Choose Photo > Edit In > Edit in Adobe Photoshop, or simply press Cmd/Ctrl-E.

If the file you selected is a raw file, Lightroom will process the file with your edits and create a new TIFF file, which it will stack with the original raw file, and then open in Photoshop.

If the file you selected is not a raw file, Lightroom will present the dialog box shown in Figure 17.10.

If you choose Edit Original, then the original image will be opened in Photoshop. The image will not contain any of the edits that you made in Lightroom.

If you choose Edit a Copy, then a copy of the original image will be opened in Photoshop, and like the previous option, the copy will not contain any Lightroom edits.

Edit a Copy with Lightroom Adjustments will create a new copy, in TIFF format, that includes all of the edits you've made in Lightroom. That copy will then be sent to Photoshop.

In each case, the copy will be stacked with the original image.

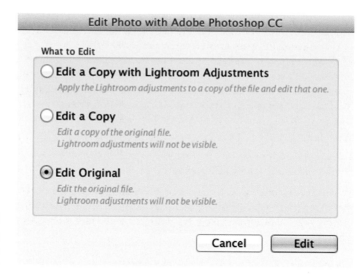

Once in Photoshop, you can work as normal, making any edits that you want. When you close the document and save it, Lightroom's previews will automatically be updated, so there's no need to reimport the adjusted image back into Lightroom.

If you go to the Photo > Edit in menu and don't see Photoshop as an option, but you have it installed, then you'll need to configure Lightroom's Preferences, as shown in Figure 17.11.

Note that you can also configure a second external editor, making it possible to launch images from Lightroom into two alternate editors.

External Editor Options

In the External Editor section of Lightroom's Preferences dialog box, you can configure some additional parameters regarding external editing. You can see these in Figure 17.11.

By default, Lightroom uses a TIFF format when it creates copies to send to Photoshop. You can change this to Photoshop format, but there's really no advantage to one format over another. TIFF files can be read by more image editors, so if you want to ensure that other people can work with your edited files, stick with TIFFs.

Bit Depth allows you to select either 8 or 16 bits per pixel. If you want to have as much editing latitude as possible—that is, to be able to make many adjustments before you see tone breaks and posterization—leave this set to 16 bits. Know, though, that the resulting files that Lightroom creates will be larger than if you had chosen 8 bits.

Earlier, you learned about color spaces. Lightroom allows you to select from three color spaces. sRGB is the smallest, while ProPhoto RGB is the largest. While you might think it's best to simply choose the largest color space possible, there are times when a larger color space can cause problems. If your image doesn't have a tremendous amount of color information in it, trying to stretch that data to fit into a larger color space can result in tone breaks and posterization. Lightroom defaults to using the ProPhoto color space, and you'll likely never have to change this. If you ever see unsightly posterization in an image, then you might consider changing Preferences to AdobeRGB before you launch the image into Photoshop.

Resolution defaults to 240, which is a good choice for many inkjet printers. If you regularly print to a printer that has a different optimum resolution, then you might want to change this. However, you can easily change this later in Photoshop.

Finally, Compression lets you specify whether you want your TIFF files compressed or not. Default is Zip, which makes for smaller files, possibly at the expense of slower save times. Realistically, on any computer that is powerful enough to run Lightroom, the loss of performance will be unnoticeable.

Selections and Masks

The terms *selections* and *masks* are actually synonymous. Photoshop has a lot of tools for creating selections, but you can also refer to a selection as a mask.

For example, in Figure 17.12, I've used the Lasso selection tool to select the horse. I did this simply by outlining the horse with the Lasso tool. On-screen, the selection is shown as a moving dotted line—usually referred to as "marching ants." If you look closely, you can see them around the edge of the horse.

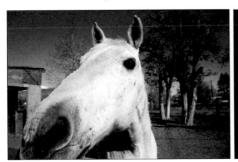 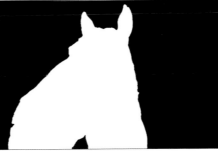

Figure 17.12

I used the Lasso tool to define a selection around this horse. Photoshop thinks of that selection as a mask. Outside the selection, things are completely masked (black), while inside they are completely unmasked (white).

Internally, Photoshop is thinking of this selection as a mask, which you can see in the right part of Figure 17.12. The black areas of the mask are completely blocked off, while the white areas are completely open. Again, it works just like a stencil with the white part representing the area that has been cut out. If I were to spray paint through such a stencil, the paint would only make it through the white areas. Similarly, in Photoshop, any operation that I make will only apply to the areas of the image that correspond to the white areas.

Photoshop has a lot of tools for making selections, and to be honest, most of them are not useful to photographers. For most everyday masking chores, I won't touch the Magic Wand, the Lasso, or the Marquee tools simply because Photoshop has gained masking tools in recent years that are far more powerful.

Basic Masking with the Quick Selection Tool

You can use selections to constrain edits and adjustments to a specific part of an image. Take a look at Figure 17.13. While the subject of this image is plainly the dog, the background details are competing for your attention. There are several things you could do to make the background less distracting. You could darken it, desaturate it, or lower its contrast. But any of these operations would require that you first create a mask to constrain your edits.

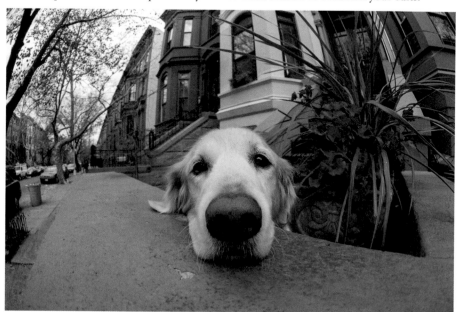

Figure 17.13

You want to make the background less distracting in this image, which you're going to do by creating a mask to protect the dog from your adjustments.

Creating a Simple Mask

The plan is pretty simple: you'll select the dog and then *inverse* the selection so that it is the *background* that ends up selected. Then you'll apply an adjustment to downplay the background.

STEP 1: SELECT THE IMAGE IN LIGHTROOM
In Lightroom, select the image dog.jpg from the Chapter 17 folder of the tutorial files and switch to the Develop module.

STEP 2: SEND THE IMAGE TO PHOTOSHOP
Press Command/Control-E to open the dog image in Photoshop. The Edit Photo with the Photoshop dialog box will appear. By default, the Edit Original option will be selected. You want to preserve your original, in case you mess things up in Photoshop, so choose Edit a Copy with Lightroom Adjustments. You haven't made any adjustments yet, but you choose this option because Lightroom will make the new copy in TIFF format. If you choose Edit a Copy, Lightroom will simply create a JPEG file, and you'd rather not work in JPEG format, because every time you save you'll run the risk of increased compression artifacts.

Click the Edit button, and you'll see Lightroom make a copy of the image; then Photoshop will launch, and the image will load.

STEP 3: CHOOSE THE QUICK SELECT TOOL
Choose the Quick Selection tool from the main tool palette (see Figure 17.14).

STEP 4: SELECT THE DOG
With the Quick Selection tool, you can paint over something in your image that you want to select. The tool employs Magic Wand–like algorithms to analyze the area you're painting and then makes a selection.

Quick Selection is a brush tool, and like all Photoshop brush tools, you can change its size using the [and] keys. Set the brush to a size slightly smaller than the dog's nose and paint over the dog's head. As you do, Photoshop should select the dog (see Figure 17.15).

Quick Selection works by analyzing the color in the areas you brush. It assumes a sudden color change is an edge, so it defines that as the edge of the selection. You might find, as in Figure 17.15, that Quick Selection sometimes selects too much. Because the color of the dog's fur is close to the color of the bricks, it selected part of the staircase behind the dog.

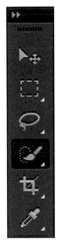

Figure 17.14

The Quick Select tool is often the easiest way to make a complex selection.

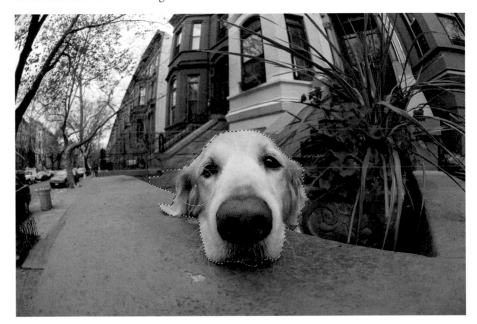

Figure 17.15

After simply brushing over the dog with the Quick Select tool, you have a good selection. It's got one flaw, which you can correct with the same tool.

STEP 5: ADJUST THE SELECTION
In the center of the Quick Selection brush, you should see a +. This indicates that, as you brush, you'll be adding to the selection. If you hold down the Option key (Alt on Windows), then the + will change to a –, indicating that the areas you brush will be removed from the selection.

If you need to remove something from the selection, hold down the Option/Alt key and brush over the selected area that you want to remove (see Figure 17.16). You might need to make the brush smaller.

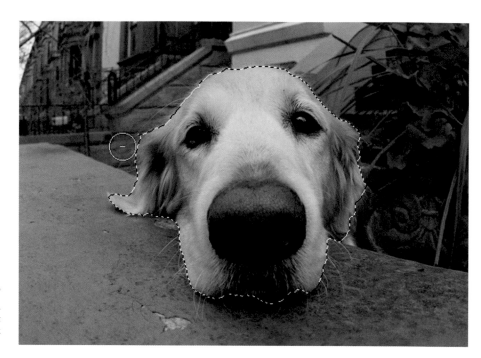

Figure 17.16

You can remove areas from a
selection by holding Option/Alt
while painting with the Quick
Select tool.

STEP 6: TEST THE SELECTION

If you want to double-check that the selection has worked, grab the Eraser tool and brush across the image. You should see the erased stroke confined to the inside of the selection (see Figure 17.17).

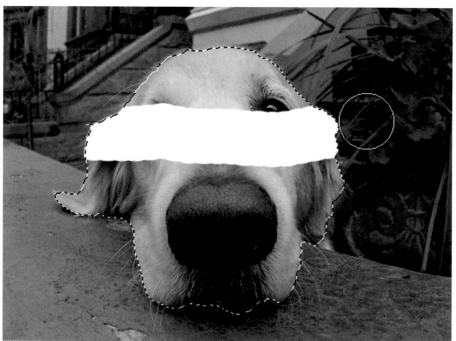

Figure 17.17

A quick test with the Eraser
shows that, in fact, the dog is
selected, while the background is
completely masked.

Note that the selection isn't perfect. There are bits of fur that aren't selected, and the boundary of the selection has a hard edge. We'll address that next.

Choose Edit > Undo to undo the erased stroke.

STEP 7: FEATHER THE EDGE OF THE SELECTION

You can soften the edge of the selection by applying a feather to it. Choose Select > Modify > Feather and enter a value of 3 into the Feather dialog box. This will add a 3-pixel-wide blur to the edge of the selection. With this blurred edge, any edits you make will have a smoother, more natural transition from the selected to unselected area.

The width of the feather is determined by how much of a transition you want from selected to unselected, and how big your image is. An image with larger pixel dimensions might need a larger feather. With experience, you'll get a better sense of how wide a feather you need on a particular selection.

STEP 8: INVERT THE SELECTION

You've got a good selection now. Unfortunately, it's the dog that's selected, and what you want to do is alter the background. Fortunately, it's easy to invert the selection.

Choose Select > Inverse.

You should still see the selection around the dog's head, but you should also see a selection around the entire border of the document. If you were to swipe with the eraser tool now, you'd see something like Figure 17.18.

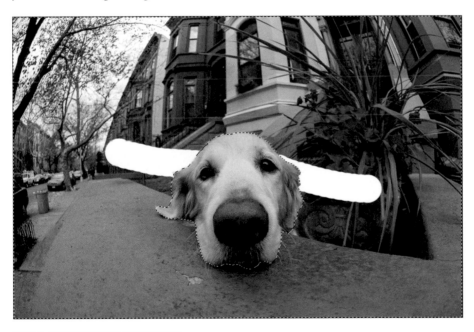

Figure 17.18

After inverting the selection, the background is now selected, and the dog is masked.

STEP 9: DESATURATE THE BACKGROUND

Now you're finally ready to make an edit. Choose Image > Adjustments > Hue/Saturation to bring up the Hue/Saturation dialog box. Drag the Saturation slider to the left to desaturate the selected area a little bit. I liked it at about –40. The goal is to make the background less distracting, but without making an edit that's too obvious.

STEP 10: HIDE THE SELECTION EDGES

With the "marching ants" tromping around, it can be hard to see whether the desaturated background looks like a conspicuous edit or not. Fortunately, Photoshop provides a way to hide the selection boundary without discarding the selection.

Choose View > Extras to hide the selection boundary.

You can also press Cmd/Ctrl-H. On a Mac, the first time you press Cmd-H, Photoshop will ask if you want to hide Photoshop or just the Extras. Choose Extras.

Note that you were able to hide the edges, even though the Hue/Saturation dialog was still visible.

STEP 11: REFINE THE SATURATION

With the selection edges hidden, you can now refine your adjustment; remember, your selection is still in place. I backed the Saturation adjustment down to –50 (see Figure 17.19). While the desaturation helps, there's one more edit you should make. Click OK to accept the Saturation change.

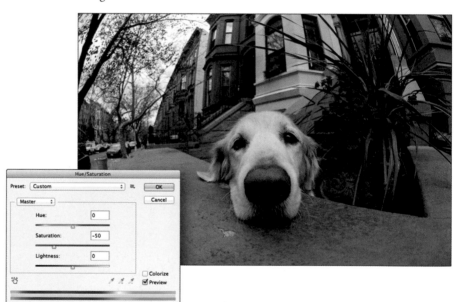

Figure 17.19

A little desaturation helps bring more attention to the dog.

STEP 12: DARKEN THE BACKGROUND

Remember—even though you can't see it, there is still a selection in place. Press Cmd/Ctrl-H to toggle the view of the selection boundary. If it's not there, then you must have accidentally deselected it somehow, and you will need to remake the selection.

If they're not hidden, hide the selection edges.

Now press Cmd/Ctrl-L to bring up the Levels dialog box. You're going to use it to add a slight darkening to the background.

Drag the midpoint to the right to darken the background. I found .75 to be about right (see Figure 17.20).

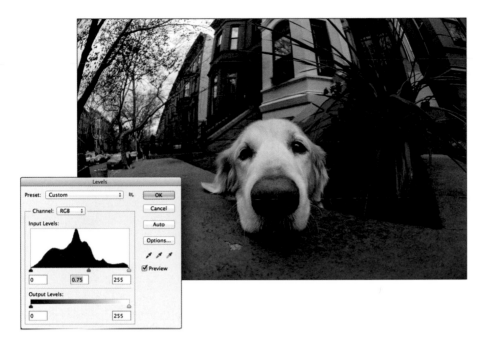

Figure 17.20

With a Levels adjustment, you can darken the background.

Again, the goal is to bring more attention to the dog, but not make a conspicuous edit. With a little bit of darkening in the background, the dog draws more focus. This is the power of selective editing and adjustment.

If you want, you can experiment with some other adjustments. For example, you might want to try increasing the saturation on the dog. You can easily do this by inverting the current selection and then applying a Hue/Saturation adjustment.

At any time, you can get rid of the current selection by choosing Select > Deselect or pressing Cmd/Ctrl-D to deselect.

STEP 13: SAVE THE IMAGE

Choose File > Save or press Cmd/Ctrl-S to save the image; then close the document. Switch back to Lightroom, and you should see the finished, edited image sitting in a stack next to your original. If you look at the file names of the images (which you can see by selecting an image and then looking at the toolbar just above the filmstrip pane), you'll see that the new image is called dog-Edit.tif.

If you had chosen Open a Copy back in Step 2, then you would have dog-Edit.jpg instead of a TIFF file. Close the stack, and you'll see only your edited version. ◄¶

Working with Virtual Copies

By now, you should be getting used to the advantages of Lightroom's nondestructive approach to editing. You've seen how it gives you the freedom to alter edits at any time and to copy edits from one image to another. But nondestructive editing offers you another great advantage: the ability to easily create multiple versions of an image without consuming lots of disk space.

As you've seen, in Lightroom (or any other nondestructive editor) edits are simply kept in a list. When Lightroom needs to display, export, or print your image, it simply looks up those edits and applies them to the original image data. But there's no reason you can't have more than one list of edits! Lightroom calls these *virtual copies*. (Yes, it's kind of a clunky name, but Apple was already using the word *versions* in Aperture, to provide the same functionality.)

In this next tutorial, you're going to create a new version of an image in preparation for a more advanced masking tutorial.

Making a Virtual Copy

STEP 1: SELECT THE IMAGE
In Lightroom, select the image Heather.jpg. Earlier, you edited this image, and in the next tutorial, you're going to edit it again in Photoshop. However, for that tutorial, you need to start with a clean version. You could simply send a copy to Photoshop, but that copy would be a JPEG file. You want the option to send a TIFF file without Lightroom edits, so you're going to create a new virtual copy.

STEP 2: CREATE A VIRTUAL COPY
Choose Photo > Create Virtual Copy. You can do this in either the Library or Develop modules. Alternately, you can press Cmd/Ctrl-'. Lightroom will immediately place a copy of the image next to the original, and will stack the two together. You can tell the Virtual Copy from the original because it has a folded up corner (see Figure 17.21).

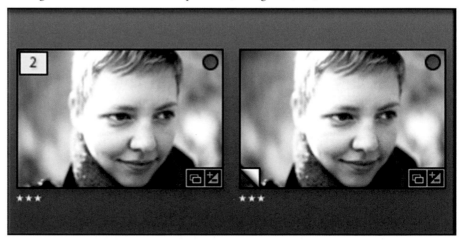

Figure 17.21

The folded up corner on the second image indicates that this is a virtual copy.

The file name for this image should read Heather.jpg/Copy 1. No new image file has been created. Instead, Lightroom has simply opened a new edit list in its internal database.

STEP 3: PREPARE THE VIRTUAL COPY
The virtual copy is truly a complete copy of the image you clicked on. All of the edits that you made in Lightroom are still there. For our purposes, you want a "clean" copy of the image, so you need to strip out all of the edits of your virtual copy.

In the Develop module, with the image selected, choose Settings > Reset All Settings, or press Cmd/Ctrl-Shift-R. You should see your image return to its original state. ◤

Virtual Copies are great for times when you want to experiment. If you've got several ideas for how you might edit an image, or if you want to play with different crops, or consider a black-and-white version, you can simply make Virtual Copies. They're quick to build, don't take up any significant disk space, and offer all the functionality of a normal image file.

Deleting Images

To delete an image—either a normal image or a Virtual Copy—simply select the image and press the Delete key. Lightroom will ask if you want to remove the images from the catalog or delete them from the disk. You can also delete images by pressing X to mark them as rejects and then later press Cmd/Ctrl-Delete to delete all rejected images.

Masking Complex Edges

While Photoshop's Feather command lets you soften the edge of a selection, the fact is a lot of things in the world don't have clearly defined edges. In fact, some edges can be extremely complex, such as hair or fluffy fur. How do you select each strand of hair?

 ## Using Refine Edge and Smart Radius

In this tutorial, you're going to use Photoshop to perform the same selective edit that you made earlier in Lightroom. This will give you the chance to feel the difference in the two programs' tools.

STEP 1: SELECT THE IMAGE AND SEND IT TO PHOTOSHOP
In Lightroom, select the virtual copy of the Heather.jpg image. If you don't have a Virtual Copy, then you need to go back and complete the last tutorial. In Lightroom's Develop module, press Cmd/Ctrl-E, and in the resulting dialog box, choose Edit a Copy With Lightroom Adjustments. In the last tutorial, you stripped all of the adjustments from this image, but you want to work in TIFF format rather than the original JPEG format of the image. This option will give you a TIFF.

STEP 2: CREATE A MASK
Using the Quick Selection tool, create a mask for the woman (see Figure 17.22). Remember, if you accidentally select part of the background, hold down the Option/Alt key and paint with the Quick Selection tool on those background areas. Holding down Option/Alt while painting with Quick Selection removes the painted area from the selection.

Changing brush size is also a good way to improve the effectiveness of the Quick Selection tool. Because the edge of her face and scarf are so blurred, you're not going to create a selection that wraps around her tightly.

STEP 3: INVERT AND HIDE YOUR SELECTION
Remember, when you painted with the Quick Selection tool, you selected the woman. But you want to operate on the background, not on her. Choose Select > Inverse to reverse the selection. You will now see that the selection traces around the edge of the background.

As you did in the last tutorial, press Cmd/Ctrl-H to hide the selection, to provide a clearer view of your edits.

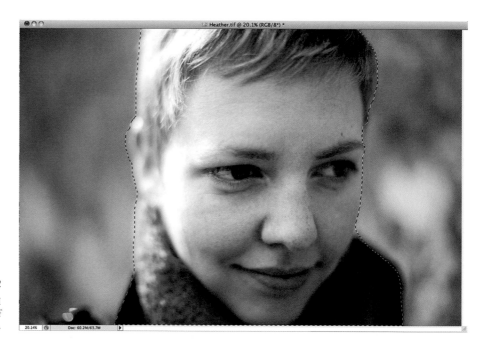

Figure 17.22

With the Quick Select tool, I created this very rough mask of the woman.

STEP 4: TRY TO DESATURATE

Choose Image > Adjustments > Hue/Saturation to bring up the now-familiar Hue/Saturation dialog box. Drag the Saturation slider all the way to the left (Figure 17.23).

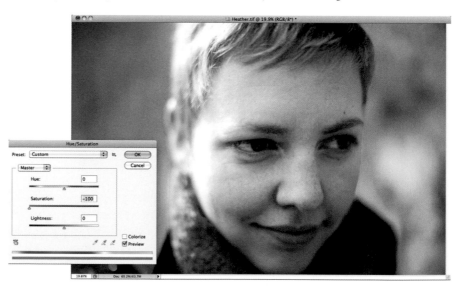

Figure 17.23

After desaturating the selected background, you get this image that doesn't look quite natural.

She's definitely standing off the background more, which is what we wanted, but the hard edge around her face—the sudden shift from color to black and white—doesn't look real. We've plainly discolored the background, and the effect is distracting.

Click Cancel in the Hue Saturation dialog box to cancel the desaturation option. You should see your full-color image again. Although you can't tell, your selection is still active.

STEP 5: INVERSE THE SELECTION AGAIN

This step isn't going to be intuitive, but trust me on this one, you want to inverse the selection again by choosing Select > Inverse. You're about to open the Refine Edge dialog box, and your Refine Edge action will be much easier if she's selected, rather than the background.

STEP 6: REFINE EDGE

Choose Select > Refine Edge to call up the Refine Edge dialog box.

By default, Refine Edge will show your selection on a completely white background. If you'd rather see it on a different type of background, you can choose a different one from the View pop-up menu at the top of the Refine Edge dialog box. White works well for this chore.

Now you can see why you needed to inverse your selection first. You need to be able to see where the edges of the woman are.

STEP 7: SMART RADIUS

Check the Smart Radius checkbox and then click on the Brush tool next to Smart Radius. Set the Radius slider to about 2 pixels.

With this brush, you're going to brush along the edges of the selection—that is, the edges of the woman. Your painting is going to give the Refine Edge function a hint as to where the edge is. It will analyze that area and calculate a new edge for the mask.

You can change the size of the Smart Radius brush with the [and] keys, just as you can with any other brush in Photoshop. I chose a diameter roughly the size of about half of one of her eyeballs. The goal is to have a brush that's as wide as the entire blurry edge that we want to refine.

Paint a stroke down her left side. When you let go of the mouse, you should see a very soft edge, as shown in Figure 17.24.

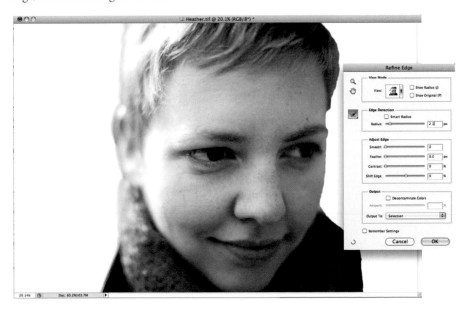

Figure 17.24

After painting with the Smart Radius brush down the left side of the selection, I have a smooth, well-masked edge.

STEP 8: PAINTING HER OTHER SIDE

Now paint her other side. In general, it's best if you can do it all in one stroke.

STEP 9: REFINE

When you painted the right side, there's a good chance that some weird stuff happened around her eye (see Figure 17.25).

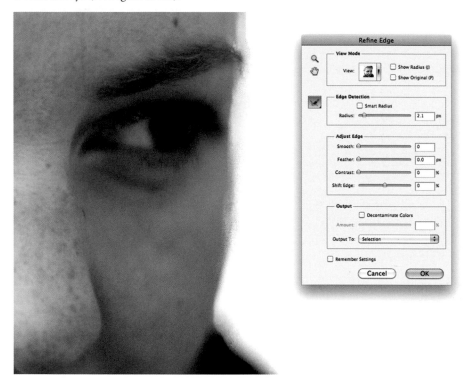

Figure 17.25

Refine Edge selected too much of her face here.

Refine Edge very likely selected too much of her face.

Click and hold on the Refine Edge brush, and a pop-up menu will appear, revealing the Erase Refinements brush. Select this brush, change to a small brush, and paint over the parts of her face that you'd like to restore. You should see them reappear.

STEP 10: ACCEPT THE SELECTION AND DESATURATE

After you've got the edges refined, press OK to make the selection. Choose Select > Inverse to inverse the selection so that the background is selected.

Invoke the Hue/Saturation dialog box and desaturate. After seeing the completely desaturated results, I decided not to desaturate entirely so that a little bit of color remains in the background. Your results should look something like Figure 17.26.

Note how the transition zones around her face look very realistic. She doesn't look "cut out" from the background, but blends with the background realistically. Refine Edge did an excellent job of masking around her hair and of creating a smooth transition along the soft edges of her face. ◥◣

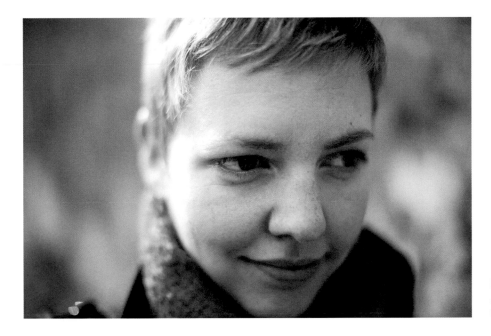

Figure 17.26
Our finished image with the background desaturated.

Masking Hair with Refine Edge

Hair is one of the most difficult masking challenges that you'll face. Consider Figure 17.27. If you wanted to create a mask around the woman, you'd have a very difficult time selecting each strand of hair.

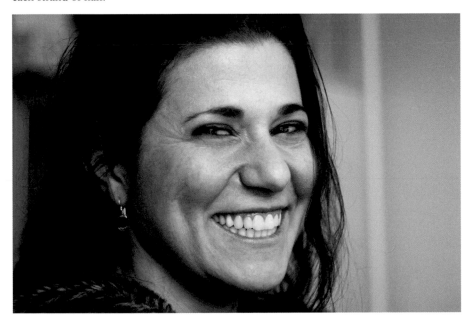

Figure 17.27

Masking successfully around all this hair is no easy task. Fortunately, Photoshop's Refine Edge feature can handle the problem.

In Photoshop CS5 and later, the Refine Edge dialog box includes all the tools you need to handle a complex masking task like this. To learn how to do this, watch the `Masking Hair.mov` tutorial, located in the Chapter 17 section of the companion website. 🖦

Saving Masks

Once you've used the various tools at your disposal to create a selection, you can save that selection as a mask for later use. In Photoshop, selections can be saved by clicking Select > Save Selection. At any time, you can use the Select > Load Selection command to restore your selection.

Earlier, you saw how separate Red, Green, and Blue channels were used to create a full-color image. You also saw that you could access those individual channels using the Channels palette. Selections, or masks, are stored in a similar fashion. When you save a selection, your image editor creates a new channel in your document—called an *alpha channel*—and stores an image of your selection (see Figure 17.28).

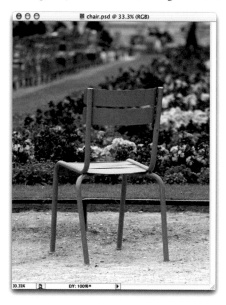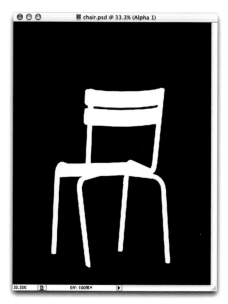

Figure 17.28

When you save a selection, Photoshop stores a grayscale, 8-bit alpha channel. Black areas of the image are masked, but white areas are not. If you load this alpha channel as a selection, the white area will be selected, just as if you had traced it with a Lasso or any other selection tool.

As you can see, any selection can be represented by a grayscale image—areas within the selection are stored as white pixels; areas outside are stored as black. (Another way of thinking of it is "black conceals, white reveals.") In Photoshop, you can create as many different selections as you want and store each in its own alpha channel. From the Channels palette, which you can open by clicking Window > Show Channels, you can access each mask by simply clicking its name (see Figure 17.29).

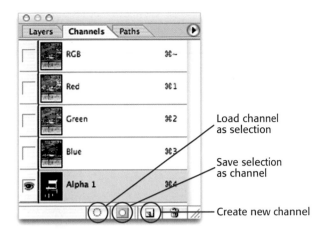

Load channel as selection

Save selection as channel

Create new channel

Figure 17.29

You can see and access the alpha channel from the Photoshop Channels palette.

A Mask by Any Other Name

"Mask," "channel," and "selection" are all synonymous, and I'll be using them interchangeably throughout the rest of this book. A selection simply creates a mask, just as any other masking tool does. All masks are saved in your document as alpha channels—8-bit channels in your image where black represents fully masked, white represents unmasked, and gray is partially masked.

Some Layer Basics

If you haven't worked with layers in Photoshop, don't worry, because they're very simple. Following are some of the basics of using the Layers control in Photoshop and Photoshop Elements. (Note that Layers weren't added to Photoshop until version 3. If you're using an earlier version, it's time to upgrade!)

Creating, Deleting, and Moving Layers

Layer management is very simple in Photoshop or Photoshop Elements—you simply use the Layers palette. On the bottom of the palette are all the controls you need to create and delete layers (see Figure 17.30). Right now, you only need to worry about the Create layer and Delete layer buttons located on the right side of the palette.

When you create a new layer, it will appear as part of the layer stack in the palette. Because new layers are empty, your image won't look any different. All edits—whether painting, filters, or image adjustments—happen in the currently selected layer, and you can select a layer by clicking it in the Layers palette. Note that you can turn off the visibility of a layer by simply clicking its eye icon.

Layers that are higher in the Layers palette obscure any lower layers, and you can rearrange layers by dragging them up or down the stacking order. Note that you cannot change the order of the lowest layer—the Background—unless you double-click it to turn it into a normal, floating layer.

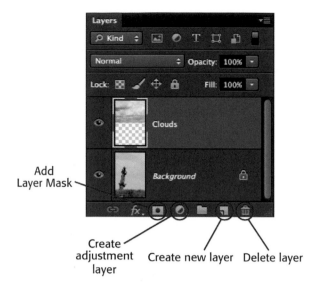

Add
Layer Mask

Create
adjustment
layer   Create new layer   Delete layer

Figure 17.30

The Photoshop Layers palette
includes simple button controls
for creating and deleting layers.

New layers are completely transparent, whereas the Background layer is completely opaque.
In the Layers palette, transparent areas of a layer appear in the layer thumbnail as a checker-
board pattern. (Obviously, as you paint into a layer, Photoshop changes the opacity of that
part of the layer so your paint is visible.)

Using a Layer Mask

In this tutorial, you're going to use a Layer Mask to apply a Shadow/Highlight adjustment
to one part of an image. You could do this same edit by making a selection and then calling
up Shadow/Highlight, but as you'll see, using a Layer Mask gets us some extra capabilities.

STEP 1: OPEN THE IMAGE
In Photoshop, open the image `boat.jpg`, located in the Chapter 17 section of the companion
website (see Figure 17.31).

While this image is generally well exposed, it would be nice to brighten up some of the shadows beneath the boat. However, I don't want to lighten the dark tones on the men near the
boat or lighten the blacks throughout the image. You've seen how the Shadows/Highlights
adjustment can be used to lighten shadows in an image.

STEP 2: APPLY SHADOWS/HIGHLIGHTS
Choose Image > Adjustments > Shadows/Highlights to bring up the Shadows/Highlights
dialog box. Set the Shadows amount to around 16. I chose this number by playing with the
slider until I got the image looking the way that I wanted (see Figure 17.32).

While the shadows under the boat definitely have more detail in them now, too many other
things in the image have been brightened also. The men are brighter, and the rocks in the
sunlight are brighter. In general, I've lost the nice contrast ratio I had before.

Click Cancel to cancel the Shadows/Highlights adjustment and restore the image to normal.

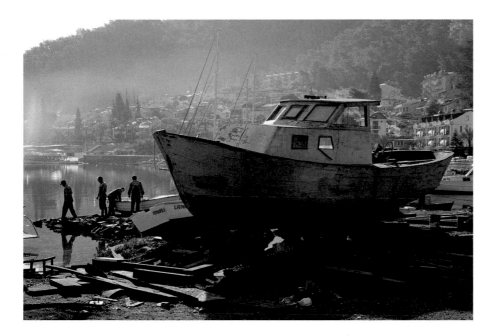

Figure 17.31

You're going to use a Layer Mask to make a localized tonal adjustment to this image.

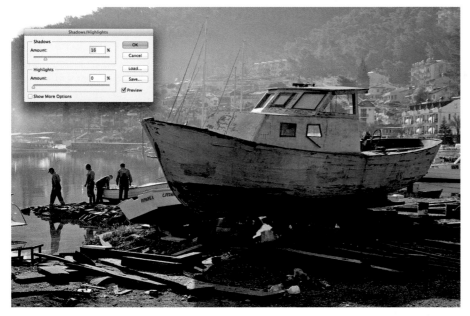

Figure 17.32

While Shadows/Highlights does make the shadows lighter, it also brightens up too many other things in the image.

What you want is to apply Shadows/Highlights to only the area under the boat. To do that, you're going to create a second copy of your original image. This second copy will get the Shadows/Highlights adjustment, and you'll use a special type of mask to composite the two images.

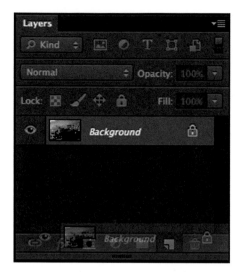

Figure 17.33

You can easily duplicate a layer by dragging it to the Create Layer button at the bottom of the Layers palette.

STEP 3: DUPLICATE THE LAYER

If the Layers palette is not visible, choose Window > Layers. In the Layers palette, you can see that your document has one layer, a layer called "Background," which contains your original image.

Duplicate the background layer by clicking on it in the Layers palette, and dragging it to the Create a New Layer button at the bottom of the palette (see Figure 17.33).

You now have two identical layers, one sitting above the other. The top layer should be highlighted, to indicate that any edits will be applied to that layer.

STEP 4: ADJUST THE TOP LAYER

Choose Image > Adjustment > Shadows/Highlights again, and again, set the Shadows level to 16; then click OK. Your entire image will be brightened.

STEP 5: ADD A LAYER MASK

Choose Layer > Layer Mask > Hide All. You will immediately see the effects of the Shadows/Highlight adjustment disappear. If you look in the Layers palette, you will see why.

On the upper layer, in addition to the image thumbnail, there is now a thumbnail showing a small black rectangle. This is a Layer Mask. Like any other mask, any part that is black indicates an area that is masked. Right now, the entire mask is filled with black. The Layer Mask controls which parts of the associated layer are visible. Since the layer is completely filled with black, the entire layer is invisible. This is why you no longer see the effects of Shadows/Highlights—it had been applied to this layer, and this layer is now invisible.

STEP 6: PAINT INTO THE MASK

Choose the Paint Brush tool and set the foreground color to white. Select a fairly large brush and begin painting into the area underneath the boat. As you paint, you should see it lighten up. But pay attention as well to what's happening to the Layer Mask (see Figure 17.34).

As you paint, you'll see white appear in the Layer Mask thumbnail in the Layers palette. So you can easily see the "hole" that you're punching in that mask. You should see the corresponding parts of your image brighten, as the adjusted layer becomes visible.

STEP 7: PAINT WITH BLACK

Now switch to black paint and paint over areas that you had previously painted. As you paint, you'll be closing up the mask and hiding the upper, brighter image. By switching between black and white paint, you can easily refine your mask and experiment with brightening and darkening different parts of the image. This flexibility is what makes this technique much better than simply making a selection and then applying the effect through the selection.

STEP 8: PAINT WITH GRAY

It's often difficult to know what the right level of adjustment is before your mask is in place. Now that you've masked off the image, it looks to me like the original Shadows/Highlight adjustment was a little too aggressive—the shadow areas are being brightened too much.

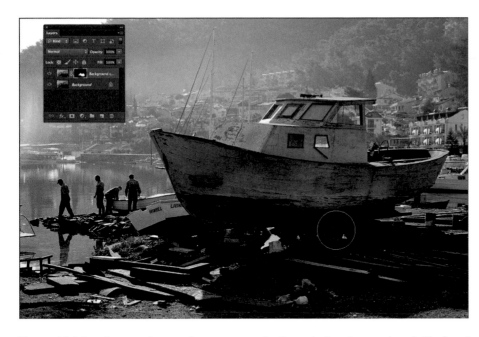

Figure 17.34

By painting white into the Layer Mask, you reveal the layer that you had adjusted with Shadows/Highlights.

You could delete the upper layer and start over—reduplicate the base layer and apply Shadows/Highlights again. In fact, this is another advantage of this technique. But there's an easier way.

Find the Swatches palette. If it's not visible, choose Window > Swatches.

Click in the Swatches palette on a middle gray tone. By default, the last swatch of the top row is 50 percent gray. Note that you can hover the mouse over a swatch to see its value.

Now paint over an area of the mask that you had previously painted white. You should see that area get darker, but not go as dark as the original (see Figure 17.35).

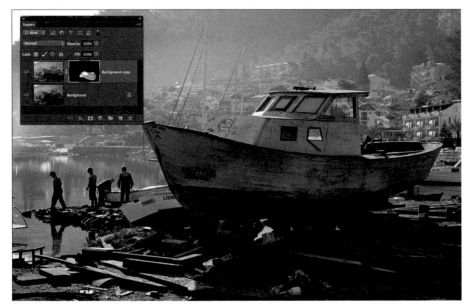

Figure 17.35

By painting into the mask with gray, you can lighten the area, but not up to the full lightness of your original adjustment.

What's happening is you're creating a semi-opaque mask. You're seeing half the value of the pixels in the upper image. This is giving you a little bit of brightness, without the full level that you originally dialed in.

This is the biggest advantage of layer masks. By painting with different shades of gray, you can paint varying amounts of one layer into another. ◥◣

Layer Masking Tip

You can select either the Layer or the Layer Mask to paint into. If you select the Layer (by clicking on the image thumbnail in the layer), then you'll actually be painting onto your image. Therefore, before you start masking, it's imperative that you ensure that the Layer Mask that you want is selected. You can tell when it's selected because it will be highlighted with white corners.

Create the Right Type of Layer Mask

When you choose to create a Layer Mask, you have the choice to "Reveal All" or "Hide All." These options simply specify if the resulting Layer Mask will be filled with black or white. You could have chosen Reveal All for your previous example, but then you would have had to paint everything *but* the area you wanted to lighten. If you want to paint *in* an effect, choose Hide All. If you want to paint *out* an effect, choose Reveal All.

Simplifying Photoshop's Interface

As mentioned earlier, one of the things that makes Photoshop so complicated is that it contains features tailored to far more than simple photography. Fortunately, in the CS and CC versions of Photoshop, you can streamline Photoshop's interface through the use of Workspaces, which allow you to highlight features tailored to a particular task.

From the Window > Workspace menu, you can select workspaces by task, or you can define your own workspace. For example, if you select the Color and Tonal Correction workspace, any menu items related to color and tonal correction will be highlighted, making it easier for you to ignore features you don't need.

Workspaces can also be used to control palette location and to hide menu items. So, for example, you could completely deactivate menu items you don't need. Consult Photoshop's Help file for more info.

Simpler Masking Using Viveza

While Photoshop provides excellent masking tools, there are also third-party plug-in mask options available for both Photoshop and Lightroom. Masking plug-ins are often tailored to specific tasks—extracting foregrounds from images shot in front of a blue or green screen, for example, or creating masks around complex subjects such as hair and transparent objects. Some programs create masks that get stored in your image as alpha channels.

The Viveza plug-in for Photoshop and Lightroom provides an exceptional tool that makes any type of masking easier than in any other image editing program (except for Nikon's Capture NX, which has these controls built-in). In Viveza, when you want to edit a particular area in your image, you click with the Color Control Point tool on the area you want to edit. Viveza analyzes the color you clicked on automatically, and then calculates and builds a mask. You can then use Viveza's tools to alter color and tone. If that sounds too good to believe, believe it! The masking tools in Viveza (and Capture NX) really work, and really are that easy to use (see Figure 17.36). Viveza is part of the Nik Collection, which is sold by Google.

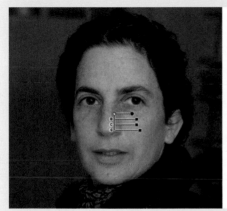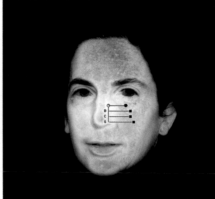

Figure 17.36 In Viveza, I created the mask shown on the right with a single click of the Control Point tool. Viveza automatically analyzes the image to create this complex mask.

Novice image editors will find masking simple to pick up in Viveza, while more experienced users will find they can create complex masks far more quickly than in any other program.

Mobile Localized Editing

Earlier, I recommended Google Snapseed for tone and color corrections. If you've been using the app, then you've hopefully already discovered its fantastic localized correction tools. Borrowing the same Control Point technology that's found in the Viveza Photoshop plug-in, Snapseed can *automatically* build very accurate, complex masks with just a simple tap or two. If you haven't explored Snapseed's Selective Adjust tools, it's worth spending some time learning about this great feature.

18

PHOTOSHOP ADJUSTMENT LAYERS

Advanced Tools for Adjustments and Corrections

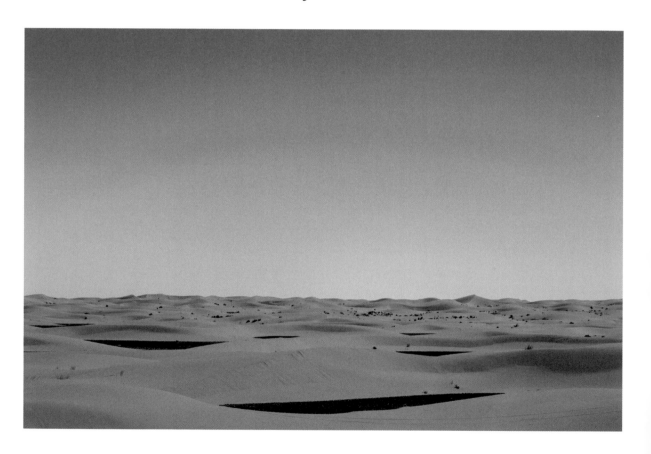

I n the last chapter, you saw how to add a mask to a layer to control which parts of a layer were visible. In Photoshop, you can also create a special type of layer called an *Adjustment Layer*, which lets you apply a nondestructive edit that can be masked in the same way that you masked a regular layer. Just like the Adjustment Brush in Lightroom, Adjustment Layers let you apply edits very selectively. However, because of Photoshop's superior masking tools, Adjustment Layers give you more control than you can get with Lightroom's Adjustment Brush. While Lightroom's tools are great for a lot of edits, I regularly find myself applying edits using Adjustment Layers.

While the edits that we've looked at so far have been destructive, Photoshop includes a powerful, flexible suite of nondestructive editing tools. Before we get to Adjustment Layers, we need to take a quick look at Photoshop's Levels control.

Levels

A Levels control provides a different interface for making the same type of edits that you made using Lightroom's Basic controls. With Levels, you can alter the value of the blackest and whitest points in your image and make the midtones brighter or darker. Most importantly, you can adjust any of your tonal ranges without affecting the others.

The Photoshop Levels control is built around a histogram of your image (Figure 18.1). The left slider shows the position of black in the histogram—that is, it points at the location on the graph that represents 100 percent black. The right slider shows the position of white, while the middle slider shows the gamma, the midpoint of the tonal range. The text fields below the histogram are simply numeric readouts of the positions of the three input sliders—0 represents black, white is represented by 255, and shades of gray are somewhere in between.

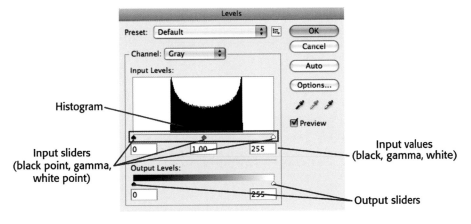

Figure 18.1

The Photoshop Levels dialog box offers a number of features. Right now, you'll be using only the histogram, input sliders, and Input Levels fields.

Adjustment Layers

Adjustment Layers let you apply certain image-correction functions as layers. For example, when you add a Levels Adjustment Layer to your document, you have access to a normal set of Levels controls (Levels is a form of exposure adjustment). But instead of applying the Levels adjustment to the image—and altering the pixels in your document—Photoshop stores the adjustment in a separate layer that appears in your Layers palette (see Figure 18.2).

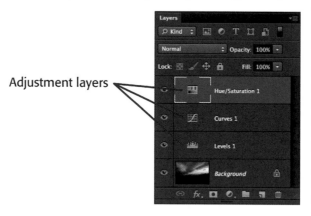

Adjustment layers

Think of an Adjustment Layer as a can of magic spray paint that you can spray onto your image. Perhaps it's a paint that increases contrast, or alters color, or converts your image to black and white. Unlike real paint, though, this is a kind of paint that you can peel off later if you don't like it.

An Adjustment Layer affects all the layers beneath it. (You can constrain the effects of an Adjustment Layer by grouping it with underlying layers; see Photoshop online Help for details.) The real strength of Adjustment Layers, though, is that you can go back at any time and change the Adjustment Layer's settings.

Figure 18.2

The top layers in this image are Adjustment Layers. They apply, respectively, Hue/Saturation, Levels, and Curves adjustments to the underlying layer. Their settings can be altered or changed at any time.

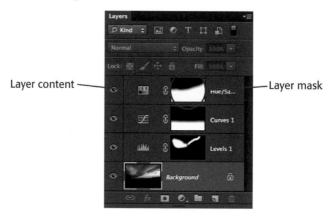

Layer content

Layer mask

One of the other great advantages of Adjustment Layers is that they have a masking capability built in. In the last chapter, you saw how Layer Masks could be used to control the visibility of an image layer. Adjustments Layers have a Layer Mask built in, which allows you to create complex localized effects very easily (see Figure 18.3).

Figure 18.3

Each of these Adjustment Layers has a Layer Mask, which constrains the effects of each Adjustment.

To continue my analogy of an Adjustment Layer being a can of paint that you spray onto your image, a Layer Mask would be a stencil that sits between that paint and your underlying print.

The easiest way to learn how Adjustment Layers and Layer Masks work is with a quick tutorial. Note that this tutorial requires either Photoshop 7 or later, or Photoshop Elements 2 or later.

Adjustment Layers

STEP 1: OPEN THE IMAGE
Download the image Snow Tree.jpg from the Chapter 18 section of the companion website. Open it in Photoshop.

STEP 2: ASSESS THE IMAGE
Choose Window > Histogram to view Photoshop's Histogram palette (see Figure 18.4).

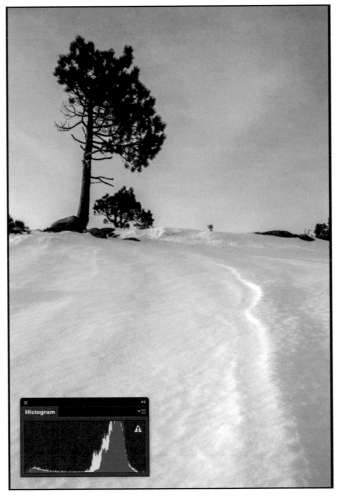

Figure 18.4

The histogram shows that this image doesn't suffer from any over- or underexposure problems, but that doesn't mean it still doesn't need some exposure adjustment.

As you can see, the news is good: there's no overexposure—something that would have been very easy to do in a bright situation like this. However, you don't perform corrections simply to correct problems. With some exposure adjustment, you can improve the contrast and texture in this image.

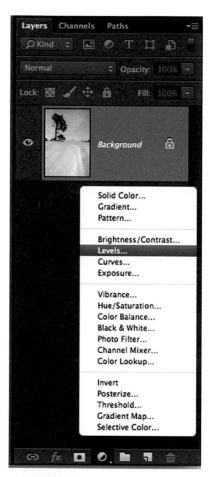

STEP 3: CREATE AN ADJUSTMENT LAYER

Make sure that the Layers palette is visible. If it isn't, choose Window > Layers. Add a new Levels Adjustment Layer by opening the Adjustment Layer pop-up menu at the bottom of the Layers palette (see Figure 18.5). You might need to open the Layers palette if it's not visible.

A Levels Adjustment Layer will be added to the Layers palette, and the Properties palette will appear. (If it doesn't appear, choose Window > Properties.) If you're using CS4 or CS5, then you'll see the Adjustments palette above the Layers palette fill with controls. Anytime you click the Levels Adjustment Layer to select it, its controls will appear in the Properties palette in CS6 or CC, or the Adjustments palette in CS4 or CS5 (see Figure 18.6).

Figure 18.5

The Layers palette includes a pop-up menu with commands for adding and managing Adjustment Layers.

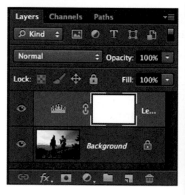

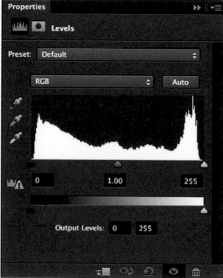

Figure 18.6

When you select an Adjustment Layer in the Layers palette, its controls appear in the Properties palette.

Another Way to Make an Adjustment Layer

The Adjustments palette (which is only available in CS4 and later) provides another way to create Adjustment Layers. Click Window > Adjustments if the Adjustments palette is not visible. When no Adjustment Layers are selected in the Layers palette, the Adjustments palette provides icons for each type of Adjustment Layer. Just click an icon to add that type of Adjustment Layer above the currently selected layer. If you hover your mouse over each icon, you'll see a Tool Tip that will tell you what type of Adjustment Layer each icon represents.

Previous Versions of Photoshop

If you're using a version of Photoshop prior to CS4 (but one that still includes Adjustment Layers), then your Adjustment Layers will work a little differently. You won't have an Adjustment palette. Instead, when you create an Adjustment Layer, the standard dialog box for that type of adjustment will appear (the Layers dialog box for a Layers Adjustment Layer, the Curves dialog box for a Curves Adjustment Layer, and so on). You can configure the controls as needed; then press OK to dismiss the box. Any time you want to alter the parameters of the Adjustment Layer, you'll double-click that layer in the Adjustment Layer palette to invoke its dialog box.

STEP 4: CONFIGURE THE BLACK POINT

By default, the Levels Adjustment Layer isn't doing anything, because its controls are set to neutral positions. Your next step, therefore, is to configure the Adjustment Layer to perform the brightening you want.

Though not overexposed, the snow is a little washed out. If it had a stronger black point, you would see more texture on it. Drag the black point to the right and watch what happens to the snow. The shadow tones and lower middle tones get darker while the whites stay white. Set the black point to around 85.

The tree is most likely represented on the histogram by that small blob of data on the left side. You've now clipped all that data to black so now the tree is too dark. Don't worry about that now because you'll fix it later (see Figure 18.7).

Double-click the name of the layer, "Levels 1," to make it editable and change the name to "Snow darken." Keeping your layers named can make things easier as you add more and more layers to your document.

Each Adjustment Layer displays an icon that tells what type of adjustment it performs. Next to this icon is another icon that represents the Adjustment Layer's mask (see Figure 18.8). This mask is just like the masks you worked with in the last tutorial. If you paint black into the mask, the Adjustment Layer will not affect those areas of the image.

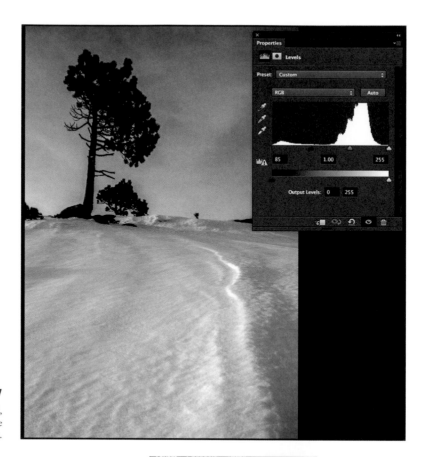

Figure 18.7

With the black point adjusted, the snow looks better, but the tree is now too dark.

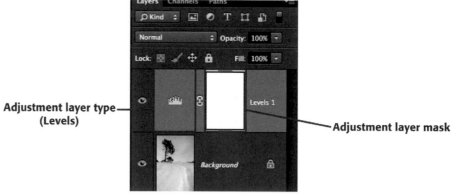

Figure 18.8

Adjustment Layers show two icons in the Layers palette: one indicates what kind of Adjustment Layer it is, and the second shows a thumbnail of the Adjustment Layer's mask.

Adjustment layer type (Levels)

Adjustment layer mask

STEP 5: PAINT THE MASK

Click the Layer Mask icon in the Levels Adjustment Layer to select it. A highlight will appear around it.

Select the Paint Brush tool and choose black as your foreground color. Because you have the Adjustment Layer's mask currently selected, painting operations will affect only the Adjustment Layer mask. With the Paint brush tool selected, paint over the tree in your image. As you brush, the tree will lighten because you will be masking it from the effects of the Adjustment Layer. When you're finished, the Layer Mask icon will show the brush strokes that you painted (see Figure 18.9).

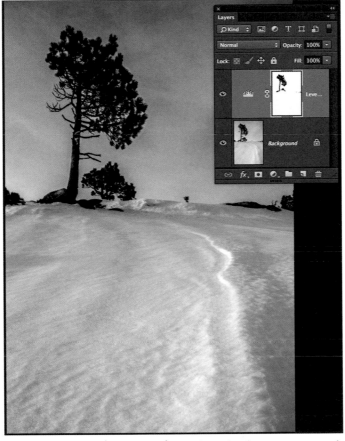

Figure 18.9

After painting into the Adjustment Layer's mask, the Layer Mask icon shows the strokes. Black areas are now completely masked out—they will not receive any of the effects of the Adjustment Layer.

(If at any time you're trying to paint a mask, you see white paint going into your canvas, it means that you've clicked on the image thumbnail in the Layers palette. Click Undo and then select the mask icon in your Adjustment Layer.)

If you make a mistake—perhaps you painted into the background—switch to white paint and paint over the mispainted areas. You may need to switch to a smaller brush for this task. You can freely switch between black and white paint to alter the mask.

STEP 6: ADJUST THE LEVELS SETTINGS
Very often, in an edit like this, after your mask is in place, you'll realize that your initial Levels settings weren't quite right. It can be difficult to assess the proper adjustment when looking at the entire image. In this case, masking out the tree lets you see that you can push the black point a little farther. Slide it over to 100. This will bring out a little more texture on the snow.

STEP 7: EXAMINE THE DIFFERENCE
Click the eyeball icon on the Levels Adjustment Layer to deactivate the layer. You should see the snow lighten. Now reactivate it to reapply the layer. This gives you a clear view of exactly what has changed. ◥

A Critical Adjustment Layer Tip

Once you start adding Adjustment Layers to your image, it becomes critical that you always pay attention to which layer is selected before you start adding adjustments and edits. This is the most common problem that I find in Photoshop classes. Students say that a particular filter or effect isn't working, and then it turns out that they have an Adjustment Layer selected, rather than their base image layer that they're trying to alter. So always be sure you're clear on which layer you're working on, and if you find that an effect doesn't seem to be doing anything, check your current layer selection before trying anything else.

 ## More Layer Masking

Because Layer Masks are so important, you're going to work with them some more. The techniques you're seeing here are everyday processes that you will use regularly, so it's important that you have a strong understanding of how all this works.

STEP 1: OPEN THE IMAGE

Download and open the image big sky.tif, located in the Chapter 18 section of the companion website. This image shows a well-exposed sky, but because this scene poses a big backlight problem, the foreground has gone way too dark (see Figure 18.10). You want to brighten the foreground without overexposing the sky.

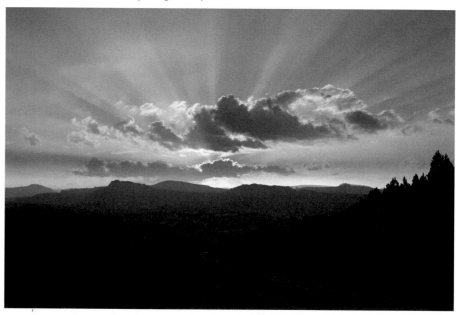

Figure 18.10

The foreground in this image is too dark. You're going to fix it with some Adjustment Layers.

Here are some handy Photoshop shortcuts. You can use Ctrl/Cmd - + to zoom in to an image and Ctrl/Cmd - - to zoom out. Ctrl/Cmd - 0 (that's a zero) will zoom the image to the largest possible size that will fit on your screen, and it's an easy way to see the whole picture.

STEP 2: ADD A LEVELS ADJUSTMENT LAYER

Using the Layers palette, add a Levels Adjustment Layer, just like you did in the last tutorial. The foreground is very dark, so you're going to need a very aggressive adjustment. Move the white point in the Levels control to the left. I set mine at 153. As before, you're not going to pay any attention to what happens to the sky because you will mask it from the effect later. You're only concerned about what the foreground looks like (see Figure 18.11).

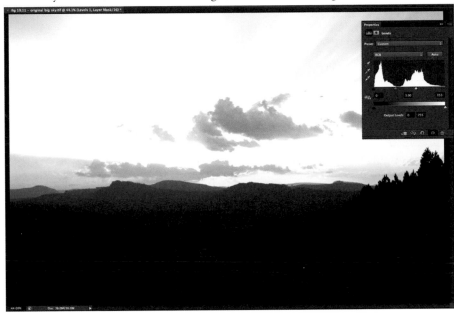

Figure 18.11

Brightening the foreground requires a very aggressive Levels Adjustment.

STEP 3: CONFIGURE THE GRADIENT TOOL

You can constrain the effects of an Adjustment Layer by painting into its mask. So, if you paint black into the area of the mask that covers the sky, the sky will be masked from the Levels Adjustment, and it will not change. The problem with trying to paint a mask of the sky is all of that detail on the horizon. It will be very difficult to paint around all of the trees and mountains. Rather than trying such refined painting, you'll use the Gradient tool to create a graduated effect.

Select the Gradient tool. By default, it's located just below the Eraser tool. However, you might see a Paint Bucket in that slot. Click and hold on the Paint Bucket, and a menu will pop out, revealing the Gradient tool. Set the foreground color to white, and set the background color to black (pressing D will set the colors for you). Open the Gradient pop-up menu on the Control Bar (see Figure 18.12) and ensure that the gradient is set to "Foreground to Background" and that you're set for a linear gradient.

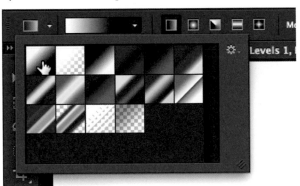

Figure 18.12

Select the Gradient tool; then, from the gradient pop-up in the Control Bar, choose Foreground to Background, which is the gradient swatch in the upper-left corner.

STEP 4: BUILD THE MASK

The Gradient tool automatically creates smooth gradients from one color to another. Since you're now configured to make a gradient from black to white, you can easily make a mask that blends from fully masked to fully unmasked.

Make sure the Levels Adjustment Layer mask is selected in the Layers palette and then click and drag in the image, as shown in Figure 18.13.

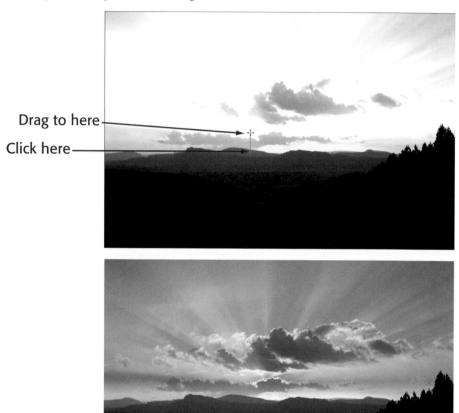

Drag to here

Click here

Figure 18.13

If you drag with the gradient as shown here, you'll get the results shown in the lower image.

With the gradient in the mask, you now have a smooth transition from the masked to unmasked areas. Look at the mask thumbnail, and you can see that about half of the mask is black because you're completely masking out the top of the image where the sky is. Then there's a very short gradient of intermediate gray tones, and the mask is completely white at the bottom of the image.

That transition zone looks natural because the sky has a gradient of its own near the horizon, so the graduated increase in brightness produced by the Levels Adjustment creates a natural looking sky.

STEP 5: IMPROVE THE FOREGROUND

With the mask in place, you can now see the relationship in brightness between the foreground and background. The foreground still looks a little dark, so you need to tweak the Layers Adjustment Layer. I set the midpoint to 1.32 and boosted the black point to 5. This midpoint adjustment brightens the midtones, while the black point adjustment makes sure I still have good contrast.

Thanks to your mask, this adjustment doesn't impact the sky at all.

STEP 6: ADJUST THE COLOR OF THE FOREGROUND

The foreground is very cool in tone. This was a tricky white balance situation, and while the sky looks okay, it would be nice if the foreground were warmer. That pinkish sky should be casting some nice warm tones on the ground.

You're going to use another Adjustment Layer to warm up the foreground, but you don't want it to affect the sky, so you'll need a mask. However, you've already created a mask for the sky, so it would be nice to reuse it.

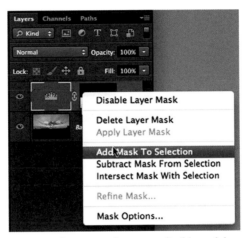

Right-click on the Layer Mask of the Levels Adjustment Layer (if you're using a Mac with a one-button mouse, then you'll need to use Ctrl-click). From the pop-up menu, choose Add Mask to Selection (see Figure 18.14).

As you've already seen, a selection can be saved as an 8-bit grayscale image, and that image can later be loaded back as a selection. That's all you're doing here: You're loading the Layer Mask that you defined earlier as a selection. Note that the menu provides some other handy utility functions: You can subtract the mask from a selection you've already got; you can select just the intersection of the Layer Mask with a current selection; and you can disable or delete the Layer Mask, refine its edge, or set some other Mask options.

Figure 18.14

Right-click on the Layer Mask of the Levels Adjustment Layer to access the pop-up menu of options.

STEP 7: ADD A PHOTO FILTER ADJUSTMENT LAYER

Photoshop provides a Photo Filter Adjustment Layer, which lets you mimic the effect of colored filters on the end of a lens. You're going to use a Photo Filter layer to create a warming effect in the image.

If you create an Adjustment Layer when you already have a selection, then that selection will automatically be defined as the Adjustment Layer's Layer Mask. Since you've already selected the selection from your previous Adjustment Layer, your new layer will get the same gradient mask that you created before.

Create a new Photo Filter Adjustment Layer.

Immediately, the road should look a little warmer, but let's warm it up even more. By default, the Photo Filter Adjustment Layer is set to use a Warming Filter equivalent to a standard 85 filter. If you open the Filter pop-up menu, you'll see four different filter colors. You can also select Color and choose a filter color by hand. We're going to stick with the Warming Filter but increase its strength.

Drag the Density slider to around 55 percent (see Figure 18.15).

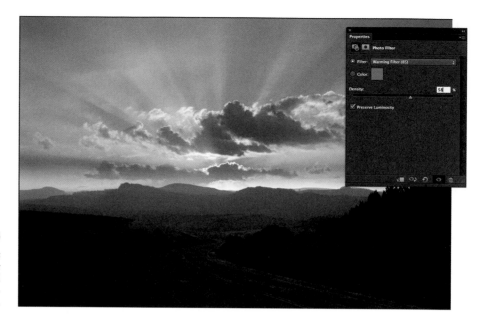

Figure 18.15

The Photo Filter Adjustment Layer provides you with an easy way to warm up the image and equalize the color of the foreground and sky.

STEP 8: MAKE FINAL TWEAKS

With all the adjustments and masks in place, you can make a final assessment of the image. Looking at it now, I think the foreground is still a little too dark, so I went back to the Levels Adjustment Layer and moved the white point to 133. Sometimes, you might need to add an additional Adjustment Layer at the top of your Layers stack, in order to adjust everything below it. Of course, printing might reveal further issues, but for now, I think this image is ready to go! ◤◣

Other Adjustment Layer Types

There are many other types of Adjustment Layers, some of which you should already be familiar with. Here's a summary of some of the most useful ones:

- ◆ **Curves.** You've already used Curves, and they work the same way when applied as an Adjustment Layer.

- ◆ **Hue/Saturation.** The Hue/Saturation dialog box that you used earlier can also be applied as an Adjustment Layer.

- ◆ **Vibrance.** If you want to alter saturation but not change skin tones, then you'll want to try a Vibrance Adjustment Layer.

- ◆ **Black and White.** We'll be looking at this adjustment in great detail in the next chapter.

More Adjustment Layer Practice

If you'd like further Adjustment Layer practice, try the following. In the Chapter 18 section of the companion website, there are two images, `cloud original.psd` and `cloud finished.psd`, both shown in Figure 18.16.

Figure 18.16 If you want more practice, see if you can make the `cloud original.psd` image look like the `cloud finished.psd` image shown below.

On your own, see if you can make the original image look like the finished image. The `finished.psd` document includes my final layered version, so you can see exactly what edits I made.

Where Should You Edit? Lightroom or Photoshop?

Obviously, there's a lot of overlap in the features of Lightroom and Photoshop. In this chapter, you saw that Photoshop offers some selective editing effects that can't be achieved in Lightroom. Obviously, when Lightroom's tools aren't up to the job of a particular selective edit, you'll need to move the image into Photoshop.

Similarly, if you need to do any retouching or painting—tasks we'll look at in later chapters—you'll need to do those edits in Photoshop, because Lightroom doesn't offer any pixel-level editing features. Through the rest of this book you're going to see other effects that can only be created in Photoshop. But before we get to those, we should address the question of *when* you make the trip into Photoshop.

The question becomes complicated by the fact that, once you send an image to Photoshop, any Lightroom edits that you've made will be permanently "baked" into the file. So you want to be sure you've finished all of the Lightroom work that you might ever want to alter. Remember, when you're in Lightroom you're working nondestructively, but once you send an image to Photoshop those nondestructive edits are combined with your original data to create a new TIFF file. Of course, you can perform additional edits on that TIFF file later, but in terms of your image data that's not as "clean" as staying in a nondestructive mode for as long as you can.

Therefore, to maintain maximum image quality and editing latitude, I recommend performing as many edits as you can in Lightroom. If you decide there are things that you need to do in Photoshop, move the image there and perform your edits. If you later decide you need to change some of the basic tonality that you altered in Lightroom, make those changes in Photoshop. As you've seen, Adjustment Layers allow you to work nondestructively in Photoshop.

If you return to Lightroom, add more Lightroom edits, and then decide that you need to go back and do more in Photoshop, then you'll have to create *another* new file with more Lightroom edits baked in. Once you move to Photoshop, it's better to just stay there until the end of your workflow.

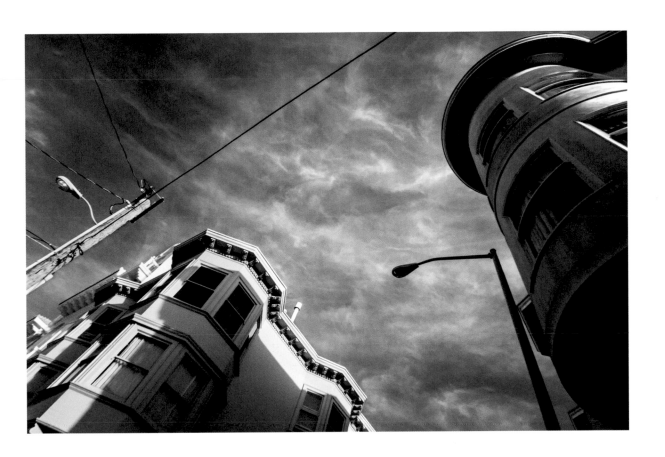

19

BLACK-AND-WHITE CONVERSION

Turning Your Color Images into
Black-and-White Images

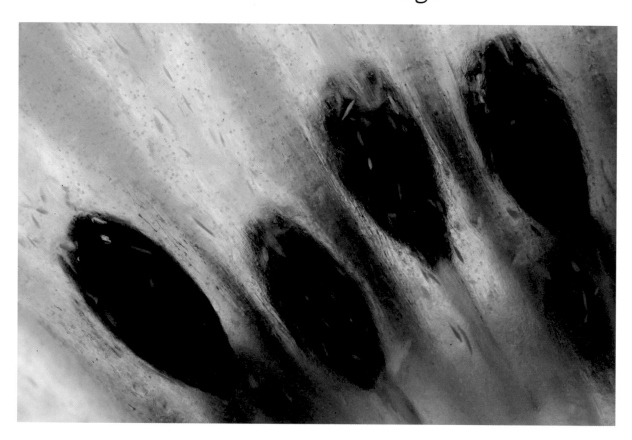

In Chapter 12, "Special Shooting," we looked fairly extensively at the process of shooting black-and-white images. Your digital camera, though, is a color device and always captures color images. (Even if you put it in a black-and-white mode, it still shoots a color image; the camera simply converts this image to black and white using its on-board computer, after the exposure has been made.)

Black-and-white conversion is the process of using your image editor to turn a color original into a black-and-white image. As you learned in Chapter 12, there is no objective "correct" correspondence between color and gray. There's no specific shade of gray that is always used to represent red, for example. So, when you perform a grayscale conversion, you are potentially facing a lot of options and decisions—you can choose to convert your image into a stark, high-contrast grayscale image with strong blacks and whites or a soft, low-contrast image with subtle shades of gray.

Because there are so many different options and interpretations that can be derived from a single color image, you'll almost always want to use a fairly manual approach to grayscale conversion, rather than a predefined "recipe," such as your camera might use internally.

In Photoshop there are many different ways to convert an image to grayscale. In this chapter, we're going to focus on grayscale conversion in Lightroom and then move on to one or two additional Photoshop techniques.

Back Up Your Original

If you're using a destructive grayscale conversion method, you should make a backup copy of your original image. Although you might want a grayscale image now, you never know when you might need to go back to your original color version.

Lightroom B&W Controls

Earlier, you saw the HSL/Color/B&W toolbox. While we looked at the HSL and Color controls, we didn't look at that last tab, which provides powerful black-and-white conversion controls.

 ## Using the Black-and-White Adjustment

In this tutorial, we're going to use the B&W controls to perform a complex grayscale conversion.

STEP 1: SELECT THE IMAGE
In Lightroom, select the image black and white tree.tif, located in the Chapter 19 folder and then switch to the Develop module (see Figure 19.1). When I shot this image, there were a lot of birds flying around the trees, but what struck me about the scene was the light tree in front of the darker green trees. Because of this tonal difference, I figured that this was a

good candidate for a black-and-white image. Therefore, our goal in the conversion will be to figure out how much that brightness difference can be played up, and whether or not it's interesting.

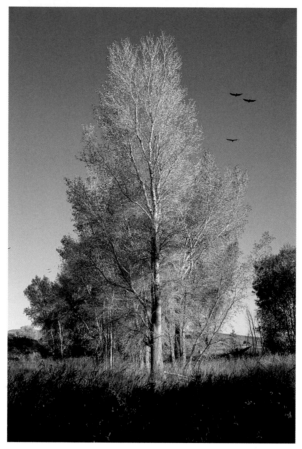

Figure 19.1

You're going to convert this image to black and white, with an eye toward emphasizing the brightness difference between the foreground and background trees.

STEP 2: ACTIVATE THE BLACK-AND-WHITE ADJUSTMENT
Scroll down the right-hand pane until you see the HSL/Color/B&W toolbox. Click on the B&W tab. The image will immediately switch to monochrome, and the sliders in the B&W tab will change positions. The black-and-white conversion that you're seeing is a default one—a stock conversion recipe that serves most images pretty well.

STEP 3: TRY A SLIDER
Drag the Blues slider to the right, and you'll see the sky get brighter (see Figure 19.2).

When you drag a particular slider, the Black-and-White adjustment finds all of the tones in the image that are within the color range of that slider. If you've dragged the slider to the right, those tones will get brighter; if you drag to the left, they'll get darker.

STEP 4: USE TARGETED ADJUSTMENT
Click on the small circular target icon in the upper-left corner of the B&W panel and then move the mouse over the image. The pointer should change to the same shape you saw earlier in the HSL tutorial. Click in the sky, near the top of the image, and drag down. Watch the sky, as well as the Blues slider in the Black-and-White dialog box (see Figure 19.3).

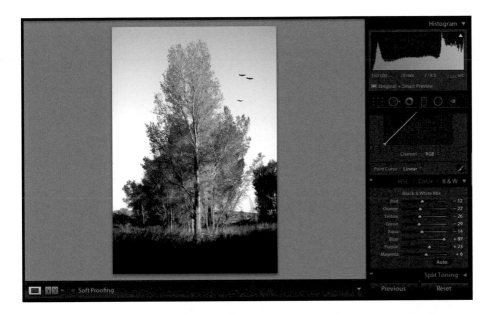

Figure 19.2

Here I've dragged the Blues slider to the right, resulting in a lightening of the sky (because it's blue).

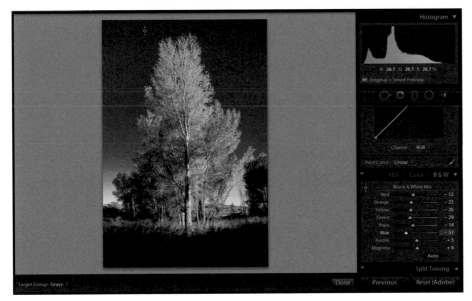

Figure 19.3

In addition to moving sliders, you can brighten or darken tones simply by dragging on them with the targeted adjustment.

As you drag with this tool, Lightroom automatically analyzes the original color of the area you clicked on and adjusts the appropriate slider as you drag. So when you click on the sky and drag down, the sky darkens, and the Blues slider moves to the left.

Note that *anything* else in the image that is blue will also get darker. The edit is not constrained to just the sky. Just as with the HSL controls, you can't make localized adjustments with the Black-and-White controls.

STEP 5: ADJUST THE TREES

As I mentioned, my original impulse with this shot was driven by the difference in brightness between the foreground tree and the darker green trees in the background. Right now, they're kind of all uniformly gray. Let's darken the greener trees.

Using the targeted adjustment tool, click one of the green trees in the background and drag down. It turns out that the trees are more yellow than green, so you should see the Yellows slider move to the left and the trees darken (see Figure 19.4).

Figure 19.4

You can darken the trees to help them stand out more behind the light tree in front.

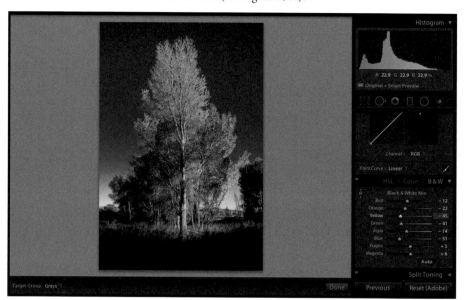

STEP 6: SWITCH BACK TO COLOR

Click on the HSL tab, and your image will change back to color. Now click on the B&W tab again, and you'll be back to black and white, but all of your black-and-white adjustments should still be there. Note that changes that you make in the HSL tab have no impact on your black-and-white conversion.

If you're not sure if you want an image in black and white or color but would like to experiment with both options, consider making a virtual copy of your original color image. You can then perform color and black-and-white experiments on different copies.

Black-and-White Adjustment Layers

Photoshop provides a Black-and-White Adjustment Layer that offers the same functionality that you've just seen in Lightroom. In addition to providing you with a great way to do black-and-white conversion in Photoshop, you also get the advantage of having a Layer Mask to play with. This gives you a way to create a black-and-white image that preserves a color element (see Figure 19.5).

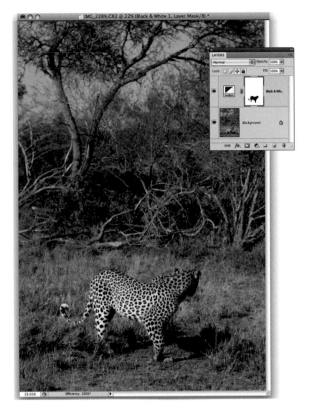

Figure 19.5

Here I've added a Black-and-White Adjustment Layer to convert this image to black and white. By painting into the Layer Mask, I've limited the black and white conversion to only the background, leaving the cat in color.

If you're using Photoshop CS4 or later, when you add a Black-and-White Adjustment Layer, its controls will appear in either the Adjustments or Properties panel, just as with any other Adjustment Layer. If you want to be able to click and drag in your image to alter tones, then you must first click on the modify button in the upper-left corner of the Adjustments palette (see Figure 19.6).

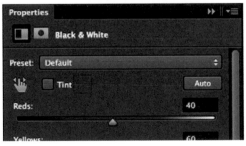

Figure 19.6

After adding a Black-and-White Adjustment Layer, you can click this tool in the Adjustments palette, and then click and drag in your image to adjust tones.

Sepia Toning

In the old days, photographic paper would turn a yellowish-brown as it aged. This sepia tone is now generally recognized as the look of a very old, antique photo. Sepia toning your grayscale prints is a nice way to give them a bit of atmosphere, and it's easy enough to do in Photoshop, with a simple Adjustment Layer.

To add a sepia tone to an image:

◆ Open the image in Photoshop and then add a Photo Filter Adjustment Layer.

◆ Select the Photo Filter Adjustments Layer, and its controls will appear in the Adjustments panel. Change the Filter pop-up menu to Sepia.

◆ Dial in the amount of toning you want by using the Density slider (see Figure 19.7).

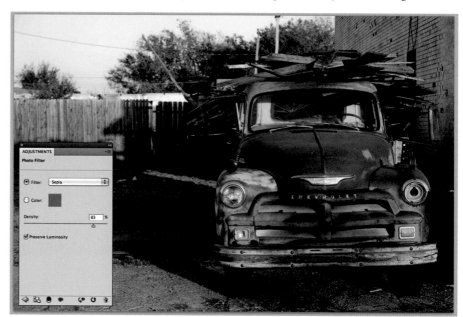

Figure 19.7

Using the Photo Filter Adjustment Layer, you can easily add a sepia tone to an image, which will create a traditional, antique look.

You can also apply the Photo Filter destructively by choosing Image > Adjustments > Photo Filter. The Photo Filter dialog box will provide the same controls that you saw in the Adjustments panel.

Other Black-and-White Conversion Techniques

There are lots of other ways to convert images to black and white. You can learn about them in the BlackAndWhiteConversion.pdf available in the Chapter 19 section of the companion website.

Split Toning

Earlier, you saw how to add a sepia toning effect, which adds a yellowish-brown cast to your entire image. Lightroom and Photoshop Camera Raw also provide a split toning effect, which allows you to add separate color tones to the shadow and highlight areas of your image.

After converting to grayscale in Lightroom, scroll down to the Split Toning toolbox, which sits just below the HSL/Color/B&W toolbox.

Set the color of the highlight tone that you want by adjusting the Hue slider in the Highlights area. You can control the degree of toning with the Saturation slider under Highlights.

Next, set the color of the shadow tone that you want by adjusting the controls in the Shadows area. The Balance slider controls whether midtones are shifted more to the highlight or shadow tone.

Figure 19.8 shows an image that has been split-toned. The shadow areas have been toned with a light blue, while the highlights have been toned with a rust color.

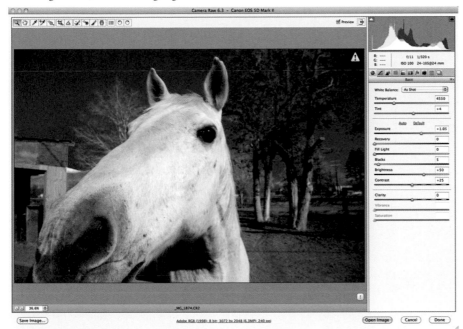

Figure 19.8

Split toning tones the shadow areas a light blue, while rendering the highlights in rust.

Black-and-White Plug-ins

Black-and-white conversion is such a critical task for the black-and-white shooter that there are programs and plug-ins dedicated entirely to the process of converting images from color to monochrome. Most of these tools ship as plug-ins, and they work with Photoshop and Lightroom.

Alien Skin Exposure is a nice plug-in for Photoshop and Photoshop Elements that provides very good black-and-white conversions. In addition, Exposure provides presets for emulating specific types of film. Choose a preset—Fuji Velvia, for example—and Exposure will adjust the tone and contrast in your image automatically to mimic the properties of Fuji Velvia film. In addition, it will try to simulate the grain of each film.

Silver Efex Pro, part of the Google Nik Collection, is a plug-in for Photoshop and Lightroom. Like Exposure, it provides a full library of stock film types, and can emulate their tonal characteristics, as well as grain and texture. Silver Efex also offers localized toning tools in the form of the same automatic masking tools found in the Viveza plug-in mentioned in Chapter 17. These tools make it simple to brighten or darken specific parts of an image without having to craft complex masks (see Figure 19.9).

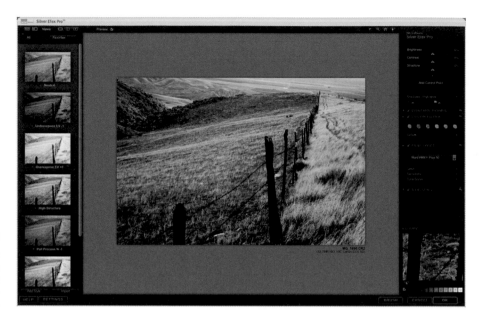

Figure 19.9

Google's Nik Silver Efex Pro
provides sophisticated black-and-
white toning tools, as well as the
ability to mimic the characteristics of real-world film types.

Refining a Grayscale Image

You might not always be able to get the tonal relationships in your image exactly the way you want during the conversion process. However, using the tonal adjustment tools you've already learned about, you can easily refine your grayscale images.

For example, consider the tree image you worked with earlier. As discussed, one of the goals was to play up the difference in tone between the foreground and background trees. While Lightroom's Black-and-White adjustment allowed you to adjust the tones of the yellow/green trees in the background, you still couldn't get a huge differentiation between the foreground and background.

But with a simple Levels Adjustment Layer and some Layer Mask painting in Photoshop, you can perform a localized brightening to make the front tree "pop" a little more (see Figure 19.10).

Experiment with your saved version of this image and see if you can create an Adjustment Layer and mask that brighten the foreground tree.

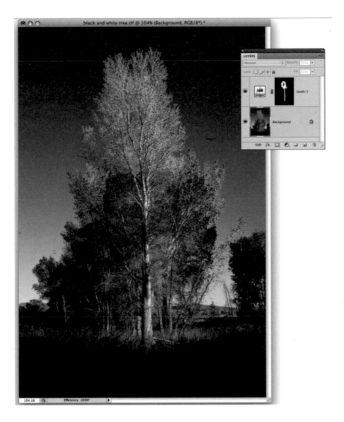

Figure 19.10

With a Levels Adjustment Layer to perform a little brightening, you can make the front tree stand out a little more.

Getting a Silver Look

Traditional black-and-white printing in a darkroom uses a silver halide process that can yield images with a beautiful range of what appear to be silvery tones. "Silvery" tones are really just different shades of gray. Simply converting your image to grayscale (using any conversion method) is usually not enough to get that traditional silver look.

Consider Figure 19.11. I used a Black-and-White Adjustment Layer to convert this image to grayscale. Adjusting the Adjustment Layer sliders let me alter my toning, and overall, it's an okay image.

The image has a wide range of gray tones, and my histogram shows a decent contrast spread, but overall it's a flat image that doesn't have any of the quality of a traditional silver print. However, with the application of some Levels Adjustment Layers, each with its own Layer Mask, I can selectively tone the image to produce the result shown in Figure 19.12.

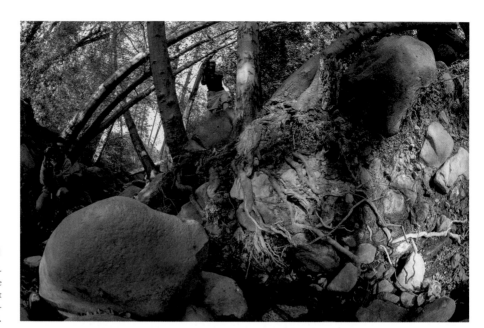

Figure 19.11

After a black-and-white conversion, I have an image with a wide range of grays, but it lacks that "silvery" quality of a good black-and-white print.

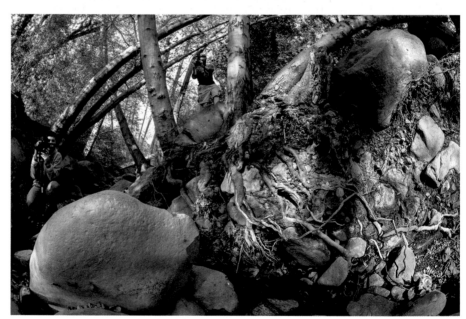

Figure 19.12

With a stack of Levels Adjustment Layers and some corresponding Layer Masks, I can pull a more silvery tone out of this picture.

When performing tonal corrections on grayscale images, consider the following:

◆ **Every image needs true black and true white.** For the most part, there should be something in your image that is true white and something that is true black. However, there shouldn't be a lot of either of these things. Typically, you'll aim for the specular highlights in your images to be true white (bright glints off water or the brightest point or face of a shiny or brightly lit object). You'll also want the very deepest part of the darkest shadow to be true black. When you look at the histogram, you should see data at white and black, but not a lot of it.

◆ **Midtones are where the "silver" lies.** While we call it "black and white" what makes a successful black-and-white print are the grays. Usually, you want as many different shades of gray as you can get. Very often, it's an adjustment to the middle tones of an area that will shift things from drab grays to sheeny silver. I often find that expanding the brightest parts of the lower quarter tone and the lower parts of the upper quarter tone yield a more silvery look.

◆ **Different areas need different adjustment.** There's almost never a single tonal adjustment that will fix an entire image. Instead, you must go through and tone specific parts of an image to bring out the right contrast for that specific area. In Figure 19.12, I used nine different Levels Adjustment Layers, each with its own Layer Mask, to get the image toned the way I wanted.

◆ **Work by the numbers.** Keep your Histogram palette open and pay attention to the black-and-white points. Remember: you can't always trust the on-screen image.

See for Yourself

I've put the layered Photoshop document, `Figure 19.12.psd`, on the companion website, at *www. completedigitalphotography.com/CDP8*. Download it now and take a look at it. When you open it, you'll find all of the Levels Adjustment Layers turned off—you'll be seeing the image you saw in Figure 19.11. Working one layer at a time from the bottom of the Layers palette up, make a layer visible, and then click on it to see its adjustment settings. By doing this, you'll be able to see what areas I chose to tone and how I chose to alter them.

Low-Contrast Images

Throughout this book, you've been learning about the importance of contrast, and you've seen how to use various tools to "properly" set the black and white points on your images. But while we've been focusing on adding more contrast to images, there are times when the best choice for an image is *less* contrast. For example, Figure 19.13 shows an image that I intentionally adjusted to have low contrast.

The lack of strong blacks creates a dreamier, more abstract feel. Also, the original color image was not shot under especially interesting light, and a faint cloud cover meant the sky was a featureless white. With a low-contrast approach, the white sky doesn't look out of place.

Lowering contrast in Photoshop is easy. Open the Levels dialog box (Image > Adjustment > Levels). You'll find a Levels interface very similar to the controls you've been using in Lightroom. Below the main controls, though, are the Output sliders (see Figure 19.14). These offer the easiest way to lower the contrast in an image. Move the Blacks output slider to the right and the blacks will get lighter and lighter. The overall tonal relationships in your image will remain the same, but the resulting image will have less contrast.

Figure 19.15 shows the original color image and a typical conversion with more normal contrast.

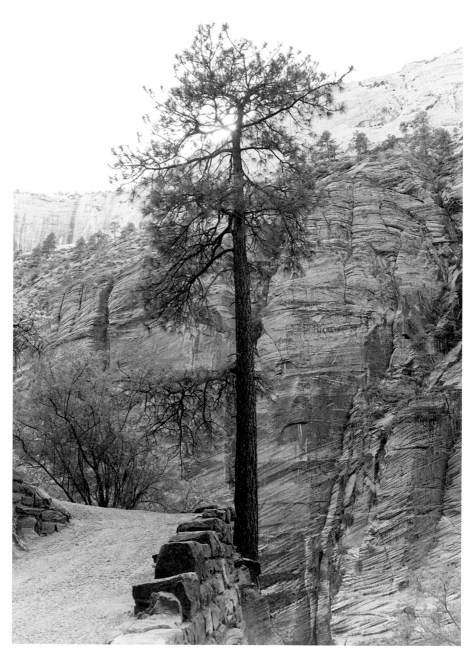

Figure 19.13

A low-contrast black-and-white conversion of this image makes for a nice result that's dreamy and abstract.

When working with grayscale conversions, don't just always go by the numbers and construct conversions that yield "correct" histograms and tonal ranges. Remember that blown-out or low-contrast images are often the best choice for some subject matter. As you've seen here, a little stylization can save an otherwise boring, unusable image.

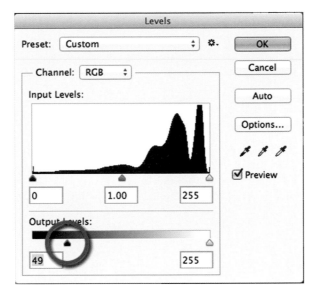

Figure 19.14

The output sliders in Photoshop's Levels dialog box let you redefine white and black in your image. In this case, I've used it to redefine black as a lighter gray, thus lowering the contrast in the image.

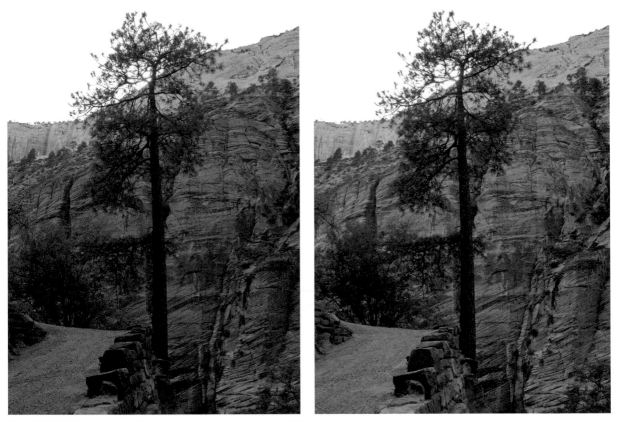

Figure 19.15 Here you can see the original color image and a more typical grayscale conversion.

20

LAYERS, RETOUCHING, AND SPECIAL EFFECTS

Additional Editing Tools and Concepts
for Improving Your Images

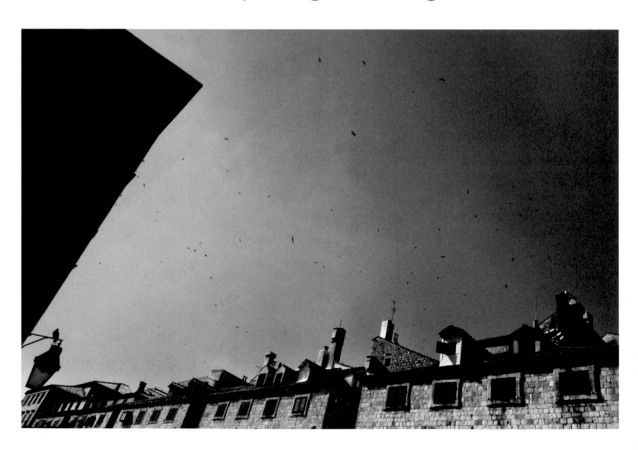

The tools you've learned to use so far are essential, everyday tools that you'll use on many (if not most) of the images that you shoot. Of course, every shoot yields its own editing challenges and problems, which is why an image editor like Photoshop is loaded with so many tools, commands, and features.

Photoshop can be intimidating because it presents so many options, but one of the first things you need to understand is that you *don't* have to know how to use every tool and feature of the program to get good results. One of the great things about Photoshop is that there are many different ways to achieve the same edit, meaning you can pick the one that makes sense to you, but you don't have to know how to do them all. It's also important to realize that many of its tools are not designed for the working photographer. Web slicing tools, scientific analysis tools, the Animation palette—these are all for other professions, and you don't have to worry about them for the type of work that we're doing.

In this chapter, we're going to look at some additional tools and processes. These are tools that you won't use every day, but they are still essential features for times when you encounter certain problems. Some of the capabilities we'll look at here will be targeted at solving specific problems, while others will be combined with other things we've learned, to provide more flexibility with the tools you've already learned about.

About the Images in This Chapter

You'll be working exclusively in Photoshop in this chapter, and the tutorials direct you to open images directly in Photoshop using any of the normal Open mechanisms. If you want, you can load the images into Lightroom and launch into Photoshop from there. It won't make any difference to the actual work.

Layers

In Chapter 17, "Selective Editing and Masks," you used multiple layers with a Layer Mask to selectively apply a Shadows/Highlight adjustment to an image. Of course, there are many other uses for Layers, the most common being to composite two different images together (see Figure 20.1).

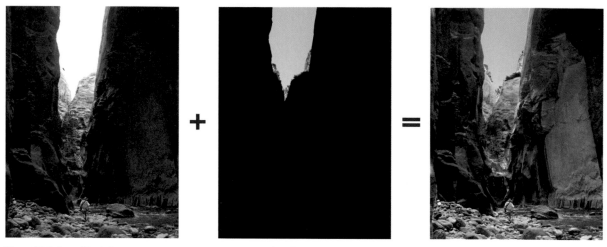

Figure 20.1 I combined these two exposures to create a composite that allows you to see both the sky and the dark tones at the bottom of the canyon.

Layers are pretty easy to understand. If your image editor provides a layer facility, you'll be able to stack images—and parts of images—on top of each other within a document. A robust layer facility provides you with the capability to make complex edits and composites easily.

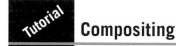 **Compositing**

Compositing is the process of stacking layers of images on top of each other to create a final result. There are a lot of reasons to create composites. Sometimes you'll create composites to keep different edits isolated in separate layers so that you can manipulate each layer without affecting the others.

In this tutorial, we're going to look at a fairly practical example of compositing and explore some essential layer and compositing techniques. Because Lightroom lacks compositing tools, you'll be performing these tutorials in Photoshop, and they should work in any version since CS3.

STEP 1: OPEN THE IMAGES

Download the images `Palace of Fine Arts1.jpg`, `Palace of Fine Arts 2.jpg` and `Palace of Fine Arts 3.jpg` from the Chapter 20 section of the companion website at *www.completedigital photography.com/CDP8*. Place them all in a folder and drag and drop that folder onto Bridge. This is a quick way to get Bridge to show you the contents of a specific folder. If you haven't used Bridge before, you should find it in the same directory as Photoshop.

These pictures were shot at the Palace of Fine Arts in San Francisco (see Figure 20.2). I wanted to get a shot of the rotunda without any people in it, but it was a nice day, and lots of visitors were milling around the area. I shot a whole bunch of images, figuring that there would be some time when every part of the structure was unobscured by a person. Using some simple layering techniques, you can combine the images to create a final version that doesn't show any people.

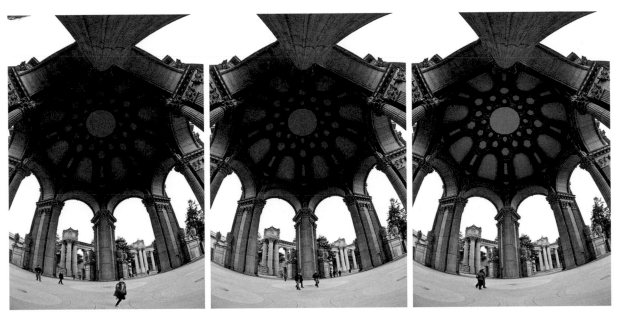

Figure 20.2 I want a shot of this rotunda, but I don't want any people in it. Fortunately, between these three images, it's possible to see every part of the rotunda. You'll composite them to yield a final image without people in it.

STEP 2: PREPARE THE IMAGES

Select all three images in Bridge by choosing Edit > Select All or by pressing Cmd/Ctrl-A. You're going to ask Bridge to automatically open all three images into a single Photoshop document. Each image will appear in its own layer.

In Bridge, choose Tools > Photoshop > Load Files into Photoshop Layers. Photoshop will activate, and a new document will appear. As you watch, you should see each layer load. When Photoshop is done, your Layers palette should look like the one in Figure 20.3.

Make sure the layers are ordered as they are in Figure 20.3, with Palace of Fine Arts 1 on top, then Palace of Fine Arts 2, and the third file on the bottom.

STEP 3: EXAMINE THE NEW DOCUMENT

Turn off the visibility of the top layer by clicking the eyeball icon. As the layer hides to reveal the layer beneath it, you'll see some people disappear, and some others appear.

Now turn off the visibility of the middle layer. In addition to the people shuffling around, you should see the rotunda shift a little bit. Despite the fact that I was shooting on a tripod, the images are still not perfectly aligned. This could be because of

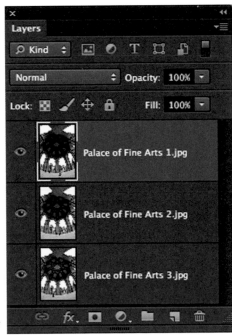

Figure 20.3

After telling Bridge to Load Files into Photoshop Layers, you should have a single document with three layers.

wind, or because I bumped the camera. Whatever the cause, you need better alignment for this to work. Because individual layers can be moved and rotated, there's no reason you can't register the images in Photoshop and then perform your compositing operations.

Fortunately, Photoshop provides an automatic way to do this.

STEP 4: ALIGN THE LAYERS

With the upper layer selected in the Layers palette, hold down the Shift key and click the other two layers. All layers should now be selected.

Now choose Edit > Auto-Align Layers. The Auto-Align Layers dialog box will appear (see Figure 20.4). All layers have to be selected before Auto-Align Layers will be active.

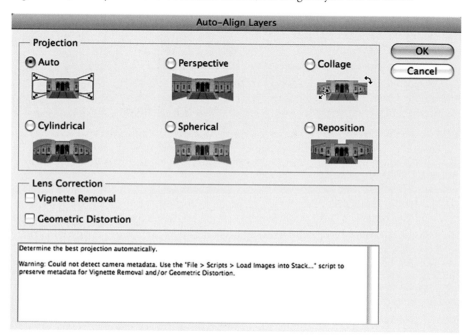

Figure 20.4

The Auto-Align Layers command automatically examines the selected layers and aligns them into perfect registration.

In the Projection section of the dialog box, click Auto and press OK.

Photoshop will think for a while and then present its results. The images didn't need a tremendous amount of movement, but as you can see, some distortions were added which have caused the edges of the images to bow inward. You can crop this out later.

If you manipulate the visibility of the layers, you should see that the images are in alignment, and that the people appear and disappear.

STEP 5: CREATE A LAYER MASK

You're going to use Layer Masks to remove people from the upper image. Select the upper layer by clicking on it.

There are many ways to add a Layer Mask. You can choose Layer > Layer Mask > Reveal All, or you can simply click on the Add Layer Mask button at the bottom of the Layers palette (see Figure 20.5).

A Layer Mask icon will appear next to the layer in the Layers palette, and it will be filled with white, indicating that all parts of the associated layer are visible.

STEP 6: REMOVE THE FIRST PEOPLE

Choose the Brush tool and set the foreground color to black. (There are many ways to do this, including clicking on the foreground swatch and selecting black from the resulting color picker.)

In the Layers palette, click the Layer Mask of the upper layer to ensure that it's selected. Then choose an appropriate brush size and paint over the people in the frame. (You can change brush size using the [and] keys.)

After painting, you should see a small black circle in the Layer Mask that's shown in the Layers palette (see Figure 20.6).

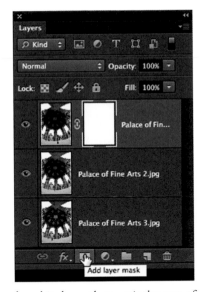

Figure 20.5

You can add a Layer Mask to any layer in the Layers palette. With it, you can selectively hide and show different parts of each layer.

This black blob corresponds to the area you just painted, and it shows that particular area of the upper layer is masked out, in order to reveal the underlying layers. When you paint out some of the people from the upper layer, you'll reveal people in the middle layer. Don't worry about that, you'll deal with them next.

STEP 7: REMOVE EVERYONE ELSE

Now switch to the middle layer, add a Layer Mask, and paint out any people you see. There are no people in the third layer revealed, so you're done! You've successfully created an image of a crowded space that lacks any crowd.

STEP 8: CORRECT THE DOME

If you hide the upper two images, you'll notice one other difference between them and the lowest image. The lower image has a better exposure on the inside of the dome. Paint into the upper two masks to reveal the dome from the bottom layer. It will be easiest to do this one layer at a time: activate the middle layer, paint its mask, then activate the upper layer and mask it.

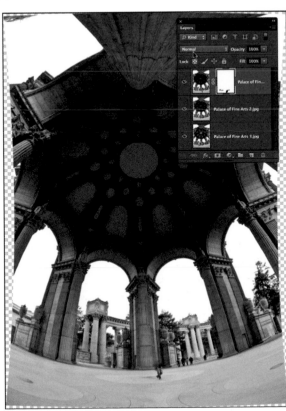

Figure 20.6

After painting, a small black circle will appear in the Layer Mask.

STEP 9: FINISH THE IMAGE

Now you can crop, straighten, add additional tonal adjustments, and perform any other edits that you want to make to the image (see Figure 20.7). You might also want to flatten the image to reduce it to a single layer. You can flatten an image by choosing Layer > Flatten Image or by choosing Flatten Image from the menu in the upper-right corner of the Layers palette.

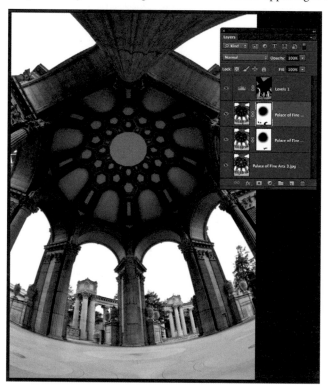

Figure 20.7

The final image, after all the masking, tone adjustments, and cropping are finished.

Sometimes, you'll want to save a layered version of a document so that you can go back and refine masks or edit individual layers later. Both Photoshop and TIFF format support multiple layers with masks.

You could have performed this same edit by stacking the layers and then using the Eraser tool to erase the people from the upper layer. However, erasing is a destructive edit because once you erase those pixels, they're gone. By using a Layer Mask, you can go back and restore the masked elements, or paint with shades of gray to partially mask an area. Overall, using masks—rather than altering layers—is always a better way to work. ◤

Opacity and Transfer Modes

You can change the opacity of the currently selected layer by simply sliding the Opacity control in the Layers palette back and forth.

You can also change how the currently selected layer interacts with layers that are lower in the stacking order by selecting a Blending (or Transfer) mode from the pop-up menu in the Layers palette. Normally, the pixels in a layer simply overwrite any pixels that are lower down the stack. By changing the Blending mode, you tell Photoshop to mathematically combine pixels, instead of simply replacing lower pixels with higher pixels (see Figure 20.8).

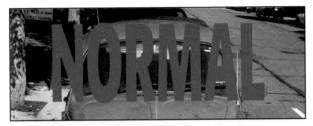

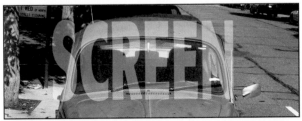

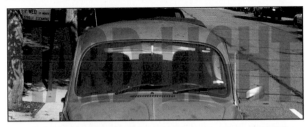

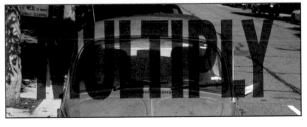

Figure 20.8

A few of Photoshop's Blending modes, which control how one layer—in this case, the text mixes with a lower layer.

As you work more with Blending modes, you'll get a better idea of what they do. At first, don't worry about being able to predict their results. Just start playing around with them until you find the effect you like. You can lessen the effect of a mode by lowering that layer's opacity.

Blending modes are essential for creating some types of compositing effects. Figure 20.9 shows the creation of a virtual tattoo. When the tattoo image was layered directly on top of the body image, it looked like a simple overlay. Changing the tattoo layer's opacity helps some, but to create a realistic blending of the colors, you need to change the tattoo's Transfer mode to Multiply.

In addition to compositing, you can use Layer modes for hand-coloring grayscale images (see Figure 20.10) and creating certain types of color corrections.

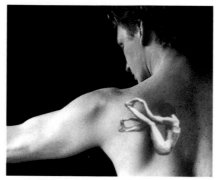

100% Opacity, Normal Transfer

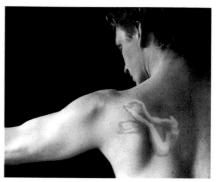

48% Opacity, Normal Transfer

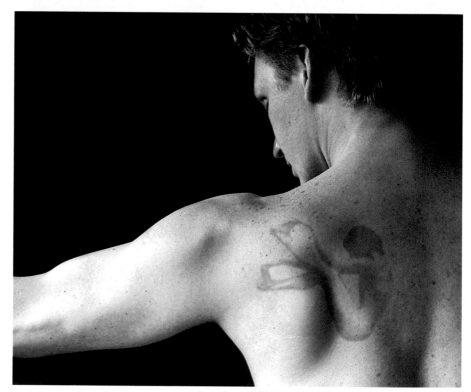

Figure 20.9

To create this tattoo effect, I used a combination of an opacity change with a Multiply Transfer mode to blend the tattoo layer with the skin.

48% Opacity, Multiply Transfer

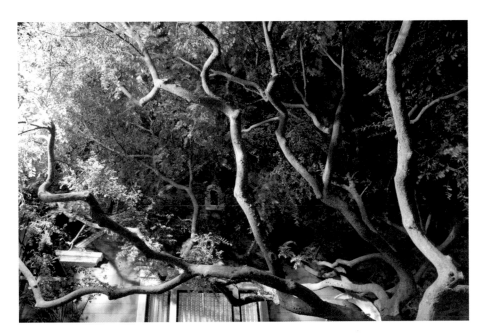

Figure 20.10

I created this hand-painted image by converting my photo to grayscale and then hand-painting color into a new layer that was blended with my grayscale image using a Transfer mode.

Watch That RAM!

As you add layers to your image, its RAM requirements will skyrocket quickly. Nothing affects Photoshop's performance as much as RAM, so if you find your computer getting sluggish, it might be that Photoshop is running out of memory. The easiest way to shrink the RAM requirements of your document is to eliminate extra layers. If you think you've finished editing an individual layer, consider merging it with other layers using the Merge Linked or Merge Visible commands, located in the Layers menu.

To Flatten or Not to Flatten

If you're performing a lot of complex, layer-based edits and effects, your document will quickly get overloaded with layers. In addition to possibly slowing your computer, extra layers can make it trickier to understand how a particular adjustment is achieved. As mentioned previously, merging layers that you're through editing can keep your documents from getting swollen with layer bloat.

The Flatten command (which you can get from the Layer menu, or from the pop-up menu in the upper-right corner of the Layers palette) combines all layers in your document into a single layer. This can be a way to dramatically reduce file size, but when you "bake" your edits this way, you can't go back and adjust them later.

I typically save my documents layered, so that I know I always have access to my edits and adjustments. If I need to send a copy of an image to someone else, then I flatten and do a Save As into a new document. That way, I have my original, layered version and a flattened copy.

Note that if you're using a version of Photoshop prior to CS5, then you must flatten before you can save into a format that doesn't support layers, such as JPEG. With CS5 and later, Photoshop will take care of the flattening step for you.

Brushes and Stamps

Many of the retouching and editing tasks performed in a real darkroom are dependent on brushes, masks, and paint. Your image editor is no different, except that your brushes and tools are digital. To get good results from them, you still need a good hand, a trained eye, and well-designed tools, just as in a real darkroom.

The documentation that came with your image editor should offer plenty of information on how to use your editor's tools. In this section, you're going to learn what each tool is good for. You'll need to refer to your image editor's manual to learn the details of how to modify and adjust each tool. Being able to identify the right tool for a particular job will often save you a lot of time.

Brushes

Hopefully, your image editor includes a good assortment of paintbrushes and airbrushes. A good Brush tool offers an easy way to select different brush sizes and shapes, has antialiased (smooth) edges, pressure sensitivity when used with a drawing tablet, and variable opacity (see Figure 20.11).

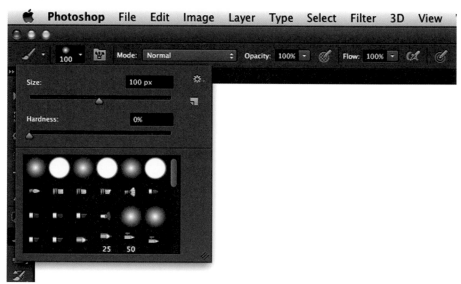

Figure 20.11

The Photoshop Brush controls—scattered between the Brush palette and the toolbar—let you select Brush size, Transfer mode, and Opacity. As you've already seen, you'll use these tools for painting masks, retouching, color correction (certain types), and many other image editing and correction tasks.

To use a Brush tool well, you need good hand-eye coordination and a feel for the brush. Your brush skills will develop over time and will be aided greatly by the use of a drawing tablet. In addition to providing a more intuitive interface, a drawing tablet is *much* easier on your hand than a mouse is. If you plan to do a lot of image editing, consider investing in an inexpensive pressure-sensitive drawing tablet such as the Wacom tablet shown in Figure 20.12. At the time of this writing, you could get a good Wacom pressure-sensitive tablet for around $80.

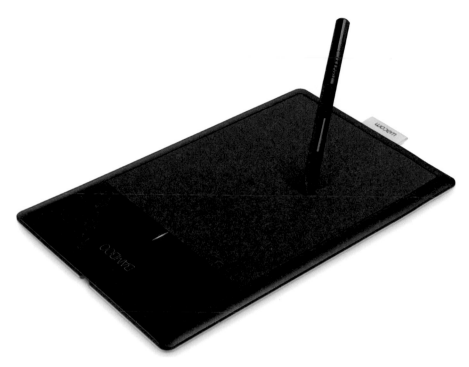

Figure 20.12

A pressure-sensitive drawing tablet such as this Wacom Bamboo is a must-have for serious image editing.

You'll also want to spend some time learning the different keyboard shortcuts that augment your Brush tool. Learn your brush's features, including parameters such as opacity, spacing, and repeat rate.

If you're using Photoshop, you'll quickly become dependent on these brush-related keyboard shortcuts:

- ◆ **B:** Selects the Brush tool.
- ◆ **Shift-B:** Toggles between the Brush and the Pencil tools.
- ◆ **[:** Shrinks the size of the current brush.
- ◆ **]:** Enlarges the size of the current brush.

Rubber Stamp or Clone

One of the most powerful—and seemingly magical—tools in your image editing toolbox is a Rubber Stamp tool (also known as a *Clone* tool), which provides a brush that performs a localized copy from one part of your image to another as you brush (see Figure 20.13).

You'll use the Rubber Stamp tool for everything from removing dust and noise to painting things out of and into your image. The advantage of a Rubber Stamp tool over normal copying and pasting is that the tool's brush-like behavior lets you achieve very smooth composites and edits.

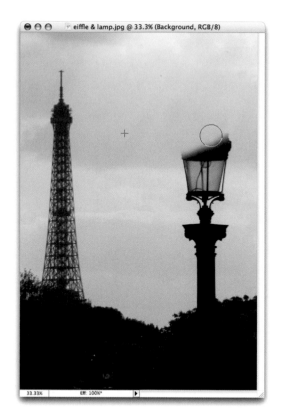

eiffle & lamp.jpg @ 33.3% (Background, RGB/8)

33.33%   Eff: 100%

Figure 20.13

When you paint with a Rubber
Stamp (Clone) tool, your image
editor copies paint from your
source area (the crosshairs) to
your target area (the circle).

In Photoshop, Change Your Painting Cursor

You'll have a much easier time with the Rubber Stamp tool, and all of Photoshop's Brush tools, if you
make a simple change to Photoshop's preferences. In the Preferences dialog (Photoshop > Preferences), select Cursors (in previous versions of Photoshop, this was Display and Cursors) and then
change Painting Cursors to Normal Brush Tip. This will show a cursor that's the exact size of your
chosen brush, making it much easier to see the effect your brush strokes will have.

If you're using something besides Photoshop, you'll need to study your Rubber Stamp tool's
documentation to learn the difference between absolute and relative cloning, and how to set
the tool's source and destination points. When you rubber-stamp an area, you want to know
how to select a source area quickly, so it's imperative to learn the tool's controls.

Your image editing application provides many more tools and functions, but you'll use the
brushes and stamps the most. These are also tools that will not be heavily discussed or documented in the rest of this book.

Cloning Video Tutorial

To learn more about cloning, watch the `Cloning Tutorial` movie located in the Chapter 20 section of the companion website (see Figure 20.14). ◄▮

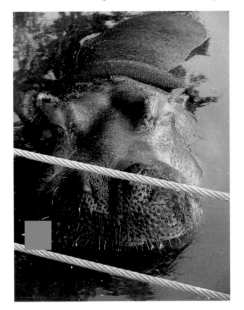

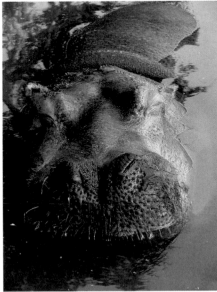

Figure 20.14

I used nothing more than the Photoshop Rubber Stamp (or Clone) tool to remove the wires from the front of this hippo. A Clone tool is a must-have for even the simplest touch-ups, so make sure you know how to use one.

Patch and Heal

Photoshop CS and later, and some versions of Elements, include special variations on the normal Rubber Stamp tool. The Healing Brush works just like the Rubber Stamp tool, but with a bit more intelligence. Rather than copying pixels directly from the source location to your brush position, copied pixels are adjusted automatically for texture, lighting, transparency, and shading, so that your cloned pixels blend more seamlessly with the surrounding parts of your image. You can achieve the same results with a regular Rubber Stamp tool, but the Healing Brush is much easier to use. The Spot Healing Brush tool lets you instantly repair spots, dust, and other small, localized troubles with a single click. The Spot Healing Brush is especially useful for removing dust, slight lens flares, stuck pixels, and certain types of noise, and is also great for removing skin blemishes and spots.

The Patch tool uses the same underlying technology as the Healing Brush tool, but it lets you patch an area by drawing around it with a lasso and then dragging that area over a part of your image that contains the texture you'd like to have in your selection. That texture is copied and blended automatically into your selection.

Video Tutorial: Painting Light and Shadow

No matter what tools or procedures you choose to use when making your edits and corrections, one of the most important things to learn is to recognize the effect of light and shadow on your images. A photo is a flat object; the sense of depth in your scene comes from the interplay of light and dark. As you learn to think more like a painter who wrestles with adding or subtracting light from specific areas in a work, you'll find yourself creating more compelling adjustments and corrections. Located in the Chapter 20 section of the companion website is a tutorial movie, Color Correction.mov, which walks you through the process of adjusting the top image in Figure 20.15 so it looks like the bottom image. This tutorial will introduce you to the idea of thinking about your image edits in terms of placement of light and shadow. ◥◤

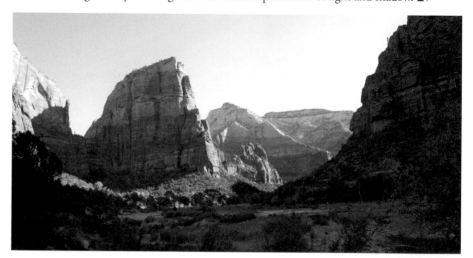

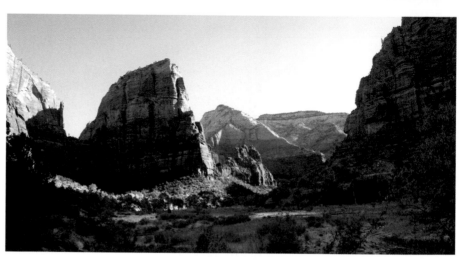

Figure 20.15

The top image doesn't look bad, but with some subtle color corrections, you can make it look much better. To learn how, watch the Color Correction video in the Tutorials/Chapter 20 folder located on the companion website at *www.completedigital photography.com/CDP8*.

Applied Editing Techniques

With the adjustment tools, layering features, and masking capabilities that you've learned about, there are a number of other edits that you can pull off. In this section, we're going to solve some different types of problems by mixing and matching some of the techniques you've learned. These are not everyday adjustments and problems, but you might occasionally need to tackle a situation similar to what you'll find in this section.

Retouching with Content-Aware Fill

Photoshop versions CS5 and later provide an astonishing technology that can greatly simplify certain types of retouching. For a lot of edits, Content-Aware Fill is faster and much easier than using a cloning tool.

STEP 1: OPEN THE IMAGE

Open the Stop Sign.jpg image, located in the Chapter 20 section of the companion website (see Figure 20.16). There's some extra junk in this image that you'd like to remove to clean up the composition. The bright bit in the lower-left corner and the bright pole next to the stop sign are both distracting. You could remove these with the Clone Stamp tool, but Content-Aware Fill is going to be a little easier, especially because of the repeating patterns on the wall.

You're going to select the areas that you want to get rid of and then automatically fill those areas with appropriate content.

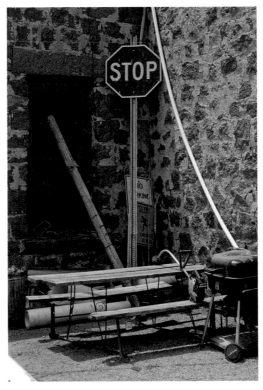

Figure 20.16

You're going to use Content-Aware Fill to remove the white pipe and the bright thing in the lower-left corner.

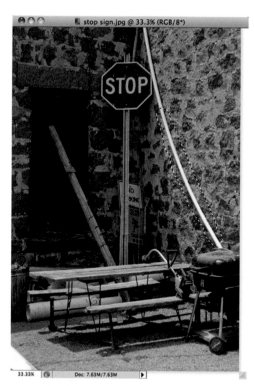

Figure 20.17

Using the Lasso tool, select the lower part of the pipe.

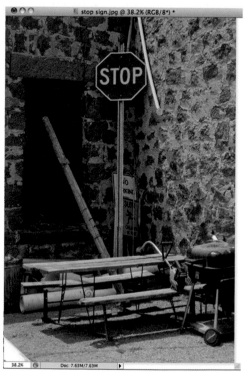

Figure 20.18

After Content-Aware Filling, the lassoed area is filled with wall texture.

STEP 2: LASSO THE PIPE

Select the Lasso tool from the Photoshop toolbox or just press L to select it. Drag a rough circle around the lower part of the pipe (see Figure 20.17).

Before you can use Content-Aware Fill, you have to select the area that you want to fill. We've selected only the lower part of the pipe because Content-Aware Fill often works better on smaller areas.

STEP 3: FILL THE SELECTION

With the pipe selected, you're ready to fill it. Choose Edit > Fill or press Cmd/Ctrl-Delete. The Fill dialog should appear. Change the Use pop-up menu to Content-Aware. Click OK, and the lassoed area should be filled with the appropriate wall texture (see Figure 20.18).

Content Aware Fill analyzes the area around the selection and attempts to concoct appropriate content to fill the selection. As you can see here, it did a great job of creating stone texture that looks natural.

STEP 4: SELECT AND FILL THE OTHER AREAS

Continue to make selections and fill them with Content-Aware. If you find a fill doesn't work, undo it and then select a smaller area and try again. For the little bit where the white pole falls along the stop sign, I used the Rubber Stamp tool. But 95 percent of the correction was performed with Content-Aware Fill (see Figure 20.19).

As you work with Content-Aware Fill, you'll probably be amazed at how good a job it's capable of. It can copy complex textures with amazing accuracy. At other times, like in my example here, you'll probably have to try a few times to get a good fill and possibly augment the job with other retouching tools.

Because it's so easy to use and easy to undo, it's always worth taking an initial stab at retouching with Content-Aware Fill, before trying the more labor-intensive Clone tool.

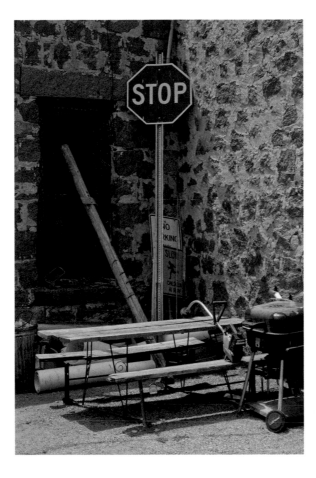

Figure 20.19

The finished image, after lots of Content-Aware Filling.

Cleaning Portraits

No matter how young and fit your portrait subjects may be, there will be times when a little digital makeover is just the thing to turn a decent portrait into an exceptional one. Facial retouching can include everything from removing wrinkles and blemishes to altering shadow details to making facial contours less pronounced. As you've probably already guessed, Photoshop provides excellent tools for this type of cleanup. If you're using a different image editor, it probably has tools similar to the ones described here.

You'll use two tools for the majority of your facial retouchings. The Rubber Stamp (or Clone) tool is good for completely removing features like dark wrinkles, assuming there's enough clear facial tone around the wrinkle to get a good clone. For the rest of your touch-ups, you'll use the Dodge tool (see Figure 20.20).

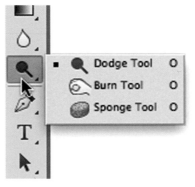

Figure 20.20

The Dodge and Burn tools in Photoshop and Photoshop Elements are essential retouching tools for removing lines and blemishes.

The Dodge and Burn tools let you brush lighter or darker "exposure" into any part of your image. With a few simple dodges, you can usually lighten wrinkles or other fine lines to make them less pronounced, or to completely eliminate them. Dodge can also be used to lighten shadow areas to make contours less extreme (see Figure 20.21).

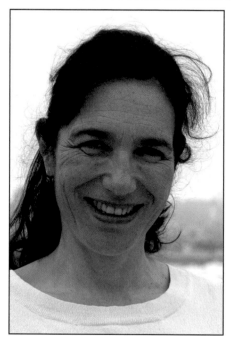 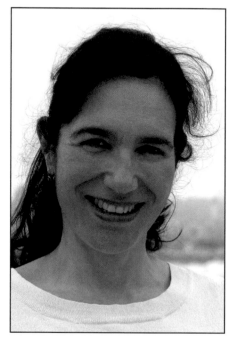

Figure 20.21

Using a combination of the Rubber Stamp and Dodge tools and a separate blur layer, I retouched the image on the left to produce the result on the right.

For the retouching shown in Figure 20.21, blemishes and discolorings were removed with the Dodge tool, as were most faint wrinkles. For larger wrinkles, the Dodge tool was used to lighten the wrinkle, and then the Clone tool was used to paint over the wrinkle with an appropriate skin tone. The Dodge tool was also used to balance color overall. The whites of the eyes were dodged, and the teeth were whitened by using a Hue/Saturation layer. Finally, to selectively soften some skin tones, a copy of the image was created in a second layer and blurred with the Gaussian Blur filter. A Layer Mask was applied to the blurred layer, allowing me to paint blurred texture into some areas, leaving other details (eyes and eyebrows) sharp. The entire process took about 45 minutes.

Nondestructive Dodge and Burn

The downside to dodging and burning is that, like any of Photoshop's painting tools, once you make the stroke, your pixels are altered, and there's no way to change your mind if you decide you need more or less of an effect. As you saw earlier, many effects can be isolated in individual layers, allowing you to paint effects into your image in a nondestructive manner that allows you to re-edit your image later.

Dodging and burning effects are no exception. To create a dodging and burning layer, add a new layer above the layer you want to edit and change the layer's blending mode to Overlay. Painting into the layer with a color that's darker than 50 percent gray darkens the underlying image; painting with colors that are lighter than 50 percent gray will lighten the underlying image.

To remove a wrinkle, select a color that's lighter than 50 percent gray and begin brushing into your Overlay layer. For more control, it's best to lower the opacity of your paintbrush to around 20 or 30 percent, so you can paint in your effects gradually. If you make a mistake, you can simply use the eraser to erase your brushstrokes.

Healing Brush

If you're using a copy of Photoshop or Photoshop Elements that has a Healing Brush tool, you might find that it works very well for correcting certain types of facial blemishes. As you've seen, Lightroom's Spot Correction tool is also effective at removing simple spots and blemishes.

Better Skin Through Plug-ins

If you do a lot of portrait work, then you might want to consider investing in a plug-in designed specifically for improving skin tones. Imagenomic's Portraiture is one such plug-in, and it does an exceptional job of improving skin tones with just a single click (see Figure 20.22). Check out *www.imagenomic.com* for more details.

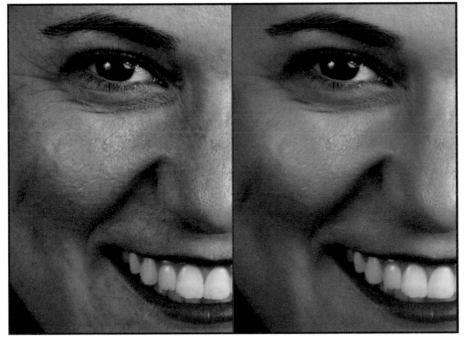

Figure 20.22 Imagenomic's Portraiture makes skin retouching a snap, offering incredible ease of use and a lot of customizability.

Noise

Of all the retouching chores that you'll come across, noise will be the most troublesome artifact to get rid of. Although modern digital cameras are extremely good in their ability to produce images with low noise, many will still generate some noise, particularly in shadow areas and bright skies, and especially when you shoot at higher ISOs.

Noise is produced by any number of components in your camera, ranging from the image sensor to the support circuits to the analog-to-digital converter. Earlier, you learned how image sensors represent light exposure as variations in voltages across the surface of the sensor. Unfortunately, the semiconductors used in your camera can generate electrical signals that are indistinguishable from the signals produced by your camera's sensor. These extra signals can leak into your image in the form of noise.

In Chapter 7, "Program Mode," you saw that there are two types of noise, luminance and chrominance. Luminance is the more attractive of the two. *Chrominance noise* is more troublesome. If you see blue or red dots in an image—and these will be especially prevalent in low-light/high-ISO images—you have some chrominance noise to deal with. Many image sensors, especially CCDs, are more sensitive to red and infrared light than to blue light, so special filters are used to cut certain frequencies of red light to improve the blue response. Unfortunately, because the sensor is weak in its blue perception, the blue channel is often the first thing to be compromised when you start amplifying the sensor signal to increase ISO. Consequently, on many cameras, you'll see pronounced noise in the Blue channel of an image. As such, chrominance noise is sometimes referred to as *Blue channel noise*.

The problem with trying to remove noise from an image is that there's no way to do it without altering your image. Removing luminance noise will tend to soften and smooth fine details, whereas trying to eliminate chrominance noise can alter the colors in your image. Noise reduction also often results in a loss of saturation.

Nevertheless, a slightly softer or less-saturated image is often preferable to an image covered with distracting, ugly noise.

Fortunately, with each new generation of digital camera, noise becomes less and less of a problem, even at high ISOs. Even better, noise reduction software has improved tremendously. Lightroom and Photoshop Camera Raw both have excellent noise reduction tools built in, and if your image editor of choice doesn't have one, you might be able to add noise reduction tools via plug-ins such as Noise Ninja and Neat Image.

Bad On-Screen Noise May Not Transfer to Print

Be careful about evaluating noise on-screen. The only way to truly judge noise is in the final output, be it a print or an electronic image at your final size. So, before you panic about noise, try some sample output in your chosen medium and decide if the noise is truly bad. You may find that what you thought was a terribly noisy image is actually acceptable in your final delivery.

Reducing Noise in Lightroom

Lightroom and Photoshop Camera Raw both provide excellent tools for battling chrominance and luminance noise.

STEP 1: SELECT THE IMAGE

If you haven't imported the sample images for this chapter in Lightroom, you should at least import the Ron Miles.jpg image from the Chapter 20 folder. Once it's imported and selected, switch to the Develop module.

STEP 2: ASSESS THE NOISE

In the Develop module, press the spacebar to zoom in to 100 percent on the image. The luminance noise should be readily apparent, and if you look very closely at some of the highlights on his face, you'll see some faint purple pixels (see Figure 20.23).

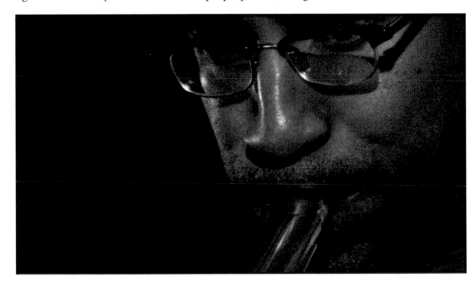

Figure 20.23

This image has some noise issues. Note that the noise might be more pronounced on your screen because some of it will be hidden by the printing process used to make this book. As mentioned earlier, you need to be careful when evaluating noise on-screen, especially at 100 percent. You're now looking at individual pixels. When printed, an individual pixel will hardly be visible, so if you print this image, the noise may not be as bad as it appears here.

STEP 3: LOWER THE NOISE

Scroll down to the Detail toolbox and find the Noise Reduction sliders. You should see two sections, one for luminance noise and one for chrominance noise. Slide the Luminance slider to the right, and you should see the luminance noise fade away. Set the Luminance slider to 50.

STEP 4: RESTORE DETAIL

While the Luminance slider has done a great job of reducing the noise, it's also cost you some detail. Drag the Detail slider to the right, and you should see some detail return to the image, but you might also find the noise coming back. Your goal is to aim for a balance of these two sliders. Noise reduction sometimes results in a reduction of contrast in the image. The Contrast slider lets you put some of that back (see Figure 20.24).

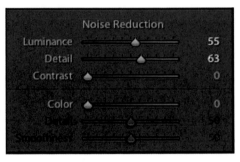

Figure 20.24

Your noise reduction efforts will involve a balance of all of the noise reduction sliders as you try to compromise noise reduction and detail loss.

STEP 5: ELIMINATE CHROMINANCE NOISE

This is very subtle, but watch the highlight on the man's cheek as you drag the Color slider to the right. You should see a slight change in the color on his skin. Some slight purple artifacts are being removed. As with luminance noise, the color noise reduction sliders need to be used in concert to balance noise reduction with detail loss. ◥◀

Vignetting

While vignetting is something you usually try to avoid by investing in good lenses, there are times when an intentional vignette will help you bring more attention to your subject.

For example, consider Figure 20.25, a fairly boring shot of a tree in the middle of nowhere. With a little color adjustment and a strong vignette, the image becomes far more compelling.

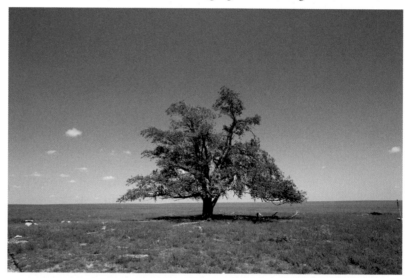

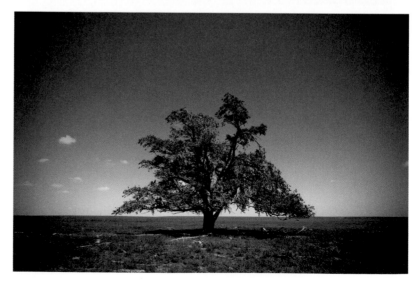

Figure 20.25

A little color and tone adjustment, and a strong vignette turns this otherwise boring shot of a tree into something more compelling.

Vignettes help guide the viewer's eye and bring more attention to the center of your image.

To add a vignette in the Lightroom Develop module, scroll down to the Effects toolbox. In the Post-Crop Vignetting section, slide the Amount slider to the left to darken the corners of the image; slide it to the right to lighten, or burn, the corners. Midpoint, Roundness, and Feather let you control the shape of the vignette, while the Highlights slider lets you control how much the highlights can shine through the vignette (see Figure 20.26).

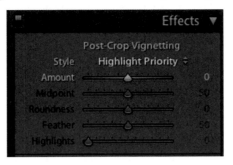

Figure 20.26

You can add vignettes using Lightroom's Effects toolbox.

Correcting Wide Angle Distortion

Earlier, you worked on a picture of a dog, which was shot with a fisheye lens. The fisheye left some fairly serious geometric distortion in the images. Lines that should have been horizontal were curved. If you're using Photoshop CS6 or later, then you have a powerful tool for correcting these types of problems.

Wide Angle Correction

STEP 1: OPEN THE IMAGE
If you have the final dog image that you created earlier, open it now. If you don't have a saved version, then download dog.tif from the Chapter 17 section of the companion website.

STEP 2: ACTIVATE ADAPTIVE WIDE ANGLE
Choose Filter > Adaptive Wide Angle. Photoshop will present the Adaptive Wide Angle dialog box, which gives you a large preview window and a few tools to work with (see Figure 20.27).

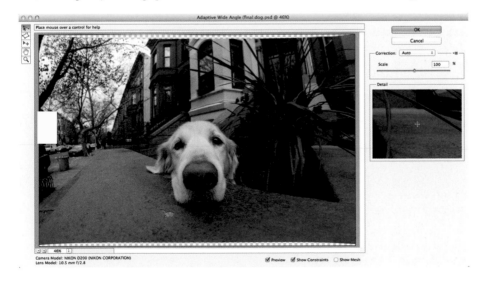

Figure 20.27

The Adaptive Wide Angle controls let you correct the weird distortions caused by the fisheye lens that was used to shoot this image.

STEP 3: CONFIGURE AUTOMATIC CORRECTION

On the right side of the dialog box, change the Correction pop-up menu to Fisheye. This will automatically correct some of the problems in the image. Photoshop reads the lens metadata in the image and tries to set the focal length automatically. If it doesn't say 10.50mm, then move the Focal Length slider until it does.

STEP 4: MAKE A MANUAL CORRECTION

By default, you should already have the Constraint Tool selected. (It's the top one in the toolbar.) Click at the far end of the inside edge of the wall (the side the dog's leaning on) and move your mouse to the near edge (see Figure 20.28). As you move the mouse, you'll see a line being drawn that should precisely match the edge of the wall. Click at the near end, and Photoshop will straighten the line that you just defined.

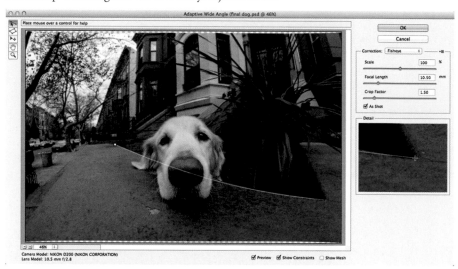

Figure 20.28

This corrects the curvature of the wall.

The image will warp along the edges, but you can crop and fill things later. The important thing is that the edge of the wall is no longer bent.

STEP 5: MAKE A SECOND CORRECTION

Now click to define a line along the outside edge of the wall.

Note that when you create a line, a circle appears around its center. This circle lets you correct for any rotation in the image that might have occurred because of the distortion. The dog's head is a little crooked now. Click on one of the control points where the circle intersects the line you created and drag to rotate the image (see Figure 20.29). When you release the mouse, the image will straighten.

STEP 6: ADD ANOTHER CORRECTION

Finally, add a line along the top of the row of buildings in the background. They're a little curved, so it's worth straightening them out. The image might rotate a little bit when you're done (keep an eye on the dog's eyes and ensure they're roughly level), but you can straighten it back out with the rotation control on the line you just made.

Note that the toolbar contains a second tool that lets you create constraints around polygonal objects. If there's a building or something in your image that's a complete polygon, then you can outline it with this tool to correct it.

Press OK to process the image.

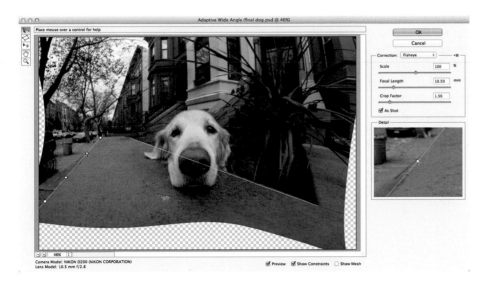

Figure 20.29

The rotation controls on the correction line let you spin the image back to true.

STEP 7: CROP AND FILL TO TASTE

Because of the distortions, your image has a lot of extra space around it, so it needs to be cropped. You also, of course, have the option of using Content Aware Fill to fill in some of the extra space. The wall fills in very nicely with Content Aware Fill, but I found a simple crop was enough to finish the image (see Figure 20.30). ◣◥

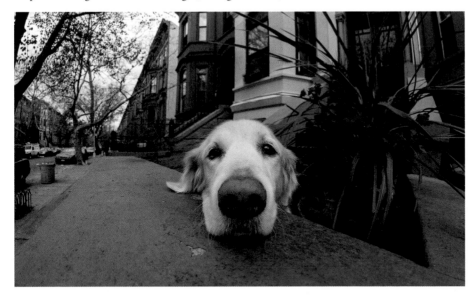

Figure 20.30

With a crop, the image is complete.

The Image Isn't Flat

Note that the single layer in your final dog image doesn't say "Background." This indicates that the image is not actually flattened. If you choose to save as a TIFF file, Photoshop will warn you that working with layers will increase file size. Simply choosing to flatten the image will turn the layer into a normal, anchored background layer.

Where to Go from Here

As mentioned before, Photoshop is a very deep program. There are lots of tools and many ways to achieve the same adjustments or edits. However, for the typical edits that you'll make to most of your images—that is, the type of edits photographers make—then you should do fine with the tools and techniques we've covered here. If you want to create "special effects" type images, then you'll want to dig into more complicated techniques, which are covered in a huge array of readily available Photoshop books.

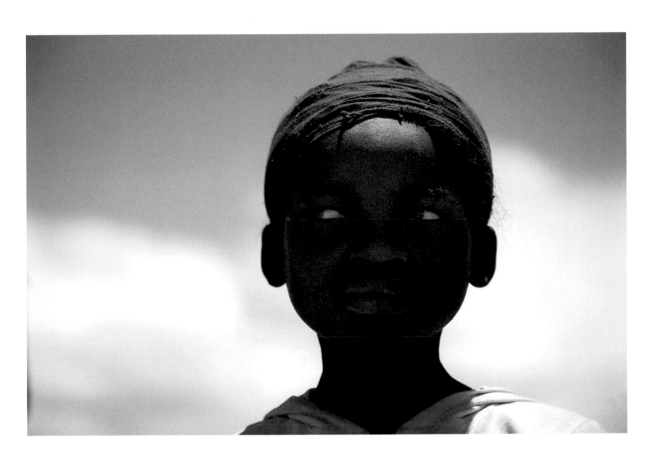

21

PANORAMIC STITCHING AND HDR MERGING

How to Process These Multi-Shot Effects

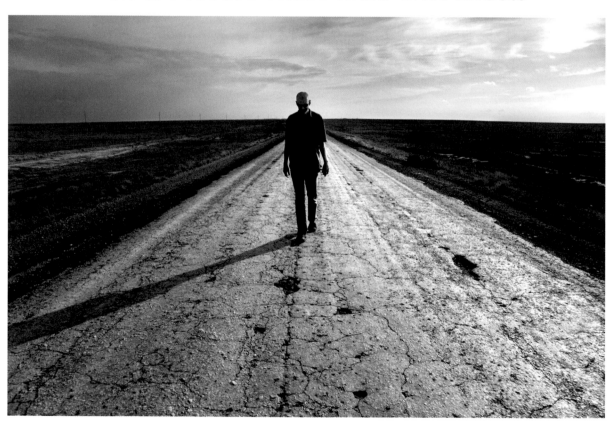

In Chapter 12, "Special Shooting," you learned about two special shooting processes: panoramas and high-dynamic range imaging, or HDR. Panoramic shooting allows you to capture a very wide field of view by shooting a series of overlapping images. HDR shooting enables you to capture a scene with a very high dynamic range by shooting a series of identical compositions, each with a different exposure.

To produce a final image, both of these techniques require you to process your source frames using special software. Photoshop CS6 (and some earlier versions of Photoshop) provides built-in facilities for both panoramic stitching and HDR processing. In addition, there are lots of third-party plug-ins and add-ons that allow you to perform these tasks.

Stitching Panoramas

As you saw in Chapter 12, the process of making a panorama begins when you shoot a series of overlapping images, each with the same exposure. If you've panned, exposed, and overlapped properly, your stitching software can take those images and merge them together into a seamless, wide image.

Every image has a vanishing point, which is a single point that all lines converge on. Panoramic stitching software corrects the perspective differences in each shot so that the resulting image has correct perspective. The images are then blended and combined along their seams to create a single, finished shot (see Figure 21.1).

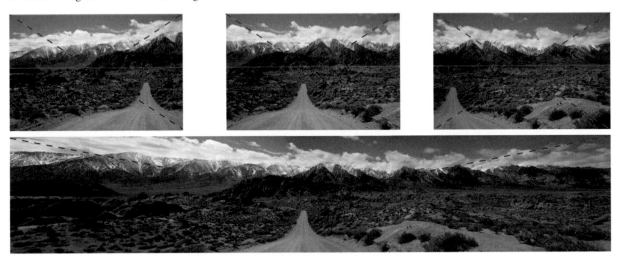

Figure 21.1 Every source image in a panorama has its own vanishing point where all lines in the image recede to this point. During the stitching process, the source images are warped so that the resulting image has a common vanishing point.

Stitching Workflow

Shooting panoramas involves creating a lot of different images. If you normally rename your images on import, you'll want to be very careful to ensure that you maintain the original shooting order; otherwise, it will be very difficult to determine which images go together to create a finished panorama.

Here's how I usually handle panoramas.

◆ After uploading all of the images from a particular shoot into a folder, I work through the folder using my workflow software of choice. Anytime I find a set of images that go together to make a panorama, I group them into a Stack (see Figure 21.2.). Adobe Photoshop Lightroom and Adobe Bridge support stacking.

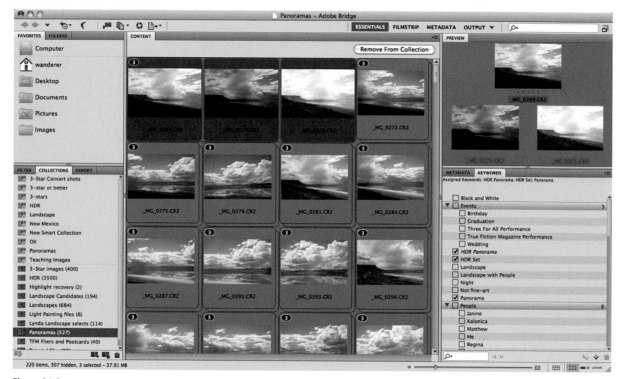

Figure 21.2 You can use Bridge's Stacks feature to keep panoramic source images and final results grouped together. This makes it easier to stay organized.

◆ Next, I add a Panorama keyword to each image, as this makes it easier for me to search for panoramas later.

◆ I then stitch the images together, which I'll cover in the next section.

◆ Finally, I add the finished, stitched image to the top of the relevant stack.

Even if I have a number of panoramic sets from the shoot, this process allows me to keep everything fairly well organized.

Launching a Stitch from Within Lightroom

While Lightroom has no stitching capability of its own, it does have tight integration with Photoshop, which has a built-in stitching facility called *Photomerge*. You can easily launch a panoramic stitch from within Lightroom.

To do so, select the images you want to merge and then choose Photo > Edit In > Merge to Panorama in Photoshop. I'll cover the Photomerge dialog in the next section.

When you save the final stitched image from Photoshop, it will be placed in the same folder as your source images and automatically added to your Lightroom catalog.

Launching a Stitch from Within Bridge

You can also launch a Photomerge stitch from within Bridge:

◆ Select the images you want to stitch. If you've already grouped the images into a stack, open the stack and select all of the images within. If you don't know how to select multiple images, check out the tutorials in Chapter 13, "Workflow."

◆ If you're using Bridge, choose Tools > Photoshop > Photomerge to launch the images into Photoshop's Photomerge feature (see Figure 21.3).

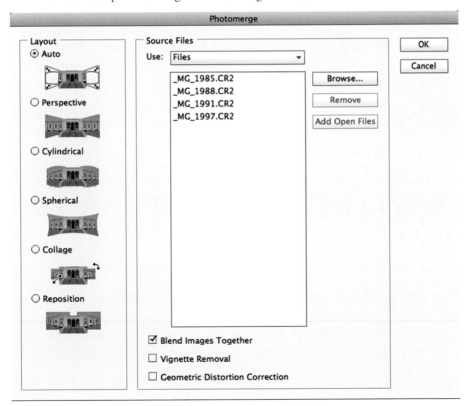

Figure 21.3

Photoshop's Photomerge dialog lets you select images to stitch and choose parameters for stitching. You can load images into Photomerge directly from Bridge.

Launching a Stitch from Within Photoshop

Of course, you can also launch a panoramic stitch from within Photoshop. The easiest way to do this is to first open all of the images you want to stitch, but *only* the images you want to stitch. Make sure that you don't have any other images open.

Choose File > Automate > Photomerge to bring up the Photomerge dialog box.

The Source Files list will be empty. If you click the Add Open Files button in the Photomerge dialog box, then all of your current images will be added to the Source Files list. This is why it is essential that you do *not* have any additional images open.

Alternatively, you can open the Photomerge dialog box and then use the Browse button to add files that you want to stitch.

You can use any Photoshop-compatible file format with the Photomerge feature. After you've selected the files that you want to turn into a panorama, you're ready to configure the rest of Photomerge's options.

Configuring Photomerge in the Layout section of the Photomerge dialog, you'll find six different options that allow you to specify how you want the source images in your panorama overlapped and distorted. As you'll see, there's no one, single approach to panoramic layout that's best for all images. However, the Auto feature almost always does a good job of selecting a layout that will be best for your particular panorama. So you'll usually have the easiest time with your stitching efforts by trying an initial stitch with the Auto layout option. If the result is distorted in a way that you don't like, or will require you to crop out an essential element, then you'll want to consider selecting a different option manually.

Photomerge's Layout options are as follows:

◆ **Auto.** Analyzes your image and tries to automatically choose an appropriate method from one of the following.

◆ **Perspective.** This layout tells Photomerge to choose one of your source images—almost always the center image—and leave it "flat" or undistorted. It will then bend, warp, stretch, and skew the other images and place them alongside the initial image to create a finished layout. What's nice about the Perspective layout is that the first image remains largely undistorted. The disadvantage is that the resulting panorama will probably require a lot of cropping (see Figure 21.4).

◆ **Cylindrical.** This layout maps individual images to the inside of a cylinder, which is then unwrapped. Cylindrical layout greatly reduces the "bow tie" distortion that you'll see with Perspective layout, and it is ideal for extremely wide panoramas.

◆ **Spherical.** This layout tells Photomerge to map source images to the inside of a sphere. This option is best for 360° panoramas, but occasionally offers good results with panoramas that don't cover a full circle.

◆ **Collage.** This layout does just what you might think: images are overlapped, collage style, and are rotated or scaled, if necessary, to create good overlap. However, after layout, the images are not blended together, as with the other layouts, so seams might be visible.

◆ **Reposition.** This layout is like Collage, but images are not scaled or rotated. Photomerge simply overlaps them to the best of its ability. As with Collage, no blending is performed.

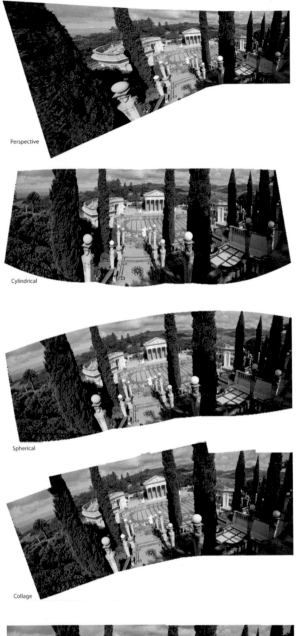

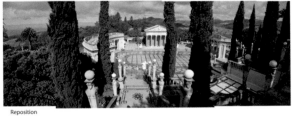

Figure 21.4

Here you can see the effect of different Photomerge layouts on the same set of panoramic source images.

Those last two options allow you to create more traditional "David Hockney" type photo collages. They're great for times when blended stitches aren't working because your exposure was off, so seams are visible. Sure, you won't end up with a seamless, perfect image, but you still might get a very usable result.

Other Photomerge Options

Beneath the Source area of the Photomerge dialog box, you'll find a few additional options.

♦ **Blend Images Together.** This layout uses a number of complex processes to reduce seams and create a more seamless panorama. If you turn this option off, Photomerge will still try to eliminate seams, but will use a less sophisticated algorithm. Turning this option off might be a better choice if you want to manually retouch your seams, something we'll discuss in the next section. For the most part, the only time you'd uncheck this is if you've got difficult source images that aren't blending, and you need to take matters into your own hands.

♦ **Vignette Removal.** This layout does just what it says—removes vignettes from source images before stitching, which can greatly reduce the threat of visible seams.

♦ **Geometric Distortion Correction.** This layout corrects barrel, pincushion, and fisheye distortion. Like Vignette Removal, this can help reduce the visibility of seams, and it is particularly useful when working with wide-angle lenses.

Correcting Stitched Panoramas

When Photomerge is done stitching your source images, a final panoramic document should be open. Take a look at the Layers palette, and you should see a separate layer for each source image, each with a Layer Mask (see Figure 21.5).

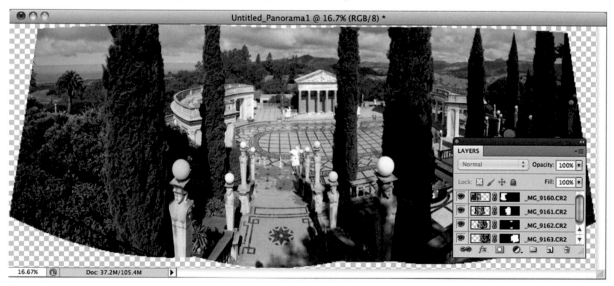

Figure 21.5 Once Photomerge has finished stitching, it will open the final, layered document. Because the document is unflattened, you can manually edit the merging of the different source images.

If you worked through the Layer Mask tutorials earlier, you should have a pretty good idea of what is going on. Photoshop has aligned and stacked all of your source images, and it has created Layer Masks to control which parts of the image are visible and which are masked out to reveal underlying layers.

If the stitch has worked well, then you shouldn't see any seams. But if seams are visible, you can try to minimize them by manually editing the Layer Masks. Use the Brush tools, Smudge and Smear, to move or refine the seams.

Before you spend too much time meticulously hand-correcting seams, try to assess why the seams are visible. Is it because your exposure wasn't even across your frames? Is it because there was vignetting on the edge of a frame? If it was the latter, make sure that Vignette Removal was turned on in the Photomerge dialog box. If it was the former, then you might be able to adjust the exposure in your original source images. If you can make the exposures more equal, then you might get a better stitch.

Cropping and Filling

All panoramas will need to be cropped. There's simply no way to stitch a panorama without creating distortions that result in a nonrectangular final image. Ultimately, you may end up making your Photomerge layout choice based on which method requires the least cropping.

There are no tricks to cropping a panoramic image. Because of their wide field of view, you most likely won't be cropping a panoramic image to a standard frame size, so be sure that your crop tool is not set to perform any constraining of aspect ratio.

Cropping a panorama can be frustrating, depending on how much distortion has occurred in your final panorama. An image that is wildly distorted, such as the Perspective example in Figure 21.4, requires such a dramatic crop that you might lose image details that you like (see Figure 21.6).

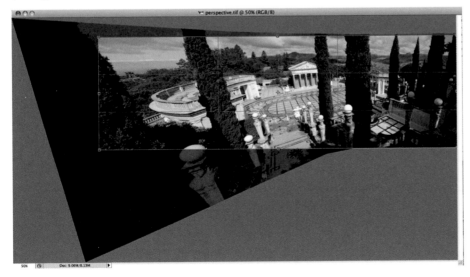

Figure 21.6

Because of the distortion in this image, I have to perform a dramatic crop—one that cuts out a fair amount of the sidewalk, a pillar, and other details.

Obviously, in Figure 21.6, I could switch to a layout that yielded a more rectangular image, but if it's critical that the center of the image remains undistorted, this may not be an option.

Fortunately, in Photoshop CS5 and later, you have another option, Content Aware Fill. While Content Aware Fill can't fill the empty parts of an image like the one in Figure 21.6, it can often do an astonishing job of filling in the corners (see Figure 21.7).

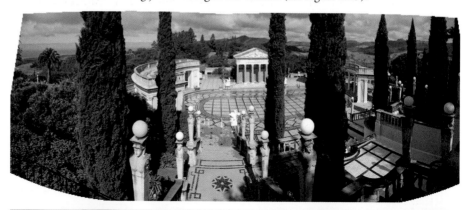

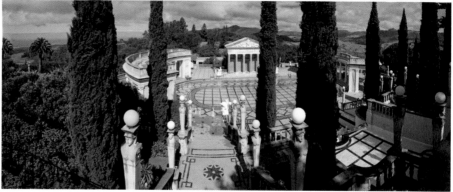

Figure 21.7

The upper image shows my initial crop, which left my image with some empty corners. The lower image shows what Content Aware Fill came up with when I selected the corners and filled them.

Content Aware Fill is great because it's so easy to use. The fixes in Figure 21.7 took under a minute! However, there will be times when Content Aware Fill can't fill the empty spaces in your cropped panorama. Or you might be using an image editor that doesn't have such a feature. For these times, you can often fill empty areas with the Rubber Stamp (Clone) tool. Skies, especially, are often fillable with some creative cloning. When choosing a crop, you'll want to consider how much of an image you can realistically fill and repair.

Retouching

Panoramas often need the same types of retouching that "normal" images do. You might have dust spots, lens flares, and other items that you want to remove. Because you don't know which ones might make it into the final panorama (one might fall on a seam and be hidden, for example), there's no reason to bother retouching your source images. Perform your merge and then retouch the finished panorama.

Similarly, color and tone correction should be performed on your final image. If you exposed your source images properly, then you won't want to alter their exposure until after you've stitched; doing so might create an uneven exposure from one image to another.

Stitching Raw Images

When you pass a raw file to the Photomerge feature, it first processes the raw files and then merges the results. For the conversion, it uses whatever settings are currently stored for the file. If you haven't made any adjustments to the file, then it uses the standard, stock conversion—the same one you'd see if you opened the image in Camera Raw.

So, if you want to perform highlight recovery or white balance adjustments, you need to do those to the original source images, before you merge. Remember, after you merge, you'll no longer be dealing with a raw file, so you will be unable to perform these edits.

To ensure that you alter each image identically:

◆ Open the source raw files in Camera Raw.

◆ Click the Select All button.

◆ Click the Synchronize button to bring up the Synchronize dialog box.

◆ Click OK to accept the default settings. Now any adjustments will be made to all the images.

When you're finished, you can either open the images and activate Photomerge from within Photoshop or click Done to close the files; then launch Photomerge. In either case, your settings will be stored in sidecar XMP files. Photomerge will process the images according to the settings you just defined.

Alternately, in Lightroom, you can make corrections to the first image and then copy and paste them to the rest of the images in your set.

Again, if you exposed the images properly when you shot, you shouldn't need to do too much to the exposure. Make your white balance adjustments and do enough highlight recovery to get the overexposed bits back to where they should be.

Speeding Up Stitching

Panoramic stitching is a computationally intensive process, and it can sometimes take awhile. However, there are some things you can do to speed up the process. Obviously, buying a faster computer will speed up all of your Photoshop operations, as will adding more RAM.

But considering image size can also make a difference. If you're shooting 20 megapixel images and then stitching them together, you're possibly ending up with huge final panoramas— panoramas that are much bigger than you'll ever actually print. So you can speed up your stitching operation by first resizing your images. Creating copies at 50 percent of the original size will give you source files that will merge much more quickly than giant originals, yet they'll still yield a panoramic result with plenty of size.

If you're working with raw files, open the original files in Camera Raw and click the Workflow Options link at the bottom of the Camera Raw dialog box. Here, you can specify a smaller-than-original size. Also, if you normally set Camera Raw to output 16-bit files, you can consider switching Depth to 8-bit. If you're not planning on performing a lot of edits on the final panorama, then you may not need the extra bit depth. After configuring these options, click Done to save them, and you'll be ready to stitch.

Stitching Vertical Panoramas

As you saw in Figure 12.23, panoramic shooting is not just for shooting really wide fields of view. You can also use the technique for shooting really tall things. You'll tilt up and down while shooting, rather than panning left and right.

When it comes time to stitch these images, first rotate them 90° and then pass the rotated results to Photomerge. Your resulting panorama will be lying on its side, but you can easily rotate it back to vertical.

Mobile Panoramic Stitching

Both the iPhone and many Android phones offer a "real-time" Panorama mode that lets you shoot panoramas simply by panning the camera in an arc. There's no stitching involved in this process, the phone simply builds the panorama on the fly. These modes require you to shoot in portrait orientation, though, which doesn't always yield the best coverage of your scene.

You can use a regular stitching workflow by taking overlapping images with your phone, just as you would with a normal camera. For the actual stitching, you can move the images into your favorite desktop stitching software or stitch them on the phone itself. There are a number of panoramic stitching apps available for both platforms.

Merging High-Dynamic Range (HDR) Images

In Chapter 12, you learned how you can shoot the same image multiple times, with varying exposures, to capture an image with much more dynamic range than what your camera can capture in a single shot. Of course, as with panoramas, shooting these frames is simply the first part of the process. When you get home, you need to process them into a finished HDR shot (see Figure 21.8).

Figure 21.8

This image was merged from three identical shots, each captured with a separate exposure. This is an example of the type of work you can get from an HDR process.

Photoshop includes a built-in HDR merging feature called *HDR Pro*. It can take care of aligning your source images, to ensure they're registered properly, and then will build them into a single, finished HDR image.

HDR shooting offers some of the same organizational challenges as panoramic shooting, so you might want to employ some of the same organizational strategies discussed earlier in the panorama section. Make sure your images stay sequentially named and consider stacking HDR sets.

What HDR Merging Does

As mentioned in Chapter 12, there's no actual way to expand the dynamic range of a monitor or a piece of paper. But, if you've shot multiple frames with different exposures, you can use HDR merging software to compress the wide dynamic range captured by your multiple exposures to fit into the limited dynamic range of your chosen output media.

It does this through a process called *tone mapping*. Super bright tones are dulled to the level of the brightest tone that your piece of paper, or monitor, can display. Similarly, super dark tones might be brightened to reveal more detail than just pure black shadows. In the midtones, lots of subtle variations might be made, as dark and light shades are remapped to different tonal values to bring out more details.

You've already seen how brightening an image can reveal more details in shadow areas or how darkening an image can reveal more highlight detail. This is what happens with tone mapping, but it happens at tiny, localized amounts that vary throughout your image. What's more, because you start with multiple images exposed in different ways, the tone mapping process doesn't have to rely on brightening or darkening existing tones. Instead, when the tone mapping algorithm needs a brighter tone, it can go to the image with a brighter exposure and copy that tone from there.

You've seen how brightening a dark image can often make it noisier. Because tone mapping routines can pull brighter tones from another image, rather than having to brighten dark tones and risk exaggerating noise, HDR images are often free of noise. However, they sometimes have their own set of troublesome artifacts.

Launching HDR Merge from Lightroom

Lightroom has no HDR merging features of its own, but you can launch a Photoshop HDR merge from within Lightroom.

◆ Select the images that you want to merge.

◆ Choose Photo > Edit In > Merge to HDR Pro in Photoshop.

Next, you'll configure the HDR Pro dialog box. When you save your final image, it will automatically be placed in the same folder as your source images and will be added to your Lightroom catalog. Stacking the result with the original is an easy way to stay organized.

Launching HDR Merge from Bridge

As with panoramic stitching, you can easily launch into an HDR merge process by selecting the images you want to merge in Bridge and then activating Photoshop's HDR feature.

To start an HDR merge in Bridge:

◆ Select the images that you want to merge. If you don't know how to select multiple images, check out the tutorials in Chapter 13. If you've already grouped the images into a stack, open the stack and select all of the images within.

◆ Choose Tools > Photoshop > Merge to HDR Pro.

Next, you'll configure the HDR Pro dialog box.

Launching HDR Merge from Photoshop

To start an HDR merge from within Photoshop:

◆ Choose File > Automate > Merge to HDR Pro.

◆ The Merge to HDR Pro dialog box will open. This simple box lets you select the files that you want to merge.

◆ Add files. If your source files are already open in Photoshop—and they're the only files that are open—then you can simply click the Add Open Files button to add those images to the merge. Alternately, you can select individual files or a folder full of files.

◆ Click OK when you've selected your merge files.

Now the actual merge will begin.

Configuring Merge to HDR Pro

After you've selected the files you want to merge, either from Bridge or from the initial Merge to HDR dialog box, the actual merge will begin. Photoshop will open your source images, copy them each into their own layer in a single document, and then align the layers. Finally, it will present the Merge to HDR Pro dialog box (see Figure 21.9).

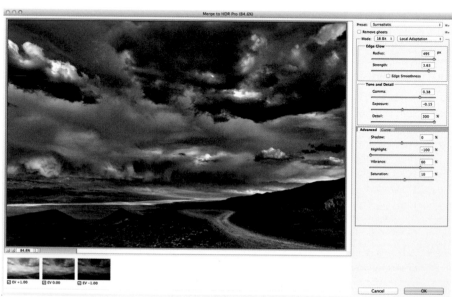

Figure 21.9

Photoshop's Merge to HDR Pro dialog box gives you a fairly thorough set of controls for configuring your HDR merges.

The large preview display can be zoomed and panned, just like the previews in most Photoshop dialog boxes. Beneath the preview display, you'll see a thumbnail strip of source images. You can turn these images on and off to expand or limit the dynamic range in the image. In general, you probably won't find a huge effect from deactivating images.

At first, the preview image may look a little flat or unimpressive—not the HDR extravaganza that you were hoping for. Don't give up; different images may need radically different settings to pull correct detail into every part of the tonal range.

At the top of the HDR Merge Pro window is a Presets pop-up menu. Working through the presets is a great way to zero in on the type of look that you might want. If a preset doesn't get your image exactly the way you want it, it might still be a good starting point. After you've chosen a preset, you can refine it using Merge to HDR Pro's other controls.

◆ **Remove Ghosts.** One of the tricky parts about HDR shooting is that you have to take multiple frames to generate source material. If something in your image moves between frames—a walking person, a blowing tree, and so on—then this can create trouble when it comes time to merge. Since there are multiple copies of the moving object, in different places in each picture, strange ghosting affects can appear. Remove Ghosts does a very good job of removing these artifacts.

◆ **Mode.** You can choose the bit-depth of the final HDR image—8, 16, or 32. Unless you have a specialized application, such as video compositing or 3D modeling, there's no need to ever choose 32 bit. In fact, your monitor can't display the full dynamic range of a 32-bit image. You'll find that 16 bit is the best way to go, as you'll be able to make adjustments without concern for certain types of artifacting, and you can always convert to 8 bit later.

◆ **Local Adaptation.** Next to the Mode menu is a pop-up menu that defaults to Local Adaptation. If you open this up, you'll see some other HDR conversion algorithms, which each bring up their own set of controls. These are older methods that rarely yield good results and are difficult to control, so you'll probably never need to change this setting.

◆ **Edge Glow.** These controls are somewhat akin to sharpening. They exaggerate edges by putting slight halos of tone around them. Fortunately, they're subtle tools, so while they can add a nice level of detail to your image, you usually don't have to worry about them introducing ugly artifacts.

◆ **Tone and Detail.** These tonal controls should already be familiar to you, as we've worked with similar controls in other places in Photoshop. The advantage of these adjustments is that they have such a large amount of source data to work with—the combined dynamic range of your multiple exposures. Note that, unlike other Photoshop controls, these sliders don't have a live update. To see their effects, you have to let go of the mouse. This is simply because Photoshop has to do so much calculation to render a change to one of these sliders. In general, it's better to do as much editing as you can with these sliders before moving on to Photoshop. Because of the large pool of data that the HDR Merge feature has to work with, you can get cleaner adjustments than what you might get in Photoshop.

◆ **Advanced and Curve.** The Advanced tab gives you Shadow, Highlight, Vibrance, and Color sliders, while the Curve tab provides a standard tone curve. Note that the curve in the Merge to HDR dialog box is very "fine." Even a slight adjustment can yield big results.

When you're done adjusting, click the OK button, and Photoshop will process your final image and open it in a new window. Your original source images will no longer be open, and the final image will be flattened. At this point, your image has not been saved. From here, you can perform additional adjustments if you couldn't get things precisely how you wanted them using the Merge to HDR Pro controls.

Other HDR Tools

Photoshop is not the only program that offers HDR merging. Stand-alone HDR merging packages offer more features and sometimes a finer degree of control. Perhaps the most popular of these is HDRsoft's Photomatix. HDR Efex Pro, part of the Google Nik Collection is also a great option. If you're serious about HDR imagery, then you'll want to look closely at these packages. Photoshop's HDR Merge is capable but limited in its controls and effects.

Aesthetic Considerations

High Dynamic Range Imaging is a fantastic tool, and one of the great photo breakthroughs of the last few years. However, as with any tool or effect, it needs to be used thoughtfully. A little HDR can go a long way, and it's not hard to turn an otherwise nice image into a garish monstrosity.

Traditionally, the photographic vocabulary is built from light and shadow, and we've explored this idea in some detail in these pages. Knowing when to let an area plunge into shadow or when to overexpose a highlight—these are all parts of your imaging vocabulary, and they are essential skills for creating images that lead the viewer's eye through your composition.

One of the great pitfalls about HDR images is that everything in them can be perfectly exposed and easily visible. While you might think "Great, I want everything in my image to be easily visible," the fact is that's not always true. When everything is equally visible, nothing stands out, and images can look dull and flat (see Figure 21.10).

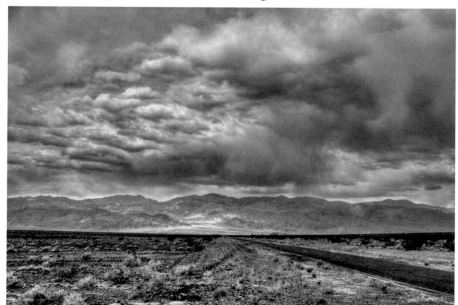

Figure 21.10

While this image has some dramatic textures in it, overall it's very flat. Your eye doesn't quite know how to make its way through the scene. Compare this to the image in Figure 21.8, which has similar subject matter, but isn't so flat and evenly exposed.

Early HDR merging programs were, well, early. It was a new technology, and the processing techniques weren't as sophisticated and refined as they are now. Consequently, early HDR images had a very particular look, which is now known as "that HDR look" (see Figure 21.11). Unfortunately "that HDR look" has become something of an aesthetic. People intentionally aim for the effect not, I think, because it looks good, but because "that's what HDR is supposed to look like."

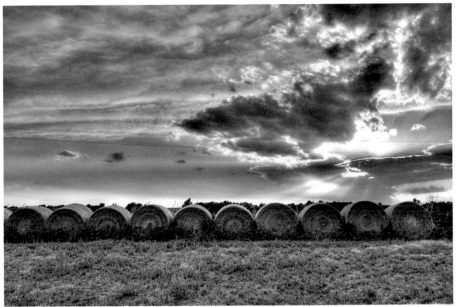

Figure 21.11

While this image may look like a typical HDR shot, I can't recommend that you aim for this effect. Garish and overwrought, it's an image that says "HDR!" more than it says anything else.

Here's a tip for applying any type of effect, be it HDR, a Photoshop filter, a dramatic color or tone adjustment, retouching, or whatever. If the effect you apply upstages the content of your image, then it's not a well-applied effect. In other words, if people look at your image and say, "Wow, look at that HDR" rather than "Wow, look at that scene/whatever," then you have not created a successful image. A good edit is seamless, subtle, and serves to help deliver impact, not to be impactful itself.

Because the HDR process has such a distinctive look and can easily wreck your image, it's important to keep that concept in mind when performing your HDR merges.

HDR Panoramas

There's no reason you can't combine both of the techniques shown in this chapter to create HDR panoramic shots. The process is pretty simple, as long as you keep track of what you're doing along the way.

To shoot your HDR panorama, plan out your pan ahead of time, just as you would with a regular panorama, but when you shoot your first frame, shoot a bracketed set, just as you would with a regular HDR shot. Then pan your camera and shoot your next bracketed set, and so on.

The trickiest thing about HDR panoramas is to stay organized during postproduction. Collect all of your source images and group them into sets for HDR processing. Perform an HDR merge on each individual set, being careful to use precisely the same settings for each merge. Save each merged image as a TIFF or Photoshop document.

Once all your merging is done, use your panoramic stitching software of choice to merge the HDR merges into a single panorama, as shown in Figure 21.12.

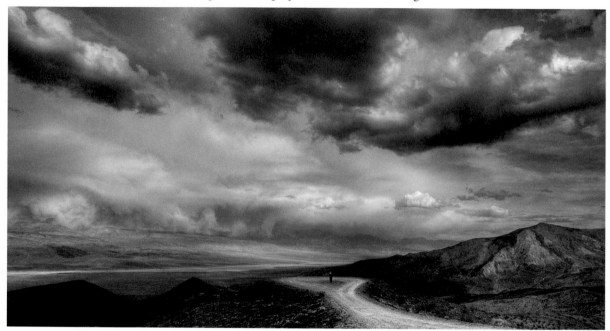

Figure 21.12 This panorama is composed of three different HDR sets. I merged the HDR files, stitched the output into a final panorama, and then adjusted and edited that panorama in Photoshop.

Mobile HDR

There are two approaches to HDR on SmartPhones. The first is a traditional "shoot and merge later" approach. With these types of apps, you shoot and merge images in separate steps, just like you do with a normal camera and computer.

Other apps take care of the entire process for you, shooting and merging with a single button press. There's no exact science to HDR merging and different apps yield very different results. For example, the built-in HDR merging on Apple's iPhone is not very good, whereas the third-party app ProHDR yields excellent results and provides a fine level of control. You might have to try multiple apps before you find a solution that you like.

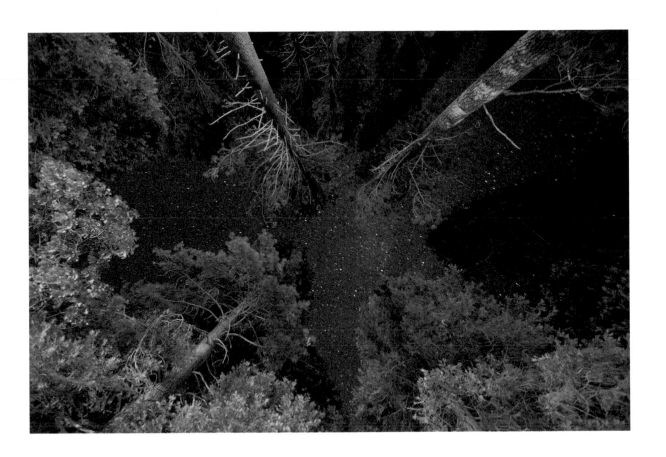

22

OUTPUT

Taking Your Images to Print or Electronic Output

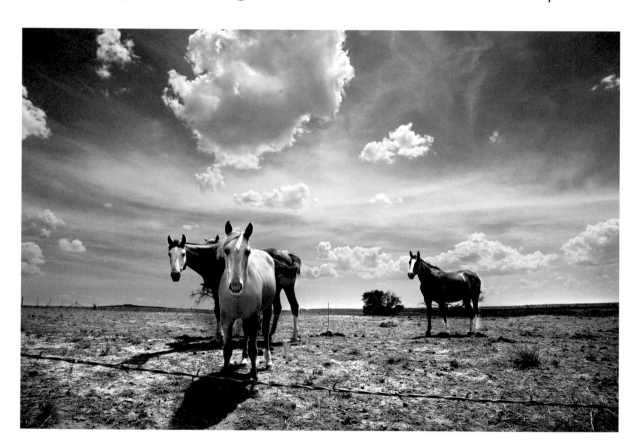

You can perform a lot of tweaking, correcting, adjusting, and editing of your images, but none of it does any good if you can't get your results out into the world for other people to see. In general, output falls into two categories: printed output and electronic output. Printed output is just what it sounds like: putting your images onto some kind of paper. Electronic output can include posting images to the Web, emailing, delivering to a client, via physical media, or sending to a photo printing service.

Earlier, output was listed as the last step in your workflow. Obviously, you have to have your image adjusted and edited to your liking before you worry about letting it loose in the world. However, like editing, your output process has its own workflow considerations. You'll need to get your image sized appropriately, possibly sharpened, and then output according to your specific delivery needs. Finally, you'll probably want to save your new resized, sharpened, ready-for-output version so you can output it again later. Along the way, you'll want to be sure to preserve a copy of your original full-resolution version in case you ever need to make changes.

In Photoshop (and many other image editors), you'll need to perform these steps in the order just described. You'll resize first because resizing can affect sharpness. Only after your image is your desired output size do you need to consider additional sharpening actions.

If you're using Lightroom or iPhoto, you won't necessarily need to perform separate resizing steps. These programs handle resizing on their own when you choose an output method. However, Lightroom *does* provide sharpening that performs the same types of tricks we'll discuss here.

One advantage to a nondestructive editor like Lightroom is that its resizing and sharpening operations are also nondestructive, so you can always undo or change them later.

We're going to look at these operations in the typical order you'll perform them.

Resizing

Your camera probably captures far more pixels than you need for typical output. If you're exporting for the Web or email, or printing out a 4″ × 6″ print, you'll need to reduce the pixel count of your image (unless you have a very old camera, or have configured your camera to shoot at a low pixel count). If your camera yields images with a very high pixel count—8 megapixels or higher—you might even need to resize when printing out to 8″ × 10.″ Similarly, if you're delivering images to a client for use in a publication, they may have specific size and resolution requirements.

If you're printing at very, very large sizes, you might need to enlarge your image. In either case, understanding the nature of image sizing is an important first step in your output workflow.

Resolution

Although your camera may capture millions of pixels, it doesn't necessarily create files that are configured with a resolution that is appropriate for your intended output. In imaging terms, resolution is simply the measure of how many pixels fit into a given space. For example, if your image has a resolution of 72 pixels per inch (ppi), the pixels in the image are sized and spaced so that 72 of them lined up alongside each other cover a distance of one inch.

Resolution is a term that is usually misused. People speak of a camera having a "6-megapixel resolution," but a camera doesn't actually *have* a specific resolution, unless you want to talk about the pixel density on the camera's sensor itself. A camera produces a certain number of pixels—we call this *pixel dimensions* or *pixel count*. How you choose to space those pixels is up to you, and we refer to that amount as *resolution*.

The resolution of an image file is simply a tag that is stored in the header information of the file. You can create two copies of the same image file and set one to 72 ppi and the other to 300 ppi, but the size of the file *will not change*! Both files will contain the same number of pixels; they will simply be tagged so that the pixels are spaced closer together or farther apart.

Different programs will choose to use this resolution setting or not. For example, a presentation program like Microsoft PowerPoint or Apple Keynote doesn't care about resolution, so it ignores the setting. These programs are only concerned with pixel dimensions, and they usually display one image pixel per screen pixel (unless you shrink the image within the application, so you can fit more image area on-screen). The average computer screen has a resolution somewhere between 72 and 96 ppi, so many digital cameras output files at 72 pixels per inch. At 72 ppi, an image from a four- or five-megapixel camera will have an area of several square feet. That is, if you line up those four or five million pixels so that 72 of them take up one inch, then your image will end up being several feet long.

When viewing on-screen in your image editor, this huge size isn't a problem because the computer can zoom in and out of the image to fit it onto your screen. For printing, though, this is far too large an area to fit on a typical printer, and 72 ppi is too low a resolution to yield good quality.

If your goal is to post the image to a website, then resolution is completely irrelevant—the only thing you care about is pixel count. A monitor has a fixed resolution. That is, the number of pixels that cover one inch is always the same. So the only thing you need to concern yourself with is how many total pixels there are.

PPI Versus DPI

Pixels (short for *picture elements*) are the colored dots that appear on your computer screen. It's very important to understand that, when speaking of printing from your computer, there is a difference between the pixels on your screen—which are measured in pixels per inch—and the dots of ink your printer creates, which are measured in dots per inch. We'll be discussing this in more detail later. For now, take note that you'll be measuring your images in pixels per inch or ppi.

When you resize an image, you will have to decide whether you want to change the number of pixels in the image (to change its pixel dimensions), and whether you want to change the resolution setting of the file.

How to Resize

Most image editing applications let you resize an image in two ways: by changing how closely the pixels are spaced or by changing the total number of pixels. In other words, by changing the resolution or by changing the pixel count. When you change resolution, the overall pixel count doesn't change. When you change the pixel count, you'll either have to throw out some original pixels or make up some additional ones.

Let's say that you have a 10-megapixel digital camera that outputs an image with dimensions of 3648 × 2736 pixels and a resolution of 72 ppi. That is, if you line up 72 of your image's pixels side by side, you will cover one inch of space. At this resolution, 3648 × 2736 pixels will take up 72″ × 38″. Obviously, this is too big to fit on a piece of office paper.

If you want to print this image on an 8″ × 10″ piece of paper, while preserving its original resolution, you could tell your computer to throw out enough pixels so it only has 8″ × 10″ worth of pixels at 72 ppi. It would then discard every third pixel or so, to reduce the pixel dimensions of the image from 2736 × 3648 pixels to 576 × 720 pixels (see Figure 22.1). This process of changing the amount of data in the image is called *resampling* (or, more specifically, *downsampling*), because you are taking a sample of pixels from your original image to create a new, smaller image.

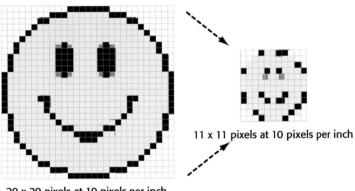

11 x 11 pixels at 10 pixels per inch

29 x 29 pixels at 10 pixels per inch

Figure 22.1

To resize an image down to a smaller size with the same resolution, you have to throw out some pixels (or resample) to fit your image into the smaller size.

The problem is that 72 ppi is too low a resolution to get a good print. After you've spent all that money for all those millions of pixels, the last thing you want to do is to throw out a bunch of them. Rather than resampling your image from 20″ × 30″ down to 8″ × 10″, it's better to change the resolution of your image so the dots are closer together, allowing you to cram more of them onto a page.

Imagine the same 72″ × 38″ image printed on a sheet of rubber graph paper. If you wanted to shrink this image to 8″ × 10″, you could simply squeeze down the sheet of paper. You would not throw out any pixels, but now your pixels would be much smaller and more of them would fit into the same space. That is, the resolution of your image—the number of pixels per inch—would have increased. This is what happens when you resize your image without resampling (see Figure 22.2).

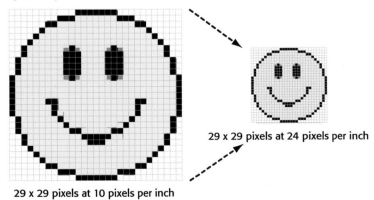

29 x 29 pixels at 24 pixels per inch

29 x 29 pixels at 10 pixels per inch

Figure 22.2

If you don't resample an image when you resize, all its pixels are kept, but they're squeezed closer together, resulting in a smaller, higher-resolution image composed of smaller pixels.

Resampling can also be used to scale up images, but just as downsampling requires your computer to throw away data, upsampling requires your computer to make up data.

For example, if you have an image that is 4" × 6" at 200 ppi, and you want to enlarge it to 8" × 10" at 200 ppi, you'll need to resample it upward, which will force the computer to generate new pixels. This process is called *interpolation*, and most applications offer a variety of interpolation techniques. Photoshop, for example, offers five interpolation methods: nearest neighbor, bilinear, bicubic, bicubic smoother, and bicubic sharper. When sampling up, it's best to use bicubic smoother, while bicubic sharper is best for sampling down. If your image editor doesn't offer these choices, bicubic is fine. Also, different vendors have their own implementation of bicubic resampling, so even if your image editor of choice doesn't offer separate bicubic sharper and bicubic smoother, it might have a bicubic algorithm that has this functionality built in.

If you have a 4" × 6" image with a resolution of 200 dpi and you scale it up to 8″ × 10″ *without* resampling, you're effectively stretching the image. Its pixels get larger, and fewer of them fit into the same space—that is, the resolution goes down as the image gets larger. This is what happens when you resize up without resampling.

Most of the time, when you scale up, you'll want to resize without resampling to prevent the computer from making up new data. However, a printer requires a certain number of pixels to be able to make a sharp print at a given size. If your camera did not produce a big enough image to start with, you might not be able to achieve the size you want with the resolution you need unless you resample.

 ## Understanding Resolution

In addition to providing controls for resizing your images, Photoshop's Image Size dialog box provides a great tool for understanding the relationship between pixel dimensions, resolution, and image size. In this tutorial, you're going to take a quick look at this feature, and hopefully arrive at a better understanding of resolution, size, and resampling.

Resizing in Lightroom

There are no size and resolution controls in Lightroom. Instead, you specify pixel dimensions and resolution when you export an image.

STEP 1: OPEN THE IMAGE
In Photoshop, open the flower.jpg image, located in the Chapter 22 section of the companion website, *www.completedigital photography.com/CDP8.*

Note: the picture on the website is too small, so it needs to be upsampled to match the dimensions in the dialog boxes in this tutorial.

STEP 2: OPEN THE IMAGE SIZE DIALOG BOX
From the Image menu, select Image Size (or Image > Resize > Image Size if you're using Elements). See Figure 22.3. For the purpose of this step, make sure the Resample Image checkbox is unchecked. Take a moment to familiarize yourself with the contents of this dialog box. In the Pixel Dimensions section, you can see the actual pixel dimensions of the image—in

this case, 3900 × 2600—and the total size of the image, 29MB. Note that right now, these pixel values are not editable.

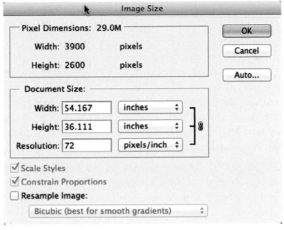

Figure 22.3

The Photoshop Image Size dialog box shows the actual pixel dimensions of an image and the print size at the current resolution.

The Document Size section of the dialog box shows the resolution of the image in pixels per inch and the resulting print size in inches.

STEP 3: RESIZE THE IMAGE WITHOUT RESAMPLING

Notice that width, height, and resolution are linked by a thick, black line. This indicates that you cannot change one of these values without changing the others. For example, if you enter 10 in the Width field, Photoshop will automatically calculate a new height of 6.667" at 390 pixels per inch (see Figure 22.4).

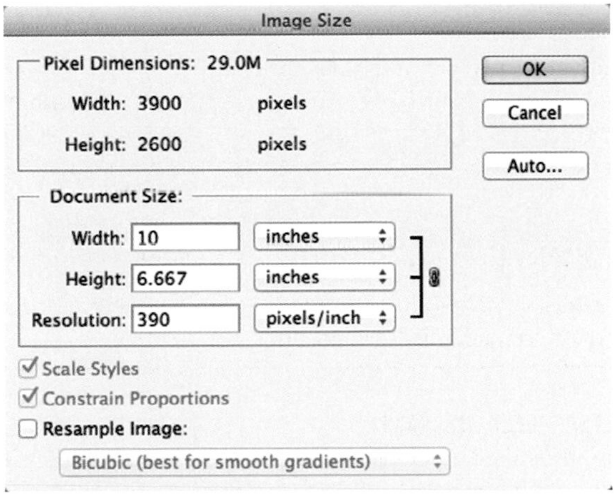

Figure 22.4

After entering 10 in the Width field, Photoshop automatically calculates a new height and resolution, as indicated by the linking bars next to the pop-up menus.

Photoshop has automatically adjusted the height to preserve the aspect ratio of the image and has calculated a new, higher resolution. Because Resample Image is *not* checked, Photoshop is not allowed to add or remove any data, so the only way it can fit the image into your requested size is to raise the resolution—that is, cram the pixels closer together.

When Resample Image is unchecked—when Photoshop is not allowed to add or remove data—it is as if your image is on a giant rubber sheet that can be stretched and compressed. As it gets compressed, resolution goes up because the pixels get pushed closer together. As it stretches, resolution goes down because the pixels get pulled farther apart.

STEP 4: RESIZE WITH RESAMPLING

As you'll learn later, the optimum image resolution for printing on many ink-jet printers is 240 pixels per inch. Enter 240 into the Resolution field. At that resolution, Photoshop calculates an image size of 16.25" × 10.83" for your image. Or maybe you want to print the image at 3" × 5". Enter 5 into the width field and press Tab. Photoshop calculates a new height of 3.3" and a resolution of 780.

This resolution is too high for your printer, but if you enter 240 in the Resolution field, your print size will change back to 16.25 by 10.83. This image simply has too much data to print 3" × 5" at 240 pixels per inch.

Click the Resample Image checkbox. Note that the Width and Height fields in the Pixel Dimensions area are now editable. With Resample Image checked, it is now possible to change the number of pixels in the image. Note, too, that Resolution is no longer linked to Width and Height. You're now allowed to change the resolution independently of the width and height, because it is now possible for Photoshop to throw out data if it needs to.

With your Document Size width still at 5" × 3.3", change your resolution to 240 (see Figure 22.5).

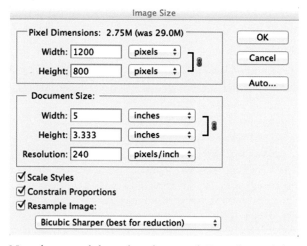

Figure 22.5

With the Resample Image checkbox selected, resolution is no longer tied to print size because Photoshop is free to add or remove pixels. This lets you change resolution independently of print size.

Note that several things have happened. First, the pixel dimensions dropped to 1200 × 800. Your file has gone from 29MB to 2.75MB. More importantly, your print size did not change. You now have the width, height, and resolution you want.

Note, too, that you changed the Resample Image pop-up menu to Bicubic Sharper, since this is the best mode to use when resampling down.

When using the Image Size dialog box, pay attention to which fields are editable and which are linked. This will give you a better understanding of how pixel dimensions, print size, and resolution are all interrelated. ◢◣

Printing with More Pixels Than You Need

If the optimum resolution for your printer is 240, what happens if your document has a higher resolution at your target print size? For the most part, nothing, in terms of image quality. But your document will be larger than it needs to be, and might take longer to print. In addition, the printer will downsample it to the pixel count that it wants. This could end up altering the effectiveness of any sharpening you've applied. In general, it's just easier to work with an image that's been scaled properly for your target size. As long as you don't overwrite your original image, you can always return to your original, full-pixel-count version.

Scaling Styles

In Photoshop, Styles are special predefined image editing effects that add drop shadows, emboss-ing, and other effects to a graphic element. Styles are targeted more toward graphic designers than photographers, so we haven't looked at them in this book. If you check the Scale Styles checkbox in the Image Size dialog box, then any styles that you've used will get scaled properly. For our uses, it won't matter if this box is checked or not.

When Should You Resample?

You should resample your image any time you have an image with more pixel data than you need for your intended output (downsampling) or not enough pixel data for your intended output (upsampling).

Downsampling

If you're outputting for the Web or email, you will definitely have to resample, unless you shot your images at a small size (640 × 480, for example). Similarly, if you're delivering elec-tronic files for print and your camera produces more pixel data than your printer needs, you'll need to downsample. If you're printing to your own desktop printer, you might also have to downsample if your image has more pixels than you need for your desired print size. If you're preparing images for use in a video, or for a DVD menu, or another electronic application, you'll almost certainly need to downsample.

Downsampling your image data is a fairly pain-free process. In fact, downsampling tends to improve sharpness and contrast in your image.

The Photoshop bicubic sharper interpolation algorithm does a very good job of downsam-pling. If you're using an earlier version of Photoshop, then the regular Bicubic method is also a good choice.

Upsampling

As you learned earlier, many digital cameras use interpolation to increase the resolution of their images. As explained, these interpolation schemes often degrade the quality of an image by introducing artifacts. Simply put, calculating new image data is a tricky, difficult thing to do. When it's done poorly, aliasing artifacts, loss of sharpness, and other image problems can appear. The same holds true when upsampling an image using an image editor.

The most basic rule of thumb for upsampling is that you want to do as little as possible. So you'll want to think very carefully about the precise print size and resolution you need, and upsample to exactly those pixel dimensions. Any more, and you'll run the risk of increased artifacts.

We'll discuss print size and resolution choice in the "Printing" section, later in this chapter.

As with downsampling, in more recent versions of Photoshop, you have several different algorithm choices you can use when upsampling. While bicubic interpolation can work very well, bicubic smoother will usually yield results with fewer artifacts.

When resampling with bicubic interpolation, it's best not to make any single resizing step greater than 10 percent. If you need to enlarge by *more* than 10 percent, use multiple 10 percent steps. This is not a concern when you are using bicubic smoother; with this algorithm, you can perform a single resizing step of any kind.

There are several products on the market designed specifically for enlarging images for print. Alien Skin's Blow Up and OnOne Software's Perfect Resize (formerly Genuine Fractals) are two Photoshop plug-ins that use proprietary algorithms for making enlargements. While these products sound great in theory, in practice, you'll usually see little difference between them and Photoshop's bicubic smoother interpolation. In fact, in some instances, you'll find you get *better* results with Photoshop, even when performing very large enlargements.

Saving a Resized Version

If you're resampling your image in Photoshop, either up or down, you'll want to perform a Save As to create a separate, resized version. Since downsampling throws out data, and upsampling creates new, possibly soft pixels, it's important to preserve a copy of your original file. By doing a Save As either before or after you perform your resizing, you'll create a second version of your document with your new sizing. You can return to your original full-size version at any time.

Sharpening

With all your edits and corrections made, and with your image at its final output size, you're finally ready to apply any necessary sharpening. As with resizing, you don't want to sharpen too early because you'll run the risk of accentuating noise and other unwanted artifacts. Also, you won't know how much sharpening you need until you've adjusted the image's contrast (after all, an image with more contrast looks sharper) and until you've resized the image. If you downsample an image, it's going to get sharper; if you upsample it, it will almost always get softer. Consequently, sharpening should be the last step you take before outputting the image.

Photoshop includes a number of sharpening filters. In addition to these, there are third-party sharpeners and procedural techniques you can use to sharpen your image. Unfortunately, Photoshop does not offer editable sharpening layers. Once you apply your sharpening effects, that's it. Consequently, it's a good idea to save a copy of your image before you sharpen it or duplicate a layer before you sharpen it. By sharpening a duplicate, you can always throw it out and go back to your original if you discover later that you need a different level of sharpening.

In Lightroom, sharpening—like every other edit—is nondestructive. You can change or remove it at any time.

Your biggest concern when you sharpen, however, is not to sharpen too much. While it may seem like sharper is always a good thing, oversharpening can create a number of undesirable artifacts, because a digital sharpening process does not actually increase the sharpness in an image. Rather, it creates an illusion of sharpness by making the edges in your image more acute.

How Sharpening Works

Photoshop, like most image editors, has several sharpening filters: Sharpen, Sharpen More, Sharpen Edges, and Unsharp Mask can all be found under the Filter > Sharpen menu. However, the Unsharp Mask (USM) filter is the only one you ever need to consider. If you're using Photoshop CS2 or later, you'll also have a Smart Sharpen option in the Sharpen menu. This is a variation of the standard Unsharp Mask filter. Sharpen, Sharpen More, and Sharpen Edges are simply too uncontrollable and destructive for quality sharpening.

Unsharp Mask gets its name from a darkroom sharpening technique where a blurry copy of a negative (an "unsharp" copy) is stacked with the original negative, and a print is made using a doubled exposure time. The Unsharp Mask negative and lengthened exposure time serve to darken the dark side of an edge and lighten the light side, causing the edge to exhibit a halo. This renders the edge more pronounced, and the image appears sharper.

The USM filter works the same way. When you apply the filter, your image is examined one pixel at a time. Obviously, the filter can't really tell what counts as an edge in your image, so it looks for sudden changes in contrast. If there is a sudden change in value between two adjacent pixels, it's safe to assume that represents an edge. The darker of the two pixels will be darkened, and the pixels around it will be ramped down, while the lighter pixel will be lightened, and the pixels around it ramped up.

If you look at an edge in an image that has had a USM filter applied, such as the one in Figure 22.6, you'll see that one side of the edge is darker and the other side is lighter. The result is a bit of a halo. As long as this halo isn't distractingly strong, the image will appear sharper.

The key to good Unsharp Masking is to know when to quit. Too much sharpening, and your image will appear unrealistically sharp, and the edge halos will be bright enough to be distracting. Your final picture will have too much contrast, and the preponderance of halos will add a type of visual noise to your image.

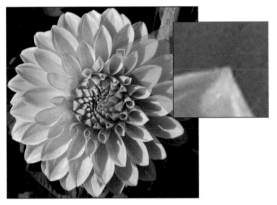

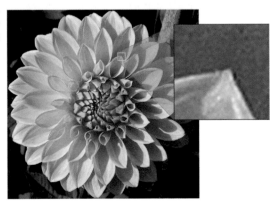

Figure 22.6

If you look closely at a sharpened image, you can see the halos that the Unsharp Mask process creates along the edges of shapes to make them appear sharper. Notice that the sharpened version also has more noticeable noise and texture, as these elements have also been sharpened.

The Photoshop Unsharp Mask tool provides three controls: Amount, Radius, and Threshold (see Figure 22.7). This is typical of USM controls, so even if you're using a different image editor, its Unsharp Mask tool probably offers the same options.

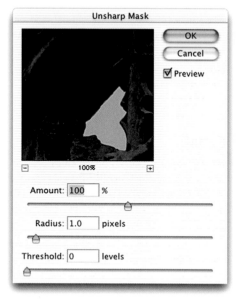

◆ **Amount.** Controls how much the pixels along an edge will be darkened and lightened. The higher the number, the more the USM filter will change the pixels. If you have too much of a change, your edge will become unnaturally contrasted and will possibly posterize.

◆ **Radius.** Determines the width of the halo that will be created. The wider the radius, the more pixels that will be altered around an edge to create a halo.

◆ **Threshold.** Determines what the filter will consider to be an edge. A higher threshold value requires more contrast between two pixels before the filter will consider it an edge that can be sharpened. With a higher threshold, USM will find fewer edges and perform less sharpening.

Figure 22.7

The Photoshop Unsharp Mask tool provides three simple controls for sharpening your images.

To learn what makes good sharpening, it's worth spending some time looking at some professional photos. Notice that even images that have lots of detail and contrast are not necessarily razor sharp. Your image editor can actually sharpen an image far beyond what looks realistic, so it's important to pay attention when sharpening.

When you use a USM filter, start with a high Amount setting—100 percent or higher—and a small Threshold. Then try to find a Radius that produces minimal halos (see Figure 22.8). Sharpening is a subjective process, so find a level of halo that suits you. However, be sure to consider your entire image.

Amount: 100
Radius: 1
Threshold: 1

100 1 1

Amount: 100
Radius: 2
Threshold: 1

100 2 1

Amount: 200
Radius: 2
Threshold: 1

200 2 1

Amount: 200
Radius: 4
Threshold: 1

200 4 1

Figure 22.8

The right level of sharpening is a balance of all three Unsharp Mask parameters.

Amount: 400
Radius: 2
Threshold: 1

400 2 1

Amount: 400
Radius: 4
Threshold: 1

400 4 1

After you've found a Radius that is right, you can back off the Amount and increase the Threshold. Your goal is to use these two sliders to apply your desired radius to the appropriate amount of edge detail in your image.

Always Sharpen at 100 Percent

Be sure that you're looking at your image at 100 percent, or 1:1, when sharpening. If you've zoomed out from your image, your image editor is already downsampling its screen image, which will serve to render the image sharper. Consequently, accurate sharpening may not be visible.

Not All Sharpness Is Created Equal

Note that some subjects can withstand more sharpening than others. Foliage and small, very detailed background elements, as well as skin tones, usually don't stand up to a good deal of sharpening, whereas simple shapes with well-defined edges do. If these types of objects are mixed together, you might be better served by selectively applying different amounts of sharpening to different parts of your image.

Based on the techniques you've learned so far, there are a number of ways you can selectively apply sharpening. You can, for example, create selections using selection tools. Or, because sharpening is an effect you want to apply to edges, you can use the luminance masking technique we learned earlier to build a mask from the image's edge detail and then apply sharpening through that mask. For the next tutorial, though, we're going to apply sharpening by painting.

Selective Sharpening

Figure 22.9 shows an original, unsharpened image that was pulled directly from a Canon digital SLR. Like most digital SLRs, Canons do not apply much sharpening to an image, leaving you in complete control of the sharpening process. After all, you can't remove sharpening once it's there, so it's often better for a camera to err on the side of too soft, since you can always sharpen later.

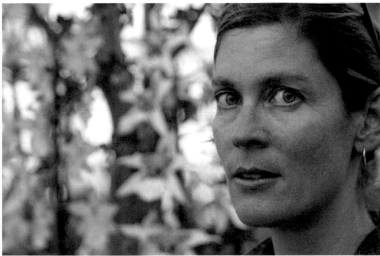

Figure 22.9

This image was taken with a Canon SLR. By default, most SLRs apply very little sharpening. Here I want to sharpen some areas but not others.

Because this image was shot with a shallow depth of field, there's really no reason to apply any sharpening to the background. There's no edge detail there anyway, so sharpening would only serve to exaggerate any noise or artifacts that might be lurking in the image. The woman's face, on the other hand, could definitely use some sharpening. However, her face doesn't need equal sharpening all over.

Eyes are the most important part of any portrait, so you want to sharpen them quite a bit. Skin tones, however, can suffer from sharpening, because sharpening intensifies pores and wrinkles, so it's better to apply less sharpening to those areas.

Fortunately, applying sharpening selectively is pretty easy using some techniques you've already learned. For a selective sharpening tutorial, download the Selective Sharpening.pdf located in the Chapter 22 section of the companion website.

Don't Get Too Hung Up on Sharpening

As with any edit, bear in mind that it's the *content* of your image that matters. Some of the most famous photographers in the world shot images that were, by today's standards, very soft. But because they were composed and exposed well, the images remain evocative and effective.

Smart Sharpening in Photoshop

Photoshop CS2 and later include a variant of the standard Unsharp Mask filter called *Smart Sharpen*. Smart Sharpen does the same thing that Unsharp Mask does—finds edges and lightens and darkens the pixels on either side to make the edge more pronounced—but adds a few additional controls (see Figure 22.10).

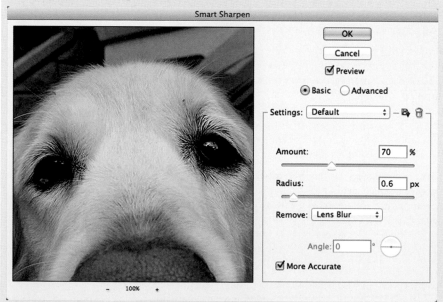

Figure 22.10 Photoshop CS2 and later provide a Smart Sharpen filter, which performs an Unsharp Mask operation, but provides more control and allows for more subtle, controlled effects.

Smart Sharpening in Photoshop (continued)

◆ **Remove.** Defines exactly which blurring algorithm is used to create the "unsharp" copy of your image that is used internally by the filter. Gaussian Blur yields the same type of sharpening as Unsharp Mask. Lens Blur will provide finer detail sharpening and possibly yield fewer halos. Motion Blur (and the accompanying Angle parameter) can yield better sharpening, depending on the image. Experiment to determine which algorithm is best for your image.

In the Advanced section of the dialog box, you'll find some additional parameters.

◆ **Fade Amount** (under the Shadow and Highlight tabs). Adjusts the amount of sharpening that is applied to highlights and shadows.

◆ **Tonal Width.** Controls the range of shadow and highlight tones that are affected by the filter.

◆ **Radius.** Controls the size of the area that is analyzed to determine if a pixel is a shadow or a highlight.

In general, when you use Smart Sharpen, you'll use the same methodology and need to keep an eye out for the same types of artifacts as when you use Unsharp Mask. You'll probably find that Smart Sharpen does a better job of constraining its sharpening effects to edges. This makes it especially useful for sharpening portraits.

Web and Email Output

Web output is very simple. Unfortunately, this is partly because there are no color management controls for the Web. Since there's nothing you can do but post your images and hope your viewers are using decent monitors, you don't need to spend time trying to tweak your final image to look good on a particular monitor or paper type.

Your main concern when you prepare an image for the Web (or for email) is file size. You probably already know what it's like to wait for a large image to download, either from the Web or from your mail server. Don't inflict the same data glut on other people by posting or emailing really large files. Obviously, if you and your recipient have high-speed connections, you can probably get away with creating larger files. Be aware, however, that the mail servers provided by many Internet service providers put a limit on the maximum size of an email attachment. If you absolutely *have* to email a large image to someone, consider segmenting it by using a file-compression utility.

Fortunately, images for the Web tend to be very small. You can safely assume that most users have a screen that's 800–1,000 pixels wide. Of course, some users will have much larger screens, and if you know your intended recipient does, then you can send a larger image. In general, most Web and email images clock in around 300 to 600 pixels wide. Save a copy of your image (be careful not to recompress it) and resize it to an appropriate pixel size.

The two most common graphics file formats on the Web are GIF and JPEG. For photos, JPEG is really the only format you need to use. Fortunately, Photoshop offers an excellent Save for Web and Devices command (under the File menu) that lets you experiment with different JPEG compression ratios and compare the effects of different compression settings side by side (see Figure 22.11).

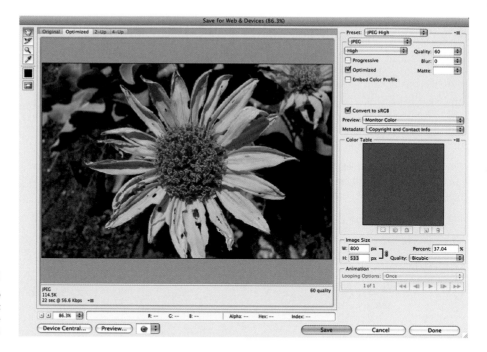

Figure 22.11

The Photoshop Save for Web and Devices command makes it simple to try different JPEG settings to balance size and quality.

In the Save for Web dialog box, you can select different compression types and play with different settings to see how image quality is affected. You can even view two- and four-up comparisons, so that you can see different compression settings side by side.

Save for Web also includes a set of Image Size controls, which let you resize the image upon output and give you the option to convert to the sRGB color space.

If you're sending images to post on another person's website, consider sending an uncompressed image. That person may have his or her own size and compression requirements and will want to perform custom resizing and compression. If you send an uncompressed file, he'll be able to compress it to custom specifications without introducing further image degradation.

If you'd like to have your own photo website but don't have access to any Web space, consider using a photo-sharing website, such as Flickr. Many online printing services (see the "Printing" section) include photo-sharing features that allow you to post images for other people to see. They can even order their own prints.

While there's no standard color management system for the Web, there is a color space that many Web browser makers try to respect and optimize for. Before outputting, if you convert your images to sRGB, there's a good chance your results will be a little more predictable and consistent from browser to browser. In Photoshop, you can convert to sRGB by choosing Edit > Assign Profile and then selecting the sRGB profile in the resulting dialog box. You can also convert to sRGB from directly within the Save for Web dialog box.

Automatic Web Photo Galleries

If you're using Photoshop CS through CS3, you can create your own online photo gallery using the Web Photo Gallery feature. In Photoshop CS, click File > Automate > Web Photo Gallery. In Elements 2, click File > Create Web Photo Gallery.

The Web Photo Gallery plug-in has been removed from Photoshop CS4 because a similar function has been added to Bridge, as you'll see in the next section. If you're really attached to the Photo Gallery (or Contact Sheet II), you can download it from this site: *www.adobe.com/support/downloads/detail.jsp?ftpID=4047*.

In Photoshop CS4 and later, you can create Web galleries from within Bridge by clicking on the Output tab at the top of the window. The Output tab lets you export PDF contact sheets or Web galleries. Click on either option at the top of the Output palette.

You'll find a number of prebuilt templates and controls for customizing and altering the template designs. Both options will construct their results using the images in the folder you're currently browsing (see Figure 22.12).

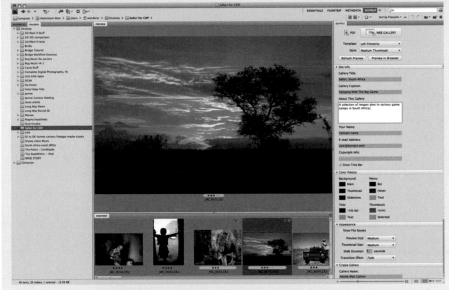

Figure 22.12 Bridge's Output tab provides a simple, powerful facility for creating Web galleries from a folder full of images.

Lightroom also provides automatic Web gallery features that make it simple to output a selection of images as an easily navigable Web album. These programs (as well as Apple iPhoto) also provide custom Export plug-ins for automatically outputting images to photo-sharing services such as Flickr.

If you're using Lightroom or iPhoto, and you need to output files for use on the Web (without creating a full-blown Web gallery), you'll simply use those programs' Export facilities to create JPEG images at a smaller size. All three apps allow you to choose an output size at the time of export. Lightroom and iPhoto also provide special email functions that automatically create a small, email-ready image and then automatically attach this to an email in your chosen email client.

Don't Forget Your Copyright

Before posting your images to the Web, use your image editor to fill in the Copyright IPTC metadata field to include your name and the copyright year. For example "Copyright © 2014 by Joe Kodak." This information will stay in the file even if people download a copy of it from your Web gallery. They can change it using their own metadata editor, but willfully changing a piece of copyright metadata can be construed as a copyright violation, so ensuring a good copyright tag can afford a good amount of protection. Note that your camera may let you enter your name and copyright information. It will then embed this automatically into every image that you shoot.

Outputting Electronic Files

While Web and email outputs are technically electronic files, there will be other times when you need to output full-res electronic files. Maybe you need to deliver images for printing to an electronic printing service or simply create a file that someone else can edit. In any case, there are a few things to consider.

- ◆ **Outputting for delivery to a printing service.** If you plan to do your printing through an online service, camera store, or drug store, you'll need to output in a specific way. We'll discuss this in detail when we cover these services in the printing section, later in this chapter.

- ◆ **Outputting for delivery to a designer or printer.** If you're producing images that will be used by a graphic designer or printer, you'll need to check with them to find out exactly what their specifications are. They will probably need an image sized to very specific pixel dimensions and with a very specific resolution. They might also need an image that has been converted to CMYK (something you cannot do in Photoshop Elements, Lightroom, or iPhoto), and they'll probably have specific file format requirements. Finally, they might also have specific color space requirements. They should be able to provide you with detailed instructions on exactly how to save the file, and can probably do any necessary CMYK conversions for you, although they may charge a fee for this service. You'll also want to find out what file format they expect for delivery. In many cases, a high-quality JPEG file will be fine, although some printers will insist on an uncompressed format such as TIFF, PSD, or possibly EPS.

- ◆ **Outputting for delivery to a retoucher or photographer.** Many photographers prefer to work with a professional retoucher, rather than perform retouching and editing on their own. There might be other times when you simply need to deliver an editable file for someone else because she needs a copy for her own use. In these instances, you'll want to deliver a full-res file, possibly with any layers you've created, and usually at the highest possible bit depth. So, if you've been shooting raw, you'll want to deliver a 16-bit file, while JPEG images will have to be sent at 8 bits. If possible, you'll want to send it in an uncompressed format such as TIFF or PSD.

Photoshop's Image Processor

Photoshop CS2 and later include a handy feature that makes it easy to convert batches of files from one format to another. If you choose File > Scripts > Image Processor, you'll be presented with the Image Processor dialog box, which lets you select a folder full of images, a destination location, and then configure checkboxes to select the file format of your output files (see Figure 22.13).

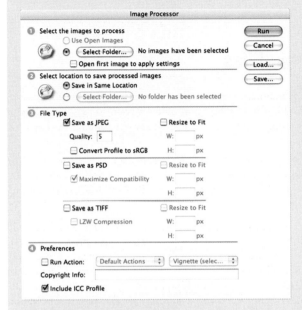

Figure 22.13

The Photoshop Image Processor lets you easily batch process entire folders full of images into different file formats.

In addition, you can opt to resize your files at the time of output, and you can even output in JPEG, PSD, and TIFF files simultaneously. Finally, using the Preferences section at the bottom of the window, you can choose an Action to run on the processed images (an action you've defined in the Actions palette) and a Copyright tag to embed in the file's IPTC info.

Note, too, that you can launch the Image Processor from within Bridge. Say there are some images that you want to resize and save as JPEGs for uploading to a website. Select the images in Bridge and then choose Tools > Photoshop > Image Processor. Configure the Image Processor dialog box accordingly, and your new files will be created.

If you need to convert many images to TIFF or JPEG very quickly, the Image Processor is an easy way to do so.

Choosing a Printer

With the pixel counts of cameras climbing ever higher and prices continuing to drop, it's not hard to see that digital camera technology is constantly improving by leaps and bounds. But desktop printing technology has been making equally impressive advancement, as evidenced by the fact that you can now buy a printer that delivers photo-lab-quality prints for under $100. For years, longevity and durability of prints was the Achilles' heel of desktop printing, but new pigment ink formulations have addressed this problem, and desktop ink-jets are now capable of producing prints that are *more* durable than traditional film printing processes.

Many new users are quick to point out that although the printers are cheap, ink cartridges are very expensive, and therefore, digital printing is a rip-off. This may be true when compared to having your film processed at your local Walmart, but you need to remember that you get what you pay for. Odds are, you'll get better-looking prints from your desktop printer than you'll ever get from a cheap photo lab.

If you tend to want prints of most of the pictures you shoot, a desktop printer will be more expensive per print than if you print using a printing service. If this sounds like you, you will want to use a photo printing service for the bulk of your images and think of your desktop printer as a replacement for the custom photo lab you would go to for those times when you want enlargements, special prints, or precise control over color. Or you might think of it as a replacement for a color darkroom you'd normally have to keep in a closet or bathroom. When viewed this way, you'll see that desktop printing is much cheaper than using a custom lab, and definitely cheaper than the equipment and materials required for a wet darkroom.

What you may find is that the ideal printing solution is a combination of mail-order printing for your everyday prints and a desktop printer for larger prints or for times when you want to tweak and adjust the color of a print.

We'll discuss both technologies in this chapter. Fortunately, all the work you've done in the preceding pages should leave you well prepared for a discussion of printing. Most of the color theory you learned when you were working with your camera will apply to your printer as well. This section begins with a discussion of the issues and questions you'll face when you buy a printer. Following that, you'll learn more about how to adjust and prepare your images for printing.

Ink-Jet Printers

The best photo-printing solution is a color ink-jet printer. Ink-jets work by shooting tiny drops of ink out of a nozzle (*really* tiny—most ink-jets use a drop that is only a few picoliters). As with any color-printing technology, different colored drops are combined to create full-color images.

Ink-jet printers have a number of advantages over other printing technologies. They have larger color gamuts, better sharpness, produce prints that are more durable, and provide much greater media flexibility than any other printing technology. With the right paper, a good ink-jet printer can create an image that's indistinguishable from a photographic print.

Ink-jet printers are typically far cheaper to buy than any other type of printer, although their cost per print can be expensive—up to $2 per page for a photo-quality 8″ × 10″ print. However, because of their ability to handle different media, you can also create lower-quality, less-expensive prints by using cheaper paper.

You might already have an ink-jet printer that you use for printing letters and other "office" type documents. The typical office ink-jet printer has four ink colors: cyan, magenta, yellow, and black. Just as your camera and computer create other colors by combining the red, green, and blue primary colors of light, your ink-jet printer combines its four primaries to create all other colors.

An office printer is suitable for printing text at reasonable speeds and will do a capable job of printing color photos. (HP even makes a three-color printer that uses cyan, magenta, and yellow inks, and then mixes these together to create black.)

A serious photo printer, though, uses more colors of ink. At the bottom end, a photo printer will have at least six colors, while a more sophisticated one might have as many as 13. For example, six-color photo printers usually add extra light cyan and light magenta cartridges to the four primaries, which allow the printer to reduce the visible printer dots that can appear in highlight areas and make it possible to create smoother color transitions and gradients. The extra colors also help improve fade resistance. Some primary colors fade faster than others, so by mixing colors from different, sturdier primaries, the printer can produce prints with better fade resistance.

Seven-color printers use those same six colors, but usually add an additional black cartridge specifically for printing on glossy paper. Several vendors make eight-color printers, but choose different mixes to achieve different results. For example, some printers use the same six colors as a six-color inkjet and add red and green ink to yield prints with better reds and greens. Other printers start with the usual six-color mix and add two lighter shades of gray to produce truly neutral gray tones.

There are even more complex ink systems, but they're all designed to do the same thing: expand the gamut and improve neutrality—the capability to print a grayscale image without a color cast.

Additional inks are also employed to help reduce metameric shift, a property of some inks that can cause them to appear different in different types of light. A print that suffers from bad metameric shift might appear fine in bright daylight but have a greenish cast under tungsten light. Metameric shift (sometimes referred to, incorrectly, as *metamerism*) is usually caused by a slight color cast in the black ink of a printer. To combat metameric shift, many printers mix a primary color with the black ink.

Ultimately, you don't need to concern yourself with the specifics of your printer's color mix. You simply want to find the printer that produces the best output. However, paying attention to the color mix in a printer can give you a good idea of what qualities to look for in a print.

With the jump from an office printer to a quality photo printer, you'll use almost twice as much ink per print. A printer that uses eight, nine, or more inks will suck up more ink per print than a six-color printer, but not substantially more.

To learn more about how to choose an inkjet printer and what separates one type from another, check out the `Ink-jet Printer Buyer's Guide.pdf`, located in the Chapter 22 section of the companion website.

Media Selection

You can stick any old paper in your inkjet printer, including the normal 20-pound copier paper typically used for office correspondence. But paper choice can have a huge bearing on the appearance of your final image.

Glossy, or "luster" papers, for example, will deeply saturate colors but exhibit weaker blacks than a matte paper. Weaker blacks will mean a cost of overall contrast ratio and shadow detail. Matte papers, meanwhile, will be able to display a greater color range but at the cost of deeply saturated colors. Which choice is right depends on the image you're printing, what type of look you're going for, and how you will display the image. So, if a particular image is dependent on supersaturated colors, you'll want to go with a glossier paper, while an image with a very broad tonal range and lots of fine detail will need a matte-finish paper. If an image is going to be displayed under glass, you may find that the paper finish is less relevant because the glass obscures a lot of gloss and adds an apparent finish of its own.

Finally, you may make your decision purely on cost. Some papers are much cheaper than others. If you simply need to get some sample images to someone or want to print out some snapshots, you might be best served by an inexpensive matte-finish paper.

In general, you'll want to experiment with your paper selections to find out what works best for your intended output. Be certain to read your printer's manual before you shove an experimental piece of paper through your printer. Most printers have thickness limits, and many printers—particularly archival-quality printers—can be damaged if you use media that wasn't specifically designed for the printer. Some types of handmade papers can produce lots of dust and particulate matter that can be hard on a print head, resulting in clogs and frequent cleanings.

Ink Choice

In general, you should always buy ink made and certified by your printer manufacturer. There might be cheaper, third-party inks available for specialized printing applications, such as high-quality grayscale printing, and these often work just fine. Be aware, though, that it is possible for your printer head to be damaged by noncertified inks. More important, to get accurate color, your printer driver needs to know that the ink formulations in your printer will mix and blend in a particular way. If you use a third-party ink, there's no guarantee that they will have mixed their ink correctly, and you'll rarely have any idea of the archival qualities of third-party inks.

Printing

In an ideal world, once you have finished correcting and adjusting your images, you would simply click the print button and out of your printer would pop a print that looked exactly like it did on-screen. In the real world, printing is a bit more involved than that.

Earlier, we discussed the processes of resizing and sharpening. What we *didn't* discuss, though, was how to determine an appropriate resolution when resizing. You want to be sure you're using all the pixels in your image to your maximum advantage. Therefore, choosing a resolution is your first major decision when preparing to print.

Choosing a Resolution

Before you can resize an image, you need to know the resolution that is best for your printer. Different printing technologies have different resolution requirements, so calculating optimal resolution differs from printer type to printer type.

If you've ever looked at a black-and-white newspaper photo up close, you've seen how dot patterns of varying size can be used to represent different shades of gray (see Figure 22.14). This type of image is called a *halftone* and traditionally was created by rephotographing a picture through a mesh screen.

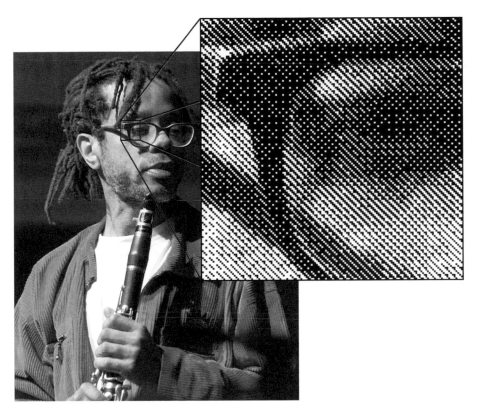

Figure 22.14

Like all of the images in this book, this figure is a halftone. In a black-and-white halftone, patterns of differently sized black dots are combined to create the appearance of various shades of gray.

The color photos in this book are printed using a similar process. To create a color halftone, four halftones are created, one each for cyan, magenta, yellow, and black. When layered on top of each other, these four halftones yield a full-color image.

All color printing processes use variations on this practice of combining groups of primary colored dots to create other colors. Nowadays, halftones are usually created digitally by scanning an image into a computer (if it didn't start out as a digital image in the first place) and then letting the computer create a halftone. In the old days, you created a halftone by photographing an image through a screen.

Your computer monitor works differently. A CRT monitor has three electron guns that light up three different colors of phosphor—red, green, and blue. An LCD monitor uses light sources with the same three colors. Liquid crystals sit in front of the light sources and act as shutters, which can be opened by varying amounts to blend and mix the three component colors.

In other words, there is not a one-to-one correspondence between a pixel on your screen and a dot printed on paper. While a pixel on your screen is made up of three component light sources, your printer might have to print a combination of 50 different cyan, magenta, yellow, and black dots to reproduce that one purple dot from your monitor. Although your printer may claim to have 1,400 dots per inch of resolution, those are 1,400 *printer dots,* not 1,400 pixels. It might take a whole lot of printer dots to reproduce one pixel from your image. Choosing a resolution, then, is dependent on how much information your printer needs to do its job.

Choosing a Resolution for an Ink-Jet Printer

All ink-jet printers have a native resolution, measured in pixels per inch (ppi). If you send an image to the printer at some other resolution, then the printer will up- or downsample that image to the printer's native resolution before printing. So, for example, if your printer has a native resolution of 300 ppi, and you send an image with a resolution of 600 ppi, at your desired output size, the printer will automatically downsample the image to that same size, at 300 ppi. In Photoshop, this is the same thing as resizing the image with Resample Image checked in the Image Size dialog box.

There are two potential problems that occur when the printer does this. First, if your printer's interpolation software is not as good as what's included in your image editor, then it's possible that you might see some image degradation when the printer performs this resizing.

More importantly, if you've sharpened your image and the printer resamples it, the result could have either too much or too little sharpening. For both of these reasons, it's best to resample the image yourself to the printer's native resolution before printing.

Unfortunately, printer vendors are not diligent about publishing native resolutions, so it can be difficult to determine what the native resolution for a particular printer might be. In general, Epson printers typically have a native resolution of 360 ppi, while Canon and HP printers typically have a native resolution of 300 ppi.

Color Management

If you've ever printed a photo from your computer you've probably already encountered the fact that prints don't usually—if ever—look like the image does on-screen. There are several reasons for this.

First, your monitor creates an image by shining light directly into your eyes. When you look at a printed picture, you're looking at light that is reflected by a piece of paper into your eyes. These are very different mediums for transmitting a visual image, and they simply have very different qualities.

Second, your monitor makes a color by mixing the additive primaries of light, while pigments are mixed using subtractive primaries. Translating between these two systems is complex.

Finally, it's extremely difficult to build two monitors to precisely the same specifications. The same holds true for cameras and printers. Stack all of these variables together and you have a hugely complex problem. In this section, we're going to look at two different approaches to getting accurate prints from your printer, and while these approaches can yield great results, it's also important to realize that, because of the different nature of light and pigment, an image on paper will simply *never* look like it does on-screen. Despite this, it is possible to get predictable results.

Managed vs. Unmanaged

In a color managed workflow, your monitor and printer paper are both *profiled*. Profiles are small text documents that are stored in your operating system. Generated by special hardware, these documents contain details of specific traits and properties of your monitor and specific printer/paper combination. When you print, software in your operating system or image editor (or sometimes a combination of both) uses these profiles to alter the color in your image as it passes to the printer and monitor. If everything goes well, the two adjusted images will match. Note that the original image data is not altered at all.

To run a color managed system, you need to have good profiles. In Chapter 4, "Image Transfer," we looked at how to make a monitor profile, and in the next section we're going to discuss printer profiles. However, for color management to work you also need a room where you can carefully control the lighting. Profiles are built with the assumption that you will be using them in a very specific kind of ambient light. If the ambient light in the room you're printing in changes, your profiles may lose accuracy, leaving you with a bad screen/printer match. Finally, even if you have good profiles for your monitor and full control of the lighting in the room, you still may not get a good match. Based on your monitor profile, your computer alters the color in your image to force the monitor to display it a particular way. However, just because the computer sends particular data to the monitor doesn't mean the monitor can accurately display that data. If your monitor is old or simply lower-quality, it won't matter how good the profile is, because you may simply not have a monitor good enough to represent the color in your image.

So before you invest in lots of expensive profiling hardware, it's worth playing with some stock monitor and printer profiles to get a feel for whether your environment and monitor are good enough to pull off a full color managed workflow. If they're not, then you'll want to go unmanaged, which we'll discuss at the end of this section.

Printer Profiles

For color management to work, you need to have a good printer profile. Just as you need to have an ICC profile for your monitor (see Chapter 4), you also need to have an ICC profile for your printer. More specifically, you need one for the particular type of paper you're going to print with in your particular type of printer.

When you installed your printer software, a collection of profiles should have been installed for each paper type your printer vendor sells. There may even be several profiles for each paper: some profiles are for specific viewing conditions (daylight, tungsten, etc.) or ink types (glossy, matte).

Unfortunately, not all vendor-supplied printer profiles are reliable. One reason is that some printers are easier to control with profiles than others. For example, some higher-end printers include sensors that carefully monitor ink flow through the print head to determine exactly how much ink is being delivered to the paper. Some printers are carefully calibrated as soon as they leave the assembly line. On the flip side, less-expensive printers often vary significantly from one unit to the next, meaning a generic, vendor-supplied profile may be of little use.

When you use a paper sold by someone other than the company that makes your printer, you'll need to make or find a profile for it. Many third-party paper vendors provide free profiles for download. Crane has an extensive profile collection, as do Hahnemühle and Ilford. Finally, you can often find free profiles on the Web simply by searching.

If you're not getting good output with vendor-supplied profiles, or if you're using a paper you can't find a profile for, it's time for a custom job. Several services, such as Inkjetart.com, make custom profiles for around $25. Simply download the supplied profile target, print it out on your printer, and mail it back. The company then sends you a standard color profile. When printing the target, be sure to set your printer settings to the ones you typically use and turn off the printer's built-in correction.

While $25 is cheap, you may find that as you change ink cartridges, your profile becomes less accurate. Continually regenerating a profile can become expensive. If you regularly create paper profiles, you may want to invest in your own profiling hardware. To create a profile, you first print test target images, which are color swatches that come with the paper profiling system. Then you measure these targets with the included hardware. The XRite Pulse Color Elite is one such system. It ships in various configurations that can include a monitor calibrator as well.

However, paper-profiling systems are not cheap. Expect to spend at least $600 for an entry-level system. Such a system can pay for itself in saved ink and paper costs if you regularly use third-party papers, but if you only occasionally need to make a profile, it's probably not worth it.

On the Mac OS, you can install printer profiles in the Library > ColorSync > Profiles folder. On Windows, you should install your printer profiles in WINDOWS\system32\spool\drivers\color. You might need to relaunch your image editing application to see the new profiles.

If you don't have a profile for the specific paper you're using, you might be able to get away with a similar one that's already in your driver. For example, if you have an HP printer that includes a profile for an HP semi-gloss paper, you might find that it works okay when printing on an Epson semi-gloss paper. It still won't be as good as a dedicated profile, but it might be good enough to get you started, and as you gain more experience with the paper, you may learn how to compensate for inaccuracies between the monitor and paper.

Soft Proofing

Simply installing profiles for your monitor and printer doesn't mean that the computer is now showing you an accurate image. Color management is not an automatic process that's always on. Adobe Photoshop CC and Lightroom offer special *soft proofing* modes, which use a color-management system and installed profiles to simulate on-screen what a print will look like when output to a specified printer.

To generate a soft proof, be sure your most recent monitor profile is active. Your profiling package should have installed it for you. If it's been more than a month since you profiled the monitor, do it again. It's best to profile your monitor at least once a month—more often if it's an older monitor.

If all of your profiles are in place, then you're ready to create a soft proof. Check out the Soft Proofing.pdf, located in the Chapter 22 section of the companion website for a detailed tutorial.

 Color Managed Printing from Photoshop

Once you soft proof your image, you might see tonal adjustments and color shifts that need to be made, and we'll discuss how to handle that shortly. First, let's see how a color-managed printing process works in Photoshop. This tutorial assumes that you have opened an image that you want to print in Photoshop, that you have a printer installed and connected, that you have monitor and printer profiles installed, and that you have performed the Soft Proofing tutorial from the previous section.

STEP 1: OPEN THE PRINT DIALOG BOX
If you're using Photoshop CS4 or later, choose File > Print. (With some earlier CS versions, you'll choose Print with Preview.) Photoshop will show you a thumbnail view of your chosen paper size, with your image positioned as it will appear when printed (see Figure 22.15).

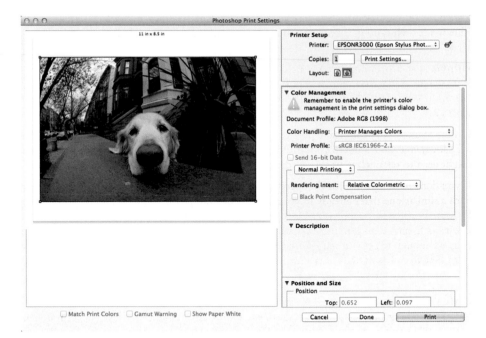

Figure 22.15

The print dialog box in Photoshop CS4 and later provides all the controls you need to run a color-managed print process. In earlier versions of the Photoshop Creative Suite, you'll get the same types of controls from the Print with Preview dialog box.

If this is your first time printing, then you'll need to configure the Printer Setup section of the dialog box. Select your target printer from the Printer pop-up menu. If it's not there, then you'll need to go through any steps required by your operating system to install and add a printer.

STEP 2: CHOOSE THE PAPER SIZE AND ORIENTATION

Click the Print Settings button to change the current paper size and orientation, as well as to select paper type and other printer-specific features. When those are configured, click Save to return to the Photoshop Print Settings dialog box.

You'll need to tell the printer what type of paper you're printing on. This allows the printer to position the print head an appropriate distance from the paper, depending on how thick the paper is.

Use the Position and Scaling controls to change how your image will be positioned and sized on the page. We're assuming you've already resized your image to your desired print size and resolution. If you haven't, you can use the Scaled Print Size controls to tell Photoshop to re-size the image now. However, you'll have no control over the interpolation method, whether the image is resampled, or of final sharpening, so this is not the best resizing option.

STEP 3: TELL PHOTOSHOP TO TAKE CONTROL OF THE COLOR

When you print, you can have Photoshop manage the color, or you can let the printer man-age the color. You want Photoshop to manage the color so that it can generate the same colors for your print that it calculates for your soft proof. If you let the printer manage the colors, there's no guarantee it will make the same color decisions.

In Photoshop CS4 and later, change the Color Handling pop-up menu to Photoshop Man-ages Color.

In Photoshop CS and CS2, click the More Options button (if it's not already clicked) and then change the Color Handling pop-up menu to Let Photoshop Determine Colors.

STEP 4: SET THE RENDERING INTENT

As you learned when you generated your soft proof, rendering intent is simply the method that Photoshop uses to cram the large color space your camera captures into the smaller space provided by your paper. You want to set the Print dialog to use the same rendering intent you chose when you soft proofed. In my soft proofing example, I used Relative Colorimetric, so set the Rendering Intent pop-up menu to Relative Colorimetric.

STEP 5: CHOOSE A PAPER PROFILE

Now set the Printer Profile pop-up menu to the same profile you chose when you soft proofed. This will be the paper profile you selected in step 2 of the previous tutorial.

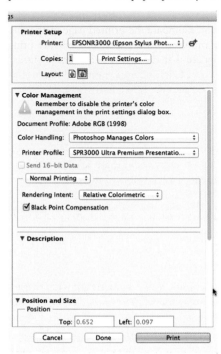

STEP 6: BLACK POINT COMPENSATION

If you chose Black Point Compensation when you configured Proof Setup, you need to activate it in the Print dialog. As you'll recall, I chose to enable Black Point Compensation, so check it now (see Figure 22.16).

STEP 7: PRINT

Now, click the Print button. Next, you might see your operating system's normal Print dialog box. From here, you can select the printer you want to print to and configure the printer driver's controls. Finally, find the control in the printer driver that turns *off* color management. Most printer drivers have their own color-management routines that try to correct an image's color for printing. However, you're asking Photoshop to take care of managing color, so you don't want the printer driver to be involved. If both systems mess with the color in your image, things get very unpredictable.

Figure 22.16

Photoshop's Print dialog should look something like this.

Printer Color Management May Be Disabled Automatically

Some newer operating systems allow programs like Photoshop to disable color management automatically in a printer driver. For example, on Mac OS X 10.7 and later, there's no need to go through this step of disabling color management—Photoshop takes care of that for you when you select Photoshop Managed Color.

If your OS requires you to deactivate printer color management manually, then you'll have to search in the Print dialog box for the appropriate control. For example, in most Epson printers, you'll find a Color Management option in the Printer dialog, which looks something like the controls shown in Figure 22.17.

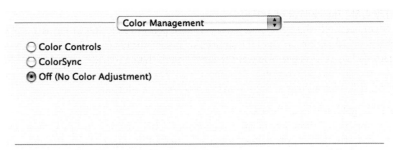

Figure 22.17

It is essential that you disable your printer's built-in color management, using the Printer Driver dialog.

Click the Print button, and your image should print. Compare the printed page to the soft proof on your screen. If you have a good-quality monitor, printer, and profiles, the print should match the screen fairly well. You'll probably see that the blacks and overall contrast range are a little different. The monitor image is probably a little more saturated because of the nature of a self-illuminated display, but the overall hues should be fairly close. ◢◣

Improving Your Print

Unfortunately, color management is not a magic bullet. Your final print will never exactly match the image that appears on your screen. However, soft proofing can allow you to get your prints and screen to a pretty close match, and reduce the number of test prints required to get a good print.

If you're sorely disappointed with the results of your print, there are a few things you can do to improve your output quality.

Change Your Rendering Intent

As you've seen, when you soft proof and print, you must select a rendering intent; that is, you tell the printer how to map "illegal" (out-of-gamut) colors to the color space of your printer—and, more specifically, to the color space of your paper.

In the Soft Proofing and Printing tutorials, you selected Relative Colorimetric as your rendering intent because it's a good, general-purpose intent. It maps the white in your image to the white of your paper profile, so the whites in the print are represented by the white of the paper, not by ink. The Relative Colorimetric rendering intent doesn't touch any other color that falls within the gamut of your ink and paper. Illegal colors are mapped to the nearest in-gamut color. If you're a stickler for color accuracy, you'll probably prefer Relative Colorimetric.

Because your eyes are far more sensitive to contrast and the relationships between colors than to absolute hues, the Perceptual intent tries to compress all the colors in your image to fit within the color gamut of your paper, while preserving the relationships between those colors. If your image has many out-of-gamut colors, Perceptual intent creates a nice-looking image, although your colors may not be especially accurate.

You'll use the Relative Colorimetric and Perceptual rendering intents the most. If your image doesn't have out-of-gamut colors, you probably won't find much difference between the two. Occasionally, you may find that one intent yields more "pop" than another. You can usually see this difference when soft proofing, so let soft proofs be your guide as to which rendering intent to use. In Photoshop's Customize Proof Condition dialog box, you can select the rendering intent you'll ultimately print with, and you can see on-screen how it will affect your image. When you find the intent you like best, take note of it and select that same intent when you print.

Photoshop has two more rendering intents. Saturation produces as much saturation as possible and is intended for illustrations and business graphics. Absolute Colorimetric is similar to Relative Colorimetric in that it clips illegal colors; however, it doesn't remap the whites in an image. If the whites in a picture have a slight cast, a printer will print the whites with that cast, rather than leave them as paper white. In other words, Absolute Colorimetric never alters any legal colors in your image.

Many people say that you should never use Absolute Colorimetric for photo printing, but on images with a large dynamic range, you might find that Absolute Colorimetric is actually the best choice. It sometimes provides a brightness that is missing from other intents. However, when Absolute Colorimetric is wrong for your image, it tends to be wrong in a very ugly way. You'll blow out an image's highlights or cause dark shadows to turn splotchy and weird. Pay close attention to these areas when soft proofing to determine if it's the right intent.

Perceptual and Relative Colorimetric also include the option of Black Point Compensation. In most cases, activating this feature is good, but again you should preview it in your soft proofs to be sure. Take note of your final choice because you'll need to select this as your intent in the Print with Preview dialog.

Finally, there's another option for improving the quality of your prints, which is to ignore Photoshop's color management altogether and let your printer handle your color. Depending on your printer, this may actually produce the best results, and you'll see how to do this in the next section.

Soft Proofing in Lightroom

Lightroom provides soft-proofing tools that are very similar to Photoshop's, and you should be able to find your way through its controls easily, based on what you've learned in the last two tutorials. The program has a simpler interface to its soft-proofing and print features than Photoshop does.

Printing with Driver Color

In the previous printing example, you let Photoshop calculate the color values sent to the printer. In the Photoshop Print dialog box, you chose Let Photoshop Determine Colors in the Options panel and then turned off Printer Color Management in the printer's driver dialog box. This left Photoshop in charge of all color calculations.

Now you're going to look at another way to print: change the Color Handling pop-up menu in the Photoshop Print Settings dialog box to Printer Manages Color. If you leave Color Management turned on in your printer's driver dialog, all color calculations will be performed by your printer. It's helpful to try this alternate method because you may find that your printer's included driver yields better results than Photoshop-managed color.

If I had suggested such a notion a few years ago, angry mobs of color geeks and printing nerds would have pelted me with empty ink cartridges. However, nowadays, printer vendors are engineering very good drivers that can often outperform Photoshop's built-in color handling.

This is especially true for black-and-white output on some printers. Some printers from both Epson and HP yield substantially better black-and-white output if you use the driver's built-in grayscale modes rather than letting Photoshop determine colors.

With color images, when you let the printer driver control color, you might notice improvements in everything from overall cast, highlight or shadow detail, certain color ranges, and even continuous tone.

Now the bad news: Printer driver color has nothing to do with Photoshop's soft-proofing feature. In other words, there's no reason to bother with soft proofing in any soft-proof-enabled application if you're going to print with driver color. So you may find that there's less of a match between your screen and printer when using driver color. On the other hand, on some images, you might find a better match and overall better quality.

So, does this mean you need to use even more ink and paper by printing every image using both methods? Probably not. You'll need to experiment a little, but what you'll likely find is that the differences between Photoshop and printer-generated color are very slight, and you can easily alter one to look like the other. With a little initial trial and error, you might also come to understand which types of images work better with a specific method.

Correcting Your Images

After enabling soft proofing or printing a test print, you can think about correcting your image to fix any tone or color problems you found in your initial test print.

In Photoshop, the easiest way to make corrections is via Adjustment Layers. Since your corrections will be specific to the type of paper you're printing on, you can create separate Adjustment Layers for each paper type and activate them as needed. In addition, with the masks built-in to Photoshop's Adjustment Layers, you can constrain adjustments to particular areas in an image.

Many color problems will be the result of your image editor remapping out-of-gamut colors to fit them into the target color space. You can solve some color problems simply by bringing these colors back to legal. Choose View > Gamut Warning, and Photoshop will display out-of-gamut colors as gray pixels. (You can use this feature with Soft Proofing on or off.)

In most cases, you can bring illegal colors back into gamut by using a Hue/Saturation Adjustment Layer. Simply lower the Saturation level, and the gray gamut warning pixels disappear.

If you're using an editing system that supports multiple versions—like Adobe Lightroom—you can create multiple versions tailored for printing on different paper types.

Tweak Your Viewing Conditions

When you build a monitor profile using a monitor calibrator, you tell the calibration software some of the details of the ambient lighting situation in your room. The ideal room has a fairly low level of ambient light, with no bright lights or colors in your field of view.

To make the most accurate assessment of your printer's output, view images under the ambient lighting conditions specified by your paper profile. For most paper profiles, this means daylight or artificial lighting that has the same color temperature as daylight. (Some vendors create multiple profiles for each paper, each tuned for different viewing conditions.)

If your print-viewing lighting is less than ideal, you'll want to consider getting some D50 lighting. D50 lights shine at 5000°K and are good matches for daylight.

If you happen to have a lot of cash lying around, you might want to spend it on a viewing station, such as a GTI Graphic Technology Professional Desktop Viewer. GTI makes all types of well-constructed viewing stations, from large stand-up units to collapsible, portable stations, and you can learn more about them at *www.graphiclite.com*.

A less-expensive option is the Ott-Lite, a 5300°K lamp that sits on your desk. You can order one for about $60 from Lumenet, and you can find details at *www.lumenlight.com*.

The cheapest D50 lighting option is to build your own. SoLux manufactures D50 lamps that start at $6.95 each. You'll need your own fixtures, which are easy to find at any hardware store. Check out *www.usalight.com* for a full assortment of SoLux lamps.

Web-Based Printing

A number of websites offer photo-printing services. After you upload your images to these sites, they will print the images and mail them back to you. These services typically use pictographic processes—traditional chemical-based printing processes that expose a piece of photographic paper using a laser or LED device.

The advantage to these services is that they're very simple to use. The downside is that you have to wait for your prints, and you don't know what sort of color and tone corrections the service will make to your images. In other words, what you see on your screen may not be close to what you get in your prints. Typically, a particular printing service will be consistent about the type of adjustments they make to their images. Once you've figured out a particular service's idiosyncrasies, you can adjust your images accordingly before you submit them.

Pay close attention to a service's cropping guidelines. Some services will blow up your image to fill an entire print. If your original was a different aspect ratio than the final print, your image will be cropped. Most services allow the option of blowing up to full print size or padding the image to preserve your original aspect ratio.

Most services also provide photo-sharing facilities, which allow you to create one or more online photo albums. You can send the address of these albums to other people who can view your images and, if they want, order prints. Posting images to a website is convenient because you only have to upload your pictures and then send out a link. Finally, some services offer much more than simple paper printing. Coffee mugs, T-shirts, banners, cakes, and cookies can all be adorned with your photographs.

In general, these services expect images in an sRGB color space. If you were shooting with your camera set to Adobe RGB (which you should be), you'll need to tag the images as sRGB RGB before you upload them. In Photoshop, you use the Edit > Assign Profile command to assign a new color space.

These services also expect images to be delivered as JPEGs, and many will have specific size and resolution requirements. Consult each service's guidelines for more details.

Conclusion

While you've worked on both ends of the arts and craft spectrum, and you've practiced some very specific techniques and learned to ask some very particular questions, the best thing you can do to improve as a photographer is to get out and take pictures! Your skill with both your camera and image editor will greatly improve as you practice, and you will begin to notice images where you possibly didn't see them before. Take your camera with you wherever you go and don't hesitate to fire away.

If you would like more video tutorials, check out my photo courses on *Lynda.com* at *www.lynda.com/benlong*. There, you'll find courses on everything from exposure and composition to macro, landscape, low light, and HDR, as well as road-trip courses that let you tag along as I shoot in various locations around the world. And finally, *www.completedigital photography.com* offers more articles, camera reviews, image galleries—and even free software.

Index

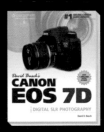 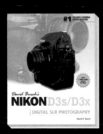 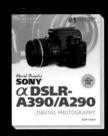 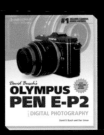 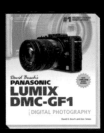
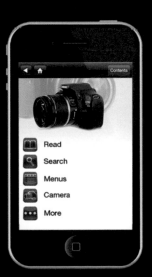
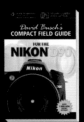
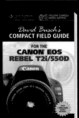
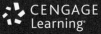

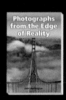

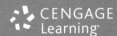